THE AMERICANA ANNUAL

2004

AN ENCYCLOPEDIA
OF THE EVENTS OF 2003

YEARBOOK OF THE
ENCYCLOPEDIA AMERICANA

GROLIER

Published 2004 by Grolier Incorporated

Library of Congress Control Number: 23-10041
ISBN: 0-7172-0244-5
ISSN: 0196-0180

This annual is also published under the title *The 2004 World Book Year Book*
© 2004 World Book, Inc.

Printed in the United States of America.

STAFF

EDITORIAL

Managing Editor, Annuals and General Publishing
Maureen Mostyn Liebenson

Managing Editor, The Year Book
Scott Thomas

Senior Editors
Timothy D. Frystak
Kristina A. Vaicikonis

Staff Editors
Andrew Davis
Christine Sullivan
Carol Yehling

Contributing Editors
Dan Blunk
Robert Knight
Barbara A. Mayes
Vicky Vasconcellos

Editorial Assistant
Ethel Matthews

Cartographic Services
H. George Stoll, Head
Wayne K. Pichler, Manager, Digital Cartography
John M. Rejba, Staff Cartographer

Indexing Services
David Pofelski, Head
Aamir Burki, Staff Indexer

Permissions Editor
Janet Peterson

ART

Manager, Graphics and Design
Sandra M. Dyrlund

Senior Designer, The Year Book
Brenda B. Tropinski

Designer
Anne Fritzinger

Contributing Designer
Sandy Newell

Photographs Editor
Sylvia Ohlrich

Contributing Photographs Editors
Kathryn Creech
Cathy Melloan

Production and Administrative Assistant
John Whitney

RESEARCH SERVICES

Manager, Research Services
Loranne K. Shields

Researchers
Madolynn H. Cronk
Lynn Durbin
Cheryl Graham
Karen A. McCormack
Hilary Zawidowski

Library Services
Jon Fjortoft, Head

PRODUCTION

Director, Manufacturing and Pre-Press
Carma Fazio

Manufacturing Manager
Barbara Podczerwinski

Senior Production Manager
Madelyn S. Underwood

Production/Technology Manager
Jared Svoboda

Proofreading
Anne Dillon, Head

Text Processing
Curley Hunter
Gwendolyn Johnson

MARKETING

Director, Direct Marketing
Mark R. Willy

Marketing Analyst
Zofia Kulik

President and Publisher
Robert C. Martin

Vice President, Editorial
Dominic J. Miccolis

Editor in Chief
Dale W. Jacobs

General Managing Editor
Paul A. Kobasa

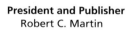

CONTRIBUTORS

Contributors not listed on these pages are members of the editorial staff.

ANDREWS, PETER J., B.A., M.S.; free-lance writer. **[Chemistry]**

APSELOFF, MARILYN FAIN, B.A., M.A.; Professor Emerita of English, Kent State University. **[Literature for children]**

ASKER, JAMES R., B.A.; Washington Bureau Chief, *Aviation Week & Space Technology* magazine. **[Space exploration]**

BARNHART, BILL, B.A., M.S.T., M.B.A.; financial markets columnist, *Chicago Tribune.* **[Stocks and bonds]**

BARRETT, NORMAN, M.A.; free-lance writer. **[Soccer]**

BAYNHAM, SIMON, B.A., M.A., Ph.D.; Senior Research Associate, Centre for Defence & International Security Studies, University of Lancaster, U.K. **[Africa and African country articles]**

BERGER, ERIC R., B.A, M.A.; science writer, *Houston Chronicle.* **[Houston]**

BOULDREY, BRIAN, B.A., M.F.A.; Assistant Professor of English, Northwestern University. **[Literature, American; Literature, World; Poetry; Prison; Pulitzer Prizes; San Francisco]**

BOYD, JOHN D., B.S.; Managing News Editor, *Transport Topics.* **[Economics; International trade; Manufacturing]**

BRADSHER, HENRY S., A.B., B.J.; foreign affairs analyst. **[Asia and Asian country articles]**

BRETT, CARLTON E., B.A., M.S., Ph.D.; Professor of Geology, University of Cincinnati. **[Paleontology]**

BUERKLE, TOM, B.A.; European Editor, *Institutional Investor.* **[Europe and Western European country articles]**

CAMPBELL, GEOFFREY A., B.J.; free-lance writer. **[U.S. government articles]**

CARDINALE, DIANE P., B.A.; Public Information Manager, Toy Industry Association, Incorporated. **[Toys and games]**

CARLSON, ROB, B.A., M.S.; Deputy Executive Director, Library and Information Technology Association, American Library Association. **[Library]**

CASEY, MIKE, B.S., M.A.; Assistant Editor, *Kansas City Star.* **[Automobile]**

DE LA ROSA, JEFF, B.A.; Subject Editor, *The World Book Encyclopedia.* **[Literature, World,** Special Report: **The Power of the Ring Draws Another Generation]**

DEEB, MARIUS K., B.A., Ph.D.; Professor, School of Advanced International Studies, Johns Hopkins University. **[Middle East and Middle Eastern country articles; North African country articles]**

DEEB, MARY-JANE, B.A., Ph.D.; Arab World Area Specialist, Library of Congress. **[Middle East** Special Report: **The War in Iraq; Middle East and Middle Eastern country articles; North African country articles]**

DeFRANK, THOMAS M., B.A., M.A.; Washington Bureau Chief, *New York Daily News.* **[Armed forces]**

DILLON, DAVID, B.A., M.A., Ph.D.; architecture and design editor, *The Dallas Morning News.* **[Architecture]**

ELLIS, GAVIN, Editor in Chief, *The New Zealand Herald & Weekend Herald.* **[New Zealand]**

FARR, DAVID M. L., D.Phil., LL.D.; Professor Emeritus of History, Carleton University. **[Canada; Canada, Prime Minister of; Canadian provinces; Canadian territories]**

FERRELL, KEITH, free-lance writer. **[Computer; Electronics]**

FISHER, ROBERT W., B.A., M.A.; free-lance writer. **[Labor and employment]**

FITZGERALD, MARK, B.A.; editor at large, *Editor & Publisher* magazine. **[Magazine; Newspaper]**

FOX, THOMAS C., B.A., M.A.; Publisher, *The National Catholic Reporter.* **[Roman Catholic Church]**

FRIEDMAN, EMILY, B.A.; health policy and ethics analyst. **[Health care issues]**

GADOMSKI, FRED, B.S., M.S.; Meteorologist, Pennsylvania State University. **[Weather]**

GATTY, ROBERT C., Executive Editor and Publisher, *Advantage* magazine. **[Food]**

GOLDEN, JONATHAN J., B.A., M.J.Ed.; Chair, History Department at the Gann Academy, New Jewish High School of Great Boston. **[Judaism]**

GOLDNER, NANCY, B.A.; free-lance dance critic. **[Dance]**

GOLDSMITH, DONALD W., B.A., PH.D., author and free-lance writer. **[Astronomy** Special Report: **Space Telescopes: Seeing the Universe in a Different Light]**

HARAKAS, STANLEY SAMUEL, B.A., B.Th., Th.D.; Archbishop Iakovos Professor (Emeritus) of Orthodox Theology, Holy Cross Greek Orthodox School of Theology. **[Eastern Orthodox Churches]**

HAVERSTOCK, NATHAN A., A.B.; affiliate scholar, Oberlin College. **[Latin America and Latin American country articles]**

HENDERSON, HAROLD, B.A.; staff writer, *Chicago Reader.* **[Chicago]**

HOFFMAN, ANDREW J., B.S., M.S., Ph.D.; Associate Professor of Organizational Behavior, Boston University. **[Environmental pollution]**

JOHANSON, DONALD C., B.S., M.A., Ph.D.; Director and Professor, Institute of Human Origins, Arizona State University. **[Anthropology]**

JOHNSON, CHRISTINA S., B.A., M.S.; free-lance science writer. **[Ocean]**

KATES, MICHAEL, B.S.J.; Associate Sports Editor, *Chicago Tribune.* **[Sports articles]**

KENNEDY, BRIAN, M.A.; free-lance writer. [Australia; Australia, Prime Minister of; Australian rules football]

KILGORE, MARGARET, B.A., M.B.A.; free-lance writer, Kilgore and Associates. [Los Angeles]

KING, MIKE, reporter, The (Montreal) Gazette. [Montreal]

KLINTBERG, PATRICIA PEAK, B.A.; Director of Constituent Affairs, Office of Communications, U.S. Department of Agriculture. [Agriculture]

KRONHOLZ, JUNE, B.S.J.; staff reporter, The Wall Street Journal. [Education Special Report: No Child Left Behind; Education]

LAWRENCE, ALBERT, B.A., M.A., M.Ed.; Executive Director, World Chess Hall of Fame. [Chess]

LEWIS, DAVID C., M.D.; Professor of Medicine and Community Health, Brown University. [Drug abuse]

LIEBENSON, DONALD, B.A.; free-lance writer. [Deaths Special Report: Bob Hope; Popular music; Television]

LYE, KEITH, B.A., F.R.G.S.; free-lance writer and editor. [Cricket]

MARCH, ROBERT H., A.B., M.S., Ph.D.; Professor Emeritus of Physics and Liberal studies, University of Wisconsin at Madison. [Physics]

MARSCHALL, LAURENCE A., B.S., Ph.D.; W.K.T. Sahm Professor of Physics, Gettysburg College. [Astronomy Special Report: Space Telescopes; Astronomy]

MARTY, MARTIN E., Ph.D.; Fairfax M. Cone Distinguished Service Professor Emeritus, University of Chicago. [Protestantism]

MAUGH, THOMAS H., II, Ph.D.; science/medical writer, Los Angeles Times. [Biology]

MAY, SALLY RUTH, B.A, M.A.; free-lance art writer. [Art]

McWILLIAM, ROHAN, B.A., M.A., D.Phil; Senior Lecturer in History, Anglia Polytechnic University, Cambridge, U.K. [Ireland; Northern Ireland; United Kingdom; United Kingdom, Prime Minister of]

MINER, TODD J., B.S., M.S.; Meteorologist, Pennsylvania State University. [Weather]

MORITZ, OWEN, B.A.; urban affairs editor, New York Daily News. [New York City]

MORRIS, BERNADINE, B.A., M.A.; free-lance fashion writer. [Fashion]

MULLINS, HENRY T., B.S., M.S., Ph.D.; Professor of Geology, Syracuse University. [Geology]

NGUYEN, J. TUYET, M.A.; United Nations correspondent, Deutsche Presse-Agentur. [Population; United Nations]

OGAN, EUGENE, B.A., Ph.D.; Professor Emeritus of Anthropology, University of Minnesota. [Pacific Islands]

PAETH, GREGORY, B.A.; business writer, The Cincinnati Post. [Radio]

REINHART, A. KEVIN, B.A., M.A., Ph.D.; Associate Professor of Religious Studies, Dartmouth College. [Islam]

RICCIUTI, EDWARD, B.A.; free-lance writer. [Conservation; Zoos]

ROSE, MARK J., B.A., M.A., Ph.D.; Executive Editor, Archaeology magazine. [Archaeology]

RUBENSTEIN, RICHARD E., B.A., M.A., J.D.; Professor of Conflict Resolution and Public Affairs, George Mason University. [Terrorism]

SARNA, JONATHAN D., Ph.D.; Joseph H. & Belle R. Braun Professor of American Jewish History, Brandeis University. [Judaism]

SAVAGE, IAN, B.A., Ph.D.; Assistant Professor of Economics and Transportation, Northwestern University. [Aviation; Transportation]

SHAPIRO, HOWARD, B.S.; staff writer and travel columnist, The Philadelphia Inquirer. [Philadelphia; Washington, D.C.]

SOLNICK, STEVEN L., B.A., M.A., Ph.D.; Moscow representative, The Ford Foundation. [Russia and other former Soviet republic articles]

STEIN, DAVID LEWIS, B.A., M.S.; former urban affairs columnist, The Toronto Star. [Toronto]

STOCKER, CAROL M., B.A.; reporter, The Boston Globe. [Gardening]

STUART, ELAINE, B.A.; free-lance public policy writer and editor. [State government]

TANNER, JAMES C., B.J.; former news editor—energy, The Wall Street Journal. [Energy supply]

TATUM, HENRY K., B.A.; Associate Editor, The Dallas Morning News. [Dallas]

THOMAS, PAULETTE, B.A.; free-lance writer. [Bank]

VAN, JON, B.A., M.A.; technology writer, Chicago Tribune. [Telecommunications]

von RHEIN, JOHN, B.A.; classical music critic, Chicago Tribune. [Classical music]

WILSON, DAVE, B.A.; Producer, Cable News Network. [Internet]

WOLCHIK, SHARON L., B.A., M.A., Ph.D.; Professor of Political Science and International Affairs, George Washington University. [Eastern European country articles]

WRIGHT, ANDREW G., B.A.; Managing Senior Editor, Engineering News-Record magazine. [Building and construction]

WUNTCH, PHILIP, B.A.; film critic, The Dallas Morning News. [Motion pictures Special Report: Katharine Hepburn; Motion pictures]

YEZZI, DAVID, B.F.A., M.F.A.; Director, Unterbeerg Poetry Center. [Theater]

CONTENTS

From a United States-led campaign to expel Saddam Hussein from Iraq to the launch of China's first manned spacecraft, 2003 was a year of extraordinary events. On these three pages are stories the editors picked as some of the most important of the year, along with details on where to find more information about them in this volume.

The Editors

2003

THE WAR IN IRAQ

United States President George W. Bush orders U.S. armed services deployed in Kuwait and the Persian Gulf to launch an attack on Iraq on March 20 (March 19 in the United States). Baghdad falls to coalition forces on April 9, and on May 1, President Bush declares that major combat operations in Iraq have ended. See **Armed forces,** page 54; **Iraq: A Special Report,** page 221; **United States, Government of the,** page 398; **United States, President of the,** page 408.

SARS OUTBREAK

The outbreak and rapid spread throughout Southeast Asia and into North America of severe acute respiratory syndrome (SARS) forces the World Health Organization to issue a rare world-wide health alert in March. See **Asia,** page 58; **Aviation,** page 87; **China,** page 120; **Public health and safety,** page 325; **Taiwan,** page 372; **Toronto,** page 384.

CHINA PUTS MAN IN SPACE

China launches its first manned spacecraft on October 15, becoming the third nation, after Russia and the United States, to put a human being into space. See **Space exploration,** page 353.

MASSIVE ELECTRICAL BLACKOUT

A massive electrical blackout in the northeastern United States and southeastern Canada in August leaves 50 million people—including residents of New York City, Detroit, and Toronto—without power. See **Energy supply,** page 184; **New York City,** page 291; **Toronto,** page 384.

WILDFIRES IN CALIFORNIA

Wildfires in California in September and October burn across 750,000 acres (306,000 hectares) and destroy more than 3,500 structures. See **Los Angeles,** page 272; **Weather,** page 411.

NEW EU MEMBERS

Ten Eastern European nations—Czech Republic, Cyprus, Estonia, Hungary, Latvia, Lithuania, Malta, Poland, Slovakia, and Slovenia—sign treaties in April to join the European Union (EU) in 2004. The EU is an organization of European countries that promotes cooperation among member nations. See **Europe,** page 187.

HOSTILITIES CONTINUE IN IRAQ

United States soldiers are killed on a nearly daily basis from May through December in a guerrilla war in Iraq in which civilians, both Iraqi and foreign, are also targets. See **Armed forces,** page 54; **Iraq: A Special Report,** page 221; **United States, Government of the,** page 398; **United States, President of the,** page 408.

9

SPACE SHUTTLE DISASTER

The space shuttle Columbia disintegrates as it re-enters Earth's atmosphere on February 1, killing all seven astronauts on board and sending debris over several states. See **Space exploration**, page 353.

CALIFORNIA GOVERNOR

California voters recall Democratic Governor Gray Davis and replace him with film star Arnold Schwarzenegger, a Republican, in a special election in October. See **Elections,** page 182; **State government,** page 361.

EUROPEAN HEAT WAVE

A prolonged summer heat wave in Europe results in the deaths of some 20,000 people, primarily the elderly. See **Europe,** page 187; **France,** page 198; **Weather,** page 411.

COURT DECISION

The U.S. Supreme Court strikes down a Texas law on June 26 that made sexual acts between people of the same sex a crime. Legal experts describe the decision as having profound legal and political implications, including invalidating laws in 13 Western and Southern states that criminalized sexual acts that do not result in *procreation* (reproduction). See **Supreme Court of the United States,** page 366.

2003

YEAR IN BRIEF

A month-by-month listing of the most significant world events that occurred during 2003.

JANUARY 2003

1 Luiz Inacio Lula da Silva is inaugurated president of Brazil in the capital, Brasilia. Lula da Silva, the leader of the Workers Party, is Brazil's first president to come from the working class and the first candidate representing a left-wing party to win a presidential vote.

5 President Valdas Adamkus of Lithuania is defeated in a runoff election against Rolandas Paksas, a former prime minister and mayor of the capital, Vilnius. Paksas ran a populist campaign in which he promised to renegotiate the terms of Lithuania's membership in the European Union, particularly rules that would result in cutting subsidies to Lithuania's agricultural sector.

6 Several thousand members of the U.S. Army's 3rd Infantry Division (Mechanized) leave the United States for the Middle East in preparation for possible war against Iraq. Military experts estimate that approximately 50,000 U.S. troops are already in the Middle East, with another 50,000 soldiers either on the way or preparing for transport. An additional 20,000 British troops are preparing to join U.S. forces in the Middle East by late February or early March, according to defense analysts.

7 U.S. President George W. Bush proposes a new round of tax cuts designed to stimulate the sluggish U.S. economy. The plan includes, among other provisions, cuts of personal tax rates for 2003—particularly for married couples and for people at upper income levels—and provides a $400-per-child rebate to many U.S. families.

8 U.S. President George W. Bush signs into law legislation extending unemployment benefits for about 2.5 million U.S. citizens. The bill, passed on January 7, is the first enacted by the new Republican-controlled Congress.

9 Bank employees in Venezuela begin a two-day strike, shutting down all banking services in the country and sending the bolivar, the Venezuelan currency, tumbling on international markets. The strike is a show of solidarity with a nationwide strike launched as an economic offensive against the government of President Hugo Chavez.

10 The government of North Korea, citing provocations by the United States, pulls out of the nuclear non-proliferation treaty, an international agreement among 187 nations that attempts to prevent the spread of nuclear weapons. North Korea is the first country to withdraw since the treaty went into effect in 1970.

14 At least 70,000 Turkish Cypriots take to the streets of Nicosia, the capital, to demonstrate in favor of accepting a United Nations plan to reunite Cyprus before its entry into the European Union in 2004. Cyprus has been divided into two republics since Turkish forces invaded in 1974 and occupied the island's northern half.

17 Saddam Hussein, addressing the Iraqi nation in a television address, calls on his people to defend their country against an attack led by the United States, which he refers to as the "Mongols of this age." He also asks the Arab world to "mobilize and defeat the enemy at the gates of Baghdad."

18 Four people are killed and about 500 houses destroyed when strong winds fan fires burning out of control in forests south of Canberra, Australia, into suburban areas around the capital, triggering what authorities described as the worst fire emergency in the city's history. Dozens of other brush fires are also burning out of control in the Snowy Mountains southwest of Canberra, in the state of Victoria, and in areas north of Sydney.

21 Hispanics have surpassed African Americans as the largest minority group in the United States, announce officials with the U.S. Census Bureau. Hispanics in July 2001 comprised nearly 13 percent of the U.S. population of 284.8 million people.

22 The U.S. Senate confirms Tom Ridge as the first secretary of the U.S. Department of Homeland Security, which is responsible for preventing terrorist attacks within the United States. The new department formally opens for business on January 24.

23 The first of some 2,000 Australian troops and defense personnel sail from Australia for the Persian Gulf to join U.S. and British forces assembling for a possible war with Iraq.

Members of the U.S. Army's 3rd Infantry Division depart Hunter Army Airfield in Savannah, Georgia, on January 6 as part of a mass deployment of troops to the Middle East.

25 An extremely fast-growing, viruslike computer worm—a program that makes copies of itself—infects nearly 40,000 corporate computers, disrupting hundreds of thousands of computer systems around the globe and overwhelming Internet data pipelines.

President Laurent Gbagbo of Cote d'Ivoire accepts a peace plan to end his country's civil war, which began with a failed *coup* (overthrow) in September 2002. The plan includes the appointment of a new prime minister, former Prime Minister Seydou Diarra, with whom Gbagbo is to share power in a coalition government.

26 The Tampa Bay Buccaneers win the National Football League's Super Bowl XXXVII in San Diego in a 48-21 victory over the Oakland Raiders.

Serena Williams wins her fourth consecutive Grand Slam singles championship, becoming only the fifth woman in tennis history to hold all four Grand Slam titles at once.

27 Chief United Nations (UN) weapons inspector Hans Blix informs the UN Security Council that Iraq is resisting international efforts to ensure that it disarms itself of weapons of mass destruction. Blix concludes, however, that UN weapons inspectors should have more time to complete their work.

28 Israel's conservative Likud Party crushes the rival Labor Party in parliamentary elections. Political experts suggest that Israeli voters believe that Likud's hard-line prime minister, Ariel Sharon, is the most dependable leader in Israel's bitter conflict with the Palestinians.

30 Richard C. Reid, a member of the al-Qa'ida terrorist network who attempted in December 2001 to blow up a trans-Atlantic flight with explosives concealed in his shoes, is sentenced to life in prison by Federal District Court Judge William G. Young.

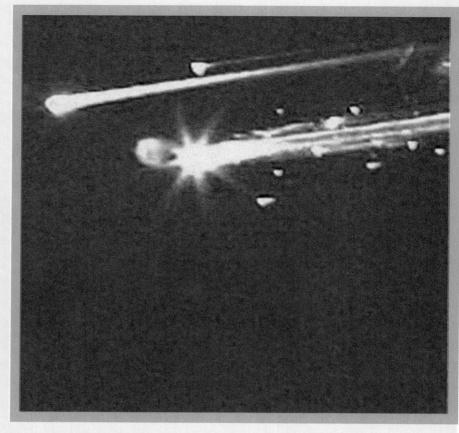

Debris from the space shuttle Columbia streaks across the sky above Tyler, Texas, on February 1. All seven astronauts aboard the shuttle were killed.

1 The space shuttle Columbia explodes above east Texas, killing all seven astronauts aboard. The Columbia was only 16 minutes away from completing a science mission that began on January 16.

2 Vaclav Havel steps down as president after leading first Czechoslovakia and then the Czech Republic for nearly 13 years.

3 U.S. President George W. Bush proposes a $2.23-trillion budget for 2004 with a 4.2-percent increase in military spending and $1.3 trillion in new or accelerated tax cuts over the next 10 years. The budget projects a deficit for 2004 of $307.4 billion.

4 Lawmakers in the Serbian capital of Belgrade dissolve the nation of Yugoslavia in favor of a loose union to be known as Serbia and Montenegro. The accord, brokered by the European Union, gives near total sovereignty to the two republics, which remain linked by joint defense and foreign affairs administrations.

5 U.S. Secretary of State Colin Powell delivers a speech before the United Nations Security Council in which he unveils top-secret U.S. intelligence that he claims provides "irrefutable and undeniable" proof of Iraqi defiance of UN disarmament resolutions. Powell challenges the Security Council to respond.

The government of North Korea announces that it has restarted its nuclear facilities, confirming what U.S. intelligence agents had concluded after observing satellite images.

10 U.S. citizens should stock plastic sheeting and duct tape to seal windows and doors in case of a chemical, biological, or radiological terrorist attack, announce officials with the U.S. Department of Homeland Security. The department also recommends that people keep three days' worth of bottled water and canned food on hand as well as scissors, a manual can opener, blankets, flashlights, radios, and spare batteries.

11 An Arab television network airs a tape purportedly made by Osama bin Laden in which the head of the al-Qa'ida terrorist network calls on all Muslims to come to the aid of Iraq in the current crisis with the United States. Bin Laden urges Muslims to launch suicide attacks against Western targets should the United States initiate a war against Iraq.

12 The International Atomic Energy Agency, the United Nations' (UN) Vienna-based nuclear watchdog agency, informs the UN Security Council that North Korea is in violation of its promise not to pursue atomic weapons.

13 Enron Corp., the failed Houston-based energy trading company, paid no income tax from 1996 through 1999, reveals a joint Congressional committee report on taxation.

14 The cloned sheep Dolly is put to death because of premature aging and disease that marred her short life, announces a spokesperson for the Roslin Institute, the Scottish laboratory where she was created in 1996.

17 A brawl in an overcrowded second-story nightclub in Chicago sets off a deadly stampede toward the club's single exit fronting on the street. Pepper spray used by security guards to break up a fight at the E2 club in Chicago's South Loop triggered panic in a crowd of some 1,100 people. A pile-up halfway down a steep and narrow stairwell leaves 21 people dead and more than 50 others injured. Authorities claim the club, which city inspectors had cited for numerous code violations, was operating illegally.

18 French President Jacques Chirac publicly warns the countries of Central and Eastern Europe to keep their opinions regarding a possible U.S.-led war on Iraq to themselves or risk losing their chance to join the European Union.

20 Nearly 2,000 U.S. Army and Marine troops are to be sent to the Philippines to assist in putting down an insurgency by the Islamic extremist group Abu Sayyaf, announces the U.S. Department of Defense.

Ninety-eight people are killed and at least 200 others are injured when a fire ignited by a pyrotechnic display during a rock concert sweeps through an overcrowded nightclub in West Warwick, near Providence, Rhode Island.

21 The United Nations (UN) delivers an ultimatum that Iraq's arsenal of missiles exceeding a specified range must be destroyed by March 1. Chief UN weapons inspector Hans Blix notes that if Iraqi President Saddam Hussein refuses to comply, Blix will declare Iraq in "material breach" of a UN resolution that it disarm itself of all weapons of mass destruction.

24 The United States submits a proposal to the United Nations Security Council asking for a resolution authorizing war against Iraq on the grounds that Iraq has failed to disarm itself of weapons of mass destruction.

British Prime Minister Tony Blair announces plans to combat global warming by cutting carbon dioxide emissions in the United Kingdom (U.K.) by 60 percent over the next 50 years. The prime minister criticizes the government of the United States, the U.K.'s chief ally, for backing out of the Kyoto Protocol of 1997, a treaty designed to minimize carbon dioxide emissions around the world.

26 North Korea has reactivated a nuclear reactor, announce officials with the administration of U.S. President George W. Bush.

The price of crude oil on world markets climbs to its highest level since Iraq invaded Kuwait in 1990. On the New York Mercantile exchange, the price of a barrel of oil hits $37.70. Analysts connect the spike in oil prices to a U.S. Energy Department report showing a sharp decline in U.S. inventories of oil and refined petroleum products.

27 Israeli Prime Minister Ariel Sharon presents the members of his new, right-wing coalition government to the Knesset and declares that the government's chief aim is economic recovery. He informs the Knesset that he will not enter into peace negotiations with the Palestinian Authority until all violence is halted and Yasir Arafat is replaced as its leader.

28 Vaclav Klaus, a former prime minister of the Czech Republic, is elected the country's president.

MARCH

2003

1 The Turkish parliament rejects a measure allowing U.S. troops to use the country as a base from which to launch operations in a northern front in a possible war with Iraq. Officials at the U.S. Department of Defense, confident that the Turkish parliament would pass the measure, had shipped military equipment to Turkish ports.

4 U.S. President George W. Bush proposes comprehensive prescription drug coverage for elderly Americans, but only if they switch from Medicare to private insurance plans, which would receive government subsidies.

5 A mysterious respiratory ailment that has caused at least five deaths in Canada and several Asian countries is declared a "worldwide health threat" by the World Health Organization (WHO), an agency of the United Nations. WHO officials characterize the hard-to-treat ailment as an atypical pneumonia, which they believe first appeared in Guangzhou, China, in November 2002 and was spread by international air travel. The ailment has been named severe acute respiratory syndrome, or SARS.

7 Members of Actors' Equity in New York City refuse to cross the picket line of striking members of Musicians Local 802, shutting down all Broadway musicals for the first time in 43 years. Performers claim to be incensed by attempts by Broadway producers to replace live orchestras with "virtual orchestras," computer-generated accompaniments that require no musicians.

10 United Nations (UN) Secretary General Kofi Annan warns U.S. President George W. Bush that the United States will be in violation of the UN charter if it carries out its threat to invade Iraq without the backing of the world body.

The Palestinian parliament grants responsibility for the day-to-day running of the Palestinian Authority to the newly created position of prime minister. The legislation gives Palestinian leader Yasir Arafat the right to nominate or remove the prime minister from office.

11 A permanent world court, called the International Criminal Court, opens in The Hague, Netherlands, to try individuals for such offenses as genocide and crimes against humanity.

12 The prime minister of Serbia, Zoran Djindjic, who in 2000 spearheaded the revolt against former President Slobodan Milosevic, is assassinated in the capital, Belgrade. Experts on Serbian politics suggest that the murder was carried out by Serbia's criminal underworld and Milosevic loyalists.

14 U.S. President George W. Bush announces that he intends to adopt a peace plan for the creation of a Palestinian nation as soon as a new Palestinian prime minister is chosen. The plan calls on the Palestinians to curb terrorism and on Israel to withdraw forces from Palestinian areas, ease restrictions on the movement of Palestinian people, and stop further Israeli settlements in the West Bank and Gaza.

15 Hu Jintao formally takes office in Beijing, China's capital, as head of the Communist Party and, therefore, head of the government. He succeeds Jiang Zemin, who remains in control of China's enormous army.

16 The leaders of the United States, the United Kingdom, and Spain issue an ultimatum to the United Nations (UN) Security Council, declaring that diplomatic efforts to disarm Iraq will end on March 17. President George W. Bush and Prime Ministers Tony Blair and Jose Maria Aznar give the Security Council 24 hours to pass a resolution approving a combined military action to depose Iraqi President Saddam Hussein.

18 United Nations (UN) weapons inspectors leave Iraq ahead of a possible U.S.-led attack. UN Secretary General Kofi Annan on March 17 ordered all UN employees to leave Iraq.

Serbia's parliament approves the nomination of Zoran Zivkovic, a loyal ally of former Prime Minister Zoran Djindjic, as prime minister.

19 U.S. President George W. Bush orders U.S. armed services deployed in Kuwait and the Persian Gulf to launch an attack on Iraq (March 20 in Iraq). More than 250,000 U.S. troops are joined by some 50,000 British soldiers and Marines. President Bush announces his decision to go to war minutes after U.S. Tomahawk missiles

United States Marines take cover during a battle on March 23 in the southern Iraq city of An Nasiriyah. More than 250,000 U.S. troops and 50,000 British soldiers and Marines launched an attack on Iraq on March 19 (March 20 in Iraq) to remove Iraqi President Saddam Hussein from power.

and bombs from Stealth bombers strike Baghdad, the Iraqi capital.

21 Stocks soar on U.S. markets, sending the Dow Jones industrial average on 30 stocks traded on the New York Exchange up 8.4 percent for the week, its best weekly performance in more than 20 years. Standard & Poor's index of stock prices for 500 companies traded on the New York Stock Exchange jumps 7.5 percent, its best weekly performance since the rebound after the terrorist attacks on the United States in September 2001.

24 Russian officials in Chechnya announce that Chechen voters approved a March 23 referendum on a new constitution that keeps the republic within the Russian federation. Human rights organizations question the legitimacy of the vote.

The price of crude oil jumps on world markets, climbing by $1.74 to $26.09 a barrel in London trading. Market analysts suggested the price hike was triggered, in part, by fears that the war in Iraq may take longer than anticipated.

25 A coalition of Democrats and moderate Republicans in the U.S. Senate slices out half of the $700 billion tax cut proposed by President George W. Bush, an action that political experts describe as a major blow for the president.

27 U.S. forces in Iraq open a second front, in the north.

31 A ban on smoking in all New York City restaurants and bars goes into effect. The ban, which was created to protect the health of employees from secondhand smoke, extends to the city's many private clubs.

Iraqis pull down a statue of former Iraqi President Saddam Hussein following the fall of Baghdad on April 9.

1 British forces in southern Iraq come under Iraqi missile attack for the first time since the war began on March 19. The attacks at Umm Qasr are made as British forces attempt to consolidate their positions in the south.

2 At least 21 people are killed when a bomb explodes outside a ferry terminal in Davao City on the island of Mindanao in the southern Philippines. Terrorism experts attribute the explosion to the Jemaah Islamiyah, an Islamic militant group believed to have ties to the al-Qa'ida terrorist network.

3 Afghan troops, backed by U.S. special forces, arrest 13 men suspected of being members of the al-Qa'ida terrorist network.

4 The U.S. economy lost 108,000 jobs in March, announces the U.S. Department of Labor. Employment in the United States has declined by more than 2 million jobs since the first quarter of 2001.

5 United Nations (UN) military observers in Congo (Kinshasa) verify that nearly 1,000 civilians were killed on April 3 in attacks on 15 villages in the northeastern part of the country. The

UN officials have yet to determine who carried out the attacks.

6 The number of people in state and federal jails and prisons in the United States topped 2 million in 2002, announces a spokesperson for the U.S. Department of Justice.

7 The Syracuse University Orangemen capture the team's first NCAA men's basketball championship, beating the Kansas Jayhawks 81–78 in New Orleans.

8 The University of Connecticut (UConn) women's basketball team beats the University of Tennessee 73–68 to claim UConn's fourth NCAA championship at the 2003 finals in Atlanta.

9 The government of Iraqi President Saddam Hussein collapses, and much of Baghdad, the capital, falls to U.S. forces. Allied tanks and armored vehicles meet no resistance as they sweep across the Tigris River into Baghdad's eastern sector. U.S. soldiers are greeted by cheering crowds of Iraqis attempting to topple an enormous statue of Saddam Hussein that dominates one of the city's public squares. In Baghdad's heavily populated southeastern neighborhoods, throngs of Shiite Muslims, long oppressed by the Hussein regime, cheer U.S. Marines as they push toward the center of the city. U.S. Brigadier General Vincent Brooks, speaking at a press briefing in Qatar, announces that Baghdad had been added to the list of places no longer under the control of Hussein's government.

10 Air France and British Airways announce the retirement of trans-Atlantic flights aboard the supersonic Concorde, which flew from London to New York City in 3.5 hours at a cost of $7,000 per passenger.

11 The mystery virus that killed more than 100 people worldwide since it emerged in China in November 2002 appears to be a mutant cold virus, announces an international team of scientists.

14 The pro-Canada Liberal Party wins a majority in Quebec's provincial assembly, taking 76 seats, compared with the former majority party, Parti Quebecois, which takes 45 seats. During its nine years in power, Parti Quebecois campaigned for Quebec's independence from Canada.

16 European leaders gather in Athens, Greece, where 10 nations sign treaties to join the European Union (EU). The expansion—the largest in EU history—will add 75 million people to the EU and increase EU territory by 23 percent.

17 Documents filed with the Securities and Exchange Commission reveal that top executives at AMR Corp., parent company of Dallas-based American Airlines, fashioned financial packages for themselves that were designed to protect them in the event of the airline's bankruptcy. The top six executives planned to give themselves "retention bonuses" of twice their annual salaries as a reward for staying with the company through 2004. They also funded a trust that protects the pension benefits of the top 45 executives. The revelation comes one day after American Airlines' flight attendants and other union employees agreed to wage cuts to stave off the company's bankruptcy.

18 A spokesperson for North Korea announces that his government either is about to begin, or has begun, reprocessing more than 8,000 spent nuclear fuel rods, a significant step toward producing nuclear weapons.

The March 2003 federal budget deficit hit $58.7 billion, announces the U.S. Treasury Department. The March figure brings the deficit for the first six months of fiscal year 2003 (September 2002–October 2003) to $252.6 billion, nearly twice the total for the same period one year earlier.

19 Olusegun Obasanjo is reelected president of Nigeria with 62 percent of the 42 million votes cast. His opponents allege massive vote fraud.

22 At least 1 million Shiite Muslims throng the streets of Karbala, in central Iraq, for a religious pilgrimage that former Iraqi President Saddam Hussein had banned for some 25 years.

28 Ten of the largest U.S. securities firms agree to pay approximately $1.4 billion in fines to end federal and state investigations into whether the companies gave customers misleading stock recommendations during the boom of the late 1990's.

29 The Palestinian parliament confirms Mahmoud Abbas as prime minister, clearing the way for a U.S.-backed Mideast peace plan to end Israeli-Palestinian violence.

30 A diplomatic coalition made up of the United States, Russia, the European Union, and the United Nations presents a detailed peace plan to leaders of Israel and the Palestinian Authority. The seven-page document, known as the road map, is designed to end more than 30 months of Israeli-Palestinian violence and restart peace negotiations.

1 U.S. President George W. Bush declares that the military phase of the war in Iraq is at an end. He describes the victory as a single battle in "a war on terror that began on September 11, 2001," the day militant Islamic terrorists attacked the United States. Speaking before a large group of sailors aboard the aircraft carrier U.S.S. *Abraham Lincoln,* the president brands former Iraqi leader Saddam Hussein an ally of leaders of the al-Qa'ida terrorist network, and the president vows to keep weapons of mass destruction out of the hands of terrorists.

Mechanical problems aboard a conventionally powered Chinese submarine off China's coast east of the Neichangshan islands resulted in the deaths on April 16 of all 70 officers and seamen, report military officials in Beijing, the capital. They describe the incident as the worst naval accident in modern Chinese history.

3 President Bashar al-Assad of Syria begins closing down the headquarters of militant Palestinian groups in Damascus as a first step in fostering a new Mideast peace process.

Funny Cide pulls ahead of two far better known and highly regarded horses, Empire Maker and Peace Rules, to win the 129th running of the Kentucky Derby by 1 ¾ lengths in a stunning upset. Funny Cide, a 12.8-1 long shot, is the first gelding to win the Derby since 1929 and the first New York State-bred horse to ever win the race.

6 U.S. President George W. Bush announces the appointment of L. Paul Bremer III as the president's special envoy to Iraq. Bremer, a retired diplomat and an expert on counter-terrorism, is to take charge of rebuilding the Iraqi government and infrastructure.

7 The estimated overall death rate from severe acute respiratory syndrome (SARS) is approximately 15 percent, announce officials with the World Health Organization (WHO), an agency of the United Nations. Earlier WHO estimates of the overall death rate were as low as 2 percent.

11 Lithuanians overwhelmingly vote in favor of joining the European Union (EU). More than 90 percent of voters approve the referendum, making Lithuania the first former Soviet republic to move toward EU membership.

12 Suicide bombers attack Western targets in Saudi Arabia's capital, Riyadh. Groups of terrorists shoot their way into three residential compounds and detonate car bombs that kill 25 people, not including the 9 people believed to be the suicide bombers. The bombings occur only two weeks after the United States announced it was withdrawing its troops from Saudi Arabia.

The U.S. National Weather Service reports that more than 412 tornadoes have been reported across the Midwest since the beginning of May, a record number.

13 U.S. military personnel in Iraq have been authorized to shoot to kill looters on sight, announce U.S. officials in Baghdad, the capital.

The U.S. trade deficit widened to $43.46 billion in March, the second largest deficit in history, announce officials with the U.S. Department of Commerce.

15 Industrial fishing fleets have stripped the world's oceans of as much as 90 percent of all big fish, including the giant tuna, swordfish, and marlin, announce biologists at Dalhousie University in Halifax, Nova Scotia.

17 Funny Cide, winner of the 2003 Kentucky Derby, wins the Preakness Stakes, the second leg of the Triple Crown, at Pimlico race track in Baltimore. Ridden by jockey Jose Santos, the New York-bred gelding completes the 1.53-mile (2.4-kilometer) course in 1 minute and 55.6 seconds.

18 Israeli Prime Minister Ariel Sharon shuts down the Middle East peace plan after a series of Palestinian suicide bombings are carried out in a single 12-hour period.

19 U.S. President George W. Bush reconfirms his commitment to send U.S. troops to the Philippines to help the Philippine government root out Muslim militants. Speaking at a joint White House press conference with Philippine President Gloria Macapagal-Arroyo, President Bush publicly acknowledges Macapagal-Arroyo's commitment to crushing international terrorism.

A young woman surveys what remains of her grandparents' house in East Pekin, Illinois, after powerful tornadoes ripped through the community on May 10 and May 12. The U.S. Weather Service reported that a record number of tornadoes had been reported across the Midwest since the beginning of May.

21 Officials with the U.S. Department of Agriculture order a temporary ban on the importation of cattle and animal feed from Canada in response to an announcement by the Canadian government that a cow had tested positive for mad cow disease in the province of Alberta.

22 Fourteen of the 15 members of the United Nations (UN) Security Council vote to lift economic sanctions against Iraq and give UN backing to a U.S.-led administration there. Representatives from Syria boycott the meeting.

25 Nestor Kirchner is sworn in as Argentina's 49th president, the 6th in less than two years.

27 The use of hormone therapy by women over the age of 65 appears to double the risk of Alzheimer's disease and other forms of dementia, announces Marilyn Albert, a professor of neurology at Johns Hopkins University in Baltimore.

28 Officials with the U.S. Fish and Wildlife Service announce that the agency will temporarily stop designating critical habitats under the Endangered Species Act because there is no money to fund the program in fiscal 2003.

30 Scientists at the University of Idaho and Utah State University report that they have cloned a mule.

31 Suspected serial bomber Eric Rudolph is captured in western North Carolina after eluding arrest for more than five years. Authorities believe that he hid out in the Great Smoky Mountains.

JUNE

2003

A U.S. soldier from the U.S. Army's 1st Armored Division keeps a wary eye during a raid in Baghdad, the Iraqi capital, on June 29. The raid was an effort to halt increasingly frequent guerrilla attacks on coalition forces.

1 China's vast, new Three Gorges Dam, scheduled to be completed in 2009, halts the flow of the Yangtze River, creating what will become the world's largest reservoir. The $24-billion dam is being constructed to provide clean electrical energy and to control flooding, which has wreaked havoc in central China for centuries.

2 The Federal Communications Commission votes 3 to 2 to eliminate long-standing rules regarding the number of media outlets a single corporation can own in a region. Media experts describe the deregulations as far-reaching and suggest that they will encourage further consolidation of the communications industry, limiting competition and the expression of diverse public opinion.

Queen Elizabeth II of the United Kingdom celebrates the 50th anniversary of her coronation with a service at Westminster Abbey in London.

3 Arab leaders pledge to stop support for terrorist organizations in the Middle East, announces Egyptian President Hosni Mubarak at a summit in the Egyptian resort of Sharm el-Sheikh.

4 Israeli Prime Minister Ariel Sharon announces at the conclusion of an Israeli-Palestinian summit that Israel endorses the U.S.-backed peace plan for the Middle East and will immediately begin to remove unauthorized Israeli settlement outposts in the West Bank and Gaza Strip.

A federal grand jury in New York City indicts lifestyle expert Martha Stewart on charges that she committed securities fraud, lied to federal investigators, and obstructed justice. Stewart denies any wrongdoing.

5 U.S. Attorney General John Ashcroft, testifying before the House Judiciary Committee, defends the record of the U.S. Department of Justice in the wake of the terrorist attacks on the United States in 2001. Ashcroft "makes no apologies" for keeping 762 illegal immigrants in custody for several months before releasing them for lack of evidence.

The executive editor and managing editor of *The New York Times* resign in the wake of a scandal involving journalistic fraud at the newspaper.

7 Empire Maker wins the 135th running of the Belmont Stakes, ruining Funny Cide's bid for a Triple Crown victory.

9 The United Kingdom is not ready to adopt the euro, the currency of the European Union, announces the chancellor of the exchequer, Gordon Brown. Brown tells the House of Commons that the euro has not yet passed four key economic tests set by the government of Prime Minister Tony Blair to make sure its adoption was "in the British national economic interest."

The leader of Zimbabwe's opposition movement, Morgan Tsvangirai, is charged with treason and remanded into custody without bail. The charges of treason are based on accusations that he attempted to oust Zimbabwe President Robert Mugabe by leading a general strike on June 2.

The New Jersey Devils regain the Stanley Cup for a third time in nine seasons by beating the Anaheim Mighty Ducks 3 to 0 in Game 7 of the National Hockey League championship.

11 Three fossilized skulls—two adults and a child—recently found in Ethiopia are among the most important discoveries ever made in the search for the origin of humans, announces paleoanthropologist Tim White of the University of California at Berkeley. White, who co-led the U.S.-Ethiopian research team that made the discovery, notes that the skulls, which are between 160,000 and 154,000 years old, are the oldest known fossils of modern humans, or *Homo sapiens.*

15 Jim Furyk wins the U.S. Open golf tournament at the Olympia Fields Country Club in Olympia Fields, Illinois, by tying the Open's scoring record of 272 strokes. The victory is Furyk's first major championship.

The San Antonio Spurs win the 2003 National Basketball Association championship by beating the New Jersey Nets 88-77 in Game 6 of the finals.

17 The government of Canada will redefine marriage to recognize same-sex matrimony, announces Canadian Prime Minister Jean Chretien.

21 Fire officials estimate that at least 200 structures have burned since a forest fire broke out on June 17 in the Coronado National Forest on Mount Lemmon near Tucson, Arizona.

22 A record-breaking 10.15 inches (26 centimeters) of rain has fallen at the U.S. Weather Bureau station in New York City's Central Park since the beginning of June, announce meteorologists. No June in New York City has been rainier since record keeping began in 1869.

23 The U.S. Supreme Court, in a 5-to-4 ruling, upholds the admissions policy of the University of Michigan law school, declaring that the applications of minority students may be given an edge over those of non-minority applicants.

25 The Federal Reserve System (the Fed), the central bank of the United States, cuts a key short-term interest rate by a quarter percentage point. The Fed reduces the federal funds rate—the interest rate on overnight loans between banks—from 1.25 percent to 1 percent, the lowest level since 1958.

27 More than 735,000 people register with the Federal Trade Commission in a single day in order to be placed on a national list of people whom telemarketers are not to call.

JULY

2003

3 The Iraqi National Museum, which was looted of certain antiquities in the aftermath of the war in Iraq, reopens with a show featuring the treasures of Nimrud, a collection of gold jewelry and vessels from the Assyrian Empire. Authorities currently believe the museum lost about 12,000 items, mostly pottery shards and individual decorative beads fashioned from semiprecious stones. Only 32 objects of extreme quality remain unaccounted for.

The discovery of a solar system similar to that of Earth is announced by a team of Australian, British, and U.S. astronomers. The leader of the team, Hugh Jones of Liverpool John Moores University in the United Kingdom, states that the solar system is 90 light-years away in the constellation Puppis. He describes it as consisting of a Jupiter-like planet that circles a sunlike star.

5 Serena Williams of the United States takes her second successive Wimbledon women's singles championship by beating sister Venus 4-6, 6-4, 6-2.

6 Roger Federer of Switzerland wins the Wimbledon men's singles championship by beating Mark Philippoussis 7-6 (5), 6-2, 7-6 (3). Martina Navratilova of the United States captures her 20th Wimbledon title by winning the mixed doubles with partner Leander Paes of India.

7 Spokespersons for various Iraqi political groups that opposed the Saddam Hussein regime and supported the U.S.-led war to topple the Iraqi president announce that they will join an interim Iraqi government.

9 U.S. military costs in Iraq are nearly twice the original U.S. Department of Defense estimates. Secretary of Defense Donald Rumsfeld informs the Senate Armed Services Committee that the monthly cost of maintaining the current force level in Iraq is $3.9 billion.

11 George Tenet, director of the Central Intelligence Agency (CIA), accepts full responsibility for claims made by U.S. President George W. Bush, in his State of the Union address in January, that the government of Iraq had attempted to purchase uranium in Africa in order to make nuclear weapons. Political experts note that President Bush used the claim that Saddam Hussein was "reconstituting" his nuclear weapons program as a primary rationale for launching an attack against Iraq in March.

12 U.S. President George W. Bush ends his five-nation tour of Africa with a pledge of $100 million to help the nations of East Africa combat various terrorist groups bent on destabilizing the governments of the region. The president also affirms that the United States will provide greater assistance to end wars in Sudan, Congo (Kinshasa), and Cote d'Ivoire.

13 A group of 25 prominent Iraqis meet in Baghdad and declare themselves Iraq's first interim government since the fall of former President Saddam Hussein. As its first act, the Governing Council abolishes national holidays associated with Hussein's 24-year rule and creates a new national holiday, April 9, to celebrate his downfall.

15 Hurricane Claudette slams into Texas with winds gusting up to 90 miles (145 kilometers) per hour. The hurricane hits land near Port O'Connor, 110 miles (177 kilometers) southwest of Houston.

North Korea has informed the government of the United States that North Korean scientists have produced enough plutonium to start making nuclear bombs, announces a spokesperson for U.S. President George W. Bush. The spokesperson, Scott McClellan, confirms that the Bush administration considers the claim to be of "serious concern."

16 At least 100 people are killed in India when a flash flood sweeps through a laborers' tent village near the resort town of Kulu in the northern state of Himachal Pradesh.

20 Ben Curtis, a relatively unknown U.S. golfer, outdistances Tiger Woods, Davis Love III, and Vijay Singh to win the British Open at Royal St. George's golf club near Sandwich, England.

22 Saddam Hussein's sons, Uday and Qusay, are dead, announce U.S. military officials in Iraq. They were killed in an intense, four-hour firefight with U.S. forces at a house belonging to a cousin of Hussein in the northern city of Mosul, 280 miles (450 kilometers) north of Baghdad.

Iraqis gather in a Baghdad electronics shop to watch a broadcast showing the remains of Saddam Hussein's sons, Uday and Qusay. They were killed on July 22 following a battle with units of the U.S. 101st Airborne Division in the northern Iraq town of Mosul, 280 miles (450 kilometers) north of Baghdad.

25 U.S. President George W. Bush orders ships carrying American troops to coastal waters off Liberia after the U.S. Embassy in Monrovia, the capital, is pounded by 20 rounds of mortar shelling. The residents of Monrovia have asked the United States for two months to send troops to Liberia to bring about a cease-fire in the three-year rebellion to drive President Charles Taylor from office.

27 U.S. cyclist Lance Armstrong wins his fifth consecutive Tour de France in the 100th anniversary of the world's premier bicycle race.

28 Two New York banks, Citigroup Inc. and J.P. Morgan Chase & Co., agree to pay $305 million to settle federal charges that they helped the failed Houston-based energy-trading company Enron Corp. defraud investors through the creation of highly complex financial arrangements.

29 Israeli Prime Minister Ariel Sharon informs U.S. President George W. Bush, during a meeting at the White House in Washington, D.C., that the Israeli government will not halt construction of a security fence on the West Bank.

30 U.S. President George W. Bush defends his decision to go to war with Iraq and accepts full responsibility for the decision to reveal in his State of the Union address in January that Iraq was seeking to buy uranium from Niger to fuel a nuclear weapons program.

31 Pope John Paul II calls on Roman Catholic politicians worldwide to oppose the passage of laws that would grant legal recognition to same-sex marriages and to the adoption of children by gay or Lesbian couples. The pope labels support for such legislation "highly immoral."

25

AUGUST

2003

Office workers pour into the streets surrounding Grand Central Station in New York City on August 14 after a power blackout struck the city. The blackout, the most widespread in U.S. history, plunged large areas of the northeastern and midwestern United States and portions of southeastern Canada into darkness.

1 North Korea is ready to take part in multinational talks on the revival of its nuclear weapons program. North Korea's news agency announces that the government of North Korean leader Kim Chong Il is prepared to participate in a six-nation summit in an attempt to resolve a crisis that has led to mounting insecurity among its neighbors, particularly South Korea and Japan.

4 California Governor Gray Davis files a lawsuit with California's Supreme Court in an attempt to delay his recall election until March 2004, the time of the state's next regularly scheduled balloting. In the suit, the governor's lawyers argue that the combination of consolidating polling places, the use of outdated punch-card machines, and a general lack of time to prepare for the election could confuse many voters.

5 A bomb explosion at the Marriott Hotel in Jakarta, Indonesia, kills 12 people and injures some 150 others.

Unusually high temperatures leave much of Europe sweltering. The heat, combined with months of drought, trigger hundreds of forest fires and widespread crop damage. Temperatures hit 95 °F (35 °C) in London and Paris, cities where air conditioning is rare; 98.6 °F (37 °C) in Rome; and 104 °F (40 °C) in Florence.

6 Actor Arnold Schwarzenegger, a star of action films and a former champion bodybuilder, announces his intention of running for governor of California in the upcoming recall election. He joins some 130 other candidates, including magazine publisher Larry Flynt and former child star Gary Coleman. California's lieutenant governor, Cruz Bustamante, also announces his intention to run despite the fact that he lacks the support of Democratic Party leaders, who continue to endorse Governor Gray Davis.

7 At least 11 people are killed and more than 40 others wounded in an explosion outside the Jordanian embassy in Baghdad, the Iraqi capital.

The Liberian legislature accepts the resignation of President Charles G. Taylor, who withdraws in favor of the vice president, Moses Blah.

10 The temperature at Gravesend-Broadness in Kent in southern England hits 100.6 °F (38 °C), the highest temperature ever recorded in the United Kingdom. Another record is broken in Germany, where temperatures reach 104 °F (40 °C) in Roth.

11 Liberian President Charles Taylor, under pressure from the international community and from rebel forces surrounding the capital, Monrovia, leaves office, and Vice President Moses Blah assumes the presidency.

13 More than 50 people are killed in Afghanistan in a series of bombings and raids, which Afghan officials attribute to Taliban guerrillas.

14 The largest power failure in U.S. history leaves 50 million people in the United States, primarily in the Northeast and Midwest, and in one Canadian province without electricity. A cascading blackout, beginning midafternoon, plunges cities from New York and Toronto to Cleveland and Detroit into darkness, leaving thousands of people stranded at airports, in trains and subways, and aboard elevators.

About 200 United States Marines land in Liberia to assist peacekeepers from West Africa to bring order to Monrovia, the capital, and distribute humanitarian aid to the starving nation.

15 Electric service is restored to New York City and much of the northeastern United States but hundreds of thousands of people in the Midwest remain without power.

16 Power is restored in Detroit, the last major metropolitan area to recover from the blackout that left 50 million people without electricity on August 14. Electrical engineers confirm that the blackout was caused by a sudden electric surge and grid shutdown in the so-called Lake Erie Loop, the part of the electrical grid that includes Detroit, Cleveland, Buffalo, New York, and Toronto, Ontario. Experts note that the U.S. power grid is outmoded.

17 Shaun Micheel wins the 2003 Professional Golfing Association (PGA) Championship, played in Rochester, New York, by two strokes over Chad Campbell and by three over Tim Clark. The victory marks 2003 as the first year since 1969 that all four majors—the Masters, the U.S. Open, the British Open, and the PGA—were captured by first-time winners.

19 An extremely powerful bomb explodes outside the United Nations (UN) headquarters in Baghdad, killing 22 people, including the top UN envoy to Iraq. Dozens of UN employees are injured. According to one eyewitness account, the bomb was detonated inside a cement mixer driven by a suicide attacker.

21 The Palestinian militant groups Hamas and Islamic Jihad declare an end to the Palestinian-Israeli cease-fire, which began on June 29. The announcements come shortly after an Israeli helicopter strike in Gaza City killed a senior Hamas leader, Ismail Abu Shanab.

27 The orbit of Mars brings the red planet to within 34.6 million miles (55.7 million kilometers) of Earth. This is the closest Mars has been to Earth in about 60,000 years, according to calculations by international astronomers. The average distance between Mars and Earth is approximately 50 million miles (80.5 million kilometers).

28 North Korea's deputy foreign minister, Kim Yong Il, tells diplomats from the United States, China, South Korea, Russia, and Japan that North Korea plans to declare that it has nuclear weapons and may test an atomic bomb.

29 More than 11,000 people died in a heat wave in France in August, announce officials with the French health ministry in Paris. France, which usually has August temperatures in the upper 80's °F (20's °C), was hit with temperatures as high as 104 °F (40 °C) during the first three weeks of the month.

1 Iraq's governing council appoints a 25-member cabinet that is to eventually assume day-to-day control of the government from allied forces in Iraq.

2 A bomb planted in a pickup truck explodes outside the office of Baghdad's police chief, Hassan Ali, missing him but killing one Iraqi officer and wounding at least 25 other people.

U.S. Senator John Kerry (D., Massachusetts) announces that he is running for president of the United States in the 2004 election.

3 A Polish-led international force of 9,000 soldiers assumes control of part of central Iraq in a move designed to relieve the burden on Allied troops.

5 Hurricane Fabian slams into Bermuda with heavy rain and winds of 115 miles (185 kilometers) per hour. The Category 3 storm is the most powerful to hit the island chain since 1963.

6 Palestinian Prime Minister Mahmoud Abbas resigns after four months in office. Experts on the Middle East suggest that a prolonged power struggle between Abbas and Palestinian leader Yasir Arafat triggered the resignation.

7 U.S. President George W. Bush, in a prime-time address to the nation, asks Congress to allocate an additional $87 billion to cover the costs of pacifying and rebuilding Iraq.

8 Ahmad Quray, speaker of the Palestinian Parliament, accepts Yasir Arafat's nomination to become the next Palestinian prime minister. Quray is a leading member of the mainstream Fatah faction.

10 A man who appears to be Osama bin Laden, the person blamed for the terrorist attacks on the United States on Sept. 11, 2001, appears on al-Jazeera network television on the eve of the second anniversary of the attacks. The video purportedly shows bin Laden and his top deputy, Ayman al-Zawahiri. Intelligence analysts believe the tapes are genuine and were recorded in late April or May.

11 The members of Israel's security cabinet vote to expel Palestinian leader Yasir Arafat from the West Bank and instruct Israeli Defense Forces to put together an expulsion plan. The cabinet issues a statement describing Arafat as an "absolute obstacle to the process of reconciliation between Israel and the Palestinians" and announces that "Israel will act to remove this obstacle."

Sweden's foreign minister, Anna Lindh, dies as a result of stab wounds she suffered on September 10 when an unidentified assailant attacked her with a knife in a department store in central Stockholm. Swedish authorities speculate that the foreign minister's strong support for Swedish adoption of the European Union currency, the euro, may have led to her death.

14 The Swedish people vote overwhelmingly against joining the European single currency, the euro. Political analysts consider the outcome of the referendum a major defeat for the prime minister, Goran Persson, who campaigned vigorously for the adoption of the euro.

General Verissimo Correia Seabra, chief of staff of the Guinea-Bissau Army, declares himself interim president after the Army staged a *coup* (overthrow) and ousted President Kumba Yala.

16 The U.S. Senate votes 55-40 to undo new Federal Communications Commission (FCC) regulations governing the ownership of media outlets.

17 Wesley Clark, a retired U.S. Army general and a former supreme commander of NATO, announces that he is a candidate for the Democratic presidential nomination in 2004.

18 Hurricane Isabel slams into the East Coast of the United States with heavy rain and winds of up to 100 miles (161 kilometers) per hour, packing enough punch to knock out electric power to hundreds of thousands of households in North Carolina and Virginia.

19 The fossil remains of a rodent that looked like a gigantic guinea pig have been found in northern Venezuela, announces an international team of scientists. *Phoberomys pattersoni* was about the size of an American bison and probably weighed as much as 1,500 pounds (680 kilograms).

21 NASA engineers bring an end to the 14-year, $1.5-billion Galileo mission

Residents of Kitty Hawk, North Carolina, watch Hurricane Isabel make landfall on September 18. Hurricane Isabel carried winds as high as 100 miles (161 kilometers) per hour, knocking out electric power to thousands of houses. The eyewall, carrying the strongest winds, hit land at North Carolina's Outer Banks between Morehead City and Cape Hatteras.

by deliberately plunging the unmanned spacecraft toward Jupiter.

22 The Detroit Tigers set an American League record with their 118th loss, falling to the Kansas City Royals 12-6.

26 The number of U.S. citizens living in poverty rose and income levels declined in the United States in 2002 for the second straight year, reports the U.S. Census Bureau.

28 A massive power failure in Italy, the largest in the country's history, leaves 50 million people without power, from Milan in the north to Sicily in the south. A minor accident on a power line in Switzerland appears to have triggered the blackout by causing a domino effect in France. France sells Italy large amounts of electricity, which is then transported into Italy through the Swiss power grid.

30 The U.S. Department of Justice opens an investigation into whether officials with the administration of President George W. Bush revealed to a newspaper writer the identity of an undercover Central Intelligence Agency (CIA) agent. In July, Robert Novak disclosed in his syndicated column that a woman named Valerie Plame was an agent with the CIA. Plame is the wife of former diplomat Joseph C. Wilson IV, whom the CIA sent to Africa in 2002 to investigate whether Iraq had attempted to buy uranium in Niger for a nuclear weapons program. Wilson later disputed President Bush's claims that Iraq had purchased the uranium, forcing the president to admit that he had no basis for the assertion made in his 2003 State of the Union address.

OCTOBER

2003

A wildfire burns out of control near Descanso, California, approximately 45 miles (72 kilometers) east of San Diego. Wildfires in California burned across an area as large as the state of Rhode Island.

1 The Israeli Cabinet approves the construction of additional fencing around Israeli settlements on the West Bank. The fences, which in some areas are actually concrete walls, are designed to protect Israelis from Palestinian suicide bombers.

2 U.S. troops in Iraq are being attacked 15 to 20 times a day on average, and 3 to 6 soldiers are being killed per week, announces the commander of American forces in Iraq, Lieutenant General Ricardo Sanchez.

5 Israel bombs what the Israeli government describes as a "Palestinian terrorist camp" in Syria, 10 miles (16 kilometers) northwest of Damascus, the capital.

The Chicago Cubs beat the Atlanta Braves, 5-1, in Game 5 of the National League division series, giving the team its first postseason victory since winning the World Series in 1908.

7 The Turkish parliament authorizes the government to send troops to join coalition forces in Iraq. A force of as many as 10,000 Turkish soldiers may be sent into Iraq as early as November to help stabilize the country.

The California electorate votes overwhelmingly to recall Governor Gray Davis and replace him with film star Arnold Schwarzenegger. In the two-part ballot, California voters were asked if they wanted to recall the governor and to indicate whom they preferred as his replacement. More than 54 percent vote to remove Davis from office. Schwarzenegger, an Austrian-born bodybuilder who immigrated to the United States, took 48 percent of votes cast in a field of 135 candidates.

8 A young person is infected with HIV, the virus that causes AIDS, every 14 seconds, reports the United Nations (UN) Population Fund. Every day, some 6,000 people between the ages of 14 and 24 are infected. The majority of these are women living in developing countries.

9 The new Palestinian prime minister, Ahmed Quray, who was sworn in as head of an emergency cabinet on October 5, threatens to resign over whether he or Yasir Arafat will control Palestinian security forces.

14 Gyude Bryant, a veteran campaigner against the warlords who have plagued Liberia, is sworn in as president in a ceremony in Monrovia, the capital.

15 China launches its first manned spacecraft with Yang Liwei, a former jet pilot, aboard the Shenzhou V. The craft, which lifts off from the Gobi Desert, is to orbit Earth 14 times during a 21-hour journey.

The Florida Marlins, playing at Wrigley Field in Chicago, beat the Cubs 9-6 in Game 7 of the series to take the National League championship. The loss costs the Cubs their first chance at a World Series in 58 years.

16 Permanent and representative nations on the United Nations Security Council vote in favor of a revised resolution on Iraq. The resolution, backed by the United States, confirms that the U.S.-led coalition will remain in power in Iraq for an unspecified period. However, the resolution stresses that sovereignty is to be transferred to a government representing the Iraqi people as soon as practicable.

Canada's two conservative parties, the Canadian Alliance and the Progressive Conservative Party, agree to unite in an effort to give the governing Liberal Party a competitive race in national elections in 2004.

17 Bolivia's president, Gonzalo Sanchez de Lozada, resigns amid enormous antigovernment demonstrations in La Paz, the capital. The new caretaker president, Carlos Mesa, calls for immediate elections.

18 The al-Jazeera satellite television network broadcasts a videotape of Osama bin Laden calling on all Muslims to enter into an Islamic "holy war" against the United States and its allies in the war in Iraq.

21 Iran agrees to suspend production of enriched uranium, which is used in the production of nuclear weapons, and to allow United Nations officials to inspect its nuclear sites.

The United Nations General Assembly passes a resolution condemning a security barrier that Israel is constructing in the West Bank. The government of Israel responds that the project, which is designed to protect Israelis from Palestinian suicide bombers, will continue.

25 The Florida Marlins win the World Series by defeating the Yankees 2-0 in Game 6 at Yankee Stadium in New York City.

26 Guerrillas fire a barrage of air-to-ground missiles at Baghdad's Al-Rashid Hotel, where U.S. Deputy Secretary of Defense Paul Wolfowitz is staying during a three-day trip to Iraq. A senior U.S. Army officer is killed and 17 other people are wounded.

28 Serious crime in the United States remained largely steady in 2002, dropping 1.1 percent below 2001 rates, announce officials with the Federal Bureau of Investigation. During the same period, the murder rate increased by 1 percent. However, the 2002 murder rate remains 34 percent below the 1992 rate, reflecting a drop in serious crimes.

29 Wildfires in California have burned across 675,000 acres (273,000 hectares), an area as large as the state of Rhode Island, in what officials describe as the most costly disaster in state history.

30 Russian authorities seize control of the oil company Yukos less than one week after the company's chief executive, Mikhail Khodorkovsky, was arrested and charged with seven counts of tax evasion and fraud. The seizure, an unprecedented act since the collapse of the Soviet Union in 1991, is made after the Yukos board voted shareholders a $2-billion dividend payout, one of the largest in Russian corporate history.

31 Malaysia's prime minister, Mahathir bin Mohamad, steps down after 22 years in power. Mahathir is credited with transforming Malaysia from a third-world country into a highly industrialized economic powerhouse. Mahathir's deputy, Abdullah Badawi, is sworn in as the country's new leader.

1 Wildfires in southern California have largely burned themselves out or have been contained within manageable zones, announce state and federal officials. The fires burned over 750,000 acres (303,500 hectares) since October 21.

3 The U.S. Congress approves $87 billion for U.S. military operations in Iraq and Afghanistan and aid for both countries.

4 President Chandrika Kumaratunga of Sri Lanka suspends the Parliament and dismisses three key ministers on the grounds that they have given too much ground to the Tamil Tiger rebels during negotiations to end the country's long civil war.

Republican candidates capture the office of governor in Kentucky and Mississippi.

5 The Environmental Protection Agency is dropping investigations into 50 power plants for past violations of the Clean Air Act. The agency based its decision to drop the cases on new, less stringent rules that go into effect in December.

6 Productivity of U.S. companies climbed in the third quarter to its highest level since early 2002, reports the U.S. Department of Labor.

A U.S. soldier and a Polish soldier are killed in Iraq. The American is killed by a land mine on Iraq's border with Syria. The Pole dies after being shot by unknown assailants near Al Mussayyib, a city south of Baghdad. The soldier is his country's first fatality since Polish forces took command of a multinational force in Iraq in September.

7 The government of Turkey announces that it will not send troops into Iraq to relieve U.S. forces.

11 Japan and the European Union threaten the United States with billions of dollars in sanctions one day after the World Trade Organization (WTO) ruled that U.S. steel tariffs are illegal. South Korea and China, the world's largest steel producers, are also threatening to place sanctions on U.S. imports if the tariffs remain in place. On November 10, the WTO confirmed an earlier ruling that U.S. steel tariffs went beyond WTO rules that allow countries to protect their industries from sudden surges of imports.

12 A suicide bombing at the headquarters of Italian forces in Iraq kills at least 28 people—19 Italians and 9 Iraqis—in the city of An Nasiriyah.

13 The government of Japan announces that it is delaying sending troops to join the U.S.-led coalition in Iraq because of the worsening security situation there.

14 Canada's governing Liberal Party chooses former Finance Minister Paul Martin as its new leader, taking over from Prime Minister Jean Chretien.

15 The United States will hand over power to a transitional government in Iraq in 2004, announces a member of the Iraqi Governing Council.

Voters in Louisiana elect the state's first female governor. Democratic candidate Kathleen Blanco takes 52 percent of the vote against Bobby Jindal, the Republican candidate.

16 Serbia fails to elect a president for the third time in just over a year because of low voter turnout. Serbia's Constitution specifies that at least 50 percent of eligible voters must cast ballots for a presidential election to be valid. Unofficial results indicate that nationalist candidate Tomislav Nikolic leads Dragoljub Micunovic, the candidate sponsored by the current government.

17 A jury in Virginia Beach, Virginia, finds John Allen Muhammad, one of the men accused of the Washington, D.C.-area sniper killings in 2002, guilty of murder, terrorism, conspiracy, and lesser charges. Muhammad may face the death penalty.

Actor Arnold Schwarzenegger is sworn in as the 38th governor of California. Schwarzenegger promises to tackle California's enormous budget deficit without raising taxes.

18 Canadian Prime Minister Jean Chretien announces that he will step down as prime minister on December 12. Chretien, who has led the government since 1993, will be replaced by Paul Martin.

21 Evidence shows that an asteroid hit Earth about 250 million years ago, announce scientists, who believe the impact and its aftermath wiped out most life on the planet. Geochemists at the University of Rochester in

A terrorist bomb explodes at the headquarters of the London-based HSBC Bank in Istanbul, Turkey, on November 20. The attack and a nearly simultaneous second bombing outside the British consulate in Istanbul left at least 25 people dead and hundreds of others wounded. Turkish authorities blamed an Islamic militant organization.

New York have found geological evidence of the asteroid in dozens of rare mineral grains in ancient rocks in Antarctica. Many scientists believe that a similar asteroid impact ended the era of the dinosaurs 65 million years ago.

23 Georgian President Eduard Shevardnadze resigns in the face of massive popular protests in Tbilisi, the capital. Shevardnadze's claim of victory in parliamentary elections on November 2 set off a widespread movement against him in parliament.

24 Croatia's prime minister concedes defeat in the country's general election. Ivica Racan's Social Democrats lost out to the Croatian Democratic Union, the hard-line nationalist party of the late President Franjo Tudjman, which took about 75 of the 140 seats in the parliament.

25 Every day some 14,000 people are infected with HIV, the virus that causes AIDS, announce officials with UNAids and the World Health Organization.

The U.S. Senate, in a 54-to-44 vote, passes a sweeping Medicare bill that adds new prescription drug benefits for millions of senior U.S. citizens.

27 U.S. President George W. Bush, in a dramatic surprise, arrives in Baghdad to spend Thanksgiving with U.S. troops in Iraq. He also meets with members of the Iraqi Governing Council before flying back to the United States.

2003

Saddam Hussein, the former president of Iraq, is found on December 13 hiding in a tiny "spider hole" below a farmhouse approximately 10 miles (16 kilometers) from Tikrit, his hometown. He was betrayed by a member of his own clan, who tipped off U.S. officials on Hussein's whereabouts.

3 Productivity of U.S. companies climbed to a 9.4-percent annual rate in the third quarter of 2003, the highest rate in 20 years, announces the U.S. Department of Labor.

The Environmental Protection Agency proposes dropping strict limits on mercury air pollution from power plants. Environmental groups accuse the agency of sidestepping the Clean Air Act, which mandates that utilities install the strictest controls possible on mercury pollution.

4 U.S. President George W. Bush lifts tariffs on foreign steel. Political experts note that removing the tariffs will hurt steelmakers in states critical to the president in the 2004 election.

7 Russian voters deliver a clear victory to allies of Russian President Vladimir Putin in elections to the State Duma, the lower half of the parliament. The pro-Putin United Russia Party leads with 37.1 percent, more than three times the number of seats taken by any other party.

8 President George W. Bush signs a new prescription drug benefit into law in the largest overhaul of Medicare since the health care program for seniors went into effect in 1965.

The U.S. dollar falls to a record new low against the euro, the currency of the European Union. In late trading, the value of a euro climbs to $1.2241. Economists point to growing U.S. deficits and low interest rates for the decline of the dollar.

9 A suicide car bombing outside a U.S. Army base west of Mosul in northern Iraq leaves 31 American soldiers injured. The attack is the third on the 101st Airborne in Mosul in three days. In Baghdad, the capital, a bomb explodes in the courtyard of a Sunni mosque, killing three Iraqis and wounding two others. West of Baghdad, a U.S. helicopter is forced to make an emergency landing after being hit by a rocket-propelled grenade.

More than one-third of Iraqi soldiers belonging to the first battalion of the new Iraqi Army have abandoned their posts one week before the battalion was to begin working alongside U.S. forces in Iraq, confirm U.S. military officials. According to the officer in charge of the U.S. division responsible for training the Iraqis, low salary—not fear of guerrilla attack—is the primary reason.

10 France, Germany, and Russia are barred from multibillion-dollar contracts for the reconstruction of Iraq, announces a U.S. Department of Defense spokesperson, who notes that only those countries that had sent troops to Iraq are eligible to bid for reconstruction work.

The U.S. government is paying the Halliburton Company of Houston, Texas, an average of $2.64 a gallon to import gasoline and other fuel to Iraq from Kuwait. Iraqis pay an average of 5 cents to 15 cents a gallon for the same fuel. A Halliburton spokesperson defends the company's profits as small considering the "hazardous and hostile environment."

Two U.S. soldiers die in the northern Iraqi city of Mosul in separate attacks. Both soldiers are killed in drive-by shootings at gas stations. The U.S. Army is posting soldiers at Iraqi gas stations because shortages have led to lines miles in length.

12 Jean Chretien steps down after 10 years as Canada's prime minister. He is replaced by Paul Martin, a former finance minister.

13 U.S. forces in Iraq capture former Iraqi President Saddam Hussein, who was hiding in a tiny "spider hole" below a farmhouse approximately 10 miles (16 kilometers) from Tikrit, Hussein's hometown. The most-wanted man on the list issued by U.S. authorities in Iraq, Hussein had not been sighted since Baghdad fell to U.S. troops in April.

18 The Second U.S. Circuit Court of Appeals rules, in a 2-to-1 decision, that the president of the United States does not have the power to indefinitely detain U.S. citizens captured or arrested as enemy combatants. The decision involves a U.S. citizen arrested in 2002 in connection with a possible terrorist attack, who was designated an enemy combatant and held without being formally charged.

The Ninth U.S. Court of Appeals in San Francisco rules that prisoners from the war in Afghanistan in 2001 being held at a U.S. Naval base at Guantanamo Bay in Cuba may use the U.S. court system to challenge their detention.

20 Libyan leader Muammar al-Qadhafi agrees to abandon the country's weapons of mass destruction program and open weapons facilities to inspections by the International Atomic Energy Agency.

21 Tom Ridge, secretary of the U.S. Department of Homeland Security, raises the national terrorism alert rating to orange, or high risk, warning that the threat of a terrorist attack on the United States is greater than at any time since the attacks on Sept. 11, 2001.

23 The U.S. gross domestic product grew at an annual rate of 8.2 percent in the third quarter of 2003, the best showing in nearly 20 years, announce officials with the U.S. Department of Commerce.

23 A sick cow slaughtered on December 9 in Washington State tested positive for mad cow disease in early laboratory results, announces the U.S. Department of Agriculture. The case is the first in the United States, according to Secretary of Agriculture Ann M. Veneman, who assures the public that the meat supply is safe.

26 An earthquake registering 6.6 devastates the ancient Iranian city of Bam, which is about 600 miles (965 kilometers) southeast of the capital, Tehran. Officials estimate that at least 25,000 people are killed in the quake, and more than 70 percent of the city is leveled.

27 A series of coordinated car bombings and mortar and machine-gun attacks in and around the Iraqi city of Karbala leave 19 people dead, including 7 coalition soldiers, 11 Iraqi policemen, and an Iraqi civilian. The victims include 5 soldiers from Bulgaria and 2 from Thailand. At least 100 people are injured in the attacks on the office of the city governor, the main police station, and military headquarters around the city.

29 The United States requires foreign airlines to carry armed law-enforcement officers on certain flights bound for the United States, announces a spokesperson for the U.S. Department of Homeland Security.

35

2003 UPDATE

The major events of 2003 are summarized in more than 230 alphabetically arranged articles, from "Afghanistan" to "Zoos." Included are Special Reports that offer in-depth looks at subjects ranging from education to the Iraq War of 2003. The Special Reports are found on the following pages.

SPECIAL REPORTS

FOCUS ON

PORTRAITS

Afghanistan in 2003 experienced its worst fighting since United States-led troops overthrew the Taliban rule in 2001. Hundreds of people were killed in attacks by guerrillas and in ethnic uprisings in 2003. The violence threatened international efforts to establish a stable central government and to root out terrorists within the country's borders.

Escalating violence. From the mid-1990's until 2001, Afghanistan was ruled by the Taliban, an extremist Islamic group. The Taliban allowed international terrorist organizations—including al-Qa'ida, a network headed by Saudi-born millionaire Osama bin Laden—to establish and run training camps in Afghanistan. Following terrorist attacks against the United States on Sept. 11, 2001, the United States and allied troops joined with anti-Taliban forces within Afghanistan to drive the Taliban from power.

An international peacekeeping force arrived in Afghanistan in late 2001 and early 2002. However, violence continued as warlords and tribal groups competed for territory and power. Also, small groups of Taliban and al-Qa'ida forces continued to battle U.S., Afghan, and allied troops.

In May 2003, U.S. Secretary of Defense Donald Rumsfeld visited Kabul, the capital, and announced that major combat operations were completed in Afghanistan. However, U.S. troops remained in the country, and at least 10 U.S. soldiers were killed in fighting in 2003.

In an effort to stabilize the country, the North Atlantic Treaty Organization (NATO), a defense alliance between 17 Western European countries, Canada, and the United States, planned to extend the jurisdiction of the International Security Force (ISA). NATO took command of ISA in August and, in October, officials discussed expanding the 5,500-member force to major cities beyond Kabul.

Some military leaders said the escalation in violence was the result of an influx of Taliban guerrillas from Pakistan. Lieutenant General John Vines, the top U.S. commander in Afghanistan, said in September that the guerrillas were trained by al-Qa'ida in Pakistan and then crossed the border into Afghanistan to sabotage peacekeeping efforts. Pakistani officials denied the charges.

Holy war. In February, a council of Islamic clerics denounced the Taliban's call for a *jihad* (holy war) against U.S.-led forces in Afghanistan. In response, the Taliban, which offered between $5,000 and $100,000 to anyone who killed or captured a U.S. soldier, assassinated several Muslim clerics who disputed the religious validity of the jihad.

In August, the spiritual leader of the Taliban, Mullah Mohammed Omar, attacked Western charities as the "greatest enemies of Islam and humanity." The statement sparked violence against aid workers in Afghanistan. By the end of 2003, many aid agencies had pulled out of the country, jeopardizing efforts to recover from decades of drought and war that left many Afghans homeless and in danger of starvation.

New constitution. Deteriorating security conditions threatened, but did not derail, the Afghan interim government's slow progress toward democracy in 2003. In November, a 35-member commission released a proposed constitution that promised to pave the way for national elections. The document attempted to balance the competing demands of Islamic and secular values.

The document specified that Afghanistan would be governed by civil laws as long as the laws were in keeping with Islam. It called for a directly elected president, supported by a vice president; a strong central government; and a two-chamber parliament. It also offered guarantees protecting human rights and civil rights.

A traditional Afghan council known as a loya jirga, meeting in Kabul, ratified the new constitution on Jan. 4, 2004. Hamid Karzai, the president of Afghanistan, was to hold office until mid-2004, when Afghans were scheduled to democratically elect a permanent government.

Karzai struggled in 2003 to control local warlords, who used extortion, intimidation, and violence to maintain power in most regions outside of Kabul. Many warlords were provincial governors, but they ignored the authority of the central government. In May, Karzai threatened to resign if the warlords did not begin cooperating with the government. The warlords agreed to turn over some local tax revenue, but they kept most of the money to fund their private armies.

In August, Karzai fired three provincial governors and stripped a powerful warlord, Mohammad Ismail Khan, of his title of regional military commander. Khan continued to serve as governor of the western city of Herat, and he retained a private army, which outnumbered the government's army of 5,000 troops.

Foreign aid. The United States, Afghanistan's largest aid donor, pledged approximately $1.2 billion to the war-ravaged country in 2003. Afghan officials said the government needed to raise $30 billion by 2008.

Opium. The UN reported in 2003 that opium production made up 50 percent of the Afghan economy. The report warned that if the poppy crops were not replaced with alternate crops, Afghanistan—the world's leading producer of opium—would become a "narco-mafia state."

◼ Henry S. Bradsher

See also **Asia; Pakistan; Terrorism.**

AFRICA

The president of the African Development Bank, Omar Kabbaj, speaking at a June 2003 summit in Addis Ababa, Ethiopia, told African finance ministers that Africa was the only region of the world that was not likely to meet the millennium development goal (MDG) of reducing extreme poverty by half by 2015. A September 2000 summit of world leaders sponsored by the United Nations (UN) in New York City had adopted eight MDG's to guide world leaders, including the goal for reducing poverty.

According to Kabbaj, African economies need to sustain annual growth rates of at least 8 percent to substantially reduce poverty. The average growth rate for the continent in 2003 was well below 4 percent, he noted. However, Kabbaj did point out that high growth rates in some parts of the continent had reduced poverty during the 1990's. In Uganda, for example, a sustained high rate of economic growth had reduced that nation's poverty rate from 56 percent of the population in 1992 to 35 percent in 2000.

Nonetheless, a UN report released in May 2003 revealed that 54 developing countries, the majority of them in Africa, entered the 21st century poorer than they had been 10 years earlier. The authors of the report noted that a child in Africa had only a one in three chance of completing primary school. They also reported that an African woman was 100 times more likely to die in childbirth than her counterpart in any industrialized Western nation.

The African Union (AU), an organization of 53 African nations established in July 2002, held its second annual summit in Maputo, Mozambique, July 10 to 12, 2003. The meeting's agenda included discussion of conflicts in African countries, including Congo (Kinshasa), Liberia, and Cote d'Ivoire (Ivory Coast), but omitted consideration of the civil and economic decline in Zimbabwe under President Robert Mugabe. Critics claimed that the AU's failure in 2003 to address the alleged abuses of power by Mugabe fatally undermined the AU's New Partnership for Africa's Development (NEPAD), an initiative in which African nations pledged to commit themselves to good governance and the rule of law in return for international financial aid.

At a May meeting in Addis Ababa, African defense chiefs endorsed a plan for an AU military intervention force to prevent conflict and genocide in African countries. The AU force would be ready for deployment as early as 2005. The European Union (EU) in November 2003 approved a grant of 250 million euros ($294 million) to the AU for development of the intervention force.

Bush visit. On a five-nation African tour in July 2003, U.S. President George W. Bush visited Senegal, South Africa, Botswana, Uganda, and Nigeria. Topping the agenda in Bush's discussions with African leaders were strife in Liberia and Zimbabwe, trade relations, and the AIDS crisis.

AIDS. The ongoing AIDS *pandemic* (widespread epidemic) in 2003 threatened the "very existence of whole countries," said Stephen Lewis, UN Secretary-General Kofi Annan's special envoy for HIV/AIDS in Africa. Health experts estimated that 25 percent of South African adults were infected with HIV, the virus that causes AIDS, and that HIV infection rates approached 40 percent in neighboring Botswana and Swaziland.

At a Franco-Africa Summit in Paris on February 20, Secretary-General Annan noted that for the first time women made up half of the total of HIV-positive people worldwide. In sub-Saharan Africa, women account for 58 percent of the total. He noted that the disease had orphaned 11 million African children and that as many as 20 million African children could be orphaned by 2010.

On May 27, 2003, President Bush signed into law a U.S.-government commitment to provide up to $15 billion to fight AIDS, mostly in Africa. The battle against AIDS received another boost on August 30, when the World Trade Organization (WTO, an organization that promotes trade among nations) agreed to let poorer nations import drugs to fight deadly diseases such as AIDS and malaria at reduced prices.

Africa Malaria Day on April 25 marked the third anniversary of a "Roll Back Malaria" (RBM) campaign launched in Abuja, Nigeria, in 2000. RBM is a global partnership supported by the World Health Organization (WHO), a UN agency. The program aims to reduce the global incidence of malaria by half by 2010.

Over 300 million cases of malaria occur worldwide each year, resulting in more than 1 million deaths, 90 percent of them in sub-Saharan Africa. Young children and pregnant women are especially vulnerable. The authors of a joint UN Children's Fund (UNICEF) and WHO Africa Malaria Report, issued on April 25, 2003, noted that the 2010 target was realistic but that more funds and stronger political commitment would be required to meet it. The report stressed that proper use of highly effective insecticide-treated mosquito nets, combined with prompt treatment, could reduce transmission by up to 60 percent. In 2003, however, only a tiny proportion of at-risk African children slept under such nets.

Southern Africa. Drought, compounded by the human toll of AIDS and, in some cases, government mismanagement, resulted in poor harvests in southern Africa in 2003. According to UN sources, 16 million people in southern Africa were in urgent need of food aid during 2003. Economic experts said that President Mugabe's highly disruptive land redistribution program in Zimbabwe had crippled that country's agricultural sector and threatened nearly half of Zimbabwe's 13 million people with starvation. Over 8 million more people needed food aid in Lesotho, Malawi, Mozambique, Swaziland, and Zambia.

In South Africa, harvests also were poor due to drought. While South Africa did not face famine, agricultural exports to neighboring countries declined, aggravating regional food shortages. South African President Thabo Mbeki faced criti-

cism in 2003 for his silence regarding Zimbabwe President Robert Mugabe's land policy, which experts claim has resulted in widespread famine in a country once known as the "breadbasket" of southern Africa.

Africa's last feudal monarch, King Mswati III of Swaziland, came under domestic fire in 2003 for insisting that his government buy him a $50-million private jet while 250,000 Swazis—a quarter of his subjects—faced starvation. A *polygamist* (a man with more than one wife at a time), the king was also criticized for taking a new teen-age wife in 2003, while also promoting a teen-age chastity campaign to curb AIDS.

Zambian officials on August 5 arrested former Zambian President Frederick Chiluba and charged him with stealing more than $30 million during his 10 years in office. In 2001, Chiluba attempted to cling to power by changing the constitution to allow him to run for a third term as president. Public protests, however, led Chiluba to hand power to his chosen successor, Levy Mwanawasa,

A child soldier with a teddy bear backpack takes aim on a street in Monrovia, Liberia, in June 2003, when rebels attacked the capital. Both rebel forces and forces loyal to Liberia's president, Charles Taylor, kidnapped children into their armies during the country's 14-year civil war. The conflict came to an end in August with Taylor's departure into exile in Nigeria.

Country	Population	Government	Monetary unit*	Foreign trade (million U.S.$) Exports[†]	Imports[†]
Algeria	32,480,000	President Abdelaziz Bouteflika; Prime Minister Ali Benflis	dinar (76.94 = $1)	19,500	10,600
Angola	14,777,000	President Jose Eduardo dos Santos	readj. kwanza (78.81 = $1)	8,600	4,100
Benin	7,007,000	President Mathieu Kerekou	CFA franc (566.80 = $1)	207	479
Botswana	1,575,000	President Festus Mogae	pula 4.63 = $1)	2,400	1,900
Burkina Faso	12,988,000	President Blaise Compaore	CFA franc (566.80 = $1)	250	525
Burundi	7,154,000	President Domitien Ndayizeye	franc (1,056.00 = $1)	26	135
Cameroon	16,191,000	President Paul Biya	CFA franc (566.80 = $1)	1,900	1,700
Cape Verde	473,000	President Pedro Pires; Prime Minister Jose Maria Pereira Neves	escudo (108.95 = $1)	30	220
Central African Republic	3,967,000	President Francois Bozize	CFA franc (566.80 = $1)	134	102
Chad	8,899,000	President Idriss Deby	CFA franc (566.80 = $1)	197	570
Comoros	631,000	President of the Union Assoumani Azali	franc (454.33 = $1)	16	40
Congo (Brazzaville)	3,401,000	President Denis Sassou-Nguesso	CFA franc (566.80 = $1)	2,400	730
Congo (Kinshasa)	58,103,000	President Joseph Kabila	CFA franc (566.80 = $1)	1,200	890
Cote d'Ivoire (Ivory Coast)	17,381,000	President Laurent Gbagbo	CFA franc (566.80 = $1)	4,400	2,500
Djibouti	658,000	President Ismail Omar Guelleh; Prime Minister Mohamed Dileita Dileita	franc (175.00 = $1)	70	255
Egypt	72,534,000	President Hosni Mubarak; Prime Minister Atef Mohammed Obeid	pound (6.15 = $1)	7,000	15,200
Equatorial Guinea	511,000	President Teodoro Obiang Nguema Mbasogo; Prime Minister Candido Muatetema Rivas	CFA franc (566.80 = $1)	2,500	562
Eritrea	4,037,000	President Isaias Afworki	nafka (13.55 = $1)	20	500
Ethiopia	69,195,000	President Girma Wolde Giorgis	birr (8.55 = $1)	433	1,630
Gabon	1,357,000	President El Hadj Omar Bongo; Prime Minister Jean-Francois Ntoutoume-Emane	CFA franc (566.80 = $1)	2,600	1,100
Gambia	1,432,000	Head of State Yahya Jammeh	dalasi (29.75 = $1)	138	225
Ghana	20,087,000	President John Agyekum Kufuor	cedi (8,538.00 = $1)	2,200	2,800
Guinea	8,648,000	President Lansana Conte	franc (1,990.00 = $1)	835	670
Guinea-Bissau	1,319,000	President Kumba Yala	CFA franc (566.80 = $1)	71	59
Kenya	31,524,000	President Mwai Kibaki	shilling (78.45 = $1)	2,100	3,000
Lesotho	2,297,000	King Letsie III; Prime Minister Pakalitha Mosisili	maloti (6.88 = $1)	422	738
Liberia	3,415,000	President Moses Zeh Blah	dollar (1 = $1)	110	165

*Exchange rates as of Oct. 3, 2003, or latest available data.   [†]Latest available data.

Country	Population	Government	Monetary unit*	Foreign trade (million U.S.$)	
				Exports[†]	Imports[†]
Libya	5,771,000	Leader Muammar Muhammad al-Qadhafi; General People's Committee Secretary (Prime Minister) Shukri Muhammad Ghanim	dinar (1.36 = $1)	11,800	6,300
Madagascar	17,856,000	President Marc Ravalomanana	franc (5,920.00 = $1)	700	985
Malawi	11,293,000	President Bakili Muluzi	kwacha (107.20 = $1)	435	505
Mali	12,731,000	President Amadou Toumani Toure; Prime Minister Ahmed Mohamed Ag Hamani	CFA franc (566.80 = $1)	680	630
Mauritania	2,995,000	President Maaouya Ould Sid Ahmed Taya	ouguiya (259.50 = $1)	355	360
Mauritius	1,199,000	President Sir Anerood Jugnauth; Prime Minister Paul Berenger	rupee (28.65 = $1)	1,600	1,800
Morocco	32,063,000	King Mohamed VI; Prime Minister Driss Jettou	dirham (9.40 = $1)	7,500	10,400
Mozambique	19,614,000	President Joaquim Alberto Chissano; Prime Minister Pascoal Manuel Mocumbi	metical (23,343.00 = $1)	680	1,180
Namibia	1,844,000	President Sam Nujoma; Prime Minister Theo-Ben Gurirab	dollar (6.85 = $1)	1,210	1,380
Niger	12,493,000	President Mamadou Tandja; Prime Minister Hama Amadou	CFA franc (566.80 = $1)	293	368
Nigeria	136,769,000	President Olusegun Obasanjo	naira (131.10 = $1)	17,300	13,600
Rwanda	8,272,000	President Paul Kagame	franc (536.85 = $1)	68	253
Sao Tome and Príncipe	160,000	President Fradique de Menezes	dobra (8,700.00 = $1)	6	25
Senegal	10,403,000	President Abdoulaye Wade; Prime Minister Idrissa Seck	CFA franc (566.80 = $1)	1,150	1,460
Seychelles	84,000	President France Albert Rene	rupee (5.18 = $1)	235	380
Sierra Leone	5,261,000	President Ahmed Tejan Kabbah	leone (2,368.00 = $1)	35	190
Somalia	10,352,000	Interim President Abdikassim Salad Hassan; Interim Prime Minister Hassan Abshir Farah	shilling (2,620.00 = $1)	126	343
South Africa	44,552,000	President Thabo Mvuyelwa Mbeki	rand (6.96 = $1)	31,800	26,600
Sudan	34,056,000	President Umar Hasan Ahmad al-Bashir	dinar (261.35 = $1) pound (2,610.00 = $1)	1,800	1,500
Swaziland	1,030,000	King Mswati III; Prime Minister Barnabas Sibusiso Dlamini	lilangeni (6.88 = $1)	820	938
Tanzania	38,493,000	President Benjamin William Mkapa; Prime Minister Frederick Sumaye	shilling (1,042.00 = $1)	863	1,670
Togo	5,007,000	President Gnassingbe Eyadema	CFA franc (566.80 = $1)	449	561
Tunisia	9,898,000	President Zine El Abidine Ben Ali; Prime Minister Mohamed Ghannouchi	dinar (1.26 = $1)	6,800	8,700
Uganda	26,418,000	President Yoweri Kaguta Museveni; Prime Minister Apollo Nsibambi	shilling (1,995.00 = $1)	476	1,140
Zambia	11,320,000	President Levy Mwanawasa	kwacha (4,695.00 = $1)	709	1,123
Zimbabwe	13,524,000	President Robert Mugabe	dollar (815.00 = $1)	1,570	1,739

in December 2001 elections, which international observers described as neither free nor fair. At the time of Chiluba's arrest in 2003, President Mwanawasa abandoned his former ally, allowing prosecution to go ahead.

West Africa. Rebels in Cote d'Ivoire signed a power-sharing deal with Cote d'Ivoire's president, Laurent Gbagbo, in Paris on Jan. 25, 2003. The pact, which led to the establishment of a new coalition government in April, brought a shaky end to a bloody uprising that erupted on Sept. 19, 2002, resulting in over 500 deaths and the intervention of 2,500 French peacekeepers.

The French-brokered agreement sparked a series of riots over several weeks in Abidjan, Cote d'Ivoire's chief port and commercial capital, when thousands of Gbagbo's supporters took to the streets to protest participation of the rebels in a power-sharing government. In early February 2003, France dispatched 600 additional troops to Abidjan to protect French citizens there.

Rebel factions formally joined in the power-sharing government in July. Though the peace generally held, a December gunbattle in Abidjan threatened renewal of hostilities, and the plight of 1 million Ivorian and Liberian refugees in the rebel-dominated northwest remained unresolved at the end of the year.

Regional stability in West Africa was also threatened during the first half of 2003 by an escalation of fighting in neighboring Liberia, where rebel action mainly by the Liberians United for Reconciliation and Democracy (LURD) forced President Charles Taylor to resign. Besieged by LURD forces in the capital, Monrovia, and indicted for war crimes in Sierra Leone by a UN-backed tribunal, Taylor departed for exile to Nigeria on August 11, ending 14 years of conflict estimated to have cost 200,000 lives. The UN Security Council on September 19 approved sending a 15,000-strong peacekeeping force to Liberia. The UN force began deploying in the country on October 1. On October 14, an interim administration consisting of representatives of the government and rebel groups came to power, headed by Gyude Bryant, a business leader. The new government promised to hold elections by 2005.

In May 2003, Niger's government made owning slaves a crime punishable by 10 to 30 years in jail. Timidria, a human rights organization in Niger, released a report in 2003 claiming that 870,000 people in Niger—about 7 percent of the population—were slaves. According to the report, slavery in Niger, bolstered by centuries of tradition, mainly involved forced labor in agriculture.

Central Africa. On April 7, a new power-sharing government took office in Kinshasa, capital of the Democratic Republic of Congo (DRC), in accordance with a peace agreement signed under South African auspices. The peace pact was to end a five-year civil war that had claimed up to 3 million lives and destabilized the Great Lakes region of central Africa. However, violent power struggles in the northeastern part of DRC broke out immediately after the pact was signed, dimming hopes of a stable peace.

On April 30, President Pierre Buyoya of Burundi, a member of the minority Tutsi tribe, handed over power to his deputy, Domitien Ndayizeye, a member of the Hutu ethnic majority. The transfer of office proceeded according to terms of a November 2001 power-sharing pact mediated by Nelson Mandela, former president of South Africa. Under those terms, the two leaders were each to serve 18 months as transitional president.

Diplomats welcomed the formal power transfer as a milestone in Burundi's history after 10 years of civil war that had resulted in the deaths of as many as 300,000 people. However the peace was shattered in July 2003, when heavily armed Hutu rebels attacked the capital, Bujumbura, and killed at least 200 people. The rebels accused Ndayizeye and his ethnically mixed government of selling out to the Tutsis, who controlled the tiny nation for all but four months since Burundi became independent from Belgium in 1962.

Rwanda's long-time president, Paul Kagame, won his first democratic election on Aug. 15, 2003. In polls which fell short of meeting "free and fair" election standards, according to EU observers, Kagame amassed over 95 percent of the vote, compared with his nearest rival Faustin Twagiramungu's 3.6 percent. Kagame, a member of the minority Tutsi tribe, has ruled Rwanda since his rebels toppled an extremist Hutu regime in 1994 after the massacre of up to 1 million Tutsis and moderate Hutus.

In the Central African Republic, General Francois Bozize on March 15, 2003, led a *coup* (overthrow) that toppled the government of President Ange-Felix Patasse. Bozize, who had organized previous coup attempts during Patasse's 10-year rule, declared himself head of state of a transitional government and promised to hold elections in 2004.

Eastern Africa and the Horn. Drought and the human toll inflicted by HIV/AIDS contributed to severe food shortages in the Horn of Africa in 2003. Ethiopia faced its worst drought since 1985, when almost 1 million people died of starvation. In September 2003, humanitarian officials said that 13 million Ethiopians were dependent on international food aid. Serious famine conditions also developed in neighboring Eritrea, where an estimated 1 million people—almost a third of the population—were dependent on food aid. The UN's World Food Program (WFP), which had launched an "Africa Hunger Alert" campaign in

December 2002, mounted emergency relief operations in the region in 2003.

In October, an official of the UN's Mission in Ethiopia and Eritrea (UNMEE) warned that the peace process between the two countries was under "severe stress." UNMEE officials accused Ethiopia of illegally sending military personnel into a 15-mile- (25-kilometer) wide temporary security zone in violation of a 2000 cease-fire, which ended a two-year border conflict that resulted in the deaths of at least 100,000 people.

Both countries had agreed to submit border claims to an independent commission for arbitration. However, Ethiopia rejected the commission's April 2002 decision, which awarded contested territory to Eritrea. A UN force of 4,200 peacekeepers remained deployed in the security zone through 2003.

In June, the Inter-Governmental Authority on Development (IGAD), an organization of seven East African nations, approved a plan to combat international terrorism by implementing stricter border controls and pooling intelligence. The IGAD area—especially Kenya, Tanzania, and Somalia—had suffered a number of terrorist incidents since the 1998 attacks on U.S. embassies in Kenya and Tanzania. ■ Simon Baynham

See also **AIDS; Terrorism; United Nations;** various African country articles.

Agriculture.

Agriculture. The United States harvested its largest corn crop ever in 2003, while South America continued to outstrip the rest of the world in soybean production. Trading partners around the world slammed their borders shut to U.S. and Canadian beef imports after single cases of mad cow disease were discovered in both countries in 2003.

World crop production. According to a U.S. Department of Agriculture (USDA) report released in November, world production of small grains, oilseeds, rice, wheat, and cotton in 2003 varied only slightly from 2002. The real story was weather-driven changes in crop production.

World wheat production was the most striking example. Although world production was down 3 percent at 548 million metric tons, the easing of a drought in North America increased wheat production 45 percent in the United States and 36 percent in Canada. Wheat production in Australia increased by 140 percent as weather there returned to more normal patterns. However, drought took hold in Russia, Kazakhstan, and Ukraine, cutting production in those countries to 50 million metric tons, down from 84 million metric tons a year ago. Europe also suffered a 12-percent decline in wheat production due to extreme heat, causing some countries to suspend exports briefly to meet domestic demand.

Production of small grains—corn, rye, sorghum, barley, oats, and millet—totaled 884 million metric tons in 2003, up 2 percent from 2002. Good weather in Australia, Canada, and the United States replenished stocks depleted by the drought of 2002. However, lingering dryness in Argentina caused farmers to plant less acreage in corn and sunflowers and more in soybeans, because the beans can be planted later in the season. In China, rains and floods in the months before harvest cut the corn crop 6 percent and reduced corn exports by nearly 50 percent.

Oilseed production, including soybeans, sunflower seeds, cottonseed, rapeseed, and peanuts, rose 6 percent to 348 million metric tons. Argentina, with 36 million metric tons of soybeans, and Brazil with 60 million metric tons, had record crops in 2003. India, with 6.2 million metric tons, also harvested a record crop of soybeans.

The 2003 world rice harvest, at 391 million metric tons, was up 3 percent from the 2002 harvest. India's 2003 crop, at about 89 million metric tons, was up 17 percent from 2002. By contrast, the 2003 rice crop in China, the world's largest producer, was 118 million metric tons, down 3 percent from the 2002 crop. The 2003 rice crops in the Philippines and Indonesia were larger than crops in 2002, while Japan and the United States experienced declines in their rice crops. The U.S. crop in 2003 was about 6 million metric tons, down nearly 8 percent from 2002.

World cotton production in 2003 was 92 million bales, up 5 percent from the 2002 harvest. One bale is equivalent to 480 pounds of cotton. Big harvests in the United States, Brazil, and India offset China's flood-damaged cotton crop.

U.S. crop production. United States farmers harvested a record 10.3-billion-bushel corn crop in 2003, 14 percent above the 2002 harvest. Weather deteriorated later in 2003, however, stressing the soybean crop, which at 2.45 billion bushels was the smallest since 1996 and down 11 percent from 2002. Reduced supplies and heavy export demand raised soybean prices above $7.00 per bushel, compared with the 2001 average price of $4.38. Higher prices and tighter supplies of U.S. soybeans were expected to encourage more soybean planting in South America, where spring begins as the American harvest ends.

The U.S. wheat crop also flourished in 2003, amounting to 2.37 billion bushels, 44 percent above the drought-reduced crop of 2002. Cotton production, at 18 million bales, was up 6 percent from the 2002 harvest. However, strong export demand—nearly 60 percent of the crop was exported—caused prices to rise above levels that would trigger extra payments under the most recently enacted farm subsidy bill, the Farm Security and Rural Investment Act of 2002.

Genetically modified (GM) crops. U.S. farmers continued to increase plantings of crops genetically modified to resist herbicides and insects. Acreage planted in GM corn rose to 40 percent from 34 percent in 2002. GM soybean acreage increased to 81 percent from 75 percent, and GM cotton plantings increased 2 percent in 2003 over 2002 levels.

In 2003, the European Union continued its five-year-old ban on imports of new GM varieties. On May 13, the United States, Argentina, Canada, and Egypt filed a case with the World Trade Organization (WTO) to protest the ban, which costs U.S. farmers $200 million a year in lost exports, trade experts estimate. The WTO, located in Geneva, Switzerland, is the arbiter of trade disputes among member countries.

Organic crops and food. Global sales of organic foods—those grown without pesticides, chemical fertilizer, or GM seeds—were estimated at between $23 billion and $25 billion in 2003, according to the International Trade Centre (ITC) of the United Nations Conference on Trade and Development.

The group's estimate of 2003 sales in the United States, the world's largest organic food market, was $11 billion to $13 billion. That estimate compared to U.S. sales of $9.5 billion in 2001. In 2002, fruits and vegetables accounted for nearly 50 percent of U.S. organic food sales, while organic meat, fish, and poultry made up only 3 percent of sales.

Mad cow disease. Canada on May 20, 2003, reported a case of bovine spongiform encephalopathy (BSE), or mad cow disease, in a cow in Alberta. BSE, also known as "mad cow disease," destroys brain tissue in cows. Scientists believe that people who eat meat from BSE-infected cows can acquire Creutzfeldt-Jakob disease, a fatal disease of the central nervous system.

Within hours of the report, major importers of Canadian beef closed their borders. What had been a $4-billion (in Canadian dollars) market in beef sales collapsed. In September, the United States opened the border to imports of Canadian boxed boneless beef from cows less than 30 months of age. In order to resume imports of live animals, the USDA in October proposed grouping countries that have BSE safeguards in place into minimum risk regions. Should a case occur within such a region in the future, trade would not stop.

On December 13, the USDA reported that a sick cow slaughtered in Washington State had tested positive for BSE in early laboratory results, the first case of the disease in the United States. Japan, Mexico, Russia, South Korea, and Thailand immediately banned U.S. beef imports.

U.S. food aid. The U.S. donated 4.5 million metric tons of food worth $1.3 billion to a number of countries. Ethiopia and Iraq each received more than $100 million in aid, the largest donations. Included in the 2003 total were 130,000 metric tons of commodities donated to food-deficit countries under the McGovern-Dole International Food for Education and Child Nutrition Program. Authorized by the 2002 Farm Bill, the program is named in honor of Ambassador and former U.S. Senator George McGovern (D., South Dakota) and former U.S. Senator Robert Dole (R., Kansas). In 2003, the program benefited about 2.25 million children and mothers worldwide.

Trade and the WTO. In 2003, the value of U.S. exports of agricultural products rose to $56 billion, 5 percent more than in 2002. At the same time, the value of agricultural imports rose to $46 billion as imports of wine, coffee, cocoa, rubber, and tobacco increased.

On Sept. 17, 2003, the 146 member countries of the WTO met in Cancun, Mexico, for a mid-term meeting on the Doha Development Agenda (the name of the round of world trade talks begun in 2001 in Doha, Qatar). However, attempts to reach agreement on nonagricultural issues dealing with trade and investments failed., The meeting adjourned without addressing measures to make agricultural trade flow more freely.

■ Patricia Peak Klintberg

See also **Food; International trade.**

AIDS. The first annual increase in the number of newly diagnosed cases of AIDS in the United States in 10 years, announced in July 2003, led U.S. public health officials to express concern that the disease may be making a comeback. The U.S. Centers for Disease Control and Prevention (CDC) in Atlanta, Georgia, reported that the number of new cases of AIDS in 2002 rose to 42,136, a 2.2-percent increase over 2001 figures. From 1993 to 2000, the AIDS rate had declined.

CDC officials also reported the third consecutive yearly increase in the number of gay and bisexual men newly infected with HIV, the virus that causes AIDS. The infection rate for these two groups, which are considered at high risk of contracting the virus, rose a total of 7.1 percent from 2001 to 2002. Since 1999, cases of HIV infection among gay and bisexual men in the United States jumped 17.7 percent.

CDC officials speculated that the increase may have resulted, in part, from a false sense of safety created by new drugs that slow the development of AIDS. They also noted, however, that the increase may reflect a rise in the number of gay and bisexual men being tested for the virus.

Despite the rise in new AIDS cases, the U.S. death rate from AIDS fell by 6 percent in 2002, to 16,371. Public health officials attributed the decline chiefly to improved medical treatment.

Drug-resistant HIV. About 10 percent of all Europeans newly infected with HIV contract a strain of the virus that is resistant to at least one of three main types of drugs used to suppress the virus, according to a July 2003 study. The study, led by researchers at the University of Utrecht in the Netherlands, involved about 1,600 newly diagnosed but untreated patients from 17 European countries. The researchers said the findings suggest that many AIDS patients undergoing treatment returned to sharing needles and engaging in unsafe sex, major ways of contracting HIV.

AIDS pledge. In January, U.S. President George W. Bush pledged $15 billion over five years to combat AIDS in African and Caribbean countries most heavily ravaged by the disease. According to the Joint United Nations Programme on HIV/AIDS, about 70 percent of people with AIDS or HIV worldwide live in sub-Saharan Africa. AIDS groups, however, criticized Bush for requesting only $2 billion in his budget for fiscal year 2004, two-thirds of the yearly amount authorized. The U.S. Congress increased funding for the initiative by $400,000.

■ Barbara A. Mayes

See also **Africa; Drugs; Public health and safety; South Africa.**

Air pollution. See Environmental pollution.

Alabama. See State government.

Alaska. See State government.

Albania.
Voters went to the polls on Oct. 12, 2003, to elect local officials in towns and municipalities across Albania. The ruling Socialist Party maintained a slight edge over the opposition Democrats.

The election was closely watched by international observers, notably the Organization for Security and Cooperation in Europe (OSCE), an association of more than 50 Eastern and Western nations that work for international security. In initial reports, OSCE monitors noted shortcomings in the election process but described the election as generally fair. However, disputes between the two major parties delayed official publication of the election results until mid-November, prompting the head of the OSCE team to issue a more negative evaluation.

Albania's gross domestic product—the value of all goods and services produced in a country in a year—grew by 6 percent in 2003, up from 4.7 percent in 2002. The rate of inflation declined gradually from a peak of 7 percent early in 2003.

At the urging of United Nations (UN) officials, Albanian leaders signed a free trade agreement with Kosovo in July. The nominally Serbian province with an Albanian ethnic majority continued to be administered by UN officials in 2003.

■ Sharon L. Wolchik

See also **Europe.**

Algeria.
French President Jacques Chirac and his wife Bernadette made a state visit to Algeria in March 2003. Although this visit was not the first visit by a French head of state to independent Algeria, it was the most official, highlighted by the signing of a formal declaration of friendship between France and Algeria. The Chiracs were accompanied by a large delegation of ministers, business leaders, and artists, including Foreign Minister Dominique de Villepin, the heads of corporate giants such as TotalFinaElf, and French cultural figures. As President Chirac rode in an open car through the streets of Algiers, the capital, with Algerian President Abdelaziz Bouteflika by his side, he was welcomed by the people, who showered him with confetti and flowers.

Earthquake. A major earthquake measuring 6.7 struck northern Algeria on May 21. The earthquake was the most serious to hit North Africa in more than 20 years. The epicenter was in Thenia, about 40 miles (64.4 kilometers) east of Algiers. According to final government reports, more than 2,200 people died and thousands more were injured.

Buildings, telecommunications, roads, and bridges suffered serious damage. In addition, tens of thousands of Algerians were left homeless. President Bouteflika visited quake survivors three times, only to be greeted by insults and stone-throwing crowds who perceived the government's response to the situation as slow.

Releases. In late June, the two top leaders of Algeria's banned fundamentalist group Islamic Salvation Front were released. They had been jailed in 1992, after the election their party had been set to win was annulled. Abassi Madani, who had been under house arrest for a number of years, was set free and eventually allowed to travel abroad. The more radical Ali Belhadj was jailed for 11 years before being released. Both were issued court orders banning them from participating in any kind of political activity.

Kidnappings. In February and March 2003, 32 Europeans were kidnapped in separate incidents in southern Algeria by the Islamic militant organization Salafist Group for Preaching and Combat (GSPC). In May, Algerian commandos freed 17 of the hostages, killing several of the abductors in the process. A hostage then died in captivity from heatstroke. Germany decided to negotiate with the GSPC for the release of the other 14 hostages and sent its Deputy Foreign Minister on a number of missions to Algeria and Mali, where the hostages were moved. In August, the remaining hostages were finally released and flew home to Germany, Switzerland, and the Netherlands.

■ Mary-Jane Deeb

Angola. See Africa.

Animal. See Conservation; Zoos.

Anthropology. Archaeologist Robert Blumen-schine of Rutgers University in New Brunswick, New Jersey, and his team announced in February 2003 their 1995 discovery of a 1.8 million-year-old upper jaw from Olduvai Gorge, Tanzania, a ravine made famous by Louis and Mary Leakey's finds of *Homo habilis* fossils.

The upper jaw, catalogued as Olduvai Hominid 65 (OH 65), preserved a complete set of worn adult teeth and portions of the lower face. The shape of the palate and anatomical features of the lower face resembled previous finds made at Olduvai Gorge and assigned to *H. habilis* ("the handy man"), widely thought to have been the maker of crude stone tools found in abundance at the gorge.

However, Blumenschine and his team also noted similarities with another early human ancestor, sometimes called *Homo rudolfensis,* found at Lake Turkana, Kenya. Some scientists consider *H. rudolfensis* a separate species from *H. habilis,* but Blumenschine suggested that if the Turkana species is the same as the *H. habilis* from Olduvai, then the species name *rudolfensis* should be dropped.

OH 65 was uncovered during archaeological excavations in the western part of Olduvai Gorge, which also yielded stone artifacts and tools that date from 2.5 to 1.5 million years ago. The scientists found the quartzite tools near fossil remains of several species of antelopes. Some of the antelope bones show stone-tool cut marks suggesting that early hominids included meat in their diet.

Ethiopia's *H. sapiens*. A team of anthropologists led by Tim D. White of the University of California, Berkeley, reported in June 2003 the recovery of fossil *crania* (skulls minus the lower jaw) of two adults and a child from the site of Herto in the Middle Awash region of Ethiopia. The geological deposit that yielded the specimens is dated to 160,000 years ago.

The two adult crania, because of their large size, were most likely males. Scientists estimated the age of the child's cranium at 6 to 7 years, too young to indicate gender. All the crania show overwhelming similarities with modern *H. sapiens* specimens. However, because of some anatomical differences from living humans, the Herto finds were designated a subspecies—*Homo sapiens idaltu* (idaltu means "elder" in the language of the local Afar people).

The highest level of genetic variation among modern humans is found in African populations, suggesting that *H. sapiens* initially arose in Africa between 250,000 and 150,000 years ago and migrated to Europe and Asia to give rise to all modern humans.

New York City's American Museum of Natural History in January unveils the world's most complete and accurate skeleton of a Neandertal (foreground), displayed beside the skeleton of a modern human being. Anthropologist Gary Sawyer led a team that constructed the new skeleton from casts of fossils of different specimens found in Europe and the Middle East. Neandertals, a relative of modern human beings, became extinct about 35,000 years ago.

The Herto discoveries strengthened this view.

Stone tools found near the skulls were less advanced than typical hand axes from the Middle and Lower Paleolithic Age and more sophisticated than African Middle Stone Age tool collections, which are dominated by stone flakes. This suggests a culture in transition. Most interesting to anthropologists were superficial cut marks in the crania that could only have been made by stone tools. The scientists suggested that the crania were defleshed as some sort of mortuary practice.

DNA from early *H. sapiens*. Giorgio Bertorelle of the University of Ferrara, Italy, and his co-workers announced in May 2003 the recovery of DNA from early *H. sapiens* specimens from southern Italy. Dating to roughly 24,000 years ago, the finds are from the Upper Paleolithic Age.

The scientists compared a sequence of mitochondrial DNA (the DNA found in the "power houses" of the cell) from these early *H. sapiens* with similar DNA stretches in modern humans as well as in Neandertals. The comparison showed that the 24,000-year-old *H. sapiens* DNA was unlike that of the Neandertals and similar to that of modern day humans. These results indicated that Neandertals were not ancestral to *H. sapiens* but probably were a separate species, *Homo neanderthalensis,* that became extinct. ■ Donald C. Johanson

See also **Archaeology.**

Archaeology.

The National Museum of Baghdad through the second half of 2003 recovered many of the artifacts that disappeared during the fall of Baghdad in April. Initially, museum officials feared that much of the museum's collection had been looted, but in June, United States Customs agents and officials from the U.S. Defense Department's Office of the Coalition Provisional Authority found many of the most important pieces in a basement vault under Baghdad's demolished central bank. A burst water pipe had flooded the vault, soaking five crates in which the collection known as the Treasure of Nimrud had been stored. The crates held smaller boxes containing 613 pieces of gold jewelry, precious stones, and ornaments dating from 800 B.C.

Weeks later, unidentified men returned the 5,200-year-old Vase of Warka, the world's oldest carved limestone vessel. It was in pieces, but experts hoped to restore it. In September, the Lady of Warka, a marble mask of the same period and from the same site as the vase, was also recovered from a farmer who had buried it in an orchard outside Baghdad. The sculpture is one of the earliest artistic representations of the human face and has been called the "Mona Lisa of Mesopotamia."

Two other items from the "30 most wanted" list of artifacts stolen from the museum, a copper sculpture from 2300 B.C. and a bronze brazier from Nimrud, were recovered in early November. Many important items were returned under a no-questions-asked amnesty program, and other artifacts were seized in raids. More than 10,000 objects remained missing at the end of 2003.

Donner Party. Excavations at a site 30 miles (48 kilometers) west of Reno, Nevada, in August 2003 yielded artifacts and possible human remains from the ill-fated Donner Party. In 1846, a wagon train carrying the Donners and other families headed west to California from Illinois. They were stopped by snowstorms in the Sierra Nevada in October and November. After running out of food, some members of the party turned to cannibalism, eating the flesh of those who had perished from starvation or the cold. About half of the 81 people who were trapped survived the winter.

Excavations in the 1980's by archaeologists at the University of Nevada, Reno, found 1840's-era artifacts at a site near Donner Lake, where several families endured the winter in three cabins. The archaeologists also found artifacts at a camp on Alder Creek, which they identified as the place George and Jacob Donner had camped. Some historians, however, argued that the Alder Creek location was too far from the wagon trail. Portland State University archaeologists returned to Alder Creek in 2003 to dig, and they used ground-penetrating radar to find more evidence. They discovered a hearth and fire-cracked rock, ceramic and pipe-bowl fragments, lead musket balls, and bone fragments of a large mammal, some of which were charred and had cut marks from an ax. Tests were planned to determine if the bone fragments were human. If so, DNA comparisons with descendants of the Donner family might confirm Alder Creek as the site of the camp.

Roman make-up. Excavations at a Roman temple some 2 miles (3.2 kilometers) south of London revealed a sealed tin box in July. When a Museum of London conservator opened the box, she found it was still half filled with a cream that smelled "sulfurous" and "cheesy." The cream still had the finger marks of the person who last used it some 2,000 years ago. Chemical analysis will determine the cream's composition, but it is most likely a face cream or face paint. Romans used various substances as make-up, such as white lead to create a fair complexion, red ochre to stain the lips, and lamp soot for eyeliner.

James ossuary a fake. The Israel Antiquities Authority (IAA) concluded in June that two artifacts with inscriptions linking them to the Bible were fakes. One of the artifacts was an *ossuary* (a limestone box in which the bones of a deceased person are stored). The other was a slab of gray stone on which were engraved instructions on the care of the main Jewish temple in Jerusalem. The IAA team concluded that the box, which dates

Chinese officials in January 2003 announced the discovery of a royal tomb in the Weshan excavation site in China that holds hundreds of 1-foot (0.3-meter) terra cotta soldiers with horses and chariots. Archaeologists believe that the Chinese of the Qin (226-221 B.C.) and Han (202 B.C.-A.D. 220) dynasties buried royalty with a symbolic military escort into the afterlife. This tomb dates from the first half of the Han period.

Hebei Province

Bo Gulf

Grand Canal

Huang He

Jinan

Weifang

Shandong Province

Qingdao

Jining

Weishan

Weishan Lake

Weishan
Excavation site of archaeological discovery

Yellow Sea

C H I N A

Grand Canal

Anhui Province

Jiangsu Province

Chang Jiang

0   100 Miles
0   100 Kilometers

A S I A

Russia

Mongolia

Beijing

N. Korea

Area of detail

C H I N A

S. Korea

Japan

Nepal

Bhutan

Shanghai

Pacific Ocean

India

Myanmar

Laos

Taiwan

from 2,000 years ago, had a forged inscription identifying it as the ossuary of James, the brother of Jesus. However, some scientists, speaking at a conference of the American Academy of Religion and the Society of Biblical Literature in Atlanta in November, argued that the finding may be premature. The IAA had not yet released a full report.

Welcome to the New World. The latest evidence for when the New World was colonized suggests that human beings arrived from Asia 18,000 years ago, at the earliest. Researchers from the University of Oxford in England and the Harvard School of Public Health at Cambridge, Massachusetts, reached this conclusion based on their study of the Y chromosome, which passes only from father to son. They identified the same *mutation* (a random change) in the Y chromosomes of both Siberian and Native American populations. Since both peoples have the mutation, it must have occurred before Asians migrated across the land bridge known as Beringia, which once existed between Siberia and Alaska. According to the researchers, the mutation occurred no more than 18,000 and likely only 15,000 years ago. This date coincides with the date of the earliest widely accepted archaeological site in the New World, Chile's Monte Verde, which has been radiocarbon dated at about 15,000 years old.   ■ Mark Rose

See also **Anthropology; Iraq: A Special Report.**

Architecture.
The redevelopment of New York City's World Trade Center dominated architectural news in 2003. In February, Daniel Libeskind won an international competition to plan the 16-acre (6.5-hectare) site. His winning proposal called for a museum dedicated to the terrorist attacks of Sept. 11, 2001; a sunken memorial space framed by the slurry walls of the twin towers; and a 1,776-foot (541.3-meter) Freedom Tower that was to be the world's tallest building. However, because Libeskind had never designed a skyscraper, developer Larry Silverstein and the Lower Manhattan Development Corporation (LMDC), which was overseeing the redevelopment, hired David Childs of Skidmore, Owings, and Merrill to collaborate on the design of the Freedom Tower. Silverstein and LMDC then brought in other architects to design other buildings while relegating Libeskind to the role of consulting architect. A revised model of the Freedom Tower was unveiled on December 19. Childs redesigned various features of Libeskind's original concept.

In November, the LMDC unveiled eight competing designs for the September 11 memorial, the emotional and symbolic centerpiece of the redevelopment. These ranged from a cloud of lights floating above Ground Zero to a pair of sunken memorial rooms marking the footprints of the Twin Towers.

Walt Disney Concert Hall opens. The $274-million Walt Disney Concert Hall in Los Angeles, designed by Frank Gehry, opened in October. The opening concluded a 16-year ordeal for the architect, during which he was forced to redesign the project, and construction halted several times because of economic and political problems. Critics compared the hall's swooping stainless steel facade to an unfolding flower, ship sails, or wind-blown drapery. The 2,265-seat auditorium is paneled in Douglas fir, a wood commonly used for violins and cellos. The complex also includes a two-story administrative building, a public garden, a restaurant, a cafe, and two amphitheaters seating 350 and 150 people. The hall is the new home of the Los Angeles Philharmonic, as well as several other performing arts groups.

Gehry also designed the Richard B. Fisher Center for the Performing Arts, which opened in April at Bard College in Annandale-on-Hudson, New York. It incorporates handsome theater and dance spaces as well as a 900-seat concert hall, all tucked under a folding metal roof that resembles a dropped handkerchief. Yasuhisa Toyota served as the acoustician for both Gehry buildings.

Nasher Sculpture Center. The Nasher Sculpture Center, designed by Italian architect Renzo Piano and U.S. landscape architect Peter Walker, opened in October in downtown Dallas. This spare *travertine* (marble) pavilion, with an intricate glass roof and five vaulted galleries, opens out to a lush garden. The center is home to one of the finest private collections of modern sculpture in the world, including major works by Rodin, Picasso, Miro, Henry Moore, and Richard Serra. The $70-million project was funded entirely by Raymond D. Nasher, a Dallas developer.

Rosenthal Center. Iraq-born architect Zaha Hadid completed her first building in the United States, the Rosenthal Center for Contemporary Art in Cincinnati, Ohio, which opened in April. The building is as edgy and confrontational as the art it contains. A curving street facade rolls into the lobby, where visitors encounter a Rubik's cube of interlocking squares and rectangles and a zigzagging central staircase. The center was created for traveling exhibitions, rather than a permanent collection.

Price Tower renovation. For sheer exoticism, nothing tops the renovation of Frank Lloyd Wright's Price Tower in Bartlesville, Oklahoma, completed in October. It is Wright's only skyscraper, and when it first opened in 1956, it contained shops, apartments, and the headquarters of Harold Price's oil pipeline company. The tower had deteriorated badly before New York City architect Wendy Evans Joseph was commissioned to convert it into an art center and a 21-room luxury hotel and restaurant. Even in modernized

In February 2003, architect Daniel Libeskind's design for rebuilding New York City's World Trade Center won a competition to which seven world-renowned architectural groups submitted designs for the 16-acre (6.5-hectare) site where nearly 3,000 people died in the terrorist attack on Sept. 11, 2001. Rick Bell, executive director of the New York chapter of the American Institute of Architects, said that Libeskind's plan for the memorial space distinguished it from the other plans and was the primary reason for its selection. Chairman of the Lower Manhattan Development Corporation (LMDC) John C. Whitehead commented, "It succeeds both when it rises into the sky and when it descends into the ground." Libeskind's design, which addressed many of the demands of people involved in the tragedy, effectively ended the debate about whether the center should be rebuilt, but sparked new debate on its future.

In July 2002, LMDC, the governmental board charged with overseeing the site's redevelopment, and city planners held a town hall meeting attended by 4,000 people. The LMDC examined six designs and then rejected all six as boring and too crammed with office space. The LMDC then put out a call to some of the world's most noted architects to partici-

PUSHING GROUND ZERO TO GREAT HEIGHTS

pate in a design competition. All plans were to incorporate a memorial, office and commercial space, parks, a hotel, a pedestrian mall, and a commuter train station. From the nine designs submitted by the seven participants, the judges chose THINK Group, led by Fred Schwartz and Rafael Vinoly, and Studio Daniel Libeskind as the finalists. Libeskind gave an impassioned final presentation showing how his design symbolized the hopes and dreams of the nation. The presentation convinced the judges and gained the support of New York Governor George Pataki and New York City Mayor Michael Bloomberg.

Daniel Libeskind was born in Poland in 1946 and came to the United States with his family in 1959 on the S.S. *Constitution.* As the ship entered the New York City harbor, he saw the Statue of Liberty and the Manhattan skyline for the first time, which made a great and lasting impression that would later influence his designs for the World Trade Center site. His family settled in the Bronx, where he graduated from Bronx High School of Science. He became a U.S. citizen in the mid-1960's. He studied at New York City's Cooper Union for the Advancement of Science and Art and decided to make architecture his life's work.

Critics consider Libeskind a leading architectural theorist and educator. In 1989, he won a design competition for the Jewish Museum Berlin for which he received the German Architecture Prize. He since has received commissions to design buildings in London and Manchester, England; San Francisco, California; Dresden, Germany; Guadalajara, Mexico; and Denver, Colorado.

Libeskind's winning proposal for the World Trade Center site included a 1,776-foot (541.3-meter) spire, called the Freedom Tower, which echoes the upraised arm of the Statue of Liberty. The tower's height, a reference to the year of the Declaration of Independence, would make it the tallest building in the world. Libeskind's plan included six acres (2.4 hectares) of memorial space that incorporated a 70-foot- (21.2-meter-) deep section of the concrete foundation walls—the so-called "bathtub"—that survived the

Architect Daniel Libes-
kind explains details of
his plan for the new
World Trade Center to
New York City Mayor
Michael Bloomberg (left)
and New York Governor
George Pataki at a press
conference on Feb. 27,
2003. Libeskind's design
was chosen over eight
other proposals submit-
ted in a competition
sponsored by the Lower
Manhattan Redevelop-
ment Corporation.

collapse of the twin towers. Libeskind also envisioned a space designed to
capture a wedge of unobstructed sunlight each year on September 11 from
the time that the first plane hit until the time the last tower fell, as well as
a 100-foot (30.5-meter) waterfall, and a Park of Heroes.

Although Libeskind's design won the competition, not everyone
involved was happy with the choice. Developer Larry Silverstein, who held
a 99-year lease on the World Trade Center property, did not approve of
the Libeskind plan and hired his own architect, David Childs, of Skidmore,
Owings, and Merrill (SOM). Childs and the SOM team had a great deal of
experience designing enormous skyscrapers, such as the Sears Tower in
Chicago—experience that Libeskind lacked. Libeskind and Childs eventually
compromised on a design for the Freedom Tower, which was revealed to
the public on December 19.

The Port Authority of New York and New Jersey, the agency that owns the land on which the new World Trade Center will stand, also expressed concern about the reduced office and commercial space in Libeskind's design. The Port Authority then hired Spanish architect Santiago Calatrava, known for his designs of rail stations in Lyon, France, and Lisbon, Portugal, to design the commuter train station, under Libeskind's guidelines. Proposed changes to the buildings and underground space in turn affected the plans for the memorial space. Libeskind agreed to raise the floor of the memorial site from 70 feet (21.3 meters) below ground level to 30 feet (9.1 meters) to accommodate the expanded transportation hub and pedestrian concourses. The increased office space significantly reduced the amount of space available for parks.

Libeskind's design flexibility is likely to be tested further before the groundbreaking, tentatively scheduled for the summer of 2004, as he tries to meet the goals and visions of families of the victims, neighborhood residents, the landowner, the leaseholder, and city planners.   ■ Carol Yehling

An artist's rendering of Daniel Libeskind's plan for the new World Trade Center shows the "Wedge of Light." Buildings are arranged at certain angles to capture a wedge of unobstructed sunlight every September 11 between 8:46 a.m., when the first plane struck the twin towers, and 10:28 a.m., when the last tower collapsed.

form, it remains one of the most romantic and fiercely individualistic works of U.S. architecture.

McCormick Tribune Campus Center. At the McCormick Tribune Campus Center, which opened in September 2003 at the Illinois Institute of Technology in Chicago, Dutch architect Rem Koolhaas faced off against modernist master Ludwig Mies van der Rohe, who designed the original campus in the 1940's. Koolhaas's new student center is a one-story steel and glass rectangle topped by a 530-foot (161-meter) steel tube that encloses an elevated train line. The tube dampens the roar of the trains while challenging Mies's pristine campus grid. The result is a clash between order and fragmentation that Koolhaas sees as the essence of contemporary life.

Pritzker Prize. The 2003 Pritzker Prize, architecture's most prestigious award, went to 84-year-old Jorn Utzon of Denmark, whose renowned Sydney Opera House was designed in the 1950's but not completed until the 1970's. The building helped to define a city, a country, and a continent, and reacquainted architects with the sculptural and lyrical possibilities of their art. The Pritzker Prize is an award given annually to a living architect who has made "consistent and significant contributions to humanity and the environment." ◼ David Dillon

See also **Building and construction; Los Angeles.**

Argentina. Nestor Carlos Kirchner was sworn in for a four-year term as president in May 2003. He pledged to revive an economy that was just emerging from the worst depression in Argentine history. He promised to reestablish the country's credit rating, but not "at the cost of the hunger and exclusion of the Argentine people." In 2003, half of all Argentinians lived below the poverty line.

Kirchner, of German-Swiss-Croatian ancestry, was governor of Santa Cruz, Argentina's sparsely populated, southernmost province, for 12 years. During his tenure as governor, Kirchner handled the privatization of the local oil industry. To promote the province's stability in troubled times, he banked the proceeds, estimated at $500 million, abroad, where it was safe from the turmoil that affected the Argentine economy in 2001.

In staffing his new administration, Kirchner relied heavily on trusted friends. He named four people to his Cabinet from Santa Cruz, including one of his closest associates, to head the state intelligence agency, and his older sister, Alicia Kirchner, as minister of social development.

Reform of armed forces. Kirchner quickly purged Argentina's armed forces, forcing about half of the top officers in the army, navy, and air force into retirement, including many officers associated with past human rights violations. In

May 2003, he named Roberto Bendini, a young commander of a Santa Cruz brigade, as army chief. Kirchner also appointed relatively inexperienced officers to head the navy and air force.

Kirchner dismissed 8 of the 10 senior commissioners of Argentina's 32,000-member federal police force in June. He also fired the head of the Buenos Aires police force, which was alleged to be highly corrupt.

Kirchner also asked the Argentine Congress to impeach members of the Supreme Court, another institution widely regarded as corrupt and politicized. Seeing the handwriting on the wall, Chief Justice Julio Nazareno resigned in June, weeks before his own impeachment trial.

Economic upturn. Kirchner was fortunate that, by the time he took office, there were signs of a recovery in Argentina's agricultural sector. The 70 percent devaluation of the Argentine peso in January 2002 had made Argentine crops a bargain for foreign buyers.

To exploit this advantage, farmers planted a record 64 million acres (25.9 million hectares) in soybeans in 2003, making soybeans Argentina's most valuable export crop. World market prices for wool, three times higher than three years previously, also helped stimulate the economic revival of Argentina's historically important sheep industry. Argentine mutton exports, which had doubled in 2002 to nearly $500 million, doubled again in the first quarter of 2003, as compared with the same period of the previous year.

Deal with the IMF. On September 10, Kirchner and Horst Kohler, managing director of the International Monetary Fund (IMF), a United Nations affiliate, announced an agreement on refinancing $21.6 billion in debt over the next three years. The accord was seen by economists as a victory for Argentina, which had successfully insisted on maintaining social welfare spending in rebuilding its society and economy.

Under the arrangement, Argentina will enjoy greater flexibility in the management of its own economy than any other Latin American nation that had previously received IMF assistance. In a deviation from past practices, the IMF refrained from imposing a timetable on Argentina for repaying its debts. This development enabled the government to work out, on a case-by-case basis, compensation due foreign banks and owners of Argentine utilities, which, like the Argentine people, were hard-hit by the devaluation of the peso in January 2002. Moreover, Kirchner also moved ahead with a $2.8-billion program to jump start the economy by creating jobs in road and public housing construction. ◼ Nathan A. Haverstock

See also **Latin America.**

Arizona. See **State government.**

Arkansas. See **State government.**

Armed forces. United States military affairs in 2003 were dominated by a war against the forces of Iraqi President Saddam Hussein. Unlike the Persian Gulf War of 1991, which liberated Kuwait from Iraq's military occupation, the Iraq War of 2003 was designed to topple Hussein and his regime from power. Following only six weeks of fighting, U.S. President George W. Bush on May 1 declared that the war was essentially over. However, at the end of 2003, more than 130,000 U.S. soldiers remained on occupation duty in Iraq, and more than 200 had died in guerrilla attacks since the end of major combat operations.

The war and its aftermath placed significant strains on the U.S. military, which was already heavily engaged in antiterrorism operations in Afghanistan. Iraqi combat tours were extended to one year, and tens of thousands of reserve soldiers were called to active duty to serve in Iraq.

War begins. After months of diplomatic maneuvering designed to persuade Saddam Hussein to leave voluntarily, President Bush ordered the start of combat operations on March 20 (March 19 in the United States). An initial missile strike targeted a leadership bunker in Baghdad where Hussein and many of his senior assistants were thought to have been hiding.

Within hours, two major columns of U.S. ground forces, which had been massing in Kuwait for several months, invaded Iraq from the south. The columns were led by the Army's Third Infantry Division and the First Marine Expeditionary Force, which was joined by a British division. A reinforced airborne infantry brigade attacked from the north, while special operations forces secured Iraqi airfields in the west. Ground forces were accompanied by a massive air campaign featuring B-1, B-2, and B-52 heavy bombers, and hundreds of air force and navy carrier-based attack aircraft.

Despite encountering occasional pockets of fierce resistance from Iraqi army units and irregular forces, most major Iraqi units were either quickly destroyed or disbanded and fled the U.S. offensive. By mid-April, most major population centers were under the control of the U.S.-British coalition, and Baghdad was surrounded.

Four days after the start of the war, an Army transportation company from Fort Bliss, Texas, suffered heavy casualties after taking a wrong turn in southern Iraq. Eleven members of the unit were killed and six others were taken prisoner, including Private First Class Jessica Lynch. On March 30, special forces commandos stormed a hospital in An Nasariyah and rescued Lynch, who had suffered severe injuries. The other five prisoners of war (POW's) were rescued in northern Iraq.

"One victory." Baghdad fell to U.S. forces on April 9, and on May 1, in a speech on the deck of the U.S.S. *Abraham Lincoln,* President Bush declared the end of major combat operations. "The Battle of Iraq is one victory in a war on terror that began on Sept. 11, 2001, and still goes on," Bush said.

Friendly fire. Despite technological advances since the 1991 Gulf War, several "friendly fire" incidents occurred during the Iraq War of 2003. On March 23, a U.S. Patriot missile shot down a British Tornado jet, killing the two crew members. U.S. officials reported on April 4 that another Patriot missile shot down a Navy F/A-18 jet fighter and that an Air Force F-15E jet fighter mistakenly fired on U.S. soldiers, killing three and wounding several others. Several other U.S. servicemen were reported killed during the course of the war.

Casualty report. Officials with the U.S. Department of Defense reported that during the combat phase of the war, 138 U.S. soldiers died, with 115 killed in action. Approximately 550 were reported wounded. U.S. military commanders did not release estimates of Iraqi civilian casualties in 2003. However, an Associated Press investigation concluded in June that more than 3,200 Iraqi civilians had died during the war, including about 1,900 people killed in Baghdad.

End of the Husseins. Saddam Hussein's sons, Qusay and Uday, were killed in July 2003 following a battle with units of the 101st Airborne Division in the northern Iraq town of Mosul, 280 miles (450 kilometers) north of Baghdad. The brothers both had $15-million bounties on their heads. U.S. Army troops captured Saddam Hussein on December 13 near Tikrit, his hometown.

Occupation difficulties. Throughout 2003, both supporters and critics of military action in Iraq admitted that winning the war proved easier than winning the peace. Efforts to establish governmental authority in Iraq, revive the Iraqi economy, and restore basic services, such as water, electricity, and medical care proved more difficult than the Bush administration had anticipated. Guerrilla units continued to attack U.S. patrols, resulting in more casualties throughout the year.

In an address to the United States on September 7, President Bush acknowledged that significant numbers of U.S. troops would remain in Iraq far longer than envisioned and that the rebuilding of the country would be far more expensive than anticipated.

Rebuilding efforts. In November, the U.S. Congress approved a request from President Bush for $87.5 billion for the continued occupation and rebuilding of Iraq and Afghanistan. The amount included approximately $66 billion designated for military operations and $21 billion for reconstruction activities. In 2003 the United States had spent approximately $79 billion on the war in Iraq and its aftermath and was spending about $3 billion a month for ongoing operations.

Death toll. By the end of 2003, the U.S. death toll in Iraq stood at more than 470 troops, including more than 2,300 wounded in action.

Global redeployments. As part of Secretary of Defense Donald Rumsfeld's effort to transform the U.S. military into a more mobile fighting force, the Bush administration announced in February that it was considering a major redeployment of military units based in foreign countries. Under the plan, the U.S. military presence in Germany, where approximately 70,000 troops were stationed in 2003,

A sailor aboard the U.S.S. *Abraham Lincoln* waves a U.S. flag as the aircraft carrier arrives in San Diego in May 2003. The Navy vessel and its 5,000-member crew was the first carrier to return from the war in Iraq.

would undergo a radical alteration. Part of the plan included transferring the troops to military bases in Poland, Hungary, and the Czech Republic and reducing European tours of duty from three years to six months.

In June, Deputy Secretary of Defense Paul Wolfowitz announced that several thousand U.S. troops would be transferred from Seoul, South Korea, to bases in the southern part of the country in an attempt to lessen tensions with North Korea. North Korean and U.S. officials were at odds in 2003 over North Korea's revival of its nuclear weapons program.

Weapons systems. Officials at the Department of Defense announced in May that they would purchase 11 more V-22 Osprey aircraft for the U.S. Marine Corps. The Osprey is a tilt-wing aircraft that lands and takes off like a helicopter but flies like an airplane. Military experts viewed the $817-million contract as an indication that a redesign had solved the mechanical problems that had plagued the aircraft.

Personnel developments. In March, Air Force officials announced plans to remove four senior commanders from the U.S. Air Force

Academy in Colorado Springs, Colorado, amid allegations that they had ignored cadets' complaints of sexual harassment. Lieutenant General John D. Dallagher, the academy superintendent, and three top subordinates were reassigned. Dozens of former female cadets said that they had been reprimanded or ignored by academy officials after reporting instances of sexual abuse.

On June 19, the Air Force released an internal review that found "no systemic acceptance of sexual assault at the academy, no institutional avoidance of responsibility or systemic maltreatment of cadets who report sexual assault." But it singled out "a gender climate in which instances of negative comments and some other forms of sexual harassment have existed despite programs to eliminate them."

Defense budget. On February 3, the Defense Department proposed spending $379.9 billion for the U.S. military for fiscal year 2004 (Oct. 1, 2003 to Sept. 30, 2004). The request of more than $1 billion a day reflected a 4.2-percent increase from fiscal year 2003. The request, which did not include funds for operations in Iraq, would sustain a military of 1.4 million active duty soldiers.

Officials with the U.S. Department of Defense in 2003 requested $9.7 billion for ballistic missile defense; $5.1 billion for 22 F-22 Raptor air superiority fighter jets; $4.6 billion for development of the Joint Strike Fighter; $3.7 billion for 11 C-17 jet cargo planes; $3.4 billion for 3 Burke-class Aegis missile destroyers; $3.2 billion for 42 F/A-18 Hornet fighter jets; $2.6 billion for a Virginia-class attack submarine; $1.7 billion for 11 V-22 Osprey; $1.4 billion for 28 Predators and other unmanned aerial vehicles; $1 billion for 301 Stryker armored vehicles; and $780 million for 12 Trident II submarine-launched ballistic missiles.

On September 25, the U.S. Congress approved a $368.2-billion defense appropriations bill. The legislation included a 4.1-percent military pay raise.

Command changes. Secretary of the Air Force James P. Roche, a retired naval officer, was nominated for the position of secretary of the Army on May 7. The former secretary, Thomas White, was dismissed in April after a series of policy disagreements over the Army's future with Defense Secretary Rumsfeld. President Bush nominated Barbara McConnell Barrett to succeed Roche as Air Force secretary.

President Bush nominated Colin McMillan, an assistant secretary of defense in the administration of President George H. W. Bush, as secretary of the Navy in May to replace Gordon England. McMillan died in July before being confirmed to the post. On August 22, the president nominated England to return to his position as secretary of the Navy.

In an unprecedented development, Rumsfeld recalled a retired general to active duty and named him Army chief of staff. The appointment of General Peter Schoomaker was announced on June 10, the day before his predecessor, General Eric K. Shinseki, retired.

In July 2003, Air Force General Richard B. Myers was reappointed to a second two-year term as chairman of the Joint Chiefs of Staff. Army General John P. Abizaid was named commander of the U.S. Central Command, succeeding General Tommy R. Franks, who retired in July.

Vice Admiral Rodney P. Rempt was named superintendent of the U.S. Naval Academy on August 4. He replaced Vice Admiral Richard J. Naughton, who resigned on June 3 after a naval investigation criticized his command style.

■ Thomas M. DeFrank

See also **Congress of the United States; Iraq; Iraq: A Special Report; Korea, North; Korea, South; People in the news** (L. Paul Bremer, Paul Wolfowitz); **United States, Government of the; United States, President of the.**

Armenia. Robert Kocharian was reelected president of Armenia on March 5, 2003, defeating challenger Stepan Demirchian in a run-off with 67 percent of the vote. The election closely paralleled the presidential election of 1998, in which Kocharian similarly defeated Demirchian's father, Karen Demirchian, in a second round of balloting.

International observers expressed concerns about voting irregularities during the presidential election, including ballot-box stuffing, voter intimidation, repeated balloting, and other forms of voting manipulation. Demirchian's supporters staged a series of rallies in Yerevan, the capital, to protest the outcome of the vote, and Demirchian appealed to the Armenian Constitutional Court, demanding that the official election results be invalidated. The Court declined to annul the vote but sharply criticized the government's handling of the election.

The governing Republican Party of Armenia (HHK) triumphed in parliamentary elections, with 24.5 percent of the vote in May. Demirchian's opposition Artarutiun (Justice) Party won 14.5 percent of the vote. The remainder was split among smaller parties. The HHK sought to form a coalition with some of the smaller parties to make up at least 50 percent of the seats in parliament.

■ Steven L. Solnick

See also **Asia.**

Art. The art world, especially art museums, suffered from the weak economy in 2003. Museums nationwide reacted to state and local funding cutbacks and a decrease in private and corporate donations with layoffs, closings, and cancellations of exhibits. Financial problems were compounded by increasing insurance premiums to cover the risk of terrorist activity.

In New York City, the Metropolitan Museum of Art lost millions of dollars in donations and faced a reduction of $1.5 million in city financing during 2003. As a result, the museum raised its suggested admission fee by 20 percent to $12 and began admitting members at $50 each to large, special exhibitions on Mondays, the day the museum was traditionally closed.

The Philadelphia Museum of Art laid off 28 staff members and froze the salaries of employees making $50,000 or more. The staff cuts were expected to save the museum $1.4 million.

The Winterthur Museum outside Wilmington, Delaware, cut 15 full-time staff members, reduced salaries 2 to 5 percent, raised admission fees, and closed the museum on Mondays. The Winterthur also closed its historic houses in Odessa, Delaware, for at least a year.

Terrorism insurance. Insurance costs to cover damage and loss of art from acts of terrorism have skyrocketed since the terrorist attacks on the

A "saliera," or salt cellar, by famed Renaissance sculptor Benvenuto Cellini (1500- 1571) was stolen from the Kunsthistorisches Museum in Vienna in May 2003. The famed gold, ebony, and enamel piece was the only work of its kind by Cellini known to have survived into modern times.

United States in 2001. U.S. President George W. Bush signed a Terrorism Insurance Act in November 2002 requiring commercial insurance companies to make terrorism coverage available, but the legislation placed no limit on the cost of premiums, which have doubled or tripled in some cases. To help defray the rising costs, many museums turned for help to the federal Arts and Artifacts Indemnity Program, a plan created by Congress in 1975 to minimize the costs of insuring international exhibitions. The program was so swamped with requests that it depleted its 2003 budget of $5 billion within the first six months of the fiscal year, which began on October 1, 2002. The National Endowment for the Arts, which runs the program, lobbied for an additional $3 billion, but Congress did not act on the proposed legislation in 2003.

Without increased terrorism insurance, many owners of art, both private and public, were hesitant to lend major works for museum exhibitions during 2003. European museums expressed doubts about lending works for three major exhibitions at the Metropolitan Museum and the Museum of Modern Art (MoMA). Directors of the New York City institutions visited museum officials in Paris to negotiate an agreement, which included the purchase of additional terrorism insurance and increased security measures.

Economic difficulties resulted in a number of museum closings and exhibition cancellations across the United States. The Solomon R. Guggenheim Foundation closed the larger of its two museums at the Venetian Resort-Hotel-Casino in Las Vegas less than 18 months after its opening. In New York City, the Guggenheim Foundation shelved plans to build an enormous museum on the East River, which experts estimated would have cost nearly $1 billion. The Whitney Museum of American Art canceled plans for a $200-million addition by Dutch architect Rem Koolhaas.

New and renewed museums. Despite the poor economy, several museums opened or launched renovation programs during 2003. In March, the Asian Art Museum of San Francisco reopened in the city's former Main Library following a three-year, $160.5-million renovation. The museum has a permanent collection of more than 14,000 objects and is one of the largest institutions in the Western world devoted solely to Asian art. The renovation increased the museum's overall space by approximately 75 percent.

Dia: Beacon became the world's largest museum for contemporary art when it opened in May in Beacon, New York. The project was completed by the New York City-based Dia Art Foundation, which converted nearly 250,000 square feet (23,000 square meters) in a former Nabisco factory to show U.S. and European Minimal, Conceptual, and Post-Minimal art of the 1960's and 1970's.

The Contemporary Arts Center in Cincinnati, Ohio, moved into its first free-standing exhibition space in May 2003, the Lois and Richard Rosenthal Center for Contemporary Art, with a group show of international artists. The museum, designed by architect Zaha Hadid, offers temporary exhibitions, site-specific installations, and performances.

The opening of the Peabody Essex Museum in June culminated a $125-million expansion project that integrated 24 historic properties and gardens owned by the Salem, Massachusetts, museum, founded in 1729. The new space includes a Chinese merchant's house from the 1800's with furniture and decorative objects that illustrate 200 years of Chinese family life and culture.

Cellini theft. Thieves broke into the Kunsthistorisches Museum in Vienna, Austria, in May 2003 and stole a rare sculpture dating from the 1500's by Renaissance master Benvenuto Cellini. The sculpture, valued at $58 million, is a gold, ebony, and enamel "saliera," or salt cellar, that stands 10 inches (25.4 centimeters) tall. The only sculpture of its kind by Cellini to have survived, it features two reclining figures symbolizing the sea and the earth.

Exhibitions. Over 400,000 people attended "Leonardo da Vinci: Master Draftsman" at the Metropolitan Museum of Art, a show of 120 drawings by the Renaissance master. It was the first comprehensive survey of da Vinci's drawings ever exhibited in the United States. Crowds also flocked to the Metropolitan to see "Manet/Velazquez: The French Taste for Spanish Painting." This exhibit was the first to examine the impact of Spanish painting of the 1600's—particularly Diego Valesquez—on French artists of the 1800's, especially Edouard Manet. The show featured more than 200 paintings and works on paper by Spanish painters Velazquez, Bartolome Estaban Murillo, and Jose de Ribera.

"Matisse Picasso" was a record-breaker at MoMA in Queens, the museum's temporary exhibit space during the expansion of its midtown Manhattan facility. The show, the first exhibition dedicated to the lifelong dialogue between the two giants of art, Pablo Picasso and Henri Matisse, included 133 masterpieces that had rarely been loaned and had never before been seen together.

The National Gallery of Art in Washington, D.C., presented an exhibition of some 230 paintings, drawings, graphics, and photographs by Edouard Vuillard, the French artist of the 1800's. At the Museum of Fine Arts in Boston, "Thomas Gainsborough, 1727-1788" featured the English master's celebrated portraits, landscapes, and drawings.   ■ Sally Ruth May

See also **Architecture**.

ASIA

Terrorist activity in 2003 threatened economic and political stability in many Asian countries. In addition, a highly contagious disease spread across Southeast Asia, killing hundreds of people and costing the region millions of dollars in lost tourism revenue.

Terrorist attacks in countries from Afghanistan to Indonesia wreaked destruction and left hundreds of people dead in 2003. Most of the terrorist activity was caused by Islamic extremist groups targeting Western interests in Asia. Asian countries harbored many such organizations, including Jemaah Islamiyah, a militant Islamic group closely linked to al-Qa'ida, an international terrorist network.

Asian officials accused Jemaah Islamiyah of organizing suicide bombings that killed dozens of people in 2003. Bombings in the southern Philippines in March and April killed 39 people, and a hotel bombing in Jakarta, the Indonesian capital, killed 12 people in August. Officials also accused Jemaah Islamiyah of plotting to bomb Western embassies in Singapore and to hijack airplanes departing from Asian countries.

Asian governments attempted to secure the region. However, efforts to crack down on extremist groups produced mixed results. Several international terrorist suspects were arrested in Pakistan, Afghanistan, Indonesia, Singapore, the Philippines, and Malaysia, but international observers agreed that the arrests did little to hinder militant networks rooted in Asia.

In March, Pakistani officials arrested Khalid Shaikh Mohammed, a senior al-Qa'ida leader, in Islamabad, Pakistan's capital. Khalid was suspected of planning the terrorist attacks on the United States in 2001. In August 2003, United States Central Intelligence Agency agents captured Riduan Isamuddin, an Indonesian better known as Hambali, in Thailand. Officials said that Hambali, one of the most wanted terror suspects in Southeast Asia, organized the Indonesian hotel attack in August and was the architect of the October 2002 bombings on the Indonesian resort island of Bali that killed more than 200 people.

Highly publicized trials for several members of Jemaah Islamiyah took place in Indonesia in 2003. Indonesian courts sentenced three men to death and one to life in prison for their involvement in the 2002 Bali bombings. More than 30

Bathers wade into the reservoir behind the Three Gorges Dam on the Yangtze, China's longest river. The dam, designed to produce hydroelectric power, began to retain water in June 2003. When completed, the dam will be the largest in the world.

other Bali bombing suspects awaited trial at the end of 2003. An Indonesian court in September acquitted Abu Bakar Bashir, leader of Jemaah Islamiyah, of charges he ordered a series of terrorist attacks in Indonesia. However, he was found guilty on charges of treason. His sentence was overturned on appeal.

In the Philippines, Fathur Rohman al-Ghozi, a Jemaah Islamiyah bomb-making expert, escaped from jail in July. Philippine authorities found and killed al-Ghozi in October.

Epidemic. Severe acute respiratory syndrome (SARS), a highly contagious disease that was first diagnosed in late 2002, raced across China and other areas of Southeast Asia in 2003. The epidemic, which began in southern China, killed more than 700 people. In China, more than 5,300 people contracted the disease, and nearly 350 people died from it.

Scientists suspected that people in the Guangzhou area of China first contracted the virus from eating animals carrying it. The disease then infected people in Hong Kong and quickly spread to Vietnam, Singapore, and Taiwan. Travelers also carried the virus to Europe and North America.

A number of governments moved quickly to

contain the virus, issuing quarantines and restricting travel. However, Chinese officials were widely criticized for concealing true infection rates and preventing international health groups from investigating the epidemic in Taiwan.

During the height of the epidemic, tourism in Asia came to a virtual halt, slowing economic progress in the region. Travel to Asia began to rebound in July and August after international health officials announced that the epidemic had been contained.

Economy. Many Asian countries experienced economic growth in 2003. However, countries were still struggling to recover from a global downturn, and widespread poverty remained a major issue in the region.

China's economy grew at a dazzling rate of 9.9 percent in the first half of 2003, outpacing every other major world economy. Asian governments feared that China would use its economic power to capture manufacturing jobs that once fueled neighboring economies.

The World Trade Organization, a United

FACTS IN BRIEF ON ASIAN COUNTRIES

Country	Population	Government	Monetary unit*	Foreign trade (million U.S.$) Exports†	Imports†
Afghanistan	25,150,000	President Hamid Karzai	afghani (43.00 = $1)	1,200	1,300
Armenia	3,465,000	President Robert Kocharian	dram (558.14 = $1)	525	991
Azerbaijan	8,232,000	President Ilham Aliyev	manat (4,923.00 = $1)	2,000	1,800
Bangladesh	131,035,000	President Iajuddin Ahmed; Prime Minister Khaleda Zia	taka (58.35 = $1)	6,200	8,500
Bhutan	2,312,000	King Jigme Singye Wangchuck	ngultrum (47.63 = $1)	154	196
Brunei	352,000	Sultan Sir Hassanal Bolkiah	dollar (1.73 = $1)	3,000	1,400
Cambodia (Kampuchea)	13,210,000	King Norodom Sihanouk; Prime Minister Hun Sen	riel (3,835.00 = $1)	1,380	1,730
China	1,319,377,000	Communist Party General Secretary Hu Jintao; Premier Wen Jiabao	yuan (8.28 = $1)	325,000	295,300
East Timor	828,000	President Jose Alexander Gusmao Prime Minister Mari Bin Amude Alkatiri	dollar (1 = $1)	8	237
Georgia	5,151,000	Acting President Nino Burjanadze	lari (2.09 = $1)	515	750
India	1,075,516,000	President Abdul Kalam; Prime Minister Atal Behari Vajpayee	rupee (45.33 = $1)	44,500	53,800
Indonesia	213,483,000	President Megawati Sukarnoputri; Vice President Hamzah Haz	rupiah (8,368.00 = $1)	52,300	32,100
Iran	74,293,000	Supreme Leader Ayatollah Ali Hoseini-Khamenei; President Mohammed Khatami-Ardakani	rial (8,335.00 = $1)	24,800	21,800
Japan	127,638,000	Emperor Akihito; Prime Minister Junichiro Koizumi	yen (110.88 = $1)	383,800	292,100
Kazakhstan	14,433,000	President Nursultan Nazarbayev	tenge (148.52 = $1)	10,300	9,600
Korea, North	22,880,000	Korean Workers' Party General Secretary Kim Chong-il	won (2.20 = $1)	842	1,314
Korea, South	47,986,000	President Roh Moo-hyun; Prime Minister Ko Kon	won (1,147.00 = $1)	162,600	148,400
Kyrgyzstan	5,153,000	President Askar Akayev	som (46.09 = $1)	488	587
Laos	5,782,000	President Khamtai Siphandon; Prime Minister Boungnang Volachit	kip (7,600.00 = $1)	345	555

Nations affiliate, removed quotas for textile exports in 2003, which sparked protests from business owners in Vietnam, Bangladesh, and Sri Lanka. Textile manufacturers in those countries said that quotas protected them from losing business to China, which could produce textiles at lower prices.

Diplomacy. Several governments made efforts to improve relations between Asian countries in 2003. For example, in June, Indian Prime Minister Atal Behari Vajpayee signed a declaration to improve political and economic cooperation between India and China.

Indian diplomats attempted to normalize relations with Pakistan, India's long-time adversary. The countries agreed to restore full diplomatic relations in 2003 and, in October, India announced proposals to reestablish transportation and sporting links between the countries. Indian and Pakistani military commanders agreed in November to a cease-fire in the Himalayan state of Jammu and Kashmir, which both countries claimed.

Officials in North Korea announced in 2003 that the country had developed nuclear weapons and had stockpiled enough material to build sev-

Country	Population	Government	Monetary unit*	Foreign trade (million U.S.$) Exports[†]	Imports[†]
Malaysia	23,786,000	Paramount Ruler Sultan Syed Sirajuddin Syed Putra Jamalullail; Prime Minister Abdullah Ahmad Badawi	ringgit (3.80 = $1)	95,200	76,800
Maldives	303,000	President Maumoon Abdul Gayoom	rufiyaa (12.80 = $1)	110	395
Mongolia	2,484,000	President Natsagiyn Bagabandi; Prime Minister Namburiin Enkhbayar	tugrik (1,126.00 = $1)	501	659
Myanmar (Burma)	50,003,000	State Peace and Development Council Chairman Than Shwe; Prime Minister Khin Nyunt	kyat (6.20 = $1)	2,700	2,500
Nepal	25,257,000	King Gyanendra Bir Bikram Shah Dev; Prime Minister Surya Bahadur Thapa	rupee (74.50 = $1)	720	1,600
Pakistan	156,164,000	President and Chief Executive Pervez Musharraf	rupee (57.87 = $1)	9,800	11,100
Philippines	82,351,000	President Gloria Macapagal-Arroyo	peso (54.85 = $1)	35,100	33,500
Russia	141,802,000	President Vladimir Putin	ruble (30.45 = $1)	104,600	60,700
Singapore	4,305,000	President Sellapan Rama Nathan; Prime Minister Goh Chok Tong	dollar (1.73 = $1)	127,000	113,000
Sri Lanka	19,646,000	President Chandrika Kumaratunga; Prime Minister Ranil Wickremesinghe	rupee (94.60 = $1)	4,600	5,400
Taiwan	22,912,000	President Chen Shui-bian; Vice President Lu Annette	dollar (33.80 = $1)	130,000	113,000
Tajikistan	6,298,000	President Emomali Rahmonov; National Assembly Chairman Makhmadsaid Ubaydulloyev	somoni (3.00 = $1)	710	830
Thailand	63,418,000	King Phumiphon Adunyadet; Prime Minister Thaksin Shinawatra	baht (39.57 = $1)	67,700	58,100
Turkmenistan	5,103,000	President Saparmurad Niyazov	manat (5,200.00 = $1)	2,970	2,250
Uzbekistan	26,293,000	President Islam Karimov	som (902.70 = $1)	2,800	2,500
Vietnam	82,280,000	Communist Party General Secretary Nong Duc Manh; President Tran Duc Luong; Prime Minister Phan Van Khai	dong (15,557.00 = $1)	16,500	16,800

*Exchange rates as of Oct. 3, 2003, or latest available data.
[†]Latest available data.

eral more. At a meeting with diplomats from the United States, Japan, South Korea, Russia, and China in August, North Korean officials said that the country would not give up its weapons until the United States agreed to sign a nonaggression treaty and provided economic aid to the poverty-stricken nation.

In September, U.S. President George W. Bush said that the United States was prepared to ease economic sanctions on North Korea and would work toward a peace treaty if North Korea agreed to begin destroying its nuclear arsenal.

Nepal. Maoist rebels withdrew from peace talks with Nepal officials in November and declared the end to a cease-fire brokered in January 2003. The announcement led to a resumption of a seven-year insurgency that left more than 7,000 people dead and damaged Nepal's economy, which relied heavily on tourism.

The rebels began fighting in 1996 to replace Nepal's constitutional monarchy with a Communist government. By early 2003, the rebels controlled several districts and were active throughout much of the country. In January, a secretly negotiated cease-fire went into effect between the government and the rebels. Low-level clashes between government forces and the rebels resumed after the agreement, and the rebels withdrew from peace talks in August. Maoists called a three-day strike in September, which led to escalating violence. In response, the government banned public protests. Police arrested hundreds of people who marched in protest against King Gyanendra Bir Bikram Shah Dev. The protesters demanded that the king restore parliament, which he had dissolved in 2002.

The Maldives, an island nation off India, was shaken in September 2003 by public riots in protest of police brutality. In November, Maumoon Abdul Gayoom began his sixth term as president by firing officials who tried to start an opposition political party.

East Timor, Southeast Asia's most impoverished country, celebrated its first anniversary of independence from Indonesia on May 20, 2003. The country, which occupies the eastern side of the island of Timor, was a Portuguese colony until 1975, when Indonesia seized control of the region. Many people resisted Indonesian rule, and in 1999, the East Timorese voted for independence. After the vote, a militia assisted by the Indonesian military launched a campaign of terror against the East Timorese. The United Nations (UN) sent a peacekeeping force to the region to stop the violence.

Attacks by Indonesian guerrillas continued after East Timor's independence. In 2003, guerrillas from Indonesian West Timor attacked the East Timorese. As a result, the UN delayed plans to withdraw peacekeeping troops.

In March, East Timor signed an agreement with Australia to divide large oil and gas reserves lying under the Timor Sea. Political observers accused Australia of bullying the fledgling East Timor government into accepting a less than equitable deal.

Laos. Fighting between Hmong guerrillas and Laotian troops resulted in several deaths in 2003. The Hmong, an ethnic minority in Laos, had been fighting against the Communist regime since 1975. In June 2003, Laotian government troops captured two European journalists following a firefight between the troops and guerrillas. The reporters were later sentenced to 15 years in prison, but Laos released the journalists in July.

AIDS. The director of the U.S. Centers for Disease Control and Prevention warned in July that China, India, and Cambodia faced an AIDS catastrophe unless the countries developed adequate public health measures to combat the epidemic. According to UN estimates, approximately 1.5 million people in China had HIV, the virus that causes AIDS, and the number could reach 10 million by 2010.   ■ Henry S. Bradsher

See also various Asian country articles.

Astronomy. Mars approached closer to Earth in 2003 than it has in thousands of years. Astronomers found new moons around Jupiter; a ring of stars around the Milky Way Galaxy; a very ancient planet orbiting another star; and evidence about the structure, age, and history of the universe.

Mars' close approach. On the morning of August 27, Mars came closer to Earth than at any time in the past 60,000 years, approaching to within 34,646,418 miles (54,716,200 kilometers). Close approaches of Mars are called oppositions because Mars appears opposite the sun in the sky as seen from Earth. During an opposition, Mars is one of the brightest objects in the heavens.

The Hubble Space Telescope took detailed pictures of Mars during the opposition, and two Mars Rover spacecraft designed to orbit and land on Mars were launched as well. The next very close opposition of Mars will be on Aug. 28, 2287.

New moons. At least 21 previously unknown satellites of Jupiter were discovered in February 2003 by astronomers at the University of Hawaii at Hilo. The new-found moons showed up on images taken by the world's two largest digital cameras on telescopes at Mauna Kea, Hawaii. The finding brought the total number of known moons of Jupiter to 61.

The University of Hawaii astronomers also announced that they had discovered a new moon of Saturn in February, bringing the total of Saturn's known moons to 31. The number of Jupiter and Saturn moons may change again as the astronomers continue to analyze the images.

Oldest planet. Astronomers in July announced the discovery of an extremely old planet around another star. They found the planet in a cluster of stars named M4 in the constellation Scorpius. This group of about 1 million stars formed between 13 billion and 12.5 billion years ago, just about 1 billion years after the big bang, which most astronomers believe gave rise to the universe.

The newly discovered planet orbits around a pair of burned-out stars. Astronomers at Pennsylvania State University in College Park and the University of British Columbia in Vancouver found the faint pair of stars in an image taken by the Hubble Space Telescope. One of the stars is a white dwarf and the other a pulsar, which emits regular pulses of radio waves. The white dwarf and the pulsar are about as far apart as Earth and the sun. Astronomers first suspected there was a planet around these old stars in 1988, when they observed irregularities in the timing of the radio pulses emitted by the pulsar. An orbiting planet could cause these irregularities.

The discovery of the ancient planet suggests that planets were able to form only a few billion years after the big bang. Previously, astronomers

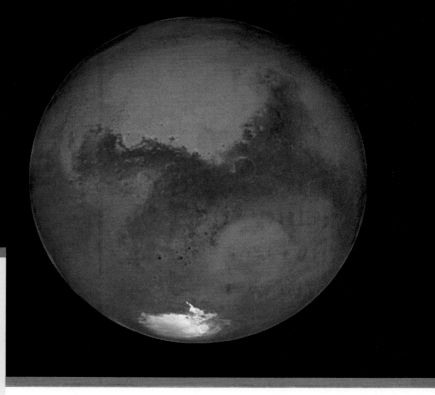

In August, Mars makes its closest approach to Earth in 60,000 years, enabling the Hubble Space Telescope to take highly detailed pictures of the red planet, less than 35,000,000 miles (55,000,000 kilometers) away.

had thought that planets could only form around older generations of stars like our sun, which had formed such heavy elements as iron, magnesium, and silicon in their interiors.

Infrared space observatory. The National Aeronautics and Space Administration in August launched the Space Infrared Telescope Facility, later named the Spitzer Space Telescope for astronomer Lyman Spitzer. The Spitzer carried a reflecting telescope designed to take pictures and analyze light in the infrared region of the electromagnetic spectrum. Because infrared radiation comes from relatively cool objects, Spitzer will be especially useful for studying young stars and clouds of cool gas and dust in the Milky Way and enable astronomers to study the earliest galaxies, which move away as the universe expands.

A huge ring of stars encircles the Milky Way Galaxy, the galaxy in which our sun resides, according to a January announcement by astronomers at Rensselaer Polytechnic Institute in Troy, New York, and Fermi National Accelerator Laboratory in Batavia, Illinois. The astronomers used data collected with the Sloan Digital Sky Survey, a telescope designed to take images and spectra of vast numbers of stars.

The huge ring is more than 120,000 light-years across. A light-year is the distance light travels in one year, or about 5.88 trillion miles (9.46 trillion

kilometers). Further evidence that the stars are part of a ring, not just an isolated group, was announced at the same time by a group of European astronomers. The astronomers think the ring of stars was produced when a smaller galaxy collided with the Milky Way billions of years ago.

New clues about the universe. NASA scientists in February announced the first results from the Wilkinson Microwave Anisotropy Probe (WMAP), a satellite launched in June 2001 to survey cosmic microwave background radiation. This faint radiation is the glow produced by hot gas in the universe just a few hundred thousand years after the big bang. The WMAP satellite mapped the microwave variations all over the sky in finer detail than any previous study, enabling scientists to draw some firm conclusions about the universe.

They concluded that the universe is 4 percent normal matter, 23 percent *dark matter* (not-yet identified particles), and 73 percent *dark energy*, a strange energy that speeds up the expansion of the universe. Scientists also concluded that the big bang occurred about 13.7 billion years ago; the first stars formed between 400 million and 100 million years after the big bang; and the theory of cosmic inflation, which proposes that the universe underwent a mammoth expansion during the first fraction of a second after the big bang, is probably correct.　■ Laurence A. Marschall

See also **Astronomy: A Special Report.**

Space Telescopes:

Seeing the Universe in a Different Light

By Laurence Marschall
and Donald Goldsmith

NASA launches the fourth of the "Great Observatories" that have redefined how scientists view the cosmos.

The National Aeronautics and Space Administration (NASA) launched the fourth and last of its satellites known as the "Great Observatories," the Space Infrared Telescope Facility—named the Spitzer Space Telescope after astronomer Lyman Spitzer—in August 2003. NASA scientists designed the Spitzer, which detects and records cosmic sources of infrared radiation, to complement the Hubble Space Telescope (HST), the Compton Gamma Ray Observatory (CGRO), and the Chandra X-ray Observatory, which have opened new windows to the cosmos in visible light, gamma rays, and X rays, respectively.

The concept of the space telescope originated in 1923, when Hermann Oberth published a book that proposed using a rocket to propel a

Images of Saturn, taken by the Hubble Space Telescope over several years, provide astronomers with information about the formation, composition, and longevity of the planet's rings.

telescope into space. Oberth was one of the fathers of rocketry and a mentor to Wernher von Braun, the first director of the NASA Marshall Space Flight Center in Huntsville, Alabama. Oberth's idea was to place a telescope beyond Earth's atmosphere, which blurs visible light and hinders or even absorbs other wavelength ranges. A telescope in space could collect images of cosmic objects in a variety of wavelengths, including infrared, visible light, X ray, and gamma ray.

Shortly after World War II (1939-1945), a group of astronomers expanded on Oberth's concept. Led by Lyman Spitzer of Princeton University in Princeton, New Jersey, the scientists suggested putting a space telescope into orbit above Earth's atmosphere. They thought that, guided

The authors:
Laurence Marschall is the W. K. T. Sahm Professor of Physics at Gettysburg College in Pennsylvania and the Deputy Press Officer of the American Astronomical Society. Donald Goldsmith has written 20 books about astronomy.

GLOSSARY

Black hole: a region of space whose gravitational force is so strong that nothing—not even light—can escape, rendering it invisible

Cosmic: having to do with the whole universe

Cosmos: the universe as a whole

Electromagnetic wave: a type of radiation that travels at the speed of light through a vacuum and includes gamma rays, X rays, ultraviolet, visible light, infrared, microwaves, and radio waves

Galaxy: a system of stars, dust, and gas held together by gravity

Gamma ray: a form of electromagnetic radiation with the highest energy and the shortest wavelength

Gyroscope: a device that uses a rotating object to specify a stable direction in space

Infrared radiation: electromagnetic radiation with wavelengths longer than those of the red part of the visible spectrum

Microwave: a short-wavelength radio wave with a wavelength that varies from 0.04 to 12 inches (1 to 300 millimeters) in length

Nebula: a cloud of dust and gas in space

Neutron star: a dense star, as massive as the sun, that is composed of neutrons

Photometer: an instrument that measures the intensity of light

Pulsar: a rapidly spinning neutron star that produces regular pulses of radio waves and occasionally produces visible light and X rays

Quasar: an extremely luminous object at the center of some distant galaxies

Spectrograph: an instrument for photographing a spectrum

Spectrometer: an instrument that spreads out light and other types of electromagnetic waves into a spectrum and displays it for study

Spectrum: electromagnetic radiation arranged in order of wavelength or frequency

Supernova: an exploding star that can become billions of times as luminous as the sun before gradually fading from view

White dwarf: the contracted core of a former star that shines dimly due to stored energy

X ray: electromagnetic radiation with very short wavelengths that can pass through substances that ordinary light cannot penetrate

by commands from the ground, the telescope could return its results to Earth by *telemetry*. Telemetry is the process of gathering and transmitting data automatically over great distances.

Spitzer was instrumental in the planning of the first such telescope—the Hubble Space Telescope. He lobbied enthusiastically for its development throughout the 1960's and 1970's with both the United States Congress and the scientific community. In 1977, Congress approved the funding for Hubble, which NASA launched in April 1990. Named for Edwin Hubble, the U.S. astronomer who discovered the ongoing expansion of the universe in 1929, the Hubble telescope photographs visible-light images of cosmic objects.

The Hubble Space Telescope

Hubble has a primary mirror about 8 feet (2.4 meters) in diameter. This mirror is much smaller than the primary mirrors on the largest Earth-bound telescopes, which are as much as 33 feet (10.2 meters) across. However, free from the blurring effects of Earth's atmosphere, Hubble produces far sharper images than ground-based telescopes. Hubble is equipped with cameras and spectrographs. A spectrum enables astronomers to identify the chemical elements in a celestial object as well as the temperature, density, and other physical conditions of the material emitting the radiation.

Hubble has a nearly circular orbit 365 miles (600 kilometers) above Earth's surface, the greatest distance that the space shuttle could carry the instrument. Hubble sends its data back to Earth through a network of satellites known as the Tracking and Data Relay Satellite System (TDRSS), which relays it to Earth's ground stations.

The Hubble Space Telescope was launched with a flaw. Soon after Hubble began to relay data to Earth, astronomers discovered that the telescope's primary mirror was incorrectly shaped. The flaw was the result of an error in the instruments that checked the mirror-grinding process. Astronomers quickly realized that the flaw could be corrected if HST's mirror could be fitted with correcting lenses that would function in the same role that spectacle lenses do for human eyes. In December 1993, astronauts on a servicing mission successfully installed the corrective optics. The telescope has performed perfectly since the installation. Astronauts on another servicing mission in March 2002 added an improved cam-

THE ELECTROMAGNETIC SPECTRUM

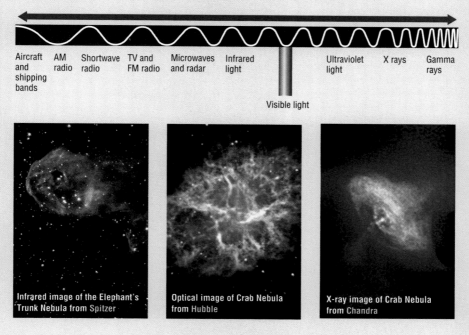

Aircraft and shipping bands | AM radio | Shortwave radio | TV and FM radio | Microwaves and radar | Infrared light | | Ultraviolet light | X rays | Gamma rays

Visible light

Infrared image of the Elephant's Trunk Nebula from Spitzer

Optical image of Crab Nebula from Hubble

X-ray image of Crab Nebula from Chandra

Light waves are forms of electromagnetic radiation. Electromagnetic radiation is basically a series of waves that includes radio waves, infrared (IR) light, ultraviolet (UV) light, X rays, and gamma rays. All electromagnetic radiation consists of streams of tiny particles called photons.

Each photon has a frequency and wavelength. The frequency describes the number of photon vibrations per second, and the wavelength specifies the distance that the photon travels as it makes a single vibration. The frequency and wavelength relate to the speed of light in empty space, which is equal to approximately 186,000 miles (300,000 kilometers) per second.

Frequencies and wavelengths distinguish different types of photons. Gamma rays have the highest frequencies and shortest wavelengths while radio waves have the lowest frequencies and longest wavelengths. The energy of a photon is directly proportional to the photon's frequency—that is, high-energy photons have high frequencies.

A person's eyes can detect visible-light photons. People perceive the differences in frequency and wavelength among visible-light photons as differences in color. Red photons have the lowest frequencies and longest wavelengths, whereas violet photons have the highest frequencies and shortest wavelengths.

Each type of photon requires different types of detectors to capture it and analyze its radiation because each kind affects the matter that it encounters differently. X-ray photons, for example, easily penetrate the human body while UV, visible-light, and IR photons do not.

Astronomers know that high-energy explosions typically produce gamma rays and X rays. Ordinary stars such as the sun emit large numbers of UV and visible-light photons while relatively cool objects, such as planets, produce mainly IR photons.

When scientists study the electromagnetic radiation produced by cosmic objects, they attempt to measure the amount of radiation at each frequency and wavelength. These amounts, typically shown in the form of a graph, furnish the object's spectrum. Every detail in the spectrum carries information about the processes that produce or remove electromagnetic radiation. These details also reveal the types and amounts of atoms and molecules within the material that has produced the electromagnetic radiation as well as the material's temperature and density.

HUBBLE SPACE TELESCOPE

The Hubble Space Telescope circles Earth above the atmosphere, providing astronomers with infinitely sharp images of planets, stars, and other celestial objects. Launched in 1990, the Hubble Space Telescope is slated to remain in space until the 2010's.

The Helix Nebula, in a composite picture taken by the Hubble Space Telescope and telescopes at Kitt Peak National Observatory in Arizona, is one of the closest planetary nebulas to Earth. A planetary nebula is the glowing gas surrounding a dying, sunlike star. Its shape is produced when the star expels outer gases in the form of a coil, or helix, into space.

A dusty spiral galaxy (below) appears to be rotating on edge as it slides through a larger, bright galaxy in an image taken by the Hubble Space Telescope. The photograph reveals the galaxy's spiral structure accompanied by dramatic lanes of dust. The bright blue areas mark regions of active star formation.

A colorful expanse of hydrogen gas, along with trace amounts of other elements, such as oxygen and sulfur, glows in the Swan Nebula. Ultraviolet radiation lights the wavelike patterns of gas.

An ultraviolet image of Saturn taken by the Hubble Space Telescope reveals auroral curtains of light that encircle both poles more than 1,000 miles (1,600 kilometers) above the planetary clouds. Saturn's auroral displays, which are similar to Earth's auroras, are caused by an energetic wind from the Sun sweeping over the planet.

era system and a new set of detectors for that portion of the infrared region that HST can observe. The telescope's solar panels and gyroscopes have also been replaced. As a result of these missions, the HST has greater capabilities than its designers envisioned.

Since its launch, Hubble has produced images that led to a number of crucial insights—the collision of Comet Shoemaker-Levy with Jupiter; the blasts of supernovae; and the births of stars from clouds of gas and dust throughout the Milky Way Galaxy. Moreover, scientists have combined Hubble's images with those of other observatories to create multifaceted views of cosmic objects. Perhaps the most important scientific breakthrough connected with Hubble was the discovery that the universe is expanding at an accelerated rate.

The Compton Gamma Ray Observatory

Space shuttle Atlantis placed NASA's second Great Observatory, the Compton Gamma Ray Observatory (CGRO), into a circular orbit 270 miles (450 kilometers) above Earth in April 1991. CGRO was named after Nobel Prize honoree Arthur Holly Compton, who provided experimental proof that electromagnetic radiation could exhibit the characteristics of particles as well as waves. CGRO's solar panels spanned 70 feet (21.3 meters). It weighed 17 tons (15.4 metric tons) and was the heaviest civilian spacecraft ever carried by a space shuttle. CGRO ceased operation in 2000.

The primary goals of the Compton Gamma Ray Observatory were to generate a map of the cosmos at gamma-ray wavelengths and to gather information from gamma-ray sources of particular interest. To carry out these tasks, CGRO carried four instruments—the Imaging Compton Telescope (COMPTEL), the Oriented Scintillation Spectrometer Experiment (OSSE), the Energetic Gamma Ray Experiment Telescope

COMPTON GAMMA RAY OBSERVATORY

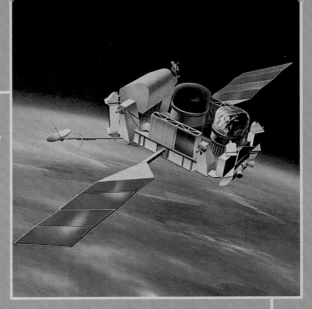

The Compton Gamma Ray Observatory, in orbit between 1991 and 2000, carried instruments called scintillators that detected gamma rays, measured their intensity, and located their sources.

A Compton Gamma Ray Observatory map of the cosmos (top) charts the distribution of the radioactive isotope aluminum 26, which scientists believe to be associated with supernovae. Another map of the cosmos (bottom) shows a gamma-ray glow from the Milky Way Galaxy, which is in the middle of both diagrams.

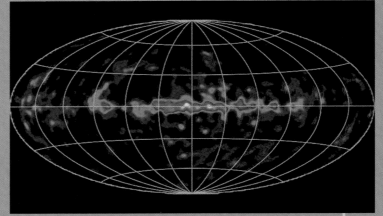

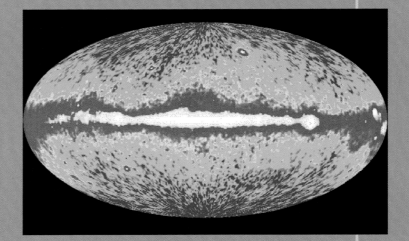

(EGRET), and the Burst And Transient Source Experiment (BATSE).

COMPTEL was a camera sensitive to gamma-ray wavelengths. Researchers could assemble COMPTEL's photographs into a gamma-ray diagram that mapped the universe. OSSE was a spectrometer that measured the range of energies of gamma rays from various sources. EGRET detected the direction and spectrum of gamma rays in the highest energy ranges—that is, with the shortest wavelengths and highest frequencies.

Of all the instruments on CGRO, BATSE was the most unusual. BATSE scanned space for sudden, brief explosions of mysterious origin. Earlier satellites that carried radiation counters had detected a few of these explosions, called gamma-ray bursts. However, since they appeared and disappeared so quickly and unpredictably, no one knew if they originated within the Milky Way Galaxy or beyond. After analyzing data from BATSE, scientists concluded that supernovae outside the galaxy probably generate these phenomena. Further observations of the bursts in visible light and X-ray wavelengths confirmed the scientists' conclusion.

Data from CGRO also allowed scientists to plot gamma-ray maps of the Milky Way Galaxy. These diagrams revealed how chemical elements are formed in stars. Moreover, CGRO's observations of galaxies led to the understanding of how black holes power their cores and produce extremely bright centers called quasars.

Astronomers could not simply turn off CGRO once its mission ended. CGRO's orbit was close enough to Earth that Earth's atmosphere exerted a tiny amount of drag, or resistance. This drag slowed the craft and made it gradually descend until it disintegrated at lower altitudes. To avoid the possibility that CGRO's debris might hurt people or damage property, NASA deliberately lowered the satellite's orbit so that reentry would occur over unpopulated areas. In June 2000, CGRO disintegrated harmlessly.

The Chandra X-ray Observatory

The space shuttle Columbia carried the third of NASA's Great Observatories, the Chandra X-ray Observatory, into outer space in July 1999. This telescope was named for the late astrophysicist and Nobel laureate Subrahmanyan Chandrasekhar, who studied the physical processes important to the structure and evolution of stars. The observatory was designed to study objects that emit large amounts of X rays. These objects include highly energetic objects such as supernovae and quasars as well as extremely hot stars, the cores of white dwarfs, and black holes.

Unlike Hubble and CGRO, which were designed to move in orbits that are roughly circular and close to Earth, Chandra was boosted into a much larger, elliptical orbit. Every 64 hours the satellite approaches within about 10,000 miles (16,000 kilometers) of Earth and then slowly drifts to nearly 90,000 miles (140,000 kilometers) away, almost one-third of the distance to the moon. Chandra's high orbit allows it to function largely outside the Van Allen belts, areas of charged particles that are trapped by Earth's magnetic field. These charged particles make Chandra's sensitive detectors useless in the lowest areas of its orbit.

CHANDRA X-RAY OBSERVATORY

The Chandra X-ray Observatory, in an artist's rendering, was launched by space shuttle Columbia in 1999. Chandra was designed to detect X rays from high-energy areas of the universe.

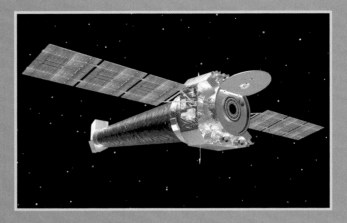

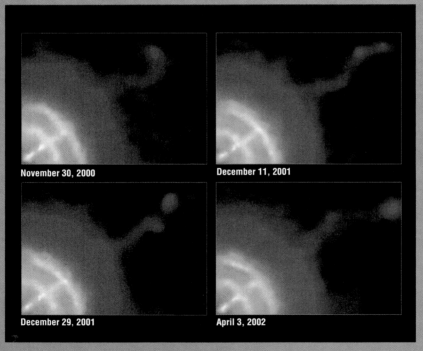

November 30, 2000

December 11, 2001

December 29, 2001

April 3, 2002

A jet of high-energy particles emanates from the Vela pulsar and whips about at the speed of light. This series of photographs taken by the Chandra X-ray Observatory provided scientists with new insight into the nature of pulsars and black holes.

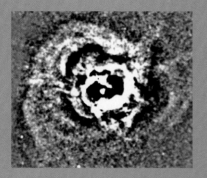

A Chandra observation of the central region of the Perseus Galaxy cluster reveals features that appear to be sound waves. These sound waves are thought to have been produced by explosive events occurring around a supermassive black hole.

However, since the observatory spends 85 percent of its time outside Earth's radiation belt, it can make uninterrupted observations of space for as long as 55 hours before the charged particles interfere again.

To collect radiation at X-ray wavelengths, Chandra carries a telescope with the largest and smoothest mirrors ever created, including one that is 48.4 inches (1.23 meters) in diameter. These highly precise mirrors enable Chandra to clearly detect and examine very distant objects.

Four instruments analyze X rays collected by Chandra's telescope. A high-resolution camera records images in X-ray wavelengths. The pictures help astronomers investigate the brightness, size, and shape of distant X-ray sources, such as the centers of galaxies and the remains of supernovae. The three other instruments aboard Chandra are spectrometers that produce spectra at X-ray wavelengths.

Chandra is an ideal counterpart to Hubble. Scientists often coordinate and compare X-ray data from Chandra with Hubble's images and spectra of the same objects.

Chandra has made major contributions to the study of the evolution of the stars, the nature and importance of black holes, the physics of pulsars, and the structures of galaxies. Chandra has collected X rays emitted by the gaseous remnants of supernovae, which have enabled astronomers to identify which chemical elements these explosions produce and in what amounts. Chandra took pictures of one such remnant, the Crab Nebula, that show spectacular waves of gas moving outward, powered by a pulsar.

Chandra has also pro-

The spiral galaxy NGC 3079 is revealed in a photograph released in February 2003 that combines Chandra's X-ray image (blue) and Hubble's optical image (red and green). The juxtaposition of warm and hot filaments suggests that they were formed by intense cosmic winds, which scientists believe play key roles in the evolution of galaxies.

SPITZER SPACE TELESCOPE

The Spitzer Space Telescope is shown here in an artist's rendition. The Spitzer was launched in August 2003 with the goal of providing data about black holes, stars' life cycles, and galaxy evolution.

Stars and galaxies glow in an early test image taken by the Spitzer in September 2003. During its mission, the Spitzer will obtain images and spectra by detecting the infrared energy, or heat, radiated by objects.

vided evidence that massive black holes reside in the cores of most galaxies. The larger of these black holes appear to have a mass a billion times larger than that of the sun.

The Spitzer Space Telescope

The fourth Great Observatory, the Spitzer Space Telescope, observes cosmic sources of infrared radiation. Scientists prefer using infrared radiation to study objects—such as planets, moons, and stars—with temperatures less than 3,500 °F (1927 °C). It uses three instruments to analyze infrared radiation—a camera, a spectrograph, and a photometer.

The heart of the Spitzer is a reflecting telescope with a mirror 33.5 inches (85 centimeters) in diameter. The mirror is equipped with a shield to block the sun's radiation, which would otherwise overwhelm the instrument. Because infrared from the telescope can interfere with observations, the Spitzer carries 95 gallons (360 liters) of liquid helium; its temperature of -450 °F (-267.8 °C) cools the instruments to limit the telescope's infrared output. There is enough liquid helium aboard the Spitzer to cool the observatory for a life span of five years.

Two earlier infrared-observing satellites were launched in January 1983 and November 1995. The Spitzer's design allows it to have a larger telescope mirror and more precise instruments than its predecessors, while weighing less. The Spitzer's greatest improvement over the other infrared observatories is its superior instruments. Not only can the Spitzer's instruments make more accurate measurements, but they can do so over a wider range of infrared frequencies and wavelengths.

The future

The three space observatories currently in orbit should operate for years, furnishing astronomers with a host of observations. Hubble, though functioning well, will end its mission in a few years. NASA is now planning to launch an improved observatory that will be considerably larger than Hubble. This new observatory is to be named the James Webb Space Telescope, or JWST, after a former NASA administrator. The JWST will have a three-mirror design with a collecting area equivalent to that of a 256-inch (6.5-meter) circular primary mirror. The JWST will orbit far from Earth, avoiding the planet as well as interfering radiation from Earth.

Once the JWST orbits sometime during the 2010's, NASA must determine whether to bring Hubble safely back to Earth. NASA may decide to attach a rocket booster to the telescope. The rocket booster would steer Hubble into Earth's atmosphere to burn up over the ocean.

FOR ADDITIONAL INFORMATION ■

Web sites

The Hubble Space Telescope Project— http://hubble.nasa.gov/
CGRO Science Support Center—http://cossc.gsfc.nasa.gov/
The Chandra X-Ray Observatory Center—http://chandra.harvard.edu/index.html
The Spitzer Space Telescope—http://sirtf.caltech.edu/

AUSTRALIA

Australian troops joined the United States military and other coalition forces in overthrowing Iraqi President Saddam Hussein's regime in 2003. Although most Australians supported the war during the active period of combat, there were protests both inside and outside Parliament House in Canberra, the capital, during U.S. President George W. Bush's visit in October. The Australian economy remained strong, but the year was marred by fires that cost lives and destroyed many houses in Canberra.

International relations. Iraq dominated the headlines in Australia throughout 2003. In January, the Opposition Australian Labor Party criticized the Liberal-National Party coalition's decision to send the transport ship HMAS *Kanimbla* to the Persian Gulf before the United Nations (UN) had acted upon a resolution on a possible U.S.-led war on Iraq. When the war was launched in March, Australia sent more than 2,000 military personnel to the Persian Gulf, spurring the largest peace protests in Australia since the Vietnam War (1957-1975). An Australian journalist, Paul Moran, was killed in March 2003 by a suicide bomber in northern Iraq. However, no Australian soldiers had been killed in Iraq when Australia withdrew most of its troops after the official end of the fighting in May.

In February, an international survey showed that only 12 percent of Australians agreed with taking unilateral action against Saddam Hussein's regime, but 56 percent were in favor if the UN supported the plan. By September, the public mood had shifted. A poll revealed that 68 percent of Australians believed that Australian Prime Minister John Howard had misled them on the reasons for going to war with Iraq.

When President Bush addressed the Australian Parliament in October, he praised Howard's support for the war in Iraq. Two Australian Greens Party senators, Bob Brown and Kerry Nettle, interrupted Bush's address by calling for fair treatment of two Australian citizens held by the United States as enemy combatants without being charged at Guantanamo Bay, Cuba. Prime Minister Howard acknowledged that Australians were divided on the Iraq war but insisted that his government's decision to send troops was correct. Australian Labor Party leader Simon Crean explained his party's opposition but stressed that it did not harbor anti-U.S. beliefs.

The trials for several Indonesians accused of the October 2002 terrorist attack in Bali that killed 202 people, including 88 Australians, began in May 2003. The accused were said to belong to Jemaah Islamiyah, a terrorist organization with links to the al-Qa'ida terrorist network. The first of the offenders, Amrozi bin Nurhasyim, dubbed the "smiling bomber" for his defiant approach to police and the court system, was sentenced in August to death by firing squad for supplying the chemicals and the van used in the blast. His brother Ali Imron bin Nurhasyim, who gave evidence against Amrozi, and his other brother Mukhlas, was sentenced to life imprisonment in September. Mukhlas was sentenced to death in October. Later in October, Prime Minister Howard traveled to Bali to mark the anniversary of the bombings.

In June, the federal Parliament passed counterterrorism legislation called the Australian Security Intelligence Organisation Legislation (ASIO) Amendment Bill 2002. The bill gave ASIO unprecedented powers to detain and question people believed to have data about terrorist attacks.

In July 2003, Australia responded to calls for help in restoring law and order in the Solomon Islands. A military and police force joined other Pacific nations in subduing rebel leaders. Prime Minister Howard attended a meeting of Pacific nations in August in Auckland, New Zealand, to discuss the Solomons and other matters.

The Australian carrier HMAS *Sydney* prepares to dock at Garden Island Navy Base in Sydney Harbor in August 2003, after spending several months in the Persian Gulf during the Iraq War of 2003. Australian participation in the U.S.-led coalition also included sending more than 2,000 military personnel to the Persian Gulf region.

Fires and drought. In January, fires burned over half of Kosciuszko National Park as they raged across 3 million acres (1.2 million hectares) of eastern Victoria and adjacent regions. The fires reached Canberra, located in nearby Australian Capital Territory, in January, where they destroyed 500 houses and killed four people.

The fires were fueled by extremely dry vegetation caused by the worst drought in 100 years. In February, heavy rain fell in areas of New South Wales that had not received adequate rainfall since 2001. Despite more rains in August 2003, the drought was so severe that farms in many areas continued to suffer. In October, authorities in Sydney joined those in other cities in imposing water restrictions on residents.

Governor general troubles. Political foes of Australian Governor General Peter Hollingworth called for his resignation through much of 2003. Although the position is largely ceremonial, the governor general is the local representative of Queen Elizabeth II, who is Australia's head of state. In May, the Anglican Church released the findings of an inquiry regarding Hollingworth's

handling of several complaints when he was archbishop of Brisbane. The inquiry found that Hollingworth made serious errors of judgment by failing to dismiss two priests guilty of child sexual abuse. Prime Minister Howard continued to support Hollingworth, telling the media that he did not regret the appointment. However, a new controversy broke out when Hollingworth was accused of rape, which allegedly happened in the 1960's. Hollingworth denied the charges but stepped aside until the case could be heard. After the accuser died, her family withdrew the case. Hollingworth nevertheless announced his resignation as governor general in May, saying that the ongoing controversy prevented him from performing his duties properly. Major General Michael Jeffery replaced Hollingworth in August. Jeffery was an honored soldier who had been governor of Western Australia in the 1990's.

Politics. In March 2003, Bob Carr won another term as premier of New South Wales when the Labor Party returned to power in state elections. In December, Australian Labor Party leader Simon Crean resigned his post after two years. The party replaced Crean with right-wing politician Mark Latham. Latham defeated former leader Kim Beazley by two votes to win the seat. Latham then named Crean deputy manager of Opposition business in the House of Representatives.

Controversy broke out in September when the Tasmanian Labor government announced the appointment of Richard Butler as governor, a position in which he would represent the monarchy. Butler, who had gained an international reputation for his work as a UN envoy, was an outspoken republican, that is, an opponent of Australia continuing as a monarchy.

Pauline Hanson, the founder of One Nation, a party known for its radical views on immigration and race, attracted more attention than any other Australian politician in 2003. Hanson, a former member of the Australian federal Parliament, unsuccessfully ran for a seat in the upper house of the New South Wales state Parliament in March. On August 20, she and David Ettridge, a cofounder of One Nation, were sentenced to prison for three years for electoral fraud connected with the party's registration in Queensland in 1997. In November 2003, the Court of Appeal division of the Queensland Supreme Court quashed the convictions and released Hanson and Ettridge.

Two other prominent Australians were sent to prison in 2003. Di Fingleton, the chief magistrate of Queensland, was sent to jail for 12 months in June for threatening a witness. Rene Rivkin, a well-known Sydney stockbroker, was found guilty of insider trading in June. He was sentenced to nine months of weekend detention but only served one night before going into a hospital to have a benign brain tumor removed. At subsequent court hearings, he continued his appeals to stay out of prison on health-related grounds.

In April, Philip Ruddock, the federal minister who was then in charge of indigenous affairs, took steps to remove financial control from the Aboriginal and Torres Strait Islander Commission, which is headquartered in Woden, Australian Capital Territory. Accusations of unacceptable behavior by the elected aboriginal leaders of the group motivated Ruddock to act. Deputy chairman Ray Robinson, who was accused of financial irregularities, resigned in June. In August, Ruddock suspended Geoff Clark from the board and from his position as chairman because of his conviction for obstructing police and behaving in a riotous manner after a pub brawl in Victoria.

Economics. Australia enjoyed a robust economy in 2003, with unemployment falling below 6 percent and inflation remaining under 3 percent. When Treasurer Peter Costello delivered his budget report in May, he forecast that economic growth would slow to 3.25 percent, maintaining that while Australia's economy was sound, the international outlook was hazy. The budget provided more money for defense and security, but the biggest changes were made in the fields of health and university education, for which the government emphasized user-pays principles.

The trade deficit, that is, the fact that Australia imported more than it exported, proved to be the government's primary economic problem in 2003. The increase in the Australian dollar—from the equivalent of 55 U.S. cents in 2002 to 70 cents in October 2003—did not help the farmers and miners, the nation's leading exporters. According to the National Farmers Federation, every 1-percent increase in the Australian dollar cost Australian farmers $115 million.

Two world leaders talked about trade when they visited Australia in October. President Bush continued discussions with Prime Minister Howard over a possible free-trade agreement between Australia and the United States. The major hurdles involved accessibility for Australian agricultural products to U.S. markets, local rules affecting Australian content for television programs, and Australian government subsidies for pharmaceutical drugs. Chinese President Hu Jintao announced details of the single biggest export contract in Australia's history during his October visit. As part of the $21.7-billion liquid natural gas deal, China agreed to buy a substantial stake in the Gorgon Development on Barrow Island off Australia's northwest coast.

Tourism, which accounted for 5 percent of the Australian economy in 2003 and provided over 500,000 jobs, was badly affected by the Iraq war

MEMBERS OF THE AUSTRALIAN HOUSE OF REPRESENTATIVES

The House of Representatives of the 40th Parliament first met Feb. 12, 2002. As of Aug. 1, 2003, the House of Representatives consisted of the following members: 68 Liberal Party of Australia, 64 Australian Labor Party, 13 National Party of Australia, 3 independents, 1 Northern Territory Country Liberal Party, and 1 Australian Greens. This table shows each legislator and party affiliation. An asterisk (*) denotes those who served in the 39th Parliament.

Australian Capital Territory
Annette Ellis, A.L.P.*
Bob McMullan, A.L.P.*

New South Wales
Tony Abbott, L.P.*
Anthony Albanese, A.L.P.*
John Anderson, N.P.*
Peter Andren, Ind.*
Larry Anthony, N.P.*
Bruce Baird, L.P.*
Bob Baldwin, L.P.
Kerry Bartlett, L.P.*
Bronwyn Bishop, L.P.*
Laurie Brereton, A.L.P.*
Alan Cadman, L.P.*
Ross Cameron, L.P.*
Ian Causley, N.P.*
John Cobb, N.P.
Janice Crosio, A.L.P.*
Pat Farmer, L.P.
Laurie Ferguson, A.L.P.*
Joel Fitzgibbon, A.L.P.*
Joanna Gash, L.P.*
Jennie George, A.L.P.
Sharon Grierson, A.L.P.
Jill Hall, A.L.P.*
Luke Hartsuyker, N.P.
Michael Hatton, A.L.P.*
Kelly Hoare, A.L.P.*
Joe Hockey, L.P.*
John Howard, L.P.*
Kay Hull, N.P.*
Julia Irwin, A.L.P.*
Jackie Kelly, L.P.*
Peter King, L.P.
Mark Latham, A.L.P.*
Sussan Ley, L.P.
Jim Lloyd, L.P.*
Robert McClelland, A.L.P.*
Leo McLeay, A.L.P.*
Daryl Melham, A.L.P.*
Frank Mossfield, A.L.P.*
John Murphy, A.L.P.*
Gary Nairn, L.P.*
Brendan Nelson, L.P.*
Michael Organ A.G.
Tanya Plibersek, A.L.P.*
Roger Price, A.L.P.*
Philip Ruddock, L.P.*
Alby Schultz, L.P.*
Ken Ticehurst, L.P.
Mark Vaile, N.P.*
Danna Vale, L.P.*
Tony Windsor, Ind.

Northern Territory
Warren Snowdon, A.L.P.*
David Tollner, C.L.P.

Queensland
Arch Bevis, A.L.P.*
Mal Brough, L.P.*
Steven Ciobo, L.P.
Peter Dutton, L.P.
Kay Elson, L.P.*
Craig Emerson, A.L.P.*
Warren Entsch, L.P.*
Teresa Gambaro, L.P.*
Gary Hardgrave, L.P.*
Michael Johnson, L.P.
David Jull, L.P.*
Robert Katter, Ind.*
De-Anne Kelly, N.P.*
Peter Lindsay, L.P.*
Kirsten Livermore, A.L.P.*
Ian Macfarlane, L.P.*
Margaret May, L.P.*
Paul Neville, N.P.*
Bernie Ripoll, A.L.P.*
Kevin Rudd, A.L.P.*
Con Sciacca, A.L.P.*
Bruce Scott, N.P.*
Peter Slipper, L.P.*
Alexander Somlyay, L.P.*
Wayne Swan, A.L.P.*
Cameron Thompson, L.P.*
Warren Truss, N.P.*

South Australia
Neil Andrew, L.P.*
David Cox, A.L.P.*
Alexander Downer, L.P.*
Trish Draper, L.P.*
Martyn Evans, A.L.P.*
Christine Gallus, L.P.*
Christopher Pyne, L.P.*
Rodney Sawford, A.L.P.*
Patrick Secker, L.P.*
Andrew Southcott, L.P.*
Barry Wakelin, L.P.*
Trish Worth, L.P.*

Tasmania
Dick Adams, A.L.P.*
Duncan Kerr, A.L.P.*
Michelle O'Byrne, A.L.P.*
Harry Quick, A.L.P.*
Sid Sidebottom, A.L.P.*

Victoria
Kevin Andrews, L.P.*
Fran Bailey, L.P.*
Phillip Barresi, L.P.*
Bruce Billson, L.P.*
Anna Burke, A.L.P.*
Anthony Byrne, A.L.P.*
Bob Charles, L.P.*
Ann Corcoran, A.L.P.*
Peter Costello, L.P.*
Simon Crean, A.L.P.*
Michael Danby, A.L.P.*
Martin Ferguson, A.L.P.*
John Forrest, N.P.*
Petro Georgiou, L.P.*
Steve Gibbons, A.L.P.*
Julia Gillard, A.L.P.*
Alan Griffin, A.L.P.*
David Hawker, L.P.*
Greg Hunt, L.P.
Harry Jenkins, A.L.P.*
David Kemp, L.P.*
Catherine King, A.L.P.
Jenny Macklin, A.L.P.*
Stewart McArthur, L.P.*
Peter McGauran, N.P.*
Brendan O'Connor, A.L.P.
Gavan O'Connor, A.L.P.*
Sophie Panopoulos, L.P.
Chris Pearce, L.P.
Nicola Roxon, A.L.P.*
Bob Sercombe, A.L.P.*
Tony Smith, L.P.
Sharman Stone, L.P.*
Lindsay Tanner, A.L.P.*
Kelvin Thomson, A.L.P.*
Maria Vamvakinou, A.L.P.
Christian Zahra, A.L.P.*

Western Australia
Kim Beazley, A.L.P.*
Julie Bishop, L.P.*
Graham Edwards, A.L.P.*
Barry Haase, L.P.*
Sharryn Jackson, A.L.P.
Carmen Lawrence, A.L.P.*
Jann McFarlane, A.L.P.*
Judi Moylan, L.P.*
Geoffrey Prosser, L.P.*
Don Randall, L.P.
Stephen Smith, A.L.P.*
Wilson Tuckey, L.P.*
Mal Washer, L.P.*
Kim Wilkie, A.L.P.*
Daryl Williams, L.P.*

and the outbreak of severe acute respiratory syndrome (SARS) epidemic in Asia. In June, Minister for Tourism Joe Hockey announced a 10-year program to encourage tourism. The plan included reducing Australia's tourist regions from 500 to a more manageable and marketable 30.

The Therapeutic Goods Administration (TGA), a division of Australia's Department of Health and Ageing, suspended the license of Pan Pharmaceuticals Limited of Sydney to manufacture medicines between April and October 2003. The watchdog organization had serious concerns about the quality and safety of the company's products. The TGA also ordered the company to remove more than 1,500 products from shops and pharmacies.

In August, Saudi Arabia refused a shipment of more than 55,000 sheep aboard the carrier *Cormo Expresso*, claiming that 6 percent of the animals had scabby mouth disease, which was above an agreed level of 5 percent. About 10 percent of the sheep died as other countries also refused to take them. Eritrea, one of Africa's poorest nations, finally came to Australia's rescue in October by agreeing to take the sheep along with 3,000 tons (2721.6 metric tons) of feed and approximately $1 million to meet transport and slaughter costs.

The arts. The Sydney Opera House in October 2003 marked the 30th anniversary of its opening but Jorn Utzon, the building's Danish designer, did not attend the celebration. Utzon, who won a 1957 competition for his boldly original design, left Australia in 1966 after a major disagreement with the New South Wales state government. Despite this development, Utzon agreed to oversee a major renovation of the building, which began in 2003 and was slated to be completed in early 2004. Utzon received the 2003 Pritzker Architecture Prize in April for his body of work.

Australian movie actress Nicole Kidman won the Academy Award for best actress in 2003 for her role as Virginia Woolf in *The Hours*. Two motion pictures, *Japanese Story* and *Gettin' Square*, received a number of awards during the year, while New Zealand-born, Australia-based director Jane Campion received attention for her internationally released film *In the Cut*. Australian actor Russell Crowe won praise for his role as British captain Jack Aubrey in *Master and Commander: The Far Side of the World*. On the New York City stage, Australian actor Hugh Jackman won raves for portraying Australian entertainer Peter Allen in the musical *The Boy From Oz*.

Artist Geoff Dyer won the Archibald Portrait Prize in March for his portrait of author Richard Flannagan. In June, Alex Miller won his second Miles Franklin Award for his novel *Journey to the Stone Country*. In October, Australian-born writer Peter Finlay won the prestigious British Booker Prize for his first novel, *Vernon God Little*, which he wrote under the pseudonym D. B. C. Pierre.

Australian country singer David Gordon Kirkpatrick, known to most Australians as Slim Dusty, was honored with a state funeral in September. The Dean of Sydney's St. Andrew's Cathedral led the singing of Slim's most famous song, "A Pub With No Beer." ■ Brian Kennedy

See also **Africa; Architecture; Australia, Prime Minister of; Economics; Iraq: A Special Report; Literature, World; Motion pictures; People in the news** (Nicole Kidman).

Australia, Prime Minister of. John

Howard in 2003 ended speculation about his possible retirement as leader of the Liberal Party. He announced in June that he planned on remaining prime minister as long as his party wanted him to occupy the post. A Newspoll survey conducted in June showed that 65 percent of Australian voters wanted Prime Minister Howard to remain head of the government.

Talks, mostly about Iraq, took Prime Minister Howard to the United States and Indonesia in February and to New Zealand in March. Australia's support for U.S. action in Iraq earned Prime Minister Howard a warm welcome from U.S. President George W. Bush during a visit to Texas in May. Prime Minister Howard then traveled to New York City for talks with United Nations Secretary-General Kofi Annan. The prime minister visited Australian troops in the Persian Gulf in September to thank them for their contribution to the Iraq War of 2003. In October, Howard attended a ceremony to mark the one-year anniversary of a Bali nightclub bombing that killed 88 Australians. Later in the month, he welcomed President Bush and Chinese President Hu Jintao. In November, the prime minister traveled to London to help open the Australian War Memorial. ■ Brian Kennedy

See also **Australia; Iraq: A Special Report.**

Australian rules football. The Brisbane

Lions in 2003 provided fans with a strong argument for declaring their team the greatest in Australian Football League (AFL) history. On September 27, the Lions crushed the Collingwood Magpies 20 goals, 14 behinds (134 points) to 12 goals, 12 behinds (84 points) in Melbourne, Australia.

With this victory, the Lions became the first team to win three consecutive premierships. The last team to perform a similar feat—Melbourne—won five Victorian Football League (VFL) premierships in the 1950's. Brisbane's Simon Black won the Norm Smith medal for the best player on the ground.

The Brownlow Medal for the best and fairest player of the season ended in a three-way tie. Collingwood's Nathan Buckley, Adelaide's Mark Ricciuto, and Sydney's Adam Goodes shared the honor.

Regionals. In the Victorian Football League, Williamstown defeated Box Hill 13.14 (92) to 9.9 (63). In the Western Australia Football League, West Perth beat Subiaco 13.9 (87) to 9.10 (64). In AFL's Queensland competition, the Morningside Panthers beat Mt. Gravatt 17.13 (115) to 7.10 (52). In Tasmania's Southern Football League, North Hobart crushed Hobart 21. 20 (146) to 5.6 (36). In the South Australia National Football League, Central District defeated West Adelaide 17.9 (111) to 11.11 (77). ■ Brian Kennedy

Austria. Chancellor Wolfgang Schuessel

formed a new conservative government in 2003 and embarked on a program of radical market-oriented reforms. Schuessel's conservative People's Party had won the largest share of the vote in the country's general election in November 2002. He sought to form a coalition government with the Social Democrats or the Green Party, but those efforts failed because of the parties' opposition to Schuessel's reform plans. The chancellor then reached an agreement with the right-wing Freedom Party. The People's Party and the Freedom Party had governed together for three years until a split inside the Freedom Party caused the government to collapse in September 2002.

The new government was sworn into office by President Thomas Klestil on Feb. 28, 2003. Joerg Haider, the controversial Freedom Party founder who espoused anti-immigrant views and praised the employment policies of Adolf Hitler's Nazi regime, did not join the government. Haider criticized some of Schuessel's policies, raising doubts about the government's stability.

Pension reform. Schuessel in April introduced legislation to overhaul Austria's state-funded pension system, which he argued would go broke unless reformed as Austrian society aged. The changes would raise the retirement age to 65 and eliminate the possibility of early retirement. The average retirement age in Austria in 2003 was 59 for men and 57 for women. The bill also would lower pension payments.

Unions protested the plan with a series of strikes, including the country's first general strike in 50 years on May 6. Nearly one-quarter of Austria's work force joined the strike, bringing trains, buses, and air traffic to a halt and disrupting banks, factories, and mail service. Despite the strikes, Schuessel used his majority in parliament to pass the pension bill in June. The government then negotiated with businesses and unions over the details of introducing the pension changes.

Railway protests. Also in 2003, the government announced plans to restructure the deficit-ridden national railway into smaller companies, saving an estimated $1.2 billion a year. Railway workers, fearing as many as 12,000 jobs could be lost, protested by going on strike for three days in November, the country's longest strike since World War II (1939-1945). Parliament approved the restructuring plan in December.

Immigration. The parliament approved new measures to restrict immigration in October, allowing Austria to deport some asylum seekers before they could appeal decisions refusing their requests to stay in the country. The United Nations High Commissioner for Refugees protested the policy. ■ Tom Buerkle

See also **Europe.**

Famed Austrian automobile engineer Ferdinand Porsche (far left) shows off his design for the Volkswagen—or people's car—to German dictator Adolf Hitler, who had ordered Porsche to design a compact, durable car that most people could afford. The first Volkswagens were built in 1945 and were used by Nazi officers during the last days of World War II (1939-1945).

Drivers say goodbye to the old-style Volkswagen Beetle, the most popular car ever produced.

Automobile. Sales of light trucks and cars in the United States remained solid in 2003, despite a year of economic uncertainties and war. By the end of September, sales of cars and light trucks totaled 12.6 million units, 1.7 percent off the sales during the same period in 2002, according to industry analysts. Analysts expected sales of cars and light trucks to total nearly 16.9 million units by the end of 2003—about the same total as in 2002.

Automakers, however, paid a steep price for those sales. The sales incentives implemented following the terrorist attacks on the United States in 2001 continued to escalate in 2003. In September, the average manufacturer incentive was $2,622 per vehicle sold, 29.4 percent higher than in September 2002, according to industry analysts. The traditional Big Three domestic automakers—General Motors (GM) Corporation of Detroit; Ford Motor Company of Dearborn, Michigan; and the U.S. division of Daimler-Chrysler AG of Germany—offered buyers the

When first introduced in the United States in 1949, the Beetle was regarded as a "second" or work car. However, it was soon adopted by the "baby boom" generation, both in the United States and abroad, and became a symbol of teen-age freedom (left) and the counterculture of the late 1960's and early 1970's. The Beetle was always "cool."

Workers in a plant in Puebla, Mexico, (above) honor the last of the 21,529,464 old-style Volkswagens, the most popular car ever built, as it rolls off the assembly line. Pollution controls and safety measures forced the company to stop production of Beetles at its German plants in 1979, but the original model remained in production in Mexico until 2003. Volkswagen began selling the New Beetle in 1998.

highest incentives, averaging $3,618 per vehicle. Japanese carmakers spent the least at $965 per vehicle. European automakers spent $1,753 per vehicle, and Korean automakers spent $1,384 per vehicle.

Sales trends. Although the traditional Big Three spent more on incentives than their competitors, the companies continued to lose market share in the United States. Through September 2003, the Big Three's market share dipped to 61.6 percent of all U.S. sales, compared with 63 percent for the same period in 2002. The Big Three held 70.5 percent of the market in 1998.

Asian automobile manufacturers proved to

be the big sales winners in 2003, with a market share of 33 percent of U.S. sales. European companies took a 5.4-percent share of the market.

Top sellers. Ford remained the top seller of light trucks during the 2003 model year. Ford's F-series pickup continued its dominance with sales totaling more than 820,000 units. The Toyota Camry captured the car sales title for the 2003 model year. The Camry sold more than 417,000 units.

The Big Three. GM's sales and market share declined during the first nine months of 2003. Sales totaled 3.5 million units, or 2.7 percent behind the first nine months of 2002. GM's market share dropped to 28.1 percent, compared with 28.4 percent for the same period in 2002. Through September 2003, GM reported a net income of $2.8 billion, compared with $716 million for the first nine months of 2002. The GM net income figures included profits from Hughes Electronics Corporation of El Segundo, California, GM's satellite broadcasting unit. GM officials announced in October 2003 that the company's stockholders had approved splitting off Hughes and allowing News Corporation, a New York City-based entertainment conglomerate, to acquire a 34-percent stake in Hughes. The transaction was to be completed in early 2004.

On the automotive side, the number-one automaker in the United States did enjoy success in 2003 with the Hummer, which posted sales of 25,453 units for the first nine months of the year. GM officials expected annual sales of Cadillac to top 200,000 units by December for the first time since 1994.

Ford sold approximately 2.6 million cars and light trucks in the first nine months of 2003, compared with 2.7 million units for the same period in 2002. Through September 2003, Ford's market share dropped to 20.7 percent, compared with 21.2 percent for the first nine months of 2002. Despite the drop in sales, the number-two U.S. automaker expected to report a better financial performance in 2003 than in 2002. The company's net income through September 2003 totaled $1.3 billion, compared with a loss of $850 million for the same period in 2002.

Bill Ford, the company's chairman and chief executive officer, attributed the improvement to cost-cutting efforts. In 2002, Ford launched a turnaround plan that included plant closings, downsizing, and efficiency improvements. The company continued the strategy through 2003. Ford officials announced the closing of an aluminum casting plant in Cleveland, Ohio; Vulcan Forge in Dearborn, Michigan; and an assembly

The boxy Toyota Scion xB miniwagon, introduced in 2003, is a relatively inexpensive and small sport-utility vehicle—12.9 feet (3.9 meters) in length—that was marketed to buyers in their teen's and 20's. It features a four-cylinder, 108-horsepower engine.

plant in Edison, New Jersey. The company also announced plans to consolidate two assembly plants in Ohio.

The Chrysler Group of DaimlerChrysler AG watched its sales decline to 1.6 million units, a 6 percent drop in the first nine months of 2003, compared with the same period in 2002. Through September 2003, Chrysler's market share fell to 12.8 percent of all U.S. sales, compared with 13.4 percent for the same period in 2002.

The corporation's financial picture for the first nine months of 2003 reflected the negative sales figures. Chrysler's operating loss was $756 million through September, compared with an operating profit of $526 million in 2002.

In 2003, Chrysler Group was in the midst of its third year of a planned three-year turn-around. The company continued streamlining with the planned closings of the McGraw Glass Plant in Detroit and the Indianapolis Foundry in Indiana. In addition, Chrysler officials announced the sales of plants in Huntsville, Alabama; New Castle, Indiana; and East Syracuse, New York.

Asian automakers. Toyota Motor Corporation, the largest automobile manufacturer in Japan, improved its sales and market share in 2003, compared with 2002. For the first nine months, the company's sales totaled 1.4 million units, or 5.3 percent more units than in 2002. Toyota's market share grew to 11.2 percent in 2003 compared with 10.4 percent in 2002. The company also revealed plans to increase the number of automobiles produced in the United States. In February 2003, Toyota executives announced that they had selected San Antonio, Texas, for an $800-million manufacturing plant for the Tundra pickup truck.

Honda increased its sales in 2003 to 1 million units in the first nine months, 11.2 percent greater than during the same period in 2002. The increase was in part due to better sales of the Accord.

Nissan also continued its turnaround, posting 595,758 units sold in the U.S. market through September 2003, or 5 percent more than the previous nine months. To further boost sales, Nissan introduced the Titan, a full-size pickup. The first model rolled off the assembly line of its new Canton, Mississippi, plant in October.

UAW contract. United Automobile Workers (UAW) union members approved new agreements with Chrysler and Ford in September and with GM in October. The contracts included a $3,000 signing bonus, a performance bonus in the second year of the contract, a 2-percent raise in the third year of the contract, and a 3-percent raise in the fourth year. ■ Mike Casey

See also **Labor and employment.**

Automobile racing. News of the continuing financial difficulties of Championship Auto Racing Teams (CART), one of the main open-wheel racing organizations, dominated the 2003 racing season. CART's financial woes increased the strain between CART and the Indy Racing League (IRL), CART's main competitor.

After CART lost many of its star drivers, engine makers, and sponsors to the rival IRL, many observers began questioning its financial future. CART officials attempted to raise cash to continue operations throughout 2003. In June, CART officials announced the company was for sale. CART officials warned investors in July that the company might not return to profitability until 2006. The reason the company went up for sale became apparent in August 2003, when officials revealed that CART had lost more than $43 million in the first half of the season. In September, CART's board accepted a bid offered by a group headed by Gerald Forsyth, a CART racing team owner.

CART. Paul Tracy won the CART driver's championship on October 26 with his victory in the Gold Coast Indy at Surfers Paradise, Australia. Tracy had won the first three races of the 19-race CART series, including back-to-back wins in July.

IRL. Sam Hornish, Jr., won his second consecutive IRL title on September 15 with his victory in the Chevy 500 at the Texas Motor Speedway in Fort Worth. The race featured 21 lead changes and was the second-closest in IRL history, with Hornish edging Helio Castroneves of Brazil by 0.0096 second.

Indianapolis 500. Gil de Ferran of Brazil returned from a serious injury suffered in a crash in March to win the Indianapolis 500 on May 25. De Ferran's victory denied his countryman and teammate, Helio Castroneves, an unprecedented third straight Indy 500 title.

De Ferran, who had suffered a concussion and broken bones in his back and neck in a crash in March, passed Castroneves on lap 170 of the 200-lap race and held him off in a very tight contest decided by only 0.299 second, the third-closest finish in Indy 500 history. De Ferran averaged 156.291 miles (251.525 kilometers) per hour, finishing in 3 hours, 11 minutes, and 56.99 seconds. De Ferran announced his retirement from racing in August.

NASCAR. Matt Kenseth won the Winston Cup Series Championship on November 9 with a fourth-place finish at the Pop Secret Microwave Popcorn 400 at North Carolina Speedway in Rockingham. He finished the season with 5,022 points, 90 points ahead of Jimmie Johnson.

Formula One. Michael Schumacher of Germany won his record-setting sixth overall world driver's title with an eighth-place finish at the Grand Prix of Japan on October 12.

Endurance. Timo Bernhard and Jorg Bergmeister of Germany and Michael Schrom of the United States easily captured the Rolex 24-hour race on February 2 in Daytona Beach, Florida. The team drove a Porsche 911 GT3 to victory, beating the next closest team by nine laps. The winning team battled back from 16th place to the lead position in the fifth hour and never trailed again. They covered 2,474.2 miles (3.980 kilometers) at an average speed on 103.012 miles (165 kilometers) per hour.

A car built by Bentley Motors of Crewe, England, won the 24 Hours at Le Mans race on June 15 in Le Mans, France. The victory was the first for a car built by Bentley since 1930. Danish driver Tom Kristensen won for a record fourth straight time. Kristensen and teammates Guy Smith of Britain and Rinoldo Capello of Italy completed a record 377 laps in 24 hours.

Dragsters. Kenny Bernstein won the 2003 National Hot Rod Association top fuel division championship; Del Worsham won the funny car division; and Greg Anderson won the pro stock division.

Death. Tony Renna, 26, died after a crash during a Firestone tire testing October 23, the first on-track fatality at Indy since Scott Brayton in 1996. ■ Michael Kates

See also **Sports**.

Juan Pablo Montoya of Colombia races to victory in the Monaco Formula One Grand Prix on June 1, 2003. Montoya edged Michael Schumacher of Germany by less than two seconds, but Schumacher went on to win his record sixth world driver's title.

Aviation. The aviation industry suffered a series of setbacks in 2003, triggered by such factors as an epidemic, a war, and a slow economy. In the spring, the severe acute respiratory syndrome (SARS) epidemic exerted a large negative impact on air travel worldwide. The flulike illness, which originated in southern China, infected passengers on international flights, who spread the disease to other parts of Asia and as far away as Toronto, Canada. The number of people traveling by air fell substantially after physicians established the connection between the spread of the disease and aviation. Airport officials began taking body temperatures in an attempt to detect those passengers who might be suffering from the disease. Officials with the International Air Travel Association (IATA), a group of international airlines headquartered in Montreal, Canada, estimated that SARS cost the airlines about $4 billion in 2003.

Speculation that war would break out in Iraq affected air travel to Europe and the Middle East in early 2003. While travel rebounded after the March-April hostilities, IATA officials estimated that the war cost airlines another $2.5 billion in lost sales.

A slow economy in 2003 had a devastating effect on the airline industry. The 30 airline members of the Association of European Airlines suffered a 12-percent drop in international traffic in March. By the last week of March, top U.S. airlines cut flight schedules by 6 to 12 percent and airline traffic decreased 10 percent.

Airline bankruptcies. US Airways of Arlington, Virginia, emerged from bankruptcy on March 31 after the airline negotiated reduced wages and benefits with its employees. US Airways raised money by selling a 37-percent stake to a pension fund, the Retirement Systems of Alabama Holding LLC. The Air Transport Stabilization Board (ATSB) guaranteed most of the loans. After the terrorist attacks on the United States in 2001, the ATSB administered a fund to guarantee loans to troubled airlines. In addition, the federal government's Pension Benefit Guaranty Corporation provided $600 million to the airline's pension plan for its pilots, after the discovery that the airline had not adequately funded the program. The bailout, however, only covered about half of US Airways' losses, which meant that retirees had to take significant pension cuts. As part of its financial restructuring, US Airways officials announced that the airline would deploy smaller regional jets that seat 30 to 100 people.

Despite the recovery of US Airways, the industry remained in dire financial straits in 2003. United Airlines, Inc., of Elk Grove Village, Illinois, the world's second-largest airline, remained in bankruptcy throughout 2003. After declaring

insolvency in December 2002, United began renegotiating contracts with suppliers and its unions.

The world's largest airline, American Airlines of Dallas-Fort Worth, Texas, came close to declaring bankruptcy in April 2003. The airline narrowly avoided insolvency by convincing employees to accept wage cuts. However, the concessions almost collapsed after it was revealed that the airline had secretly arranged bonuses and extra pensions for senior managers at the same time it was asking employees to make sacrifices. The airline's chairman and chief executive officer, Donald J. Carty, was forced to resign.

Concorde finale. The decrease in air travel in 2003 proved to be the death knell for supersonic jet passenger service. Air France and British Airways, the only two operators of Concorde supersonic jets, ended service in May and October 2003, respectively. Service aboard the Concorde began in 1976 with three-hour flights between London and New York City and Paris and New York City. While expensive to operate, the aircraft were the flagships of their airlines and provided the aviation industry's finest service. The aircraft had been withdrawn from service for 16 months following a crash in Paris in July 2000 and returned to the depressed aviation market that followed the terrorist attacks on the United States on Sept. 11, 2001.

East Coast competition. Despite financial troubles, competition heated up in 2003 between airlines flying routes along the East Coast of the United States. Officials at JetBlue of New York City announced plans in April to add aircraft to its fleet. The news preceded the announcement that JetBlue's passenger traffic had increased 61 percent in June, compared with the same month in 2002. Delta Air Lines of Atlanta, Georgia, launched a new budget carrier, named Song, in April 2003. In July, Atlantic Coast Airlines of Dulles, Virginia, announced that the company was severing its relationship with United Airlines, with whom it had operated under the United Express brand. Atlantic Coast Airlines officials planned to use the company's 50-seat regional jets to compete as an independent low-cost airline from its hub at Washington Dulles International Airport in Sterling, Virginia.

Merger. Representatives of Air France of Paris and KLM Royal Dutch Airlines of Amsterdam announced in September that the companies were merging. If the French and Dutch governments approved the deal, the new airline would be the largest in Europe and the third largest in the world. ■ Ian Savage

See also **Canada; China; Economics; France; Iraq: A Special Report; Middle East; Public health and safety; Toronto; United Kingdom; United States, Government of the.**

Azerbaijan. On Oct. 15, 2003, Azerbaijani voters elected Prime Minister Ilham Aliyev to the presidency by a landslide. Aliyev's father, Heydar Aliyev, had served as Azerbaijan's Communist Party chief in the Soviet period and as its president since 1993. The elder Aliyev had been ill for several years and had not appeared in public since entering a hospital for treatment in July 2003.

Ilham Aliyev's election was marked by widespread allegations of vote fraud and manipulation. The U.S.-based National Democratic Institute condemned the election, saying it "did not meet minimum international standards," and opposition Musavat Party leader Isa Gambar claimed he had received 60 percent of the vote. Protests over the vote erupted in violence in Baku, the capital, on October 15 and 16. In the wake of clashes between protesters and police, the government arrested hundreds of opposition politicians and ransacked the premises of leading opposition parties. By the end of 2003, the Azerbaijani political opposition was in shambles, and Ilham Aliyev appeared poised to exercise the same complete control over Azerbaijan that his father had.

■ Steven L. Solnick

See also **Asia; Turkey.**

Bahamas. See **West Indies.**

Bahrain. See **Middle East.**

Ballet. See **Dance.**

Bangladesh. Hundreds of people in Bangladesh died in ferry-boat accidents in 2003. Two separate accidents near the capital, Dhaka, on April 21 killed more than 130 people. On July 8, more than 500 people died when a large ferry sank south of Dhaka.

Ferries are the main form of mass transportation in Bangladesh, a country that sits on the delta of three large rivers. Ferries are often overcrowded and poorly maintained. As a result, hundreds of people die in ferry accidents annually.

The government continued a controversial campaign to crack down on crime in 2003. The anticrime drive began in 2002 when the army arrested nearly 11,000 people. More than 40 suspects died in custody. In February 2003, the parliament adopted a law granting troops immunity for their actions. Human rights groups criticized the law, and the European Union threatened to cut off aid unless the situation improved.

The World Bank, an affiliate of the United Nations, reported in September that Bangladesh's economy grew by more than 5 percent in 2003. The increase was short of the goal of 8 percent annual growth that economists said is needed to reduce the number of Bangladeshis living in poverty by half by 2010.

■ Henry S. Bradsher

See also **Asia; Disasters.**

Bank. In the biggest bank transaction of 2003, Bank of America and FleetBoston Financial announced on October 27 that the two institutions would merge, creating a sprawling new consumer bank with branches across the country. Officials at Bank of America, based in Charlotte, North Carolina, said the company would pay an estimated $48 billion in stock for FleetBoston, which had a stronger branch system in the Northeast and some of the wealthiest households in the United States as customers. The combined companies expected to have 5,700 branches in 29 states and about 10 percent of the nation's deposits.

With $933 billion in assets—Bank of America's $737 billion plus FleetBoston's $196 billion—the new institution would be the second largest U.S. bank in assets, after Citigroup of New York City with $1.2 trillion in assets and ahead of JP Morgan Chase of New York City with $792 billion.

Economists saw the merger as a sign that banks are retreating to less exciting business lines, such as checking accounts and car loans, which have been more reliable sources of profit than corporate loans and securities in recent years. Banks have found that depositors gained through acquiring new branches often buy other products from their bank, including mutual fund accounts, annuities, and mortgages.

Government pursuit. Bank of America in 2003 was investigated along with other mutual fund and Wall Street firms for allegedly conducting improper and illegal mutual fund trading. The bank fired several top executives, and one former broker faced criminal charges. On September 16, Theodore C. Sihpol III, a former broker at Bank of America, was charged with larceny and securities fraud and was also accused of helping a *hedge fund* (an investment fund set up as a limited partnership for investing private capital speculatively) to trade mutual fund shares after the markets closed to take advantage of after-hours market events. The case remained pending at the end of 2003.

Sihpol was just one banking executive who fell under scrutiny from government investigators. In what became one of the most closely followed trials of the year, Frank P. Quattrone, the former star technology banker at Credit Suisse First Boston, was indicted by a federal grand jury on May 12 on charges that he obstructed justice and destroyed evidence. United States District Judge Richard Owen of the Southern District of New York presided over the case.

The investigation involved the allegation that investment bankers had offered shares in hot new stocks from initial public offerings, which were not widely available to the general public. In exchange, the corporate officials moved their investment banking business to those firms.

The obstruction charge against Quattrone, who headed Credit Suisse's investment banking division for technology companies, stemmed from his December 2000 e-mail, which recommended that staffers "clean up" their files. The government alleged that the recommendation was a prompt to workers to destroy evidence of insider deals for selling stock in exchange for investment banking business. Prosecutors said that Credit Suisse lawyers warned Quattrone days earlier that regulators and prosecutors from the Southern District had issued subpoenas for documents concerning the hot stock offerings to prized corporate clients. Quattrone denied receiving the warning.

The case was also noteworthy because Quattrone, one of the most powerful Wall Street financiers to face a judge and jury on criminal charges, took the stand to testify on his own behalf. Judge Owen declared a mistrial on Oct. 24, 2003, when the jury could not reach a verdict. Government prosecutors left open the possibility that they would bring new charges.

Banks and Enron. On July 28, the nation's two largest banks agreed to pay $305 million in fines and penalties to settle accusations that they helped the Houston-based Enron Corp. in misrepresenting its financial condition for years before the giant energy trader collapsed in December 2001. The banks were involved in funding Enron ventures that were fraudulent.

The Securities and Exchange Commission (SEC), which administers and enforces federal laws governing the purchase and sale of securities, and the Manhattan District Attorney Robert Morgenthau brought the charges against J.P. Morgan Chase and Citigroup, both based in New York City. The agreement ended 19 months of scrutiny of the banks' actions. Neither bank admitted any wrongdoing under the terms of the settlement.

Morgenthau and the SEC announced that in one case, Enron accounted for money it borrowed from the banks as cash flow from operations, which made it appear that the money was actually profits, and concealed the bank debt.

The banks agreed to overhaul risk-management procedures, especially the ways they handled the most complicated transactions.

Industry earnings. Low interest rates helped banks post high profits in 2003, thanks to housing-related lending, which is very sensitive to interest rates. In the first six months of the year, commercial banks and savings institutions posted record-breaking earnings of $59.6 billion. An improving trend in loan quality that began in the fourth quarter of last year continued through the first three months of 2003, especially in business lending.

Both the first and second quarters of 2003 showed record high profits. The banks had strong gains on the sales of assets, loan growth, and declining losses on bad loans. In the second quarter, fewer U.S. banks were running at a loss than at any time in the last five years, according to the Federal Deposit Insurance Corporation.

Congress. In the early 2000's, the U.S. Congress has reviewed the deposit insurance system, which protects bank deposits for consumers up to $100,000 per account. On April 2, 2003, the U.S. House of Representatives passed a bill that reformed the deposit insurance system. A second reform bill was introduced in the Senate, but the full Senate did not vote on the measure. The two bills differed in small details, but both merged the separate insurance funds that cover deposits in banks and savings and loans. The legislation would also increase the insured amount to $130,000, tied to future increases in the rate of inflation. It would also give banks rebates of the insurance premiums that they pay, after the fund rises above a certain level.

The Senate Banking Committee on September 8 launched a year-long investigation into how terrorists finance their activities. The investigation was a bipartisan effort by Committee Chairman Richard Shelby (R. Alabama) and Paul Sarbanes (D. Maryland). ■ Paulette Thomas

See also **Crime; Economics; Stocks and bonds.**

Baseball. The Florida Marlins in 2003 won their second World Series in just their 11th year since joining Major League Baseball (MLB). In Game 6 on October 24, Marlins ace pitcher Josh Beckett, throwing on just three days' rest, led the Marlins to victory over the New York Yankees at Yankee Stadium to seal the series win.

For a time, it appeared that two of baseball's "cursed" teams—the Chicago Cubs and the Boston Red Sox—would face each other in the World Series. According to folklore, the Red Sox, who last won the series in 1918, are cursed because they traded the great Babe Ruth to the Yankees in 1920. The Cubs, who have not won a World Series since 1908 or played in one since 1945, are supposedly under a curse placed on them by a local bar owner who, along with his goat, was denied entry to a game at the 1945 World Series at Wrigley Field in Chicago.

Both teams made the play-offs and appeared destined to reverse their "curses." But in eerily similar circumstances, both teams were ahead by three runs and were five outs away from the series, with each team's pitching ace on the mound, only to lose.

The Cubs blew a three-run lead in Game 6 of the National League Championship Series (NLCS) with Mark Prior on the mound, eventually allowing eight Florida Marlins runs in one inning to score. Similarly, the Red Sox led the Yankees 5-2 in Game 7 of the American League Championship Series (ALCS), with ace Pedro Martinez on the mound. But Martinez gave up three runs, and the Yankees bumped the Red Sox out of contention.

World Series. After winning the first game in New York City, the Marlins dropped Game 2 in New York and Game 3 in Miami. Yankees starting pitcher Roger Clemens, who announced before Game 4 that he was retiring after the season, was touched for three runs in the first inning at Miami. The Yankees rallied to tie the game 3 to 3 in the top of the ninth inning and appeared poised to

take control of the series. But the Marlins' Alex Gonzalez launched a lead-off 12th-inning homer to win the game 4-3. It was the 13th game-winning home run in World Series history. In Game 5, Florida held on to win 6-4, then won the series on Beckett's brilliant complete-game 2-0 victory in Game 6.

Play-offs. In the National League (NL) Division Series, the Cubs beat the Braves 3 games to 2, while the Marlins beat the Giants 3 games to 1. In the NLCS, the Cubs took a 3-games-to-1 lead over Florida before Beckett fired a two-hit shut-out in Game 5. However, the Cubs collapsed in Game 6 at

Florida Marlins pitcher Josh Beckett tags Jorge Posada of the New York Yankees for the final out in Game 6 of the World Series in New York City on Oct. 25, 2003. The Marlins took the series by defeating the Yankees 4 games to 2, capping a tremendous second half of the season in which the Marlins had the best record in baseball.

Wrigley Field. Leading by three runs, the Cubs allowed the Marlins to score eight runs in the eighth inning for the victory. The Marlins then won Game 7, making them only the fourth team in NLCS history to rally from a 3-games-to-1 deficit.

In the American League (AL) Division Series, the Yankees defeated the Minnesota Twins 3 games to 1, while Boston rallied from a 2-game deficit to beat the Oakland Athletics in five games.

In the ALCS, the Red Sox forced a seventh game with a 9-6 victory in Game 6 in New York. In Game 7 on October 16, the Red Sox knocked Clemens out early but squandered several scoring chances and in the seventh inning were clinging to a three-run lead. The Yankees tied the game on Jorge Posada's two-run bloop double in the eighth inning and won it on Aaron Boone's lead-off home run in the 11th inning.

FINAL STANDINGS IN MAJOR LEAGUE BASEBALL

AMERICAN LEAGUE

American League champions—
New York Yankees
(defeated Boston Red Sox, 4 games to 3)

Eastern Division	W.	L.	Pct.	G.B.
New York Yankees	101	61	.623	—
Boston Red Sox*	95	67	.586	6
Toronto Blue Jays	86	76	.531	15
Baltimore Orioles	71	91	.438	30
Tampa Bay Devil Rays	63	99	.389	38
Central Division				
Minnesota Twins	90	72	.556	—
Chicago White Sox	86	76	.531	4
Kansas City Royals	83	79	.512	7
Cleveland Indians	68	94	.420	22
Detroit Tigers	43	119	.265	47
Western Division				
Oakland Athletics	96	66	.593	—
Seattle Mariners	93	69	.574	3
Anaheim Angels	77	85	.475	19
Texas Rangers	71	91	.438	25

Offensive leaders

Batting average	Bill Mueller, Boston	.326
Runs scored	Alex Rodriguez, Texas	124
Home runs	Alex Rodriguez, Texas	47
Runs batted in	Carlos Delgado, Toronto	145
Hits	Vernon Wells, Toronto	215
Stolen bases	Carl Crawford, Tampa Bay	55
Slugging percentage	Alex Rodriguez, Texas	.600

Leading pitchers

Games won	Roy Halladay, Toronto	22
Earned run average (162 or more innings)—	Pedro Martinez, Boston	2.22
Strikeouts	Esteban Loaiza, Chicago	207
Saves	Keith Foulke, Oakland	43
Shut-outs	Roy Halladay, Toronto	2
Complete games	Bartolo Colon, Chicago	9
	Roy Halladay, Toronto	9
	Mark Mulder, Oakland	9

Awards[†]

Most Valuable Player	Alex Rodriguez, Texas
Cy Young	Roy Halladay, Toronto
Rookie of the Year	Angel Berroa, Kansas City
Manager of the Year	Tony Pena, Kansas City

NATIONAL LEAGUE

National League champions—
Florida Marlins (defeated Chicago Cubs, 4 games to 3)
World Series champions—
Florida Marlins (defeated New York Yankees, 4 games to 2)

Eastern Division	W.	L.	Pct.	G.B.
Atlanta Braves	101	61	.623	—
Florida Marlins*	91	71	.562	10
Philadelphia Phillies	86	76	.531	15
Montreal Expos	83	79	.512	18
New York Mets	66	95	.410	34½
Central Division				
Chicago Cubs	88	74	.543	—
Houston Astros	87	75	.537	1
St. Louis Cardinals	85	77	.525	3
Pittsburgh Pirates	75	87	.463	13
Cincinnati Reds	69	93	.426	19
Milwaukee Brewers	68	94	.420	20
Western Division				
San Francisco Giants	100	61	.621	—
Los Angeles Dodgers	85	77	.525	15½
Arizona Diamondbacks	84	78	.519	16½
Colorado Rockies	74	88	.457	26½
San Diego Padres	64	98	.395	36½

Offensive leaders

Batting average	Albert Pujols, St. Louis	.359
Runs scored	Albert Pujols, St. Louis	137
Home runs	Jim Thome, Philadelphia	47
Runs batted in	Preston Wilson, Colorado	141
Hits	Albert Pujols, St. Louis	212
Stolen bases	Juan Pierre, Florida	65
Slugging percentage	Barry Bonds, San Francisco	.749

Leading pitchers

Games won	Roy Ortiz, Atlanta	21
Earned run average (162 or more innings)—	Jason Schmidt, San Francisco	2.34
Strikeouts	Kerry Wood, Chicago	266
Saves	Eric Gagne, Los Angeles	55
Shut-outs	Kevin Millwood, Philadelphia	3
	Matt Morris, St. Louis	3
	Jason Schmidt, San Francisco	3
Complete games	Livan Hernandez, Montreal	8

Awards[†]

Most Valuable Player	Barry Bonds, San Francisco
Cy Young	Eric Gagne, Los Angeles
Rookie of the Year	Dontrelle Willis, Florida
Manager of the Year	Jack McKeon, Florida

*Qualified for wild-card play-off spot.
[†]Selected by the Baseball Writers Association of America.

Regular season. The NL Central Division race came down to the final weekend of the season, with the upstart Cubs trying to fend off a late-season run by the Houston Astros. The Cubs clinched the division on September 26, the penultimate day of the season, by sweeping a doubleheader against the Pittsburgh Pirates. The Cubs clinched by one game, after Houston lost games on September 25 and 26.

In the NL East, Atlanta cruised to the best record in the National League at 101-61. In the NL West, San Francisco posted a record of 100-61, winning the division by 15½ games over the Los Angeles Dodgers.

In the AL, the Yankees captured the East Division by 6 games over Boston with a mark of 101-61. The Oakland Athletics overtook Seattle late in the season to win the West Division with a 96-66 mark, three games better than the Mariners. Minnesota moved past the Chicago White Sox in September to win the Central Division by 4 games with a 90-72 mark.

The Detroit Tigers won five of their last six games to finish with 43 wins and 119 losses and avoid the distinction of losing the most games ever in a single season. The 1962 New York Mets, who lost 120 games, still hold that record. However, the Tigers' 119 losses did establish a new AL record for losses in a season.

Sosa's travails. In a game against the Cincinnati Reds on April 4, 2003, Sammy Sosa of the Cubs became the 18th player—and the first from Latin America—to hit 500 home runs. However, Sosa's season took a bizarre turn on June 3 in Chicago. Umpires examining a bat that Sosa had shattered found a piece of cork just above the handle. Inserting cork inside a bat is against MLB rules because it is believed to help batters hit the ball farther. Sosa admitted the bat was his, but said it was a practice bat that he had used accidentally in the game. Sosa received an eight-game suspension that was later reduced to seven games.

Other milestones. Roger Clemens secured his 300th victory on June 13 in New York City with a 5-2 win over the St. Louis Cardinals. Clemens, the 21st pitcher to win 300 games, also struck out 10 batters to become the third pitcher to reach 4,000 strikeouts. The other two are Nolan Ryan and Steve Carlton.

On May 11, Rafael Palmeiro of the Texas Rangers joined the 500-home-run club. With his homer, Palmeiro became the 19th player to hit 500 career home runs.

San Francisco's Barry Bonds on June 24 stole second base against Los Angeles to became the founding member of the "500-500 club." Bonds was the first player to hit 500 home runs and steal 500 bases in a career. No other player has even hit 400 home runs and stolen 400 bases.

Eric Gagne, a relief pitcher with the Dodgers, completed a record 55 consecutive saves on September 2. His streak began in 2002. Gagne finished the 2003 season with a perfect record of 55 saves in 55 chances and will carry a streak of 63 consecutive saves into 2004.

Steroid usage. MLB officials announced in November 2003 that any player discovered using *steroids* (drugs that can improve athletic performance) during the 2004 season will be punished. The announcement came after evidence of steroid usage was discovered in more than 5 percent of players who were randomly tested during the 2003 season. First offenders must undergo drug treatment and a subsequent offense will result in a 15-day suspension or a $10,000 fine.

College. Rice University in Houston captured the school's first national championship in any sport on June 23, winning the National Collegiate Athletic Association World Series in Omaha, Nebraska. Rice routed Stanford 14-2 in the final game.

Youth. On August 24 in South Williamsport, Pennsylvania, a team from Tokyo captured the Little League World Series. It defeated a team from Boynton Beach, Florida, 10-1.

Death. Warren Spahn, a Hall-of-Fame southpaw who won 363 games over 21 seasons, died on November 24.   ■ Michael Kates

See also **Deaths; Sports.**

Basketball. The San Antonio Spurs won their second National Basketball Association (NBA) title in five years on June 15, 2003, defeating the New Jersey Nets 4 games to 2. Tim Duncan led the Spurs with a memorable performance in the finals, for which he was later named the play-offs' Most Valuable Player.

In college basketball, the University of Syracuse won the school's first National Collegiate Athletic Association (NCAA) men's title in 2003, and the University of Connecticut (UConn) successfully defended its title as women's champion.

King James. On June 26, the Cleveland Cavaliers made LeBron James, who stands 6 feet, 8 inches (2 meters) tall and weighs 240 pounds (108 kilograms), the top pick in the NBA draft. The selection capped off a tumultuous year for the Akron, Ohio, high school senior, nicknamed "King James." In January, the Ohio High School Athletic Association had declared James ineligible for the last five games of the season for allegedly receiving two free jerseys from a Cleveland clothing store. However, a judge later shortened the suspension to one game.

Media hype over James's amazing athletic talents began in 2002 during his junior year at St. Vincent-St. Mary High School in Akron. The attention on James, whose skills were so highly developed that some professional scouts labeled him a prodigy, led to two of his high school games being televised on

THE 2002-2003 COLLEGE BASKETBALL SEASON

COLLEGE TOURNAMENT CHAMPIONS

NCAA (Men)

	Division I:	Syracuse
	Division II:	Northeastern St. (Oklahoma)
	Division III:	Williams (Massachusetts)
(Women)	Division I:	Connecticut
	Division II:	South Dakota State
	Division III:	Trinity (Texas)

NAIA (Men)

	Division I:	Concordia (California)
	Division II:	Northwestern (Iowa)
(Women)	Division I:	Southern Nazarene (Oklahoma)
	Division II:	Hastings (Nebraska)

NIT (Men) St. John's

MEN'S COLLEGE CHAMPIONS

CONFERENCE	SCHOOL
America East	Boston
	Vermont (tournament)
Atlantic 10	Dayton (tournament)
East Division	Saint Joseph's
West Division	Xavier*
Atlantic Coast	Wake Forest
	Duke (tournament)
Atlantic Sun	
North	Belmont
South	Mercer–Troy State*
Big 12	Kansas
	Oklahoma (tournament)
Big East	
East Division	Boston College–Connecticut (tie)
West Division	Pittsburgh*–Syracuse (tie)
Big Sky	Weber State*
Big South	Winthrop
	UNC Asheville (tournament)
Big Ten	Wisconsin
	Illinois (tournament)
Big West	UC Santa Barbara
	Utah State (tournament)
Colonial	UNC Wilmington*
Conference USA	
American Division	Marquette
	Louisville (tournament)
National Division	Memphis
Horizon League	Butler
	Wisconsin-Milwaukee (tournament)
Ivy League	Pennsylvania†
Metro Atlantic	Manhattan*
Mid-American	
East Division	Kent State
West Division	Central Michigan*
Mid-Continent	Valparaiso
	Indiana-Purdue University at Indianapolis (tournament)
Mid-Eastern	South Carolina State*
Missouri Valley	Southern Illinois
	Creighton (tournament)
Mountain West	Utah–Brigham Young (tie)
	Colorado State (tournament)
Northeast	Wagner*
Ohio Valley	Austin Peay–Morehead State (tie)
	Louisville (tournament)
Pacific 10	Arizona
	Oregon (tournament)
Patriot League	Holy Cross*
Southeastern	
Eastern	Kentucky*
Western	Mississippi State
Southern	
North Division	Appalachian State–East Tennessee State*–Davidson (tie)
South Division	Charleston
Southland	Sam Houston State*
Southwestern	Prairie View A&M
	Texas Southern (tournament)
Sun Belt	
East Division	Western Kentucky*
West Division	Lafayette-Louisiana
West Coast	Gonzaga
	San Diego (tournament)
Western Athletic	Fresno State
	Tulsa (tournament)

*Regular season and conference tournament champion.
†No tournament played.
Sources: National Collegiate Athletic Association (NCAA);
National Association of Intercollegiate Athletics (NAIA);
National Invitation Tournament (NIT); Conference Web sites.

the national sports cable TV network ESPN 2.

Professional men. On June 15, 2003, in the championship game of the NBA Finals, Tim Duncan turned in one of the best performances in NBA Finals history. Duncan scored 21 points, grabbed 20 rebounds, had 10 assists, and blocked 8 shots as the Spurs rallied from a 10-point fourth-quarter deficit to beat New Jersey 88-77 and win the NBA Finals 4 games to 2. Duncan also set a record by blocking 32 shots during the finals.

The Spurs reached the finals by topping the Phoenix Suns 4 games to 2 in the first round of the play-offs. They then bounced the three-time defending champion Los Angeles Lakers 4 games to 2 in the conference semifinals and eliminated the Dallas Mavericks 4 games to 2 to capture the Western Conference and move on to the finals.

During the regular season, the Nets' record of 49 wins and 33 losses topped the Atlantic Division, while Detroit posted the best regular-season mark in the Eastern Conference with 50 wins and 32 losses. In the Western Conference, San Antonio tied Dallas for the league's best mark at 60 and 22, but San Antonio won the Midwest Division because they had a better record against Dallas in the regular season. Sacramento won the Pacific Division with a 59 and 23 mark.

Professional women. The Detroit Shock won the Women's National Basketball Association (WNBA) championship on September 16, defeating the two-time defending champion Los Angeles Sparks 2 games to 1. Ruth Riley led the Shock in the final of the three-game series, scoring a career-high 27 points.

The WNBA nearly had to cancel its seventh season because of a labor dispute. The WNBA and its players' association reached an agreement on a new contract on April 18. Nevertheless, two WNBA teams dissolved and two

Tim Duncan of the San Antonio Spurs (#21) blocks the shot of Kenyon Martin of the New Jersey Nets in Game 6 of the National Basketball Association Finals on June 15, 2003. In the game, Duncan scored 21 points, grabbed 20 rebounds, and blocked 8 shots in a great performance.

others moved to new cities in 2003.

College men. On April 7, Syracuse (30-5) held on for an 81 to 78 victory over the University of Kansas (Lawrence) to win the national championship. Freshman Carmelo Anthony, playing with a back injury, led Syracuse with 20 points, 10 rebounds, and 7 assists.

To get to the title game, Syracuse, the third seed in the East bracket, blasted the University of Texas (Austin), the top seed in the South bracket, 95 to 84 on April 5. In the other semifinal, Kansas (30-8), the second seed in the West bracket, throttled third-seeded Marquette (Milwaukee) 94-61.

College women. The (UConn) Huskies (37-1) capped off a near-perfect season on April 8 with a 73 to 68 victory over the University of Tennessee (Knoxville) in Atlanta, Georgia. The Huskies were led by national player of the year Diana Taurasi, who scored 28 points and made 8 of 15 shots from the field, including four 3-pointers.

To reach the final, UConn, the top seed in the East, rallied from a nine-point deficit to edge the University of Texas (Austin), the second seed in the West, 71 to 69 on April 6. Tennessee (33-5), the top seed in the Mideast, reached the final by beating Duke, the top seed in the Midwest.

Scandals. A wave of coaches being fired or forced to resign for their behavior rolled through college basketball in 2003. In March, University of Georgia (Athens) coach Jim Harrick resigned amid allegations of academic fraud and payments to a former player. The school banned the team from competing in the conference and NCAA tournaments in 2003.

Also in March, officials at Fresno State University at Fresno, California, banned the basketball team from competing in postseason play for four years because of allegations of academic fraud, which reportedly occurred during the 1999-2000 season under then-coach Jerry Tarkanian. Fresno State had

NATIONAL BASKETBALL ASSOCIATION STANDINGS

EASTERN CONFERENCE

Atlantic Division	W.	L.	Pct.	G.B.
New Jersey Nets*	49	33	.598	—
Philadelphia 76ers*	48	34	.585	1
Boston Celtics*	44	38	.537	5
Orlando Magic*	42	40	.512	7
Washington Wizards	37	45	.451	12
New York Knicks	37	45	.451	12
Miami Heat	25	57	.305	24

Central Division	W.	L.	Pct.	G.B.
Detroit Pistons*	50	32	.610	—
Indiana Pacers*	48	34	.585	2
New Orleans Wizards*	47	35	.573	3
Milwaukee Bucks*	42	40	.512	8
Atlanta Hawks	35	47	.427	15
Chicago Bulls	30	52	.366	20
Toronto Raptors	24	58	.293	26
Cleveland Cavaliers	17	65	.207	33

WESTERN CONFERENCE

Midwest Division	W.	L.	Pct.	G.B.
San Antonio Spurs*	60	22	.732	—
Dallas Mavericks*	60	22	.732	—
Minnesota T'wolves*	51	31	.622	9
Utah Jazz*	47	35	.573	13
Houston Rockets	43	39	.524	17
Memphis Grizzlies	28	54	.341	32
Denver Nuggets	17	65	.207	43

Pacific Division	W.	L.	Pct.	G.B.
Sacramento Kings*	59	23	.720	—
Los Angeles Lakers*	50	32	.610	9
Portland Trail Blazers*	50	32	.610	9
Phoenix Suns*	44	38	.537	15
Seattle Supersonics	40	42	.488	19
Golden State Warriors	38	44	.463	21
Los Angeles Clippers	27	55	.329	32

INDIVIDUAL LEADERS

Scoring	G.	F.G.	F.T.	Pts.	Avg.
Tracy McGrady, Orlando	75	829	576	2,407	32.1
Kobe Bryant, L.A. Lakers	82	868	601	2,461	30.0
Allen Iverson, Philadelphia	82	804	570	2,262	27.6
Shaquille O'Neal, L.A. Lakers	67	695	451	1,841	27.5
Paul Pierce, Boston	79	663	604	2,048	25.9
Dirk Nowitzki, Dallas	80	690	483	2,011	25.1
Tim Duncan, San Antonio	81	714	450	1,884	23.3
Chris Webber, Sacramento	67	661	215	1,542	23.0
Kevin Garnett, Minnesota	82	743	377	1,883	23.0
Ray Allen, Seattle	76	598	316	1,713	22.5
Allan Houston, New York	82	652	363	1,845	22.5

Rebounding	G.	Off.	Def.	Tot.	Avg.
Ben Wallace, Detroit	73	293	833	1,126	15.4
Kevin Garnett, Minnesota	82	244	858	1,102	13.4
Tim Duncan, San Antonio	81	259	784	1,043	12.9
Jermaine O'Neal, Indiana	77	202	594	796	10.3
Brian Grant, Miami	82	241	596	837	10.2
Troy Murphy, Golden State	79	228	578	806	10.2
Dirk Nowitzki, Dallas	80	81	710	791	9.9
Shawn Marion, Phoenix	81	199	574	773	9.5
Jerome Williams, Toronto	71	231	419	650	9.2
P.J. Brown, New Orleans	78	243	458	701	9.0
Donyell Marshall, Chicago	78	234	465	699	9.0

NBA champions—San Antonio Spurs
(defeated New Jersey Nets, 4 games to 2)

*Made play-offs.

won the regular season title before the three-year-old allegations came to light.

On April 17, 2003, officials at St. Bonaventure University in St. Bonaventure, New York, fired coach Jan van Breda Kolff and athletic director Gothard Lane for allowing an ineligible player to compete. St. Bonaventure President Robert Wickenheiser had already resigned after admitting to helping transfer the player, Jamil Terrell, despite the fact that he was not academically qualified.

In May, Iowa State University (Ames) coach Larry Eustachy resigned after a newspaper published photographs showing Eustachy partying with University of Missouri (Columbia) students after Eustachy's team lost at Missouri in January.

Also in May, the NCAA put the University of Michigan (Ann Arbor) men's basketball program on probation for four years, banned the team from postseason play for the 2003-2004 season, and took away one scholarship for a four-season period starting with the 2004-2005 season. The penalties were imposed because of illegal payments to players made by a prominent booster during the 1990's. The school also forfeited more than 100 victories it had won with the players involved and returned $450,000 in post-season earnings. The post-season ban was later lifted.

In August 2003, Baylor University (Waco, Texas) head coach Dave Bliss and athletic director Tom Stanton resigned after an investigation into the murder of a Baylor player Patrick Dennehy revealed NCAA rules violations. Officials alleged that Bliss had provided rent money to several players and paid for Dennehy's tuition.

Kobe Bryant. Basketball fans were shocked by the July 4 arrest of Los Angeles Lakers star Kobe Bryant for allegedly sexually assaulting a 19-year-old employee of a resort in Colorado. Bryant, who is married with an infant daughter, admitted having relations with the woman but denied assaulting her. If convicted, Bryant faced four years to life in prison or 20 years to life on probation and a fine of up to $750,000. ■ Michael Kates

See also **Sports**.

Belarus. Belarus and Russia in 2003 continued to spar over the terms of a proposed political and economic union. In July, Belarusian President Aleksandr Lukashenko postponed the introduction of the Russian ruble for noncash transactions in Belarus. He subsequently claimed as a rationale that the switch would cost Belarus more than $1 billion. Relations between the two countries worsened over the summer, when Russia announced that it would begin charging Belarus world-market prices for natural gas. In October, after two meetings with Russian President Vladimir Putin, Lukashenko declared the two sides deadlocked over the key issues in economic and political union.

In July, Lukashenko banned several foreign entities, including nongovernmental organizations, organizations supporting independent media and academic exchanges, and the Russian television station NTV. Also in July, he dismissed his prime minister and reshuffled his Cabinet, charging them with mismanaging the economy. Political analysts suggested that the moves, which deepened Lukashenko's isolation both at home and abroad, probably represented the first steps in his campaign for a constitutional amendment permitting him to seek a third presidential term in 2006.   ■ Steven L. Solnick

See also **Europe; Russia.**

Belgium became involved in a major diplomatic dispute with the United States in 2003 over a controversial war crimes law. The law, passed in 1993, gave Belgian courts the right to investigate war crimes allegations anywhere in the world.

In March 2003, a Belgian attorney filed a complaint against former U.S. President George H. W. Bush, Vice President Dick Cheney, Secretary of State Colin Powell, and retired General Norman Schwarzkopf. All were accused of war crimes in the bombing of a bunker in Iraq in which hundreds of civilians were killed during the Persian Gulf War (1991). In April 2003, a left-wing activist filed a complaint accusing General Tommy Franks, U.S. commander of coalition forces in the 2003 war in Iraq, of war crimes in that conflict.

U.S. Secretary of Defense Donald Rumsfeld protested against the complaints at a meeting of the North Atlantic Treaty Organization (NATO) in Brussels in June, calling them politically motivated. He threatened to refuse U.S. funding for a new NATO headquarters in the city unless the cases were dropped. Although Belgium had opposed the Persian Gulf War and the invasion of Iraq, the government of Prime Minister Guy Verhofstadt condemned the war crimes complaints, saying they abused the law's intent. The government amended the law so that complaints could be brought only for crimes involving citizens or residents of

Belgium. In September, Belgium's supreme court dismissed the complaints against the U.S. officials.

Al-Qa'ida trial. Eighteen suspected al-Qa'ida members were convicted of crimes in September, ending the biggest European prosecution yet against the terror network. Nizar Trabelsi, a Tunisian immigrant, was sentenced to 10 years in prison for a 2001 plot to bomb a NATO military base outside Brussels that houses U.S. troops. The other defendants were convicted of lesser crimes.

Election campaign. The Verhofstadt government won reelection in May 2003 by a wide margin. The victory was a public endorsement of the government's economic policies, which included tax cuts and a reduction of the national debt, as well as its liberal social policies, such as legalizing euthanasia. Verhofstadt's Flemish Liberal Party, based in the Dutch-speaking northern region of Belgium, won 25 seats in the 150-seat parliament. The sister Liberal Party in Wallonia, the French-speaking southern region of the country, won 24 seats. Verhofstadt formed a coalition between the Liberals and the country's two Socialist parties, which together won 48 seats.

■ Tom Buerkle

See also **Europe.**

Belize. See Latin America.
Benin. See Africa.
Bhutan. See Asia.

Biology. Biologists made a number of interesting discoveries during 2003. They found areas in the ocean where many marine species gather, discovered more types of bacteria that thrive under extreme conditions, and determined how elephants run.

Marine scientists in August reported finding undersea "Serengetis" where sharks, tuna, billfishes, and other big predators gather to feast on smaller species. The scientists compared these undersea gathering spots to Africa's Serengeti region, where animals congregate because of rich food sources and predators come to feed on them. A team led by marine scientist Boris Worm of the Institute for Marine Science in Kiel, Germany, identified the gathering spots. They studied commercial fishing records and noted several spots where at least 12 predator species were caught for every 50 other marine animals.

The major gathering spots were in waters off the east coast of Florida, south of Hawaii, and off the Great Barrier Reef and Lord Howe Island, both in Australia. Such marine gathering spots should be primary targets for conservation, environmentalists say, because they provide a wealth of species in a relatively small area.

Caribbean marine life. In a separate study in August, researchers from Conservation International, a Washington, D.C.-based environmental

The first cloned horse, Prometea, which was born in May, stands beside the mare that was both the donor of the cell that was cloned and the birth mother. Scientists at the Laboratory of Reproductive Technology in Cremona, Italy, fused the nucleus of a skin cell from the mare with a horse egg, which was then implanted in the mare's womb.

group, reported that the Caribbean, especially near the Florida coast, has the greatest concentration of marine life in the Atlantic Ocean. They analyzed 1,172 marine species and found that 22 percent of them live only in the Caribbean.

Some like it hot. A newly discovered microbe thrives at temperatures that were previously thought to kill all microorganisms, two microbiologists from the University of Massachusetts at Amherst reported in August. The microorganism, Strain 121, was collected off Puget Sound, along the Pacific Northwest coast. Researchers found the microorganism at a vent in the sea floor where boiling hot water seeps into the ocean. In the laboratory, Strain 121 can grow in temperatures of 250 °F (121 °C) or higher. Ordinarily, water boils at 212 °F (100 °C). The discovery of Strain 121 suggests that scientists looking for life elsewhere in the universe may need to study places once thought to be hostile to any life form.

The temperatures at which Strain 121 thrived were the opposite extreme of temperatures in which another microorganism survived. Researchers from the University of Illinois at Chicago in December 2002 reported finding 2,800-year-old microorganisms frozen in slushy water taken from a lake in Antarctica. The water is seven times as salty as ocean water, allowing it to remain liquid at temperatures of -10 °F (-23 °C).

Running elephants. Elephants run with a bent-legged gait, reported scientists at Stanford University in Stanford, California, in April 2003. The researchers found that elephants can run faster than previously believed, reaching speeds of at least 15 miles (24 kilometers) per hour. A number of experts on elephants had thought the animals did not really run and were capable of reaching a top speed of only about 10 miles (16 kilometers) per hour.

In reaching their conclusions, the scientists reconsidered the definition of running. Most four-footed animals gallop when they run. Both of their front limbs touch the ground at about the same time, followed by both rear limbs. At some point, all four feet are off the ground, which used to be the definition of running. Elephants never change their gait, however, and always have at least one foot on the ground.

The Stanford team found that as the elephants' speed increases, they bend their knees to improve their efficiency of movement, giving them a bouncing gait. The scientists considered that such a gait has the biomechanical qualities of running. "Walking is a stiff, pendulumlike gait; the limb stays pretty straight and swings back and forth," said one team member. "Running is a bouncing gait in which the limb actually compresses and bounces back with a spring."

First human clothing. Studies of lice provided a unique insight into the question of when human beings first started wearing clothing. Geneticist Mark Stoneking of the Max Planck Institute for Evolutionary Anthropology in Leipzig, Germany, concluded that the transition occurred between 110,000 and 32,000 years ago but was probably about 72,000 years ago. He reported his findings in August 2003.

Most biologists agree that human body lice, which feed on hairless parts of the body but reproduce in clothing, descended from head lice. Head lice live only on the scalp and glue their eggs to hair shafts. Stoneking compared the genetic blueprint of the two species and concluded that they diverged about 70,000 years ago. He assumed that after humans started wearing clothing, some head lice evolved fairly quickly to take advantage of the new ecological niche that clothing provided. Therefore, the appearance of body lice and clothing should be more or less around the same time. Anthropologists had previously believed that humans started wearing clothing long before 70,000 years ago.

Synthetic bacterium. A microorganism that can make and use an amino acid not found in nature was created by researchers at the Scripps Research Institute in La Jolla, California. The researchers announced the creation in January. Amino acids are the building blocks of proteins, large molecules that are basic components of cells. Most organisms use only 20 amino acids, but the one the researchers created used 21.

The Scripps team reported in 2001 that they had used genetic engineering techniques to modify the common bacterium *Escherichia coli*. The modified *E. coli* used an amino acid not found in nature to make certain proteins. However, the unusual amino acid had to be added to the bacterium's growth medium. In their January 2003 report, the team noted that they had further modified the mutant *E. coli* so that it could produce the amino acid by itself.

The researchers hoped that their work could lead to a better understanding of why most organisms only use 20 amino acids. They also hoped to design bacteria that can produce synthetic materials using the unusual building blocks.

Migrating monarchs. Monarch butterflies may have an accurate internal, or circadian, clock that helps them migrate from the United States to central Mexico. Researchers at the University of Massachusetts Medical School in Worcester in May provided the first strong evidence for the existence of such a clock and some hints about how it might work.

Every autumn, monarch butterflies fly thousands of miles to Mexico, where they spend the winter and then return to the North in the spring. How they navigate to the same site has been a mystery. Some researchers suggested that the butterflies navigate by the sun. But to do so, they have to have a precise internal clock that allows them to compensate for the sun's change of position in the sky during the daytime.

Monarchs have several life stages. They change from one form to another. Adult butterflies develop in a chrysalis. When they emerge from their chrysalises, it is usually morning. When the researchers exposed chrysalises to constant light, they found that the butterflies emerged at any time of the day. This was a sign some kind of internal clock had been disrupted.

The team then tested butterflies in a special flight simulator. The normal monarchs flew toward the southwest, the direction they would fly to reach Mexico. Butterflies exposed to light in such a way that their day ran from 1 p.m. to 1 a.m. failed to interpret the sun's position correctly. They flew toward the southeast. Butterflies that had been exposed to constant light simply headed straight for the sun, no matter where in the sky it was. Other scientists had found similar results with birds, indicating that birds and monarch butterflies have similar navigating systems.　■ Thomas H. Maugh II

See also **Ocean.**

Boating. Switzerland became the first European country to win the 152-year-old America's Cup on March 2, 2003. The Swiss yacht *Alinghi* swept two-time defending champion *Team New Zealand* in five straight races off the coast of Auckland, New Zealand.

Alinghi's captain, New Zealander Russell Coutts, became the first captain to skipper a winning yacht for two countries, having won the cup for New Zealand in 1995. He also became only the third captain in the race's history to win three straight America's Cup trophies. Coutts shares the distinction with Harold Vanderbilt (1930-1937) and Charlie Barr (1899-1903), both of the United States.

Team New Zealand faced difficult challenges in 2003. The team experienced several breakdowns, including having a mast snap into two pieces in the fourth race, and endured the frustration of having a number of races postponed because of bad weather. Because of the breakdowns, *Team New Zealand* was unable to finish two of the five races.

Alinghi took the lead at the start of the last race and never trailed, despite the fact that its team lost critical time replacing a spinnaker pole that snapped when the sail wrapped around it. Because Switzerland is a landlocked country, the Swiss will not host the next America's Cup competition in 2007. The race will be held from a European port.

The Swiss yacht *Alinghi* (left) maneuvers ahead of *Team New Zealand* in the fifth race of the America's Cup finals off Auckland, New Zealand, on March 2, 2003. The *Alinghi* crew, which won the race in a 5-0 sweep, became the first European team to ever take the America's Cup.

Clipper 2002 race. *Jersey* won the Clipper 2002 race on Sept. 27, 2003, sailing into Liverpool, England, ahead of second-place *Bristol* and third-place *Liverpool*. In the race, eight identical 60-foot (18-meter) yachts representing Hong Kong; London; New York; Cape Town, South Africa; Glasgow, Scotland; Bristol and Liverpool, England; and the the British island of Jersey competed in a 34,000-mile (55,000-kilometer) around-the-world race with 6 legs and 16 stopovers. Each yacht has a crew of 14 amateur racers, who pay to compete, and a professional captain. The race began on Oct. 28, 2002, with a 5,300-mile (8,500-kilometer), two-race leg from Liverpool to Cuba.

Around Alone. Bernard Stamm of Switzerland captured the 28,755-mile (46,000-kilometer) Around Alone race on May 1, 2003, in Newport, Rhode Island, about nine months after departing from New York City.

World championships. Giorgio Goldoni and Pedro Campos of Spain sailed *Telefonica Movistar* to victory in the Division A class in the Rolex IMS Offshore World Championships on May 24, 2003, off Capri, Italy.

Powerboats. Mitch Evans piloted *Miss Fox Hills* to victory in the Gold Cup race for Unlimited Hydroplanes in Detroit on August 24. Evans was the first driver since 1983 to win with a piston-powered boat. All other winning boats since 1983 had been turbine-powered. ■ Michael Kates

See also **Sports.**

Bolivia. See **Latin America.**

Books. See **Literature, American; Literature, World; Literature for children.**

Bosnia-Herzegovina. A scandal involving a Bosnian Serb company selling arms to former Iraqi President Saddam Hussein's military led to political and military consequences in Bosnia in 2003. Partly as a result of international condemnation in the wake of the "arms-to-Iraq" scandal, Bosnia's government adopted important military reforms in late 2003.

"Arms-to-Iraq" scandal. United States authorities in 2002 accused the Bosnian Serb defense firm Orao of supplying Hussein with arms, in defiance of United Nations (UN) sanctions. A North Atlantic Treaty Organization (NATO) investigation confirmed the allegations.

Orao was closely connected with the military establishment of the Republika Srpska (RS). Bosnia consists of two ministates: the Republika Srpska, run by Bosnian Serbs; and the Muslim-Croat Federation (MCF). Both states participate in a loosely configured national government, but each has had its own military establishment.

Revelation of the Bosnian Serb arms sales brought international condemnation. Under intense pressure, Mirko Sarovic, the Bosnian Serb member of Bosnia's *tripartite* (three-member) joint presidency, resigned on April 2, 2003. In mid-April, the Bosnian parliament chose Borislav Paravac to fill the position reserved for ethnic Serbs in the joint presidency. Paravac joined the Croat and Muslim presidents already in office.

Unified military command. On December 1, the Bosnian parliament enacted a military reform placing all of the country's armed forces under a central Bosnian authority, the country's joint tripartite presidency. Governments of the RS and the MCF had earlier approved the reform. According to military experts, the unified command encouraged accountability and reduced opportunities for misuse of military power such as had occurred in the "arms-to-Iraq" scandal. NATO officials said the reforms removed a barrier to Bosnia's admission to the Partnership for Peace, a first step toward full NATO membership.

Joint institutions. In January 2003, legislators from all major ethnic parties in Bosnia's parliament approved a new national government headed by Prime Minister Adnan Terzic, leader of the Muslim Party of Democratic Action. In August, officials in both parts of Bosnia agreed to create a unified school system to replace the existing, ethnically segregated, system.

Refugees. The 1992-1995 war in Bosnia drove 2.2 million Bosnians from their homeland. Peace and stability had, by mid-2003, encouraged nearly 1 million of the refugees to return to Bosnia, according to the UN High Commission for Refugees. ■ Sharon L. Wolchik

See also **Europe.**

Botswana. See Africa.

Bowling. The 2003-2004 Professional Bowlers Association (PBA) campaign was a wide-open race from the start. Seven different men won the first seven events. Patrick Allen of Tarrytown, New York, made a strong early showing through the first third of the season. Allen took the lead in earnings and was among the leaders in both the points and average categories.

The Professional Women's Bowling Association (PWBA) suffered financial difficulties that interrupted the season. In August 2003, PWBA officials canceled the PWBA fall 2003 schedule of four events, citing a lack of operating funds. In September, PWBA officials announced the organization had been sold to a new ownership group, Pinnacle Events of Syosset, New York.

Carolyn Dorin-Ballard of North Richland Hills, Texas, established herself as a leading candidate for the 2003 Women's Bowler of the Year title, winning the Greater Cincinnati Open in June. The victory was Dorin-Ballard's 20th title and gave her the lead in earnings ($53,750), competition points (5,330), and average (215.22).

PBA. On March 9, Walter Ray Williams, Jr., of Ocala, Florida, moved to second on the all-time titles list when he captured the PBA World Championship in Taylor, Michigan. Williams's victory at the event, the final competition of the 2002-2003 season, brought him within four titles of the late Earl Anthony.

The 2003-2004 PBA season began in October. Robert Smith of Thousand Oaks, California, defeated Mike Machuga of Erie, Pennsylvania, to win the Banquet Open on Oct. 12, 2003, in Council Bluffs, Iowa. Norm Duke of Clermont, Florida, captured his 21st career title on October 19. He edged out Mika Koivuniemi of Ann Arbor, Michigan, at the Greater Kansas City Open.

Seniors. Dale Eagle of Tavares, Florida, defeated Bob Glass of Lawrence, Kansas, on May 30 in Tucson, Arizona, to capture the Senior Masters title, a three-game, double-elimination, match-play tournament. In December, Eagle led the tour in earnings ($34,000), was third in average (215.92), and second in points (12,626).

PWBA. Tiffany Stanbrough of Oklahoma City, Oklahoma, was the only two-time winner on the PWBA tour in 2003. Wendy Macpherson of Henderson, Nevada, captured the Women's International Bowling Congress Queens Championship on April 11. Kelly Kulick of Union, New Jersey, won the Women's U.S. Open on June 1 in Sterling Heights, Michigan. The title was Kulick's first of her professional career.

2002 Players of the Year. Williams by April became the second man to win six PBA Player of the Year awards, joining Anthony. Michelle Feldman of Skaneateles, New York, was named PWBA Player of the Year for 2002. ■ Michael Kates

Boxing. Shane Mosley outlasted Oscar de la Hoya for the second time in three years in one of the most anticipated bouts of 2003. The fight, however, was not without controversy.

Mosley won the last four rounds and all three judges scored the fight 115 to 113 in favor of Mosley on September 13 in Las Vegas, Nevada. Mosley's victory earned him the super welterweight titles in both the World Boxing Council (WBC) and the World Boxing Association (WBA). Mosley used his quickness and stamina to wear down de la Hoya, the same strategy he used to defeat de la Hoya in 2000.

The 2003 decision outraged de la Hoya and his supporters. De la Hoya even threatened to hire lawyers to investigate the decision. Statistics did show that de la Hoya outpunched Mosley 221-127, landing 106 jabs to Mosley's 33 and 115 power punches to Mosley's 94.

However, all three of the judges and the Associated Press scored the fight in favor of Mosley. Nevada boxing officials stood by the result and de la Hoya's camp later backed down from its protests. For his win, Mosley collected $5 million, plus an additional $500,000 that de la Hoya had promised to pay out of his own guaranteed $17-million payday if Mosley won.

Holyfield goes down. Four-time heavyweight champion Evander Holyfield moved closer to retirement when he lost to James Toney on October 4 in Las Vegas. Toney, in his debut as a heavyweight, became only the second boxer—after Riddick Bowe—to stop Holyfield from finishing a fight.

In other boxing action, Floyd Mayweather, Jr., defended his WBC lightweight title on April 19, winning a unanimous decision over Victoriano Sosa of the Dominican Republic. On November 8, Roy Jones, Jr., defeated Antonio Tarver to take the WBC light heavyweight title. Jones already held the WBA heavyweight crown.

Women's boxing. In a battle between the two biggest names in women's boxing, Laila Ali, the daughter of former heavyweight champion Muhammad Ali, knocked out (KO) Christy Martin in the fourth round on August 23 in Biloxi, Mississippi. Ali improved her record to 16-0 (13 KO's) while Martin fell to 45-3-2 (31 KO's).

Tyson's troubles. Former heavyweight champion Mike Tyson, who apparently lost nearly $300 million in earnings, filed for Chapter 11 bankruptcy protection in August. According to court documents, Tyson owed more than $17 million in back taxes and more than $10 million in other debts. Earlier in the year, he had agreed to pay his ex-wife Monica $6.5 million from future earnings as part of a divorce settlement.

■ Michael Kates

Brazil. Luiz Inacio Lula da Silva of the Workers' Party was sworn in for a four-year term as Brazil's president in January 2003. Known affectionately as "Lula," Lula da Silva, a former machinist and labor leader, became his country's first elected chief executive from a leftist party. He pledged to boost Brazil's economy and wage war on poverty.

Aiding the poor. Immediately after assuming office, Lula da Silva launched "Zero Hunger," a $1.5-billion program designed to ensure that no one in Brazil suffered from hunger. By the end of February, more than 4,000 foreign and domestic corporations expressed interest in donating to the program. The Brazilian subsidiary of Nestle of Vevey, Switzerland, pledged 2.2 million pounds (1 million kilograms) of food, while Ford Brazil of Sao Paulo donated 400,000 pounds (181,437 kilograms) of food. The Brazilian food chain Pao de Acucar, headquartered in Sao Paulo, undertook to distribute the food through its national network of supermarkets.

AIDS generics. The Brazilian government authorized the import of generic versions of patented AIDS drugs in September. The action followed an impasse between the government and multinational pharmaceutical companies, which were willing to provide only a 6.7-percent discount on some of these drugs, as compared

WORLD CHAMPION BOXERS

WORLD BOXING ASSOCIATION

Division	Champion	Country	Date won
Heavyweight	Roy Jones, Jr.	United States	3/03
Light heavyweight	Silvio Branco	Italy	10/03
Middleweight	William Joppy	United States	11/01
Welterweight	Corky Spinks	United States	12/03
Lightweight	Vacant		
Featherweight	Juan Manuel Marquez	Mexico	11/03
Bantamweight	Johnny Bredahl	Denmark	4/02
Flyweight	Eric Morel	Puerto Rico	8/00

WORLD BOXING COUNCIL

Division	Champion	Country	Date won
Heavyweight	Lennox Lewis	United Kingdom	11/01
Light heavyweight	Roy Jones, Jr.	United States	11/03
Middleweight	Bernard Hopkins	United States	4/01
Welterweight	Ricardo Mayorga	Nicaragua	1/03
Lightweight	Floyd Mayweather	United States	4/02
Featherweight	Vacant		
Bantamweight	Veeraphol Nakhonluang	Thailand	12/98
Flyweight	Pongsaklek Wonjongkam	Thailand	3/01

with the 40 percent the Brazilian government demanded to stay within the $200 million budgeted annually for a program to distribute AIDS drugs free to needy sufferers.

Amazon basin development. Brazil's government in September unveiled a $66-billion, four-year effort to develop infrastructure within the Amazon basin. The program, which drew immediate fire from environmentalists, specified doubling the generating capacity of the Tucurui hydroelectric plant in the eastern Amazon; constructing a $4-billion dam on the Xingu River; and building two natural gas pipelines through part of the rain forest.

Soybeans. Brazil became the world's largest producer of soybeans in 2003, surpassing the United States. To support Brazil's soybean farmers, the Lula da Silva administration in September 2003 reversed a three-year ban on the use of genetically modified soybean seeds, which are cheaper to grow. Environmentalists were quick to warn that the planting of soybeans on huge tracts of previously uncultivated land had already become a major contributor to the destruction of the Amazon's rain forests. The damage was particularly marked in the Brazilian state of Mato Grosso, where forests of an area larger than New Jersey were felled between November 2002 and September 2003 to accommodate the crop.

Airline merger. In September, Brazil's two leading air carriers, Varig and TAM, agreed to a merger, creating Latin America's largest airline. The merger was scheduled for early 2004. Experts expected the new airline to control more than 60 percent of the Brazilian market.

Rocket accident. Brazil's space program suffered a setback when a rocket exploded during prelaunch tests in Alcantara in August 2003. The accident left 21 people dead and 20 others wounded. The explosion caused the launching pad to collapse, burying technicians who were preparing the $2.2-million rocket for a take-off later in August with two satellites aboard.

Deaths. Lula da Silva declared three days of national mourning following the August death of media magnate Roberto Marinho. Marinho built *O Globo*, the newspaper company he inherited, into Brazil's most powerful media empire.

Also in August, Sergio Vieira de Mello, a prominent Brazilian diplomat, who was the senior United Nations (UN) official in Iraq, was killed by terrorists. De Mello, the UN's High Commissioner for Human Rights, died from injuries suffered in the bombing of the UN's Baghdad headquarters. ■ Nathan A. Haverstock

See also **Iraq: A Special Report; Latin America.**

British Columbia. See Canadian provinces.

Brunei. See Asia.

Building and construction. Boston reached a milestone in the spring of 2003, when engineers opened the northbound segment of its Central Artery/Tunnel project—nicknamed the "Big Dig"—to traffic. The $14.6-billion, 12-year reconfiguration of the city's central routes—primarily from above ground to below—was one of the largest public works in history. In all, construction workers excavated enough soil to fill a football stadium 15 times over.

With the northbound lanes open, traffic could proceed on Interstate 93 from south of Boston, under the city through tunnels, and then across the Charles River on the new Leonard P. Zakim Bunker Hill Bridge, the widest cable-stayed bridge in the world. The southbound section of the roadway complex, linking Logan International Airport to Interstate 90, was scheduled to open in January 2004.

Underground concert hall. On Sept. 12, 2003, New York City's Carnegie Hall opened the Judy and Arthur Zankel Hall, a 644-seat auditorium built directly beneath the existing Isaac Stern Hall, in space hewn out of solid bedrock. The four-year, $72-million construction project posed a number of unusual engineering challenges. Excavation and removal of the rock had to be accomplished while preserving the existing masonry structure and bypassing a nearby subway tunnel.

In the first phase of construction, workers shored the ground-level structure by installing steel beams underneath. Then, to minimize disruption to ongoing performance venues, the contractor cut a hole in an adjacent sidewalk to install a 10- by 16-foot (3- by 4.9-meter) elevator. Through that elevator, workers removed nearly 7,000 cubic yards (5,352 cubic meters) of rocky debris, extracted from under the original concert hall. When the subterranean space was cleared, workers constructed a concrete "eggshell" to encompass the new hall.

Earthquake-resistant skyscraper. The Torre Mayor, a 739-foot (225-meter), 55-story office tower in Mexico City, ranked as Latin America's tallest building when it opened in June. Because the structure stands on a dry lake bed in a seismically active region, designers took special care to equip it with earthquake-resistant features, devising a novel arrangement of structural elements drawn from conventional seismic structural technology. Such elements include fluid-filled *dampers* (devices to stop or minimize vibrations) and superdiagonal bracing, a system of connecting diagonal beams aligned in a series of repeating patterns.

The way in which the superdiagonals and dampers were configured made the Torre Mayor unique. The building's bracing consists of over-

The Leonard P. Zakim Bunker Hill Bridge in Boston opens to traffic on March 29, 2003. A link in the city's massive Central Artery/Tunnel project to reconfigure express traffic through downtown Boston, the bridge is the widest cable-stayed span in the world.

lapping diamond shapes, instead of the more typical configuration of touching X's. In the overall diamond pattern, smaller diamonds are formed where the top point of one large diamond overlaps with the bottom point of the next-higher one. Dampers are concentrated in the smaller diamonds formed at the overlaps. The engineers predicted that this special configuration would enable the Torre Mayor to resist four times the seismic stress that a conventionally damped building could withstand. Their claim was put to a test on January 21, when an earthquake measuring 7.8 struck west of Mexico City and strongly shook the city. The Torre Mayor came through that quake without a scratch.

Chinese dam. After 10 years of construction, Chinese engineers in June 2003 closed the sluice gates behind the 600-foot (185-meter) Three Gorges Dam in east-central China and began flooding the Yangtze River Valley. Within two weeks, a large reservoir filled to a depth of 443 feet (135 meters). Locks bypassing the dam were opened to shipping in mid-June, and the first electrical generators went online in September.

Rebuilding Iraq. The administration of U.S. President George W. Bush, after declaring an end to the war in Iraq on May 1, turned its attention to Iraq's reconstruction. Not only had the recent hostilities inflicted damage, but years of

economic sanctions and former Iraqi President Saddam Hussein's diversion of resources had left much of the infrastructure in disrepair.

A high priority for the U.S.-led coalition in Iraq was to restore the energy infrastructure so that oil and natural gas could flow freely again and generate much-needed revenue. To that end, the U.S. Department of Defense contracted with Houston-based Halliburton KBR to repair oil fields and pipelines. According to published reports, Halliburton landed more than $1 billion in Iraq contracts during 2003. Another company, San Francisco-based Bechtel, won contracts worth $1 billion to repair Umm Qasr, Iraq's major port on the Persian Gulf, and other infrastructure throughout the country.

Critics in the United States claimed that the Bechtel and Halliburton KBR contracts were not competitively awarded. Bechtel and Halliburton representatives countered that their companies possessed the technical merit and experience to perform in the postwar Iraq environment in which crises such as oil field fires and damaged power grids had to be addressed quickly. In November, Congress approved an appropriation of $87 billion that included nearly $19 billion for infrastructure repair in Iraq. ■ Andrew Wright

See also **Architecture; Asia; China; Congress of the United States; Environmental pollution.**

Bulgaria. The government of Prime Minister Simeon Saxe-Coburg-Gotha held onto power in 2003, despite several defections from the ruling coalition. In May, the prime minister's coalition survived a no-confidence vote in parliament called by the main opposition party.

Saxe-Coburg-Gotha, who as a child reigned as king of Bulgaria before the establishment of a Communist government in 1946, heads a political party called the National Movement for Simeon II. The movement came to power in the June 2001 elections.

Bulgaria's economy grew at a rate of between 4 and 5 percent in 2003, matching the strong growth of 2002. Bulgaria's unemployment rate declined steadily in 2003, to 13.2 percent in June from nearly 18 percent in 2002.

In early 2003, Bulgaria permitted the United States and its allies to use Bulgarian air space during the U.S.-led war in Iraq. Bulgaria contributed noncombat troops to the active phase of the war in March and April and sent 500 troops in September to participate in the stabilization and reconstruction of Iraq. ■ Sharon L. Wolchik

See also **Europe.**

Burma. See Myanmar.

Bush, George W. See United States, President of the.

Business. See Bank; Economics.

Cabinet, U.S. The United States Senate on Jan. 22, 2003, voted 94 to 0 to confirm Tom Ridge as the U.S. secretary of homeland security. The new Cabinet position was to oversee domestic defense, specifically coordinating efforts to protect the United States from terrorist attack. The 170,000-employee department replaced the Office of Homeland Security and created a government agency consisting of all or parts of 22 federal agencies. It was created in response to the terrorist attacks on the United States on Sept. 11, 2001.

Department of the Treasury. The U.S. Senate, on Jan. 30, 2003, unanimously confirmed John W. Snow as the U.S. secretary of the treasury. He was sworn into office on February 3. President George W. Bush nominated Snow for the post following the resignation of Paul O'Neill in 2002. Snow had been chairman and chief executive officer of CSX Corporation, a railroad company headquartered in Richmond, Virginia.

Resignation rumors. Colin L. Powell, the U.S. secretary of state, denied a newspaper article published in August 2003 that alleged he had informed the Bush administration that he would not serve in the Cabinet if President Bush were elected to a second term in 2004. The article, published in *The Washington Post,* claimed that Powell said he would resign on Jan. 21, 2005, the day after the next presidential inauguration.

Powell denied the story and told reporters, "the president and I have not discussed anything other than my continuing to do my job for him."

Gulf War decision. Secretary of Defense Donald Rumsfeld said in October 2003 that his authority in Iraq had not been diminished, despite the creation of a committee designed to oversee rebuilding efforts in Iraq. National Security Adviser Condoleezza Rice headed the committee, which took over certain functions previously handled by Rumsfeld. Following the declared end of the war in Iraq on May 1, Rumsfeld had become responsible for overseeing the work of U.S. military commanders and civil administrators in Iraq. Some political experts claimed that Rice's Iraq Stabilization Group, created without input from Rumsfeld, amounted to an expression of dissatisfaction by the Bush administration with Rumsfeld's performance in rebuilding postwar Iraq.

Confidential memo. *USA Today* published a confidential memo from Rumsfeld on October 22 in which the defense secretary wrote that the U.S.-led war on terrorism was producing mixed results. ■ Geoffrey A. Campbell

See also **Armed forces; Congress of the United States; Iraq: A Special Report; People in the news** (John Snow; Paul Wolfowitz); **United States, Government of the; United States, President of the.**

Cambodia held National Assembly elections on July 27, 2003, its third elections since a peace agreement in the 1990's ended years of civil war. The ruling Cambodian People's Party (CPP), led by Prime Minister Hun Sen, won 47 percent of the votes, falling short of the two-thirds majority needed to form a new government. A party led by Sam Rainsy, a former finance minister, won 22 percent, and a royalist party captured 21 percent. The opposition parties charged that the elections had been rigged by the CPP and demanded that Hun Sen resign. In November 2003, however, opposition parties agreed to form a government headed by Prime Minister Hun Sen.

Cambodia signed an agreement with the United Nations (UN) in June 2003 to try former leaders of the Khmer Rouge, a Communist regime that ruled Cambodia from 1975 to 1979 and was responsible for the deaths of more than 1.5 million people. The 2003 agreement was reached six years after Cambodia asked the UN to help establish an international tribunal.

Riots destroyed Thailand's embassy and Thai-owned businesses in Phnom Penh, the capital, in January. The riots were sparked by a rumor that a Thai actress claimed that Angkor Wat, an ancient temple in northwestern Cambodia, belonged to Thailand. ■ Henry S. Bradsher

See also **Asia.**

CANADA

Canadians faced a number of challenges in 2003, including disease, natural disasters, political change, and social reform. In the spring, an outbreak of severe acute respiratory syndrome (SARS) struck Toronto, which provides 20 percent of Canada's economic output. Manufacturing slowed, and business and personal travel was disrupted. In May, mad cow disease (bovine spongiform encephalopathy, or BSE) was discovered in a cow in northern Alberta, leading to a ban on Canadian beef exports to foreign markets. A dry, hot summer led to the worst forest fires in 50 years in British Columbia, displacing thousands of people and destroying valuable timber lands. At the end of August, 835 fires burned simultaneously in the province. The eastern North American electric power outage of August 14 affected most of Ontario, leading to cutbacks in economic activity. Hurricane Juan hit the Nova Scotia coast on the night of September 28, demolishing houses, boats, and wharves, especially in lobster fishing waters. The seaport of Halifax sustained severe damage with hundreds of trees felled and its harbor battered.

In politics, Prime Minister Jean Chretien resigned from office on December 12, after the Liberal Party elected former finance minister Paul Martin as party leader.

Canada's government addressed two controversial social issues during 2003—allowing the use and possession of small amounts of marijuana for medical benefits and the legalization of gay marriages.

Political parties. Prime Minister Chretien announced in 2002 that he would retire in February 2004 after his successor had been chosen in a Liberal Party leadership convention in November 2003. The Liberal Party held 171 of the 301 seats in the House of Commons, assuring that the chosen party leader would also become Canada's next prime minister. By summer it was clear that delegates to the convention were overwhelmingly in favor of Martin as the new party leader.

One by one other candidates dropped from the race, including Deputy Prime Minister John Manley, Chretien's preferred successor. Another candidate, Minister of Canadian Heritage Sheila Copps, who represented a leftist faction of the party, had little delegate support (about 10 percent), making Martin's selection in November inevitable. On November 14, the Liberals officially

declared Martin their leader, with 94 percent of the vote. On November 18, Chretien announced that he would retire from office on December 12.

Two of the opposition parties also selected new leaders in 2003. The Progressive Conservative Party (PCP), which had held power from 1964 to 1984 when it lost to the Liberal Party, selected a member of Parliament from Nova Scotia, Peter MacKay. PCP support was thin across the country, with only 15 seats in the House of Commons. The party considered merging with the country's other conservative party, the Canadian Alliance (CA), which held 63 seats in Parliament, mostly representing western Canada. MacKay discussed the possibility of electoral cooperation with the CA party leader, Stephen Harper from Alberta. On Oct.15, 2003, they announced that the talks had been successful and a new national party was to be created, called the Conservative Party of Canada. While the details of the union were still to be worked out, a mail-in vote to approve the merger was held among the members of the two parties. In December, it was announced that 96 percent of CA members and 90 percent of PCP members voted to endorse the merger. A convention was scheduled for March 2004 to choose a leader for the new party.

Canada's socialist New Democratic Party (NDP) with 14 seats in the Commons in 2003, chose as its leader prominent community activist Jack Layton, a long-serving city councillor from Toronto. Layton was expected to appeal to urban voters, a constituency of the NDP that had been lost in recent elections, mainly to the Liberals.

The Bloc Quebecois (BQ), advocating the independence of Quebec in federal politics, held 34 seats in Parliament in 2003, all from the province. Separatism, however, seemed a waning force in Quebec, where the BQ, led by Gilles Duceppe, lost several seats to the Liberals in 2003 by-elections. Independents held four seats in Parliament.

Health care. Public health care remained a subject of concern to Canadians in 2003. Established about 40 years ago, public health care was accessible to all Canadians, with similar benefits portable across the country. It was funded jointly by the federal and provincial governments, though the delivery of services was a provincial responsibility. During the 1990's, federal funding to the program had been cut back as the Chretien government concentrated on balancing its budget. A commission of inquiry, under former Saskatchewan Premier Roy Romanow, reported in November 2002 that funding had to be improved to restore the health of the system. The commission recommended that an addi-

Canadian Prime Minister Jean Chretien brandishes a steak knife as a waitress serves him Canadian beef at an Ottawa restaurant on May 23. He ordered the sirloin steak to prove there was nothing to fear after a case of "mad cow" disease was discovered in Alberta (right), a center of the Canadian beef industry. The beef industry annually contributes over $4 billion to the economy of the province.

tional $15 billion be injected into the program through 2006. It urged more support for home care, an expansion of its drug plan, and funds to eliminate a deficiency in high-tech diagnostic equipment and services. The authors of the study also recommended that a health council be created to report on the delivery of services to Canadians and make the system more accountable. Romanow made it plain that he believed health care should remain a provincial responsibility and that medical care was cherished by Canadians and constituted "a public trust." Some provinces, however, along with some people in the medical community, advocated the expansion of private medical services to ease the financial burden on the government.

The Romanow report was discussed by provincial and territorial first ministers and the Chretien government at a 12-hour meeting in Ottawa on February 5. The provinces put up a united front, demanding that federal funding be established at the levels recommended by Romanow. Prime Minister Chretien responded with an offer of $34.8 billion over the next five years. The premiers countered that this sum included funds already embedded in the financing of the system. In the end, however, the federal offer was accepted.

Discussion of the proposed health council was heated. The council, to be made up of representatives from government, the health care community, and the public, would establish performance guidelines and report regularly on waiting times and other service issues. Some of the larger provinces feared that such a council would interfere with their area of constitutional responsibility, but in September, the federal government and the provinces agreed to create a 27-member national health council, including a chairperson, 13 government representatives, and 13 people from outside the government.

Electoral law reform. Prime Minister Chretien announced prior to 2003 that he wanted to see a series of measures enacted by Parliament that would constitute the legacy of his 40 years in public life and 10 years as head of the government. One of these items—a reform of Canada's electoral law—was brought forward in January. The proposal included a ban on contributions from corporations and unions to political parties; however, donations of up to $1,000 would be permitted from corporations and unions to individual candidates. Instead of private support for political parties, the government would offer subsidies to parties based on their performances in previous elections. Federal accountants calculated that this aid would amount to $1.75 for each vote cast. The new electoral law easily gained parliamentary approval in June.

Medical marijuana. A bill was introduced in Parliament in 2003 to decriminalize possession of small amounts of marijuana by people who use it for medical benefits. The bill also considered stiffer penalties for trafficking in larger amounts of the drug. The measure was withdrawn after the U.S. government strongly disapproved of the legalization of marijuana. Chretien declared,

2003 CANADIAN POPULATION ESTIMATES

PROVINCE AND TERRITORY POPULATIONS

Alberta	3,169,035
British Columbia	4,181,349
Manitoba	1,152,581
New Brunswick	757,352
Newfoundland and Labrador	529,383
Northwest Territories	41,581
Nova Scotia	946,650
Nunavut	29,328
Ontario	12,244,268
Prince Edward Island	140,929
Quebec	7,492,073
Saskatchewan	1,006,556
Yukon Territory	29,669
Canada	31,721,554

CITY AND METROPOLITAN AREA POPULATIONS

	Metropolitan area	City
Toronto, Ont.	5,055,096	2,521,471
Montreal, Que.	3,556,360	1,829,400
Vancouver, B.C.	2,127,412	559,116
Ottawa-Hull	1,133,055	
Ottawa, Ont.		796,801
Hull, Que.		*
Calgary, Alta.	998,035	929,571
Edmonton, Alta.	969,856	687,633
Quebec, Que.	698,564	511,237
Hamilton, Ont.	688,294	499,687
Winnipeg, Man.	685,740	619,972
Kitchener, Ont.	439,381	195,512
London, Ont.	427,722	341,032
St. Catharines-Niagara Falls	392,380	
St. Catharines, Ont.		128,477
Niagara Falls, Ont.		79,593
Halifax, N.S.	364,029	363,061
Windsor, Ont.	321,165	212,917
Victoria, B.C.	318,800	74,375
Oshawa, Ont.	311,099	140,991
Saskatoon, Sask.	231,860	198,095
Regina, Sask.	196,742	177,364
St. John's, Nfld. Lab.	177,361	98,110
Sherbrooke, Que.	156,803	75,572
Chicoutimi-Jonquiere	156,525	
Chicoutimi, Que.		58,846
Jonquiere, Que.		54,197
Greater Sudbury, Ont.	155,682	151,420
Abbotsford, B.C.	152,074	119,871
Trois-Rivieres, Que.	141,440	45,440
Saint John, N.B.	126,940	68,572
Thunder Bay, Ont.	124,981	107,234

*Hull became part of the city of Gatineau in 2002. Gatineau's projected 2003 population was 232,590.

Source: World Book estimates based on data from Statistics Canada.

however, that the bill would be reintroduced in the 2004 parliamentary session.

In July 2003, the federal government announced a plan to distribute marijuana to about 500 registered individuals who required the drug for pain relief. Physicians were to distribute the marijuana, grown especially for the program at an abandoned mine in Manitoba. The U.S. government again objected, as did the Canadian Medical Association, which declared that the efficacy of marijuana for pain relief was not definitively established. The medical distribution of marijuana nevertheless went forward.

Gay marriages. New legislation on gay marriages created controversy in Canada and around the world. The House of Commons agreed with the Ontario Court of Appeal by a 137 to 132 vote that the definition of marriage as a union between a man and a woman violated equality provisions of the Canadian Charter of Rights and Freedoms and was, therefore, unconstitutional. The Ontario ruling in June required that same-sex marriages be permitted immediately and ordered the federal government to change its definition of marriage. The government decided not to appeal this decision and instead brought forward a new marriage law that included gay and lesbian couples in its definition. The proposed bill would continue to allow churches to follow their own practices in solemnizing marriage. The government asked the highest court to review the pro-

posed law's constitutionality before the measure was placed before Parliament, where a free vote, not subject to party discipline, was to be held. The legislation created divisions even within political parties. Because the Supreme Court opinion could not be expected before early 2004, the bill would not come before Parliament until the new administration is in place.

MEMBERS OF THE CANADIAN HOUSE OF COMMONS

The House of Commons of the second session of the 37th Parliament convened on Sept. 30, 2002. As of Nov. 12, 2003, when the second session ended, the House of Commons consisted of the following members: 170 Liberal Party, 63 Canadian Alliance, 34 Bloc Quebecois, 15 Progressive Conservative Party, 14 New Democratic Party, 4 Independents, and 1 vacancy. As of December 7, 2003, the Progressive Conservative Party and the Canadian Alliance Party merged to become the Conservative Party of Canada. This table shows each legislator and party affiliation. An asterisk (*) denotes those who served in the 36th Parliament.

Alberta
Diane Ablonczy, C.P.C.*
Rob Anders, C.P.C.*
Leon E. Benoit, C.P.C.*
Rick Casson, C.P.C.
David Chatters, C.P.C.*
Joe Clark, P.C.†
Ken Epp, C.P.C.*
Peter Goldring, C.P.C.*
Deborah Grey, C.P.C.*
Art Hanger, C.P.C.*
Stephen Harper, C.P.C.
Grant Hill, C.P.C.*
Rahim Jaffer, C.P.C.*
Dale Johnston, C.P.C.*
Jason Kenney, C.P.C.*
David Kilgour, Lib.*
Anne McLellan, Lib.*
Rob Merrifield, C.P.C.
Bob Mills, C.P.C.*
Deepak Obhrai, C.P.C.*
Charlie Penson, C.P.C.*
James Rajotte, C.P.C.
Monte Solberg, C.P.C.*
Kevin Sorenson, C.P.C.
Myron Thompson, C.P.C.*
John Williams, C.P.C.*

British Columbia
Jim Abbott, C.P.C.*
David Anderson, Lib.*
Andy Burton, C.P.C.*
Chuck Cadman, C.P.C.*
John Cummins, C.P.C.*
Libby Davies, N.D.P.*
Stockwell Day, C.P.C.
Herb Dhaliwal, Lib.*
John Duncan, C.P.C.*
Reed Elley, C.P.C.*
Paul Forseth, C.P.C.*
Hedy Fry, Lib.*
Jim Gouk, C.P.C.*
Gurmant Grewal, C.P.C.*
Richard Harris, C.P.C.*
Jay Hill, C.P.C.*
Betty Hinton, C.P.C.
Sophia Leung, Lib.*
Gary Lunn, C.P.C.*
James Lunney, C.P.C.
Keith Martin, C.P.C.*
Philip Mayfield, C.P.C.*
Grant McNally, C.P.C.*
Val Meredith, C.P.C.*
James Moore, C.P.C.
Stephen Owen, Lib.
Joe Peschisolido, Lib.
John Reynolds, C.P.C.*
Svend Robinson, N.D.P.*
Werner Schmidt, C.P.C.*
Darrel Stinson, C.P.C.*
Chuck Strahl, C.P.C.*
Randy White, C.P.C.*
Ted White, C.P.C.*

Manitoba
Reg Alcock, Lib.*
Bill Blaikie, N.D.P.*
Rick Borotsik, C.P.C.*
Bev Desjarlais, N.D.P.*
John Harvard, Lib.*
Howard Hilstrom, C.P.C.*
Inky Mark, C.P.C.*
Pat Martin, N.D.P.*
Anita Neville, Lib.
Rey Pagtakhan, Lib.*
Brian Pallister, C.P.C.
Raymond Simard, Lib.
Vic Toews, C.P.C.
Judy Wasylycia-Leis, N.D.P.*

New Brunswick
Claudette Bradshaw, Lib.*
Jeannot Castonguay, Lib.
Yvon Godin, N.D.P.*
John Herron, P.C.*†
Charles Hubbard, Lib.*
Dominic LeBlanc, Lib.
Andy Savoy, Lib.
Andy Scott, Lib.*
Greg Thompson, C.P.C.*
Elsie Wayne, C.P.C.*

Newfoundland and Labrador
Rex Barnes, C.P.C.
Gerry Byrne, Lib.*
Norman Doyle, C.P.C.*
R. John Efford, Lib.
Loyola Hearn, C.P.C.
Bill Matthews, Lib.*
Lawrence D. O'Brien, Lib.*

Northwest Territories
Ethel Blondin-Andrew, Lib.*

Nova Scotia
Scott Brison, Lib.*
Bill Casey, C.P.C.*
Rodger Cuzner, Lib.
Mark Eyking, Lib.
Gerald Keddy, C.P.C.*
Wendy Lill, N.D.P.*
Peter MacKay, C.P.C.*
Alexa McDonough, N.D.P.*
Geoff Regan, Lib.
Peter Stoffer, N.D.P.*
Robert Thibault, Lib.

Nunavut
Nancy Karetak-Lindell, Lib.*

Ontario
Peter Adams, Lib.*
Sarkis Assadourian, Lib.*
Jean Augustine, Lib.*
Sue Barnes, Lib.*
Colleen Beaumier, Lib.*
Reginald Belair, Lib.*

Mauril Belanger, Lib.*
Eugene Bellemare, Lib.*
Carolyn Bennett, Lib.*
Maurizio Bevilacqua, Lib.*
Ray Bonin, Lib.*
Paul Bonwick, Lib.*
Don Boudria, Lib.*
Bonnie Brown, Lib.*
John Bryden, Lib.*
Sarmite Bulte, Lib.*
Charles Caccia, Lib.*
Murray Calder, Lib.*
John Cannis, Lib.*
Elinor Caplan, Lib.*
Aileen Carroll, Lib.*
Marlene Catterall, Lib.*
Brenda Chamberlain, Lib.*
David M. Collenette, Lib.*
Joe Comartin, N.D.P.
Joe Comuzzi, Lib.*
Sheila Copps, Lib.*
Roy Cullen, Lib.*
Paul DeVillers, Lib.*
Stan Dromisky, Lib.*
Art C. Eggleton, Lib.*
John Finlay, Lib.*
Joe Fontana, Lib.*
Cheryl Gallant, C.P.C.
Roger Gallaway, Lib.*
John Godfrey, Lib.*
Bill Graham, Lib.*
Ivan Grose, Lib.*
Albina Guarnieri, Lib.*
Tony Ianno, Lib.*
Ovid Jackson, Lib.*
Joe Jordan, Lib.*
Jim Karygiannis, Lib.*
Stan Keyes, Lib.*
Bob Kilger, Lib.*
Gar Knutson, Lib.*
Karen Kraft Sloan, Lib.*
Walt Lastewka, Lib.*
Derek Lee, Lib.*
Judi Longfield, Lib.*
Paul H. Macklin, Lib.*
Steve Mahoney, Lib.*
Gurbax Malhi, Lib.*
John Maloney, Lib.*
John Manley, Lib.*
Diane Marleau, Lib.*
Brian Masse, N.D.P.
John McCallum, Lib.*
Larry McCormick, Lib.*
John McKay, Lib.*
Dan McTeague, Lib.*
Peter Milliken, Lib.*
Dennis Mills, Lib.*
Maria Minna, Lib.*
Andy Mitchell, Lib.*
Lynn Myers, Lib.*
Robert Nault, Lib.*
Pat O'Brien, Lib.*
John O'Reilly, Lib.*

Carolyn Parrish, Lib.*
Janko Peric, Lib.*
Jim Peterson, Lib.*
Beth Phinney, Lib.*
Jerry Pickard, Lib.*
Gary Pillitteri, Lib.*
David Pratt, Lib.*
Carmen Provenzano, Lib.*
Karen Redman, Lib.*
Julian Reed, Lib.*
Scott Reid, C.P.C.
Allan Rock, Lib.*
Gary Schellenberger, C.P.C.
Benoit Serre, Lib.*
Judy Sgro, Lib.*
Alex Shepherd, Lib.*
Bob Speller, Lib.*
Brent St. Denis, Lib.*
Paul Steckle, Lib.*
Jane Stewart, Lib.*
Paul Szabo, Lib.*
Andrew Telegdi, Lib.*
Tony Tirabassi, Lib.
Alan Tonks, Lib.
Paddy Torsney, Lib.*
Rose-Marie Ur, Lib.*
Tony Valeri, Lib.*
Lyle Vanclief, Lib.*
Joseph Volpe, Lib.*
Tom Wappel, Lib.*
Susan Whelan, Lib.*
Bryon Wilfert, Lib.*
Bob Wood, Lib.*

Prince Edward Island
Wayne Easter, Lib.*
Lawrence MacAulay, Lib.*
Joe McGuire, Lib.*
Shawn Murphy, Lib.*

Quebec
Carole-Marie Allard, Lib.
Mark Assad, Lib.*
Gerard Asselin, B.Q.*
Andre Bachand, P.C.*†
Claude Bachand, B.Q.*
Eleni Bakopanos, Lib.*
Gilbert Barrette, Lib.
Stephane Bergeron, B.Q.*
Robert Bertrand, Lib.
Bernard Bigras, B.Q.*
Gerard Binet, Lib.
Diane Bourgeois, B.Q.
Serge Cardin, B.Q.*
Jean-Guy Carignan, Ind.
Martin Cauchon, Lib.*
Yvon Charbonneau, Lib.*
Jean Chretien, Lib.*
Denis Coderre, Lib.•
Irwin Cotler, Lib.•
Paul Crete, B.Q.*
Madeleine Dalphond-Guiral, B.Q.*
Odina Desrochers, B.Q.*
Stephane Dion, Lib.*

†These members have not agreed to the Conservative Party of Canada merger.
They have announced that they will serve out their terms and will not seek reelection.

Nick Discepola, Lib.*
Claude Drouin, Lib.*
Gilles Duceppe, B.Q.*
Claude Duplain, Lib.
Georges Farrah, Lib.
Raymonde Folco, Lib.*
Ghislain Fournier, B.Q.*
Liza Frulla, Lib.
Christiane Gagnon, B.Q.*
Marcel Gagnon, B.Q.
Sebastien Gagnon, B.Q.
Roger Gaudet, B.Q.
Michel Gauthier, B.Q.*
Jocelyne Girard-Bujold, B.Q.*
Monique Guay, B.Q.*
Michel Guimond, B.Q.*
Andre Harvey, Lib*.
Marlene Jennings, Lib.*
Christian Jobin, Lib.
Mario Laframboise, B.Q.
Francine Lalonde, B.Q.*
Robert Lanctot, Lib.
Ghislain Lebel, Ind.*
Clifford Lincoln, Lib.*
Yvan Loubier, B.Q.*
Richard Marceau, B.Q.*
Serge Marcil, Lib.
Paul Martin, Lib.*
Real Menard, B.Q.*
Gilbert Normand, Lib.*
Massimo Pacetti, Lib.
Pierre Paquette, B.Q.
Denis Paradis, Lib.*
Bernard Patry, Lib.*
Gilles-A. Perron, B.Q.*
Pierre Pettigrew, Lib.*
Pauline Picard, B.Q.*
Louis Plamondon, B.Q.*
David Price, Lib.*
Marcel Proulx, Lib.*
Lucienne Robillard, Lib.*
Yves Rocheleau, B.Q.*
Jean-Yves Roy, B.Q.
Jacques Saada, Lib.*
Benoit Sauvageau, B.Q.*
Helene Scherrer, Lib.
Caroline St-Hilaire, B.Q.*
Diane St-Jacques, Lib.*
Guy St-Julien, Lib.*
Yolande Thibeault, Lib.*
Suzanne Tremblay, B.Q.*
Pierrette Venne, Ind.*

Saskatchewan
David Anderson, C.P.C.
Roy Bailey, C.P.C.*
Garry Breitkreuz, C.P.C.*
Brian Fitzpatrick, C.P.C.
Ralph E. Goodale, Lib.*
Rick Laliberte, Lib.*
Lorne Nystrom, N.D.P.*
Jim Pankiw, Ind.*
Dick Proctor, N.D.P.*
Gerry Ritz, C.P.C.*
Carol Skelton, C.P.C.
Maurice Vellacott, C.P.C.*
Lynne Yelich, C.P.C.

Yukon Territory
Larry Bagnell, Lib.

THE MINISTRY OF CANADA*

Paul Martin—prime minister
Jacob Austin—leader of the government in the senate
David Anderson—minister of the environment
Ralph Goodale—minister of finance
Anne McLellan—deputy prime minister and minister of publc safety and emergency preparedness
Lucienne Robillard—minister of industry and minister responsible for the Economic Development Agency of Canada for the Regions of Quebec
Pierre Pettigrew—minister of health, minister of intergovernmental affairs, and minister responsible for official languages
James Scott Peterson—minister of international trade
Andrew Mitchell—minister of Indian affairs and Northern development
Claudette Bradshaw—minister of labour and minister responsible for homelessness
Denis Coderre—president of the Queen's Privy Council for Canada; Federal Interlocutor for Metis and Non-Status Indians; minister responsible for La Francophonie; and minister responsible for the Office of Indian Residential Schools Resolution
Rey D. Pagtakhan—minister of Western economic diversification
John McCallum—minister of veterans affairs
Stephen Owen—minister of public works and government services
William Graham—minister of foreign affairs
Stan Kazmierczak Keyes—minister of national revenue and minister of state (sport)
Robert Speller—minister of agriculture and agri-food
Joseph Volpe—minister of human resources and skills development
Reg Alcock—president of the Treasury Board and minister responsible for the Canadian Wheat Board
Geoff Regan—minister of fisheries and oceans
Tony Valeri—minister of transport
David Pratt—minister of national defence
Jacques Saada—leader of the government in the House of Commons and minister responsible for democratic reform
Irwin Cotler—minister of justice and attorney general of Canada
Judy Sgro—minister of citizenship and immigration
Helene Chalifour Scherrer—minister of Canadian heritage
John Efford—minister of natural resources
Liza Frulla—minister of social development
Ethel Blondin-Andrew—minister of state (children and youth)
Andy Scott—minister of state (infrastructure)
Gar Knutson—minister of state (new and emerging markets)
Denis Paradis—minister of state (financial institutions)
Jean Augustine—minister of state (multiculturalism and status of women)
Joseph Comuzzi—minister of state (Federal Economic Development Initiative for Northern Ontario)
Albina Guarnieri—associate minister of national defence and minister of state (civil preparedness)
Joseph McGuire—minister of Atlantic Canada Opportunities Agency
Mauril Belanger—deputy leader of the government in the House of Commons
Carolyn Bennett—minister of state (public health)
Aileen Carroll—minister of international cooperation

*As of December 31, 2003

PREMIERS OF CANADIAN PROVINCES

Province	Premier
Alberta	Ralph Klein
British Columbia	Gordon Campbell
Manitoba	Gary Doer
New Brunswick	Bernard Lord
Newfoundland and Labrador	Danny Williams
Nova Scotia	John Hamm
Ontario	Dalton McGuinty
Prince Edward Island	Patrick George Binns
Quebec	Jean J. Charest
Saskatchewan	Lorne Albert Calvert

GOVERNMENT LEADERS OF TERRITORIES

Northwest Territories	Joe Handley
Nunavut	Paul Okalik
Yukon Territory	Dennis Fentie

Economy. Canada led the Group of Eight (G-8) industrialized nations (Canada, France, Germany, Italy, Japan, Russia, the United Kingdom, and the United States) in economic growth at the beginning of 2003. Chretien pursued financial policies that helped his administration achieve a balanced budget for the sixth year in succession. The rate of debt to gross domestic product (GDP)—the value of all goods and services produced in a country during a given period—continued to fall, job growth was strong in 2003, and inflation remained under control. All these factors contributed to a rise in the value of the Canadian dollar against its U.S. counterpart. Between January and October, the value of the Canadian dollar rose 20 percent.

During the second half of 2003, Canada ended its four-year run of faster economic growth than the United States. The predicted rate of growth was revised downward from 3.2 percent to 2.2 percent in late September. The economy suffered the effects of the SARS outbreak, mad cow disease, the rapidly appreciating Canadian dollar, and generally weak economies around the world, especially in the United States, which purchases about 85 percent of Canada's exports.

Minister of Finance John Manley delivered a "spending budget" on February 18, in contrast to the previous years of cost-cutting budgets presented by the Chretien administration. A substantial part of the budget included increased federal contributions to public health care and an expansion of foreign aid, half of it directed to Africa. Money also was allocated to implement provisions of the Kyoto Protocol, an international agreement to decrease the rate at which carbon dioxide and five other gases are released into the atmosphere. In 2003, for the first time in Chretien's administration, more money was allocated for the strengthening of defense forces, though defense outlays were still lower than when the Chretien government took power. Funds also were designated for cities for the improvement of infrastructure. Although the spending budget was 11 percent higher than in 2002, Manley estimated a budget surplus of $3 billion during fiscal year 2003-2004, which began on April 1.

Foreign policy. A long tradition of basic agreement between Canada and the United States on foreign policy ended in 2003 as the two neighbors differed on how to deal with Iraq as the alleged possessor of weapons of mass destruc-

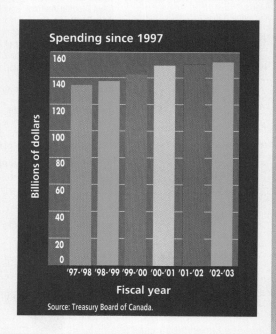

FEDERAL SPENDING IN CANADA
Estimated budget for fiscal 2003-2004*

Department or agency	Millions of dollars†
Agriculture and agri-food	1,756
Canada customs and revenue agency	3,662
Canadian heritage	3,289
Citizenship and immigration	1,165
Environment	733
Finance	67,183
Fisheries and oceans	1,468
Foreign affairs and international trade	4,022
Governor general	19
Health	3,437
Human resources development	29,219
Indian affairs and northern development	5,263
Industry	5,045
Justice	1,330
National defence	12,265
Natural resources	1,109
Parliament	419
Privy Council	254
Public works and government services	2,424
Solicitor general	3,645
Transport	3,902
Treasury board	2,411
Veterans affairs	2,498
Total	**156,518**

Spending since 1997

Billions of dollars

'97-'98 '98-'99 '99-'00 '00-'01 '01-'02 '02-'03

Fiscal year

Source: Treasury Board of Canada.

* April 1, 2003, to March 31, 2004.
† Canadian dollars; $1 = U.S. $0.74 as of Oct. 3, 2003.

tion (WMD, biological, chemical, or nuclear weapons). Canada maintained that armed intervention to force the removal of Saddam Hussein's regime in Iraq should only be carried out with the authorization of the United Nations (UN) Security Council. Canadian representatives to the UN sought to draft a resolution setting a deadline for the report of weapons inspectors assigned to find WMD's. The resolution was intended to provide a compromise among positions adopted by the United States and the United Kingdom, which favored immediate armed intervention, and European nations, such as France and Germany, which opposed war and wanted to give the inspectors more time. Canada's efforts were sidelined when U.S. President George W. Bush led his country into a war against Iraq without UN sanction.

The Canadian government announced on February 13 that it would send a military force to Afghanistan to help establish security during its reconstruction. This action, combined with peacekeeping commitments already assumed in Bosnia and Kosovo, meant that Canada could not take part in military operations in Iraq. Public controversy on the Iraq issue may have contributed to President Bush's decision to postpone a visit to Ottawa planned for May 5. International affairs experts noted that President Bush was not likely to reschedule his visit until after Chretien's retirement from office. In October, the Canadian government pledged $150 million toward the rebuilding efforts in Iraq.

A force of 1,900 Canadian soldiers arrived in Afghanistan in August to take up positions in and around the capital, Kabul. The troops formed part of the International Security Assistance Force under North Atlantic Treaty Organization control. Two soldiers were killed and three others injured in a land mine explosion while on a routine patrol of Kabul in early October. The Canadians' tour of engagement was to end in August 2004.

Defense. On May 15, 2003, the Canadian government endorsed the construction of a missile shield to protect North America from rocket strikes that might be launched by "rogue states"—essentially, countries hostile to the United States and suspected of pursuing weapons of mass destruction. The decision received a mixed reception in Canada, but the government went ahead with negotiations during the summer. However, the government did make it clear that it opposed the deployment of missile-launching sites in outer space and pressed for joint control of the shield.

Trade and commerce. Trade and commerce were deeply affected by the SARS epidemic and a single case of mad cow disease found in Alberta. The SARS virus struck Toronto, Canada's financial capital, in March, prompting the World Health Organization (WHO) to place the city on its travel-warning list. The travel and hospitality industries were hit hardest. A total of 375 people were infected with the disease in Toronto, of whom 44 died. WHO lifted the travel advisory in early July.

A case of mad cow disease discovered in May in Alberta led to trade difficulties with several countries. The United States moved quickly to ban Canadian beef, of which U.S. imports annually run in excess of $2.2 billion. Over 30 other countries followed suit. The Japanese threatened to shut off U.S. beef imports as well, unless it could be shown that no beef from Canada was included in the shipments. This proved an impossible task, since Canadian and U.S. cattle pass back and forth across the border before coming to market. In August, the United States eased its ban, allowing imports of Canadian cattle under 30 months of age.

Death. Robert Lorne Stanfield, former leader of the Progressive Conservative Party (1967-1976), died in Ottawa Dec. 16, 2003, at age 89. He also served as premier of Nova Scotia (1956-1967), but his attempts to break into national politics were overshadowed by Prime Minister Pierre Trudeau. Stanfield was often called "the best prime minister Canada never had."   ■ David M. L. Farr

See also **Afghanistan; Canada, Prime Minister of; Canadian provinces; Canadian territories; Iraq: A Special Report; Montreal; Public health and safety; Toronto.**

Canada, Prime Minister of. Cana-

dian Prime Minister Jean Chretien retired from office on Dec. 12, 2003, after serving 10 years as prime minister. During his term, he faced the challenges of a separatist movement in the province of Quebec, and he was credited with preserving a united, bilingual Canada. Chretien also established a healthy financial system for the country, with a balanced federal budget, large tax cuts, and six successive budget surpluses.

Chretien's successor was his political rival Paul Martin, who served for over eight years as finance minister under Chretien until the prime minister ousted him in June 2002 for launching a leadership campaign against Chretien. Martin's popularity led Chretien to announce that he would leave office in February 2004. At a conference in November 2003, the Liberal Party formally elected Martin as its leader. Shortly after the election, Chretien announced his December departure. As leader of the majority party in the the House of Commons, Martin automatically became prime minister.

Martin said that he would try to repair U.S.-Canadian relations, which had deteriorated under Chretien, who declined participation in the U.S.-led intervention in Iraq because it lacked UN authorization.   ■ David M. L. Farr

See also **Iraq: A Special Report; Canada; Canadian provinces; Canadian territories.**

Canadian provinces. Natural disasters severely battered Canada's 10 provinces during 2003. These included forest fires and floods in British Columbia, drought on the prairies, disease in Ontario, and a tropical hurricane in Nova Scotia and Prince Edward Island.

Political change was as unpredictable as the weather. In the country's two largest provinces, Ontario and Quebec, long-sitting governments were replaced, and the Atlantic province of Newfoundland and Labrador voted a different party into power. The three other Atlantic provinces and Saskatchewan reelected sitting governments.

Alberta. Mad cow disease, or bovine spongiform encephelopathy (BSE), was discovered in a single cow on May 20 at a farm near Wanham, Alberta. People who consume beef products tainted with BSE are at risk for acquiring the human form of the disease, known as Creutzfeldt-Jakob disease. The United States and about 30 other countries immediately closed their borders to Canadian beef exports, which earn $2.2 billion annually. (All amounts are in Canadian dollars.) Federal and provincial governments provided assistance to farmers, but there was anxiety over the future of the beef industry.

Canadian Natural Resources Ltd., an independent oil and natural gas exploration and development company based in Calgary, announced in August that it would proceed with the $8.5 billion Horizon project to recover light crude oil from the oil sands in northern Alberta. The project was stalled while the federal government defined emission targets under the Kyoto Protocol. The protocol is an international agreement to decrease the rate at which carbon dioxide and five other gases are released into the atmosphere. Hearings began in September for regulatory approval, which would allow construction to begin on the project in mid-2004. The first recovered oil was expected in 2008, and the project was to produce 110,000 barrels a day in the beginning, increasing to 155,000 barrels in 2010, and 233,000 barrels a day in 2012.

Soaring revenues from strong oil and gas production allowed the province on April 8, 2003, to achieve its 10th consecutive balanced budget. Economic growth for 2003 was about 3 percent, and unemployment was the second-lowest in the country at 5.3 percent.

British Columbia in 2003 experienced one of the hottest and driest summers in recorded provincial history. Hundreds of forest fires, most resulting from lightning strikes, occurred across the province. At Kamloops, 150 miles (240 kilometers) northeast of Vancouver, fires burned both north and south of populated areas. At Kelowna, on Lake Okanagan, 30,000 people were forced from their residences, 250 of which were destroy-

ed. The fires also consumed all but four of 18 historic wooden trestle bridges in the mountains. Fighting forest fires normally costs the provincial government about $58 million a year. In 2003, the cost rose to $545 million.

The International Olympic Committee on July 2 awarded Vancouver the honor of hosting the 2010 Winter Games. Six new venues were to be constructed in the city and its nearby ski resort at Whistler, at a cost of $620 million.

The provincial budget, tabled in the legislature on Feb. 12, 2003, showed a deficit of $3.5 billion. In spite of efforts to control spending, the deficit raised the province's accumulated public debt to $41 billion, the largest in provincial history. British Columbia's growth rate for 2003 was 1.2 percent, the lowest of any provincial economy. An ongoing decline in forestry and fisheries, and the devastating fires, affected the growth rate.

Manitoba. In spite of adverse weather and low grain prices, the agricultural economy in Manitoba remained satisfactory in 2003. Real economic growth was forecast in October at 2.3 percent for 2003. The unemployment rate, at 4.9 percent, was the lowest in the nation.

The Asper Foundation, established by Manitoba publishing and broadcasting empire CanWest Global Communications, along with local, provincial, and federal governments, announced plans to build a national human rights museum in Manitoba. The $270-million project was to be the first of its kind in Canada and was slated to be constructed at the junction of the Red and Assiniboine rivers in downtown Winnipeg, the capital. The museum was intended to be an education center to promote understanding of and respect for ethnic, religious, and racial diversity. The Asper Foundation launched an architectural design competition for the 240,000-square-foot (22,000-square-meter) building, with the winning design to be chosen in the spring of 2004 and the museum scheduled to officially open in 2008.

New Brunswick. In a June 9, 2003, election, members of the Progressive Conservative Party (PCP), led by Bernard Lord, had expected to win an easy victory. The party took power in 1999, holding 44 of the 55 seats in the legislature. During the 2003 election campaign, the problem of soaring automobile insurance costs became an issue that caused voters to turn against the PCP, which won only 28 seats, some by very narrow margins. The Liberal Party took 26 seats, and the New Democratic Party (NDP) won the remaining seat. Since one PCP member became speaker of the house, the party was left with only a one-vote majority.

Lord moved immediately to deal with the auto insurance problem. Premiums had been increasing because of the high levels of compensation paid for nonserious injuries. The provincial government passed legislation that imposed a cap of $2,500 on temporary injuries and promised to reduce insurance rates by 20 percent.

Violence erupted on May 4 at Shippagan, a Gulf of St. Lawrence fishing port, when quotas for the snowcrab fishery were reduced because of diminishing supply. A crab-processing plant, warehouses, and four boats were burned, leaving one in three of the town's 2,800 residents without employment. Anger was sharpened by the fact that recent quotas for about one-quarter of the $105-million annual catch had been given to *aboriginal* (native Canadian) fishermen.

Newfoundland and Labrador. After nearly 15 years of rule by the Liberal Party, the people of Newfoundland voted on October 21 to bring in a new PCP government, headed by Danny Williams. The PCP won 34 of the 48 seats in the legislature. The Liberal Party won 12 seats, and the New Democratic Party retained their 2 seats. The election focused on economic issues. While Newfoundland had experienced impressive growth in the energy sector, the decline in the fisheries led to a severe drop in employment. The province's jobless rate ran as high as 16.7 percent, the highest in Canada.

Cod fishing, once the backbone of the island's economy, officially ended in April when Federal Fisheries Minister Robert Thibault closed the three largest fishing districts. He claimed the stocks of cod were at record low levels and showed no signs of recovery, despite conservation efforts during the 1990's. Officials expected that 900 licensed fishermen would be affected, as well as thousands of processing plant workers throughout the Atlantic provinces.

Fishermen in southwest Newfoundland and a part of the Labrador coast south of Cape Harrison also felt the effects of quota cuts in snow crab fishing announced in April. Snow crab had replaced cod as the most important sector of the Newfoundland fishing industry, with a catch valued at $435 million in 2002. Quotas were cut by 40 percent.

Inco Ltd., the world's second largest nickel producer, based in Toronto, unveiled its new nickel mining technology in October. The technology will be used on the Voisey's Bay nickel project on the coast of Labrador. Inco officials expected the mine and its concentrator to begin production in 2006.

Nova Scotia. Hurricane Juan slammed ashore in central Nova Scotia on Sept. 28, 2003. The province's capital, Halifax, was hit hard, with extensive damage to wharves, boats, and lobster traps at numerous fishing harbors, estimated at $140,000. The storm's winds, at 87 miles (150 kilometers) per hour, wrecked farms, killed livestock, and flattened crops. Electric power was cut in many communities for several days. Damages exceeded $100 million.

In an election on August 5, the PCP, under the leadership of John Hamm, won 25 seats. The NDP won 15 seats, and the Liberals took 12 seats. Hamm, therefore, returned to power with a minority government. Steeply rising auto insurance rates, for some drivers by as much as 66 percent, were a key issue in the election, just as they had been in neighboring New Brunswick.

Ontario. On October 2, voters decisively rejected the PCP government, which had been in office for eight years. The Liberal Party, under Dalton McGuinty, swept into power with promises of increased social spending, a balanced budget, and a tax freeze. The Liberals won 72 seats in the 103-seat assembly, the PCP won 24 seats, and the NDP elected 7 members. Dissatisfaction with the delivery of public health care and cost-cutting in education appeared to be the main issues that swayed voters. McGuinty and 22 cabinet ministers were sworn into office on October 23.

Toronto, Canada's largest city, suffered an outbreak of severe acute respiratory syndrome (SARS) in 2003, which was carried into Canada from Asia in mid-March. The virus was confined to patients in hospitals and nursing homes, and 10,000 individuals were quarantined and a number of hospitals closed. On April 23, the World Health Organization (WHO), the United Nations specialized agency for health headquartered in Geneva, Switzerland, advised travelers not to visit Toronto, a ruling that hurt the tourism and hospitality industries. The travel advisory was lifted on April 30 but reinstated on May 27, when a second outbreak occurred in a convalescent home. The advisory again was lifted on July 3, when Canadian health officials reported no new SARS cases since June 12. The disease affected about 375 people and killed 44 in Toronto. To improve the morale of residents and encourage more travel to the city, a concert featuring the Rolling Stones was held on July 30. About 500,000 people attended the event, held on an abandoned airfield north of the city.

The PCP government under Premier Ernie Eves had announced in May 2002 that the government would privatize Hydro One, the part of the electricity system responsible for transmission and distribution. On Jan. 20, 2003, Eves changed his mind and declared that Hydro One would remain a provincial corporation. After residents and businesses experienced large increases in electricity rates in March, Eves imposed a rate cap of 4.3 cents per kilowatt hour for consumers, to last until 2006. Taxpayers were to pay about half the difference between the frozen consumer price and fluctuating market prices. The remainder was to be covered by a special levy on all power users.

Prince Edward Island. Buffeted by the tail end of tropical Hurricane Juan, the residents of Canada's smallest province went to the polls on Sept. 29, 2003, to give Premier Pat Binns and his PCP government a third consecutive majority victory. The PCP won 23 seats in the assembly, and the Liberals won 4. In spite of power failures, blocked roads, and heavy winds and rain, 83 percent of voters cast ballots.

The Confederation Centre in Charlottetown, which houses a theater and art gallery, was designated a National Historic Site in August 2003. It was the first modern-era building to receive this designation. The center was built in 1964 to commemorate the first of the 1864 conferences that lead to the formation of Canada.

Quebec. The electoral defeat on April 14, 2003, of the separatist Parti Quebecois (PQ) strengthened the Liberal Party's control of government in Quebec. During the campaign, the PQ avoided the issue of separatism and concentrated on everyday matters important to Quebecers, but the party was soundly defeated by the Liberal Party under Jean Charest, a leader committed to federal unity. The Liberals won 76 seats, the PQ won 45, and a newer third party, Action Democratique du Quebec, won 4 seats in the assembly. Charest was sworn in as Quebec's 29th premier on April 29, with 24 ministers, a cabinet one-third smaller than the previous PQ cabinet. After his election, Charest cut taxes on small businesses and curbed spending on nearly every government program except health care, the environment, and education. Early in his term, Charest attempted to separate previously merged towns and cities of the province, reversing an unpopular action taken by the PQ to combine smaller communities into larger municipalities. Charest found that administratively and financially the mergers could not be undone and called on Quebecers to lend their support to the new regional organization.

Quebec received two budgets in 2003. The first, presented by the PQ government on March 11, was a cautious document showing large spending on social programs. When the Liberals took office in April, a budget misrepresentation was discovered, meaning that a budget that the PQ had declared to be balanced actually contained a deficit, perhaps as high as $4 billion. Charest's government presented a second, more restrained budget on June 13. It slashed subsidies and tax credits to businesses to begin dismantling the high level of state intervention in the economy.

Saskatchewan. The NDP was reelected for the fourth time on November 5. The victory was a narrow one, with Premier Lorne Calvert's party winning 30 seats and 44 percent of the popular

The worst forest fires in 50 years rage in the mountains overlooking Kamloops, British Columbia, in August 2003. The smoke and flames drove thousands of people from their residences; shut down a major highway and rail services; and destroyed houses, businesses, and lumber mills.

vote. A newer party advocating free enterprise, the Saskatchewan Party, captured 28 seats and 39 percent of the popular vote. The Liberals were shut out of the assembly. The role of private business in Saskatchewan's future proved to be the primary election issue. In 2003, the province had a larger number of provincial corporations than any other region in Canada. The Saskatchewan Party, appealing to the rural vote, promised to challenge public enterprise in Saskatchewan life. The prevailing NDP, drawing on urban support, vowed to leave the public role as strong as ever.

The prairie province received more favorable weather for its chief crop, wheat, in 2003, but lower prices guaranteed no improvement in farm incomes. Livestock sales also suffered from the loss of markets caused by the mad cow disease discovered in neighboring Alberta.

Saskatchewan's government delivered the province's 10th consecutive balanced budget on March 28. Although health care spending rose to a record $2.5 billion, there were no tax increases or higher health premiums. The budget included a plan to index personal taxes for inflation beginning in January 2004, lowering taxes paid in the future by every individual in the province.

■ David M. L. Farr

See also **Canada; Canadian territories; Food; Montreal; Public health and safety; Toronto.**

Canadian territories. The territories
experienced political and economic growth in 2003, with the prospect of a new oil pipeline, increases in the caribou harvest, and the assignment of authority for taxation and land use to an aboriginal government.

Northwest Territories. An unprecedented agreement signed in June gave the native inhabitants of Canada's northern territory up to a one-third share in an 800-mile (1,300-kilometer) pipeline along the Mackenzie River that carries natural gas from the Arctic coast to markets in the United States and Canada. The Aboriginal Pipeline Group received financial backing from a consortium of five companies, headed by TransCanada Corporation, a pipeline industry giant. The loan would be repaid with the profits of the project, expected to be completed by 2008. Other members of the consortium involved in the $5-billion project included Imperial Oil Ltd., ConocoPhillips Canada, Shell Canada Ltd., and Exxon Mobil Canada Ltd. (All amounts are in Canadian dollars.)

On Aug. 23, 2003, Canadian Prime Minister Jean Chretien signed a landmark document that transferred authority for taxation and land use to an aboriginal government for the first time in Canadian history. In 2003, the Tli Cho native group, the Dogrib, included 3,000 people living in four communities in a 39,000-square-mile

(101,000-square-kilometer) area, about the size of Belgium, between Great Slave Lake and Great Bear Lake. Under the agreement, the Dogrib would own the area's resources. They would govern themselves and have control over hunting, fishing, and industrial development. The four communities would elect their councillors and chiefs, at least half of whom must be Dogrib. The federal government would continue to enforce criminal law, and the Northwest Territories would continue to manage health and education programs. Parliament and the Northwest Territories Legislative Assembly were expected to ratify the agreement in the spring of 2004.

Aber Diamond Corporation sold its first diamonds from the territory's Diavik mine in April 2003 for $4.1 million, at an average price of $96.22 per carat. About one-quarter of the sale went to Tiffany & Co. of the United States. The rest were sent to the open diamond market in Antwerp, Belgium. In November, Tiffany opened its Laurelton Diamonds cutting and polishing center in Yellowknife, the capital of the Northwest Territories.

The residents of the territory elected 19 new members of the legislature on November 24. Most of the representatives in the previous assembly were returned, five by *acclamation* (oral vote). The new legislature chose Joe Handley as premier on December 10.

Nunavut. Nunavut's sealskin industry continued to grow in 2003. In 1995, the territorial government started a program of buying skins from hunters and selling them at auction. Nearly 10,000 pelts were sold in 2002 through the annual fur auction at North Bay, Ontario. Most of the skins went to buyers from Denmark. The best earned prices as high as $63 a pelt, while in the mid-1990's a good sealskin sold for $5. In 2003, the program paid $500,000 to hunters throughout Nunavut.

The commercial caribou hunting industry also experienced growth in 2003. A caribou harvest program was initiated in 1994 to control over 60,000 caribou on Southampton Island because the herd was seriously depleting food resources. Hunters harvested 250,000 pounds (113,400 kilograms) of caribou meat and exported it to international markets. According to conservation experts, the controlled hunt has maintained the herd at a sustainable level.

A government study showed that another caribou population, the Bathurst herd, was diminishing. The herd, which ranges over the Northwest Territories-Nunavut border, fell from 350,000 head to about 186,000 in 10 years. Researchers said that the numbers were within the normal range of caribou fluctuations, but the counts raised a flag that the herd was vulnerable.

Prime Minister Chretien opened a new national park, Ukkusiksalik, the second in Nunavut, in August. The park's 8,500 square miles (22,000 square kilometers) lie around a saltwater inlet, Wager Bay, on the northwest coast of Hudson Bay. The area is now home to a wide variety of animal life and holds deposits of soapstone, a traditional Inuit carving material.

Yukon. The Yukon government feared that when the last census was tallied, the territory would owe money to the federal government. The federal government bases annual payment amounts on population growth compared with the rest of the country. Since the last census in 1996, Yukon's population has dropped, and officials set aside $15 million in expectation that the territory had received too much money over the past five years and would have to repay it. However, the results of the census showed that Yukon owed no money and, in fact, was underpaid by $15 million between 1996 and 2002.

Gemologists in November 2003 confirmed the 2002 discovery of a gemstone, beryl, in Yukon by True North Gems Inc. of Vancouver. Beryl resembles aquamarine but is a unique stone, native to Canada. Its color is a deep blue, which comes from its high iron content. True North is exploring the possibility of mining the gem commercially.   ■ David M. L. Farr

See also **Canada.**

Cape Verde. See Africa.

Census. The United States Census Bureau continued painting a complex portrait of the United States in 2003, releasing a number of statistics from surveys conducted following the 2000 census. The Census Bureau data showed a growing foreign-born population, a shift in the minority population, and changes in educational backgrounds and the make-up of families.

Foreign-born population. The foreign-born population of the United States reached an estimated 33 million people in 2002, the bureau reported on Sept. 3, 2003. The Census Bureau's American Community Survey showed that in 2002, the foreign-born population grew by 1.6 million people. According to the study, 52 percent were born in Latin America, 27 percent were born in Asia, and 15 percent were born in Europe.

The survey revealed that 28 percent of the foreign-born population reported living in California. Miami, Florida, had the highest reported foreign-born population of any city, with 60.6 percent.

Minority groups. Census Bureau officials announced in June 2003 that Hispanics had surpassed African Americans as the largest minority group in the United States. The Hispanic population of the United States grew to 38.8 million people in July 2002, up 9.8 percent from April 2000. The African American population increased

to 38.3 million people, up 2 percent during the same period. The bureau reported that about 53 percent of the Hispanic population's growth was linked to immigration.

Education. On March 21, 2003, the Census Bureau released figures that showed the high school graduation rate for women had edged ahead of that for men. It marked the first time since 1989 that there was such a statistical difference between the sexes. The bureau reported that the graduation rate for women was 84.4 percent. The rate for men was 83.8 percent. The report also revealed that in 2002, 27 percent of adults aged 25 or older were college graduates, approximately 1 percent higher than in 2001.

The Census Bureau found that higher education levels had a significant impact on the earnings potential of U.S. residents. Adults aged 18 and older with advanced college degrees earned an average of $72,869 in 2001. Graduates with a bachelor's degree earned an average of $50,623. Adults who had earned only a high school diploma had an average salary of $26,795. Adults without a high school diploma earned an average of $18,793.

Families. The number of unmarried couples in the United States who live together increased between 1990 and 2000, according to 2000 census data released in March 2003. The number of unmarried couples living together grew from 3.2 million in 1990 to 5.5 million in 2000, according to the report. Married couples still make up the majority of U.S. households, the bureau reported, with 55.4 million, or 52 percent of households.

The Census Bureau revealed in a separate report issued on June 12, 2003, that about 70 percent of the nation's 72.3 million children under age 18 lived with two parents, making two-parent households the national norm. The bureau found that 19.8 million children under age 18 lived with one parent. Of those, 16.5 million children lived with their mothers and 3.3 million children with their fathers.

Adjusted count. The Census Bureau announced in March that it had overcounted the U.S. population by 1.3 million people in the 2000 census. Some politicians had claimed that the 2000 census missed 3.2 million people. As a result, many communities lost federal funding that is awarded based on population.

The findings revealed an overcount of whites, Asians, and American Indians living on reservations. Bureau officials said that whites were overcounted by 1.1 percent. Asians and American Indians were overcounted by less than 1 percent. Officials said that the new figures would not alter the official population count of 281.4 million people in 2000.   ■ Geoffrey A. Campbell

See also **Population.**

Chemistry. A simple, sensitive test for detecting lead was announced in May 2003 by chemists Yi Lu and Juewen Liu at the University of Illinois in Urbana-Champaign. The chemists said the test they created could be used by homeowners. Basically, the test is similar to using litmus paper to test for acids or bases in a solution. If vinegar containing dissolved paint chips turns a red color, it means there is lead present. If it turns blue or purple, lead is not present.

Exposure to lead can do a great deal of harm, especially to the brains of children. Manufacturers have taken steps to remove lead from gasoline, water pipes, and paint. However, a huge amount of paint and pipes containing lead remain in older houses and other buildings.

The first step toward dealing with the lead risk is to determine when it is present, but lead is not easy to find or identify. Chemists consider most lead-paint test kits unreliable. The alternative is a technique called X-ray fluorescence spectroscopy, which requires expensive equipment and trained inspectors.

To create a test as simple and reliable as a litmus test, the scientists manipulated tiny molecular segments of several substances. They found a single strand of DNA (deoxyribonucleic acid) that can attach to lead. Then they selected nanoparticles, with just a few molecules each, of gold. The particles turn blue when put together and red when separated. The chemists linked the gold particles with the DNA to make a test strip.

Testing for lead in paint only required dissolving some paint flakes in vinegar and dripping it on the test strip. In the presence of lead, the DNA separated the gold particles, turning the strip red. If no lead was present, the strip turned blue.

The chemists also learned to fine-tune the test by varying the types of DNA in the mix. This gave the test the potential to show not only that lead was there, but to tell how much. The basic test also had the potential to look for other environmental *toxins* (poisons). The chemists were trying to develop a test with different color schemes that could detect a variety of poisonous metals, including mercury, chromium, and arsenic.

A fine mesh. The development of new bandages based on materials the human body uses to heal itself was announced by biomedical engineer Gary L. Bowlin of Virginia Commonwealth University, Richmond, in February. He reported that bandages he developed offered the potential for better wound treatment and more effective ways to reduce bleeding during emergency treatment and surgery. Scabs dissolve and come off on their own, but bandages must be ripped away and may cause more injury to the patient.

Bowlin created his bandages using mats made of long strands of fibrinogen, a *soluble* (dissolvable) protein found in blood. The body breaks down fibrinogen to form the stringy protein fibrin, which is the basis for blood clots.

Bowlin formed the fibrinogen strands, which are a thousand times finer than a human hair, using a process called electrospinning. A tiny nozzle blew out a solution of the protein, which was attracted to an electrically charged piece of metal. The protein solidified into fibers as it moved through an electric field. The result was a mat of fibrinogen that clumps together like spaghetti. The body treats this mat as natural material similar to the body's own protein.

Medical researchers imagine many uses for the fibrinogen mats, from covering wounds of accident victims to stopping bleeding in blood vessels during surgery. The material would not need to be removed. The body would simply dissolve it or let it drop off.

The bandages were successfully tested on small animals. Scientists next planned to test them on humans.

Sticky lessons of how tapeworms use the chemical compound cyclic guanosine monophosphate (cyclic GMP) may cut the costs of some medicines and reduce damage to the environment. This conclusion was reported in March by pharmacologist Paul Bass and bioscientist John Oaks at the University of Wisconsin-Madison.

The researchers found that cyclic GMP helps the tapeworm by slowing down the digestive system of the host animal in which the tapeworm is living. The parasite invades the intestines and holds on with hooks and suckers. Bass and Oaks analyzed a variety of biochemicals produced by the tapeworm and found that cyclic GMP actually slows or turns off the body's natural flushing mechanism. This allows the tapeworm to more easily stick to the intestines of its host.

The researchers speculated that cyclic GMP could increase the time it takes for medicines to pass through the human intestine so that the body derives more value from them. Today, up to 50 percent of an oral medication may pass through the body without being absorbed. In the case of the common drug used to treat osteoporosis, Fosamax, 99 percent of the medicine is wasted. This result makes it difficult to prescribe the right dosage and increases the amount—and cost—of medicines.

Cyclic GMP may also help with an environmental concern. Medications given to farm animals pass through the animals and wind up in the environment. Antibiotics, hormones, and other drugs get into ground water, where they can add to such problems as bacterial resistance to antibiotics. Giving cyclic GMP to farm animals may slow their digestion and reduce the amount of drugs they excrete.   ■ Peter Andrews

Chess. Garry Kasparov of Russia was the world's top-rated chess player in 2003, maintaining a lead over countryman Vladimir Kramnik, who defeated Kasparov in 2000 for the now-defunct Brain Games World Chess Championship.

World championship. Two world champions were recognized in 2003. Kramnik was the Einstein Classical World Chess champion, and 20-year-old Ruslan Ponomariov of Ukraine, ranked 12th in the world, was the official champion of the Federation Internationale des Echecs (FIDE), the governing body of international chess. The world title was split in 1993, when then-world champion Kasparov broke away from FIDE. After more than 10 years of dual champions, FIDE tried to unify the titles even though Ponomariov refused to play Kasparov in September 2003.

World Chess Hall of Fame inductions. On March 1, FIDE inducted several former world champions into its Hall of Fame in Miami, Florida. The inductees—Mikhail Botvinnik, Vassily Smyslov, Mikhail Tal, Tigran Petrosian, and Boris Spassky—hailed from the former Soviet Union and, along with U.S. citizen Bobby Fischer, dominated chess from 1948 to 1972. Spassky, now retired, attended the ceremony. On the same day, the U.S. Chess Federation inducted former U.S. champions Lev Alburt, Walter Browne, and Donald Byrne into its Hall of Fame, located in the same rook-shaped building in Miami.

Human vs. computers. Kasparov played against two computer programs in 2003. Both matches were televised from New York City, and both were draws. In the first match, the FIDE Man vs. Machine World Chess Championship, Kasparov played against Deep Junior from January to February. Sanctioned by FIDE, the contest offered $500,000 in prizes, with Kasparov earning $250,000 in addition to his $500,000 fee. In November, Kasparov faced the top-rated computer program Fritz, playing four games against the program in a 3-D format by sitting in front of a computer with special electronic glasses.

Other players and events. Hungary's Judit Polgar sustained her claim of being the game's best-ever female player by ranking 11th in the world—notably, just above FIDE champion Ponomariov. Alex Shabalov of Pittsburgh, Pennsylvania, became U.S. men's champion, while Anna Hahn, of Jersey City, New Jersey, became U.S. women's champion at a competition held in Seattle in January. At the National Elementary Chess Championship in May in Nashville, Tennessee, 10-year-old Fabiano Caruana of New York City won. Kazim Gulamali of Forest Park, Georgia, took the junior high division as National Scholastic Chess Champion. Three students tied for top honors in the National High School Chess Championship in March in Columbus, Ohio. ■ Al Lawrence

Chicago. Richard M. Daley was reelected to a fifth term as mayor of Chicago with 79 percent of the vote on Feb. 25, 2003. He was first elected mayor in 1989. Because of Daley's popularity and longevity in office, he continued in 2003 to wield considerable power.

Airport controversy. Daley displayed that power in late March when city crews, at his behest, began tearing up runways at Meigs Field, a downtown airport, in the middle of the night of March 30. The move effectively shut down the small airfield, which is located on an island in Lake Michigan. Daley had long wanted the island reclaimed for parkland, a move opposed by many state officials, who accused the mayor of arrogance.

Building disasters. Three disasters that attracted national attention turned Chicago's building code and its enforcement into major political issues. On February 17, patrons at the E2 nightclub panicked when a chemical spray was used to stop a fight on the crowded dance floor. As patrons tried to flee the second-story club, they were trapped in a stairwell and unable to escape. The incident left 21 people dead and more than 50 others injured. A housing court judge had previously ordered the club closed because of code violations. The owners had ignored the order and continued to hold events. Critics argued that the city should have enforced the building codes more aggressively. On September 23, a grand jury handed down indictments for the four men who owned or managed the club, charging them with involuntary manslaughter.

On June 29, an apartment porch collapsed under a large group of partygoers, killing 13 people and injuring some 50 others. Investigations determined that the porch had not been built to the city's code requirements. On September 4, Mayor Daley announced that building inspectors would become more active in the neighborhoods and perform fewer inspections in professionally managed buildings in the downtown area.

The third incident, however, involved fire-safety codes and occurred in just such a downtown high-rise building. On October 17, a fire at the Cook County Administration building left 6 people dead and 11 others seriously injured. The victims were fleeing the building via an internal fire escape. For security purposes, doors in the stairway had been fitted with locks that permitted entrance, but did not allow reentry from the stairs onto the floors. When some workers found they were unable to evacuate the building on the ground floor, they tried to return to their offices but were trapped in the stairwell, where they were overcome by smoke inhalation.

Schools. In autumn 2003, many low-perform-

Chicago's Soldier Field reopened on Sept. 29, 2003, after a major renovation that included fitting an entirely new stadium inside the walls and colonnades of the original amphitheater. The new design sparked considerable controversy.

ing city schools found it difficult to comply with federal education reform requirements, which mandated that students attending schools with poor standardized test results be allowed to transfer to better-performing schools. More than 19,000 students applied for transfers, but only around 1,000 places were available.

Sports. A renovated Soldier Field opened on September 29 for a game between the Chicago Bears and the Green Bay Packers football teams. Some critics complained that the addition looked like a spaceship that had landed in the old, colonnaded stadium. The designers claimed the new addition allowed fans to be much closer to the action on the field.

Both of the city's major-league baseball teams were in contention for playoff spots late in the season. The Cubs advanced to their first playoff appearance since 1998, but neither the White Sox nor the Cubs made it to the World Series.

Deaths. Well-known Chicago columnist Irv Kupcinet died in November 2003. In 1943, he began writing "Kup's Column" for the paper that would become the Chicago Sun-Times. The 91-year-old was still writing his column in the weeks before his death. ■ Harold Henderson

See also **Aviation; Baseball; Education.**

Children's books. See Literature for children.

Chile. A free-trade pact between Chile and the European Union (EU) went into effect in February 2003. The pact boosted noncopper exports, including grapes and farm produce, to EU members by 27.4 percent in the first quarter of 2003.

Chilean officials hoped that a treaty signed with the United States in June would lead to comparable increases in the country's export trade. The treaty abolished tariffs on 85 percent of consumer and industrial products traded with the United States beginning in January 2004, with the balance phased out over a 12-year period. Economists estimated that the agreement would help increase Chile's exports by nearly 16 percent and its gross domestic product (the value of all goods and services produced in a country in a given year) by more than 2 percent.

Corruption. Scandals erupted in January 2003 when Carlos Cruz, a former public works minister, revealed that agency officials received payments from private contractors who won public awards. Although Cruz defended the practice, nearly 30 government workers were in jail by August.

In January, President Ricardo Lagos Escobar proposed 49 bills to deter corruption after the theft of some $110 million from Chile's development bank. The legislation would end secretive campaign financing. ■ Nathan A. Haverstock

See also **Latin America.**

China. Hu Jintao was elected president of China on March 15, 2003, by the National People's Congress (NPC), China's parliament. Hu, who replaced Jiang Zemin as China's leader, assumed the role of general secretary of the ruling Chinese Communist Party (CCP) in 2002. The 2003 election completed the first orderly transition of power in China's modern history.

The NPC also chose Wen Jiabao as prime minister. Wen, a former deputy premier, succeeded Zhu Rongji, a dynamic reformer who was the architect of China's rapid economic growth in the 2000's. The NPC reelected Jiang as head of the Central Military Commission and named Jiang's longtime ally, Zeng Qinghong, as vice president. As supreme military commander, Jiang was second in power only to Hu.

Power struggle. Political observers claimed that Jiang's continuing role in government caused tension among high-ranking officials. Before stepping down as president, Jiang placed allies in strategic positions, which allowed him to retain his political clout. Hu attempted to consolidate power by replacing some of Jiang's allies and cautiously pushed the government toward a more liberal political system.

On July 1, the 82nd anniversary of the founding of the CCP, Hu called for new policies to tackle China's growing gap in personal wealth, including fighting rural and urban unemployment, and improving health care and social security. He stressed, however, that changes must come gradually. The speech was Hu's first major national address, and many observers had expected him to announce plans to move the country to a more democratic form of government. However, Hu did not announce any bold reform plans. Political analysts said that Hu would institute major political and economic reforms only after a long process of consensus building among party liberals and conservative officials loyal to Jiang.

Wen, who handled agriculture and banking reforms as deputy premier, vowed to continue Zhu's policies, which had made China's economy the sixth largest in the world. In his first national address in March, Wen promised to make rural and urban development a priority and talked about the urgent need to fight corruption.

SARS. Hu faced his first international crisis in early 2003 when his government bungled the handling of severe acute respiratory syndrome (SARS), a highly contagious disease. The epidemic, which began in China in 2002, spread across Southeast Asia and into North America, and killed more than 800 people by July 2003. In China, more than 5,300 people contracted the disease, and nearly 350 people died from it.

Chinese authorities learned of the disease by early 2003, but they did little to deal with it. Instead, health officials attempted to hide the growing epidemic by refusing to correctly diagnose patients. They also lied to international health groups about the number of infected people in China. After a Chinese physician accused the government of lying about SARS figures in March, the World Health Organization (WHO), a United Nations (UN) affiliate, demanded access to hospitals in Beijing, the capital, and found that SARS was far more prevalent than Chinese officials had previously admitted.

The Chinese government then acknowledged that it had covered up the extent of the disease and fired two top officials. In April, China's health minister and the mayor of Beijing were fired on charges that they contributed to the spread of SARS by insisting that health officials lie about infection rates.

After admitting the extent of the epidemic, China's government acted to contain the disease. Officials imposed quarantines and reduced the May Day holiday from one week to one day to discourage people from traveling and spreading the disease. In June, WHO lifted its warning against travel to China, after it determined that the epidemic had declined significantly and was not a significant threat to visitors.

AIDS. China continued to grapple with a growing AIDS epidemic in 2003. UN officials urged the Chinese government to spend more on education and prevention and complained that many Chinese officials were not committed to fighting the disease. In June, police stormed a small village and attacked residents infected with HIV, the virus that causes AIDS, who were staging a protest to demand better health care.

Economy. The SARS crisis did little to slow China's dazzling economy, which was the world's fastest-growing in 2003. The economy grew at a rate of 9.9 percent in the first quarter of 2003. The negative effects of SARS were limited primarily to tourism and the travel sector. By October, however, tourism rebounded. The World Travel and Tourism Council, a private organization, predicted that tourism to China would grow 22 percent annually through 2012.

Government officials enacted policies in 2003 designed to narrow the gap between rich and poor in China. In January, the government changed regulations that discriminated against approximately 94 million migrant workers who struggled to survive in China's urban slums.

The government continued a series of economic reforms started in the 1980's that led to less government control over some business activities. In 2003, the government ended the guarantee of lifetime jobs for 30 million employees of state-owned industries, and it encouraged greater investment in Southeast Asia by Chinese companies. Trade between China and the 10 Southeast Asian countries grew by more than 55 percent in 2003.

Space. In October, China became only the third nation to send a person into space. The Chinese spacecraft Shenzhou 5 launched from the Gobi Desert on October 15 carrying a single astronaut, Lieutenant Colonel Yang Liwei. It orbited Earth 14 times before returning after a voyage of approximately 21 hours.

China began a secret program to send a person into space in the 1970's. However, domestic turmoil obstructed the program, and it was not revived until 1992, when Jiang put China on the path toward exploration. China launched four unmanned spacecraft between 1992 and 2002. Chinese officials announced after the 2003 mission that China intended to explore space and the moon for energy resources, launch a space telescope, and construct a space station.

The Three Gorges Dam, which was designed to control flooding and improve navigation on the Yangtze, China's longest river, and to generate hydroelectric power, began to retain water in 2003. On June 1, the dam's sluice gates were closed and water began filling the reservoir behind the dam. The boat locks were also opened

to shipping traffic. The first of the dam's working generators began producing commercial electric power in August.

Construction of the dam began in 1994. When completed, the Three Gorges will be the world's largest dam. The dam's huge reservoir has forced the resettlement of more than 1 million people. The project had many critics, who charged that it would create environmental problems, cover some of China's best farmland, and destroy thousands of historical sites. Supporters say the dam will save lives by preventing floods on the eastern Yangtze and that the electric power the project generates will help reduce the use of coal and decrease air pollution.

Missile program. China accelerated production of short-range ballistic missiles to threaten Taiwan, the United States Department of Defense reported in July 2003. China already had approximately 450 short-range missiles aimed at Taiwan, an island-state regarded by China as a province. The new missiles would complicate the U.S. military's efforts to protect Taiwan from a Chinese invasion, according to the report. Chinese officials responded by charging that the United States issued the report to justify its intentions of selling weapons to Taiwan.

The Chinese and U.S. governments also

Newlyweds kiss through surgical masks during a wedding photo session in Beijing in May. Many people in China wore masks in public to protect themselves against severe acute respiratory syndrome (SARS), a highly contagious respiratory disease that killed nearly 350 people in China in 2003.

debated Chinese weapons exports in 2003. In May, U.S. officials accused one of China's largest conglomerates of assisting in the Iranian missile program and banned exports by the firm to the United States.

A proposed security bill for Hong Kong, a special administrative district of China, triggered massive demonstrations and calls for free elections in 2003. The security bill, proposed by the government's chief executive, Tung Chee-hwa, introduced stringent definitions of treason, *sedition* (an act that stirs up discontent against established government authority), and other crimes. On July 1, 500,000 people carried out a peaceful demonstration against the bill. Tung responded by removing most of the measure's controversial provisions and delaying a vote on it.

A submarine sank in April during training exercises in the Bohai Gulf. All 70 crew members aboard the vessel died in the accident. It was China's worst acknowledged military accident in modern Chinese history. The Navy replaced its two top commanders following the accident.

Olympics. The International Olympic Committee selected Beijing as the host for the 2008 summer games. China budgeted $34 billion to prepare for the games.   ■ Henry S. Bradsher

See also **Asia; People in the news** (Hu Jintao); **Public health and safety; Taiwan.**

City. Cities in the United States faced serious financial problems in 2003. Increased spending for public safety and antiterrorism measures, a floundering national economy, and reductions in state aid all squeezed city budgets, according to the National League of Cities (NLC). The NLC is a Washington, D.C.-based organization that seeks to improve the quality of life in U.S. cities.

Falling state aid. Pressured by their own budget shortfalls, states cut revenues to cities for fiscal year 2004 by a total of $2.3 billion, a 9.2-percent drop over fiscal 2003 levels, the NLC reported in September. (The 2004 fiscal year for states runs from July 1, 2003, to June 30, 2004.) The NLC criticized the decline as an "unraveling of the intergovernmental partnership" that "threatens to undermine government's ability to deliver the goods and services Americans need."

According to the report, the revenues of cities in 24 states declined for fiscal year 2004. Cities in Kansas experienced the worst drop, after that state cut all its general revenue-sharing funds. State aid also plummeted in California (60 percent), Texas (47 percent), and West Virginia (39 percent). The cuts included revenue-sharing programs and general purpose and project grants.

The NLC report noted that the new cuts followed previous declines in state aid in recent years, some of them dramatic. From fiscal year 1999 to fiscal 2003, state revenues to cities dropped by 68 percent in North Carolina, 49 percent in West Virginia, 38 percent in Alaska, and 33 percent in Washington. The NLC also noted that since 1977 the federal share of total city revenues had fallen from 15 to 5 percent. Some states attempted to compensate for the cuts by increasing cities' authority to levy taxes.

Fiscal struggle. Four out of five cities reported being less able to meet their financial needs in 2003 than they were in 2002, according to the NLC's annual survey of city finance managers, released in May 2003. The NLC said the results revealed the worst fiscal conditions for cities since the organization began its poll in 1985. In the survey, which covered 330 U.S. towns and cities, 79 percent of managers reported deteriorating fiscal conditions in 2003, up from 55 percent in 2002. The findings also revealed that cities faced a 4-percent gap between revenues and spending—a 1-percent drop in revenues and a 2.9-percent increase in spending. Nearly 40 percent of managers reported that the quality of life in their city had declined because of a worsening financial climate.

In a related NLC study issued in March 2003, more than one-third of finance managers blamed state funding cuts for declining revenues. The NLC said the driving force behind cities' spending increases was higher expenditures for public safety, including antiterrorism measures. More than 80 percent of cities reported increased spending in this area in 2003.

In response to these problems, 61 percent of cities raised fees or imposed new fees, 54 percent drew on financial reserves, and 25 percent increased property taxes. In addition, about 17 percent of cities laid off staff, including firefighters and police officers. Cities also slashed spending on infrastructure and maintenance.

Fastest-growing cities. Five suburbs in the Southwest captured the top spots in a list of the fastest-growing U.S. cities by population, released by the U.S. Census Bureau in July 2003. They included Gilbert, Arizona; North Las Vegas and Henderson, in Nevada; and Chandler and Peoria, in Arizona. Gilbert, Chandler, and Peoria are suburbs of Phoenix. North Las Vegas and Henderson lie outside Las Vegas. Other cities in the top 10 included Irvine, Rancho Cucamonga, Chula Vista, and Fontana, all in California, and Joliet, Illinois.

Quality of life. Cities in Australia, Canada, New Zealand, and western Europe won the highest ratings in the 2003 worldwide quality of life survey of cities, conducted annually by Mercer Human Resource Consulting in New York City. The survey, released in February, evaluated

215 cities on the basis of 39 criteria, including political, social, economic, and environmental conditions. New York City served as the bench mark for the survey.

Zurich, Switzerland, placed first in the ratings. Vancouver, Canada; Vienna, Austria; and Geneva, Switzerland, tied for second place. Sydney, Australia, and Bern, Switzerland, came in third. Auckland, New Zealand; Copenhagen, Denmark; and Frankfurt, Germany, tied for fourth place. Brazzaville, capital of the Republic of the Congo in west-central Africa, ranked last.

North American cities that placed in the top 50 included Vancouver, Toronto, and Ottawa, all in Canada, followed by San Francisco and Honolulu, Hawaii. Canadian cities Montreal and Calgary also made the list.

Mercer also ranked cities by personal safety, based on crime levels, law enforcement, and internal stability. Luxembourg, capital of the small European country of the same name, placed first. Five cities tied for second place: Bern, Geneva, and Zurich, all in Switzerland; Helsinki, Finland; and Singapore, capital of the island country of Singapore. The lowest-ranking city was war-torn Bangui, capital of the Central African Republic.

The Canadian cities of Calgary, Montreal, Ottawa, Toronto, and Vancouver also ranked among the 50 safest cities. Honolulu, Houston, and San Francisco outscored all other U.S. cities for personal safety. The survey named Washington, D.C., as the least safe city in North America.

City honors. Six U.S. cities won awards from the NLC in 2003 for their efforts to enhance their community's quality of life. The winners among cities with a population of 150,000 or more were Tempe, Arizona, for transforming a dried-out riverbed into a tourist destination, and St. Petersburg, Florida, for a program that encourages community members to renovate and repair the houses of the poor, elderly, and disabled.

The winners among cities with a population of 50,000 to 150,000 were Bellevue, Washington, for developing a strategy for reclaiming neighborhoods threatened by aging, growth, and change; and Roanoke, Virginia, for a water conservation education campaign. The winners among cities with a population under 50,000 were Tupelo, Mississippi, for the construction of a community center in a needy area, and Coralville, Iowa, for creating a sense of place in a community with a "drive-thru" image.

Traffic congestion. Traffic congestion in U.S. urban areas continued to worsen, according to the annual Urban Mobility Study by the Texas Transportation Institute at Texas A&M University in College Station, released in October 2003. The researchers noted, however, that urban traffic

50 LARGEST URBAN CENTERS IN THE WORLD

Rank	Urban center	Population
1.	Tokyo, Japan	26,683,000
2.	Sao Paulo, Brazil	18,916,000
3.	Mexico City, Mexico	18,580,000
4.	Mumbai, India	17,384,000
5.	New York City, U.S.	16,979,000
6.	Dhaka, Bangladesh	14,414,000
7.	Delhi, India	14,067,000
8.	Calcutta, India	13,784,000
9.	Los Angeles, U.S.	13,541,000
10.	Shanghai, China	13,023,000
11.	Buenos Aires, Argentina	12,271,000
12.	Jakarta, Indonesia	12,234,000
13.	Karachi, Pakistan	11,058,000
14.	Osaka, Japan	11,013,000
15.	Rio de Janeiro, Brazil	10,958,000
16.	Beijing, China	10,486,000
17.	Manila, Philippines	10,380,000
18.	Lagos, Nigeria	10,034,000
19.	Seoul, Republic of Korea	9,888,000
20.	Cairo, Egypt	9,833,000
21.	Paris, France	9,702,000
22.	Istanbul, Turkey	9,529,000
23.	Tianjin, China	9,269,000
24.	Moscow, Russia	8,506,000
25.	Lima, Peru	7,875,000
26.	Bangkok, Thailand	7,819,000
27.	London, U.K.	7,640,000
28.	Bogota, Colombia	7,249,000
29.	Tehran, Iran	7,161,000
30.	Chicago, U.S.	7,103,000
31.	Hong Kong, China	7,102,000
32.	Madras, India	6,683,000
33.	Essen, Germany	6,543,000
34.	Bangalore, India	6,119,000
35.	Lahore, Pakistan	5,982,000
36.	Hyderabad, India	5,850,000
37.	Kinshasa, Congo	5,716,000
38.	Santiago, Chile	5,702,000
39.	Wuhan, China	5,647,000
40.	Chongqing, China	5,356,000
41.	Baghdad, Iraq	5,152,000
42.	Riyadh, Saudi Arabia	5,135,000
43.	Toronto, Canada	4,990,000
44.	Shenyang, China	4,880,000
45.	Ho Chi Minh City, Vietnam	4,854,000
46.	Ahmedabad, India	4,853,000
47.	St. Petersburg, Russia	4,725,000
48.	Yangon, Myanmar	4,724,000
49.	Belo Horizonte, Brazil	4,529,000
50.	Philadelphia, U.S.	4,513,000

Source: 2003 estimates based on data from the United Nations.

50 LARGEST CITIES IN THE UNITED STATES

Rank	City	Population*
1.	New York, N.Y.	8,106,667
2.	Los Angeles, Calif.	3,846,740
3.	Chicago, Ill.	2,877,945
4.	Houston, Tex.	2,036,964
5.	Philadelphia, Pa.	1,482,746
6.	Phoenix, Ariz.	1,396,908
7.	San Diego, Calif.	1,272,954
8.	San Antonio, Tex.	1,218,092
9.	Dallas, Tex.	1,217,063
10.	Detroit, Mich.	914,363
11.	San Jose, Calif.	894,739
12.	Indianapolis, Ind.	782,882
13.	Jacksonville, Fla.	775,956
14.	San Francisco, Calif.	752,303
15.	Columbus, Ohio	729,340
16.	Austin, Tex.	670,774
17.	Memphis, Tenn.	649,563
18.	Baltimore, Md.	631,992
19.	Charlotte, N.C.	590,058
20.	Milwaukee, Wis.	588,705
21.	Boston, Mass.	586,865
22.	El Paso, Tex.	583,905
23.	Fort Worth, Tex.	582,054
24.	Seattle, Wash.	571,360
25.	Washington, D.C.	567,989
26.	Denver, Colo.	557,606
27.	Nashville, Tenn.	545,335
28.	Portland, Ore.	543,724
29.	Oklahoma City, Okla.	525,654
30.	Las Vegas, Nev.	518,460
31.	Tucson, Ariz.	510,914
32.	Long Beach, Calif.	478,368
33.	Albuquerque, N. Mex.	473,849
34.	New Orleans, La.	468,982
35.	Cleveland, Ohio	463,708
36.	Fresno, Calif.	454,244
37.	Sacramento, Calif.	448,826
38.	Kansas City, Mo.	444,336
39.	Virginia Beach, Va.	438,697
40.	Mesa, Ariz.	436,963
41.	Atlanta, Ga.	427,074
42.	Omaha, Nebr.	403,668
43.	Oakland, Calif.	400,930
44.	Tulsa, Okla.	391,410
45.	Honolulu, Hawaii	382,356
46.	Miami, Fla.	381,072
47.	Minneapolis, Minn.	371,797
48.	Colorado Springs, Colo.	370,801
49.	Arlington, Tex.	357,884
50.	Wichita, Kan.	357,806

*2003 World Book estimates based on data from the U.S. Census Bureau.

50 LARGEST METROPOLITAN AREAS IN THE UNITED STATES

Rank	Metropolitan area*	Population†
1.	Los Angeles-Long Beach, Calif.	9,732,235
2.	New York City, N.Y.	9,567,989
3.	Chicago, Ill.	8,564,013
4.	Washington, D.C.-Md.-Va.-W.Va.	5,172,418
5.	Philadelphia, Pa.-N.J.	5,156,220
6.	Atlanta, Ga.	4,611,001
7.	Houston, Tex.	4,509,410
8.	Detroit, Mich.	4,496,406
9.	Dallas, Tex.	3,862,324
10.	Phoenix-Mesa, Ariz.	3,714,128
11.	Riverside-San Bernadino, Calif.	3,512,272
12.	Boston, Mass.	3,463,351
13.	Minneapolis-St. Paul, Minn.-Wis.	3,121,883
14.	Orange County, Calif.	3,003,657
15.	San Diego, Calif.	2,921,542
16.	Nassau-Suffolk, N.Y.	2,799,603
17.	St. Louis, Mo.-Ill.	2,638,914
18.	Baltimore, Md.	2,608,537
19.	Seattle-Bellevue-Everett, Wash.	2,553,377
20.	Tampa-St. Petersburg-Clearwater, Fla.	2,512,113
21.	Oakland, Calif.	2,501,106
22.	Miami, Fla.	2,365,357
23.	Pittsburgh, Pa.	2,348,097
24.	Denver, Colo.	2,304,869
25.	Cleveland-Lorain-Elyria, Ohio	2,265,759
26.	Portland, Ore.-Vancouver, Wash.	2,075,174
27.	Newark, N.J.	2,070,420
28.	Las Vegas, Nev.-Ariz.	1,987,392
29.	Kansas City, Mo.-Kan.	1,841,862
30.	Fort Worth-Arlington, Tex.	1,834,078
31.	Orlando, Fla.	1,819,657
32.	San Francisco, Calif.	1,773,065
33.	Fort Lauderdale, Fla.	1,769,902
34.	San Jose, Calif.	1,745,957
35.	Sacramento, Calif.	1,735,490
36.	San Antonio, Tex.	1,690,844
37.	Indianapolis, Ind.	1,687,878
38.	Cincinnati, Ohio-Ky.-Ind.	1,685,724
39.	Charlotte-Gastonia, N.C.-Rock Hill, S.C.	1,633,551
40.	Norfolk-Virginia Beach-Newport News, Va.	1,611,343
41.	Columbus, Ohio	1,608,130
42.	Milwaukee-Waukesha, Wis.	1,522,456
43.	Austin-San Marcos, Tex.	1,437,270
44.	Salt Lake City-Ogden, Ut.	1,433,958
45.	Bergen-Passaic, N.J.	1,403,877
46.	New Orleans, La.	1,354,248
47.	Raleigh-Durham-Chapel Hill, N.C.	1,332,036
48.	Nashville, Tenn.	1,325,987
49.	Greensboro-Winston-Salem-High Point, N.C.	1,324,989
50.	West Palm Beach-Boca Raton, Fla.	1,239,679

*The U.S. Bureau of the Census defines a metropolitan area as a large population nucleus with adjacent communities having a high degree of economic and social integration.

†2003 World Book estimates based on data from the U.S. Census Bureau.

would be even more sluggish if cities had not implemented some measures to speed traffic flow. The study analyzed information collected from 75 cities in 2001.

The Texas researchers found that U.S. traffic congestion accounted for 5.7 billion gallons (21.6 billion liters) of wasted fuel and 3.5 billion hours of lost productivity. The lost hours cost businesses and individuals $69.5 billion, an increase of $4.5 billion over 2000 levels. Cities with the worst traffic, measured in hours of extra travel time during rush hour per commuter, included Los Angeles (90 hours); San Francisco-Oakland (68); Denver (64); Miami, Florida (63); Chicago (61); Phoenix (61); and San Jose, California (60). Commuters in Boston; Portland, Oregon; and Washington, D.C., endured an average of 58 hours of extra travel time each.

In 2003, for the first time, institute researchers calculated the effect of "congestion remedies" on travel times. These remedies included public transportation systems; special lanes for buses and car poolers; and devices to coordinate traffic signals and regulate traffic flow on highway ramps. They found that a combination of the three cut the national average annual congestion delay per commuter from 58 hours to 50.5 hours.   ■ Barbara A. Mayes

See also **Chicago; Los Angeles; New York City.**

Civil rights. The United States-led war against terrorism ignited a firestorm of controversy in 2003. Many civil rights activists and some U.S. politicians argued that increased government powers to combat terrorism intruded on individual rights and curtailed civil liberties. Supporters of the legislation argued that the federal government required more stringent powers to investigate and detain suspected terrorists.

The USA PATRIOT Act, passed in October 2001, was at the heart of the debate. The act gave law enforcement the power to detain for seven days—or in some cases indefinitely—any noncitizen suspected of being a risk to national security. The act also granted authorities greater freedom to conduct searches. In some cases, the searches were carried out without notifying the subject of the search.

Many people maintained that the USA PATRIOT Act threatened the privacy and civil rights of U.S. residents. By the end of 2003, several states and more than 150 communities in the United States had approved resolutions opposing the act. In July, the U.S. House of Representatives approved legislation preventing the federal government from conducting any further secret searches of terrorism suspects.

In July, a report by the Office of the Inspector General, a division of the U.S. Department of Justice, identified more than 30 cases in which department employees had been accused of civil rights and civil liberties violations involving the enforcement of the act. The Office of the Inspector General's report revealed that by June 2003, 34 complaints had been filed that investigators considered credible. The report cited several accusations made by Arab and Muslim immigrants who claimed to have been beaten while held in federal detention centers.

Supporting the act. Growing criticism aimed at the USA PATRIOT Act and the way in which it was being used by the administration of U.S. President George W. Bush led officials to launch an unusual public relations campaign. In August, Attorney General John Ashcroft began a multi-state speaking tour in support of the act. Among other things, Ashcroft argued that the enhanced powers the act granted to federal authorities were essential to prevent future terrorist attacks on the United States. He added that the act had led to the arrests of a number of terrorism suspects. The Justice Department also announced in August the launching of a Web site—www.lifeandliberty.gov—that provided information on key elements of the act and positive articles about the law.

Guantanamo Bay detainees. Justices on the U.S. Supreme Court announced on November 10 that they would hear two appeals over whether hundreds of terrorist suspects held in custody in a prisoner-of-war camp at the U.S. Navy base at Guantanamo Bay, Cuba, were being held unlawfully. The court was expected to begin hearing the cases in 2004.

More than 600 people from about 40 countries were detained at Guantanamo Bay in 2003. According to civil rights advocates, they were denied access to their families or attorneys without being charged with formal crimes. Federal officials had interrogated the detainees—who were believed to be Taliban fighters or members of al-Qa'ida, a terrorist organization—off and on since they were captured in Afghanistan or across the border in Pakistan. Most of the detainees were captured in 2001.

Secret detentions upheld. The U.S. Court of Appeals for the District of Columbia ruled on June 17, 2003, that the federal government can withhold the names of people it has detained on suspicion of terrorism. In his decision, U.S. Circuit Judge David Sentelle ruled that requiring the government to release the identities of detainees could give terrorists information they could use to intimidate witnesses and fabricate evidence. Civil liberties groups argued that the secrecy violated the civil rights of detainees and withheld information that traditionally has been made public.

Presidential powers. The U.S. Court of Appeals for the Fourth Circuit in Richmond, Virginia, on July 9 upheld the power of President Bush to indefinitely detain enemy combatants and deny them access to legal representation, even if they are U.S. citizens. Voting 8 to 4, the court upheld a ruling by a court panel in January.

On December 18, a three-judge panel of the 2nd U.S. District Circuit Court of Appeals in New York City voted 2 to 1 that the president does not have the power to detain U.S. citizens captured as enemy combatants on the battlefield. The court ruled that citizens can be tranferred to civilian authorities who can then file criminal charges.

Racial profiling. The Justice Department on June 17, 2003, issued guidelines that effectively banned the use of racial profiling by federal law enforcement officials. Racial profiling is the act of targeting a person for criminal investigation primarily because of racial or ethnic characteristics. The Justice Department's ban meant that federal law enforcement officials could not use race as a factor when deciding whether to stop motorists and could not rely on generalized racial or ethnic stereotypes when investigating crimes.

■ Geoffrey A. Campbell

See also **Courts; Human rights; Supreme Court of the United States; United States, Government of the.**

Classical music. Like a virus with no

immediate cure, the economic downturn that began infecting musical organizations across the nation several years ago continued to undermine the fiscal health of these institutions in 2003. In certain cases, it proved fatal. By the end of 2003, nearly a dozen debt-ridden American orchestras had either disbanded or were in danger of doing so. The list included the Florida Philharmonic Orchestra of Ft. Lauderdale, San Jose (California) Symphony, Tulsa (Oklahoma) Philharmonic, San Antonio (Texas) Symphony, Colorado Springs (Colorado) Symphony, Savannah (Georgia) Symphony, Louisville (Kentucky) Orchestra, and Rochester (New York) Philharmonic Orchestra. Even those orchestras not on the endangered list battled lagging ticket sales and attendance as well as declining contributions. The worth of their endowment funds also slipped as the stock market declined in 2002 and early 2003.

The musicians of the Houston Symphony Orchestra went on strike for three weeks in March and April and, in the end, were forced to settle for a contract that cut back sharply on their wages and benefits. The musicians of the Pittsburgh (Pennsylvania) Symphony Orchestra, St. Paul (Minnesota) Chamber Orchestra, Oregon Symphony, and the Florida Orchestra of Tampa Bay, also agreed to pay cuts. (The St. Paul players

The Polish opera company Dolnoslaska gives a June performance of *La Gioconda,* written in the 1600's by Italian composer Amilcar Ponchielli. The amphitheater used by the company for its summer opera program, which is built on a peninsula along the Odra River in Wroclaw, Poland, has a three-level stage that extends over the river.

accepted a reduction in salary in return for being given a greater voice in artistic decisions.) Some critics blamed the musicians' union for having pushed management down the road of spiraling deficits. These orchestras, they argued, now find themselves having to pay their musicians top salaries to present more concerts than a shrinking classical music market can support.

Some arts groups cut back on programming to stem the rising red ink. The San Francisco Opera, which faced a $9.2-million deficit in 2003, scaled back from 88 performances of 11 or 12 operas to 65 performances of 9 operas.

Meanwhile, a nationwide crisis in state budgets created what one arts executive called a "devastating" impact on state arts agency funding. As of June, 42 states had cut their funding to the arts, eliminating 13 percent from the $354 million that arts organizations receive in grants from public money.

Music and the mind. Learning music for six years or less can boost verbal memory in children, and the longer the training, the better the memory. That conclusion was the finding of a report in the July issue of the journal *Neuropsychology,* published by the American Psychological Association, based in Washington, D.C. Psychologists at the Chinese University of Hong Kong studied 90 boys, ages 6 to 15. Half of them had been given up to five years of music lessons and training. The other half had no training. Researchers gave them verbal memory tests to see how many words they recalled from a list. The students with

musical training recalled significantly more words than the untrained students. The study also suggested that learning music could help people recovering from brain injuries.

Merger called off. The classical music world was startled by the announcement in June that the boards of directors of the New York Philharmonic and Carnegie Hall, two of New York's oldest and most important cultural institutions, had agreed to merge. Much debate ensued, in and out of the media, as to how Carnegie Hall could find room in its crowded concert schedule to accommodate the Philharmonic, which presents roughly 130 concerts each season. Four months later, the two boards issued a joint statement saying that they had "unanimously agreed to end discussions toward a merger of the two institutions." No reason was given for the collapse of the plan.

New orchestral works. The celebration of Ned Rorem's 80th birthday brought numerous retrospective concerts of the Pulitzer Prize-winning American composer's music, but it also added several new scores to his sizable output. His *Cello Concerto,* written for soloist David Geringas, made its debut in March with the Kansas City Symphony under Michael Stern. The

Philadelphia Orchestra introduced Rorem's *Flute Concerto* with principal flutist Jeffrey Khaner as soloist, Roberto Abbado conducting, in December.

Another distinguished senior American composer, Elliott Carter, had two major premieres. They included his *Boston Concerto,* written for and performed by the Boston Symphony Orchestra under Ingo Metzmacher in April, and *Of Rewaking,* a song cycle on poems by William Carlos Williams, sung by mezzo-soprano Michelle De Young with the Chicago Symphony Orchestra, Daniel Barenboim conducting, in May.

John Adams won the 2003 Pulitzer Prize for his 2002 work, *On the Transmigration of Souls,* a symphonic meditation on the terrorist attacks on the United States in 2001. Conductor Michael Tilson Thomas and the San Francisco Symphony gave the premiere of Adams's orchestral piece, *My Father Knew Charles Ives,* in May. Another new Adams work, *The Dharma at Big Sur,* inspired by the writings of author Jack Kerouac, became the first work to receive its premiere in the new Walt Disney Concert Hall in Los Angeles in October. Esa-Pekka Salonen conducted the Los Angeles Philharmonic, which commissioned the score.

New operas. *Madame Mao,* by the Chinese American composer Bright Sheng, premiered at the Santa Fe Opera in July, with John Fiore conducting. The opera is a largely fictitious musical drama about Jiang Ching, the wife of Chinese ruler Mao Zedong and leader of the infamous Cultural Revolution of 1966-1969, which banned Western influences in China. The Houston Grand Opera in May gave the premiere of *The Little Prince,* with music by Rachel Portman and libretto by Nicholas Wright. The opera is based on the popular 1943 children's novel, *Le Petit Prince,* by French aviator Antoine de Saint-Exupery.

Notable deaths. Luciano Berio, Italy's most important composer of the late 20th century, died in May 2003 at age 77. Lou Harrison, one of the last rugged individualists among U.S. composers, who drew connections between various Western and Eastern cultures, died in February at age 85. Franco Corelli, one of the most exciting operatic tenors of the 1950's and 1960's, died in October at age 82. Rosalyn Tureck, the American pianist and harpsichordist whose more than six decades of performing, researching, and teaching revived an interest in Johann Sebastian Bach's music, died in July at age 88. John Browning, a gifted American pianist who sprang to prominence during the 1950's, died in January at age 69. Harold C. Schonberg, the retired chief music critic of *The New York Times* and an influential voice in arts criticism, died in July at age 87. ■ John von Rhein

See also **Deaths; Los Angeles; Popular music.**

Clothing. See Fashion.

Coal. See Energy supply.

Colombia. The Colombian government made gradual progress in the war against insurgency during 2003, as attested by fewer acts of rebel terrorism than in previous years. Analysts credited the hard-line policies of Colombian President Alvaro Uribe for the reduction in activity. In his first year in office, Uribe deployed more than 45,000 additional soldiers and police officers and was backed by large-scale military assistance from the United States.

Reports of human rights violations by the United Self-Defense Forces, right-wing paramilitary units alleged to have committed numerous past atrocities, also declined in 2003. In November, 800 members of these groups voluntarily surrendered their arms in Medellin in return for entrance into programs aimed at helping people to become productive members of Colombian society.

Referendum fails. Uribe welcomed these positive developments as he wrestled with the daunting task of reducing escalating deficits caused by increased government spending to achieve a military victory in Colombia's 39-year-old war against insurgency. In October, Uribe asked Colombians to approve a referendum that would allow him to freeze government spending for two years. The bill would have also given Uribe the power to make additional cuts to a public sector debt of more than $40 billion.

Despite Uribe's continued popularity with voters for his handling of the war against Marxist insurgents, Colombians did not approve the referendum, forcing the president to accommodate his political opponents in Congress to obtain the necessary cost-cutting powers. In November, Uribe accepted the resignations of three key members of his Cabinet and the commanders of the armed forces and national police, whose unpopularity with legislators helped defeat the October referendum.

Coca eradication. Because of U.S. military assistance of more than $2.7 billion from 2000 to 2002, Uribe predicted that the acreage devoted to the cultivation of coca, the source of cocaine, would be cut in half by the end of 2003. He attributed this success to an ongoing aerial spraying campaign conducted with the help of more than 1,000 U.S. civilians under contract to the U.S. Department of Defense.

Casualties. At least five U.S. military, law enforcement, or contract civilian employees were killed in Colombia in 2003. Three other Americans were taken hostage by the Revolutionary Armed Forces of Colombia (FARC), a Marxist rebel movement, after their helicopter crashed in the mountainous terrain of the southern Caqueta province in February. They remained FARC hostages at the end of 2003.

Apple Computer, Inc., of Cupertino, California, in January 2003 introduced a laptop with a large, 17-inch (43-centimeter) screen. Apple simultaneously came out with a miniature laptop with a 12-inch (30-centimeter) screen.

In February, all 23 Colombian soldiers aboard a Black Hawk helicopter provided to Colombian antidrug forces by the United States were killed when it crashed in bad weather near the town of Curumani, about 300 miles (483 kilometers) northeast of Bogota, the capital. The soldiers belonged to an elite unit that pursued Colombian rebels in mountainous terrain.

Urban violence. A powerful car bomb detonated in the garage of an exclusive social club in Bogota in February 2003, killing 36 people and wounding more than 160 others. A similar bombing in Medellin later in February killed at least 4 people and wounded 32 others. Colombian authorities attributed both bombings to the FARC terrorist rebel organization.

Another bomb exploded in February in Neiva, 145 miles (233 kilometers) south of Bogota, in what was believed to be an assassination attempt on President Uribe. He escaped unscathed, but 16 people were killed and 30 others were injured in the attack.   ■ Nathan A. Haverstock

See also **Latin America.**

Colorado. See State government.
Common Market. See Europe.
Commonwealth of Independent States. See Asia; Azerbaijan; Belarus; Georgia; Kazakhstan; Russia; Ukraine.
Comoros. See Africa.

Computer. A series of computer viruses concerned the computer industry and law enforcement agencies during 2003. The virus infections peaked in August, according to Central Command, Inc., a maker of virus protection software in Medina, Ohio. The bulk of the attacks stemmed from viruses called SoBig and MS Blaster. SoBig was known as a worm because of its ability to "worm" into unprotected computers and copy any e-mail addresses on the machines. At its peak, the worm created millions of e-mailed copies of itself daily, resulting in a measurable slowdown of Internet traffic.

The viruses took advantage of security holes in the Microsoft Windows computer operating system. Microsoft Corporation of Redmond, Washington, offered rewards for information leading to the arrest of virus developers.

Open source ownership lawsuit. A legal challenge to the rights of open source Linux came in March 2003 from The SCO Group of Linden, Utah. "Open source" software is based on underlying programming, or code, that is free to the development industry. Linux is free, but various companies sell applications—programs designed for specific uses, such as word processors and databases—that are built on it.

A key part of SCO's suit stems from the fact that Linux was derived from an older program called Unix. SCO, which claimed it had the rights to Unix, sued International Business Machines (IBM) of Armonk, New York, for $1 billion, charging that IBM had violated SCO's Unix copyright by sharing code with the Linux development community. IBM countersued SCO, arguing that the essence of an open source arrangement is the ability to share software without restraint.

Legal experts believed it would take years for a court ruling on the case. Nevertheless, the ramifications for the open source software development community concerned many developers and enthusiasts.

Takeover battle. A bitter takeover battle was fought throughout the second half of 2003 by Oracle Corporation, a database company in Redwood Shores, California, and PeopleSoft, Inc., of Pleasanton, California. Oracle attempted a hostile takeover of PeopleSoft by purchasing the software company against the wishes of PeopleSoft's executives. PeopleSoft rejected an initial offer of $5.1 billion in early June. Oracle responded by offering ever-larger purchase prices, reaching $7.5 billion by late July. The takeover battle was not resolved by the end of 2003. Industry analysts speculated that Oracle would purchase some other company if the PeopleSoft acquisition did not go through.   ◾ Keith Ferrell

See also **Internet; Telecommunications.**

Congo (Kinshasa).

On April 2, 2003, representatives of all major parties to the five-year civil war in the Democratic Republic of Congo (DRC) signed a comprehensive peace agreement in a ceremony hosted by South African President Thabo Mbeki in Sun City, South Africa. The historic agreement finalized a preliminary pact approved in December 2002. Officials of the Kinshasa government, members of opposition political parties, and rebel leaders agreed to a blueprint for a power-sharing transition government in the DRC and eventual free elections. On April 7, DRC President Joseph Kabila was sworn in as head of the transitional government. The civil war had begun in 1998, with Angola, Namibia, and Zimbabwe on the side of the government in Kinshasa, and with Rwanda and Uganda on the side of competing rebel groups. Aid agencies estimated that the conflict claimed up to 3 million lives.

Massacres. One day after the formal signing of the DRC peace agreement, violence erupted in Congo's troubled Ituri province. United Nations (UN) officials reported that on April 3, 2003, Lendu tribal militias massacred as many as 300 men, women, and children of the Hema tribe near Bunia, the provincial capital. Hema-Lendu ethnic tensions resulted in hundreds of additional killings in Bunia through April and May. At the same time, Uganda withdrew its troops from the

region in accordance with terms of the peace agreement, leaving behind a power vacuum.

UN role. The rapidly deteriorating situation in Ituri prompted widespread criticism of MONUC, the UN peacekeeping force in the DRC. Equipped for peacekeeping duties rather than a combat role, the MONUC soldiers had been unable to stop the killings in Bunia.

To quell further violence in the Bunia region, the UN on May 30 authorized deployment of a European Union-sponsored combat force. The 1,400 heavily armed French-led troops began arriving in Bunia in mid-June and remained until September. On July 28, the UN extended MONUC's mandate in the DRC for one year and increased troop strength from 8,700 to 10,800.

Disaster. At least 120 passengers fell to their deaths over south-central Congo on May 8 when they were sucked out of a Russian-made Ilyushin 76 airplane when the cargo bay door flew open. Hundreds of people had jammed into the modified cargo plane, but the exact number of passengers—and thus the death toll—would never be known, authorities said. At least 180 people were killed on November 26, when high waves driven by a sudden storm caused a dangerously overcrowded ferry to founder on a lake in western Congo.   ◾ Simon Baynham

See also **Africa.**

Congress of the United States.

The U.S. Congress focused its attention on the economy, terrorism, and a war against Iraq during 2003. Lawmakers also considered a wide range of legislation, including bans on certain forms of junk mail and a sweeping change in the Medicare program, which provides health care benefits for elderly persons in the United States.

Economic issues. In an effort to boost a slowly growing economy, both the U.S. House of Representatives and the U.S. Senate approved, on May 23, a bill providing $330 billion in tax cuts and $20 billion in federal aid to states. Among other provisions, the bill accelerated some previously enacted tax cuts, including the child tax credit. The law increased the child tax credit from $600 to $1,000 per child in 2003 and 2004 and authorized the Internal Revenue Service (IRS) to make advance refund payments to the estimated 25 million middle-income families in the United States earning between $27,000 and $110,000 annually. During the summer, the IRS mailed out refund checks for the difference between the old $600 child tax credit and the new $1,000 per child credit. Supporters of the legislation argued that the advance payment of the refund would stimulate the economy. Critics claimed that the measure was unfair because it excluded low-income families with annual

MEMBERS OF THE UNITED STATES SENATE

The Senate of the second session of the 108th Congress consisted of 48 Democrats, 51 Republicans, and 1 Independent when it convened on Jan. 20, 2004. The first date in each listing shows when the senator's term began. The second date in each listing shows when the senator's term expires.

STATE	TERM
Alabama	
Richard C. Shelby, R.	1987-2005
Jeff Sessions, R.	1997-2009
Alaska	
Theodore F. Stevens, R.	1968-2009
Lisa Murkowski, R.	2003-2005
Arizona	
John McCain III, R.	1987-2005
Jon Kyl, R.	1995-2007
Arkansas	
Blanche Lambert Lincoln, D.	1999-2005
Mark Pryor, D.	2003-2009
California	
Dianne Feinstein, D.	1992-2007
Barbara Boxer, D.	1993-2005
Colorado	
Ben N. Campbell, R.	1993-2005
Wayne Allard, R.	1997-2009
Connecticut	
Christopher J. Dodd, D.	1981-2005
Joseph I. Lieberman, D.	1989-2007
Delaware	
Joseph R. Biden, Jr., D.	1973-2009
Thomas Carper, D.	2001-2007
Florida	
Bob Graham, D.	1987-2005
Bill Nelson, D.	2001-2007
Georgia	
Zell Miller, D.	2000-2005
Saxby Chambliss, R.	2003-2009
Hawaii	
Daniel K. Inouye, D.	1963-2005
Daniel K. Akaka, D.	1990-2007
Idaho	
Larry E. Craig, R.	1991-2009
Mike Crapo, R.	1999-2005
Illinois	
Richard J. Durbin, D.	1997-2009
Peter Fitzgerald, R.	1999-2005
Indiana	
Richard G. Lugar, R.	1977-2007
Evan Bayh, D.	1999-2005
Iowa	
Charles E. Grassley, R.	1981-2005
Tom Harkin, D.	1985-2009
Kansas	
Sam Brownback, R.	1996-2005
Pat Roberts, R.	1997-2009
Kentucky	
Mitch McConnell, R.	1985-2009
Jim Bunning, R.	1999-2005

STATE	TERM
Louisiana	
John B. Breaux, D.	1987-2005
Mary L. Landrieu, D.	1997-2009
Maine	
Olympia Snowe, R.	1995-2007
Susan M. Collins, R.	1997-2009
Maryland	
Paul S. Sarbanes, D.	1977-2007
Barbara A. Mikulski, D.	1987-2005
Massachusetts	
Edward M. Kennedy, D.	1962-2007
John F. Kerry, D.	1985-2009
Michigan	
Carl Levin, D.	1979-2009
Debbie Stabenow, D.	2001-2007
Minnesota	
Mark Dayton, D.	2001-2007
Norm Coleman, R.	2003-2009
Mississippi	
Thad Cochran, R.	1978-2009
Trent Lott, R.	1989-2007
Missouri	
Christopher S. (Kit) Bond, R.	1987-2005
Jim Talent, R.	2003-2009
Montana	
Max Baucus, D.	1978-2009
Conrad Burns, R.	1989-2007
Nebraska	
Chuck Hagel, R.	1997-2009
Ben Nelson, D.	2001-2007
Nevada	
Harry M. Reid, D.	1987-2005
John Ensign, R.	2001-2007
New Hampshire	
Judd Gregg, R.	1993-2005
John E. Sununu, R.	2003-2009
New Jersey	
Jon S. Corzine, D.	2001-2007
Frank R. Lautenberg, D.	2003-2009
New Mexico	
Pete V. Domenici, R.	1973-2009
Jeff Bingaman, D.	1983-2007
New York	
Charles E. Schumer, D.	1999-2005
Hillary Rodham Clinton, D.	2001-2007
North Carolina	
John Edwards, D.	1999-2005
Elizabeth Dole, R.	2003-2009
North Dakota	
Kent Conrad, D.	1987-2007
Byron L. Dorgan, D.	1992-2005

STATE	TERM
Ohio	
Mike DeWine, R.	1995-2007
George V. Voinovich, R.	1999-2005
Oklahoma	
Don Nickles, R.	1981-2005
James M. Inhofe, R.	1994-2009
Oregon	
Ron Wyden, D.	1996-2005
Gordon Smith, R.	1997-2009
Pennsylvania	
Arlen Specter, R.	1981-2005
Rick Santorum, R.	1995-2007
Rhode Island	
Jack Reed, D.	1997-2009
Lincoln D. Chafee, R.	1999-2007
South Carolina	
Ernest F. Hollings, D.	1966-2005
Lindsey Graham, R.	2003-2009
South Dakota	
Thomas A. Daschle, D.	1987-2005
Tim Johnson, D.	1997-2009
Tennessee	
Bill Frist, R.	1995-2007
Lamar Alexander, R.	2003-2009
Texas	
Kay Bailey Hutchison, R.	1993-2007
John Cornyn, R.	2003-2009
Utah	
Orrin G. Hatch, R.	1977-2007
Robert F. Bennett, R.	1993-2005
Vermont	
Patrick J. Leahy, D.	1975-2005
James M. Jeffords, I.	1989-2007
Virginia	
John W. Warner, R.	1979-2009
George F. Allen, R.	2001-2007
Washington	
Patty Murray, D.	1993-2005
Maria Cantwell, D.	2001-2007
West Virginia	
Robert C. Byrd, D.	1959-2007
John D. Rockefeller IV, D.	1985-2009
Wisconsin	
Herbert Kohl, D.	1989-2007
Russell D. Feingold, D.	1993-2005
Wyoming	
Craig Thomas, R.	1995-2007
Mike Enzi, R.	1997-2009

MEMBERS OF THE UNITED STATES HOUSE OF REPRESENTATIVES

The House of Representatives of the second session of the 108th Congress consisted of 205 Democrats, 229 Republicans, and 1 Independent (not including representatives from American Samoa, the District of Columbia, Guam, Puerto Rico, and the Virgin Islands) when it convened on Jan. 20, 2004. This table shows congressional district, legislator, and party affiliation. Asterisk (*) denotes those who served in the 107th Congress; dagger (†) denotes "at large."

Alabama
1. Jo Bonner, R.
2. Terry Everett, R.*
3. Mike Rogers, R.
4. Robert Aderholt, R.*
5. Bud Cramer, D.*
6. Spencer Bachus, R.*
7. Artur Davis, D.

Alaska
†Donald E. Young, R.*

Arizona
1. Rick Renzi, R.
2. Trent Franks, R.
3. John Shadegg, R.*
4. Ed Pastor, D.*
5. J.D. Hayworth, R.*
6. Jeff Flake, R.*
7. Raul Grijalva. D.
8. Jim Kolbe, R.*

Arkansas
1. Marion Berry, D.*
2. Vic Snyder, D.*
3. John Boozman, R.*
4. Mike Ross, D.*

California
1. Mike Thompson, D.*
2. Wally Herger, R.*
3. Douglas Ose, R.*
4. John Doolittle, R.*
5. Robert T. Matsui, D.*
6. Lynn Woolsey, D.*
7. George E. Miller, D.*
8. Nancy Pelosi, D.*
9. Barbara Lee, D.*
10. Ellen Tauscher, D.*
11. Richard Pombo, R.*
12. Tom Lantos, D.*
13. Pete Stark, D.*
14. Anna Eshoo, D.*
15. Mike Honda, D.*
16. Zoe Lofgren, D.*
17. Sam Farr, D.*
18. Dennis Cardoza, D.
19. George Radanovich, R.*
20. Calvin Dooley, D.*
21. Devin Nunes, R.
22. Bill Thomas, R.*
23. Lois Capps, D.*
24. Elton Gallegly, R.*
25. Howard McKeon, R.*
26. David Dreier, R.*
27. Brad Sherman, D.*
28. Howard Berman, D.*
29. Adam Schiff, D.*
30. Henry Waxman, D.*
31. Xavier Becerra, D.*
32. Hilda Solis, D.*
33. Diane Watson, D.*
34. Lucille Roybal-Allard, D.*
35. Maxine Waters, D.*
36. Jane Harman, D.*
37. Juanita Millender-McDonald, D.*
38. Grace Napolitano, D.*
39. Linda Sanchez, D.
40. Ed Royce, R.*
41. Jerry Lewis, R.*
42. Gary Miller, R.*
43. Joe Baca, D.*
44. Ken Calvert, R.*
45. Mary Bono, R.*
46. Dana Rohrabacher, R.*
47. Loretta Sanchez, D.*
48. Christopher Cox, R.*
49. Darrell Issa, R.*
50. Randy Cunningham, R.*
51. Bob Filner, D.*
52. Duncan Hunter, R.*
53. Susan Davis, D.*

Colorado
1. Diana DeGette, D.*
2. Mark Udall, D.*
3. Scott McInnis, R.*
4. Marilyn Musgrave, R.
5. Joel Hefley, R.*
6. Tom Tancredo, R.*
7. Bob Beauprez, R.

Connecticut
1. John Larson, D.*
2. Rob Simmons, R.*
3. Rosa DeLauro, D.*
4. Christopher Shays, R.*
5. Nancy L. Johnson, R.*

Delaware
†Michael Castle, R.*

Florida
1. Jeff Miller, R.*
2. Allen Boyd, D.*
3. Corrine Brown, D.*
4. Ander Crenshaw, R.*
5. Virginia Brown-Waite, R.
6. Clifford B. Stearns, R.*
7. John Mica, R.*
8. Ric Keller, R.*
9. Michael Bilirakis, R.*
10. C. W. Bill Young, R.*
11. Jim Davis, D.*
12. Adam Putnam, R.*
13. Katherine Harris, R.
14. Porter J. Goss, R.*
15. Dave Weldon, R.*
16. Mark Foley, R.*
17. Kendrick Meek, D.
18. Ileana Ros-Lehtinen, R.*
19. Robert Wexler, D.*
20. Peter Deutsch, D.*
21. Lincoln Diaz-Balart, R.*
22. E. Clay Shaw, Jr., R.*
23. Alcee Hastings, D.*
24. Tom Feeney, R.
25. Mario Diaz-Balart, R.

Georgia
1. Jack Kingston, R.*
2. Sanford Bishop, Jr., D.*
3. Jim Marshall, D.
4. Denise Majette, D.
5. John Lewis, D.*
6. Johnny Isakson, R.*
7. John Linder, R.*
8. Mac Collins, R.*
9. Charles Norwood, R.*
10. Nathan Deal, R.*
11. Phil Gingrey, R.
12. Max Burns, R.
13. David Scott, D.

Hawaii
1. Neil Abercrombie, D.*
2. Ed Case, D.

Idaho
1. C.L. Otter, R.*
2. Mike Simpson, R.*

Illinois
1. Bobby Rush, D.*
2. Jesse L. Jackson, Jr., D.*
3. William O. Lipinski, D.*
4. Luis Gutierrez, D.*
5. Rahm Emanuel, D.
6. Henry J. Hyde, R.*
7. Danny Davis, D.*
8. Philip M. Crane, R.*
9. Janice Schakowsky, D.*
10. Mark Kirk, R.*
11. Gerald Weller, R.*
12. Jerry F. Costello, D.*
13. Judy Biggert, R.*
14. J. Dennis Hastert, R.*
15. Timothy Johnson, R.*
16. Donald Manzullo, R.*
17. Lane A. Evans, D.*
18. Ray LaHood, R.*
19. John Shimkus, R.*

Indiana
1. Peter J. Visclosky, D.*
2. Chris Chocola, R.
3. Mark Souder, R.*
4. Steve Buyer, R.*
5. Dan Burton, R.*
6. Mike Pence, R.*
7. Julia Carson, D.*
8. John Hostettler, R.*
9. Baron Hill, D.*

Iowa
1. Jim Nussle, R.*
2. Jim Leach, R.*
3. Leonard Boswell, D.*
4. Thomas Latham, R.*
5. Steve King, R.

Kansas
1. Jerry Moran, R.*
2. Jim Ryun, R.*

3. Dennis Moore, D.*
4. Todd Tiahrt, R.*

Kentucky
1. Edward Whitfield, R.*
2. Ron Lewis, R.*
3. Anne Northup, R.*
4. Kenneth Lucas, D.*
5. Harold (Hal) Rogers, R.*
6. Ernie Fletcher, R.*

Louisiana
1. David Vitter, R.*
2. William J. Jefferson, D.*
3. W. J. (Billy) Tauzin, R.*
4. Jim McCrery, R.*
5. Rodney Alexander, D.
6. Richard Hugh Baker, R.*
7. Chris John, D.*

Maine
1. Thomas Allen, D.*
2. Michael Michaud, D.

Maryland
1. Wayne T. Gilchrest, R.*
2. C. A. "Dutch" Ruppersberger, D.
3. Benjamin L. Cardin, D.*
4. Albert Wynn, D.*
5. Steny H. Hoyer, D.*
6. Roscoe Bartlett, R.*
7. Elijah Cummings, D.*
8. Chris Van Hollen, D.

Massachusetts
1. John W. Olver, D.*
2. Richard E. Neal, D.*
3. James McGovern, D.*
4. Barney Frank, D.*
5. Martin Meehan, D.*
6. John Tierney, D.*
7. Edward J. Markey, D.*
8. Michael Capuano, D.*
9. Stephen F. Lynch, D.*
10. William Delahunt, D.*

Michigan
1. Bart Stupak, D.*
2. Peter Hoekstra, R.*
3. Vernon Ehlers, R.*
4. Dave Camp, R.*
5. Dale Kildee, D.*
6. Frederick S. Upton, R.*
7. Nick Smith, R.*
8. Mike Rogers, R.*
9. Joseph Knollenberg, R.*
10. Candice Miller, R.
11. Thaddeus McCotter, R.
12. Sander M. Levin, D.*
13. Carolyn Kilpatrick, D.*
14. John Conyers, Jr., D.*
15. John Dingell, D.*

Minnesota
1. Gil Gutknecht, R.*
2. John Kline, R.

3. Jim Ramstad, R.*
4. Betty McCollum, D.*
5. Martin O. Sabo, D.*
6. Mark Kennedy, R.*
7. Collin C. Peterson, D.*
8. James L. Oberstar, D.*

Mississippi
1. Roger Wicker, R.*
2. Bennie Thompson, D.*
3. Charles Pickering, R.*
4. Gene Taylor, D.*

Missouri
1. William Clay, D.*
2. Todd Akin, R.*
3. Richard A. Gephardt, D.*
4. Ike Skelton, D.*
5. Karen McCarthy, D.*
6. Samuel Graves, R.*
7. Roy Blunt, R.*
8. Jo Ann Emerson, R.*
9. Kenny Hulshof, R.*

Montana
†Dennis Rehberg, R.*

Nebraska
1. Doug Bereuter, R.*
2. Lee Terry, R.*
3. Tom Osborne, R.*

Nevada
1. Shelley Berkley, D.*
2. Jim Gibbons, R.*
3. Jon Porter, Sr., R.

New Hampshire
1. Jeb Bradley, R.
2. Charles Bass, R.*

New Jersey
1. Robert E. Andrews, D.*
2. Frank LoBiondo, R.*
3. H. James Saxton, R.*
4. Christopher H. Smith, R.*
5. Scott Garrett, R.
6. Frank Pallone, Jr., D.*
7. Mike Ferguson, R.*
8. William Pascrell, Jr., D.*
9. Steven Rothman, D.*
10. Donald M. Payne, D.*
11. Rodney Frelinghuysen, R.*
12. Rush Holt, D.*
13. Robert Menendez, D.*

New Mexico
1. Heather Wilson, R.*
2. Steve Pearce, R.
3. Thomas Udall, D.*

New York
1. Tim Bishop, D.
2. Steve Israel, D.*
3. Peter King, R.*
4. Carolyn McCarthy, D.*
5. Gary L. Ackerman, D.*
6. Gregory Meeks, D.*
7. Joseph Crowley, D.*
8. Jerrold Nadler, D.*
9. Anthony Weiner, D.*
10. Edolphus Towns, D.*
11. Major R. Owens, D.*
12. Nydia Velazquez, D.*
13. Vito J. Fossella, R.*
14. Carolyn Maloney, D.*
15. Charles B. Rangel, D.*
16. Jose E. Serrano, D.*
17. Eliot L. Engel, D.*
18. Nita M. Lowey, D.*
19. Sue Kelly, R.*
20. John Sweeney, R.*
21. Michael R. McNulty, D.*
22. Maurice Hinchey, D.*
23. John McHugh, R.*
24. Sherwood Boehlert, R.*
25. James Walsh, R.*
26. Thomas Reynolds, R.*
27. Jack Quinn, R.*
28. Louise M. Slaughter, D.*
29. Amo Houghton, R.*

North Carolina
1. Frank Ballance, Jr., D.
2. Bob Etheridge, D.*
3. Walter Jones, Jr., R.*
4. David Price, D.*
5. Richard Burr, R.*
6. Howard Coble, R.*
7. Mike McIntyre, D.*
8. Robin Hayes, R.*
9. Sue Myrick, R.*
10. Cass Ballenger, R.*
11. Charles H. Taylor, R.*
12. Melvin Watt, D.*
13. Brad Miller, D.

North Dakota
†Earl Pomeroy, D.*

Ohio
1. Steve Chabot, R.*
2. Rob Portman, R.*
3. Michael Turner, R.
4. Michael G. Oxley, R.*
5. Paul E. Gillmor, R.*
6. Ted Strickland, D.*
7. David L. Hobson, R.*
8. John A. Boehner, R.*
9. Marcy Kaptur, D.*
10. Dennis Kucinich, D.*
11. Stephanie Tubbs Jones, D.*
12. Pat Tiberi, R.*
13. Sherrod Brown, D.*
14. Steven LaTourette, R.*
15. Deborah Pryce, R.*
16. Ralph Regula, R.*
17. Timothy Ryan, D.
18. Bob Ney, R.*

Oklahoma
1. John Sullivan, R.*
2. Brad Carson, D.*
3. Frank Lucas, R.*
4. Tom Cole, R.
5. Ernest Jim Istook, R.*

Oregon
1. David Wu, D.*
2. Greg Walden, R.*
3. Earl Blumenauer, D.*
4. Peter A. DeFazio, D.*
5. Darlene Hooley, D.*

Pennsylvania
1. Robert Brady, D.*
2. Chaka Fattah, D.*
3. Philip English, R.*
4. Melissa Hart, R.*
5. John Peterson, R.*
6. Jim Gerlach, R.
7. W. Curtis Weldon, R.*
8. Jim Greenwood, R.*
9. Bill Shuster, R.*
10. Donald Sherwood, R.*
11. Paul E. Kanjorski, D.*
12. John P. Murtha, D.*
13. Joseph Hoeffel, D.*
14. Michael Doyle, D.*
15. Patrick Toomey, R.*
16. Joseph Pitts, R.*
17. Tim Holden, D.*
18. Tim Murphy, R.
19. Todd Platts, R.*

Rhode Island
1. Patrick Kennedy, D.*
2. James Langevin, D.*

South Carolina
1. Henry Brown, Jr., R.*
2. Joe Wilson, R.*
3. J. Gresham Barrett, R.
4. James DeMint, R.*
5. John M. Spratt, Jr., D.*
6. James Clyburn, D.*

South Dakota
†William Janklow, R.**

Tennessee
1. William Jenkins, R.*
2. John J. Duncan, Jr., R.*
3. Zach Wamp, R.*
4. Lincoln Davis, D.
5. Jim Cooper, D.
6. Bart Gordon, D.*
7. Marsha Blackburn, R.
8. John S. Tanner, D.*
9. Harold E. Ford, Jr., D.*

Texas
1. Max Sandlin, D.*
2. Jim Turner, D.*
3. Sam Johnson, R.*
4. Ralph M. Hall, D.*
5. Jeb Hensarling, R.
6. Joe Barton, R.*
7. John Culberson, R.*
8. Kevin Brady, R.*
9. Nick Lampson, D.*
10. Lloyd Doggett, D.*
11. Chet Edwards, D.*
12. Kay Granger, R.*
13. Mac Thornberry, R.*
14. Ron Paul, R.*
15. Rubén Hinojosa, D.*
16. Silvestre Reyes, D.*
17. Charles W. Stenholm, D.*
18. Sheila Jackson Lee, D.*
19. Randy Neugebauer, R.
20. Charlie Gonzalez, D.*
21. Lamar S. Smith, R.*
22. Tom DeLay, R.*
23. Henry Bonilla, R.*
24. Martin Frost, D.*
25. Chris Bell, D.
26. Michael Burgess, R.
27. Solomon P. Ortiz, D.*
28. Ciro Rodriguez, D.*
29. Gene Green, D.*
30. Eddie Bernice Johnson, D.*
31. John Carter, R.
32. Pete Sessions, R.*

Utah
1. Rob Bishop, R.
2. Jim Matheson, D.*
3. Christopher Cannon, R.*

Vermont
†Bernard Sanders, Ind.*

Virginia
1. Jo Ann Davis, R.*
2. Edward Schrock, R.*
3. Robert Scott, D.*
4. J. Randy Forbes, R.*
5. Virgil Goode, Jr., R.*
6. Robert Goodlatte, R.*
7. Eric Cantor, R.*
8. James P. Moran, Jr., D.*
9. Rick C. Boucher, D.*
10. Frank R. Wolf, R.*
11. Tom Davis, R.*

Washington
1. Jay Inslee, D.*
2. Rick Larsen, D.*
3. Brian Baird, D.*
4. Doc Hastings, R.*
5. George Nethercutt, Jr., R.*
6. Norman D. Dicks, D.*
7. Jim McDermott, D.*
8. Jennifer Dunn, R.*
9. Adam Smith, D.*

West Virginia
1. Alan B. Mollohan, D.*
2. Shelley Moore Capito, R.*
3. Nick J. Rahall II, D.*

Wisconsin
1. Paul Ryan, R.*
2. Tammy Baldwin, D.*
3. Ron Kind, D.*
4. Gerald D. Kleczka, D.*
5. James Sensenbrenner, Jr., R.*
6. Thomas E. Petri, R.*
7. David R. Obey, D.*
8. Mark Green, R.*

Wyoming
†Barbara Cubin, R.*

Nonvoting representatives

American Samoa
Eni F. H. Faleomavaega, D.*

District of Columbia
Eleanor Holmes Norton, D.*

Guam
Madeleine Bordallo, D.

Puerto Rico
Anibal Acevedo-Vila, D.*

Virgin Islands
Donna M. Christensen, D.*

**Announced resignation effective
Jan. 20, 2004.

incomes below $27,000. Republicans in the House and Senate also suggested that the slow growth of the U.S. economy in 2003 could have potentially negative implications during the 2004 presidential and congressional elections.

The 2003 tax cut bill also accelerated an earlier tax law to eliminate what is commonly called the "marriage penalty," anomalies in the tax structure that result in married couples paying higher taxes than single taxpayers. Futhermore, the legislation reduced taxes on dividends and *capital gains* (a tax on income from the sale of capital assets, which include stocks, bonds, real estate, and partnerships).

Electronic commerce. The House voted in August to renew a ban on Internet access taxes. The legislation was designed to prohibit states and other political jurisdictions from taxing Internet access or imposing discriminatory taxes on e-commerce. E-commerce, also called electronic commerce or e-business, is the electronic exchange of money or other valuables for goods and services. The ban, which was first passed in 1998, expired in November 2003. The Senate was expected to vote on the bill when Congress reconvened in 2004.

USA PATRIOT Act. The U.S. House of Representatives in July 2003 overwhelmingly approved legislation to roll back some provisions of the USA PATRIOT Act. The act was approved following the terrorist attacks on the United States on Sept. 11, 2001, and had been designed to give the government greater resources to combat terrorism. The 2003 rollback legislation would prevent the federal government from funding secret government searches of terrorism suspects.

Terrorism. A congressional investigative panel on July 24 criticized the U.S. intelligence community for failing to piece together information it had about a terrorism plot that only came to light following the 2001 terrorist attacks. The report, the result of an investigation by the Senate Select Committee on Intelligence and the House Permanent Select Committee on Intelligence, laid much of the blame for the intelligence breakdown on poor communications between the Federal Bureau of Investigation (FBI) and the Central Intelligence Agency (CIA). The report concluded that both the FBI and the CIA had amassed a large amount of information about terrorist activity in 2001, but did not recognize the significance of the information.

War. In October 2003, the House and the Senate approved an $87-billion spending package for Iraq and Afghanistan military and reconstruction efforts as well as other emergency programs in both countries. Congress overwhelmingly approved the funds despite widespread concerns that the request was excessive at a time when the federal deficit was already soaring and funding for domestic programs was tight. However, many in Congress decided to back the funding to support U.S. troops occupying Iraq and to assist the Iraqi people. Other lawmakers opposed the funding as a show of opposition to the war itself. President George W. Bush signed the funding package on November 6.

Iraqi weapons. Congress received a classified briefing on October 2 on the CIA's efforts to find *weapons of mass destruction* (biological, chemical, or nuclear weapons) in Iraq. David Kay, the chief weapons inspector in Iraq, told Congress that a three-month search of the country had yielded no illegal weapons. However, Kay told lawmakers that inspectors had found some evidence that Iraq had intended to develop weapons of mass destruction and had the capability to make them. CIA Director George Tenet appointed Kay to lead the weapons inspection team. The CIA later provided the press with a declassified version of Kay's congressional briefing.

Medicare. Congress in late November gave final approval to a sweeping change in the Medicare program, which provides health care benefits for the nation's elderly. The Senate, in a 54 to 44 vote on November 25, gave final approval to changes in the program that would provide prescription benefits to an estimated 40 million elderly citizens in the United States. The House had approved the plan on November 22.

The prescription benefit, which was scheduled to start in 2006, would cover approximately 75 percent of drug costs up to $2,250 a year. The program would pay 95 percent of the cost of drugs when a person had spent $3,600 out of pocket for drugs.

Taxpayer protection. The House approved legislation on June 19, 2003, designed to protect taxpayers and reform the IRS. Among other things, the legislation authorized the IRS to allow taxpayers to make installment payments and to accept less than taxpayers owe in cases in which full and immediate payments would be ruinous.

Partial-birth abortions. Congress in 2003 approved legislation making it illegal for a physician or any other person to perform partial-birth abortions, except in cases where the procedure is necessary to save the life of a mother. Partial-birth abortions involve a procedure known as *intact dilation and extraction* that is typically carried out in the latter half of a pregnancy. President George W. Bush signed the legislation on November 5.

Do-not-call registry. On September 25, Congress approved legislation specifically authorizing the Federal Trade Commission (FTC) and the Federal Communications Commission (FCC) to establish a national "do-not-call" registry, which in effect would shield those on the list from telephone calls from telemarketers. The bill passed 95 to 0 in the Senate and 412 to 8 in the House.

Some 50 million people in the United States subsequently signed up to be placed on the do-not-call registry. However, the U.S. District Court in Oklahoma City, Oklahoma, ruled in September that the FTC overstepped its authority when it set up the anti-telemarketing system. Several telemarketing companies filed lawsuits claiming that the list violated their constitutional right of free speech. The lawsuits also challenged the authority of the FTC and the FCC to enforce the controversial list.

The 10th U.S. District Court of Appeals in Denver, Colorado, set aside the district court's decision on October 7. The appellate court justices ruled that the FTC could run the program while the appellate justices continued to hear telemarketers' appeals. The registry went into effect in October.

E-mail "spam." The House passed legislation on December 8 that would ban companies from sending unsolicited e-mail advertisements to a person's computer. The messages, known as "spam," are the electronic equivalent of junk mail. Spam messages often use misleading subject lines to entice unwary users to open them. The Senate approved the legislation in November. Some computer experts said that the legislation could lead to a "do-not-spam" registry similar to the do-not-call registry.

Spending bills. President Bush presented his federal budget to Congress on February 3. The proposed $2.25-trillion budget for fiscal year 2004 (Oct. 1, 2003 to Sept. 30, 2004) included tax refunds and more money for the armed forces, domestic security, medical research, and foreign aid. However, Congress approved only 5 of the required 13 spending bills in 2003, notably the Defense appropriation bill, which was signed into law on September 30, and the Homeland Security budget, which was signed into law October 1. Congress approved several temporary spending measures to keep the government running without a budget and was expected to pass the remaining measures when the body reconvened in 2004.

Nomination filibusters. In mid-November 2003, Senate Democrats successfully filibustered to prevent a vote on three of President Bush's nominees to federal appellate courts. Filibustering is the practice by which a minority in a legislature uses extended debate to block or delay action on a proposed bill.

In response to the Democrats' nearly 40-hour filibuster, Senate Republicans made certain that the Senate remained in session. The tactic forced Democrats to stay on the floor at all times to keep the filibuster going. The marathon session began on November 12 and lasted until the early morning of November 14.

The Republicans, who with 51 votes hold only a slim majority in the Senate, were unable to muster the 60 votes necessary to break the filibuster and vote on three of the president's judicial nominees—California Supreme Court Justice Janice Rogers Brown, who was nominated for the U.S. Court of Appeals for the District of Columbia; Carolyn B. Kuhl, a trial judge in California nominated for the U.S. Court of Appeals for the Ninth Circuit in San Francisco; and Texas Supreme Court Justice Priscilla R. Owen, who was nominated for the U.S. Court of Appeals for the Fifth Circuit in New Orleans, Louisiana.

Energy plan. The House reached a compromise in November on a bill to provide a new national energy policy. The plan, which the House passed by a vote of 246 to 180, would give tax breaks to energy producers and create new rules that supporters believe would help reduce the chances of massive power blackouts such as those that hit the northeastern and midwestern United States on August 14. The legislation marked the first overhaul of U.S. energy policy since the 1990's and would provide $23 billion in energy-related tax incentives over 10 years. About two-thirds of the tax incentives would go to coal, oil, and natural gas industries. The legislation would also double the use of corn-based ethanol for gasoline and impose federal rules on the operators of high-voltage power lines to reduce the risk of another massive blackout. The Senate was expected to debate the issue in 2004.

Guilty verdict. Representative Bill Janklow (R., South Dakota) announced on Dec. 8, 2003, that he would resign from office on Jan. 20, 2004. The announcement came hours after a jury convicted Janklow of second-degree manslaughter, reckless driving, running a stop sign, and speeding for an accident in August 2003 that killed a Minnesota man riding a motorcycle. ■ Geoffrey A. Campbell

See also **Armed forces; Cabinet, U.S.; Courts; Democratic Party; Economics; Elections; Immigration; Iraq: A Special Report; People in the news** (Bill Frist); **Republican Party; State government; Taxation; Terrorism; United States, Government of the; United States, President of the.**

Connecticut. See State government.

Daniel Patrick Moynihan:
Death of a Statesman

Daniel Patrick Moynihan, a former United States senator, official in four presidential administrations, diplomat, author, and academic, died on March 26, 2003, at the age of 76. Moynihan was highly regarded by members of both the Democratic and Republican parties and was the only person to ever hold cabinet or subcabinet positions under four successive presidents and in both Democratic and Republican administrations.

Moynihan was born in Tulsa, Oklahoma, on March 16, 1927, the oldest of three children. His father, a newspaper reporter, eventually took a job as an advertising copywriter in New York City. After Moynihan's father deserted the family, his mother moved them to Hell's Kitchen, which was then considered one of Manhattan's poorest neighborhoods. Pat, as he was generally known, went to work at an early age, shining shoes and selling newspapers to help his mother support the family. He graduated from high school and then worked on the docks while attending the City College of New York.

After serving in the U.S. Navy as a gunnery officer from 1944 to 1947, Moynihan attended Tufts University in Medford, Massachusetts, on the G.I. Bill. He studied at the London School of Economics and Political Science as a Fulbright fellow and earned a Ph.D. degree from Tufts University's Fletcher School of Law and Diplomacy in 1961.

Moynihan began his academic career at Syracuse University in Syracuse, New York, where he taught political science. He also taught political science and urban studies at Wesleyan University in Middletown, Massachusetts; Harvard University in Cambridge, Massachusetts;

and the Massachusetts Institute of Technology in Cambridge. Over the years, Moynihan wrote or co-wrote 19 books, including *Family and Nation* (1986), *On the Law of Nations* (1990), and *Secrecy* (1998).

In 1955, Moynihan married Elizabeth Brennan. The couple had three children.

Moynihan entered politics in 1955 as an aide to New York Governor W. Averell Harriman. Through Harriman, Moynihan became involved in John F. Kennedy's presidential campaign. President Kennedy subsequently appointed Moynihan assistant secretary of the Department of Labor. He served in the same position in President Lyndon B. Johnson's administration. Moynihan also served under presidents Richard M. Nixon and Gerald R. Ford.

In 1973, President Nixon appointed Moynihan U.S. ambassador to India, a post he held until 1975. President Ford named Moynihan U.S. ambassador to the United Nations (UN). During his UN tenure (1975–1976), he gained a reputation for being outspoken and even provocative. Moynihan once branded Ugandan President Idi Amin a "racist murderer" after Amin called for the "extinction" of Israel.

In 1976, Moynihan, a Democrat, was elected to the U.S. Senate from the state of New York. He was reelected in 1982, 1988, and 1994. Throughout his years in the Senate, Moynihan focused on work and family issues, on which he had taken controversial stands in the mid-1960's. A work he co-wrote, *The Negro Family: A Case for National Action* (1965), proposed that despite large federal expenditures in the 1960's aimed at reducing poverty in African American families, little significant progress had been made. According to Moynihan, the fact that many such families were headed by single mothers played a significant role. At the time, many liberals denounced Moynihan as a racist. However, many sociologists later noted the same connection between poverty and families headed by single mothers in white as well as African American families.

In 1988, Moynihan was instrumental in enacting the Family Support Act, a revision of U.S. welfare laws. The act provided federal funds to families living in poverty to pay for job and day care programs.

Moynihan expressed a strong interest throughout his political career in preserving architectural landmarks. In the 1960's, he became involved in a project in Washington, D.C., to revitalize and restore Pennsylvania Avenue from the U.S. Capitol to the White House. The redevelopment, which restored office buildings and replaced pawn shops and boarded-up buildings with luxury hotels, shops, and restaurants, was completed in 1989, in time for the inaugural procession of President George H. W. Bush.

Moynihan was also instrumental in the effort to convert the landmark James Farley Post Office building in Manhattan into a new Pennsylvania Station. The old station, which was long considered a gateway for rail passengers arriving in and departing from New York City, had been torn down in 1963. Critics called the decision "one of the great cultural sins of our time." The outcry resulted in the passage of a law to prevent further destruction of historic structures. After Moynihan's death, New York Governor George Pataki and New York City Mayor Michael Bloomberg announced that the new Pennsylvania Station would be called the Daniel Patrick Moynihan Station. It was scheduled to open in 2008.

Upon Moynihan's death, Senate Minority Leader Tom Daschle (D., South Dakota) quoted a description of Moynihan published in the *Almanac of American Politics*—Moynihan was "the nation's best thinker among politicians since Lincoln and its best politician among thinkers since Jefferson." ■ Kristina Vaicikonis

Conservation. Coral reefs and their inhabitants received a lot of attention from conservationists in 2003. The news concerning reefs was both good and bad. Divers found a previously undiscovered reef with an area of 46.3 square miles (120 square kilometers) in Australia's Gulf of Carpentaria in May. The reef was almost 100 feet (30 meters) beneath the surface of the ocean. Scientists believed the formation to be as much as 80,000 years old and filled with many forms of marine life.

The bad news involved studies released in July that showed that coral reefs in the Caribbean Sea were dying. Scientists from the University of East Anglia, in Norwich, England, compiled data from 263 separate reef sites in what they called the most extensive coral study ever conducted in the region. The study revealed that, in some places, up to 80 percent of reefs may have disappeared since the 1980's. The scientists concluded that both disease and weather conditions had damaged the reefs, as well as pollution and overfishing.

The study revealed that coral reefs harbor thousands of species of animals that do not live anywhere else. Destruction of the reefs threatens many species with extinction.

Tropical fish trade. In September 2003, a United Nations (UN) Environment Program study reported that more than 20 million fish were harvested annually to supply the booming marine aquarium trade in Europe and the United States. Scientists concluded that the trade did not threaten fish species with extinction, but could upset the balance of reef communities.

On the other hand, the director of the UN program also stated that the aquarium industry, if managed properly, could support long-term conservation and a sustained use of coral reefs in areas where other options for generating revenue were limited. In Sri Lanka, 50,000 people capture and export ornamental fish yearly. The economic benefits of a responsible trade motivated the residents to keep the coral reefs healthy.

Parks. Representatives from around the world met in September 2003 at the World Parks Conference in Durban, South Africa, to discuss the state of parks and reserves. At the conference, officials of the Brazilian state of Amazonas announced the creation of a 9.4-million acre (3.8-million hectare) reserve in the heart of the Amazon basin.

Ministers from Nigeria and Cameroon agreed to protect the Cross River gorilla, the world's rarest subspecies of gorilla, by jointly enforcing laws against poachers. According to officials with the Wildlife Conservation Society (WCS), based in New York City, fewer than 300 of these gorillas remain alive in the wild.

In March, officials at the Pelican Island National Wildlife Refuge in Florida, the first federal bird reservation, marked the park's 100th anniversary. As of 2003, there were more than 540 national wildlife refuges, including the Mountain Longleaf National Wildlife Refuge in Alabama and Georgia, which U.S. Secretary of the Interior Gale A. Norton established on May 29.

West Nile virus. West Nile disease was increasingly threatening animals in 2003, announced officials with the U.S. Centers for Disease Control and Prevention in Atlanta, Georgia, and the U.S. Department of Agriculture. Scientists said the disease was infecting—and killing—thousands of animals both in the wild and in captivity. These creatures ranged from a wolf in the Denver (Colorado) Zoo to birds of prey in several parts of the United States. The real danger, said scientists, was that the disease could spread among endangered species, such as the California condor. Scientists have also concluded that some mammals, in addition to certain birds, can carry the virus.

Poaching polar bears. Authorities with the U.S. Fish and Wildlife Service reported in 2003 that poachers have ignored the Russian ban on killing polar bears. Illegal hunting may have resulted in the deaths of more than 200 polar bears annually in the area of the Chukchi Sea, between Alaska and far eastern Russia. The law allowed native people in the region to kill a lim-

In January, U.S. Park Service employees herd bison that wandered out of Yellowstone National Park. The Yellowstone herd, the only free-ranging bison in the country, numbers 4,000—1,000 more than the park can bear, according to conservationists. Thinning the herd of the once-endangered species sparked controversy.

hoped that the new visitors would breed with the wild alligators living in the lake and increase the population.

Hippos in trouble. In August, the WWF released an alarming report about the state of hippos in Virunga National Park in Congo (Kinshasa). According to the study, only 1,300 hippos remained of the 30,000 animals that lived there 30 years ago. Scientists blamed poachers, who hunt hippos for their teeth, for the decline in numbers. Environmentalists were concerned that the loss of hippos would skew the ecological balance in the region.

Logging in national forest. In December, the administration of U.S. President George W. Bush set aside rules established in 1997 by U.S. President Bill Clinton that had barred road building in much of Alaska's Tongass National Forest. The Clinton rules also placed 9.3 million acres (3.8 million hectares) of the forest's 17 million acres (6.8 million hectares) off limits to vehicles, effectively barring logging. The Bush administration decision to set aside the roadless rule opened 9 million acres (3.6 million hectares) to road building and 300,000 acres (120,000 hectares) of old growth forest to logging.   ■ Edward R. Ricciuti
See also **Biology; Zoos.**

Costa Rica. See Latin America.
Cote d'Ivoire. See Africa.

ited number of bears for food. However, it appeared to the officials that much of the hunting was being carried out with the aim of selling polar bear hides. Department officials were concerned about a drastic drop in the population if poaching persisted.

Illegal logging. In July, the U.S. Department of State announced it had initiated an effort to help developing countries stop illegal logging, which destroyed wildlife habitats in many parts of the world. U.S. Secretary of State Colin Powell announced the plan with Kathryn Fuller, president of the WWF, formerly known as the World Wildlife Fund. According to a WWF report, illegal logging had decimated forests in more than 70 countries in recent years. The program aimed to help countries stop unlawful logging and trade by promoting good business practices.

"Muddy dragon." In China, they call the alligator "Tu Long," or "muddy dragon." The animal is the only other alligator besides the species found in North America, and destruction of the its habitat has brought the reptiles to the brink of extinction. Only about 130 of them survive in the wild, according to the WCS. In June, three of the Chinese alligators were released into a lake in China by a group of WCS and Chinese scientists. The alligators were fitted with radio collars so scientists could track them. Conservationists

Courts. Questions over religious freedoms
protected by the United States Constitution and the separation of church and state led to several controversial legal rulings in 2003. Courts also continued to sift through the legal fallout from the U.S.-led war on terrorism.

The Ten Commandments. On August 21, the Alabama Supreme Court ordered a 5,280-pound (2,394-kilogram) granite monument inscribed with the Ten Commandments removed from the court's lobby in Montgomery, the state capital. In 2002, the U.S. District Court in Montgomery had ruled that the monument was an unconstitutional endorsement of religion and had to be removed. Alabama Chief Justice Roy Moore, who had the monument installed, appealed the decision. On Aug. 20, 2003, the U.S. Supreme Court refused to stay the ruling requiring the monument's removal. Moore was suspended on August 21 for failing to obey the order. The monument was removed from view on August 27. Alabama's judicial ethics panel removed Moore from the bench in November.

Pledge of Allegiance. In a decision handed down in February, the U.S. Court of Appeals for the Ninth Circuit in San Francisco voted 15 to 9 to uphold a 2002 decision that declared that requiring public school students to recite the Pledge of Allegiance was unconstitutional. A three-judge panel of the appeals court in June 2002 found that the words "under God," which were added by the U.S. Congress in 1954, violated the Constitution's requirement of separation between church and state. On Oct. 14, 2003, the U.S. Supreme Court agreed to hear arguments in early 2004 on the question of whether the Pledge of Allegiance constituted an endorsement of religion.

Secret detention. The U.S. Court of Appeals for the District of Columbia ruled on June 17 that the government of the United States could legally withhold the names of people detained in the U.S. war against terrorism. The court ruled that requiring the government to release the identities of those detained could provide terrorists with information they could use to intimidate witnesses and fabricate evidence, thus reducing national security. Civil liberty groups argued that the secrecy violated the civil rights of detainees.

Presidential powers. On July 9, the U.S. Court of Appeals for the Fourth Circuit in Richmond, Virginia, upheld the power of U.S. President George W. Bush to indefinitely detain enemy combatants and deny them access to legal representation, even if they are U.S. citizens. On December 18, the Second U.S. Circuit Court of Appeals in New York City overturned the decision, ruling that the president does not have the power to detain U.S. citizens captured as enemy combatants.

Also on December 18, the Court of Appeals for the Ninth Circuit ruled that prisoners taken in the war in Afghanistan in 2001 and held at a U.S. Naval base at Guantanamo Bay in Cuba may use the U.S. court system to challenge their detention. In a 2-to-1 decision, Judge Stephen Reinhardt wrote that the assertion of the Bush administration that detainees at Guantanamo Bay may not challenge their detention in U.S. courts is "inconsistent with fundamental tenets of American jurisprudence" and raises "most serious concerns" under international law.

WorldCom settlement. United States Bankruptcy Judge Arthur Gonzalez on Aug. 6, 2003, approved a record $750-million settlement between the U.S. Securities and Exchange Commission (SEC) and WorldCom, Inc., a telecommunications company headquartered in Clinton, Mississippi. The settlement resolved the largest fraud case ever filed by the SEC, which enforces federal laws governing the purchase and sale of *securities* (stocks and bonds). The SEC claimed WorldCom officials had used improper accounting techniques that allowed the company to fraudulently overstate its earnings by more than $11 billion. WorldCom filed for bankruptcy in 2002.

"Do-not-call" list. The Tenth U.S. District Court of Appeals in Denver, Colorado, in late 2003 continued to hear arguments on a national "do-not-call" registry. The list, designed to stop unwanted calls from telemarketers, went into effect in October, but several telemarketing companies filed lawsuits claiming that the list violated their constitutional right of free speech. The lawsuits also challenged the authority of the Federal Trade Commission (FTC) and the Federal Communications Commission to enforce the list. The U.S. District Court in Oklahoma City, Oklahoma, ruled in September that the FTC overstepped its authority when it set up the anti-telemarketing measure, but the appeals court ruled in October that the list could go forward while justices listened to objections.

Same-sex marriage. The Massachusetts Supreme Judicial Court ruled on Nov. 18, 2003, that same-sex couples are legally entitled to wed under the state's constitution. The court ordered the state legislature to draft a law under which same-sex couples could be joined in union.

The International Criminal Court, responsible for trying people accused of war crimes, genocide, crimes against humanity, and other offenses, opened on March 11 in The Hague, Netherlands. The court is the first permanent world body for trying individuals for crimes of concern to the international community.

■ Geoffrey A. Campbell

See also **Crime; Popular music; Supreme Court of the United States; United Nations.**

Cricket. Fears over players' security continued to create problems in international cricket in 2003. In August, Bangladesh became the first cricket side to tour Pakistan since a suicide bomb attack in Karachi in May 2002. During the tour, Pakistan defeated Bangladesh in three tests and five one-day international events.

In September 2003, South Africa initially canceled its tour of Pakistan after another bombing in Karachi, but South African officials changed their minds when Pakistan moved the matches to other parts of the country. Pakistan won the two-match test series, but South Africa won the one-day internationals by 3 matches to 2.

In late October, a junior cricket team from India arrived in Pakistan to participate in a three-nation tournament despite years of very tense relations between the two countries due to a bitter border dispute. It was the first time that a team from India had played in Pakistan since 1998. In a further move toward improving relations between the two nations, India announced in 2003 that its full test side would tour Pakistan early in 2004.

World Cup. Australia defeated India by 125 runs to win the International Cricket Council (ICC) World Cup in Johannesburg, South Africa, on March 23, 2003. Australia reached the finals by defeating Sri Lanka by 48 runs on March 18, while India defeated Kenya by 91 runs on March 20.

The World Cup event was marred by security fears and political problems between February and March in venues in Kenya, South Africa, and Zimbabwe. All 10 match-playing countries participated, in addition to Canada, Kenya, Namibia, and the Netherlands. The 14 teams were split into two groups and were to play 42 matches in the first round. However, because of concerns over security, England declined to play in Harare, Zimbabwe, and New Zealand refused to play in Nairobi, Kenya. By forfeiting its match, England enabled Zimbabwe to take its place in the second round, known as the Super Sixes. New Zealand's decision to forfeit enabled Kenya to reach the Super Sixes stage.

Two of Zimbabwe's top players, Andy Flower and Henry Olonga, created a stir when they wore black arm bands during their opening match against Namibia in protest over the administration of Zimbabwe President Robert Mugabe. They later issued a statement saying that they were "mourning the death of democracy in our beloved Zimbabwe." Following the World Cup, both players sought new careers outside their country.

Other one-day internationals. Australia beat England in the final of the Victoria Bitter series, contested by Australia, England, and Sri Lanka in January.

In May and June, Australia took a 4-0 lead in a seven-match series against the West Indies cricket side. However, the West Indies fought back and won the last three games. England staged two one-day internationals during its summer season. England defeated Pakistan 2-0 in the first match in June and then won the triangular NatWest series against South Africa and Zimbabwe in July.

Test cricket. In January, Australia, the world's top cricket side, won the 2002-2003 Ashes against England by a score of 4-1. Australia won the first four matches, but England salvaged the final match in January, winning by 228, thanks mainly to the fine play of opener Michael Vaughan. Australia's Matthew Hayden topped the batting averages, and Glenn McGrath headed the bowling averages.

In April and May, Australia toured the Caribbean, comfortably defeating the West Indies in the first three tests. However, like England in January, West Indies made a comeback in the fourth and final test, compiling a remarkable 418-7 in the final innings of the match. West Indies won the game by seven wickets. In July, Australia again proved its skill by defeating Bangladesh, winning both tests by an innings.

In October, Australia overwhelmed Zimbabwe in two tests. Matthew Hayden scored 380 on the second day of the first test, the highest individual test score ever, out of a total of 735-6 declared. Hayden struck 38 fours and 11 sixes in his spectacular innings, which broke the record of 375 set by West Indies' Brian Lara in 1994.

South Africa, ranked second among the test-match playing countries, defeated Pakistan in January 2003, winning both tests. South Africa and Zimbabwe later toured England. England won the two tests against Zimbabwe in May and June, but only managed to draw the five-match series with South Africa, both sides winning two tests with one match drawn. Graeme Smith, the South African captain, who was little-known in England at the start of the series, scored two double centuries in his series aggregate of 714 runs. Nasser Hussein resigned as captain of the England side in July after the first test, though he kept his position in the side. Under Hussein, who had taken over in 1999, England compiled a record of 17 test victories, 15 losses, and 13 draws.

Michael Vaughan, who had been the one-day internationals captain, succeeded Hussein. Vaughan led England to Bangladesh in October and November 2003, winning both of the tests over the woefully bad Bangladesh side.

Twenty20. English officials introduced a shortened, 20-over version of cricket in 2003, with the 18 first-class counties competing for the so-called Twenty20 Cup. This spectacle proved to be highly popular, averaging more than 5,000 spectators per match. Several cricket writers predicted that Twenty20 cricket could one day become part of the international game. ■ Keith Lye

Crime. The incidence of serious crime in the United States continued to rise slightly, the Federal Bureau of Investigation (FBI) announced in October 2003. The FBI's 2002 Crime Index reported an estimated 11.88 million serious offenses in 2002, an increase of about one-tenth of one percent over 2001 levels and about 2 percent over 2000 figures. Despite the increases, the crime rate in 2002 was still much lower than it was in the 1990's—4.9 percent below 1998 figures and 16 percent below 1993 statistics.

The annual Crime Index lists reported incidents of four types of violent crime—murder and non-negligent homicide; forcible rape; robbery; and aggravated assault—and three types of property crime—burglary, larceny-theft, and motor vehicle theft. It includes statistics from more than 12,000 law enforcement agencies nationwide.

Violent crimes accounted for 12 percent of the total offenses reported in 2002. According to the FBI, violent crime dropped by 2 percent over 2001 levels, though the number of murders rose by 1 percent and the incidence of rapes jumped by 4.7 percent. Robberies and aggravated assaults fell by 0.7 percent and 1.6 percent, respectively. Aggravated assaults accounted for 63 percent of the violent crimes in the index, the largest single category.

The number of reported property crimes committed in 2002 rose by 0.1 percent over 2001 levels. Burglary was up by 1.7 percent, with motor vehicle theft rising 1.4 percent. Larceny-theft, which includes such crimes as purse-snatching, shoplifting, and bicycle theft, fell by 0.6 percent. Larceny-theft accounted for the largest number of property crimes, 60 percent.

Geographical differences. The southern United States, the nation's most populous region, had the highest overall crime rate, with 41 percent of total offenses reported. Western states, however, showed the largest increase over 2001 levels, 3.3 percent. Murder rates rose there by nearly 6 percent.

Cities with a population of 250,000 or more experienced a 1.8-percent decrease in serious crime, the largest for any population group, the FBI reported. Suburban and rural areas reported slightly higher crime rates.

Hate crimes. The number of hate crimes reported in the United States fell 23 percent in 2002, according to a November 2003 report by the FBI. According to the study, 7,462 incidents involving 9,222 victims were reported to about 12,000 local and state law enforcement agencies, compared with a record 9,730 incidents in 2001. Of the 2002 offenses, 49 percent resulted from racial bias; 19 percent were motivated by religious bias; 17 percent resulted from bias against a sexual orientation; 15 percent were caused by bias against an ethnic group or national origin; and 0.6 percent were motivated by bias against a disability. Eleven percent of the victims were killed.

The largest drop occurred in crimes involving bias against an ethnic group or national origin. That number fell from 2,098 in 2001 to 1,102 in 2002. The number of reported anti-Islamic incidents also fell significantly, from 481 in 2001 to 155 in 2002.

Beltway sniper verdict. A jury in Virginia Beach, Virginia, on Nov. 17, 2003, convicted 42-year-old John Allen Muhammad of murdering 1 of 10 people killed in a three-week spate of shootings in the Washington, D.C., metropolitan area in October 2002. Muhammad was found guilty of shooting Dean Meyers, an engineer from Gaithersburg, Maryland, while Meyers was filling his car's gas tank in Virginia. Three other people suffered serious wounds in the seemingly random shootings, which were committed with a long-distance rifle. The shooters became known as the Beltway snipers. On November 25, the jury sentenced Muhammad to death for the killing.

Muhammad was one of two men accused in the attacks. Lee Boyd Malvo, 18, an illegal immigrant from Jamaica who was arrested with Muhammad, was found guilty in December and sentenced to life in prison for killing another of the victims, Linda Franklin of Arlington, Virginia.

Rudolph captured. A five-year manhunt by hundreds of federal law enforcement agents for alleged bomber Eric R. Rudolph ended in May 2003 with Rudolph's capture by a local police officer in Murphy, North Carolina. Rudolph was a suspect in four bombings, including a deadly attack at the 1996 Olympic Games in Atlanta, Georgia, in which one woman was killed and more than 100 people were injured. Rudolph also was a suspect in two 1997 bombings in the Atlanta area and in the 1998 bombing of a family planning clinic in Birmingham, Alabama. The Birmingham attack claimed the life of an off-duty police officer working as a clinic guard. In June 2003, authorities decided to try Rudolph first in Birmingham.

Green River killer. Gary Leon Ridgway pleaded guilty on Nov. 5, 2003, to murdering 48 women in the Seattle area between 1982 and 1998. The murders were known as the Green River slayings after the river where the first victim was found. Ridgway, who was linked to seven of the murders by DNA and other evidence, admitted to the killings in return for a sentence of life without parole. Prosecutors agreed to forgo seeking the death penalty in order to obtain information about murders in which Ridgway was a suspect but for which they had little physical evidence linking him to the crimes.   ■ Barbara A. Mayes

See also **Civil rights; Prison; Terrorism.**

Croatia. Parliamentary elections on Nov. 23, 2003, ended the three-year moderate coalition government of Prime Minister Ivica Racan. The nationalist Croatian Democratic Union (HDZ), which had governed prior to an election defeat in 2000, won 66 parliamentary seats. Racan's Social Democrats (SDP) took 34 seats, giving the SDP-led coalition a total of 58. HDZ leader Ivo Sanader became the new prime minister.

The HDZ was founded by Franjo Tudjman, Croatia's first president. Although revered by many Croatians for guiding the nation successfully through its war of independence from the Yugoslav federation in the early 1990's, Tudjman drew international criticism for his failure to deliver indicted Croatians to the War Crimes Tribunal in The Hague, Netherlands. Analysts speculated that the return of HDZ nationalists to power could impede Croatia's progress toward European Union (EU) membership, a prime objective of the outgoing SDP-led government.

Application for EU membership. Croatia in February 2003 submitted its application for EU membership. EU officials welcomed the application but admonished Croatian officials to cooperate more fully with the War Crimes Tribunal and said that Croatia's chances for EU admission, possibly as early as 2007, would depend in part upon such cooperation.

The case of retired General Ante Gotovina was key among European leaders' concerns. In July 2001, the tribunal indicted Gotovina on charges related to a 1995 mass killing of ethnic Serbs in Croatia. European authorities kept up pressure on Croatia in 2003 to deliver Gotovina.

Relations with the United States cooled in early 2003 over Iraq. In March, Prime Minister Racan criticized the administration of U.S. President George W. Bush for going to war in Iraq without United Nations (UN) approval, and Croatian President Stipe Mesic said the war "lacked legitimacy." The U.S. ambassador to Croatia, Lawrence Rossin, responded that Croatia might suffer unspecified consequences for its stance. Nonetheless, Croatia permitted overflights of U.S. and British warplanes during Iraq hostilities.

Relations with neighbors. In a historic September visit to Belgrade, President Mesic met with Svetozar Marovic, president of Serbia and Montenegro, the successor state to Yugoslavia. The two leaders mutually apologized for their nations' actions during the 1991–1995 Croatian war and pledged to work for the return of ethnic Serb refugees still displaced from Croatia. According to the UN refugee agency, about 180,000 such refugees remained at large in late 2003.

◾ Sharon L. Wolchik

See also **Europe; Iraq: A Special Report.**

Cuba. Cuban President Fidel Castro was warmly received when he attended the 2003 inaugurations of new presidents in Brazil, Ecuador, and Argentina, whose voters had elected leftist leaders. Castro, the world's longest-ruling leader, was also pleased by the way the new presidents pushed for continental unity in confronting a global trade system that Castro had often criticized as being unjust.

Crackdown on dissidents. Cuban authorities arrested nearly 100 dissidents and independent journalists on various charges of subversion in March 2003. Many of them were summarily sentenced to lengthy prison terms. The Cuban government blamed United States diplomats for helping dissidents on the island to foment a counterrevolution and restricted the movements of all U.S. envoys to Havana, the capital.

United States President George W. Bush retaliated by ordering similar restrictions on Cuban envoys in the United States. He also ordered an end to the granting of licenses, which had enabled U.S. students, educational organizations, and religious groups to travel to Cuba legally despite the continuing U.S. trade embargo.

Trade embargo. The wave of repression in Cuba and the April execution of three Cubans who hijacked a commuter ferry in Havana Bay in an unsuccessful attempt to reach the U.S. mainland halted efforts by U.S. lawmakers who wanted to allow U.S. companies to sell agricultural products to Cuba. Some U.S. political leaders felt that, unless the Cuban regime reversed course, peaceful political and economic change would be an impossibility.

Verdict for family. A court in Miami, Florida, awarded the family of Howard Anderson, a U.S. businessman executed by a Cuban firing squad in 1961, $67 million in damages in April 2003. The family hoped to collect the money from frozen Cuban assets in U.S. banks.

Tourism boom. Despite the setbacks in U.S.-Cuba relations, tourism surged in 2003. Nearly 800,000 tourists visited Cuba between January and April, a 19-percent increase over the same period in 2002. Forty percent of the tourists hailed from European Union nations. To accommodate those visitors, Cuba accorded official status to their new currency, the euro.

Deaths of legends. In 2003, the musical world mourned the deaths of musicians Compay Segundo and Ruben Gonzalez, who were in the 1999 film *Buena Vista Social Club,* a documentary about surviving pre-Castro regime musicians. The album of the same name sold over 2 million copies worldwide. ◾ Nathan A. Haverstock

See also **Deaths; Latin America.**

Cyprus. See Middle East.

Czech Republic. In February 2003, the Czech Republic chose a new president, marking what many observers viewed as the end of an era. Vaclav Klaus was elected to replace President Vaclav Havel, the internationally acclaimed Communist-era dissident who became president in 1989, after the fall of Communism. As president of Czechoslovakia and later the Czech Republic, Havel guided the nation through a difficult transition to a free-market economy and democracy. In 2003, the Czech Republic won approval for entry into the European Union (EU) in 2004.

Presidential succession. In a hard-fought contest requiring three rounds of parliamentary voting, Vaclav Klaus, a former finance minister of Czechoslovakia and a former prime minister of the Czech Republic, won election on Feb. 28, 2003, as president of the Czech Republic. The Czech president is elected by parliament.

Klaus, leader of the center-right Civic Democratic Party, had been prime minister in the mid-1990's but resigned in 1996 due to a fund-raising scandal. As finance minister in the early 1990's, Klaus championed market-oriented policies.

Klaus defeated Jan Sokol, the candidate of Prime Minister Vladimir Spidla's ruling coalition. The coalition received a further blow in July 2003, when a coalition member in parliament defected, erasing Spidla's one-vote majority.

Vaclav Havel reviews an honor guard during a ceremony marking his retirement as president of the Czech Republic. Havel stepped down on Feb. 2, 2003, after more than 10 years as president, first of Czechoslovakia and then of the Czech Republic.

Economic growth in the Czech Republic failed to match forecasts made early in 2003. Growth in the nation's *gross domestic product* (GDP, the value of all goods and services produced in a year) held at just over 2 percent through August. Inflation remained low, but the rate of unemployment held at about 10 percent.

In order to accommodate EU targets, Prime Minister Spidla endorsed austerity measures intended to lower the budget deficit from 6 to 4 percent of the GDP by 2006. The budget cuts sparked a protest demonstration in which more than 10,000 union activists paraded through Prague, the capital, in mid-September, 2003.

Foreign policy. EU and Czech officials signed an accession treaty in April, and Czech voters approved EU membership in June, setting the stage for the Czech Republic's formal entry into the EU in 2004. However, the nation's new status as an EU member-to-be complicated its foreign relations. The United States-led war in Iraq in early 2003 put Czech leaders in the position of trying to maintain good relations both with the United States and EU members critical of the war, such as France and Germany. During the Iraq war, Czech leaders permitted overflights of U.S. and British warplanes and sent a field hospital unit to Iraq. ■ Sharon L. Wolchik

See also **Europe; Iraq: A Special Report.**

Dallas voters went to the polls on May 3, 2003, and reelected Mayor Laura Miller to a full four-year term. Miller took 56 percent of the vote, compared with her main challenger, council member Mary Poss, who received 40 percent. Miller was first elected mayor in January 2002 in a special election necessitated by the resignation of Mayor Ron Kirk.

Voters also approved a $555-million municipal bond issue in 2003. Bonds were issued to provide $199 million for street repairs, $43.2 million for parks, $11.5 million toward a performing arts center, $3 million for a homeless assistance center, $11.8 million for an animal shelter, and $3.2 million to upgrade the city's farmers' market.

Police chief fired. Dallas City Manager Ted Benavides dismissed Police Chief Terrell Bolton on August 26. Benavides cited 20 reasons for the firing, but analysts speculated that the release of a report by the Federal Bureau of Investigation showing Dallas with the highest per capita crime rate among large cities for the sixth straight year may have been the primary cause. Bolton, the city's first African American police chief, had served four years in the post.

Nasher Sculpture Center opens. The $70-million Nasher Sculpture Center opened on October 20 in the downtown Arts District, providing a public venue for a collection that experts have described as one of the finest in the world. The center, funded by Dallas developer and collection owner Raymond Nasher and designed by architect Renzo Piano, features works by Picasso, Matisse, Rodin, Henry Moore, and others. The collection is valued in excess of $400 million.

Performing arts center plan. On Sept. 10, 2003, the Dallas Center for the Performing Arts Foundation released a plan for a new $250-million performing arts complex in downtown Dallas. The plan included a 2,200-seat opera house, a 600-seat theater, and a building for dance and music groups. As of September, the foundation had raised $132 million from private sources and about $20 million in government funding, including money from the May bond issue.

New football stadium? On March 23, Dallas Cowboys owner Jerry Jones unveiled plans for a Dallas-area $1-billion sports and entertainment complex that would replace Texas Stadium in suburban Irving. Sites under consideration for the project included land along the Trinity River near downtown Dallas and expansion of the Las Colinas development in Irving.

The new stadium, which as planned could hold 100,000 fans, would be part of a larger development including a hall of fame museum, entertainment district, recreation lake, and hotels. Funding would come in part from a new county tax on hotel rooms and rental cars, which would require approval by the voters.

Housing lawsuit resolved. On August 12, the city of Dallas settled a 1985 federal lawsuit that determined the city and the Dallas Housing Authority had discriminated against minorities in the placement of public housing. The lawsuit led to demolition of some public housing projects and construction of new units, including scattered-site housing in north Dallas upper-income neighborhoods. In all, the changes mandated by the court cost the city $118 million.

Dallas school lawsuit ends. The federal courts ended 33 years of oversight of the Dallas School District on June 5, 2003, after declaring the schools desegregated. The judicial oversight stemmed from a 1970 lawsuit in which the plaintiffs had argued that the schools in Dallas were segregated and did not provide equal education to minority students.

Police headquarters completed. The $58.9-million Jack Evans Police Headquarters opened on March 17, 2003. Located south of downtown Dallas as part of an economic development plan for the southern part of the city, the new headquarters enabled the Dallas Police Department to move out of the old city hall and an annex to consolidate police operations in one building.

■ Henry Tatum

See also **City.**

Dance. The challenge of maintaining the creative legacy of a master American choreographer after his death was resolved in a unique way in 2003. The company of Alwin Nikolais, the founder of multimedia dance in the United States, went out of business and his vast repertory remained unperformed after his death in 1993. However, in 2002, his long-time collaborator, Murray Louis, decided to entrust Nikolais's work to another troupe, the Ririe-Woodbury Dance Company of Salt Lake City, Utah. Louis chose the group to revive seven of Nikolais's dances, spanning 50 years, because Nikolais developed much of his unique dance vocabulary and theatrical ideas while working with Shirley Ririe and Joan Woodbury in the 1960's. The resulting *Alwin Nikolais: A Celebration Tour* kicked off on Sept. 24, 2003, in Salt Lake City, then traveled to Colorado, Virginia, California, and finally the Joyce Theater in New York City.

Two major ballet institutions. Neither the American Ballet Theater (ABT) nor the New York City Ballet produced important new works during 2003. In fact, ABT's two premieres, *Here-After* and *Artemis,* shown during the company's two-month spring season at the Metropolitan Opera House in New York's Lincoln Center, were roundly panned by the critics. As in several previous years, it was only the troupe's sensational dancers—especially the men—who kept the stage lively. The talents and personalities of four of those men—Jose Manuel Carreno, from Cuba; Angel Corella from Spain; Vladimir Malakhov from Ukraine; and Ethan Stiefel of the United States—were celebrated in a PBS documentary entitled *Born To Be Wild: The Leading Men of ABT.* Broadcast nationally in February, the show provided an intimate glimpse of the dancers in their home environments as well as on the stage. A specially choreographed piece by Mark Morris for the virtuosos concluded the film.

The New York City Ballet produced what is a rarity for the troupe, a ballet designed for children. Christopher Wheeldon's *Carnival of the Animals,* set to the popular score by French composer Camille Saint-Saens, bowed on May 14 during the company's two-month run at Lincoln Center's New York State Theater. Featuring the actor John Lithgow as the narrator with a script he had written, *Carnival of the Animals* tells of a boy who falls asleep in New York City's Museum of Natural History and dreams about his family, teachers, and friends, who curiously resemble the animals in the museum. Critics described the ballet as charming, if slight.

The Dance Theater of Harlem looked to Broadway for its major production of the year—Michael Smuin's *St. Louis Woman: A Blues Bal-*

Virginie Mecene dances the part of the bride in one of the late Martha Graham's most famous works, *Appalachian Spring*, in January at the Joyce Theater in New York City. Graham's works had not been performed for three years, as her dance company and her sole designated heir, Ron Protas, fought a court battle over ownership of her works.

let. Based on the Harold Arlen/Johnny Mercer 1946 musical *St. Louis Woman,* the ballet tells a love story set in the black underworld of a saloon in St. Louis, Missouri. After premiering on July 8, 2003, during the Lincoln Center Festival of the Arts, the company took the ballet on tour in the United States and London.

The Kennedy Center in Washington, D.C., introduced the unusual format of shared programs for its major dance events. From March 4 to 16, three companies shared each bill of the International Ballet Festival. On one program, ABT performed Jerome Robbins's *Fancy Free;* the Royal Danish Ballet, excerpts from August Bournonville's *Napoli;* and the Bolshoi, several short pieces. The Kirov Ballet, Miami City Ballet, and Adam Cooper and Company shared the second bill. (Cooper performed as the swan in an all-male *Swan Lake*.) Of special note was a Bolshoi solo, *Narcissus,* choreographed by Kasyan Goleizovsky. Goleizovsky was considered a prime influence on George Balanchine, but his work is rarely performed outside of Russia.

The Houston Ballet and the Paul Taylor Dance Company, a modern dance group, teamed up for a week of performances in April, during which Taylor premiered *In the Beginning* to music by Carl Orff. Taylor first created the work with his own dancers. However, it was performed during the premiere by the Houston Ballet. In typical

Taylor vein, this dance about the Biblical creation was both humorous and serious.

Forsythe and the Frankfurt Ballet. On September 30, the Frankfurt Ballet of Germany, directed by U.S.-born choreographer William Forsythe, began what was dubbed as its farewell engagement in North America. Although many U.S. ballet companies have regularly performed Forsythe's works, he has served as director of the Frankfurt Ballet since 1984, developing an avant-garde and controversial style of ballet that put Frankfurt in the cultural spotlight of Europe. However, in 2002, Forsythe and Frankfurt's city government, which heavily subsidized the troupe, became engaged in a bitter, publicized dispute about future funding and the company's artistic profile. Forsythe announced his decision to leave.

During the farewell tour, the Frankfurt Ballet opened the Next Wave Festival at the Brooklyn Academy of Music in New York City with four U.S. premieres. One of these pieces, "One Flat Thing, reproduced," ended with the dancers hauling 20 metal tables across the stage, releasing a thunderous clap of noise. Critics noted it was a fitting finale to Forsythe's provocative career in Germany.

Changes in artistic leadership occurred among U.S. dance companies as well. In July 2003, Stanton Welch replaced Ben Stevenson as artistic director of the Houston Ballet. Having already created several works for the company, the Australian-born choreographer was no stranger to the Texans. Also in July, Christopher Stowell, a principal dancer with the San Francisco Ballet, replaced James Canfield as head of Oregon Ballet Theater in Portland. Stowell's parents became directors of the Pacific Northwest Ballet in Seattle in 1977.

In April 2003, nationally recognized choreographer Eliot Feld announced that he was suspending operations of New York City's Ballet Tech performance company for the 2003-2004 season because of lack of financial support.

Balanchine. Celebrations marking the centennial of George Balanchine's birth (1904-1983) got a head start in 2003. From July 30 to August 5, the New York City Ballet, which Balanchine founded, performed during the White Nights Festival in St. Petersburg, Russia. The festival was staged to celebrate the city's 300th anniversary. The company danced in the Maryinsky Theater, in which Balanchine studied as a child.

A symposium on the life and work of Balanchine was held in Ann Arbor, Michigan, from October 31 to November 1. The Suzanne Farrell Ballet, directed by Farrell, a protege of Balanchine and a source of inspiration for him, performed. ■ Nancy Goldner

DEATHS

in 2003 included those listed below, who were Americans unless otherwise indicated.

Agnelli, Giovanni (1921–January 24), Italian businessman who transformed the family-owned Fiat Auto into a multinational conglomerate and became a symbol of the postwar recovery of the Italian economy.

Amin, Idi (1925?–August 16), African strongman whose reign of terror in Uganda made his name a byword for brutality.

Atkins, Cholly (Charles Sylvan Atkinson) (1913–April 19), half of the legendary dance duo of Coles and Atkins and choreographer who orchestrated the movements of such Motown groups as Smokey Robinson and the Miracles and the Supremes.

Atkins, Robert C. (1930–April 17), physician whose unorthodox diet plan made its creator a best-selling author.

Axelrod, George (1922–June 21), playwright— *The Seven Year Itch* (1952), *Will Success Spoil Rock Hunter?* (1955), *Goodbye Charlie* (1959)—who wrote the screenplays for *Breakfast at Tiffany's* (1961) and *The Manchurian Candidate* (1962).

Ballard, Hank (John H. Kendricks) (1927?–March 2), singer and songwriter whose hit song "The Twist," recorded by Ballard in 1958 and by Chubby Checker in 1959, sparked a national dance craze.

Barbieri, Fedora (1920–March 4), famed Italian mezzo-soprano whose enormous repertory included 109 roles.

Bates, Sir Alan (1934–December 27), English stage actor who became a major film star of the 1960's in *Zorba the Greek* (1964), *Georgy Girl* (1966), and *Women in Love* (1969).

Borel, Armand (1923–August 11), Swiss-born mathematician who played an important role in the evolution of modern mathematics through his study of certain mathematical symmetries, known as Lie groups.

Braidwood, Robert J. (1907–January 15) and **Linda S. Braidwood** (1909–January 15), husband-and-wife team of archaeologists who helped transform their field through investigations of humankind's transition from nomadic hunting and gathering to members of communities engaged in farming. Both died on the same day in the same hospital after 66 years of marriage.

Brakhage, Stan (1933–March 9), experimental filmmaker who revolutionized avant-garde films with the critically acclaimed *Dog Star Man* (1964).

Brinkley, David (1920–June 11), droll and iconic television newscaster who rose to national attention as half of NBC's Huntley-Brinkley anchor team.

Brockhouse, Bertram H. (1918–October 13), Canadian physicist who shared the 1994 Nobel Prize in physics for developing a technique to measure the atomic structure of matter.

Bronson, Charles (Charles Buchinsky) (1921–August 30), coal miner turned actor who became internationally known for his tough-guy roles in such films as *The Magnificent Seven* (1960) and *Death Wish* (1974).

Brooks, Herb (1937–August 11), coach who melded an unheralded group of hockey players into the "Miracle on Ice" team that won the gold medal at the 1980 Winter Olympics.

Brooks, Rand (1918–September 1), actor who played Scarlett O'Hara's hapless first husband in *Gone With the Wind* (1939) and Randy Boone on the television series "Rin Tin Tin."

Buchholz, Horst (1933–March 3), German star who appeared in *The Magnificent Seven* (1960).

Carney, Art (1918–November 9), comedic actor who played Ed Norton on the TV series "The Honeymooners" and who won the 1974 Academy Award for best actor for *Harry and Tonto*.

Carter, Benny (1907–July 12), musician and one of the preeminent alto saxophonists in jazz whose compositions and arrangements helped lay the foundation for the swing era.

Carter, Nell (1948–January 23), singer-actress who played the sassy housekeeper in the television sitcom "Gimme a Break!" and won a Tony Award in 1978 for her role in the Broadway musical *Ain't Misbehavin'*.

Cash, Johnny (1932–September 12), singer whose unmistakable baritone and highly rhythmic accounts of the struggles of everyday people made him a pop icon. Also see Popular music: Portraits.

Cash, June Carter (1929–May 15), singer and member of country music's pioneering Carter family who co-composed "Ring of Fire" and shared Grammy Awards with husband Johnny Cash for "If I Were a Carpenter" and "Jackson."

Chiang Soong Mei-ling (Madame Chiang Kai-shek) (1897–October 23), pivotal player in the struggle for control of post-imperial China who won a large U.S. following for the stand she and her husband, the leader of Chinese Nationalists, took against the Chinese Communists.

Chuganji, Yukichi (1889–September 28), retired Japanese silkworm breeder who, at 114, was the world's oldest man.

Clement, Hal (Harry Clement Stubbs) (1922–October 29), respected science

David Brinkley, newscaster

writer whose novels, notably *Mission of Gravity*, accentuated the science in science fiction.

Connor, George (1925–April 1), Hall of Fame All-American tackle (Chicago Bears 1948–1955) who was considered one of the great linebackers in professional football history.

Coors, Joseph, Sr. (1917?–March 15), brewer who turned his family's beer into a national brand and founded the Heritage Foundation, a conservative think tank.

Corelli, Franco (1921–October 29), Italian tenor whose voice and matinee-idol looks made him a favorite during his 15 seasons (1961-1976) with New York City's Metropolitan Opera.

Art Carney, comedian

June Carter Cash and Johnny Cash, country musicians

Celia Cruz, musician

Hume Cronyn, actor

Coxeter, Harold Scott MacDonald (1907–March 31), English-born Canadian mathematician and geometrician whose ideas later inspired the drawings of artist M. C. Escher as well as the architectural forms of inventor R. Buckminster Fuller.

Crain, Jeanne (1925–December 15), actress of the 1940's and 1950's who was best known for two 1949 films, *A Letter to Three Wives* and *Pinkie*.

Crenna, Richard (1926–January 17), actor who graduated from the radio and television comedy "Our Miss Brooks" to dramatic roles in such films as *Body Heat* (1981).

Cronyn, Hume (1911–June 15), Canadian-born character actor and playwright who most famously appeared with wife Jessica Tandy in such stage successes as *The Four Poster* (1951) and *A Delicate Balance* (1967) and in more than 40 films.

Cruz, Celia (1924–July 16), flamboyant Cuban musician whose role in helping to reinvent Latin music earned her the title "Queen of Salsa."

Dalzel-Job, Patrick (1913–October 12), British World War II hero who carried out daring exploits behind enemy lines and upon whom Ian Fleming based James Bond.

De Brunhoff, Cecile (1903?–April 7), French mother who created a bedtime story that her husband, artist and illustrator Jean de Brunhoff, transformed into Babar the Elephant.

DeBusschere, Dave (1940–May 14), basketball Hall of Fame forward who helped propel the New York Knicks to their only NBA championships, in 1970 and 1973, and who was the youngest coach to lead an NBA team.

Dillon, C. Douglas (1909–January 10), investment banker who served as secretary of the U.S. Treasury in the administrations of presidents John F. Kennedy and Lyndon B. Johnson.

Djindjic, Zoran (1952–March 12), pro-Western prime minister of Serbia who in 2000 spearheaded the successful revolt against former President Slobodan Milosevic.

Doby, Larry (1923–June 18), Hall of Fame outfielder with the Cleveland Indians who was named an all-star 7 times in his 13-year career and who was the first African American in baseball's American League.

Dugan, Alan (1923–September 3), poet whose ironic and unsentimental verse was awarded National Book Awards in 1962 and 2001.

Larry Doby, baseball player

Buddy Ebsen, actor

Dunne, John Gregory (1932–December 30), novelist and journalist who often collaborated with his wife, Joan Didion, on screenplays, including *True Confessions* (1981).

Ebsen, Buddy (Christian Rudolph Ebsen, Jr.) (1908–July 6), Broadway and film dancer who achieved his greatest fame in television, as Jed Clampett on "The Beverly Hillbillies" and as the aging detective "Barnaby Jones."

Ederle, Gertrude (1905–November 30), swimmer who in 1926 found herself to be a media sensation—"America's best girl"—after becoming the first woman to swim the English Channel.

Elam, Jack (1916?–October 20), lazy-eyed actor who generally played villains in some 200 television episodes and 100 films.

Fast, Howard (1914–March 12), author whose best-selling novels, including *Citizen Tom Paine* (1943) and *Spartacus* (1953), were grounded in

Althea Gibson, tennis player

Gregory Hines, actor and dancer

themes of liberty and human rights.

Fisher, Doris (1915–January 15), song-writer of a string of 1940's hits, including "That Old Devil Called Love" and "You Always Hurt the One You Love."

Foss, Joe (1915–January 1), World War II Marine fighter pilot who won the Medal of Honor and went on to become governor of South Dakota, commissioner of the American Football League, and head of the National Rifle Association.

Freeman, Orville L. (1918–February 20), former governor of Minnesota who served as secretary of the Department of Agriculture in the John F. Kennedy and Lyndon Johnson administrations.

Freestone, George F. (1898–February 8), oldest known Boy Scout. Freestone joined the Boy Scouts of America in 1910 and remained active for 92 years.

Gardner, Herb (1934–September 24), playwright whose Broadway successes included *A Thousand Clowns* (1962) and *I'm Not Rappaport* (1985).

Gelber, Jack (1932–May 9), playwright whose highly realistic work *The Connection*, produced off-Broadway in 1959, sent off shock waves that proved highly influential on contemporary American theater.

Gibb, Maurice (1949–January 12), British-born composer and one of the three Bee Gees, a group that sold 120 million records, including *Saturday Night Fever,* one of the best-selling movie soundtracks of all time.

Gibson, Althea (1927–September 28), preeminent figure in women's tennis in the late 1950's who was the first African American to win the Wimbledon and U.S. Open championships.

Gibson, Don (1928–November 17), country music singer and composer of "Sweet Dreams," "Oh Lonesome Me," and "I Can't Stop Loving You."

Gionfriddo, Al (1922–March 14), Brooklyn Dodger outfielder who made one of the great catches in baseball when he took a game-tying home run away from Joe DiMaggio in Game 6 of the 1947 World Series.

Graham, Winston (1910–July 10), British author of such popular novels as the "Poldark" series about life in Cornwall in the late 1700's and *Marnie*, upon which an Alfred Hitchcock film was based.

Hackett, Buddy (Leonard Hacker) (1924–June 30), stand-up comedian and rubber-faced clown who appeared in such films as *The Music Man* (1962) and *It's a Mad, Mad, Mad, Mad World* (1963).

Harrison, Lou (1917–February 2) influential classical composer whose innovative but melodic music bridged Eastern and Western forms.

Hatfield, Bobby (1940–November 5), half of the vocal duo the Righteous Brothers whose 1964 hit "You've Lost That Lovin' Feeling" received more airplay than any other song in U.S. radio history.

Hepburn, Katharine (1906–June 29), unique and spirited star whom many critics considered the preeminent film actress of Hollywood's golden era. Also see Motion pictures: A Special Report.

Hiller, Dame Wendy (1912–May 14), distinguished British stage and screen actress whom George Bernard Shaw chose to play Eliza Doolittle in *Pygmalion* (1936) and heiress-turned-Salvation Army officer in the film *Major Barbara* (1940).

Hines, Gregory (1946–August 9), singer and actor dubbed the greatest tap dancer of his generation who successfully crossed from musical theater to film to television.

Hines, Jerome (1921–February 4), bass who was considered one of the great opera singers of his generation and who had the longest career—41 years—of any principal singer in the history of New York City's Metropolitan Opera.

Hirschfeld, Al (1903–January 20), artist whose show business caricatures captured the glamour and spirit of the Broadway theater and the personality of its performing artists for much of the 20th century. Also see Theater: Portraits.

Hongo, Kamato (1887–October 31), Japanese woman who, at 116 years old, was believed to be the world's oldest person.

Hope, Bob (Leslie Townes Hope) (1903–July 27), English-born entertainer whose masterful delivery of the comic monologue and one-liner carried him from vaudeville to stardom on stage, radio, film, and television. Also see Deaths: A Special Report.

Jackson, Maynard, Jr. (1938–June 23), politician who, at age 35 in 1973, made history with his election as Atlanta's first African American mayor.

Janeway, Gertrude (1909–January 17), the last widow of a Union veteran of the U.S. Civil War and the last recipient of a Civil War pension. Janeway married the 81-year-old Civil War veteran in 1927.

Jeter, Michael (1952–March 30), award-winning actor who specialized in inept, nerdy characters on television—"Evening Shade," "Sesame Street"—and was featured in such films as *The Fisher King* (1991) and *The Green Mile* (1999).

Katz, Sir Bernard (1911–April 20), German-born British scientist who shared the 1970 Nobel Prize in physiology or medicine for his explanation of how the brain transmits messages to muscles.

Kazan, Elia (Elia Kazanjoblous) (1909–September 28), Turkish-born stage and screen director who was one of the most influential artists of his generation. Kazan's triumphs included the original Broadway productions of *A Streetcar Named Desire* (1947) and *Death of a Salesman* (1949)

Elia Kazan, director

and such films as *On the Waterfront* (1954) and *Splendor in the Grass* (1961).

Kelly, Craig (1966–January 20), athlete credited with making snowboarding a mainstream sport who died in an avalanche in the Canadian Rockies.

Kempson, Rachel (1910–May 24), English actress who was married to actor Michael Redgrave and was the mother of Vanessa, Lynn, and Corin Redgrave.

Kerr, Jean (1922–January 5), humorist who gained fame with the 1957 best seller *Please Don't Eat the Daisies* followed by the Broadway comedy *Mary, Mary* (1961).

King, Earl (1934–April 17), New Orleans guitarist and prolific composer of such rhythm-and-blues standards as "Those Lonely, Lonely Nights" and "Come on Baby, Let the Good Times Roll."

Lange, Hope (1931–December 19), film actress who was nominated for an Academy Award in 1957 for the role of Salena Cross in *Peyton Place*.

Long, Russell B. (1918–May 9), former U.S. senator from Louisiana who devised the "earned-income tax credit." Long was the only person ever preceded in the Senate by both parents, the legendary Huey P. Long and Rose McConnell Long.

Longden, Johnny (1907–February 14), British-born jockey who rode 6,032 winners, including Count Fleet, the 1943 Triple Crown winner, in a racing career that spanned 40 years.

Loudon, Dorothy (1933–November 14), Broadway actress and singer who won a Tony Award in 1977 for her role as a mean-spirited manager of an orphanage in the musical *Annie*.

Lubetzky, Seymour (1898–April 5), librarian whose *Rules for Descriptive Cataloging* (1949) and *Cataloging Rules and Principles* (1953) provided the foundation for the modern Anglo-American book cataloging system. Also see Library: Portraits.

Dame Wendy Hiller, actress

MacKenzie, Gisele (1927–September 5), Canadian singer and star of early 1950's television programs, including "Your Hit Parade."

Maddox, Lester (1915–June 25), Atlanta restaurateur whose refusal to serve African Americans made him a symbol of segregationist defiance and propelled him into the Georgia governor's mansion.

Makarov, Oleg (1933–May 28), Russian cosmonaut who survived when the booster rocket carrying his space capsule exploded after liftoff.

Mann, Herbie (Herbert Solomon) (1930–July 1), innovative flutist who formulated a jazz style for the flute that incorporated a wide and international range of musical influences.

Marshall, William (1924–June 11), stage and film actor who was hailed as the "best Othello of our time" and who won further renown for his characterizations of such African American leaders as Frederick Douglass and Massachusetts Senator Edward Brooke.

Mauldin, Bill (1921–January 22), Pulitzer prize-winning political cartoonist who was best known for creating, while an Army sergeant in World War II, the characters Willie and Joe, who came to symbolize the wartime spirit of the American infantryman.

McClendon, Sarah (1910–January 8), long-serving correspondent with the White House press corps who covered and lectured every president from Franklin D. Roosevelt to George W. Bush.

McCloskey, Robert (1914–June 30), award-winning author and illustrator of such classic children's books as *Make Way for Ducklings, Homer Price,* and *Blueberries for Sal.*

McDonald, Frank (1896–August 23), Australian hero who was that country's last surviving World War I veteran to have been cited for bravery.

Merton, Robert K. (1910–February 23), Columbia University sociologist and author of the highly influential *On the Shoulders of Giants* who invented the focus group and coined the terms "self-fulfilling prophecy" and "role model."

Modigliani, Franco (1918–September 25), Italian-born economist who won the Nobel Prize for his research on why people save money for their old age.

Moynihan, Daniel Patrick (1927–March 26), academic, diplomat, and intellectual contrarian who served as an adviser to four consecutive presidents, from John F. Kennedy to Gerald Ford, and was elected to four terms in the U.S. Senate (D., New York). Also see United States, Government of the: Portraits.

Murie, Margaret (1902–October 19), conservationist and Wilderness Society official who helped preserve millions of acres of U.S. land through her support for the Arctic National Wildlife Refuge and passage of the Wilderness Act.

Neilson, Roger (1934–June 21), highly innovative Canadian hockey coach who led eight National Hockey League teams.

O'Bannon, Frank L. (1930–September 13), governor of Indiana who entered state politics in 1970 as a Democrat who succeeded his father in the state senate.

O'Connor, Donald (1925–September 27), song-and-dance man whose career began at age 1 in vaudeville and peaked with such 1950's movie musicals as *There's No Business Like Show Business* and *Singin' in the Rain* with O'Connor's showstopping "Make 'Em Laugh" number.

Omarr, Sydney (Sidney Kimmelman) (1926–January 2), astrologer whose horoscopes were carried by more than 200 newspapers and whose books sold more than 50 million copies.

Palmer, Robert (1949–September 26), debonair British rock singer who rose to fame in the 1980's with such hits as "I Didn't Mean to Turn You On" and "Addicted to Love."

Parker, Suzy (Cecilia Anne Renee Parker) (1932–May 3), cover girl—dubbed "the" model of the 1950's —and actress whose life served as the basis for the 1957 movie musical *Funny Face.*

Paycheck, Johnny (Donald Eugene Lytle) (1938–February 19), controversial singer who became a

Suzy Parker, model

Gregory Peck, actor

major figure in country music's "outlaw" movement with such hits as "Don't Take Her, She's All I Got" and "Take This Job and Shove It."

Peck, Gregory (1916–June 12), film star whose craggy good looks and understated acting in such films as *Gentleman's Agreement* (1947), *Cape Fear* (1962), and *To Kill a Mockingbird* (1962) fostered a screen image of decency and moral courage.

Phillips, Sam (1923–July 30), Sun Records founder who was instrumental in blending blues and country music into what became known as rock 'n' roll and who launched the careers of Elvis Presley, Johnny Cash, Carl Perkins, Jerry Lee Lewis, Roy Orbison, and Charlie Rich.

Plimpton, George (1927–September 25), literary figure who cofounded and edited *The Paris Review* and wrote several books of so-called "participatory journalism," including the best-selling *Paper Lion.*

Pouch, Richard (1904–June 24), conservationist who was a founder of the Nature Conservancy and other important preservation groups.

Prigogine, Ilya (1917–May 28), Russian-born scientist who won the 1977 Nobel Prize in chemistry for his research on how life arises in apparent defiance of the laws of physics.

Ralston, Vera Hruba (1923–February 9), Czech-born ice-skating star who in the 1940's and 1950's starred in a series of "B" movies.

Reeves, Connie (1901–August 17), America's oldest working cowgirl, who died in San Antonio, Texas, at age 101—12 days after being thrown by her horse, Dr. Pepper.

Regan, Donald (1918–June 10), financier and former secretary of the U.S. Treasury who served as President Ronald Reagan's chief of staff.

Riefenstahl, Leni (1902–September 8), German filmmaker and photographer whose masterful documentaries *Triumph of the Will* (1934) and *Olympia* (1938) earned her fame as a cinematic genius and infamy as a Nazi propagandist.

Ritter, John (1948–September 11), television, film, and stage actor who found instant fame playing the lovably goofy Jack Tripper in the 1970's television sitcom "Three's Company."

Rogers, Mister (Fred McFeely Rogers) (1928–February 27), composer and ordained minister who created the quiet but revolutionary "Mister Rogers' Neighborhood," which ran on public television from 1968 to 2001. Also see Television: Portraits.

Rostow, Walt W. (1916–February 13), scholar and author who served as a key national security adviser to presidents John F. Kennedy and Lyndon B. Johnson during the escalation of U.S. participation in the Vietnam War.

Roth, William V. (1921–December 12) five-term senator (R., Delaware) for whom the Roth IRA was named.

Safar, Peter (1924–August 3), Austrian-born anesthesiologist who developed the lifesaving technique known as cardiopulmonary resuscitation (CPR).

John Ritter, actor

Said, Edward W. (1935–September 24), Palestinian-born literary critic and foremost Arab American scholar who championed the Palestinian cause while attempting to bridge Arab and Western cultures.

St. John, Robert (1902–February 6), legendary journalist who was beaten up for writing articles about Al Capone; wounded by Nazis while serving as a foreign correspondent; and scooped the end of World War II for NBC by 20 seconds.

Schlesinger, John (1926–July 25), British-born filmmaker who directed the Academy Award-winning *Midnight Cowboy* (1969), *The Falcon and the Snowman* (1985), and *Cold Comfort Farm* (1995).

Scott, Martha (1914–May 28), stage, screen, and television actress who originated the role of Emily in Thornton Wilder's *Our Town* (1938) and played Charlton Heston's mother in *The Ten Commandments* (1956) and *Ben Hur* (1959).

Scribner, Belding H. (1921–June 19), physician who

Bill Shoemaker, jockey

Robert Stack, actor

invented the Scribner shunt, a device that allowed millions of people to live on long-term kidney dialysis.

Shields, Carol (1935–July 16), Pulitzer Prize-winning Canadian novelist who wrote *The Stone Diaries* and more than 20 other critically esteemed books.

Shoemaker, Bill (1931–October 12), legendary jockey whose 8,833 victories, which included 11 Triple Crowns, made him the second most winning rider in thoroughbred racing history.

Simmons, Richard W. (1913–January 11), movie extra who enjoyed brief fame in the title role of the 1950's television adventure series "Sergeant Preston of the Yukon."

Simon, Paul (1928–December 9), highly respected former congressman (D., Illinois) who served three terms in the House and two in the Senate.

Simone, Nina (Eunice Waymon) (1933–April 21), singer-pianist who blended elements of gospel, blues, folk, and classical with and a repertoire that ranged from jazz to Broadway to protest to create a unique sound and style.

Singleton, Penny (1908–November 12), actress who brought the comic strip character "Blondie" to life in 28 films and who gave voice to Jane Jetson in the television cartoon series "The Jetsons."

Sinnott, Richard (1926–April 30), Boston bureaucrat who was the last city official to affix the infamous "banned in Boston" label on entertainment that failed to meet local standards. The practice, which dated back to the Puritan era, was eliminated in 1982.

Sisulu, Walter (1912–May 5), South African civil rights activist who brought Nelson Mandela into the African National Congress and helped lead the fight against apartheid.

Slough, Elena (1889?–October 5), woman documented as the oldest person in the United States.

Spahn, Warren (1921–November 24), Hall of Fame baseball player who, during 21 seasons, won 363 games, the major league record for a left-handed pitcher.

Stack, Robert (1919–May 14), tough-guy actor who played featured roles in many films, including *Written on the Wind* (1956), but attained stardom in the late 1950's as Eliot Ness on "The Untouchables" television series.

Nina Simone, jazz singer

Starr, Edwin (Charles Hatcher) (1942–April 2), Motown singer who produced a number of hit singles, most famously "War (What Is It Good For?)."

Steig, William (1907–October 3), author of more than 25 children's books, including *Shrek!,* and cartoonist whose "symbolic drawings" of dogs, damsels, drunks, and satyrs challenged *New Yorker* readers for more than 60 years. Steig's ironic and insightful drawings are also credited with revolutionizing the greeting card industry.

Stone, Peter (1930–April 26), writer who became the first person to win an Academy Award *(Father Goose),* an Emmy Award ("The Defenders"), and a Tony Award *(1776, Women of the Year, Titanic).*

Sunderman, F. William (1898–March 9), physician, scientist, and editor who at age 99 played his Stradivarius violin at Carnegie Hall and at age 100 was honored by Congress for being the nation's oldest full-time worker.

Taradash, Daniel (1913–February 22), screenwriter and former president of the Academy of Motion Picture Arts and Sciences who won an Academy Award in 1953 for his *From Here to Eternity* screenplay.

Teller, Edward (1908–September 9), Hungarian-born physicist who created quantum physics; helped develop both the atomic and hydrogen bombs; and played a major and controversial role in U.S. defense policies through several presidential administrations.

Thigpen, Lynne (1948–March 12), actress who appeared in the original Broadway cast of *Godspell* (1974) and a number of television series, including "Where in the World Is Carmen Sandiego?," "L.A. Law," and "The District."

Thomas, Sir Graham Stuart (1909–April 16), English gardener and author who introduced hundreds of plant varieties but was best known for propagating and preserving old varieties of climbing and shrub roses.

Strom Thurmond, senator

Thurmond, Strom (1902–June 26), history's longest-serving U.S. senator (R., South Carolina) (1955–2003) who is credited with helping to fuel the South's transition from solidly Democratic to widely Republican.

Till-Mobley, Mamie (1921–January 6), schoolteacher whose courage in the face of the racially motivated murder of her son, Emmett Till, in 1955 helped inspire the civil rights movement.

Tureck, Rosalyn (1914–July 17), pianist and harpsichordist who played a major role in reviving interest in the music of Johann Sebastian Bach.

Uris, Leon (1924–June 21), popular novelist who wrote a series of best sellers, including *Exodus* (1958), *Armageddon* (1964), *Topaz* (1967), and *QB VII* (1970).

Washington, Walter (1915–October 27), former Washington, D.C., mayor who was the first African American to become chief executive of a major U.S. city and the capital's first elected mayor in more than a century.

White, Barry (1944–July 4), singer, songwriter, and arranger whose distinctive bass voice and sensual delivery produced six Top 10 singles during the 1970's disco craze, including "Can't Get Enough of Your Love, Babe" and "You're the First, the Last, My Everything."

Wilson, Kemmons (1913–February 12), Holiday Inn founder who is credited with revolutionizing the hotel industry by providing reliably comfortable and affordable lodging.

Wilson, Sloan (1920–May 25), novelist whose *The Man in the Gray Flannel Suit* (1955) entered the American lexicon as a symbol of the drive for success and suburban conformity of the 1950's.

Winsor, Kathleen (1919–May 26), author whose banned-in-Boston best seller *Forever Amber* (1944) provided the model for a new genre—the racy historical romance novel.

Zevon, Warren (1947–September 7), singer and songwriter whose cynical "pulp fiction" brand of songs—"Werewolves of London" and "Lawyers, Guns and Money"—attracted a cult following.

Ziegler, Ron (1939–February 10), President Richard Nixon's press secretary who most famously described the 1972 break-in at the Democratic National Committee's Watergate headquarters as a "third-rate burglary."

Zindel, Paul (1936–March 27), playwright of *The Effect of Gamma Rays on Man-in-the-Moon Marigolds* (1971) and author of the young-adult novels *The Pigman* (1968) and *My Darling, My Hamburger* (1969), which introduced a new realism to teen-age literature.

Zorina, Vera (Eva Brigita Hartweig) (1917–April 9), dancer who performed in ballet, Broadway musicals, and films of the 1930's and 1940's, most successfully under the direction of George Balanchine, to whom she was once married.

A legendary entertainer dies following a career that spanned much of the 20th century.

BOB HOPE:
THANKS FOR THE MEMORIES

By Donald Liebenson

Entertainer Bob Hope died on July 27, 2003, at age 100. His show business career began in vaudeville in the 1920's and moved onto the Broadway stage. He eventually found fame in motion pictures and on radio and television. In his lifetime, he became an American institution, for whom theaters and schools were named. This acclaim was due in large part to his long dedication to American troops, particularly U.S. soldiers based overseas. Hope staged shows for the U.S. armed forces from World War II (1939-1945) to the Persian Gulf War of 1991.

Leslie Townes Hope was born on May 29, 1903, near London, the fifth of seven sons born to William Henry Hope, a stonemason, and Avis Townes Hope, a former concert singer. His family immigrated to the United States in 1907 and settled in Cleveland, Ohio, where Hope attended school. By his own admission, Hope was an indifferent student, and after graduating from high school in 1920, he tried his hand at a variety of jobs, including delivery boy and shoe salesman. He even served a stint as a boxer. Around the same time, he began taking dance lessons and discovered that he was a natural.

He first performed on stage in 1923 with a 15-year-old dancing partner, Mildred Rosequist. In 1924, Hope and a new dancing partner, Lloyd Durbin, joined silent film comedian Fatty Arbuckle's stage show, *Hurley's Jolly Follies.* Hope sang, danced, and performed a comedy routine. By 1927, he had debuted on Broadway in *The Sidewalks of New York,* and in 1928 he adopted the name Bob Hope, because he thought it sounded more "regular." Hope appeared with a succession of partners before becoming a solo performer in 1930.

By the early 1930's, Hope was on his way to stardom. He received critical praise for his featured role in the musical comedy *Roberta* in 1933, and by 1936 he received star billing with Ethel Merman and Jimmy Durante in Cole Porter's musical *Red, Hot, and Blue!*

His personal life was also on the upswing. Hope married nightclub singer Dolores Reade in 1934. The longevity of their marriage—more than 68 years—may have set a Hollywood record.

Making it big

Hope's success on Broadway attracted the attention of Hollywood, and he was cast in his first feature film, *The Big Broadcast of 1938,* in which he co-starred with fellow comedian W. C. Fields. In the film, Hope sang a bittersweet song about faded love, "Thanks for the Memory," which became his highly recognizable theme song.

In 1939, he appeared in the film *The Cat and the Canary,* a horror-comedy in which he played a mock-heroic lady's man who wisecracks his way through all situations, no matter how serious. In the film, a frightened character asks, "Don't big empty houses scare you?" "Not me," Hope replies, "I used to be in vaudeville." Hope adopted this wise-cracking character as his public persona and built one of the most durable careers in show-business history on its appeal.

In addition to his film career, Hope began hosting a popular radio program on the NBC network in 1939. "The Bob Hope Pepsodent Show," which ran until 1948, provided Hope with a public presence that was widespread and unique. Though movie actors of the era often appeared on radio, none—with the possible exception of crooner Bing Crosby—became true stars of the medium except Hope. And while such radio luminaries as Jack Benny or George Burns and Gracie Allen made movies at the height of their popularity, no one except Hope was simultaneously a true star of both mediums. In 1950, he easily moved from radio to television and appeared in a series of highly rated specials through the rest of his career. His relationship with NBC proved to be the longest in network history.

In 1940, Hope co-starred with Bing Crosby and Dorothy Lamour in the motion-picture comedy *Road to Singapore,* the first in a series of seven "Road" pictures. Hope played his usual wisecracking character—the hapless, but appealing mediocrity—who in this and other "Road" movies is constantly at the mercy of a conniving partner, Crosby. They kid each other, and speaking directly to the camera, they kid their audience. In a memorable scene from *Road to Bali* (1952), Hope warns the

The author:
Donald Liebenson is
a free-lance writer.

Bob Hope (left), Dorothy Lamour, and Bing Crosby in *Road to Morocco* (1942). The trio starred in seven of the highly popular "Road" pictures.

audience that Crosby is about to sing and suggests it may be a good time to get up for popcorn. The films, which reproduced a sense of the banter of live radio of the period, seemed so spontaneous that audiences believed Hope and Crosby were making up the jokes as they went along. According to Hope, many scenes in the motion pictures were indeed improvised.

Hope ranked among the top-ten box office stars from 1941 to 1953 and was number one in 1949. Among his more than 50 films, critics cite *My Favorite Blonde* (1942), *Monsieur Beaucaire* (1946), *The Paleface* (1948), *Fancy Pants* (1950), and *The Lemon Drop Kid* (1951) as among Hope's best solo comedy films. As a dramatic actor, he also distinguished himself in two film biographies—*The Seven Little Foys* (1955), in which he portrayed vaudeville star Eddie Foy; and *Beau James* (1957), in which he played New York City Mayor James J. "Jimmy" Walker. Hope, however, usually deprecated his abilities as an actor. "Welcome to the Academy Awards," he famously joked at the opening of one of the 18 ceremonies he hosted. "Or as it is known in my house—Passover."

Entertaining the troops

Hope performed his first show for United Service Organizations (USO), a civilian organization that serves members of the U.S. armed forces, at March Field, California in 1941—before the United States entered World War II on December 8 of that year. Hope subsequently staged USO overseas tours annually through the end of the war. The Bob Hope Christmas USO tours began in 1948 in Germany, where his group performed for troops participating in the Berlin Airlift. The Bob Hope Christmas tour became a USO tradition, and he visited military bases and veterans hospitals every December for the next 34 years. He typically performed as close to the front lines as possible and visiting the wounded in hospitals. "Don't get up," he would announce upon entering a ward to soldiers confined to their beds. President Lyndon B. Johnson awarded Hope with the Presidential Medal of Freedom for his service to the men and women of the armed forces in 1969.

Hope's considerable star power and highly public connection with the USO gained him access to world leaders and other powerful people, and Hope claimed to have kidded every president from Franklin D. Roosevelt to Bill Clinton. He also became a very wealthy man. His image as a member of the establishment and the ultimate insider became a double-edged sword during the Vietnam War (1959-1975). In the 1970's, he and his style of humor fell out of favor, particularly with a generation that was largely against that war. Younger audiences booed him and branded him as prowar. "There is no one more antiwar than me," he responded.

Despite the 1970's, Hope's overall appeal endured, particularly with the generation of Americans who had fought World War II, for whom Hope remained a hero. He entertained troops for the last time in 1990, when he was in his late 80's, during a trip to Saudi Arabia before the start of the Persian Gulf War of 1991.

Hope continued to make hundreds of appearances a year through the mid-1990's. His last television special, marking his 90th birthday, earned an Emmy Award in 1993. In 1997, the U.S. Congress passed a resolution naming him the first honorary veteran of the armed forces in recognition of his dedication to the U.S. armed services.

In his prime, Hope shaped a generation of comedians. Writer and director Woody Allen—the leading comic actor of the generation that turned its back on Bob Hope—openly acknowledges that he was greatly influenced by Hope and his extraordinary comedic timing. Allen notes, "If I wanted to have a weekend of pure pleasure, it would be to have a half-dozen Bob Hope films and watch them."

Bob Hope entertains servicemen on the island of New Georgia in the Solomon Islands during World War II (1939-1945). Hope visited the troops, often very near the front lines during wartime, for nearly 50 years.

Democratic Party. Democratic candidates lost three gubernatorial seats to Republican challengers in off-season elections during 2003. Democratic Party officials downplayed the significance of the losses, noting that all voters, Democrats and Republicans, were in the mood for change.

In the year's most high-profile election, the people of California voted on October 7 to recall Governor Gray Davis, a Democrat who had won election to a second term in 2002. California voters replaced Davis with motion-picture star Arnold Schwarzenegger, a Republican.

Davis's defeat was followed by two more gubernatorial losses on Nov. 4, 2003, when voters in Mississippi and Kentucky opted for Republican governors. In Mississippi, Governor Ronnie Musgrove, a Democrat, lost to Republican challenger Haley Barbour, a former chairman of the Republican National Committee.

In Kentucky, Democrat Ben Chandler, the state's attorney general, lost a bid to succeed Governor Paul Patton to U.S. Representative Ernie Fletcher (R., Kentucky). Patton, a Democrat, was barred from running for reelection by term limits.

Democrats declared victory in Louisiana on November 15, where Lieutenant Governor Kathleen Babineaux Blanco defeated Bobby Jindal, a Republican, in the race to succeed Governor Mike Foster. Term limits also prohibited Foster, a Democrat, from seeking reelection.

Democratic Party leaders claimed that the 2003 elections merely demonstrated that voters were unhappy with the *status quo* (the existing state of affairs). They suggested that the unsettled mood among voters could carry over into the 2004 presidential election.

Mayoral victory. Party officials were heartened by the reelection of Philadelphia Mayor John Street in November 2003. Street remained unscathed by the revelation during the campaign that he had been under federal investigation in 2003 due to irregularities in the awarding of municipal contracts. Street defeated Republican challenger Sam Katz, a Philadelphia businessman.

Fund-raising. Federally registered Democratic Party committees raised $56.4 million through June 2003, according to figures released on August 28 by the Federal Election Commission (FEC). The FEC is a U.S. government agency that enforces campaign financing regulations. The figures represented an increase for Democrats over the $40 million they raised in 2002. Though the Democrats increased their fundraising, they failed to keep pace with the Republicans. According to the FEC, federally registered Republican Party committees raised $139.1 million in the first six months of 2003. The FEC reported that Democrats had spent $39.3 million in the first six months of 2003, while Republicans had spent $106.8 million.

The FEC report revealed that individual contributions provided the majority of fund-raising for the Democratic Party. Democrats received $42.7 million from individuals and $8.1 million from political action committees (PAC's). PAC's are groups set up by a labor union, corporation, or other organization to contribute money to candidates for federal and state offices.

Soft money. The Democratic National Committee raised $220 million in "soft money" contributions in 2002, prior to changes in campaign finance law. That finding was reported in January 2003 by Common Cause, a citizens advocacy group headquartered in Washington, D.C. Soft money contributions are individual contributions to political parties that are not subject to the same restrictions placed on contributions to candidates. The changes to campaign finance law, which went into effect in November 2002, barred political parties from raising and spending soft money.

The Republican National Committee raised approximately $250.3 million in soft money contributions in 2002, Common Cause reported.

Presidential campaigns. Several candidates announced their intentions in 2003 to seek the Democratic Party's nomination for president of the United States in 2004. The candidates included Wesley Clark, a retired U.S. Army general; Howard Dean, the former governor of Vermont; U.S. Senator John R. Edwards (D., North Carolina); U.S. Representative Richard A. Gephardt (D., Missouri); U.S. Senator John Kerry (D., Massachusetts); U.S. Representative Dennis Kucinich (D., Ohio); U.S. Senator Joseph I. Lieberman (D., Connecticut), who ran for vice president in 2000; former U.S. Senator Carol Moseley Braun (D., Illinois); and Al Sharpton, a clergyman and political activist.

On Nov. 8, 2003, Dean announced that he would not accept taxpayer money but would rely on private contributors to fuel his campaign in the 2004 presidential primaries. By opting out of public financing for his campaign, Dean avoided the spending limit—about $45 million—that comes with public funds in order to compete with the heavily funded reelection campaign of President George W. Bush. By not accepting public funds Dean could spend unlimited amounts for his party's nomination.

On Nov. 14, 2003, Kerry announced that he also would reject public financing for the presidential primaries, allowing him to use more of his family's personal wealth to fund a presidential campaign.   ■ Geoffrey A. Campbell

See also **Congress of the United States; Elections; People in the news** (Wesley Clark, Howard Dean); **Philadelphia; Republican Party; State government; United States, Government of the.**

Denmark. Immigration issues dominated Danish politics in 2003. The government of Prime Minister Anders Fogh Rasmussen, which was elected on an anti-immigration platform in 2001, proposed a new law in August 2003. The law would require visitors from developing countries to obtain a visa and have a Danish sponsor pay a $7,600 deposit. The deposit would be returned when the visitor left the country. The measure was designed to prevent visitors from remaining in Denmark illegally.

The immigration debate was further enlivened by the engagement in October of Crown Prince Frederik, the heir to the Danish throne, to Mary Donaldson, a lawyer from Australia. Frederik's announcement was celebrated by thousands of cheering Danes in front of the royal Amalienborg Palace in Copenhagen, the capital. However, some critics pointed out that many Danes were unable to bring their foreign-born partners into Denmark because of tough immigration rules passed by the Rasmussen government in 2002. Those rules require both partners to be at least 24 years old, to have a permanent residence in the country, and to have spent more of their combined years in Denmark than in another country. Political parties had indicated they would support an act of parliament to grant citizenship to Donaldson, eliminating the waiting period that can stretch as long as nine years for ordinary applicants.

Economy. The Danish economy remained sluggish in 2003, affected by slow growth across Europe. The country's *gross domestic product,* (GDP, total of all goods and services produced in a year) was expected to grow by 0.8 percent.

Rasmussen indicated that he intended to hold a new referendum, perhaps in 2004, on the euro, the single European currency that Danes rejected in 2000. The prime minister contended that Denmark had lost influence in the European Union by not adopting the euro.

Iraq. The Danish government supported the United States-led war in Iraq, despite widespread public opposition. Denmark sent 400 troops to southern Iraq in June 2003, after U.S. President George W. Bush declared the war had ended, and another 90 troops in October to reinforce security.

Blackout. A fault in a transmission line connecting Denmark and Sweden caused an electrical blackout on September 23 that disrupted power to some 4 million homes and businesses in the two countries for several hours. Copenhagen and surrounding areas were shut down, including the airport and the Oresund bridge and tunnel linking Denmark and Sweden.   ■ Tom Buerkle

See also **Europe; Iraq: A Special Report.**

Dinosaur. See Paleontology.

Disability. In 2003, United States President George W. Bush proposed a number of plans to help people with disabilities who live in nursing homes or other institutions to move back into their communities. The proposals were part of a program called the New Freedom Initiative.

A plan called the "Money Follows the Individual Rebalancing Demonstration" was to provide $1.75 billion over five years to pay for such services as home modifications, including the installation of ramps. About $570 million over 10 years was earmarked for "respite" care, which allows family caregivers of disabled adults or children a temporary period of rest, or respite, from duties. Funds of $504 million over 10 years were to help residents of psychiatric facilities move to family- or community-based alternatives. Other funds were earmarked to ease the shortage of *personal assistance workers* (employees who help disabled people with daily living tasks). Funds were also provided to ensure that if a disabled person returns to work, a disabled spouse could continue to be insured through Medicaid. Previously, a working spouse's income could disqualify a disabled person from receiving Medicaid.

How small is small? The U.S. Supreme Court ruled in April that some small companies are not subject to the 1990 Americans with Disabilities Act (ADA). The ADA, which was enacted to protect people with disabilities from discrimination, applies to companies with 15 or more employees. The law requires companies to provide such accommodations as wheelchair ramps and accessible restrooms. In the case before the court, *Clackamas Gastroenterology Associates v. Wells,* the question arose whether physicians who own a medical clinic should be counted as employees. The Supreme Court ruled that they should not. The justices cited standards used by the Equal Employment Opportunity Commission, which state that an individual who cannot be discharged or who can be held liable in a malpractice suit should not be considered an employee.

Addiction and obsolescence. The Supreme Court heard two other cases related to the ADA in 2003. In *Raytheon Company v. Hernandez,* the justices determined in December that the defense contractor had not violated the ADA by refusing to rehire an employee who had been fired for illegal drug use in the workplace. The employee had undergone rehabilitation and claimed his addiction was a disability. In *Barnhart v. Thomas,* the Supreme Court in November upheld a Social Security Administration decision that an elevator operator whose occupation had been virtually eliminated was not entitled to disability payments even though she was unable to perform work in any other field.   ■ Kristina Vaicikonis

See also **Supreme Court of the United States.**

Disasters. The deadliest disaster of 2003 was an earthquake in the Iranian city of Bam that left at least 30,000 people dead. Disasters that resulted in 25 or more deaths include the following:

Aircraft crashes

January 8—Turkey. A Turkish Airlines jet, en route from Istanbul to Diyarbakir in southeastern Turkey, crashes in fog just short of the runway at the Diyarbakir airport. Five of the 75 people aboard the British Aerospace RJ 100 aircraft survive.

February 19—Iran. A Russian-built Iranian military plane crashes in eastern Iran some 50 miles (80 kilometers) northwest of the city of Zahedan, killing all 302 people aboard.

March 6—Algeria. More than 100 passengers and crew members aboard an Air Algerie jet are killed when it crashes in the Sahara Desert shortly after taking off from Tamanrasset. A young Algerian soldier is the only survivor.

May 8—Congo (Kinshasa). More than 120 people are killed when the doors of an Ilyushin 76 transport plane open mid-flight, causing passengers to be sucked out at an altitude of 7,000 feet (2,200 meters). The Russian crew, who were flying Congolese military officials and civilians from Kinshasa to Lubumbashi, manage to land the plane.

May 26—Turkey. All 75 passengers and crew members are killed when a Ukrainian-chartered Yak-42 plane crashes in northeast Turkey. The pilot of the plane, carrying Spanish peacekeeping forces home from Afghanistan, attempted to land in dense fog in order to refuel.

July 8—Sudan. A Sudan Airways jet crashes shortly after take-off from Port Sudan on the Red Sea, killing 105 passengers and 10 crew members. One passenger, a small child, survives. The Boeing 737 was en route to Khartoum, the capital.

December 25—Benin. A Boeing 727 bound for Lebanon with 161 people aboard plunges into the Atlantic Ocean, shortly after taking off from Cotonou, Benin's primary city. More than 130 people are killed in the crash.

Earthquakes

January 21—Mexico. At least 25 people are killed and more than 300 others are injured when an earthquake of 7.8 magnitude strikes the Pacific state of Colima. The effects of the quake are felt as far away as Mexico City, 300 miles (483 kilometers) to the east.

February 24—China. An earthquake with a magnitude of 6.8 rocks far western China. Chinese officials report that at least 260 people are killed and more than 4,000 others are injured in and around the city of Jiashi in Xinjiang province.

May 1—Turkey. More than 160 people are killed and at least 1,000 others are injured when an earthquake with a magnitude of 6.4, followed by 70 aftershocks, strikes the city of Bingol in southeastern Turkey. Many of the dead and injured are children trapped in a school dormitory.

May 21—Algeria. An earthquake registering a magnitude of 6.7 strikes northern Algeria, causing the deaths of more than 2,200 people and injuries to thousands of others. Most of the deaths occur just east of Algiers, the capital.

December 26—Iran. An earthquake registering 6.6 levels 70 percent of the ancient city of Bam, about 600 miles (965 kilometers) southeast of Tehran. At least 30,000 people are killed.

Explosions and fires

February 2—Nigeria. An explosion in Lagos, Nigeria, tears the front from a four-story office and residential complex, killing at least 30 people.

February 20—Rhode Island. One hundred people are killed and more than 200 others are injured when a fire ignited by a pyrotechnic display during a heavy metal band concert sweeps through a small nightclub in West Warwick, near Providence, Rhode Island.

April 10—Russia. Twenty-eight preschool children are killed and more than 100 others are injured when a fire sweeps through a boarding school for the deaf in the Caspian Sea port of Makhachkala.

June 19—Nigeria. A pipeline explodes in southeastern Nigeria, killing at least 125 people as they attempt to scavenge gasoline.

July 28—China. Twenty-nine people are killed and more than 140 others are injured when an explosion tears through a fireworks factory near the city of Tianjin in northern China.

August 3—Pakistan. A fire at a contractor's house ignites dynamite stored within the structure, setting off a series of explosions that rip through the northern village of Gayal, killing at least 50 people and injuring more than 150 others.

August 3—India. More than 40 people are killed in Surat, in western India, when a gas cylinder explodes in a diamond cutting and polishing workshop. The blast levels three buildings that housed both workshops and residences.

November 24—Russia. Thirty-six students are killed and nearly 200 others are injured when a fire sweeps through a crowded, five-story dormitory in Moscow. The building housed foreign students, primarily those from developing nations.

December 23—China. A natural gas well near Chongqing in southwestern China explodes, spewing toxic fumes over an area officials call the "zone of death." At least 200 people are killed and 10,000 others are burned or poisoned.

Heat waves

May—India. A heat wave that affected most of India throughout the month of May causes the

Patrons flee one of the deadliest nightclub fires in United States history on Feb. 20, 2003, in West Warwick, Rhode Island. The fire erupted during a pyrotechnic display during a performance by a heavy metal band. One hundred people were killed and more than 200 others were injured.

deaths of more than 1,400 people. Temperatures in the southern state of Andhra Pradesh reached a record high of 124 °F (51 °C).

August—France. Health ministry officials report that almost 15,000 people died from heat-related causes in France because of a month-long heat wave in Europe that began in July. Elsewhere across the continent, officials report about 5,000 heat-related deaths.

Mine disasters

March 23—China. Provincial officials report that more than 60 miners were killed on March 22 during a gas explosion in a coal mine in Shanxi province in northern China. The accident was the third in less than one month in which more than 10 people were killed in the province.

May 13—China. At least 82 miners are killed during a gas explosion in a coal mine near Hufei in eastern China's Anhui province.

August 19—China. The government of China's northern Shanxi province suspends nearly all coal mining operations after gas explosions cause more than 80 deaths at three mines during a 7-day period.

Shipwrecks

March 23—Burundi. A ferry overloaded with some 200 passengers capsizes in Lake Tanganyika. At least 150 people, en route from Kalemie in Congo (Kinshasa) to Uvira in Burundi, are killed.

April 16—China. Mechanical problems aboard a nonnuclear Chinese submarine off China's coast east of the Neichangshan islands result in the deaths of all 70 officers and crew members. Naval experts speculate that a malfunction in the diesel engines removed the oxygen from the sub's interior during a descent.

April 21—Bangladesh. Two ferries—one traveling on the Buriganga River near Dhaka, the capital, and the other carrying a wedding party on the Meghna River, about 50 miles (80 kilometers) northeast of Dhaka—capsize in severe tropical storms. More than 130 people are killed.

June 20—Tunisia. A Libyan vessel carrying some 250 immigrants from Africa to Italy capsizes in the Mediterranean Sea about 70 miles (112 kilometers) from Sfax, a Tunisian port. Only 41 people survive.

July 8—Bangladesh. As many as 500 people drown when a ferry carrying some 800 passengers from Dhaka to Lalmohan, in the southeast, capsizes in turbulent waters where the rivers Padma, Meghna, and Dakatia meet.

November 26—Congo (Kinshasa). At least 180 people are killed when high waves driven by a sudden storm cause a dangerously overcrowded ferry to founder on a lake off the Congo River.

Storms and floods

February 17—East Coast, United States. A powerful storm system with high winds and low temperatures races across the eastern United States, closing highways and airports and triggering widespread power outages. Several East Coast cities receive record-breaking amounts of snow. Authorities attribute the deaths of some 40 people to the storm, which began in the Midwest on February 14.

May 17–Sri Lanka. Flash floods in the Ratnapura distict in south-central Sri Lanka kill more than 200 people and force an estimated 150,000 others to evacuate. Most of the victims are killed in a landslide that wipes out an entire village.

July 16—India. A flash flood sweeps through a laborers' tent village near the resort town of Kulu in the northern state of Himachal Pradesh. At least 100 people are killed.

August 5—Pakistan. Government officials report that more than 170 people in the southern province of Sindh have died since July 8, when monsoon rains triggered 24 days of flooding. An additional 1 million people were left homeless.

September 4—China. More than 80 people are killed in two simultaneous disasters as floods, landslides, and Typhoon Dujuan—the strongest typhoon to hit China in 25 years—strike the country in the course of a week. Flooding and landslides caused by the Wei River in the northern province of Shanxi accounted for about half of the deaths, while the typhoon primarily affected people in the southern province of Guangdong.

September 13—South Korea. Government officials report that as many as 117 people were killed when Typhoon Maemi hit the South Korean port city of Pusan, 280 miles (450 kilometers) southeast of Seoul, the capital, on September 12.

September 18—Middle Atlantic states. Hurricane Isabel, with winds as high as 99 miles (160 kilometers) per hour, strikes the East Coast, ultimately taking at least 36 lives.

November 3—Indonesia. Torrential rains trigger a flash flood on the Indonesian island of Sumatra that kills more than 150 people.

December 20—Philippines. Week-long rains trigger landslides, causing the deaths of more than 200 people. Most of the victims lived in southern Leyte province, where, according to environmentalists, illegal logging may have contributed to the instability of steep hillsides.

Train wrecks

February 1—Zimbabwe. A passenger train carrying more than 1,100 people en route to the resort town of Victoria Falls in northwestern Zim-babwe collides with a freight train carrying flammable liquid near the town of Dete. More than 40 people are killed as both trains explode.

June 22—India. Fifty-one people are killed when a train traveling from the port city of Karwar on India's southwestern coast to Mumbai derails after striking boulders that recent flooding and landslides had washed onto the tracks.

Other disasters

May 1—South Africa. At least 52 members of South Africa's largest trade union are killed when the bus in which they are travelling to a May Day celebration plunges into a reservoir.

May 8—Hungary. Thirty-four German tourists are killed when their bus is struck by a train near the Hungarian resort town of Siofok on Lake Balaton. The bus was en route from Budapest to Nagykanizsa, in western Hungary.

August 27—India. Thirty-three people, most of them women and the elderly, are killed when a crowd stampedes during a Hindu festival in the Nasik, about 85 miles (137 kilometers) northeast of Mumbai. The pilgrims had gathered in the city to ritually bathe in the Godavari River.

September 7—Nigeria. At least 70 people are killed in a deadly blaze when a passenger bus and three other vehicles collide on a highway about 60 miles (100 kilometers) south of Abuja, the capital.

Drug abuse. In 2002, 120 million Americans—nearly half the U.S. population—were current drinkers, 61.1 million were current smokers of cigarettes, and 19.5 million were illegal drug users, according to the 2003 National Survey on Drug Use and Health (NSDUH). The figures were based on past-month use of the substances, according to the Substance Abuse and Mental Health Services Administration (SAMHSA), which conducts and publishes the survey annually.

Alcohol and youth. The NSDUH survey reported 10.7 million underage drinkers (people younger than 21) in the United States in 2002, or 28.8 percent of the age group. The Monitoring the Future Survey (MFS), an annual study focusing on 8th-, 10th-, and 12th-graders, reported declines in the rates of alcohol consumption among high school students. The survey is sponsored by the National Institute on Drug Abuse.

Tobacco. The number of new daily cigarette users decreased from 2.1 million in 1998 to 1.4 million in 2001, reported NSDUH. The survey noted a similar decline among youths under 18, down from 1.1 million new daily cigarette users in 1997 to 757,000 new users in 2001.

Illegal drugs. According to NSDUH, 19.5 million Americans (8.3 percent) were illicit drug users in 2002—that is, they had used an illegal drug such as ecstasy, marijuana, heroin, or crack/cocaine. Marijuana was the most widely used illegal drug in 2002, as in previous years. According to NSDUH, about 75 percent of all illicit drug users reported using marijuana. More than half said that they used the drug exclusively.

Use of ecstasy, a hallucinogen associated with a youth subculture movement known as "raves"—all-night dance parties—increased dramatically between the early 1990's and 2002. However, the Monitoring the Future Survey found that in 2002, for the first time since 1999, ecstasy use declined among high school students.

Buprenorphine. In August 2003, the New York City Department of Health and Mental Hygiene and the U.S. Center for Substance Abuse Treatment sponsored a forum in New York City on prescribing buprenorphine as a substitute for heroin. Buprenorphine is a federally approved drug that offers some advantages over methadone, the drug typically used in heroin replacement therapy. Buprenorphine gives users only a mild "high" and poses a low risk of overdosing. More importantly, buprenorphine can be prescribed by a user's own physician, whereas methadone can be obtained only in a methadone treatment clinic. Treatment experts said that the ease of using buprenorphine was likely to draw more drug users into therapy.   ■ David C. Lewis

See also **Drugs.**

Drugs. Continued illegal efforts by many United States consumers to buy less expensive prescription drugs from Canada provoked strong responses by the U.S. Food and Drug Administration (FDA) and U.S. drug companies in 2003. The U.S. Congress, however, considered several measures to legalize the drug reimports.

Lured by significant savings, millions of Americans, particularly seniors, flocked to Canada and Canadian-linked Internet pharmacies and discount drug outlets to fill their prescriptions. Unlike the United States—where drug manufacturers are free to set their own prices—Canada regulates drug costs. As a result, Canadian companies are able to buy drugs more cheaply, including drugs manufactured in the United States, and then resell them to U.S. citizens at prices lower than those charged in the United States.

In February, the FDA sternly reminded consumers and pharmacies that reimporting drugs violated U.S. law. In a widely publicized letter, the agency warned that it could not guarantee the safety of reimported drugs. Advocates of reimported drugs, however, accused the FDA, which had previously ignored cross-border sales, of caving in to pressure from U.S. drug companies.

A number of drug manufacturers also imposed new restrictions on Canadian drug retailers to halt the multimillion-dollar reimported drug trade.

These included limiting drug supplies and requiring Canadian pharmacies to promise not to export drugs and to bypass wholesalers and buy their drugs directly from the companies. The companies also threatened to halt drug sales to pharmacies whose orders exceeded local demand.

Advocates of drug reimports found support in Congress, however. Both the House of Representatives and the Senate passed measures that, if approved by the entire Congress, would permit licensed U.S. pharmacists and drug distributors to sell reimported drugs.

New AIDS drug. The first in a new class of drugs designed to combat HIV, the virus that causes AIDS, won FDA approval for use in the United States on March 13, 2003. The drug, enfuvirtide (sold under the trade name Fuzeon), is intended for people with advanced HIV infection whose blood levels of the virus continue to rise despite treatment with virus-fighting medications. Many HIV patients have developed resistance to existing medications, the FDA said.

Enfuvirtide belongs to a new class of anti-HIV drugs called fusion inhibitors. These drugs block the AIDS virus from attaching to the outer surface of and then entering certain white blood cells vital to the immune system. Other anti-HIV drugs attack the virus after it has infected the cells.

Enfuvirtide, which was codeveloped by Hoffmann-La Roche Inc. of Nutley, New Jersey, and Trimeris, Inc., of Durham, North Carolina, is the most complicated HIV-fighting drug ever marketed. Its annual cost of $20,000, twice that of any other anti-HIV drug, seriously limited its use.

Drug agreement. The world's poorest countries won the right to bypass international trade laws on patented drugs and import cheaper generic versions of drugs under an agreement announced by the World Trade Organization (WTO) on August 30. The Geneva-based WTO arbitrates disputes between member nations. African countries, in particular, had long pushed for the pact, arguing that the needs of people suffering from AIDS and other life-threatening epidemics outweighed the financial interests of drug companies.

The new plan expands an existing waiver system that permitted countries to manufacture generic drugs to fight serious epidemics. WTO rules, however, had severely restricted the export of these drugs to countries too poor to manufacture them on their own.

The WTO adopted the expanded system after the United States dropped its opposition to the measure, which was approved by all other members of the WTO in late 2002. The administration of President George W. Bush and the U.S. pharmaceutical industry had argued that export waivers should cover only a few life-threatening diseases in order to prevent the widespread distribution of illegally manufactured drugs.

The new system includes safeguards designed to limit the export of generic drugs to the least-developed countries. Many countries also agreed not to import any drugs manufactured under the system or to use the system only in emergencies.

Heartburn drug. The over-the-counter debut of Prilosec, the world's top-selling prescription drug, in September 2003 produced mixed financial results for consumers with heartburn. Some benefited from the FDA's decision in June to authorize the sale of a cheaper, easier-to-obtain version of Prilosec. Others, however, especially those in managed care plans, saw their drug costs rise, because many health insurers stopped paying for the medication. As a result, the cost of the over-the-counter version exceeded the copayment that consumers had been charged for their prescriptions. A similar situation affected some consumers who turned to Claritin in spring 2003 to relieve their seasonal allergy symptoms. The FDA approved an over-the-counter version of that drug in late 2002.

Despite the complaints about higher costs, many health care experts praised the FDA for reclassifying the two drugs. They argued that making them available without a prescription would help reduce soaring drug costs as well as unnecessary physician visits.   ■ Barbara A. Mayes

See also **AIDS; Health care issues; Medicine.**

Eastern Orthodox Churches. The

leaders of most major Orthodox Churches condemned the possibility of war between the United States and Iraq in 2003. Statements of opposition were issued in February and March by the Ecumenical Patriarchate of Istanbul, the Patriarchate of Moscow, the Church of Greece, the Serbian Orthodox Patriarchate, the Standing Conference of Canonical Orthodox Bishops in America, the Greek Orthodox Archdiocese of America, the Orthodox Church in America, and others.

Ecumenical Patriarchate. Ecumenical Patriarch Bartholomew met in August 2003 with Turkish Prime Minister Recep Tayyip Erdogan to renew his request to reopen the Halki Seminary, which was closed by the Turkish government in 1971 when religious education was put under state control. Bartholomew called the closing "a great injustice," and Erdogan told him the Turkish government would try to find a solution.

Greek Orthodox Church. Members of the European Union, in a December 2002 report, pressured the Athonite monastic establishment in Greece to abandon the 1,000-year-old tradition of not allowing women on the island of Athos because it violates international conventions on gender equality and nondiscrimination. The leadership of the 20-monastery religious community issued a statement in January 2003, saying that state intervention would violate their rights to self-governance, religious freedom, protection of property, and private asylum.

Russian Orthodox Church. In September, a Russian priest, Father Vladimir Enert, was suspended after conducting a marriage service between two men. The church condemned the action as blasphemous. According to Orthodox Church doctrine, marriage is the union of a man and a woman, and homosexuality is a mortal sin. The couple exchanged vows at a chapel in Nezhny Novgorod, east of Moscow. One of the men stated that he bribed the priest with the equivalent of $450 to perform the ceremony. The church set up a commission to investigate the incident and ultimately defrocked the priest.

Georgian Orthodox Church. An agreement between the Republic of Georgia and the Vatican regarding the rights of Roman Catholics in Georgia was canceled in September because of protests by conservative Orthodox Christians who accused the Vatican of trying to steal members of their flock. The Vatican responded with harsh criticism, and President Eduard Shevardnadze proposed ways to extend religious freedoms.   ■ Stanley S. Harakas

See also **Georgia; Greece; Roman Catholic Church; Russia.**

Economics. The world economy went

through sharp adjustments during 2003. Major industrial nations spent much of the first half of the year in a slow-growth phase that at times threatened to fall into *recession* (generally, two consecutive quarters of negative growth). In the second half of 2003, the economy strengthened, and trends pointed toward a more solid and balanced recovery in 2004.

Demand for goods and services was hampered early in 2003 by a combination of factors, including fears that the looming United States-led war against Iraq could go badly, repeated antiterrorist alerts that dampened commercial activity, soaring fuel prices, and the spread of severe acute respiratory syndrome (SARS). Companies faced slumping demand and could not increase prices to cover the higher fuel and insurance costs, so key central banks, including the U.S. Federal Reserve (the Fed), reduced interest rates to record lows. This action, along with tax cuts, helped spur recovery in the third quarter of 2003.

Oil and the war on Iraq. U.S.-led forces moved into Iraq in March 2003. By April, the coalition had taken control of Iraq's extensive oil fields without the kind of destruction that oil markets had feared. Oil prices began a long slide, and concerns of possible terrorist retaliation inside the United States and other industrial countries lessened. Consumer and business demand, however, remained weak throughout the spring, as major economies reported declines in output and business and consumer confidence.

Crude oil is a crucial commodity for industrial economic activity and a major determinant of overall fuel costs. Analysts said swings in the price of oil during 2003 had a significant impact on overall economic growth. After peaking at $34 a barrel before the Iraq War began in March, the price of crude oil fell sharply starting in April. By the end of August, the price had returned to $30 a barrel. Analysts at the International Monetary Fund (IMF), the United Nations (UN) affiliate that specializes in financial and economic restructuring of its member nations, said the late-summer rise in prices was due to several factors—Iraq's oil output did not quickly increase immediately after the war, and rising economic activity kept oil inventories low in industrial nations. In addition, later reports that Iraq was rapidly rebuilding its production capacity prompted the Organization of the Petroleum Exporting Countries (OPEC, a group of 11 countries whose economies rely on oil export revenues) to cut output. The IMF projected in September that oil prices would remain about the same through the end of 2003 and then decline to $25 a barrel by late 2004.

SARS. The spread of SARS disrupted commerce in spring 2003, as outbreaks occurred in several key commercial centers of Asia and Canada's largest city, Toronto. Commercial contacts between SARS-affected areas and other countries slowed during the first half of 2003 before authorities declared the disease under control.

The World Health Organization, a UN agency based in Geneva, Switzerland, issued an alert in March about the spread of SARS through Hong Kong. The disease had also broken out in the southern China province of Guangdong; China's capital, Beijing; Singapore; and Hanoi, the capital of Vietnam. Travel to these areas dropped sharply, affecting the transportation and hospitality industries. Many business operations were put on hold as employees were told to stay at home. Various other nations, including Canada, the United States, and Brazil, also reported cases of SARS among people who had traveled to the affected Asian countries.

The impact of SARS was one reason the IMF announced in its September *World Economic Outlook* that the volume of world trade of goods and services would grow just 2.9 percent in 2003 after a 3.2-percent growth in 2002. The IMF also hoped that global trade talks would lead to new pacts that could help spur trade in the future, but the talks collapsed.

SELECTED KEY U.S. ECONOMIC INDICATORS

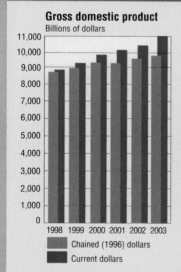

Gross domestic product
Billions of dollars

Chained (1996) dollars

Current dollars

Sources: U.S. Department of Commerce and U.S. Department of Labor, except 2003 figures, which are estimates from The Conference Board.

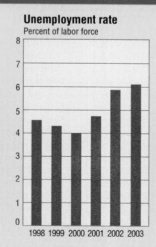

Unemployment rate
Percent of labor force

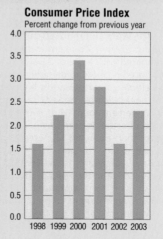

Consumer Price Index
Percent change from previous year

The gross domestic product (GDP) measures the value in current prices of all goods and services produced within a country in a year. Many economists believe the GDP is an accurate measure of the nation's total economic performance. Chained dollars show the amount adjusted for inflation. The unemployment rate is the percentage of the total labor force that is unemployed and actively seeking work. The Consumer Price Index measures inflation by showing the change in prices of selected goods and services consumed by urban families and individuals.

Rate cuts. The Fed and the European Central Bank both cut their key short-term interest rates in June 2003, after waiting for months for economic recovery to take hold. The ECB cut one-half a percentage point and the Fed, one-quarter. The cuts brought the U.S. federal funds rate on overnight market loans between commercial banks to just 1 percent, its lowest level in 45 years and lower than interest rates for most other industrial economies. The move placed the Fed in a monetary policy position in which it had little additional room to cut rates if the economy did not soon revive.

The rate cuts came just before a large new U.S. tax cut took effect and began pouring billions of dollars from the government into the hands of taxpayers. U.S. President George W. Bush had pushed Congress to advance the schedule for cuts in tax rates that it passed before the terrorist attacks on the United States on Sept. 11, 2001. Bush hoped to expand upon them and have them appear as lower tax withholding amounts in paychecks by July 2003. The tax cuts and credits boosted consumer spending, and signs increased throughout the third quarter of 2003 that the economy was strengthening in the United States, the main locomotive for world growth.

Recovery. Monthly economic data indicated stronger recovery beginning in July. The world's stock market activity showed that investors thought the low interest rates, tax cuts, unwinding of war-related uncertainties, and lowered oil prices had created the best outlook in years. Equity markets gained markedly, making 2003 the best year for investors since the stock market bubble burst in 2000, though IMF officials cautioned that the effects of that burst bubble continued.

The IMF's autumn 2003 outlook forecast world output to rise 3.2 percent by the end of the year, compared with a rise of 3 percent in 2002, with advanced economies gaining just 1.8 percent and developing countries overall growing 5 percent. The agency looked ahead to a faster global growth of 4.1 percent for 2004. However, the United States later reported its economy had grown at a much-faster-than-expected 8.2 percent annual pace in the third quarter—compared with 3.3 percent in the second quarter and 1.4 percent in the first quarter. The tax cut and the Fed's promise to keep interest rates down "for a considerable period" spurred the growth, according to many economists.

Manufacturers in the United States and countries using the euro currency reported growth continuing into October 2003. Both Australia and the United Kingdom raised interest rates to rein in their economies and the expansion of credit.

■ John D. Boyd

See also **Bank; International trade; Iraq: A Special Report; Manufacturing; Public health and safety; United States, Government of the.**

Ecuador. Lucio Edwin Gutierrez, of the Patriotic Society Party, was sworn in as president for a four-year term in January 2003. Gutierrez, a former army officer who had been imprisoned for his role in a January 2000 *coup* (overthrow), vowed to fight his country's "corrupt oligarchy."

IMF credit. Gutierrez visited New York City and Washington, D.C., in February 2003 to reassure creditors abroad that his administration would honor Ecuador's financial obligations. The International Monetary Fund (IMF), a United Nations affiliate that provides short-term credit to member nations, agreed in March to grant Ecuador a $205-million line of credit that would also give the country access to $300 million in loans from other international agencies. Gutierrez assured creditors that his support in Ecuador was strong enough for him to meet the economic conditions demanded by lenders.

Coalition collapses. Gutierrez's ruling alliance, which included the Indian movement that helped catapult him into office, began to unravel in August. Pachakutik, the left-wing faction of Latin America's only native political party, voted to defeat a bill that incorporated IMF demands. Pachakutik claimed that the president had ignored the interests of the poor in striking a deal with the IMF.   ■ Nathan A. Haverstock

See also **Latin America.**

Education. Educational institutions in 2003 struggled with the implementation of reforms, such as the No Child Left Behind program and school vouchers. They also faced budget cuts because of the ailing economy in the first half of the year, forcing schools to cut faculty and staff, course offerings, and special programs.

Enrollment. An estimated 53.7 million children enrolled in public and private elementary and secondary schools in the United States in the autumn of 2003. K-12 enrollment had been growing since 1988 and was projected to continue growing until 2006, when it was expected to begin leveling off at about 53.5 million. Elementary-school enrollment had declined slightly for three years and was about 35.3 million in the fall of 2003. Secondary-school enrollment increased by 275,000 students to 18.4 million. Private school enrollment accounted for about 9 percent of the total, the same as 10 years ago. A projected 13.6 million undergraduates enrolled in two- and four-year colleges and universities in the fall, which also was a record, with more than three-quarters of them in public institutions.

The demographic profile of U.S. students changed as the number of students continued to grow. The U.S. Department of Education reported that in 2000, 39 percent of students in public elementary and secondary schools were minorities, up from 12 percent in 1972. About 17 percent also spoke another language at home, reflecting the surge in immigration in recent years. From 1979 to 1999, the population of 5- to 24-year-olds increased by 6 percent, the department said, but the percentage of students who spoke a language other than English at home increased by 118 percent. Among college students, 11 percent of undergraduates were foreign-born, 56 percent were female, and 39 percent attended school part time. About 17 percent of children aged 5 to 17 lived in poverty, about the same as in 1979.

Budgets and spending. Schools and universities in almost every state had to cope with tight budgets brought on by the economic decline in 2002 and the first half of 2003. With state revenues down because of lower income and sales-tax receipts, the National Conference of State Legislatures, a bipartisan organization based in Washington, D.C., said 19 states cut their higher-education budgets midway through the fiscal year, which ends on June 30 in most states. Twelve states also trimmed their elementary- and secondary-school budgets, which are protected by state constitutions and generally are the last items lawmakers care to touch.

The State Higher Education Executive Officers, a group based in Denver, Colorado, said the average higher-education spending cut was about 5 percent. Universities responded by eliminating courses, laying off teachers, and raising tuition. The American Association of Community Colleges said that tuition and fees at community colleges jumped 11.4 percent nationwide during the 2003-2004 school year. The states spent $63.6 billion on higher education in the 2002-2003 school year, according to Illinois State University in Bloomington, which makes a yearly calculation.

Mid-year cuts in elementary and secondary-school budgets rippled down to the school districts. When Ohio cut $30 million from the state education department, for example, the department in turn cut back on the money it sends to the districts for buses, testing, and programs for children with behavior problems. When Oregon cut state education funding, the Portland schools eliminated sports and shortened the school year. The cuts came just as schools were beginning to tote up the costs of U.S. President George W. Bush's No Child Left Behind education plan, which required them to expand testing, meet yearly learning goals, retrain teachers, and offer private tutoring to children in failing schools.

No Child Left Behind. In 2003, parts of the Bush administration's sweeping education-reform plan of January 2002 began to phase in. For the first time, all states were required to report on student-test results. Several states did not meet the law's learning goals, and large percentages of

schools were labeled "in need of improvement." The high failure rates in some states and low rates in others were in large part the result of the Department of Education allowing states to set their learning goals. The law required states to have all their students "proficient" at reading and math by 2014, but allowed each state to define what proficient means and to decide how many students must score at proficient levels for the state to meet yearly federal goals.

Affirmative action. The U.S. Supreme Court ruled in June 2003 that colleges and universities can give some preferential treatment in their admissions processes to black, Hispanic, and Native American students. In a landmark decision likely to reach into business, civic affairs, and the military as well, the court said that affirmative action is necessary if the country is to develop "a set of leaders with legitimacy in the eyes of the citizenry."

The ruling came in two cases brought against the University of Michigan at Ann Arbor by three white students who were denied admission to the undergraduate and law schools, while minority students with similar grades and admissions-test scores were accepted. The university gave extra admissions points to minority undergraduate applications, a practice that the court struck down in a 6-3 decision. However, the court upheld, by a 5-4 vote, the admissions practice of the law school. School officials said that they considered race, but did not make it a "decisive" factor.

Vouchers. The Colorado legislature in April 2003 passed a voucher plan, the only state to do so since the U.S. Supreme Court upheld the constitutionality of vouchers in June 2002. Vouchers allow children to use taxpayer money to attend private schools, including those that are church-affiliated. Colorado's Opportunity Contract Pilot Program, scheduled to take effect in 2004, would have required school districts with eight or more low-performing schools to offer vouchers. Only children who were poor enough to qualify for the federal free-lunch program and who were performing below grade level were to be eligible for the program. In December 2003, a Denver district judge ruled that the new school voucher law violated the state's constitution by taking away the control over education from local school boards.

Supporters pushed a federally funded voucher plan for the Washington, D.C., public schools through the U.S. House of Representatives by a one-vote majority in 2003. After a week of acrimonious debate, which reflected how divided the country was on vouchers, the plan stalled in the Senate. Republican senators included it in a large government-spending bill that is expected to pass Congress in early 2004. ■ June Kronholz

See also **Education: A Special Report; State government; Supreme Court of the United States.**

The Child Left Behind

By June Kronholz

Legislation intended to help all children succeed in school became federal law in 2002. But will it work?

The learning gap—it is education's most nagging problem. When the United States Supreme Court ruled in June 2003 that colleges and universities can accept lower-scoring minority students over higher-scoring whites and Asian Americans, Sandra Day O'Connor wrote that she and other justices "expect" such racial preferences will not be needed in 25 years. Justice O'Connor's opinion was based on the assumption that African Americans, Hispanics, and Native Americans would close the education achievement gap that has separated them from white and Asian American students and that they would no longer need the added boost of affirmative action. President George W. Bush assumed the gap would close, too. His No Child Left Behind education plan, which went into effect in 2002, envisioned all children being proficient at reading and math in 12 years.

Nevertheless, the gap is so wide, so persistent, and the result of such widespread social and economic problems that many experts worry it will grow larger instead of smaller. Are 12 or even 25 years enough to close a gap that has its roots in poverty, poor schools, and family culture? For

Americans, who believe that education is the great equalizer in society, that is a troubling question.

The federal government began tracking the gap in 1971, when, on orders from Congress, it began the National Assessment of Educational Progress (NAEP). The NAEP is a test given regularly to a statistical sampling of 4th-, 8th-, and 12th-graders around the country. NAEP scores on reading, math, science, and other subjects are reported as a national average. But scores are also averaged for black, white, Asian American, Hispanic, and Native American students, as well as by family income and level of parental education. Those scores tell us much of what we know about the gap and provide researchers the data for studying it.

School districts and states also have their own testing programs, which add detail to the national picture. Beginning in 1998, Congress required that the results of those tests be *disaggregated,* or reported by gender, race, and ethnicity, as well. The purpose of that requirement was to determine whether schools are helping all of their children learn or are concentrating their efforts on just one group or another.

Further evidence of the learning gap comes from education researchers, government studies, and private testing companies. In 1998, the U.S. Department of Education began a study that tracked the learning progress of 22,000 children from kindergarten through 5th grade. At the other end of the education spectrum, SAT and ACT college admissions test scores provide additional information on the gap. The SAT (formerly known as the Scholastic Aptitude Test, owned by the New York City-based College Board) and the ACT (formerly called the American College Testing Program, administered by Iowa City, Iowa-based ACT Inc.) are each taken annually by more than 1 million high school seniors. The results of those tests are also reported by race and ethnicity.

How wide is the gap?

All of the test results and research, when taken together, paint a disturbing picture. When non-Asian minority children enter school, they are already substantially behind white youngsters in their alphabet, number, and vocabulary skills. Among kindergartners in 1998, about 18 percent of white children scored in the bottom quarter of the class on reading skills and 30 percent scored in the top quarter, the education department's kindergarten study found. But one-third of black kindergartners and 42 percent of Hispanics scored in the bottom quarter, while only 15 percent scored in the top quarter. The gap continues to grow, so that by 12th grade, the NAEP reading scores of many minority teen-agers are lower than those of white 8th-graders.

In its early childhood study, the U.S. Department of Education identified three skills, among other points, that a child must have in order to be ready to learn to read. A child should know that print is read from left to right; that a reader must look down to the next line when the print ends at the margin; and that one must turn the page to continue the story. Almost half the white children had all three "print familiarity" skills, twice as many as minority children. About one-quarter of the black and Hispanic children and more than one-third of the American Indian children did not have any of the three skills.

The author:
June Kronholz is a reporter for *The Wall Street Journal* and has written extensively on education issues.

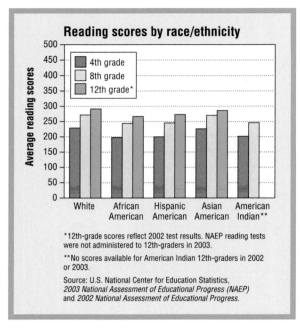

Reading scores by race/ethnicity

Average reading scores

- 4th grade
- 8th grade
- 12th grade*

White | African American | Hispanic American | Asian American | American Indian**

*12th-grade scores reflect 2002 test results. NAEP reading tests were not administered to 12th-graders in 2003.

**No scores available for American Indian 12th-graders in 2002 or 2003.

Source: U.S. National Center for Education Statistics, *2003 National Assessment of Educational Progress (NAEP)* and *2002 National Assessment of Educational Progress.*

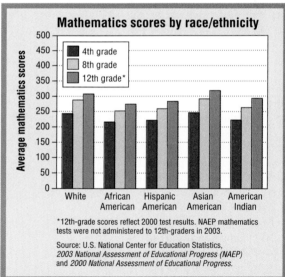

Mathematics scores by race/ethnicity

Average mathematics scores

- 4th grade
- 8th grade
- 12th grade*

White | African American | Hispanic American | Asian American | American Indian

*12th-grade scores reflect 2000 test results. NAEP mathematics tests were not administered to 12th-graders in 2003.

Source: U.S. National Center for Education Statistics, *2003 National Assessment of Educational Progress (NAEP)* and *2000 National Assessment of Educational Progress.*

National reading and mathematics test scores demonstrate the existence of a learning gap between white and non-Asian minority students. By the 12th grade, for example, the scores of many black, Hispanic, and Native American students are lower than those of white 8th-graders.

By 4th grade, teachers generally expect that children have learned to read and can begin to read to learn—that is, to use their reading skills to acquire knowledge. NAEP scores that were released in November 2003 based on tests given earlier in the year showed that reading is still a problem for many U.S. children, but a far bigger problem for minorities than for whites. Forty-one percent of white children in grades 4 and 8 (the 2003 NAEP did not test 12th-graders) were either "proficient" or "advanced" readers, terms that mean they were working at grade level or above. But only 13 percent of black children, 15 percent of Hispanic children, and about 16 percent of Native American children in those grades were proficient or advanced readers.

NAEP also looked at which children scored at "below basic" levels, or who had only minimal reading skills. Twenty-five percent of white 4th-graders scored below basic, but among blacks, the percentage was 60; among Hispanics, 56; and among Native Americans, 53. Among 8th-graders, 17 percent of whites, but 46 percent of blacks, 44 percent of Hispanics, and 43 percent of Native Americans scored below basic.

In addition to measuring proficiency levels, NAEP also measures reading scores on a 500-point scale. In 2003, among black 4th-graders, the scale score rose to 198 from 193 in 1998, but fell by 1 point from 2002. Among Hispanics, it rose to 200 from 193 in 1998, but also fell by 1 point from 2002. Among Native Americans, the score fell to 202 in 2003, from 207 in 2002 and 214 in 2000. Because the score for white 4th-graders improved, to 229 from 225, the test-score gap between white and black 4th-graders closed by only 1 point in five years. The score gap widened by 2 points between white and black 8th-graders. The gap between white and Hispanic scores narrowed by 4 points among 4th-graders but is wider than it was in 1992 among 4th-graders and 8th-graders alike. And between Native American and white 4th-graders, the gap widened, from 10 points in 2000 to 22 points in 2002 and 27 points in 2003. The gap between Native American and white 8th-grade reading scores was very similar to that of 4th-grade scores.

State test results confirm the gap. By 2003, 19 states required that high school students pass special exams before they are allowed to graduate. In Minnesota, 78 percent of white youngsters—but only 33 percent of black and 43 percent of Hispanic and Native American students—passed the exit exam in math on their first try in 2003. In South Carolina, 90 percent of whites, 66 percent of blacks, 73 percent of Hispanics, and 78 percent of Native Americans passed the 2002 math exam on the first try, according to results released in 2003. The Center for Education Policy, a Washington, D.C.-based research group that analyzed the exit exam results, reported that all 19 states had gaps.

The gap is also huge on the SAT and ACT, where high scores can give students an edge in getting into elite universities and going on to elite graduate schools and high-paying careers. In August 2003, the College Board reported an average score of 1026 points out of a possible 1600 for students who took the test as high school seniors in 2002 and entered college in fall 2003. Asian Americans scored highest at 1083 points, followed by whites at 1063. American Indians scored 962; Mexican Americans, 905; and African Americans, 857.

The combined average on the four-subject ACT test, also released in

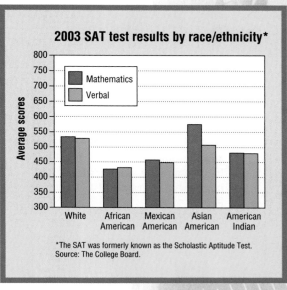

2003 SAT test results by race/ethnicity*

*The SAT was formerly known as the Scholastic Aptitude Test.
Source: The College Board.

August 2003, was 20.8 of a possible 36 points. Asians and whites scored 21.8 and 21.7, respectively, while Hispanics averaged 19.0; American Indians, 18.7; and blacks, 16.9. Based on the scores of black students, the ACT revealed that only 5 percent were ready for college biology and only 10 percent were ready for college algebra courses. By comparison, 30 percent of whites were ready for college biology and 45 percent were ready for algebra. Among Asian American students, 31 percent were ready for biology and 56 percent, for algebra.

The gap is not just evident in test scores. According to the Washington, D.C.-based research organization Child Trends, about 7 percent of whites aged 16 to 24 were high school dropouts in 2001, compared with 27 percent of Hispanics and 11 percent of blacks. Blacks accounted for about 17 percent of high school students in 2001, but only 13 percent of college students. By comparison, whites represented 61 percent of high school students and 68 percent of college students. Among people who had graduated from high school, 33 percent of whites earned a college degree in 2001, compared with 18 percent of blacks and 11 percent of Hispanics. Income generally increases with education in the United States, so those workers with the least education generally earn the lowest salaries. Thus, the learning gap eventually extends far beyond education, affecting job prospects, pay, housing, and a family's ability to care for its children.

By the time students reach college age, the learning gap has become much wider. On the SAT test, which helps determine college admissions, Asian American students scored an average of 1083 points out of a combined possible total of 1600 points in 2003. White students scored 1063; black students scored 857; Mexican American students, 905; and American Indian students, 962.

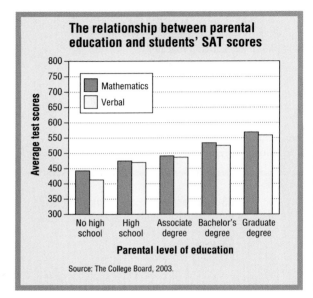

The relationship between parental education and students' SAT scores

- Mathematics
- Verbal

Average test scores

Parental level of education:
No high school, High school, Associate degree, Bachelor's degree, Graduate degree

Source: The College Board, 2003.

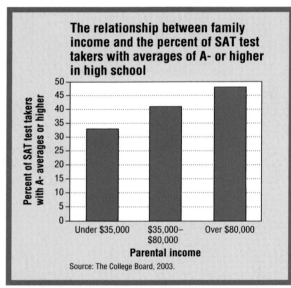

The relationship between family income and the percent of SAT test takers with averages of A- or higher in high school

Percent of SAT test takers with A- averages or higher

Parental income:
Under $35,000, $35,000–$80,000, Over $80,000

Source: The College Board, 2003.

Causes of the gap

Educational experts agree that there is no one reason for the gap and thus no one solution. However, family income and the education of a child's parents generally correlate to a youngster's educational achievement. The higher the family income and the further the parents progressed in school, the likelier the child is to be a high-achieving student. In the government's kindergarten study, for example, a child whose mother had at least a college degree was almost eight times as likely to get a top score in an early reading test as a child whose mother had not finished high school.

Similarly, NAEP found that 8th-graders whose parents have a college education scored an average 273 points on its 500-point-scale reading test in 2003. That score was 28 points higher than that of 8th-graders whose parents did not finish high school. The College Board found that SAT test takers whose parents had a college degree scored 33 points above the national average in 2003, while students whose parents did not finish high school scored 170 points below the national average.

There were similar score gaps between children from upper- and lower-income families. In the 2003 NAEP, 4th-graders whose low family incomes made them eligible for the federal lunch program scored an average of 201 on the reading test, while

Researchers have found that other factors besides race or ethnicity play a role in students' performance on tests and in school. Students whose parents held college degrees scored higher on SAT tests than those whose parents did not finish high school. Students who came from wealthier families scored higher than those from families with lower incomes.

4th-graders whose family incomes were high enough to make them ineligible scored an average of 28 points higher. The College Board reported that only about one-third of its SAT test takers who came from families earning less than $35,000 a year had high school grade averages of A-minus or higher. Among students whose families earned $80,000 or more, almost half reported A-minus averages or better.

Black, Hispanic, and Native American children are more than three times as likely as white children to live in the country's poorest and least-educated households. So, while the gap has its roots in income and family education, it shows up as a gap between children of different races.

Income and education are not the only causes. School achievement is also affected by whether a child lives in a one-parent or two-parent household, how often the family moves and whether it is homeless, the language spoken at home, and whether the child comes from a high-poverty neighborhood. In the kindergarten study, which was based on a population sample that resembled the U.S. population as a whole, 15 percent of the white children and 54 percent of the black children came from single-parent households. Those figures are significant. As the education department reported in 2001, 43 percent of children living in families with both their parents earned "mostly" A's in school, compared with 29 percent of youngsters who lived with a mother only. In addition, suspension or expulsion rates were double for children from one-parent households.

Many researchers have concluded that such social and economic factors account for about two-thirds of the learning gap. But wide debate continues on what causes the rest. Paul Barton, a senior researcher for Educational Testing Service, the Princeton, New Jersey-based test writing company, calculated in the early 1990's that five family factors account for all but about 9 percent of the difference between children who are successful in school and those who are not. Those factors include the presence of two parents in the home; the number of pages read for homework each day; the quantity and quality of reading material in the home; the number of hours spent watching television; and the number of days absent from school. Department of Education statistics support the idea that children who watch less television do better in school. White and Asian kindergartners reportedly watch about 13 hours of TV a week, compared with almost 18 hours for black kindergartners and 15 hours for Hispanics.

In *Inequality at the Starting Gate,* a report published by the Economic Policy Institute in 2002, researchers Valerie E. Lee and David T. Burkam found that white and Asian parents are more likely than black and Hispanic parents to read to their children, take them to museums and libraries, and enroll them on sports teams and in music, dance, and craft classes. The two researchers also found that white kindergartners tend to own an average 93 books each, about twice as many as owned by kindergartners who are black, Hispanic, and Asian.

In another study, conducted in the mid-1990's, researchers Betty Hart and Todd Risley observed 42 families with very young children. The study, which ran 2½ years, indicated that the more affluent a family was, the more words a child heard and the larger his or her vocabulary grew. Children in welfare families heard about 616 words an hour, compared with 2,153 words heard hourly in families where the parents were professionals. By the time the child from the family on welfare was 3 years old, the researchers calculated, he or she had a vocabulary of 525 words, compared with 1,116 words among the toddlers in professional-class families.

The education theorist E. D. Hirsch has calculated that to score well enough on an admissions test to get into an elite college, a 12th-grader needs to know between 60,000 and 100,000 words. The acquisition of a 100,000-word vocabulary requires learning 15 new words a day, more than any child is likely to learn at school alone.

Schools and the gap

Although the learning gap starts at home, it accelerates during school years because black and Hispanic children are more likely than whites and Asian Americans to attend failing schools. The Education Trust reported

in 2003 that about one-third of the classes in high-poverty or in largely minority-attended schools were taught by teachers who did not have either a college major or minor in the subject they were teaching. In low-poverty and primarily white-attended schools, only one-fifth of instructors were teaching subjects outside their college majors and minors, according to the Trust, a Washington, D.C.-based organization that advocates for better schools.

The Education Trust also calculated that school districts with the highest poverty rates have, on average, $966 less to spend on educating each child than districts with the lowest poverty rates. Those with the highest minority enrollments have $902 less than those with the fewest minority students. Thus, a class of 25 students may lose out on as much as $22,500 each year if it is located in a high-poverty district that consists primarily of minority students.

Harvard University's Civil Rights Project, which studies school integration, reported in 2001 that about 37 percent of black and Hispanic students attended schools with almost no white classmates. Minority students in segregated schools faced lower levels of competition from their classmates, more of whom lived in poverty than did the classmates of most white students, the Civil Rights Project revealed. As a result, there were often not enough students deemed ready for advanced placement or honors courses for such classes to be offered in their schools. African Americans accounted for 17 percent of public school enrollment but only 8 percent of all students enrolled in gifted-and-talented programs. They accounted for only 6 percent of all students who took advanced placement biology or English exams in 2001, the Education Trust calculated.

Those inequalities are compounded by students' own choices in school. The College Board reported that minority students tend to take fewer courses in high school and fewer of the high-level math and science courses that generally raise test scores. The Board noted that 31 percent of black test takers enroll in precalculus, half as many as Asian Americans; 13 percent take calculus, half as many as whites. The Education Trust also revealed that half of the nation's black, Hispanic, and Native American students were enrolled in Algebra II, compared to nearly two-thirds of whites and Asian Americans.

Learning English as a second language can be a huge disadvantage for many students, lowering test scores and opportunities, but it clearly does not hold everyone back. Asian Americans increased their SAT scores by 41 points from 1993 to 2003, including a 19-point gain on the verbal test, which tests vocabulary, reading skills, and grammar, among other

Social and economic factors that influence test scores

Educational researchers find that most of these factors are especially important during the prekindergarten years, ages 3 to 5.

- mother's level of education;
- parents' combined income level;
- number of parents in the home;
- whether a child has been read to;
- number of hours child watches TV;
- percentage of students at a child's school who live in poverty;
- number of children's books, records, audiotapes, or CD's in the home;
- whether a child has been taught letters, words, or numbers;
- parents' level of involvement in school;
- child's weight at birth and subsequent health;
- whether a child has regularly visited a library;
- whether stories have been told or songs sung to a child;
- whether a child has done arts and crafts.

Sources: U.S. Department of Education, National Center for Education Statistics, *National Household Education Survey, 1993 and 1999; The Condition of Education 2003.*

things. Puerto Ricans increased their verbal test scores by 13 points. By contrast, verbal test scores among Mexican Americans fell by 3 points.

The federal government's two major programs aimed at closing the learning gap, Head Start and Title 1 of the Elementary and Secondary Education Act, were passed as part of President Lyndon Johnson's Great Society program in 1965. In the 2002-2003 school year, Head Start, a child health, nutrition, and preschool program, enrolled 900,000 low-income 3- and 4-year-olds at a cost of about $7,000 per child. Head Start schools are run by community groups, churches, tribes, and local governments, rather than by state education departments. For many years, the schools focused on feeding children and providing them with day care, as well as helping their families access such services as job training and health care. Head Start workers typically had only a high school diploma and often were the parents or grandparents of Head Start children.

In 1998, as concern began to mount about the learning gap, Congress required that Head Start schools begin teaching prereading, vocabulary, such premath skills as numbers, and concepts such as "bigger than" and "smaller than." Congress also required that half of all Head Start teachers have two-year college degrees by 2003.

Despite the additional academic requirements, the U.S. Department of Health and Human Services (HHS), which runs Head Start, reported in June 2003 that Head Start children had made little progress in closing the

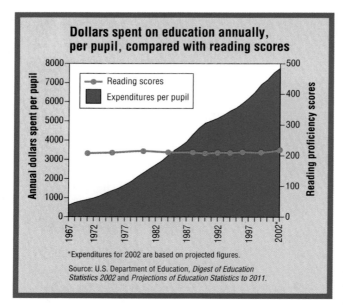

Dollars spent on education annually, per pupil, compared with reading scores

Reading scores
Expenditures per pupil

*Expenditures for 2002 are based on projected figures.

Source: U.S. Department of Education, *Digest of Education Statistics 2002* and *Projections of Education Statistics to 2011.*

Although annual per pupil expenditures have soared since the federal government increased its funding of education in 1965, reading scores have remained virtually the same. (The federal government began national testing in 1970.)

learning gap. The youngsters who entered Head Start in fall 2000 scored among the lowest 25 percent of children nationally on vocabulary, reading, and math skills. Nine months later, the Head Start children remained in the lowest 25 percent. Although the Head Start children had been learning, they could not catch up to children in private preschool programs or in state-run programs who had been learning, too.

The HHS finding fueled calls in Congress for even higher standards. Many Congressional leaders wanted Head Start children to be assessed at the beginning and at the end of each school year, so that schools in which children failed to make sufficient progress could be closed and their money shifted to others.

Head Start is open only to families living at or below the poverty line, which in 2003 was $18,400 a year for a family of four. Even with such a restriction, the program's budget covers only about one-third of eligible children. In addition to Head Start, 42 states and Washington, D.C., operate their own preschool programs, which enroll about 2 million children. These programs also are limited to the very poorest children, leaving lower- and middle-income families to find and pay for preschool on their own or do without. When upper-income children are enrolled in high-quality, expensive preschool programs, their educational advantages—and the learning gap—widen ever further.

Advocates have long called for universal, state-paid preschool, and most of the nation's governors campaigned for election in the early 2000's on promises that they would provide preschool. However, many people oppose the states' taking over early education. They claim it takes away a parent's child-rearing role. Others oppose universal preschool as too costly.

Title 1 is the federal government's program to help schools and school districts that have high numbers of children from low-income families. The funds can be used for a variety of special programs at the district's discretion. In fiscal year 2004 (which covers the period Oct. 1, 2003, to Sept. 30, 2004), the government provided about $12.4 billion in Title 1 aid, or an average of about 8 percent of the funds for school district budgets. The money gives the federal government the leverage to set learning and other standards for schools, even though education remains under the jurisdiction of state governments.

Current efforts to close the gap

In 2001, during a five-year reauthorization of the Elementary and Secondary Education Act, Congress passed the No Child Left Behind education plan. President Bush signed the bill into law in 2002. Among other directives, the plan required states to set learning standards, or detailed outlines of what each state expected its school children to learn. Each state was then required to administer yearly reading and math tests to youngsters in grades 3 through 8 to determine if they were learning the material the standards said they should know.

Test scores were to be disaggregated. Schools were required to show that students in each racial, ethnic, or other subgroup (such as special education students) were making learning progress each year and that the gaps among the subgroups were closing. The law mandated that, by 2014, all students must be "proficient" at reading and math—that is, they must meet standards set by their state in those subjects. Schools that did not show yearly student learning progress or did not narrow the gap were to receive additional money and technical help for a time but then faced an escalating series of sanctions that could result in a state take-over.

Even before Congress passed the No Child Left Behind legislation, most states had begun their own education-overhaul programs that included learning standards and yearly tests. States spent much of the first year of No Child Left Behind adapting those overhaul programs to meet federal requirements, but they also began pointing out what they saw as problems with the new law. Most states complained  that the law did not give them enough new funds to pay for the teacher training and remedial programs it required. Rural states and states with troubled inner-city school districts warned that they would not be able to meet new requirements that all teachers be "highly qualified" in the subjects they teach within three years. The law also allowed children in low-performing schools to transfer to better schools in the same school district. However, in cities such as Washington, D.C., New York, and Chicago, better schools were already overcrowded.

A Head Start teacher leads preschool children in an activity in one of the first such programs in the 1960's. The federal government began the Head Start program—a child health, nutrition, and preschool initiative—in 1965 in an attempt to bridge the learning gap.

Some states, including Texas, Florida, and North Carolina, reported that they were narrowing the learning gap, based on results of state tests. However, based on national NAEP test results published late in 2003, the gap remained as large as ever.

On the SAT, the score gap between whites and blacks widened to 206 points in 2003, up from 187 points in 1993. Whites outscored Mexican Americans by 158 points, up from 127 points. They outscored Native Americans by 101 points, up from 84 points in 1993. Blacks boosted their scores by 7 points in 10 years, but whites boosted their scores by 26 points, widening the gap further. Asian American scores increased by 41

In August 2002, U.S. President George W. Bush spoke at an Arkansas school to focus attention on his No Child Left Behind education plan, which he had signed into law in January. The legislation includes goals—and consequences for schools that do not meet the goals—that legislators hoped could help all children improve their skills.

points. Nationally, the average score improved 23 points in 10 years.

Why the gap continues to widen

The reasons that the gap exists are the same as the reasons for its widening. Harvard's Civil Rights Project reported that school segregation in the 1990's and 2000's grew as courts lifted desegregation plans they had imposed in the 1960's. One-third of black students attended majority-white schools in 1998, the latest year for which the Harvard group had figures. That proportion was down from a high of 44 percent in 1988 and about the same as it was in 1970.

An economic downturn strained state budgets in 2003. As a result, 23 states cut or slowed the growth of their preschool programs, and 21 states cut their spending on elementary and high schools, reported the National Council of State Legislatures. Indiana decreased the amount that families can earn in order for their children to be eligible for state-paid preschool from 43 percent above the poverty line in 2002 to 27 percent above the poverty line in 2003. The move reduced enrollment by 3,000 children. Meanwhile, Oregon schools closed two or three weeks early because their operating budgets were cut.

The growing number of immigrants in the United States was another factor that was causing the gap to continue and widen. Many big-city school districts reported that up to 100 different languages were spoken by students in their schools. Some immigrants from Latin America and Africa who were arriving at schools were unable to read in any language. The Census Bureau reported that 17 percent of public school children in the United States spoke a language other than English at home. For two-thirds of those children, the home language was Spanish.

Alternatives to the traditional public school

Dismay over the problems of some public schools encouraged parents, governors, and state legislators to look for alternatives to the way children are taught. Those experiments included vouchers, home schooling, and charter schools.

Vouchers are grants that allow students to attend private schools—many of which are affiliated with religious institutions—with tuition paid for by either the local school district or the state. The U.S. Supreme Count ruled in June 2002 that vouchers do not violate the principle of separation of church and state and are, therefore, constitutional. Nevertheless, vouchers remain controversial. As critics point out, vouchers take money away from public schools. In 2003, only Milwaukee, Wisconsin; Cleveland, Ohio; and Florida had voucher programs in place, all of which were limited to low-income children or to those in failing schools. Colorado voters approved a voucher program in 2003 that was to go into effect in fall 2004. However, a district court judge ruled in December 2003 that the law violates the state's constitution. The U.S. House of Representatives approved a voucher program for children in the District of Columbia in fall 2003, but the bill was deferred in the Senate. Polls showed that public opinion about vouchers was divided. In most polls, African American parents viewed vouchers far more favorably than did white parents, perhaps because inner-city schools, which are the country's most troubled, are predominantly attended by blacks.

Other parents choose home schooling as an alternative to troubled public schools. The U.S. Department of Education reported that about 850,000 children were home schooled in 1999, the last year for which federal government figures are available. Home school supporters claim the number is greater because many home schoolers do not register anywhere and, therefore, are not counted. The National Home Education Network estimated that the number of home schoolers was closer to 2 million. African Americans are estimated to make up about 10 percent of the children who are home schooled. Hispanics make up about 9 percent.

Charter schools are publicly funded schools that are operated independently of a school district by parent or community groups, churches, or education-management companies. Charters were intended to compete with traditional public schools and to be laboratories for new teaching ideas. The Center for Education Reform, a nonprofit group that tracks charters, reported that there were 2,695 charter schools enrolling 684,000 students in the 2002-2003 school year. As many as 100 additional schools were to open in the 2003-2004 school year. Although one-third of those schools had few minority students, the charter movement saw large gains in inner cities, where public schools are most troubled and minority enrollment is highest. About 40 percent of charter schools had minority enrollment of 60 percent or higher, the Center for Education Reform added. In Washington, D.C., where about 95 percent of the students are nonwhite, about 12 percent of youngsters are enrolled in a charter school.

Such alternate forms of education have created competition that education reformers hope will force the public schools to improve. Schools receive funding based on their enrollments and stand to have their budgets cut if they lose students to other kinds of schooling.

However, charters, vouchers, and home schooling accounted for fewer than 2 million children in 2002, compared with the 47.7 million enrolled in public schools. The numbers suggest that the new approaches to schooling will have little impact on most children. The job of closing the learning gap, and readying all students for college admission and jobs, still must be done in the public schools and in individual families. If no child is to be left behind, that is where the gap must be closed.

Cleveland, Ohio, city council member Fannie Lewis celebrates a Supreme Court ruling in June 2002 that voucher programs do not violate the principle of separation of church and state. Vouchers are grants funded by either the local school district or the state that allow public school children to attend private schools—often religious schools—using taxpayers' money.

Egypt. French President Jacques Chirac invited Egyptian President Hosni Mubarak to the G-8 summit in Evian, France, in June 2003. The G-8 (Group of 8) is an informal group of eight industrialized nations. The purpose of inviting Egypt and other developing countries was to discuss how to cooperate with wealthier countries in dealing with such issues as AIDS and poverty.

President Mubarak hosted an Arab-United States peace summit in Sharm al-Shaikh in June. The summit included four additional Arab leaders—Crown Prince Abdallah bin Abd al-Aziz of Saudi Arabia, King Abdullah II of Jordan, King Hamad bin Isa Al Khalifa of Bahrain, and Palestinian Prime Minister Mahmoud Abbas—and U.S. President George W. Bush. The meeting was convened to discuss the internationally sponsored "road map" for peace between the Israelis and the Palestinians.

Human rights. The Egyptian government abolished the High State Security Court in June in the name of expanding civil liberties. The state of emergency that went into effect in Egypt in 1981 gave this court and the Emergency State Security Court wide powers to investigate and prosecute individuals. Human rights groups argued that the 2003 abolition of the High Court was merely cosmetic since the parliament—controlled by President Mubarak's ruling National Democratic Party—left intact the Emergency State Security Court, from which there is no appeal. Only a presidential pardon can reverse that court's decisions.

In April, the Egyptian authorities detained without charge Ashraf Ibrahim, a political dissident who rallied opposition against the war in Iraq; criticized Egypt's economic policies; and clamored for the end of a state of emergency in Egypt. After four months in prison, Ibrahim was charged with seeking to overthrow the government and with disseminating false information abroad harmful to Egypt's interests. Ibrahim denied these charges, but his case was referred to the Emergency State Security Court. If convicted, he could face a life sentence. Human rights advocates argued that the charges were meant to silence political dissidents.

Arrests. In January, Egyptian authorities arrested 43 suspected members of al-Jihad, an Egyptian extremist group. They were charged with plotting attacks on U.S. and Israeli targets in Egypt. Although al-Jihad is led by Ayman El-Zawahri, who is associated with al-Qa'ida founder and terrorist leader Osama bin Laden, initial investigations revealed that the suspects had no direct links with bin Laden's terrorist network. However, analysts believed that the group was inspired by al-Qa'ida's ideology.

■ Marius Deeb

See also **Middle East.**

Elections. California citizens forced an unprecedented recall vote against the state's governor, Gray Davis, in October 2003. Although Californians have had the right to recall state officials since 1911, when the state constitution was modified, the 2003 recall was the first in state history. On October 7, Californians voted to recall Davis, a Democrat who had won election to a second term in 2002. Voters elected Republican Arnold Schwarzenegger, an actor and former bodybuilder, to replace Davis.

Schwarzenegger triumphed over 134 other candidates, including such minor celebrities as former child actor Gary Coleman and a star of the adult film industry. Davis became the first governor in the United States to be recalled since Governor Lynn Frazier of North Dakota was voted out of office in 1921. Schwarzenegger was sworn into office on Nov. 17, 2003.

Other gubernatorial races. On November 15, Louisiana voters elected Kathleen Babineaux Blanco, the lieutenant governor, as their first female governor. Blanco, a Democrat, defeated Bobby Jindal, a Republican, in the race to succeed Governor Mike Foster. Term limits prevented Foster, a Democrat, from seeking reelection. Blanco and Jindal were the top vote-getters of 18 candidates in a general election held on October 4. Under Louisiana law, all candidates run in the general election. If no candidate wins a majority, the top two finishers, regardless of party affiliation, advance to a runoff.

The Republican Party captured the two remaining gubernatorial elections held in 2003. On November 4 in Kentucky, Republican U.S. Representative Ernie Fletcher defeated Democrat Bill Chandler, the state's attorney general, in the race to succeed Governor Paul Patton. Patton was barred by term limits from seeking reelection.

Haley Barbour, a former chairman of the Republican National Committee and Washington lobbyist, defeated Mississippi Governor Ronnie Musgrove in his bid for reelection.

The Republican gains in 2003 built on successes in the 2002 elections, when Republican candidates prevailed against Democratic governors in Alabama, Georgia, and South Carolina. By the end of 2003, 28 of the 50 governors in the United States were Republicans.

Mayoral races. Several cities also held mayoral elections on November 4. In Philadelphia, Mayor John Street, a Democrat, defeated Republican challenger Sam Katz, a Philadelphia businessman. Street won despite being under federal investigation because of irregularities in the awarding of municipal contracts. It was revealed prior to the election that the Federal Bureau of Investigation had planted listening devices in the mayor's office as part of the probe.

The top two vote-getters in the mayoral election in San Francisco faced each other in a runoff election on December 9. Neither Democrat Gavin Newsom nor Matt Gonzalez, a member of the Green Party, received a majority of the vote in the race. Both candidates were San Francisco city supervisors. Newsom won the runoff election.

In Houston, neither Texas Democratic Party chairman Bill White nor former city councilman Orlando Sanchez captured a majority of the vote in their bids for mayor in a nonpartisan election, forcing a runoff election on December 6. Voters elected White mayor.

Campaign finance reform. In a 5 to 4 decision on December 10, the Supreme Court of the United States upheld the McCain-Feingold Law, legislation passed by Congress in 2002 to reform how federal political candidates finance their election campaigns. The court ruled that the McCain-Feingold ban on "soft-money" donations was not an unconstitutional curb on free speech. Soft money refers to unlimited contributions from corporations, labor unions, and individuals in support of a political party.

The decision also upheld the law's ban on the solicitation of soft money by federal candidates and a prohibition against political advertisements by special interest groups in the weeks leading up to a federal election.

The Supreme Court's decision overturned a May 2 ruling from a special three-judge panel in Washington, D.C., that had upheld several parts of the law while striking down other sections.

Campaign finances. The Federal Election Commission (FEC), a U.S. government agency which enforces campaign financing regulations, announced in August that federally registered Republican Party committees had raised $139.1 million and spent $106.8 million during the first six months of 2003. The FEC said federally registered Democratic Party committees had raised $56.4 million and spent $39.3 million.

Campaign contributions. Democratic presidential candidate Howard Dean announced on November 8 that he would reject taxpayer money and rely on private contributors to fuel his 2004 presidential bid, thus avoiding spending limits required by federal law. On Nov. 14, 2003, Senator John Kerry (D., Massachusetts), another presidential candidate, announced that he would reject public financing for the presidential primaries. President George W. Bush also announced in 2003 that he would not accept public money for his reelection campaign. ■ Geoffrey A. Campbell

See also **Congress of the United States; Democratic Party; Elections; Houston; People in the news** (Wesley Clark; Howard Dean); **Philadelphia; Republican Party; State government; United States, Government of the.**

Electronics. The world's electronics industry, still suffering from the effects of a worldwide slowdown in spending on consumer electronic products and related accessories, nevertheless began to see signs of recovery in mid-2003. Sales of television sets and related technologies showed sharp increases.

Sales of digital television (DTV) sets and plasma TV sets picked up speed in 2003. More than 2 million DTV units had been sold by August, according to the Consumer Electronics Association (CEA) of Arlington, Virginia.

Media Center. Additional momentum for DTV and related technology was generated by aggressive moves into the market place by companies better known for purely computer-related products. In July, Microsoft Corporation of Redmond, Washington, announced a formal commitment to its Media Center technology. Media Center links a home personal computer and a TV set. The TV or the computer can be used to manage and play video recordings, slide shows of digital pictures, live TV shows, radio programs, and computer games. A keyboard or remote control device can be used to browse through on-screen menus.

Windows XP Media Center was available only on new computers. It was not available as an upgrade to existing machines.

Videodisc recorders make headway. One of 2003's hottest consumer electronic products was the digital videodisc recorder (DVR), a device that allowed users to make, or "burn," copies of DVD's and other digital video materials, including still photos. Sales of DVR drives on laptop and desktop computers and as standalone units increased by more 500 percent during the first half of 2003, according to The NPD Group, Inc., a research firm in Port Washington, New York. By mid-2003, DVR drives were increasingly common on new computers. Standalone DVR devices benefited from price drops to well below $600 by mid-2003, from over $2,000 in the same period in 2001.

Cell phone gadgets. A walkie-talkie style cellular phone feature called "push-to-talk" was introduced in August 2003 by Verizon Wireless of Bedminster, New Jersey, to compete with Nextel Communications Inc.'s Direct Connect product. The walkie-talkie feature was aimed at business users needing rapid, brief contact with employees. The service required a specially equipped Motorola cell phone.

Cell phones that could take and send still pictures were also promoted during 2003. In August, Sanyo Electric Co. of Osaka, Japan, introduced a cell phone that could receive TV pictures.

Very small development. The creation of the world's smallest light-emitting transmitter, a device with a diameter 50,000 times smaller than that of a single human hair, was announced in May by International Business Machines (IBM) of Armonk, New York. The device was based on nanotechnology, a field that involves the manipulation of atoms to create molecule-sized devices capable of performing a variety of functions.

The IBM researchers who created the device used a carbon nanotube, a tube-shaped molecule made of carbon. Carbon nanotubes have great strength, electrical properties, and the ability to conduct heat.

The light-emitting transmitter and other such small devices could lead to better high-speed communications and smaller transistors. High-speed communications increasingly rely on light to transmit signals. The heat generated by traditional silicon-based transistors, which are at the heart of all digital electronics, ultimately limits how small such transistors can be.

Nanotube devices theoretically face no such limits. Scientists predicted the devices would lead to electronic components no bigger than a molecule or two that operate faster but require less energy than silicon devices. ■ Keith Ferrell

See also **Computer; Telecommunications.**

Employment. See Economics; Labor and employment.

Endangered species. See Biology; Conservation.

El Salvador. President Francisco Flores Perez and the conservative National Republican Alliance (ARENA) suffered a setback in mid-term elections in March 2003. The left-wing Farabundo Marti National Liberation Front (FMLN), a party of former rebels, held onto 31 of 84 seats in El Salvador's legislature. FMLN thus maintained its dominant role in the legislature, placing ARENA proposals to reform the country's health care and social security programs in jeopardy.

Political campaign. As El Salvador headed toward presidential elections in 2004, the FMLN candidate, Shafik Handal, a Communist of Christian-Palestinian origin, sought to make himself acceptable to the business sector. He pledged to encourage foreign investment if elected, though he also vowed to end the privatization of state-owned assets. Some polls in 2003 showed Handal as the front-runner.

Immigration extension. In July, the United States Department of Homeland Security granted an 18-month extension of the Temporary Protected Status program, in which 290,000 Salvadoran emigrants were permitted to live and work legally in the United States. The program was originally designed to help El Salvador recover from devastating earthquakes in 2001.

■ Nathan A. Haverstock

See also **Latin America.**

Energy supply. Global energy demand increased in 2003 due to economic recovery in the United States and other industrialized nations. However, demand increased slowly, and fuel supplies remained ample. There was even a surplus of electricity despite a huge power blackout in the northeastern United States and Ontario, Canada, in August.

Industry experts worried about possible supply disruptions throughout 2003. Petroleum was the main concern, primarily because of the war against terrorism in the Middle East and the war on Iraq. Iraq holds some of the world's largest oil fields and is a member of the Organization of the Petroleum Exporting Countries (OPEC), composed of 11 oil-producing nations.

Continuing political turmoil in other OPEC member states, such as Venezuela and Nigeria, also restricted some oil supplies. OPEC itself contributed to supply disruption fears by limiting its members' production. In addition, the expanding role of natural gas as an energy source raised supply-related fears for that fuel as well.

Price surges. These developments made fuels more expensive than expected in 2003. Crude oil hovered around $30 a barrel for much of the year, occasionally spiking higher. That rate was up sharply from the 2002 average of about $25 per barrel. Natural gas prices, approximately $4 per 1,000 cubic feet (28.3 cubic meters) in 2002, increased to over $6 in 2003.

The members of OPEC actually produced more oil in 2003 than their self-imposed quotas recommended. Moreover, natural gas shortages did not occur. Still, motorists and others felt the impact of higher fuel and electricity costs.

Regular grade gasoline, which had averaged a relatively expensive $1.44 per gallon (3.8 liters) at the pump in 2002, climbed to nearly $1.80 per gallon (3.8 liters) in 2003. Prices of other fuels processed from crude oil also jumped. Each $1 increase in a barrel of crude oil added about 2.5 cents per gallon (3.8 liters) to the price of gasoline at the pump, home heating oil, or jet fuel.

Higher petroleum and natural gas prices affected other energy costs, including electricity, which is increasingly generated by the burning of natural gas. According to the Energy Information Administration (EIA), a statistical agency of the U.S. Department of Energy, the average retail price for electricity through the first half of 2003 was 8.5 cents per kilowatt-hour. It was 8.35 cents per kilowatt-hour for the same period in 2002.

Demand. Demand for electricity was sluggish for much of 2003, which affected coal production in the United States, because coal burning generates one-half of the nation's electricity. For the first nine months of 2003, coal output totaled 802.4 million short tons (727.9 million metric tons), down from 820.1 million short tons (744 million metric tons) for the previous nine months, according to the EIA.

Aside from coal, demand for energy sources such as oil and gasoline generally continued to grow in 2003, because of better economic conditions. The Paris-based International Energy Agency, which represents the major oil-consuming nations, estimated that global demand for oil increased by more than 1 million barrels daily in 2003 to more than 78 million barrels daily. Experts expected demand to increase in 2004.

The United States continued to be the world's biggest oil consumer, accounting for more than one-fourth of petroleum use worldwide. According to the EIA, the nation used some 20 million barrels of petroleum products daily in 2003, nearly 250,000 barrels a day more than in 2002. In a November 2003 report, the EIA projected that U.S. oil demand would increase by 310,000 barrels daily in 2004, to 20.3 million barrels a day.

Gasoline was the most commonly used fuel in the United States in 2003, accounting for nearly half of all petroleum products. In September 2003, U.S motorists consumed 9 million barrels of gasoline daily, 3 percent higher than in September 2002, according to the EIA.

Conservation. The growing U.S. reliance on foreign oil, much of it imported from the Persian Gulf region, brought energy conservation to the forefront in 2003. The issue of conservation was particularly important concerning transportation, a sector of the economy in which fuel consumption has remained unaffected by recent recessions. Officials looked at the fuel consumption average of the nation's vehicles and discovered that the average number of miles per gallon was decreasing, rather than increasing, largely because of the poor fuel efficiency of highly popular sport utility vehicles (SUV's). Experts noted that the proposed Energy Policy Act of 2003, which triggered bitter debate in the U.S. Congress late in 2003, seemed to offer little toward improving the fuel efficiency of the nation's vehicles.

Analysts expected natural gas to figure more prominently in the nation's future, primarily because it causes less pollution than other forms of hydrocarbon-based energy. Hydrogen, seen by many as the hope of the future if made economically feasible as an automotive fuel, would likely be processed from natural gas. In terms of future supplies for U.S. needs, the sharply higher prices of 2003 sparked new drilling for natural gas. Also, several oil companies announced plans to build ports and plants for the shipping of liquefied natural gas to the United States from the Middle East and elsewhere. ■ James Tanner

Engineering. See **Building and construction.**
England. See **United Kingdom.**

Environmental pollution. Leaders of the European Union urged Russian government officials throughout 2003 to *ratify* (approve) the Kyoto Protocol. The protocol is an international agreement adopted in 1997 to reduce the emission of greenhouse gases—gases in the atmosphere, such as carbon dioxide, that trap heat and may be responsible for rising temperatures on Earth. Many scientists believe that global warming, as the phenomenon is called, is altering climate patterns worldwide and may devastate agriculture, society, and the environment.

By December 2003, 120 countries had ratified the protocol. However, the industrialized nations that had ratified the protocol were responsible for only 44 percent of global greenhouse gas emissions. In order for the agreement to go into effect, industrialized nations that contribute 55 percent of global emissions must ratify the accord. Because the United States (which is responsible for 36.1 percent of global emissions) refused in 2001 to ratify the accord, Russian participation would bring the treaty into force. Russia was responsible for 17.4 percent of emissions. (The remaining three industrialized countries that contribute to 55 percent of the world's emissions—Australia, Liechten-stein, and Monaco—together account for only 2.1 percent of emissions.)

In December 2003, a government adviser on economic affairs claimed that Russia would not ratify the treaty, as it ran counter to the nation's best interests. However, Russia's deputy economic minister later stated that the treaty was still under discussion.

Managing the world's water. In March, delegates from 170 countries met in Kyoto, Japan, for the World Water Forum, a conference held every three years to develop plans for managing the world's water resources. The group's goals, as established by the United Nations, were to cut by half the number of people without safe drinking water and basic sanitation by 2015.

The 2003 forum concluded that few of its short-term targets had been met and that significant additional spending was needed to meet them. The group estimated that in 2003, 1.2 billion people lacked access to clean water and 2.4 billion people had no basic sanitation.

The Equator Principles, codes of conduct to reduce environmental damage by the funding of infrastructure development, were adopted in June by 10 of the world's largest banks. Infrastructure includes, among other installations, dams, power stations, and mines. The principles were based on standards set by the International Finance Corp., a subsidiary of the World Bank. (The World Bank is a United Nations agency that provides loans to countries for development.)

The banks agreed to fund only those projects that are developed in a socially responsible manner and that adhere to sound environmental practices. The 10 signatories provided about 30 percent of the world's infrastructure financing in the early 2000's.

Easing ozone depletion. Scientists who had analyzed data gathered by U.S. National Aeronautics and Space Administration (NASA) satellites reported in July 2003 that the rate of destruction of the Earth's ozone layer had slowed. The ozone layer consists of gas that protects the Earth from the sun's harmful ultraviolet rays. Scientists credited the decline to a reduction in the use of chlorofluorocarbons, chemical compounds used in refrigeration and air conditioning before they were phased out by an international agreement ratified in 1987. Nevertheless, scientists warned that decades were still needed for the ozone layer to recover fully.

Three Gorges Dam. China's controversial Three Gorges Dam, the largest flood-control and hydroelectric project in the world, reached several milestones in 2003. On June 1, engineers closed the gates of the dam, and the reservoir behind the dam began to fill with water. By July, the water level had risen high enough to produce hydroelectric power for the first time. The dam, which was almost 1.5 miles (2.4 kilometers) wide and about 600 feet (185 meters) high, was designed to produce 84.7 billion kilowatt-hours of power per year by completion in 2009 and to control flooding on the Yangtze River. Environmentalists had long opposed the dam, which was to flood 254 square miles (658 square kilometers), submerge hundreds of small cities and villages, and displace 1.3 million people. The environmentalists claimed that industrial and residential wastewater would flow into the reservoir from new developments along its banks, turning the project into an environmental catastrophe.

Bush administration policy. During 2003, U.S. President George W. Bush's administration continued to propose controversial changes to the "new source review" (NSR) rules of the 1977 Clean Air Act amendments. The NSR provisions exempted older facilities, such as factories, power plants, and refineries—located mostly in western and midwestern states—from having to install costly, state-of-the-art emission control devices when they upgraded and expanded their operations, as long as the renovations were part of "routine maintenance." The expectation was that such acknowledged heavy polluters would eventually be phased out. However, by 2003, at least half of the power plants were still in operation, emitting most of the airborne pollutants that reached the northeastern states.

In 2003, the attorneys general of several

states most affected by the airborne emissions sued in federal court to stop the 2002 NSR reforms. Although the court would not grant a delay, it did ask the Environmental Protection Agency (EPA) to review the issue. In August 2003, the EPA issued yet another revision to NSR rules, allowing a more flexible interpretation of the term "routine maintenance." The Bush administration stated that the change would encourage older facilities to become more efficient and reliable. However, environmentalists charged that the revision hindered efforts to improve air quality, as had been intended by the Clean Air Act.

In May, the House of Representatives passed a bill that would allow the military to exempt itself from the Endangered Species Act and the Marine Mammal Protection Act if the acts' restrictions were judged to interfere with military training and readiness. The Senate had passed a version of the bill in 2002 that contained an exemption only to the Endangered Species Act. Environmentalists opposed exemptions to either law. Both laws had been passed to protect rare animal and plant species, over 300 of which rely on habitat found on military lands. In November 2003, Congress passed compromise legislation that included military exemptions to both laws as part of the 2004 defense authorization bill.

In December 2003, President Bush signed the Healthy Forests Restoration Act, an effort to reduce catastrophic forest fires. The law was to hasten the burning of underbrush and thinning of trees on federal land and represented a radical change in 25 years of forest policy. A coalition of environmental groups criticized the measure, claiming that the law directly benefited the timber industry and curtailed the ability of citizens to go to court to prevent foresters from cutting down old-growth trees. Both the Senate and the House had passed the bill in November.

Air quality at ground zero. In August, Nikki Tinsley, the Inspector General of the EPA (the agency's internal watchdog), released a report criticizing the agency for its reassurances to the public about the air quality at Ground Zero following the attacks upon the World Trade Center in New York City on Sept. 11, 2001. According to Tinsley, insufficient tests had been carried out to warrant the agency's statements that the air was safe to breathe. Tinsley suggested that the assurances were made under pressure from the Bush administration. EPA officials denied the allegations. ■ Andrew Hoffman

See also **China; Conservation; United States, Government of the.**

Equatorial Guinea. See Africa.
Eritrea. See Africa.
Estonia. See Europe.
Ethiopia. See Africa.

EUROPE

Tensions over the war in Iraq dominated the European political scene in 2003. Germany and France opposed the United States-led war, straining relations with the United States. The United Kingdom (U.K.) both supported and participated in the war, and other European Union (EU) countries—including Spain and Italy—and several Eastern European nations also supported it. These sharp differences complicated efforts to draft the first formal constitution governing the EU.

European concerns about the war first surfaced in Germany, where Chancellor Gerhard Schroeder won reelection in September 2002 after promising to keep German forces out of any such war. Polls showed a large majority of Europeans opposed the war, and large antiwar demonstrations were held across Europe. The biggest protests took place in countries whose governments supported the United States. Demonstrations on Feb. 15, 2003, drew crowds of some 1 million people in London, Barcelona, and Rome.

Antiwar stance. Schroeder and President Jacques Chirac of France worked together diplomatically in early 2003 in an attempt to prevent the war and formed a common position with President Vladimir Putin of Russia. The three leaders argued that Iraq did not pose an imminent threat to Western security. They wanted to reinforce the United Nations (UN) weapons inspection teams in Iraq and give them more time to search for *weapons of mass destruction* (chemical, biological, or nuclear weapons). The three leaders also contended that an invasion would be illegal unless it was authorized by the UN Security Council. When U.S. President George W. Bush and British Prime Minister Tony Blair lobbied for a UN resolution authorizing the war in early March, Chirac blocked their efforts by stating that France would use its veto power on the Security Council to oppose the resolution. The United States and the U.K. contended that the invasion already had UN backing under an earlier

Parisians cool off in the Trocadero fountain in Paris in August during a heat wave that gripped Europe in the first half of the month. Temperatures hovered at or above 100 °F (37.8 °C) for days throughout Europe, and about 20,000 people—mostly the elderly—died from heat-related illnesses.

Country	Population	Government	Monetary unit*	Foreign trade (million U.S.$) Exports[†]	Imports[†]
Albania	3,214,000	President Alfred Moisiu; Prime Minister Fatos Nano	lek (117.10 = $1)	340	1,500
Andorra	71,000	Co-sovereigns bishop of Urgel, Spain, and the president of France; Prime Minister Marc Forne Molne	euro (0.86 = $1.00)	58	1,077
Austria	8,041,000	President Thomas Klestil; Chancellor Wolfgang Schuessel	euro (0.86 = $1)	70,000	74,000
Belarus	9,885,000	President Aleksandr Lukashenko	ruble (2,115.00 = $1)	7,700	8,800
Belgium	10,286,000	King Albert II; Prime Minister Guy Verhofstadt	euro (0.86 = $1)	162,000	152,000
Bosnia-Herzegovina	4,160,000	Chairman of the collective presidency Dragan Covic	marka (1.67 = $1)	1,150	2,800
Bulgaria	7,742,000	President Georgi Purvanov; Prime Minister Simeon Saxe-Coburg-Gotha	lev (1.68 = $1)	5,300	6,900
Croatia	4,385,000	President Stjepan Mesic; Prime Minister Ivo Sanader	kuna (6.56 = $1)	4,900	10,700
Czech Republic	10,262,000	President Vaclav Klaus; Prime Minister Vladimir Spidla	koruna (27.53 = $1)	40,800	43,200
Denmark	5,375,000	Queen Margrethe II; Prime Minister Anders Fogh Rasmussen	krone (6.42 = $1)	56,300	47,900
Estonia	1,309,000	President Arnold Ruutel; Prime Minister Juhan Parts	kroon (13.52 = $1)	3,400	4,400
Finland	5,214,000	President Tarja Halonen; Prime Minister Matti Taneli Vanhanen	euro (0.86 = $1)	40,100	31,800
France	59,579,000	President Jacques Chirac; Prime Minister Jean-Pierre Raffarin	euro (0.86 = $1)	307,800	303,700
Germany	81,886,000	President Johannes Rau; Chancellor Gerhard Schroeder	euro (0.86 = $1)	608,000	487,300
Greece	10,953,000	President Konstandinos Stephanopoulos; Prime Minister Konstandinos Simitis	euro (0.86 = $1)	12,600	31,400
Hungary	9,770,000	President Ferenc Madl; Prime Minister Peter Medgyessy	forint (219.01 = $1)	31,400	33,900
Iceland	287,000	President Olafur Grimsson; Prime Minister David Oddsson	krona (76.67 = $1)	2,300	2,100
Ireland	3,875,000	President Mary McAleese; Prime Minister Bertie Ahern	euro (0.86 = $1)	86,600	48,600
Italy	57,231,000	President Carlo Azeglio Ciampi; Prime Minister Silvio Berlusconi	euro (0.86 = $1)	259,200	238,200 (includes San Marino)
Latvia	2,367,000	President Vaira Vike-Freiberga; Prime Minister Einars Repse	lat (0.56 = $1)	2,300	3,900
Liechtenstein	34,000	Prince Hans Adam II; Prime Minister Otmar Hasler	Swiss franc	2,470	917

resolution, passed in November 2002 that warned Iraq of serious consequences if it failed to disarm.

Political fallout. The opposition of France and Germany to the war caused serious divisions inside the North Atlantic Treaty Organization (NATO) and the European Union. In early February 2003, France blocked a U.S. request that NATO prepare to defend Turkey, an alliance member, in the event of a war in Iraq. France argued that such preparations would make war inevitable.

Divisions also erupted inside the European Union when five EU members—the U.K., Spain, Italy, Portugal, and Denmark—and three candidate countries—Poland, Hungary, and the Czech Republic—signed a letter supporting the U.S. position toward Iraq on January 30. U.S. Defense Secretary Donald Rumsfeld aggravated the internal EU divisions by dismissing France and Germany as "old Europe." At an emergency EU summit meeting about Iraq held in Brussels on February 17, Chirac criticized the Eastern European countries for siding with the United States, saying they had

Country	Population	Government	Monetary unit*	Foreign trade (million U.S.$)	
				Exports[†]	Imports[†]
Lithuania	3,661,000	President Rolandras Paksas; Prime Minister Algirdas Mikolas Brazauskas	litas (2.98 = $1)	5,400	6,800
Luxembourg	458,000	Grand Duke Henri; Prime Minister Jean-Claude Juncker	euro (0.86 = $1)	10,100	13,250
Macedonia	2,059,000	President Boris Trajkovski	denar (53.60 = $1)	1,100	1,900
Malta	396,000	President Guido De Marco; Prime Minister Eddie Fenech Adami	lira (0.37 = $1)	2,000	2,800
Moldova	4,251,000	President Vladimir Voronin; Prime Minister Vasile Tarlev	leu (13.00 = $1)	590	980
Monaco	33,000	Prince Rainier III	euro (0.86 = $1)	no statistics available	
Netherlands	16,087,000	Queen Beatrix; Prime Minister Jan Peter Balkenende	euro (0.86 = $1)	243,300	201,100
Norway	4,536,000	King Harald V; Prime Minister Kjell Magne Bondevik	krone (7.07 = $1)	68,200	37,300
Poland	38,466,000	President Aleksander Kwasniewski; Prime Minister Leszek Miller	zloty (3.91 = $1)	32,400	43,400
Portugal	10,068,000	President Jorge Sampaio; Prime Minister Jose Manuel Durao Barroso	euro (0.86 = $1)	25,900	39,000
Romania	22,206,000	President Ion Iliescu; Prime Minister Adrian Nastase	leu (33,300.00 = $1)	13,700	16,700
Russia	141,802,000	President Vladimir Putin	ruble (30.45 = $1)	104,600	60,700
San Marino	28,000	2 captains regent appointed by Grand Council every 6 months	euro (0.86 = $1)	259,200	238,200 (includes Italy)
Serbia and Montenegro	10,489,000	President Svetozar Marovic	new dinar (56.50 = $1)	2,300	6,300
Slovakia	5,416,000	President Rudolf Schuster; Prime Minister Mikulas Dzurinda	koruna (35.61 = $1)	12,900	15,400
Slovenia	1,978,000	President Janez Drnovsek; Prime Minister Anton Rop	tolar (203.61 = $1)	10,300	11,100
Spain	39,878,000	King Juan Carlos I; President of the Government (Prime Minister) Jose Maria Aznar	euro (0.86 = $1)	122,200	156,600
Sweden	8,796,000	King Carl XVI Gustaf; Prime Minister Goran Persson	krona (7.77 = $1)	80,600	68,600
Switzerland	7,153,000	President Pascal Couchepin	franc (1.34 = $1)	100,300	94,400
Turkey	71,455,000	President Ahmet Necdet Sezer; Prime Minister Recep Tayyip Erdogan	lira (1,388,889.00 = $1)	35,100	50,800
Ukraine	47,730,000	President Leonid Kuchma	hryvna (5.34 = $1)	18,100	18,000
United Kingdom	59,107,000	Queen Elizabeth II; Prime Minister Tony Blair	pound (0.60 = $1)	286,300	330,100

*Exchange rates as of Oct. 3, 2003, or latest available data.   [†]Latest available data.

missed a good "opportunity to shut up." These tensions between EU members complicated 2003 negotiations on a constitution for the bloc.

France and Germany sought to repair the rift with the United States after Bush's May 1 declaration that the war had officially ended. Chirac and Bush agreed to leave the dispute behind when they met at the summit meeting of the Group of Eight leading industrial nations in Evian, France, in June, while Schroeder held a similar meeting with Bush at the UN in New York City in September. France and Germany also supported a UN Security Council resolution in October that recognized the U.S.-led Coalition Provisional Authority as the governing power in Iraq but urged it to hand power back to the Iraqi people as soon as possible. France and Germany declined to contribute peacekeeping troops or significant aid to Iraq, however. On December 9, the U.S. Department of Defense announced it was barring French and German firms from bidding on $19 billion worth of U.S.-funded reconstruction projects in

Iraq because of their antiwar stance.

EU defense initiative. France and Germany sought to strengthen Europe's defense capabilities in response to the dispute over Iraq, believing such capability would give Europe the political and military clout to act independently of the United States in the future. In April, Chirac and Schroeder met in Brussels with the leaders of Belgium and Luxembourg and agreed to establish a joint military planning unit separate from NATO. They broadened the military discussions to other EU countries, including the U.K., later in 2003. U.S. officials expressed concern that the initiative might undermine NATO, but Chirac and Schroeder insisted they wanted to complement the alliance, not create a rival. France, Germany, and the U.K. agreed in November to propose creating an EU military planning unit inside NATO's Brussels headquarters and propose that NATO allow the EU to use its aircraft, spy satellites, and communications networks.

EU Convention. European Union nations engaged in negotiations during 2003 aimed at producing the first formal constitution for the bloc. Leaders hoped a constitution would streamline the group's rule-making procedures to ensure that the EU could continue to govern itself after it takes in 10 new members from eastern and southern Europe in 2004. They also wanted a constitution to set out in clearer terms the bloc's guiding principles and objectives.

The Convention on the Future of Europe, an assembly of 105 senior politicians led by former French President Valery Giscard d'Estaing, produced a draft constitution in July 2003. It included a charter of fundamental rights; the creation of an EU foreign minister; greater EU powers over immigration and asylum; a wider use of majority voting to reach decisions; and closer links between national parliaments and the EU Parliament.

A summit in Brussels to debate the draft constitution collapsed on December 14 in a stand-off over voting rights. Italian Prime Minister Silvio Berlusconi, the host, halted the meeting after it became clear that Poland and Spain, which had joined the U.S.-led coalition in Iraq, would not consider revisions that would weaken their voting power. Both countries—with populations of approximately 40 million people each—insisted on retaining 27 votes each; Germany and France—with populations of some 80 million each but with only 29 votes apiece—were equally insistent on stripping Poland and Spain of votes.

Enlargement. EU heads of government signed the Treaty of Accession with 10 new members at a meeting in Athens, Greece, on April 16, 2003. Under the treaty, Cyprus, the Czech Republic, Estonia, Hungary, Latvia, Lithuania, Malta, Poland, Slovakia, and Slovenia were to become EU members in May 2004. The treaty followed a decade of efforts by the candidate countries to meet EU criteria for open, democratic governments and free-market economies.

Economy. Europe suffered a second straight year of economic stagnation in 2003, though signs of recovery appeared late in the year. A sluggish world trade environment and uncertainty about the Iraq war depressed business and consumer confidence. The weakness was concentrated in larger European countries, with Germany, Italy, and the Netherlands in *recession* (two straight quarters of negative growth) in the first half of the year and France only narrowly avoiding recession. *Gross domestic product* (GDP, the value of all goods and services produced in a year) was forecast to grow by an average of just 0.8 percent in the 15 EU countries. The 2003 GDP was down from 1.1 percent growth in 2002 and was the region's worst performance since the recession of the early 1990's. Unemployment rose to 8.1 percent of the labor force in 2003, from 7.7 percent in 2002.

Several countries launched major reform initiatives during 2003 in response to the economic difficulties. Germany led the way, as Schroeder in March unveiled a package that included major cuts in government welfare, unemployment and health programs, and reductions in income taxes. In France, the government of Prime Minister Jean-Pierre Raffarin enacted reforms in June 2003 aimed at guaranteeing the solvency of the state-funded pension system by gradually raising the retirement age.

Budget dispute. The weak economy caused budget deficits to rise across the EU as tax revenues slowed and welfare spending increased. The problem was particularly acute in France and Germany, where deficits rose to an estimated 4.2 percent of GDP in 2003, the second straight year that the two countries had violated the EU's Stability and Growth Pact. The pact requires countries using the euro to keep their deficits below 3 percent of GDP to prevent budget problems in one country from affecting the entire euro zone.

The European Commission, the EU executive agency that enforces the Union's economic rules, recommended in November that France and Germany make deeper budget cuts to reduce their deficits. The commission wanted to back up its recommendation by threatening to impose multi-billion-dollar fines if they failed to comply. The French and German governments refused to make the cuts, however, arguing that such a move would merely weaken their economies further. France and Germany enlisted enough support from other EU members to block the commission's recommendation. The move angered several smaller countries, which regarded the French and

German move as evidence that big countries were powerful enough to ignore EU rules.

Central bank. Jean-Claude Trichet, the governor of the Bank of France, took over as president of the European Central Bank (ECB) in November. He succeeded Wim Duisenberg of the Netherlands, who had led the ECB since it was founded in 1998 to manage the euro. Trichet was appointed to an eight-year term.

Trade clashes. The EU adopted a more aggressive stance in international trade negotiations in 2003. It pushed to include new issues, such as antitrust policy and cross-border investment rules, during negotiations on a new global trade agreement. Developing countries opposed the EU's demands and argued instead for deep cuts in U.S. and EU farm subsidies. The ministerial meeting of the World Trade Organization (WTO) in Cancun, Mexico, in September, broke up without an agreement.

The EU succeeded in a separate trade clash with the United States. President Bush had imposed tariffs as high as 30 percent on steel imports in 2002 to help U.S. steel companies, many of which were losing money. The EU filed a complaint with the WTO, claiming the tariffs were illegal. On Nov. 10, 2003, the WTO ruled in Europe's favor. Bush lifted the tariffs in December.

Cyprus talks. Efforts to end the division of Cyprus, sparked when Turkey invaded the north of the island in 1974, failed in 2003. The UN-sponsored talks began in 2002 because many Greek and Turkish Cypriots wanted to reunite the island before it entered the EU in 2004. The talks collapsed in March 2003 after Turkish Cypriot leaders claimed the proposed settlement would require them to give up too much land. A Turkish Cypriot election on December 14 produced a stalemate as pro- and anti-settlement factions each won 25 seats in the 50-seat parliament. The collapse meant that only the Greek Cypriot part of the island would join the EU.

Heat wave. A severe heat wave hit much of Europe in late July and the first half of August 2003, causing thousands of deaths. Temperatures soared above 100 °F (37.8 °C) from the Mediterranean countries of Spain and Italy to northern France and Germany, setting records in many countries. A political controversy erupted in France after the state-run health system was caught unprepared. Authorities estimated that nearly 15,000 people in France, mostly the elderly, died because of complications brought on by the heat. The death toll was estimated at more than 4,000 in Italy and at least 1,000 in Portugal and the Netherlands. ■ Tom Buerkle

See also various European country articles; **Disasters; Economics; Iraq: A Special Report; Labor and employment; Weather.**

Fashion. The fashion frenzy that peaked in the 1990's showed no signs of reemerging in 2003. "Reality" clothes, rather than fantasy styles, were what the American public wanted to wear in a year of economic downturn.

Street fashions as a uniform. "People are dressing in uniforms," said U.S. designer Geoffrey Beene. "They are not interested in personal style. Functionalism prevails." The effect of this uniformity of style cut across gender, age, and class lines. As more people shopped at discount stores, many of the distinctions once marked by an individual's clothing were diminished. Nearly all but the very wealthy or very poor, the very young or very old, wore similar styles. Clothing, it could be said, was becoming more "democratic."

The "go everywhere" uniform for women of all ages continued to be denim or khaki pants, T-shirts, and sneakers or sandals. This trend transcended age. Mature women, who in another era might have chosen loose dresses or skirts with jackets, were now wearing jeans and T-shirts similar to those worn by teen-agers. There was one difference between the uniforms of older and younger women—the younger women almost invariably wore their pants low-slung, baring the navel.

The tendency of modern clothing to be worn by people of all ages also worked in reverse. Children of both genders, who at one time dressed differently from 20-year-olds, now wore miniature versions of the clothing worn by adults. For girls, the fashions borrowed from their elders were hip-hugger jeans or miniskirts worn with a short T-shirt. Young boys continued to wear the low-rise, baggy pants first seen in the 1990's.

Mature men proved to be the one group that defied the pattern of wearing clothing worn across a wide span of ages. While men in their 40's might wear T-shirts with straight-legged jeans just as they had in their 20's, they did not wear the urban styles worn by very young men, perhaps because of lower societal pressure to appear younger. Adult men usually wore casual attire like denim jeans and a T-shirt or, in a "business-casual" environment, khaki pants and a collared shirt. The formal business suit was seen infrequently.

Design for the masses. High fashion continued to spill into discount chains in 2003. U.S. ready-to-wear designer Isaac Mizrahi entered into a partnership with Minneapolis-based Target Corp., creating a line of colorful, quirky clothing for budget-minded women. Mizrahi was one of several designers working for the discount chain.

Manolo Blahnik. Manolo Blahnik was recognized at an exhibition of his work that ran from February to May at London's Design Museum. Blahnik began designing shoes in the early 1970's, and his creations—with starting prices at around $500—grew in popularity until celebrities and fashionable

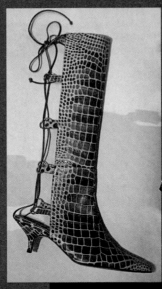

A London museum hosts a retrospective of the shoe designs of Manolo Blahnik.

Spanish-born shoe designer Manolo Blahnik (above) presides at the opening of the retrospective of his design career presented by London's Design Museum in February 2003. The show featured such "Manolos" as crocodile boots that laced up the calf (above left) and mules trimmed in ostrich feathers (below left).

women the world over were wearing his stiletto-heeled shoes. "Manolos," as the shoes were affectionately known, entered into pop culture when they were extolled by television characters on the BBC's "Absolutely Fabulous" and HBO's "Sex and the City."

The designer as a brand name. The name of a successful designer can, over time, become a very valuable brand name. Established fashion houses, therefore, often hire a new designer to continue the name after the founding designer dies or retires. American designer Calvin Klein continued to consult for the company that bears his name, but the design of his clothing line shifted in 2003 to Brazilian Francisco Costa. American Michael Vollbracht was hired in 2003 to keep Bill Blass's house in business after the designer's death in 2002. Finally, Tom Ford, the designer who had breathed new life into the long-established house of Gucci, announced he would leave that firm in 2004.

Deaths. The fashion world mourned the death of Eleanor Lambert in October 2003. Lambert founded the Council of Fashion Designers of America in 1962. She promoted American design despite the perception at that time that important fashion was created only in Paris. C. Z. Guest, a socialite whose taste and style influenced fashion and fashion designers for decades, died in November 2003.

■ Bernadine Morris

Finland experienced a politically turbulent year in 2003. The election campaign in the spring became a close contest between Finland's two biggest parties, the Social Democrats, who had led the government since 1995, and the opposition Center Party. The Social Democrats of Prime Minister Paavo Lipponen promised to maintain welfare and social service programs and increase spending on job-creation efforts. The Center Party, led by Anneli Jaatteenmaki, blamed Lipponen's government for the weak state of Finland's economy and promised to cut taxes to stimulate growth.

Jaatteenmaki also sought to take advantage of widespread opposition among Finns to the United States-led war in Iraq. She claimed that Lipponen had indicated that Finland would support a U.S.-led invasion of Iraq when he met with U.S. President George W. Bush in December 2002. Secret foreign ministry documents leaked to the press appeared to support Jaatteenmaki's position. Lipponen denied the claim, but the Iraq issue dominated the campaign.

The Center Party won 55 seats in the March 16, 2003, election, making it the largest party in parliament. The Social Democrats won 53 seats. The National Coalition, a conservative party that had governed in coalition with the Social Democrats, won only 40 seats. Jaatteenmaki

formed a coalition among her Center Party, the Social Democrats, and the small Swedish People's Party. She was elected prime minister on April 15 and took office two days later.

Shortly after the election, during a police investigation into the leak of the foreign ministry documents, Jaatteenmaki acknowledged having possession of the documents but denied leaking them to the press. Her credibility suffered when an aide to President Tarja Halonen said he sent the documents to the prime minister upon her request. Jaatteenmaki announced her resignation on June 18. A week later, the Center Party nominated Matti Vanhanen, the party's deputy leader and Finland's minister of defense, as the new prime minister. The new government promised to continue the previous government's policies, including cuts in income and corporate taxes.

Economy. Finland continued to suffer from weak economic growth in 2003. The country's main export markets in Western Europe remained depressed, and investment in important technology sectors, such as mobile telephones, was subdued. The economy was expected to grow by 1.5 percent in 2003, compared with 2.2 percent in 2002, according to the European Commission, which monitors the economies of the European Union

■ Tom Buerkle

See also **Europe; Iraq: A Special Report.**

Food. On Oct. 9, 2003, United States Secretary of Health and Human Services Tommy G. Thompson announced two new regulations by the Food and Drug Administration (FDA) to implement the Public Health Security and Bioterrorism Preparedness and Response Act. The law had been passed by Congress in 2002, giving the FDA authority to protect the U.S. food supply against terrorist acts and other food-related emergencies.

The first regulation requires food importers to give the FDA advance notice of arrival times for shipments at U.S. ports and details of the contents. The second rule requires domestic and foreign food manufacturers, processors, and shippers to register with the agency. A system for online registration was established. The regulation will allow the FDA to maintain a roster of foreign and domestic food facilities so that they can be notified of any food contamination. Both regulations went into effect Dec. 12, 2003.

On October 13, the FDA issued its "Risk Assessment for Food Terrorism and Other Food Safety Concerns." The agency concluded that "there is a high likelihood, over the course of a year, that a significant number of people will be affected by an act of food terrorism or by an incident of unintentional food contamination that results in serious food borne illness."

Food safety. On May 20, Canadian government officials announced that a laboratory had confirmed that a cow from Alberta had tested positive for bovine spongiform encephalopathy (BSE), or "mad cow disease." BSE is a fatal brain disorder in cattle that scientists believe is related to a brain degenerative disease in humans called variant Creutzfeldt-Jakob disease. BSE was first diagnosed in the United Kingdom in 1986. In 1989, the U.S. government implemented safeguards that prohibit animals, meat, meat products, and animal feed containing processed animal proteins from being imported from countries declared by the United States to be at risk for BSE. As a result, the United States banned such products from Canada. The case resulted in 2,800 animals being slaughtered and tested. No other cases were found in Canada.

In December 2003, the U.S. Department of Agriculture (USDA) announced that the first case of BSE in the United States had been discovered in a cow in Washington State. At least 25 countries responded by banning U.S. beef imports. The USDA on December 30 announced a number of new regulations to reduce the spread of BSE, including banning meat from cattle that are too sick or old to stand up. Stricter controls are also to be placed on meat packing procedures to better ensure that spinal cord tissue is not accidentally included in meat products.

On October 17, the USDA announced a 25-percent drop in the percentage of ready-to-eat meat and poultry products that contain *Listeria monocytogenes.* The bacteria can cause flulike symptoms and even death in people with weak immune systems. Of the random samples collected and analyzed between January 1 and September 30, 0.75 percent tested positive for listeria, compared with 1.03 percent in 2002. In 1995, before the USDA's Hazard Analysis and Critical Control Points system was established, 3.02 percent of samples contained listeria.

Obesity. The connection between obesity and conditions such as heart disease and diabetes attracted increased attention in 2003. U.S. Surgeon General Richard H. Carmona reported in September that nearly two of three Americans were overweight or obese, a 50-percent increase from 1993. In July 2003, Secretary Thompson announced that the FDA would require, by Jan. 1, 2006, that food labels list the amount of trans fatty acids, or trans fats. Trans fats occur in foods when manufacturers use hydrogenation, a process in which hydrogen is added to vegetable oil to turn the oil into a more solid fat. Trans fat is often found in the same foods as saturated fat, such as margarines, snack foods, and other processed foods. Trans fats raise the levels of low-density lipoprotein (LDL, or "bad" cholesterol) in the blood, which experts say increases the risk of heart disease. ■ Robert C. Gatty

See also **Agriculture; Medicine.**

Football. The organizers of the Bowl Championship Series (BCS), which is designed to determine the best college football teams in the United States, suffered a huge embarrassment in 2003. The team voted number one in both the media and coaches' polls prior to the 2003 title game—the University of Southern California (USC), in Los Angeles—was excluded from the game, a situation that had not happened since the BCS system was adopted in 1998.

Louisiana State University at Baton Rouge (LSU) claimed its first BCS national title—and topped the coaches' poll—by defeating the University of Oklahoma (Norman) 21-14 in the Sugar Bowl in New Orleans, Louisiana, on Jan. 4, 2004. However, USC remained number one in the media poll after its 28-14 victory over the University of Michigan (Ann Arbor) at the Rose Bowl in Pasadena, California, on January 1. This situation resulted in the first "split" national title since 1997, when Michigan took the media poll and the University of Nebraska (Lincoln) took the top spot in the coaches' poll. The National Collegiate Athletic Association (NCAA) created the BCS system to avoid another such occurrence.

In the National Football League (NFL), the Tampa Bay Buccaneers—for decades one of the weakest teams in the league—captured their first Super Bowl title, pummeling the Oakland Raiders 48-21 on Jan. 26, 2003, in San Diego.

BCS mess. The BCS controversy began on December 6 when Kansas State University (Manhattan) stunned then-number one Oklahoma 35-7 in the Big 12 Conference title game. Because of Oklahoma's poor showing, the media and coaches selected USC as the country's top team, dropping Oklahoma to third place, below LSU, in both polls. Oklahoma nevertheless remained number one in the BCS standings, which are determined through both polls and computer programs that examine the difficulty of schedules; win-loss records; and so-called "quality wins" against other highly ranked BCS teams. The BCS system ranked LSU second and USC third after USC came in third in computer poll average and strength of schedule. The chaos in 2003 renewed calls for a different method of selecting the nation's best teams, specifically a play-off in which the best teams would go head to head.

College. LSU's stifling defense helped the team overcome Oklahoma 21-14 in the Sugar Bowl. Oklahoma's potent offense came into the game averaging more than 45 points per game. In the Rose Bowl, USC defeated Michigan 28-14 as quarterback Matt Leinart threw three touchdowns and caught another.

In other major bowls, the University of Miami defeated Florida State (Tallahassee) 16-14 at the Orange Bowl on January 1 in Miami, Florida.

THE 2003 COLLEGE FOOTBALL SEASON

NATIONAL CHAMPIONS

NCAA Div. I-A	Louisiana State	21	Oklahoma	14
NCAA Div. I-AA	Delaware	40	Colgate	0
NCAA Div. II	Grand Valley State	10	North Dakota	3
NCAA Div. III	St. John's (Minn.)	24	Mt. Union	6
NAIA	Carroll College	41	Northwestern Okla.	28

BOWL CHAMPIONSHIP SERIES GAMES

BOWL	RESULT			
Sugar	Louisiana State	21	Oklahoma	14
Orange	Miami	16	Florida State	14
Fiesta	Ohio State	35	Kansas State	28
Rose	Southern California	28	Michigan	14

OTHER BOWL GAMES

Alamo	Nebraska	17	Michigan State	3
Capital One	Georgia	34	Purdue	27
Continental	Virginia	23	Pittsburgh	16
Cotton	Mississippi	31	Oklahoma State	28
Ft. Worth	Boise State	34	Texas Christian	31
GMAC	Miami of Ohio	49	Louisville	28
Gator	Maryland	41	West Virginia	7
Hawaii	Hawaii	54	Houston	48
Holiday	Washington State	28	Texas	20
Houston	Texas Tech	38	Navy	14
Humanitarian	Georgia Tech	52	Tulsa	10
Independence	Arkansas	27	Missouri	14
Insight	California	52	Virginia Tech	49
Las Vegas	Oregon State	55	New Mexico	14
Liberty	Utah	17	S. Mississippi	0
Motor City	Bowling Green	28	Northwestern	24
Music City	Auburn	28	Wisconsin	14
New Orleans	Memphis	27	North Texas	17
Outback	Iowa	37	Florida	17
Peach	Clemson	27	Tennessee	14
San Francisco	Boston College	35	Colorado State	21
Silicon Valley	Fresno State	17	UCLA	9
Sun	Minnesota	31	Oregon	30
Tangerine	N.C. State	56	Kansas	26

CONFERENCE CHAMPIONS
NCAA DIVISION I-A

CONFERENCE	SCHOOL
Atlantic Coast	Florida State
Big 12	Kansas State
Big East	Miami
Big Ten	Michigan
Conference USA	Southern Mississippi
Mid-American	Miami of Ohio
Mountain West	Utah
Pacific 10	Southern California
Southeastern	Louisiana State
Sun Belt	North Texas
Western Athletic	Boise State

NCAA DIVISION I-AA

CONFERENCE	SCHOOL
Atlantic 10	Delaware—Massachusetts (tie)
Big Sky	Montana—Montana State—N. Arizona (tie)
Gateway	Southern Illinois—Northern Iowa (tie)
Ivy League	Pennsylvania
Metro Atlantic	Duquesne
Mid-Eastern	N. Carolina A&T
Northeast	Albany
Ohio Valley	Jacksonville State
Patriot	Colgate
Pioneer	Valparaiso
Southern	Wofford
Southland	McNeese State
Southwestern	Southern

ALL-AMERICA TEAM (as chosen by the Associated Press)
OFFENSE

Quarterback—Jason White, Oklahoma
Running backs—Chris Perry, Michigan; Darren Sproles, Kansas State
Wide receivers—Larry Fitzgerald, Pittsburgh; Mike Williams, USC
Tight end—Kellen Winslow, Miami
Center—Jake Grove, Virginia Tech
Other linemen—Shawn Andrews, Arkansas; Alex Barron, Florida State; Robert Gallery, Iowa; Jacob Rogers, USC
All-purpose player—Antonio Perkins, Oklahoma
Place-kicker—Nate Kaeding, Iowa

DEFENSE

Linemen—David Ball, UCLA; Tommie Harris, Oklahoma; Chad Lavalais, LSU; Kenechi Udeze, USC
Linebackers—Derrick Johnson, Texas; Teddy Lehman, Oklahoma; Grant Wiley, West Virginia
Backs—Will Allen, Ohio State; Keiwan Ratliff, Florida; Derrick Strait, Oklahoma; Sean Taylor, Miami
Punter—Dustin Colquitt, Tennessee

PLAYER AWARDS

Heisman Trophy (best player)—Jason White, Oklahoma
Bednarik Trophy (best defensive player)—Teddy Lehman, Oklahoma
Lombardi Award (best lineman)—Tommie Harris, Oklahoma

On December 13, the Downtown Athletic Club of New York City awards the Heisman Trophy to University of Oklahoma quarterback Jason White as the outstanding college football player in the United States. White received 319 first-place votes, compared with 253 votes for runner-up Larry Fitzgerald of the University of Pittsburgh.

2003 NATIONAL FOOTBALL LEAGUE FINAL STANDINGS

AMERICAN CONFERENCE

North Division	W.	L.	T.	Pct.
Baltimore Ravens*	10	6	0	.625
Cincinnati Bengals	8	8	0	.500
Pittsburgh Steelers	6	10	0	.375
Cleveland Browns	5	11	0	.312

East Division	W.	L.	T.	Pct.
New England Patriots*	14	2	0	.875
Miami Dolphins	10	6	0	.625
Buffalo Bills	6	10	0	.375
New York Jets	6	10	0	.375

South Division	W.	L.	T.	Pct.
Indianapolis Colts*	12	4	0	.750
Tennessee Titans*	12	4	0	.750
Jacksonville Jaguars	5	11	0	.312
Houston Texans	5	11	0	.312

West Division	W.	L.	T.	Pct.
Kansas City Chiefs*	13	3	0	.812
Denver Broncos*	10	6	0	.625
Oakland Raiders	4	12	0	.250
San Diego Chargers	4	12	0	.250

*Made play-offs

NATIONAL CONFERENCE

North Division	W.	L.	T.	Pct.
Green Bay Packers*	10	6	0	.625
Minnesota Vikings	9	7	0	.562
Chicago Bears	7	9	0	.438
Detroit Lions	5	11	0	.312

East Division	W.	L.	T.	Pct.
Philadelphia Eagles*	12	4	0	.750
Dallas Cowboys*	10	6	0	.625
Washington Redskins	5	11	0	.312
New York Giants	4	12	0	.250

South Division	W.	L.	T.	Pct.
Carolina Panthers*	11	5	0	.688
New Orleans Saints	8	8	0	.500
Tampa Bay Buccaneers	7	9	0	.438
Atlanta Falcons	5	11	0	.312

West Division	W.	L.	T.	Pct.
St. Louis Rams*	12	4	0	.750
Seattle Seahawks*	10	6	0	.625
San Francisco 49ers	7	9	0	.438
Arizona Cardinals	4	12	0	.250

*Made play-offs

TEAM STATISTICS

Leading offenses (yards gained)	Yards	Per game
Kansas City	4,113	369.4
Indianapolis	4,289	367.1
Denver	3,126	349.9
Tennessee	4,031	343.8
Jacksonville	3,421	334.9

Leading defenses	Avg. points against	Yards per game
Buffalo	17.4	269.6
Baltimore	17.6	271.3
Denver	18.8	277.1
Jacksonville	20.7	291.1
New England	14.9	291.6

TEAM STATISTICS

Leading offenses (yards gained)	Yards	Per game
Minnesota	4,169	393.4
Green Bay	3,377	362.4
San Francisco	3,566	355.4
Seattle	3,872	351.7
St. Louis	4,287	341.1

Leading defenses	Avg. points against	Yards per game
Dallas	16.3	253.5
Tampa Bay	16.5	279.1
Carolina	19.0	295.3
San Francisco	21.1	308.0
Chicago	21.6	309.2

INDIVIDUAL STATISTICS

Leading scorers, touchdowns	TD's	Rush	Rec.	Ret.	Pts.
Priest Holmes, Kansas City	27	27	0	0	162
LaDainian Tomlinson, San Diego	17	13	4	0	102
Jamal Lewis, Baltimore	14	14	0	0	84
Clinton Portis, Denver	14	14	1	0	86

Leading kickers	PAT made/att.	FG made/att.	Longest FG	Pts.
Mike Vanderjagt, Indianapolis	46/46	37/37	50	157
Matt Stover, Baltimore	35/35	33/38	49	134
Doug Brien, New York	24/24	27/32	48	105
Gary Anderson, Tennessee	42/42	27/31	43	123

Leading quarterbacks	Att.	Comp.	Yds.	TD's	Ints.
Peyton Manning, Indianapolis	566	379	4,267	29	10
Trent Green, Kansas City	523	330	4,039	24	12
Tom Brady, New England	527	317	3,620	23	12
Jon Kitna, Cincinnati	520	324	3,591	26	15
Tommy Maddox, Pittsburgh	519	298	3,414	18	17

Leading receivers	Passes caught	Rec. yards	Avg. gain	TD's
Chad Johnson, Cincinnati	90	1,355	15.1	10
Derrick Mason, Tennessee	95	1,303	13.7	8
Marvin Harrison, Indianapolis	94	1,272	13.5	10
Hines Ward, Pittsburgh	95	1,163	12.2	10

Leading rushers	Rushes	Yards	Avg.	TD's
Jamal Lewis, Baltimore	387	2,066	5.3	14
LaDainian Tomlinson, San Diego	313	1,645	5.3	13
Clinton Portis, Denver	290	1,591	5.5	14
Fred Taylor, Jacksonville	345	1,572	4.6	6

Leading punters	Punts	Yards	Avg.	Longest
Shane Lechler, Oakland	96	4,503	46.9	73
Brian Moorman, Buffalo	85	3,788	44.6	71
Craig Hentrich, Tennessee	71	3,117	43.9	58
Micah Knorr, Denver	68	2,937	43.2	62

INDIVIDUAL STATISTICS

Leading scorers, touchdowns	TD's	Rush	Rec.	Ret.	Pts.
Ahman Green, Green Bay	20	15	5	0	120
Randy Moss, Minnesota	17	0	17	0	102
Shaun Alexander, Seattle	16	14	2	0	96
Brian Westbrook, Philadelphia	13	7	4	2	78

Leading kickers	PAT made/att.	FG made/att.	Longest FG	Pts.
Jeff Wilkins, St. Louis	46/46	39/42	53	163
John Kasay, Carolina	29/30	32/38	53	125
Paul Edinger, Chicago	27/27	26/36	54	105
John Hall, Washington	26/27	25/33	54	101

Leading quarterbacks	Att.	Comp.	Yds.	TD's	Ints.
Marc Bulger, St. Louis	532	336	3,845	22	22
Matt Hasselbeck, Seattle	513	313	3,841	26	15
Brad Johnson, Tampa Bay	570	354	3,811	26	21
Aaron Brooks, New Orleans	518	306	3,546	24	8
Daunte Culpepper, Minnesota	454	295	3,479	25	11

Leading receivers	Passes caught	Rec. yards	Avg. gain	TD's
Torry Holt, St. Louis	117	1,696	14.5	12
Randy Moss, Minnesota	111	1,632	14.7	17
Anquan Boldin, Arizona	101	1,377	13.6	8
Laveranues Coles, Washington	82	1,204	14.7	6

Leading rushers	Rushes	Yards	Avg.	TD's
Ahman Green, Green Bay	355	1,883	5.3	15
Deuce McAllister, New Orleans	351	1,641	4.7	8
Stephen Davis, Carolina	318	1,444	4.5	8
Shaun Alexander, Seattle	326	1,435	4.4	14

Leading punters	Punts	Yards	Avg.	Longest
Todd Sauerbrun, Carolina	77	3,433	44.6	64
Mitch Berger, New Orleans	71	3,144	44.3	59
Tom Tupa, Tampa Bay	83	3,590	43.3	60
Scott Player, Arizona	82	3,511	42.8	64

Also, Ohio State University (Columbus) defeated Kansas State 35-28 in the Fiesta Bowl on January 1 in Tempe, Arizona.

Tough times. Penn State (State College) finished the season with a 3-9 record, the greatest number of losses in school history. The 2003 season was the fourth losing season in head coach Joe Paterno's 38-year career, with three of those seasons in the last four years. The team's struggles prompted calls for the 77-year-old Paterno to retire. However, Paterno, whose career victories record was broken by Florida State coach Bobby Bowden on October 25, vowed to return.

In September, Ohio State suspended star running back Maurice Clarett for the entire season after a school investigation determined that he had broken NCAA by-laws concerning improper benefits and had lied to investigators. Clarett also faced criminal charges for allegedly filing a false police report.

Later in September, Clarett, who as a freshman scored the winning touchdown in Ohio State's national championship win over Miami in the 2002-2003 season, sued the NFL to allow him to enter the upcoming draft. NFL rules specify that a player must be out of high school for three years before being eligible for the draft.

Heisman Trophy. Oklahoma quarterback Jason White won the Heisman Trophy on December 13. White received 319 first-place votes, compared with 253 first-place votes for runner-up Larry Fitzgerald of the University of Pittsburgh.

NCAA milestones. Derek Abney of the University of Kentucky (Lexington) tied the NCAA career mark for kick-return touchdowns on October 25, taking a punt back 80 yards for his eighth score. He tied the 1970-1971 record of Cliff Branch of the University of Colorado (Boulder) and the 1970-1972 record of Johnny Rodgers of Nebraska. Oklahoma's Antonio Perkins became the first Division I-A player to score on three returns in one game on Sept. 20, 2003. In the same game, he also set a record for return yards in a single game—277.

NFL. Tampa Bay took its first NFL title on January 26 by routing the Oakland Raiders 48-21 in Super Bowl XXXVII. The Buccaneers' defense overwhelmed the Raiders, which had the league's top offense, led by quarterback Rich Gannon. Tampa Bay's defense intercepted Gannon five times, a Super Bowl record.

Tampa Bay's victory made Buccaneers head coach Jon Gruden, 39, the youngest coach to win a Super Bowl. To hire Gruden away from the Raiders before the start of the 2002-2003 season, the owners of the Buccaneers paid the owners of the Raiders $8 million and gave up two first-round and two second-round draft choices.

Play-offs. In the American Football Conference (AFC) wild-card play-offs, the New York Jets embarrassed the visiting Indianapolis Colts 41-0 on Jan. 4, 2003, and the host Pittsburgh Steelers overcame a 17-point deficit to defeat the Cleveland Browns 36-33 on January 5. The following weekend, the Tennessee Titans outlasted Pittsburgh 34-31 in Nashville on Joe Nedney's overtime field goal, and host Oakland scored 20 unanswered points in the second half to beat the Jets 30-10. The Raiders topped Tennessee 41-24 in the AFC title game on January 19 in Oakland.

In the National Football Conference (NFC) wild-card play-offs, the Atlanta Falcons thrashed the Green Bay Packers 27-7 on January 4. The loss snapped the Packers' streak of winning 13 consecutive home play-off games. The San Francisco 49ers advanced past the visiting New York Giants 39-38 on January 5, when the Giants botched the snap on a game-winning field goal attempt. In the next round, the host teams both prevailed as the Philadelphia Eagles belted Atlanta 20-6 and Tampa Bay flattened San Francisco 31-6. In the NFC title game, the Buccaneers beat Philadelphia 27-10 at Veterans Stadium in Philadelphia.

2003-2004 season. Neither of the teams that competed in Super Bowl XXXVII made the play-offs in the 2003-2004 season. The success of the Dallas Cowboys under new head coach Bill Parcells provided one of the biggest surprises of the season. Parcells, who led the New York Giants to two Super Bowl titles in the 1980's, inherited a team that was 5-11 the previous season and finished 10-6 the next season.

The New England Patriots, the 2002 Super Bowl champions, won 14 of 16 regular-season games in 2003, the best season in their history. Kansas City started the season 9-0 before being upset by the Cincinnati Bengals, one of the hottest teams at midseason under first-year coach Marvin Lewis. The Bengals, 2-14 last season, started the 2003-2004 season 0-3 but finished 8-8.

Quarterbacks Peyton Manning and Steve McNair shared The Associated Press's Most Valuable Player award. In just the third tie since the award began in 1957, each received 16 votes from a panel of 50 sports writers and broadcasters who cover the NFL. Manning and McNair led their teams—respectively, the Indianapolis Colts and Tennessee Titans—to 12-4 records.

NFL milestones. On Sept. 14, 2003, Baltimore Ravens running back Jamal Lewis established a single-game rushing record of 295 yards on 30 carries, including touchdown runs of 82 and 63 yards. Lewis broke the record of 278 yards set by Cincinnati's Corey Dillon in 2000.

On Dec. 28, 2003, Kansas City Chiefs running back Priest Holmes set the NFL single-season touchdown record at 27.   ■ Michael Kates

See also **Sports.**

France. The French government opposed the United States-led war in Iraq in 2003, straining relations between the two nations. French President Jacques Chirac argued that United Nations (UN) weapons inspectors should be given more time to search for *weapons of mass destruction* (biological, chemical, or nuclear weapons) in Iraq. He also contended that an invasion could worsen relations between the West and the Arab world and incite an upsurge in terrorism.

When the United States and the United Kingdom (U.K.) began lobbying the UN Security Council for a second resolution authorizing an invasion in February, Chirac made clear he would veto it. Lacking support, the United States did not put the resolution to a vote in the Security Council. Nevertheless, U.S. President George W. Bush insisted the United States had the right to invade Iraq under Resolution 1441, passed in 2002, which demanded that Iraq disarm or face serious consequences.

Chirac's stand provoked a backlash in the United States, as some congressmen called for a boycott of French goods and the number of U.S. tourists visiting France fell significantly in 2003. Bush and Chirac pledged to put the dispute behind them, however, when they met at the summit meeting of the Group of Eight leading industrial nations in Evian, France, in June. France also voted for a new UN resolution in October that gave the UN a larger role in the reconstruction of Iraq.

European defense. Chirac sought to bolster Europe's

The Eiffel Tower glows with a dazzling new display of 20,000 twinkling lights, inaugurated on June 21. The tower's new lighting was turned on for 10 minutes every hour from nightfall until 1 or 2 a.m.

defense capability in reaction to the tension with the United States. At a meeting with the leaders of Germany, Belgium, and Luxembourg in April, Chirac proposed establishing a European defense force capable of acting independently of the North Atlantic Treaty Organization (NATO), an alliance of 17 European nations, the United States, and Canada. Later in 2003, the four leaders persuaded other European countries, including the U.K., to join the effort.

The French economy stagnated on the verge of recession for a second straight year in 2003, pushing unemployment higher and swelling the country's budget deficit. France suffered from the general weakness in many European economies and a decline in business investment because of uncertainty about the war in Iraq. A rise in the value of the euro against the dollar also hurt the economy by making French goods more expensive on global markets.

European Union (EU) economists forecast that French economic output would grow by just 0.1 percent in 2003, compared with 1.2 percent in 2002. Unemployment rose to 9.4 percent in 2003, from 8.8 percent in 2002.

Deficit problems. The weak economy worsened France's budget deficit, causing political problems. The European Commission, the executive agency of the EU, forecast that in 2003 France's deficit would amount to 4.2 percent of the country's *gross domestic product* (GDP, the value of goods and services produced in a year) in 2003, the second straight year the deficit exceeded the limit of 3 percent of GDP for countries that use the euro. The commission requested that the French government make bigger cuts in its deficit in 2004 by cutting spending or raising taxes.

Finance Minister Francis Mer refused. With support from Germany, which had similar problems, Mer blocked a commission proposal that could lead to heavy fines for violating the euro rules.

Pension reform. The government passed controversial reforms to the country's state-run pension system in 2003, in an effort to curb the growing cost of the system as the population aged. The reforms forced people employed in the public sector to work longer—40 years, compared with 37 ½ years in 2003—to qualify for a full pension.

Credit Lyonnais. The troubles of the bank—which was rescued by the French government in the mid-1990's at a cost of some $36 billion, the largest bailout ever in Europe—were exposed in two separate investigations in 2003. On June 18, a French court found the bank's former chairman, Jean-Yves Haberer, and two other senior executives guilty of false accounting for covering up the bank's losses. Haberer was sentenced to 18 months in prison.

On December 18, a long U.S. investigation into Credit Lyonnais's 1991 purchase of bonds and other business from a failed California insurance company, Executive Life, ended with the largest settlement in U.S. history. Credit Lyonnais, the French government agency that bailed out the bank, and the French insurer MAAF both pleaded guilty to charges of deceiving U.S. regulators by making it appear that Lyonnais would not control Executive Life. (U.S. regulations at the time prevented banks from owning insurance companies.) The three French organizations and Artemis, a company owned by one of France's richest men, Francois Pinault, agreed to pay $771 million to compensate Executive Life policyholders.

Airline merger. Air France agreed to acquire KLM Royal Dutch Airlines in September 2003 for $900 million. The merger, which would create the largest airline in Europe, was the first between major European carriers and was intended to help the companies face growing competition in the industry. The deal was expected to close in 2004, pending U.S. and European regulatory approval. Air France also held talks with Italian carrier Alitalia about a possible acquisition.

Deadly heat wave. A scorching heat wave caused the deaths of nearly 15,000 people, mainly the elderly, in France in the summer of 2003. The heat wave, which affected much of Europe in late July and early August, sent temperatures soaring above 100 °F (37.8 °C) across much of France. The government-run health service was slow to respond to a surge in health complaints as many hospital workers and most government ministers were on vacation when the crisis hit.

■ Tom Buerkle

See also **Aviation; Europe; Iraq: A Special Report; Islam; United Nations; Weather.**

Gardening. The Conservatory of Flowers, a 12,000-square-foot (1,116-square-meter) Victorian conservatory in San Francisco's Golden Gate Park, reopened Sept. 20, 2003, after an 8-year, $25-million renovation. The 1879 structure sustained extensive damage in a 1995 storm, when wind gusts toppled large sections.

The renovation featured structural improvements, such as steel reinforcements in the building's redwood frame, and several new exhibits. Among the new exhibits is a remarkable assemblage of 700 species of high-altitude orchids.

Trends. Gardening consumers in large numbers favored container gardens and fountains in 2003. Gardening experts surmised that homeowners regarded pot gardens and fountains as high-impact, low-maintenance garden features. Plant hybridizers introduced dozens of new plants marketed especially for growing in pots. Vendors offered fountain models ranging in price from less than $100 to thousands of dollars.

Trees under attack. In October 2003, the California Department of Pesticide Regulation approved a chemical called phosphonate or phosphite for use on trees to prevent or treat infection by sudden oak death syndrome. The treatment, which was developed and tested by researchers at the University of California-Berkeley, can be applied either as a spray on tree bark or as a solution injected into tree vascular systems.

Sudden oak death syndrome, caused by a microscopic fungus called *Phytophthora ramorum,* first appeared in California in the mid-1990's. It has since been reported in Oregon, Washington State, and the Canadian province of British Columbia. The disease is known to attack and kill tan oak, live oak, and black oak.

The September discovery of an Asian longhorned beetle by a Toronto-area resident led to an intensive effort by officials in that Canadian city to identify and destroy affected trees. Prior to the Toronto find, experts believed that the beetle was confined in North America to locales in the New York City and Chicago metropolitan areas. The destructive beetle is believed to have arrived in North America in shipping containers from China.

Another deadly tree pest, the emerald ash borer, spread in 2003 from the Detroit area to Ohio, Maryland, and Ontario, killing millions of native ash trees. The borer, like the Asian longhorned beetle, can be stopped only by destroying all infected trees and cutting a wide "firebreak" area denuded of susceptible trees.

Memorial garden makeover. In January, the Battery Conservancy in New York City hired noted Dutch garden designer Piet Oudolf to replant the Gardens of Remembrance, an 820-foot (250-meter) border garden lining the city's Battery, the waterfront park at the southern tip of Manhattan Island.

The Battery Conservancy is a not-for-profit corporation created in 1994 to refurbish and preserve the Battery. The original garden was created by Saratoga Associates in 2001 and dedicated to victims of the terrorist attacks on the United States on Sept. 11, 2001. Oudolf, well known for his work in public parks in Europe, was expected to create a rich tapestry of perennials, ornamental grasses, and winding paths, according to conservancy officials.

Deaths. British horticulturist Graham Stuart Thomas died in Woking, England, on April 16, 2003, at age 94. Thomas restored more than 100 historic gardens in England and authored 19 influential gardening books but is best remembered for rescuing a number of varieties of "old roses" from oblivion. These are single-blooming shrub roses that predate the reblooming hybrid tea roses developed in the 1900's. In recent years, "old roses" have reappeared in gardens across the United States and Europe.

Robert Thomson, onetime host of Boston's WGBH television's "The Victory Garden," died on Oct. 2, 2003, in Topsfield, Massachusetts, at age 74. Thomson hosted the popular "how-to" show from 1979 to 1991.   ■ Carol Stocker

Gas and gasoline. See Energy supply.

Genetic engineering. See Biology; Medicine.

Geology. The current state of the ability to predict volcanoes, one of the most feared natural disasters on Earth, was highlighted in the March 28, 2003, issue of *Science* magazine. Volcanic eruptions throughout history have killed thousands of people. A 1997 eruption on the island of Montserrat, in the West Indies, however, caused no loss of life despite the fact that the city of Plymouth on the island was buried. The explanation for this comes from the hard and sometimes dangerous work conducted by volcanologists, coupled with better technology. Both have greatly improved the ability to predict volcanic eruptions.

Satellite-borne radar and global positioning systems can detect subtle ground swells, which often precede volcanic eruptions. Ground-based seismometers can detect the shallow earthquakes near volcanoes that often, but not always, accompany rising magma. Magma is molten rock that rides up within and then erupts from a volcano.

Volcanologists in mid-2003 for the first time began drilling into the area that conducts magma in an active volcano in Japan in an attempt to better understand volcanic eruptions. Researchers at Mount Vesuvius, Italy, were using a technique called seismic tomography to provide "CT-scans" of the interior "plumbing" of the volcano that destroyed Pompeii in A.D. 79. Scientists in Hawaii and Greece were developing special computer software that could provide three-dimensional, real-time images of volcanoes.

Despite all these advances, authors of the *Science* article concluded that predicting volcanic eruptions remained as much an art as a science.

Early greenhouse effect. Early Earth may have had a much stronger greenhouse effect than it does today. Geologists Alan Jay Kaufman at the University of Maryland in College Park and Shuhai Xiao of Tulane University in New Orleans studied the so-called faint young sun paradox and found evidence to support this conclusion. They published their findings in September 2003.

About 5 billion years ago, the sun was not as bright as it is today. Earth should have been a frozen, lifeless planet, because the sun was not producing enough energy to warm it. The geologic record, however, shows that there were liquid oceans and life on Earth at least 3.8 billion years ago. Kaufman and Xiao analyzed tiny fossil remains in 1.4 billion-year-old shale from China and used their findings to estimate the amount of carbon dioxide in the ancient atmosphere.

Carbon dioxide is a greenhouse gas in Earth's atmosphere. Like the glass in a greenhouse, carbon dioxide traps heat from the sun, making the planet warmer than it would otherwise be. Kaufman and Xiao suggest that there was between 10 and 200 times more carbon dioxide in the atmosphere about 1.4 billion years ago than there is today. So much carbon dioxide in the atmosphere would have offset the effects of the "faint young sun."

Abrupt climate change. Earth's climate may change in 10 years or less, according to an article in the March 28, 2003, issue of *Science* magazine by geologist Richard B. Alley of Penn State University in University Park and a team of his colleagues. Because human beings are adding greenhouse gases to

Formations of stones and soil look like strange donuts covering parts of the Norwegian island of Spitsbergen. The circles, as well as other patterns elsewhere, are formed by repeated cycles of freezing and thawing, according to researchers at the University of California at Santa Cruz, who reported in January 2003 that they had used computer simulations to determine how such geological patterns can arise naturally in polar and mountainous regions.

the atmosphere, there is a growing concern about climate change. Most people believe that climate change, if it occurs, will happen gradually over centuries, allowing human populations to adapt. Alley and his colleagues warn that change could occur much more rapidly.

Alley's team based its conclusion on historical and geologic records that show evidence of large, abrupt climate changes. The researchers point out that the Arctic area warmed abruptly during the 1920's. This development was followed by the Dust Bowl period of drought in the midwestern United States in the 1930's. Evidence of climate changes over the past 10,000 years also show that there were abrupt floods, droughts, and changes in global temperature. The scientists stated that all these changes are examples of "threshold behavior," which is a rapid transition between distinctly different states of climate. Abrupt climate changes may have large and unanticipated impacts on both human society and the natural world.

Acid rain. The amount of acid rainfall can affect the rate at which *calcite* (calcium carbonate) forms, reported Christopher K. Lajewski of Syracuse (New York) University and a team of U.S. and Canadian scientists in the *Geographical Society of America Bulletin* for March 2003. Pollutants from power plants combine with precipitation to form acid rain. In areas with a low capacity to neutralize acid, such as the Adirondack Mountains in New York State, acid rain acidifies lakes and damages lake ecosystems. The researchers studied how acid rain affects terrain made of limestone, which has a great capacity to neutralize acid.

They examined the sediment record of calcite formation in the Finger Lakes region of New York State and found that between about 9,000 and 5,000 years ago, when summers were warmer, there was a good deal of calcite formation caused by rain falling on limestone rocks. About 5,000 years ago, however, calcite formation abruptly stopped as temperatures cooled and weathering decreased. Calcite formation resumed again in the 1800's and increased rapidly after 1940. Apparently, acid rain falling on the limestone released large quantities of calcium and carbonate to the lakes. The scientists concluded that, unlike the Adirondacks, where acid rain acidifies lakes, acid rain falling on limestone terrain has the opposite effect by alkalizing the water. ■ Henry T. Mullins

Georgia. Parliamentary elections on Nov. 2, 2003, plunged Georgia into chaos and ultimately drove Georgian President Eduard Shevardnadze from office.

Government officials initially claimed the pro-government For A New Georgia bloc emerged with a narrow majority of the vote, but with fewer seats than the combined opposition parties. The vote tally was interrupted several times and the final results were not announced for weeks. Opposition politicians claimed that President Shevardnadze was attempting to block the victory of an opposition he charged would "devastate and destroy everything."

With each passing day in November, the scale of peaceful demonstrations in the Georgian capital Tbilisi grew, and protesters increasingly called on President Shevardnadze to resign. Finally, on November 23, Russian Foreign Minister Igor Ivanov flew to Tbilisi to broker an end to the crisis. After a short meeting with opposition leaders, Shevardnadze emerged to announce his resignation. As protesters cheered and fireworks erupted, parliamentary speaker Nino Burjanadze was named acting president. Elections to replace Shevardnadze were scheduled for Jan. 4, 2004.

■ Steven L. Solnick

See also **Asia; Russia.**

Georgia. See State government.

Germany. The government of Chancellor Gerhard Schroeder launched a program of reforms in 2003 in an effort to stimulate the economy after a decade of sluggish growth. Schroeder presented his program—called Agenda 2010 to emphasize its long-term goals—on March 14, 2003, to the Bundestag, the lower house of parliament. The reforms included measures to cut the cost of the country's generous welfare and health care systems, reduce taxes, and push some of Germany's 4 million unemployed people back to work. Critics on the left wing of the ruling Social Democratic Party argued that the proposed cutbacks went too far. However, after Schroeder threatened to resign if the party failed to support him, the cabinet approved the reform proposals in August.

Health care reform. The parliament approved the first reform measure, designed to cut the cost of the state-funded health care system, in September and October, as the opposition Christian Democrats and Free Democrats supported Schroeder. The measures, which were to take effect in 2004, required Germans to pay modest fees for physician visits, hospital treatment, and prescription drugs, which had previously been fully covered by the state-run health insurance system. The government estimated the changes would reduce health care spending by

$11.5 billion in 2004. In 2003, the German health care system was the third most expensive in the world, after those of the United States and Switzerland.

Labor reforms. In October, Schroeder won the Bundestag's approval for labor market reforms and tax cuts. The labor reforms would require people who have been unemployed for more than a year to take any available job, even if they were overqualified. Schroeder argued that existing rules that allow people to draw unemployment benefits for years were helping to keep unemployment high. The labor measure was part of a budget package for 2004 that was to cut personal income taxes by $19 billion. The Christian Democrats rejected the measures in the Bundesrat, or upper house of parliament, where they held a majority. They contended that tax cuts would only worsen the country's already-high budget deficit. The government and the opposition reached a compromise in December that halved the tax cut to $9.7 billion and approved the labor reforms.

The economy continued to stagnate for a third straight year in 2003. German industry slashed investments because of uncertainty stemming from the Iraq war and weakness in Germany's main export markets. The economy was in recession in the first half of the year as output declined. After a modest upturn in the second half, European Union (EU) economists forecast that the gross domestic product (GDP, the value of all goods and services produced in a year) would be virtually unchanged compared with 2002. Unemployment rose to 9.4 percent in 2003 from 8.6 percent in 2002.

State elections. The combination of a weak economy and the unpopularity of many of the government's economic reforms produced serious defeats for Schroeder's Social Democrats in several state elections in 2003. On February 2, the Social Democrats lost control of the legislature in Lower Saxony, Schroeder's home state, to the Christian Democrats as the party's share of the vote fell to 33 percent from 48 percent in the previous election four years earlier. On September 21, the Social Democrats were routed in Bavaria by the Christian Social Union, the sister party of the Christian Democrats. The Social Democrats won just 20 percent of the vote, their worst showing in the state since World War II (1939-1945).

Deficit dispute. The weak economy caused Germany's budget deficit to expand in 2003 and led to a conflict with the EU. The deficit was forecast to rise to 4.2 percent of GDP, up from 3.5 percent in 2002 and above the EU limit of 3 percent for countries that use the euro. The European Commission, the EU agency that applies the euro's economic rules, requested in November

Floodwaters from a storm that swept across Europe in early January inundate the Deutsches Eck (German Corner) monument at the point where the rivers Rhine and Mosel meet in Koblenz. The flooding forced the closure of several stretches of both rivers to barge traffic.

2003 that Germany make deeper cuts in its 2004 budget to reduce the deficit or face disciplinary action. Finance Minister Hans Eichel refused, however, arguing that cuts would hurt the weak economy. With support from France, which also experienced rising deficits, Eichel persuaded EU finance ministers not to take disciplinary action against the two nations. The decision was strongly opposed by smaller EU countries that had respected the deficit limits and raised doubts about the rules governing the euro.

Relations with the United States. Schroeder opposed the U.S.-led war in Iraq during 2003, straining U.S.-German relations. He allied himself with President Jacques Chirac of France and President Vladimir Putin of Russia, who favored giving United Nations inspectors more time to search for *weapons of mass destruction* (chemical, biological, or nuclear weapons). However, Schroeder met with U.S. President George W. Bush in New York City in September and offered Germany's assistance in the reconstruction of Iraq. Germany also worked closely with the United States in Afghanistan, holding a joint command with the Netherlands of a peacekeeping force before handing control over to the North Atlantic Treaty Organization in August. ■ Tom Buerkle

See also **Europe; France; Iraq: A Special Report.**
Ghana. See Africa.

Golf. In 2003, the four major tournaments of the Professional Golfers' Association (PGA) were, for the first time since 1969, won by players who had never before won a major. Women golfers made forays into men's golf in 2003, with several women participating in men's events. Eldrick "Tiger" Woods did not have his best season, but set a new mark for consistently fine play.

On October 24, Se Ri Pak of South Korea became the first woman in 58 years to *make the cut* (qualify to finish a tournament) in a men's event. Babe Didrikson was the first woman to participate in a men's tournament, doing so in 1945. Several other women golfers had played in men's tournaments earlier in the season, including Annika Sorenstam of Sweden and Suzy Whaley and Michelle Wie of the United States. However, they failed to make the cut.

PGA. Mike Weir on April 13 became the first left-handed player and the first Canadian to win the Masters Championship in Augusta, Georgia. Both Weir and Len Mattiace shot a 7-under 281 in regulation play, but Weir edged Mattiace on the first play-off hole for the victory.

Jim Furyk won the U.S. Open on June 15 in Olympia Fields, Illinois. Furyk won by three strokes and tied the lowest-ever score for a U.S. Open by turning in a mark of 8-under-par 272.

At the British Open in July, Ben Curtis, a

rookie professional from the United States, shot a 2-under-par 69 on the final day to shock the world and win the first major he had ever entered. Curtis, who finished at 1-under 283, was the only player to break par on the challenging Royal St. George's course in Sandwich, England.

Shaun Micheel of the United States won the PGA Championship on August 17 in Rochester, New York, in dramatic fashion. With a 1-stroke lead on the final hole, Micheel made one of the most amazing shots in PGA major history, dropping his approach within inches of the cup to seal his victory. Micheel finished the tournament at 4-under-par, edging Chad Campbell by two strokes.

Tiger makes cut. In October, Eldrick "Tiger" Woods tied the record for making the most consecutive cuts in tournaments, with 113. The 54-year-old record had been held by Byron Nelson.

LPGA. Patricia Meunier-Lebouc won the Nabisco Championship in Rancho Mirage, California, on March 30. She defeated Sorenstam by one stroke for her first major victory.

Sorenstam bounced back to win the LPGA Championship in Wilmington, Delaware, on June 8. Sorenstam finished regulation play tied with Grace Park, but won in a play-off.

At the U.S. Women's Open, Hilary Lunke became the first *qualifier* (player who had to play a special round to even qualify for the tournament) to win. Lunke sank a 15-foot (4.5-meter) birdie putt on the 18th hole of a three-way play-off on July 7 in North Plains, Oregon. Lunke finished the play-off one stroke ahead of Angela Stanford and three ahead of Kelly Robbins.

On August 3, Sorenstam became only the sixth woman to complete a career *grand slam* (winning all four major tournaments) when she captured the Women's British Open at Lytham St. Annes, England. Sorenstam finished with a 10-under 278, one shot better than Se Ri Pak.

Senior PGA. On the circuit for professionals more than 50 years old, John Jacobs won his first major tournament on June 8, winning the Senior PGA Championship at Newtown Square, Pennsylvania. Jacobs finished two strokes ahead of Bobby Wadkins.

Bruce Lietzke won his first major with a 7-under 277 at the U.S. Senior Open in Toledo, Ohio, on June 29. Lietzke struggled in the final round, finishing at 2-over-par. Lietzke won by two strokes.

Craig Stadler shot a 17-under 271 to capture the Senior Players Championship on July 13 in Dearborn, Michigan.

Tom Watson won the Senior British Open in Turnberry, Scotland, on July 27 in a play-off with Carl Mason. Watson and Mason finished regulation play tied at a record 17-under-par, but Watson won in the play-off.   ■ Michael Kates

See also **Sports.**

Ben Curtis of the United States finishes up a putt at the British Open in Sandwich, England, in July 2003. Curtis, a virtually unknown rookie, shocked the golf world by becoming the only player at the tournament to break par, winning by one stroke.

Greece. A trial of suspected members of Greece's most notorious terrorist group ended with the conviction of 15 people in 2003. The group was called November 17 after the date in 1973 when Greece's then-ruling military *junta* (group in power) sent tanks to crush a student protest. November 17 group members killed 23 people over a 25-year period, beginning with the assassination of the Central Intelligence Agency's Athens station chief, Richard Welch, in 1975.

The trial dominated Greek news for nine months until Dec. 8, 2003, when a panel of three judges found 15 people, including group leader Alexandros Giotopoulos and the main hit man Dimitris Koufodinas, guilty of multiple counts of murder, attempted murder, and bomb attacks. They received multiple life sentences. The verdicts were welcomed by Greek leaders, who hoped the convictions would ease concerns about potential terrorist attacks during the 2004 Summer Olympic Games, to be held in Athens.

Olympic progress. Preparations for the Olympics made progress in 2003 after several years of delays. The International Olympic Committee expressed confidence in October that sporting facilities would be ready in time, though work on the main stadium and new train lines being built for the games would continue almost until the opening ceremony in August 2004.

Parthenon controversy. Greece continued to pressure the United Kingdom to return in time for the Olympics a collection of marble plaques and statues that were once part of the Parthenon in Athens. The statues were taken by British explorer Lord Elgin in 1803 and have been displayed in the British Museum in London since 1811. The museum's director, Neil MacGregor, said in February 2003 that he would oppose any attempt to return the sculptures because the Parthenon, an ancient temple that sits atop the Acropolis, is in ruins. Nevertheless, Greek authorities continued work on an Acropolis museum intended to house the sculptures.

Greek Prime Minister Costas Simitis was criticized by political opponents for trying to use the sculptures for political gain. At a European Union summit meeting in October, Simitis asked British Prime Minister Tony Blair to support the return of the sculptures, saying it would help Simitis's campaign to win reelection in 2004.

Airline sale. The Greek parliament in September 2003 approved plans to sell 51 percent of the state-owned carrier, Olympic Airways, to private investors and to eliminate 4,300 of the carrier's 6,100 employees. The government said the cuts were necessary to avoid bankruptcy of the airline. ■ Tom Buerkle

See also **Europe.**

Grenada. See **Latin America.**

Guatemala. In December 2003, Guatemalan voters elected Oscar Berger, a pro-business, former mayor of Guatemala City, president. His election returned power to the country's traditional landed elite. Berger was a candidate of the Grand National Alliance, a coalition of political parties. The election was Berger's second try for the presidency. In 1999, he lost to Guatemala's incumbent President Alfonso Antonio Portillo Cabrera.

Election violence. The 2003 elections were the second held since peace accords were signed in 1996, bringing an end to a 36-year-long civil war. The elections marred by frequent violence, including the deaths of at least 27 people involved in campaigning. Much of the violence was attributed to General Efrain Rios Montt, a former military dictator. His supporters looted stores, burned cars, and attacked journalists in Guatemala City in early April 2003. The show of force by the general's backers influenced the subsequent decision by the nation's supreme court to approve his candidacy, despite a constitutional provision that prohibits former military dictators from becoming president. Despite the decision, the general lost in the first round of elections in November. ■ Nathan A. Haverstock

See also **Latin America.**

Guyana. See **Latin America.**

Haiti. President Jean-Bertrand Aristide failed to meet the September deadline to schedule elections in 2003 in keeping with resolutions by the Organization of American States (OAS), a 35-member regional body that promotes democracy. OAS officials had previously declared the 2000 Haitian elections fraudulent. In frustration, United States Assistant Secretary of State for Western Hemisphere Affairs Roger F. Noriega blamed Aristide for the impasse and his "inability and unwillingness to move the country along a democratic path."

Reduced international aid. In response to Aristide's hostility, the United States reduced its aid to Haiti to some $70 million in 2003. International financial agencies, which provided Haiti with about $427 million following the 1994 U.S. intervention that restored Aristide to power, also reduced their assistance. Like the U.S. government, the agencies tried to aid social impact and humanitarian programs judged free of the rampant corruption within the Haitian government. Unfortunately, the brunt of the political deadlock fell on the shoulders of Haiti's poor, most of whom were jobless or struggling to survive on less than $1 a day. ■ Nathan A. Haverstock

See also **Latin America.**

Harness racing. See **Horse racing.**

Hawaii. See **State government.**

Health care issues. The most sweeping federal health care legislation in nearly 40 years was the focus of intense political controversy in the United States for much of 2003. In November, the U.S. Congress approved a bill reshaping Medicare, the federal program that pays for many health care expenses for Americans over 65 and some other groups.

Changing Medicare. President George W. Bush, in his State of the Union speech in January, proposed that Medicare beneficiaries who do not have coverage for prescription drugs—about 33 percent of the total—obtain the benefit by joining a private insurance plan. When the idea was criticized by Democrats and even some Republicans, Senator Bill Frist (R., Tennessee) urged the Republican-controlled Congress to develop its own prescription drug benefit plan, using a "framework" provided by the Bush administration.

Intense political debate ensued, and a number of issues besides subsidies for prescription drugs were added to the legislation. The House and Senate each passed its version of the bill in June and a committee of House and Senate negotiators worked for five months to reconcile them. In a 220-215 vote, the House passed the reconciled legislation on November 23. The Senate voted 54-44 in favor of the bill on November 26. Signed into law in December, the statute provides for drug discount cards, which seniors may purchase, that would reduce the cost of any drug by 15 percent, and $600-a-year subsidies for low-income seniors' drug costs.

The law creates a Medicare-based prescription drug benefit, which will begin in 2006. Participants will pay $420 a year for the program, the first $250 of prescription drug costs, and 25 percent of costs up to a limit of $2,250, after which there is no coverage until the cost per year exceeds $5,100. After $5,100, Medicare will pay 95 percent of the cost.

The law also offers seniors the option of joining a private health plan that provides drug coverage; Medicare will pay most of the premium. However, not all drugs will be covered by these plans, and benefits will vary from one area to another. The law also gives $14 billion in subsidies to private insurers who offer coverage to Medicare beneficiaries in certain markets deemed unprofitable. It also offers tax breaks for employers who continue to pay for the drug costs of retired workers. A "demonstration project" is to be set up under which Medicare must compete with private insurers for beneficiaries in six metropolitan areas.

The law specifically prohibits the federal government from negotiating with drug manufacturers for lower prices for Medicare beneficiaries, though private insurers may do so, and the purchasing of U.S.-produced prescription drugs from Canada, unless the federal government certifies the drugs to be safe, is also prohibited.

Health insurance. In September, the U.S. Census Bureau reported that 2.4 million more U.S. citizens became uninsured in 2002, bringing the total number of people without insurance to 43.6 million. Iowa, Minnesota, Rhode Island, and Wisconsin had the lowest rates of uninsured citizens—approximately 8 percent. Texas had the highest—24.1 percent. Several states launched initiatives in 2003 designed to produce broader or universal coverage. The most ambitious were in Maine, where the state sought to subsidize coverage for all residents, and California, where the legislature passed a bill requiring most employers to provide coverage to workers.

Health care costs. Health care costs continued to rise at a near-record rate. Spending in 2002, the last year for which information was available, increased by 9.6 percent. Health costs rose by 8.7 percent in 2001, according to figures from the U.S. Department of Health and Human Services, which projected that costs would double by 2012 to $2.8 trillion a year, or 17 percent of gross domestic spending.

◼ Emily Friedman

See also **Congress of the United States; Drugs; Medicine; People in the news** (Bill Frist).

Hockey. The New Jersey Devils won their third Stanley Cup in nine seasons on June 9, 2003, defeating the Anaheim Mighty Ducks 3-0 in East Rutherford, New Jersey. The home team won every game in the seesawing series, in which the Devils topped the Mighty Ducks 4 games to 3.

The Devils, who allowed just 13 goals in the play-offs, became the first team since 1965 to win the Stanley Cup by only winning home games. New Jersey set a National Hockey League (NHL) record by winning 12 play-off games at home. Anaheim goaltender Jean-Sebastien Giguere won the Conn Smythe trophy for the most valuable player in the play-offs. He was the first player from a losing team to take the honor since 1987.

Regular season. In the Eastern Conference, Ottawa racked up the league's best record, posting 52 wins and 113 points to capture the Northeast Division. New Jersey won the Atlantic Division with 108 points, and the Tampa Bay Lightning won the Southeast Division with 93 points. In the Western Conference, Dallas (111 points), Detroit (110 points), and Colorado (105 points) captured the Pacific, Central, and Northwest divisions, respectively.

Play-offs. Anaheim swept the Minnesota Wild 4 games to 0, sending the team to its first Stanley Cup finals. The Mighty Ducks limited Minnesota to just one goal in the series. Anaheim had swept

NATIONAL HOCKEY LEAGUE STANDINGS

WESTERN CONFERENCE

Central Division	W.	L.	T.	†OTL.	Pts.
Detroit Red Wings*	48	20	10	4	110
St. Louis Blues*	41	24	11	6	99
Chicago Blackhawks	30	33	13	6	79
Nashville Predators	27	35	13	7	74
Columbus Blue Jackets	29	42	8	3	69
Northwest Division					
Colorado Avalanche*	42	19	13	8	105
Vancouver Canucks*	45	23	13	1	104
Minnesota Wild*	42	29	10	1	95
Edmonton Oilers*	36	26	11	9	92
Calgary Flames	29	36	13	4	75
Pacific Division					
Dallas Stars*	46	17	15	4	111
Anaheim Mighty Ducks*	40	27	9	6	95
Los Angeles Kings	33	37	6	6	78
Phoenix Coyotes	31	35	11	5	78
San Jose Sharks	28	37	9	8	73

EASTERN CONFERENCE

Northeast Division	W.	L.	T.	OTL.	Pts.
Ottawa Senators*	52	21	8	1	113
Toronto Maple Leafs*	44	28	7	3	98
Boston Bruins*	36	31	11	4	87
Montreal Canadiens	30	35	8	9	77
Buffalo Sabres	27	37	10	8	72
Atlantic Division					
New Jersey Devils*	46	20	10	6	108
Philadelphia Flyers*	45	20	13	4	107
New York Islanders*	35	34	11	2	83
New York Rangers	32	36	10	4	78
Pittsburgh Penguins	27	44	6	5	65
Southeast Division					
Tampa Bay Lightning*	36	25	16	5	93
Washington Capitals*	39	29	8	6	92
Atlanta Thrashers	31	39	7	5	74
Florida Panthers	24	36	13	9	70
Carolina Hurricanes	22	43	11	6	61

*Made play-offs   †Overtime losses

STANLEY CUP CHAMPIONS—New Jersey Devils
(defeated Anaheim Mighty Ducks, 4 games to 3)

LEADING SCORERS	Games	Goals	Assists	Pts.
Peter Forsberg, Colorado	75	29	77	106
Markus Naslund, Vancouver	82	48	56	104
Joe Thornton, Boston	77	36	65	101
Milan Hejduk, Colorado	82	50	48	98
Todd Bertuzzi, Vancouver	82	46	51	97

LEADING GOALIES (26 or more games)	Games	Goals against	Avg.
Marty Turco, Dallas	55	92	1.72
Roman Cechmanek, Philadelphia	58	102	1.83
Dwayne Roloson, Minnesota	50	98	2.00
Martin Brodeur, New Jersey	73	147	2.02
Patrick Lalime, Ottawa	67	142	2.16

AWARDS

Adams Award (coach of the year)—Jacques Lemaire, Minnesota
Calder Trophy (best rookie)—Barret Jackman, St. Louis
Hart Trophy (most valuable player)—Peter Forsberg, Colorado
Jennings Trophy (team[s] with fewest goals against)—Martin Brodeur, New Jersey; Roman Cechmanek, Philadelphia
Lady Byng Trophy (sportsmanship)—Alexander Mogilny, Toronto
Masterton Trophy (perseverance, dedication to hockey)—Steve Yzerman, Detroit
Norris Trophy (best defenseman)—Nicklas Lidstrom, Detroit
Pearson Award (best player as voted by NHL players)—Markus Naslund, Vancouver
Ross Trophy (leading scorer)—Peter Forsberg, Colorado
Selke Trophy (best defensive forward)—Jere Lehtinen, Dallas
Smythe Trophy (most valuable player in Stanley Cup)—Jean-Sebastien Giguere, Anaheim
Vezina Trophy (best goalkeeper)—Martin Brodeur, New Jersey

New Jersey Devils goalkeeper Martin Brodeur rejects a shot by Dan Bylsma of the Anaheim Mighty Ducks during Game 7 of the National Hockey League Finals on June 9, 2003. The Devils went on to capture the Stanley Cup 4 games to 3.

the defending champion Detroit Red Wings 4 games to 0 in the first round and defeated Dallas 4 games to 2 in the semifinals.

New Jersey beat Ottawa 4 games to 3 to win the Eastern Conference. The Devils had buried Boston 4 games to 1 in the first round and beat Tampa Bay 4 games to 1 in the semifinals.

Milestones. Brett Hull of the Detroit Red Wings scored his 700th regular-season goal on Feb. 10, 2003, becoming only the sixth NHL player to reach that mark.

Patrick Roy, who won four Stanley Cups and holds the NHL record with 551 regular-season wins and 1,029 games played, announced his retirement on May 28.

World championships. Canada won its first world hockey title in six years on May 11, 2003. The Canadians slipped past Sweden 3-2 in Helsinki, Finland, to win the title.

College. The University of Minnesota (Minneapolis) routed the University of New Hampshire (Durham) 5 to 1 on April 12 in Buffalo, New York, to take the National Collegiate Athletic Association Division I championship for the second year in a row.

Death. Dan Snyder, 25, a member of the NHL's Atlanta Thrashers, died October 5, six days after a car accident in which teammate Dany Heatley was driving. Heatley was charged with reckless driving. ■ Michael Kates

See also **Sports.**

Honduras. See **Latin America.**

Horse racing. Funny Cide, a gelding from New York state, excited racing fans in 2003 by becoming the 17th horse in history to win the first two legs of the Triple Crown—the Kentucky Derby and the Preakness Stakes—only to lose the third, the Belmont Stakes. Funny Cide was the first gelding to capture the Kentucky Derby since Clyde Van Dusen in 1929.

A minor controversy broke out after the race involving jockey Jose Santos when a published photo of the race appeared to show a dark area in the space between Santos's hand and whip as he crossed the finish line. Concerned that the dark area was an illegal device used to create an electric shock to encourage horses to run faster, race officials examined the photo and determined that the dark area was merely the strap of Santos's goggles and the silks of another jockey.

In the Breeders' Cup races on Oct. 25, 2003, in Arcadia, California, Julie Krone became the first female jockey to win a Breeders' Cup race in the 20 years of the event. High Chaparral and Johar battled to the first dead heat in Breeders' Cup history in the Turf race. Trainer Richard Mandella set a record by saddling four winning horses, with victories in the Turf, Juvenile, Juvenile Fillies, and

MAJOR HORSE RACES OF 2003

THOROUGHBRED RACING

Race	Winner	Value to Winner
Atto Mile (Canada)	Touch of the Blues	$600,000
Belmont Stakes	Empire Maker	$600,000
Blue Grass Stakes	Peace Rules	$465,000
Breeders' Cup Classic	Pleasantly Perfect	$2,080,000
Breeders' Cup Distaff	Adoration	$1,040,000
Breeders' Cup Filly & Mare Turf	Islington	$520,000
Breeders' Cup Juvenile	Action This Day	$780,000
Breeders' Cup Juvenile Fillies	Halfbridled	$520,000
Breeders' Cup Mile	Six Perfections	$780,000
Breeders' Cup Sprint	Cajun Beat	$520,000
Breeders' Cup Turf (each)	Johar-High Chaparral	$763,200
Canadian International Stakes	Phoenix Reach	$900,000
Dubai World Cup (United Arab Emirates)	Moon Ballad	$3,600,000
Derby Stakes (United Kingdom)	Kris Kin	£852,600
Haskell Invitational Handicap	Peace Rules	$600,000
Hollywood Gold Cup	Congaree	$450,000
Irish Derby (Ireland)	Alamshar	£507,931
Jockey Club Gold Cup	Mineshaft	$600,000
Kentucky Derby	Funny Cide	$820,000
Kentucky Oaks	Bird Town	$355,756
King George VI and Queen Elizabeth Diamond Stakes (United Kingdom)	Alamshar	£435,000
Oaklawn Handicap	Medaglia d'Oro	$300,000
Pacific Classic	Candy Ride	$600,000
Preakness Stakes	Funny Cide	$650,000
Prix de l'Arc de Triomphe (France)	Dalakhani	914,240 euros
Santa Anita Derby	Buddy Gil	$450,000
Santa Anita Handicap	Milwaukee Brew	$600,000
Land's End Stakes	New York Hero	$300,000
Stephen H. Foster Handicap	Perfect Drift	$531,030
Travers Stakes	Ten Most Wanted	$600,000

HARNESS RACING

Race	Winner	Value to Winner
Cane Pace	No Pan Intended	$165,500
Hambletonian	Amigo Hall	$500,000
Kentucky Futurity	Mr. Muscleman	$194,620
Little Brown Jug	No Pan Intended	$240,204
Meadowlands Pace	Allamerican Theory	$500,000
Messenger Stakes	No Pan Intended	$126,472
Woodrow Wilson	Modern Art	$320,000
Yonkers Trot	Sugar Trader	$168,614

Sources: *The Blood Horse Magazine* and U.S. Trotting Association.

Classic. Mandella also set a record for earnings in a single day, raking in more than $4.5 million.

Three-year-olds. On May 3, Funny Cide, a 12-to-1 longshot, outdueled favorite Empire Maker by 1 ¾ lengths to win the Kentucky Derby in Louisville, Kentucky. On May 17, Funny Cide easily won the Preakness Stakes, the second race in the Triple Crown, by 9 ¾ lengths, the second-largest margin in the 128-year history of the race at Baltimore's Pimlico Race Course. However, Empire Maker spoiled Funny Cide's Triple Crown bid on June 7 at the Belmont Stakes in Elmont, New York, outrunning Ten Most Wanted by ¾ of a length in the 1 ½-mile race. Funny Cide finished third.

Jockey Jose Santos aboard Funny Cide rejoices after winning the Kentucky Derby on May 3, 2003, at Churchill Downs in Louisville, Kentucky. Funny Cide, the first gelding to win the Kentucky Derby since 1929, overcame 12-to-1 odds for the victory.

International. On March 29, Moon Ballad out-ran Harlan's Holiday to capture the world's richest horse race, the $6-million Dubai World Cup held in the United Arab Emirates. Dalakhani captured the Prix de l'Arc de Triomphe on October 4 in Paris; Kris Kin won the English Derby on June 7 in Epsom, England; Alamshar won the Irish Derby on June 29 at the Curragh Racecourse in Kildare, Ireland.

Harness racing. No Pan Intended became the 10th winner of pacing's Triple Crown, winning the Messenger Stakes on October 18 at The Meadows in Meadow Lands, Pennsylvania. The 3-year-old colt previously won the Cane Pace at Freehold (New Jersey) Raceway and the Little Brown Jug in Delaware, Ohio.

Deaths. Bill Shoemaker, whose 8,833 victories made him the most successful jockey ever, died October 12. He was 72.　　■ Michael Kates

See also **Deaths; Sports.**

Hospital. See **Health care issues.**

Housing. See **Building and construction.**

Houston. The DNA division of the Houston Police Department's crime laboratory came under heavy fire in March 2003, after an external audit in January disclosed numerous problems, including unqualified staff members, poor scientific practices, and a leaky roof that may have contaminated DNA evidence. The DNA section was closed indefinitely.

The Harris County District Attorney's office ordered the retesting of DNA evidence in nearly 369 convictions. Of the 74 samples returned by November, more than a dozen possible problems were found. One test resulted in the release from prison in March of Josiah Sutton, who served four years for a rape he may not have committed.

Internal police memos suggested that department officials, including Police Chief C. O. Bradford, knew about the problems but did not correct them until after they became public. In October, the police department also closed the crime lab's toxicology division, which tests blood and urine for drugs and alcohol, after a technician failed a competency test.

In October, Irma Rios, former DNA section manager of the Texas Department of Public Safety, was named the new crime lab director. Her first priority was to correct the laboratory problems, but the DNA and toxicology divisions were not expected to reopen until some time in 2004.

New mayor. Democratic Party chairman Bill White defeated former councilman Orlando Sanchez in a nonpartisan, runoff election on Dec. 6, 2003. Neither candidate had been able to capture a majority of the vote in the initial election.

Rail system. Houston voters approved in November a $7.5-billion expansion of the city's light rail system. The vote endorsed a plan to expand the current 7.5 miles (12 kilometers) of light rail to more than 70 miles (112 kilometers) by 2025. Although the expansion had broad support from much of Houston's political leadership, critics, such as U.S. Representative John Culberson (R., Texas), sought to derail expansion plans in favor of building more highway lanes. The vote was a culmination of more than 30 years of work to bring a major light rail system to the city.

Columbia memorials. The disintegration of the space shuttle Columbia on Feb. 1, 2003, had a powerful, emotional impact on Houston and its Clear Lake suburbs, where Johnson Space Center is located. More than 15,000 public- and private-sector employees work at the space center. Many knew the astronauts aboard the shuttle or worked to ensure the vehicle's safety. United States President George W. Bush visited Houston on February 8 to lead a remembrance of the Columbia crew. In March, a Clear Lake arts center dedicated a fountain as a memorial to the seven astronauts who died.

Toyota Center. The Houston Rockets opened the $235-million Toyota Center in October, after calling the Compaq Center home for nearly 30 years. The move completed a six-year building spree in which Houston spent about $900 million on new facilities for its three major sports franchises—the Rockets (National Basketball Association), the Texans (National Football League, Reliant Stadium), and the Astros (Major League Baseball, Minute Maid Park). No other U.S. city has built as many major league sports venues in as little time. Houston's stadiums were built largely with revenues from hotel and car-rental taxes.

Enron. The reverberations from the December 2001 collapse of the Houston-based energy trading company Enron Corp. continued for a second year. The company, which once had more than 20,000 employees worldwide, had fewer than 12,000 employees in 2003, including fewer than 1,000 in Houston. Lawyers managing Enron's reorganization have billed the company more than $515 million since Enron filed for bankruptcy. By the end of 2003, more than 20 former Enron executives had been indicted for committing fraud, including former Chief Financial Officer Andrew Fastow. Prosecutors were continuing to collect evidence against former chairman Ken Lay and former chief executive Jeffrey Skilling. ■ Eric Berger

See also **Bank; Space exploration; Sports.**

Human rights. The annual conference held by the United Nations Commission on Human Rights (UNCHR) in 2003 revealed problems that many human rights advocates found troubling. Although charged with protecting and promoting human rights, the commission had grown more politicized, and a number of the nations represented on the commission had problematic human rights conditions within their own borders. In 2003, this situation was accentuated when Libya—a nation with a long history of human rights abuses—was elected to chair the conference in Geneva, Switzerland, in March and April. Libya's selection as chair by the commission's African nations was perceived as repayment for Libyan financing of the newly formed African Union.

United Nations (UN) Secretary-General Kofi Annan was critical of the maneuvering that occurred at the conference, as was the UNCHR's own high commissioner, Sergio Vieira de Mello. (Vieira de Mello was killed later in 2003 in Iraq, in a bombing attack on the UN Baghdad headquarters.)

Guantanamo. Rights groups in 2003 criticized the United States for the continuing detention of more than 600 prisoners—most of whom had been captured in Afghanistan in 2001—held in camps at the U.S. Navy base at Guantanamo Bay, Cuba. The United States denied them access to the U.S. legal system and classified them as enemy combatants. They did not, therefore, qualify as prisoners of war under the Geneva Conventions, which limited their legal rights. The Geneva Conventions are treaties that establish a code of conduct during time of war for signatory nations.

Cuba. On March 18, 2003, Cuba began a crackdown on political dissidents. Through March and April, some 50 prodemocracy reformers and around 25 journalists were arrested, tried, and given prison sentences averaging 20 years in duration. Three Cubans who had hijacked a ferry and demanded passage to the United States were executed in April after a one-day trial.

Cuban leader Fidel Castro claimed that many of the dissidents arrested were being aided by the United States, specifically by the top U.S. diplomat to Cuba, James Cason.

Trial of Slobodan Milosevic. The war crimes trial of Milosevic continued in 2003, with the prosecution expected to complete its case against the former Serbian and Yugoslavian president in early 2004. Milosevic, who represented himself at the trial, was accused of genocide and other crimes committed by Serbian troops during the Balkan wars that raged during much of the 1990's.

Nigeria. In September 2003, a Nigerian court overturned the sentence of an unmarried mother, Amina Lawal, who had been found guilty in 2002 of adultery under the Islamic law, Sharia, which is practiced in the north of Nigeria. Under Sharia,

Army engineers complete work on the "Europe Bridge" across the Danube River in Budapest in time for Hungary's National Holiday on March 15. The footbridge symbolizes Hungary's anticipated entry into the European Union.

adultery carries the penalty of death by stoning. Lawal's plight captured the sympathy of Westerners, and numerous Web sites and petitions called for her release. The Nigerian court's reversal was based on procedural issues and did not affect others in Nigeria condemned for similar crimes.

Liberia. Charles Taylor relinquished the presidency of Liberia on Aug.11, 2003, and went into exile in Nigeria. Taylor was elected in 1997 following a bloody civil war and quickly developed a reputation for brutal repression of civilians. Taylor also established so-called "Small Boy Units," squads of child soldiers, and provided support for rebels in Sierra Leone. On June 4, 2003, the UN-backed Special Court for Sierra Leone unsealed its indictment against Taylor, charging him with responsibility for murder, rape, the use of child soldiers, and other crimes against humanity.

Conflict diamonds. In 2003, the Kimberley Diamond Company, headquartered in Australia, began a certification scheme for diamonds traded and sold on the world market. The system was designed to stem the trade in "conflict diamonds," *rough* (uncut) diamonds that were being used by rebel movements to finance prolonged conflicts in such African nations as Congo (Kinshasa), Angola, and Sierra Leone.   ■ Geoffrey A. Campbell

See also **Cuba; Liberia; Nigeria; Serbia and Montenegro; United Nations.**

Hungary. The nation's pending entry into the European Union (EU), set for May 2004, dominated political and economic life in Hungary in 2003. Hungary supported the United States-led war effort in Iraq in March and April 2003.

EU member-to-be. The stage was set for Hungary's formal May 2004 entry into the EU after Hungarian voters approved EU membership by a five-to-one vote in a referendum, and Hungarian and EU officials signed an accession treaty, all in April 2003. As Hungarian leaders prepared for EU entry, they grappled with a budget deficit far exceeding EU targets. According to economists, Hungary's budget deficit had by early 2003 ballooned to more than 9 percent of *gross domestic product* (GDP, the total value of goods and services produced in a country in a year).

The need to reduce the deficit led to friction in the ruling left-of-center coalition headed by Prime Minister Peter Medgyessy of the Socialist Party (MSZP). The Free Democrats (SZDSZ), major coalition partners with the Socialists, advocated immediate income tax reforms, including a lowering of tax rates. However, Medgyessy insisted on postponing the tax cuts beyond 2003. Political experts said the dispute did not immediately endanger the governing coalition.

Status law amendments. EU and other European leaders continued to express concerns about Hungary's so-called status law. The law, passed by Hungary's parliament in 2001, extended special privileges to Hungarian minorities in six neighboring countries. Romania and Slovakia have by far the largest of these Hungarian minorities.

In May 2003, Hungary's foreign minister, Laszlo Kovacs, announced significant changes in the status law. Certain benefits previously available only to ethnic Hungarians living in neighboring countries were now extended to non-Hungarian citizens of those countries. References to extranational Hungarians as "members of a united Hungarian nation" were struck from the law. These changes, asserted Hungarian officials, removed any incompatibilities with EU principles.

Hungarian Prime Minister Medgyessy and Romanian Prime Minister Adrian Nastase signed a peace accord between their two countries in Bucharest, Romania, on September 23. The accord ratified Hungary's status law revisions.

Iraq. As war loomed in Iraq in early 2003, Hungarian leaders approved overflights by U.S. and coalition warplanes and a U.S.-sponsored program to train dissident Iraqi extranationals at Hungary's Taszar military base. In August, Hungary sent 300 peacekeeping troops to Iraq.

■ Sharon L. Wolchik
See also **Europe; Iraq: A Special Report.**

Ice skating. Michelle Kwan of the United States won her fifth world championship on March 29, 2003, tying Carol Heiss (1956-1960) and Dick Button (1948-1952) for the most titles won by U.S. skaters. Kwan also captured her seventh U.S. title in January 2003.

The International Skating Union, the sport's governing body, began to test a new computer-based scoring system on a limited basis in 2003. The new system was developed in response to a major judging scandal during the 2002 Winter Olympic Games in Salt Lake City, Utah, in which a French judge admitted she had been pressured to vote for the Russian pairs skaters.

Instead of the traditional 6.0 scale, the new system employs points, with every technical element assigned a value based on its difficulty. Judges give five marks for each performance. The points are totaled, and the skater with the highest score wins. The system could be in use at official events, including the Olympic Games, by 2004.

World championships. Michelle Kwan captured her fifth world woman's title in Washington, D.C., in March 2003, earning two perfect scores for artistic impression. Kwan edged Elena Sokolova of Russia, who took the silver, and Fumie Suguri of Japan, who won the bronze.

Canada's Shae-Lynn Bourne and Victor Kraatz won the gold medal in ice dancing on March 28.

Michelle Kwan of the United States performs her winning free skate program at the World Championships in Washington, D.C., in March 2003. With her victory, Kwan became the first woman since 1960 to claim five world titles.

Russia's Irina Lobacheva and Ilia Averbukh took silver, and Bulgaria's Albena Denkova and Maxim Staviyski won bronze.

Evgeny Plushenko of Russia captured the second world men's title of his career on March 27. Tim Goebel of the United States won the silver and Japan's Takeshi Honda took the bronze.

On March 26, Xue Shen and Hongbo Zhao of China won their second consecutive pairs title. Russians Tatiana Totmianina and Maxim Marinin settled for silver and Maria Petrova and Alexei Tikhonov of Russia took the bronze.

European Championships. Russian skaters swept the European Championships, held at Malmo, Sweden, in January. Plushenko won the men's title, Irina Slutskaya took her fifth women's title, Totmianina and Marinin defended their pairs title, and Lobacheva and Averbukh won the ice dancing crown. Russia last swept in 1999.

U.S. Championships. Kwan captured her sixth consecutive U.S. Championships crown at the competition held in Dallas in January 2003. Only Maribel Vinson, who won nine U.S. titles, has more. Michael Weiss captured his third men's title despite falling during a routine. Tiffany Scott and Philip Dulebohn won their first pairs title while Naomi Lang and Peter Tchernyshev won their fifth ice-dancing crown.   ■ Michael Kates

See also **Sports.**

Immigration.
The methods employed by the government of the United States to handle immigration changed significantly in 2003 after the U.S. Immigration and Naturalization Service (INS) was moved out of the Department of Justice and integrated into the Department of Homeland Security. Immigration experts viewed the integration of the INS into the Department of Homeland Security as one of the most important steps taken by the administration of President George W. Bush and the U.S. Congress to address problems that had plagued the INS. The INS came under intense criticism in 2002 when it was learned that officials had issued student visas to two of the highjackers who had carried out the terrorist attacks on the United States on Sept. 11, 2001.

As part of the integration process, immigration duties that had been handled by the INS were divided among two new bureaus within the Homeland Security Department. On March 1, 2003, services that had been administered by the INS were transferred to the Homeland Security Department's Bureau of Citizenship and Immigration Services (BCIS). The BCIS was responsible for overseeing immigrant visa petitions; naturalization petitions; and asylum and refugee applications. The U.S. Senate confirmed Eduardo Aguirre, Jr., as BCIS director on June 19. President Bush nominated Aguirre for the position in

February. Aguirre came to the post from the Export-Import Bank of the United States, where he had been vice chairman and chief operating officer.

Also on March 1, enforcement and border patrol functions were transferred to the Homeland Security Department's Directorate of Border and Transportation Security (BTS). The BTS assumed responsibility for securing U.S. borders and transportation systems, including 350 official ports of entry and more than 7,500 miles (12,000 kilometers) of border between the United States and Canada to the north and Mexico to the south. The BTS was also responsible for enforcing U.S. immigration laws.

Immigration ruling. The U.S. Supreme Court ruled on April 29 that the federal government can imprison immigrants it is trying to deport without giving them a chance to demonstrate that they do not pose a risk to the community or that they are unlikely to flee. In the 5-to-4 decision, the court upheld provisions of a 1996 immigration law requiring the government to detain immigrants who have been convicted of drug crimes prior to deportation. Tens of thousands of immigrants have been imprisoned under the law before being deported. A number of appeals courts had ruled the law unconstitutional.

U.S. VISIT. Homeland Security Secretary Tom Ridge on April 29, 2003, announced a new security system that he said would make it easier for foreign students, business travelers, and tourists to enter the United States. Ridge claimed that the process would also make it more difficult for people to illegally enter the United States.

The U.S. Visitor and Immigrant Status Indication Technology (U.S. VISIT) requires visitors to the United States to register with an electronic system. The system uses photographs, fingerprints, or iris scans to create an electronic check-in and check-out system for people from other countries coming to the United States to work, travel, or study. The system was scheduled to be implemented in early 2004.

Foreign health care workers who enter the United States to work on a temporary basis faced new certification requirements under a plan announced by Department of Homeland Security officials in July 2003. Foreign health care workers, except for physicians, must present a certificate granted by an approved independent crediting organization before being allowed to enter the United States. The rule is intended to ensure that all foreign nurses, physical and occupational therapists, speech pathologists, and other health care professionals who seek employment in the United States meet U.S. professional medical standards.   ■ Geoffrey A. Campbell

See also **Civil rights; Human rights.**

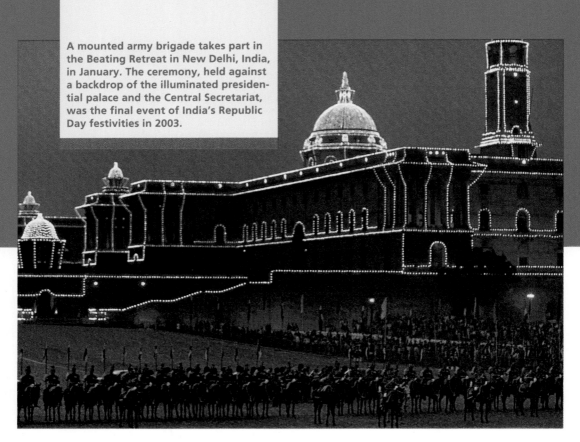

A mounted army brigade takes part in the Beating Retreat in New Delhi, India, in January. The ceremony, held against a backdrop of the illuminated presidential palace and the Central Secretariat, was the final event of India's Republic Day festivities in 2003.

India. The ruling Hindu-nationalist Bharatiya Janata Party (BJP) fought off challenges from the Congress Party, India's main opposition party, and held together its coalition government in 2003. Prime Minister Atal Behari Vajpayee's government solidified its power base in state elections when the BJP won leadership in three states held by the Congress Party.

In August, the Congress Party called for a no-confidence vote against Vajpayee's government after India's Defense Ministry refused to disclose findings of a report probing allegations of corruption during a 1999 conflict between India and Pakistan. During a raucous parliamentary debate on the no-confidence motion, Congress Party leader Sonia Gandhi accused government officials of being "brazenly corrupt." The parliament defeated the no-confidence motion.

State elections. In December 2003, the BJP won three of four state elections, which surprised many observers who predicted that the no-confidence debate would weaken the BJP's standing among voters. The BJP was swept to power in three states held by the Congress Party—Madhya Pradesh, Rajasthan, and Chhattisgarh. The Congress Party maintained control of the capital, New Delhi. Despite the successes of their party, BJP leaders ruled out the possibility of moving the 2004 general elections forward.

Economy. Budget negotiations in 2003 caused friction between the government and opposition parties. The BJP backed away from promised reforms and continued to offer tax benefits to its political supporters. Finance Minister Jaswant Singh was widely criticized for his fiscal policies, which included raising tax breaks for the middle class. In May, Singh postponed the imposition of a nationally coordinated value-added tax. Economists said the tax was needed to control India's runaway fiscal deficit, which hovered around 11 percent of domestic output in 2003 and threatened to balloon in 2004.

Singh announced in November 2003 that the government expected the economy to expand by 7 percent by March 2004. Economists said that India's target of 7 to 8 percent annual growth would be unachievable until the government took aggressive measures to cut the deficit.

Heavier-than-normal monsoon rains in 2003 increased farm production, which was devastated by a drought in 2002. In addition, India's exports surged in 2003, and many Indians living abroad invested in Indian companies. As a result, foreign exchange rose to a record $82 billion.

The influx of money from exports and investments allowed the government to reduce its dependence on foreign aid. In June, Indian officials told 22 small-donor countries that India would stop accepting aid after existing programs ended. India would still accept aid from the United Nations, which provided 60 percent of India's annual aid income. It would also accept aid from large-donor countries.

Religious violence. India struggled to deal with the aftermath of deadly riots between Hindus and Muslims in 2002 in Gujarat, a state in western India. The violence, which resulted in the deaths of at least 1,000 people, was the worst between the two religious groups since 1992, when Hindus destroyed a Muslim mosque in Ayodhya, a city in the state of Uttar Pradesh. The unrest in 2002 was sparked by Hindu preparations to build a temple on the site of the former mosque. Gujarat's Hindu-nationalist rulers and the police were accused of standing by as Muslims were killed during the riots. Hindus make up more than 80 percent of India's population. Muslims make up about 13 percent.

In May 2003, a key witness recanted her testimony at a trial of 21 Hindus accused of burning alive 14 people during the riots. The witness later claimed that she withdrew her testimony after two Hindu politicians threatened her. In July, the judge acquitted the defendants, citing a lack of evidence and shoddy police work. After India's Supreme Court questioned the willingness of Gujarat officials to prosecute the offenders, the trial was reopened and 12 Hindus were convicted of killing 14 Muslims.

Human rights groups warned that the government's inability to prosecute the offenders was driving some Muslims into extremist groups. Police said that two bombs that exploded in Mumbai on August 25 may have been planted by a Muslim group that was formed to avenge the Gujarat murders. The bombs killed 52 people.

Kashmir. Indian and Pakistani military commanders agreed in November to a cease-fire along their border, in the Himalayan state of Jammu and Kashmir, which both countries claimed. The truce was the first formal cease-fire since the early 1990's, when Indian military forces clashed with Muslim protesters in the Indian section of Kashmir.

Holidays. In August 2003, the government announced plans to reduce the number of public holidays in an effort to improve productivity. Approximately 20 million public sector workers received 201 days of paid leave in 2003.

AIDS. The director of India's National AIDS Control Organization reported in July that 4.58 million people in India were infected with HIV, the virus that causes AIDS. In 2003, India had a higher population of HIV-infected people than any country except South Africa.

■ Henry S. Bradsher

See also **Asia; Pakistan.**

Indian, American. A Hopi woman became the first female soldier to die in the war in Iraq in 2003 and the first known Native American woman to be killed in combat as a member of the United States military. U.S. Army Private First Class Lori Piestewa of Tuba City, Arizona, was killed on March 23, when the support convoy in which she was riding was ambushed near An Nasiriyah, a city southeast of Baghdad, the capital.

Arizona's State Board on Geographic and Historic Names voted in April to change the name of Squaw Peak in Phoenix to Piestewa Peak in her honor. State Route 51, known as Squaw Peak Parkway, was renamed Lori Piestewa Freeway.

Trust accounts. On September 25, a federal judge presiding over the largest class-action lawsuit ever brought against the U.S. government ruled that the U.S. Department of the Interior must provide a full accounting of the royalties earned on Indian land by 2007. In November 2003, the accounting was put on hold as an appeals court considered the legality of a bill passed by Congress that month that suspended the federal judge's ruling.

More than 300,000 Native Americans had brought the suit in 1996, demanding that the government account for money managed by the Interior Department for individual Indians and tribes since 1887. The money was generated by royalties from oil, gas, timber, and mining on Indian lands. In January 2003, lawyers for the Indians had presented private records of oil drilling and mineral mining dating to the late 1800's that indicated a total of $137 billion in funds had been mismanaged. The Interior Department acknowledged the mismanagement but claimed the losses involved only hundreds of millions of dollars. A court-appointed investigator reported in August 2003 that he had confirmed the mismanagement. Oil and gas companies had paid $432 to $455 annually to private landowners near the Navajo reservation in the southwestern United States for each 16.5-foot (5-meter) length of pipeline the companies had built across the residents' property. Navajo landowners were paid $25 to $40 for the same length of pipeline.

Sacred objects. The results of a chemical analysis published in March 2003 confirmed that many Native American sacred objects held in museums had become tainted with toxic chemicals. The artifacts, many of them made of animal hides or feathers, were in the process of being returned to Native American tribes as a result of the 1990 Native American Graves Protection and Repatriation Act.

Peter Palmer, a chemist at San Francisco State University, reported that he had tested 17 objects returned to the Hoopa tribe of northern California by the Peabody Museum at Harvard University in Cambridge, Massachusetts. The items contained mercury and pesticides in enough quantities to be dangerous to anyone who touched or wore them.

Curators revealed that most of the objects—which had been taken from various tribes over the course of 300 years—had been treated with toxic substances to preserve them. Museums had no records of which objects had been treated, and some of the institutions insisted that the expense of testing the items should be borne by the individual tribes.

Memorial. A monument in memory of the Native Americans who died in battle against the U.S. Army's 7th Cavalry, led by General George Custer in 1876, was unveiled at the Little Bighorn Battlefield National Monument in southeastern Montana in June 2003. The memorial, dedicated on June 25, was authorized by Congress in 1991.

The monument to Native Americans consists of a bronze sculpture designed by Canadian Indian artist Colleen Cutschall and a circular earthwork created by Philadelphia landscape artists John and Allison Collins. The sculpture, called Spirit Warriors, depicts three warriors on horseback, with a woman handing one of them his shield. An opening in the earthworks allows visitors to see the white obelisk erected in 1881 to honor the fallen cavalry.   ■ Kristina Vaicikonis
See also **Iraq**.

Indiana. See **State government**.

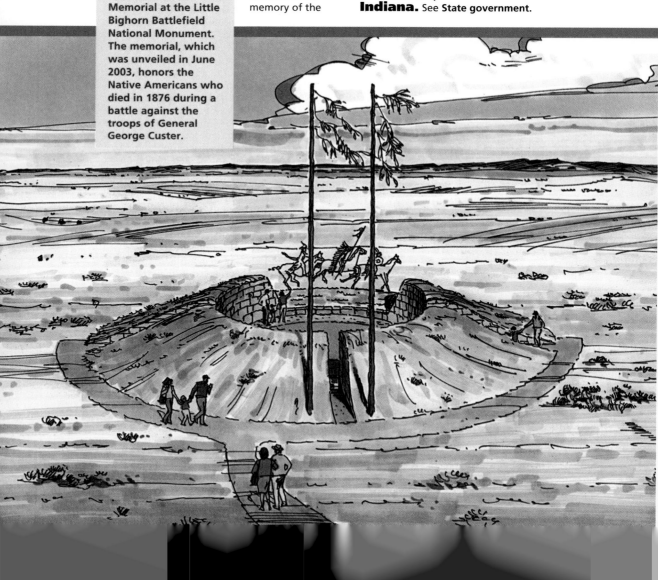

A bronze sculpture depicting warriors on horseback and an earthwork circle make up the new Indian Memorial at the Little Bighorn Battlefield National Monument. The memorial, which was unveiled in June 2003, honors the Native Americans who died in 1876 during a battle against the troops of General George Custer.

Indonesia. A terrorist attack on a hotel in the Indonesian capital, Jakarta, on Aug. 5, 2003, drew international attention to Indonesia's ongoing struggle to control militant Islamic groups. The suicide car bombing at the J. W. Marriott Hotel, which was popular with United States tourists, killed 12 people and wounded more than 150 others. The bombing was the eighth major terrorist attack against Western interests in Indonesia since 2000. Police said in 2003 that the suicide bomber was a member of Jemaah Islamiyah, a militant Islamic group closely linked to al-Qa'ida, a terrorist network headed by Saudi-born millionaire Osama bin Laden.

Less than two weeks after the attack, U.S. agents captured Riduan Isamuddin, an Indonesian better known as Hambali, in Thailand. Officials said that Hambali, one of the most wanted terror suspects in Southeast Asia, organized the hotel attack and was the architect of the October 2002 bombings on the Indonesian resort island of Bali that killed more than 200 people. Terror experts claimed that Hambali was a close associate of Osama bin Laden and served as a link between al-Qa'ida and Jemaah Islamiyah. Officials said Hambali also helped organize the terrorist attacks against the United States in 2001.

Bali verdicts. The 2003 hotel bombing took place two days before an Indonesian court sentenced Amrozi bin Nurhasyim to death for his involvement in the 2002 Bali bombings. In October 2003, a court sentenced Amrozi's older brother, Mukhlas, to death for his involvement. A third brother, Ali Imron, received a life sentence after he cooperated with authorities investigating the incident. In September, Imam Samudra, who authorities said was the mastermind of the Bali attack, was sentenced to death. All four men were suspected members of Jemaah Islamiyah. More than 30 other Bali bombing suspects were awaiting trial at the end of 2003.

An Indonesian court in September acquitted Abu Bakar Bashir, leader of Jemaah Islamiyah, of charges he ordered a series of terrorist attacks in Indonesia and of plotting to assassinate Indonesian President Megawati Sukarnoputri. The court convicted him on treason charges, but the charges were overturned on appeal. Political observers said the verdict underscored Western concerns that Indonesia was not serious about cracking down on Islamic militants.

In 2002, the People's Consultative Assembly (parliament) attempted to ease international concerns that Indonesia, the world's most populous Islamic country, was becoming a center for Islamic militants. The Assembly rejected a proposal to impose strict Islamic law on the secular country and made constitutional changes aimed at enhancing democracy in Indonesia. In 2003,

however, government officials remained reluctant to criticize radical Islamic groups because they feared alienating moderate Muslims who might be sympathetic to the militants.

Aceh battle. In May, Indonesia sent 40,000 troops to battle separatist rebels in Aceh, a province at the western tip of Indonesia, shortly after peace talks in Tokyo between the government and the rebels collapsed and Sukarnoputri declared martial law in Aceh. The talks to end a 27-year civil war between the government and the Free Aceh Movement were brokered by the United States, Japan, and the United Nations (UN). Since 1990, at least 12,000 people have been killed in the war.

Human rights. In February 2003, UN prosecutors charged General Wiranto, a former Indonesian military chief, and seven other officers with crimes against humanity for their roles in the violence following the 1999 referendum on independence for East Timor. UN officials estimated that more than 1,000 East Timorese were killed by a military-backed militia after the referendum.

U.S. officials said they would withhold military aid to Indonesia until the government investigated the 2002 murders of two U.S. teachers in Papua. U.S. officials said that Indonesian soldiers killed the teachers. ■ Henry S. Bradsher

See also **Asia; Terrorism.**

International trade expanded during 2003, but more slowly than had been expected, due to the weakening of the global economy early in the year. An increasingly angry face-off between developing nations—often led by Brazil—and industrial powers, including the European Union (EU) and the United States, became a feature of world and regional trade talks during 2003. Resentments centered on issues such as agricultural subsidies by rich countries at the expense of poorer countries, and this anger scuttled talks held in Cancun, Mexico, in September by the World Trade Organization (WTO)—a Geneva, Switzerland-based group that oversees international trade agreements and arbitrates disputes among member nations. Such resentments also contributed to an uprising that forced Bolivia's president to resign in October and set the stage for a confrontation around a Miami, Florida, conference in November that was meant to promote a special trading zone throughout the Western Hemisphere.

The WTO conference. As commercial activity steadily increased in the second half of 2003, trade ministers from around the world gathered in the Mexican resort city of Cancun on September 10 to continue the so-called Doha round of trade negotiations—named for the capital of Qatar where the negotiations were launched.

Many hoped the meeting would get the WTO talks back on track. Leaders of the Group of Eight (G-8) major industrial nations reaffirmed their commitment to the Doha Development Agenda in a June statement.

Observers noted, however, that there was a sense among developing nations that trade was of greater benefit to wealthier nations than to them. A group of developing nations, led by Brazil, China, and India, insisted that Europe and the United States take stronger action to cut domestic farm subsidies. Subsidies paid to farmers in wealthier nations make it hard for those in developing nations to compete, despite the lower production costs in developing nations. Friction arose over other issues, and on September 14, Luis Ernesto Derbez, Mexico's foreign secretary and the conference's chairman, declared an impasse and adjourned the meeting. Experts suggested that it would probably prove impossible to reach an agreement on the rules concerning trade among WTO nations by the Jan. 1, 2005, deadline. The collapse of the talks raised doubts about the future of the global trade alliance and spurred a tendency already under way for major trading zones to expand regional and bilateral agreements.

Further trade-related events. On Oct. 17, 2003, Gonzalo Sanchez de Lozada resigned as president of Bolivia following a popular revolt in which farmers, workers, and miners marched in mass demonstrations against his U.S.-backed free-market policies. Protesters blockaded the capital, La Paz, and some 80 demonstrators were killed —reportedly by gunfire from security forces. The protests had focused, in part, on Lozada's plan to sell Bolivian natural gas to the United States and Mexico.

On November 12, EU leaders and officials from the South American Mercosur trading bloc —Argentina, Brazil, Paraguay, and Uruguay— said they planned to negotiate a free-trade accord by the end of 2004. Trade policy disagreements between the United States and Brazil curbed plans to create a wide-ranging Free Trade Area of the Americas (FTAA) among 34 nations, in favor of the limited compromise pact. The United States subsequently began pursuing smaller regional trade accords and on December 17, announced a pact with four Central American nations.

Other tensions. Highly sensitive trade disputes from previous years reemerged in 2003, notably in a WTO appeals panel ruling that came down on November 10 against the United States. At issue were import fees, called duties, that had been levied by the United States in 2002 on most foreign steel entering the country. The United States claimed it was attempting to protect its ailing steel industry. Foreign competitors threatened a trade war on U.S. goods if the United States did not remove the duties within 30 days of the WTO decision. The United States removed the tariffs in early December.

Tensions also arose over currency policies as the U.S. dollar, for the second year running, weakened against many other currencies. As the largest single-nation economy, the United States had traditionally been the principal engine for world growth, with its consumers buying a huge amount of goods from other nations. A falling dollar, however, made foreign-supplied goods and services more expensive inside the United States, while making U.S. products cheaper on the world market. This development put pressure on other nations to stimulate their own economies rather than depend on U.S. trade.

Recovery. The WTO reported that a weak trade recovery during 2002 had been "followed by a near stagnation of trade flows in the first half of 2003." The U.S. and EU economies weakened during the first months of 2003 amid growing uncertainty caused by a looming U.S.-led war against Iraq.

War-related fears about potential disruption to Persian Gulf oil supplies pushed the price of crude oil and related fuels up sharply. Tensions also grew because many nations in Europe and the developing world did not support the United States and the United Kingdom in their stance against Iraq. Quick initial success by the coalition forces led to a fall in oil prices during the early summer months, but the world economy did not show much strength until midsummer, when a U.S. tax cut and cuts in interest rates by the United States, Britain, and the EU all began to take effect.

In September, the International Monetary Fund (IMF)—a United Nations-affiliated agency that provides advice and financial restructuring to member nations—said in its "World Economic Outlook" report that "growing signs of a pickup in activity" were evident, especially in the United States, Japan, and some of the emerging-market countries, such as China and India. The IMF forecast the volume of world trade in goods and services would grow by 2.9 percent in 2003, down from 3.2 percent in 2002, but an improvement over the 1-percent decrease in volume in 2001. China's trade still remained quite strong, however. The IMF estimated that the Chinese economy would grow by 7.5 percent in 2003, compared with an 8-percent increase in 2002. The 2003 growth occurred despite the economic impact of an outbreak of severe acute respiratory syndrome (SARS) in China.   ■ John D. Boyd

See also **Brazil; China; Economics; Europe; Latin America; United States.**

iTunes, Apple Computer's online music store that was introduced in April, provides a legal way to purchase music over the Internet. Users can download songs, at 99 cents each, to computers or iPod music players or burn them on CD's. Apple released free iTunes software in 2003 for both Macintosh and Windows computers.

Internet. The number of home Internet users in the United States rose slightly in 2003, reaching approximately 109 million, up from 106 million in 2002, according to Nielsen/Netratings. About 60 percent of people in the United States—about 175 million—had some form of Internet access either at home or at work.

High-speed access grows. While the portion of Americans with Internet access at home seemed to have leveled off after years of steep increases, the type of access shifted dramatically during 2003. A Pew Internet & American Life Project report in May found that the number of high-speed broadband Internet connections in U.S. households increased by 50 percent from March 2002 to March 2003. About 31 percent of U.S. home Internet users had broadband access in 2003, up from 24 percent in 2002. The increased percentage represented approximately 30 million people. Nevertheless, Canada, South Korea, and other nations were ahead of the United States, with about 50 percent of all the families having broadband Internet access in their homes.

As broadband access in the United States increased, the number of people using slower, dialup access with a modem and a telephone fell by about 12 percent in 2003. Despite that shift, there were still about twice as many dialup users as broadband users, largely because broadband

was four to six times as expensive as dialup. Many experts believed that once most U.S. consumers have high-speed Internet access at home, downloading very large files, such as motion pictures, will become common, transforming the way people work and play.

Spam also grows. The amount of *spam*, or unsolicited e-mail messages for products ranging from weight loss programs to pornography, increased dramatically in 2003. The messages may have misleading subject lines to entice an unwary user to open them. A survey of Internet users reported by the Pew Internet & American Life Project in October found that about 50 percent of those responding had between 5 and 30 spam e-mails every day. Some 15 percent said they spent one half-hour or more every day dealing with spam that they had received. Some computer scientists believed that most e-mail was junk mail by the end of 2003.

Most of the Internet-based crimes targeted by the United States Federal Trade Commission, such as offering medical treatments that do not work, are spam. But spam also slowed the Internet and drove up costs for Internet service providers, which sell Internet access to individuals and companies. The increase in spam led to the introduction of several bills in the U.S. Congress to deal with the problem.

By 2003, the spam problem had grown to such an extent that many universities, local governments, and private industries instituted strict regulations forbidding spamming by anyone using the institutions' computers.

The U.S. House of Representatives also passed legislation in December that would ban companies from sending spam to a person's e-mail. The Senate approved the legislation in November.

Internet security. The CERT Coordination Center at Carnegie Mellon University in Pittsburgh, Pennsylvania, a federally funded group charged with maintaining security on the Internet, reported in October that the number of security incidents rose steadily through 2003. CERT reported 114,855 incidences in the first nine months of 2003, compared with 82,094 in all of 2002. CERT issued several advisories during 2003 warning of attacks by small, damaging programs called viruses and worms. Microsoft Windows and Outlook e-mail programs were particularly vulnerable to attacks, according to an advisory from CERT in October.

In November, Microsoft Corporation of Redmond, Washington, took the unprecedented step of offering $5 million in rewards for information leading to the conviction of "cyberattackers." Microsoft was particularly interested in tracking down those responsible for the MS Blaster worm and the SoBig virus that attacked computers and networks in 2003. MS Blaster overloaded computer networks, leading to denial of service messages. The SoBig virus triggered mass mailings from the e-mail address books of thousands of Internet users.

Music piracy. The music recording industry tried new tactics in its ongoing battle against people who use computers and the Internet to download songs for free instead of paying for them. In April, the Recording Industry Association of America (RIAA) began suing individual consumers for allegedly violating copyright law by sharing songs with others. As the year went on, the RIAA particularly targeted students who used college and university computers to obtain songs.

In November, the International Federation of the Phonographic Industry (IFPI), an organization representing more than 1,500 music companies in 76 countries, announced a new licensing scheme for selling music on the Internet. The plan allowed Internet service providers, such as AOL, to negotiate multinational licensing agreements rather than negotiate with each country individually. The IFPI said that illegally downloaded music in 2003 exceeded legal music sales in Germany, Japan, the United States, and several other countries. ■ Dave Wilson

See also **Telecommunications**.

Iowa. See **State government**.

Iran. World leaders became concerned in 2003 that Iran was on the verge of producing a nuclear weapon. In October, French Foreign Minister Dominique de Villepin, German Foreign Minister Joschka Fischer, and British Foreign Secretary Jack Straw met with Iranian leaders to discuss the country's nuclear program, which the Iranians claimed was geared only toward energy production. On October 21, the Iranians committed themselves to signing an additional protocol of the nuclear nonproliferation treaty. The additional protocol allows for unfettered inspection of Iranian nuclear facilities by officials from the International Atomic Energy Agency (IAEA), a Vienna-based organization that promotes safe and peaceful uses of nuclear energy. The United States and the three main European powers had pushed for the additional protocol after it became evident that Iran had an advanced nuclear program. According to a confidential IAEA report released in November, Iran had breached the nuclear nonproliferation treaty by conducting a secret nuclear program for the last 18 years and by producing small amounts of enriched uranium and plutonium. Iranian leaders signed the additional protocol of the nuclear nonproliferation treaty on December 18.

Opposition. An Iranian opposition group, Mujahedin Khalq, revealed the existence of Iran's secret uranium enrichment program at Natanz in late 2002. Although the group has provided the most effective opposition to the Muslim clerics who rule Iran, it continued in 2003 to be listed as a terrorist organization by the U.S. Department of State. The military wing of Mujahedin Khalq, which came into existence in Iran in the 1980's, began coordinating activities with U.S.-led coalition forces in Iraq in 2003.

Iran and al-Qa'ida. Intelligence sources in 2003 revealed that Iran had given sanctuary to leading members of the al-Qa'ida terrorist network—including Sayf al-'Adil, an Egyptian allegedly in charge of global operations, and Sa'd bin Laden, Osama bin Laden's son and a regional al-Qa'ida commander. Experts noted that the Iran-al-Qa'ida connection was not surprising given their shared goals—to drive the West, particularly the United States, from the Middle East.

An earthquake registering 6.6 devastated the ancient city of Bam on December 26, killing at least 30,000 people. More than 70 percent of the city was leveled, including Bam's 2,000-year-old citadel, which was the largest mud-brick structure in the world. ■ Marius Deeb

See also **Iraq: A Special Report; Middle East**.

THE WAR —IN— IRAQ:

THE MILITARY CAMPAIGN AND AFTERMATH

By Scott Thomas

A United States fighter jet carrying U.S. President George W. Bush landed aboard the U.S.S. *Abraham Lincoln* on May 1, 2003. The Abraham Lincoln was in the Pacific off San Diego, California, on its way home from the Persian Gulf, where a U.S.-led coalition force had been engaged in a war with Iraq since March 20 (March 19 in the United States). Dressed in the flying gear of a U.S. Navy fighter pilot, the president announced to the assembled crew—and to the world—that the military phase of the war was essentially over. Identifying former Iraqi leader Saddam Hussein as an ally of the al-Qa'ida terrorist network,

President Bush described the victory in Iraq as a single battle in "a war on terror that began on Sept. 11, 2001"—the day militant Islamic terrorists attacked the United States. The president then vowed to keep weapons of mass destruction out of the hands of such terrorists. The declaration aboard the *Abraham Lincoln* capped a campaign in which the coalition forces, made up primarily of

One of Saddam Hussein's palaces in Baghdad burns after being targeted by U.S. missiles on March 27. Missile and other air attacks largely targeted government facilities in an attempt to limit collateral damage.

U.S. and British troops, conquered the forces of Saddam Hussein in less than six weeks. At the time, few people argued with the president's assertion that the war had been carried out "with a combination of precision and speed and boldness the enemy did not expect, and the world had not seen before." The conflict, however, proved to be far from over.

The Persian Gulf War

The war in Iraq was the second war fought between a U.S.-led coalition and the forces of Saddam Hussein. An earlier coalition, led by U.S. President George H. W. Bush, father of George W. Bush, defeated Iraq in the Persian Gulf War of 1991. That war began after Iraq invaded and occupied Kuwait, Iraq's neighbor to the south. After the invasion, the United Nations (UN) Security Council authorized the coalition to expel Iraq from Kuwait, which it did in late February 1991.

Iraq agreed, as part of the cease-fire agreement ending the 1991 war, to destroy all weapons of mass destruction—that is, biological, chemical, or nuclear weapons. However, Iraq failed to cooperate completely with UN teams sent to inspect suspected weapons sites, and beginning in 1998, Saddam Hussein refused to allow the UN inspectors into the country.

The UN and weapons of mass destruction

President George W. Bush, soon after taking office in January 2001, began to assert that Hussein continued to develop weapons of mass destruction and, therefore, posed a threat to the United States. After the terrorist attacks on the United States in September 2001, President Bush argued that Hussein supported the al-Qa'ida terrorist network responsible for the attacks. Addressing the United Nations (UN) in September 2002, President Bush announced that the United States would take the lead to disarm the Hussein regime. He warned that the UN risked becoming irrelevant by failing to enforce its own resolutions. Soon after, the U.S. Congress gave President Bush authorization to use military force against Iraq.

The UN responded to President Bush's challenge by sending weapons inspectors into Iraq in November 2002. In the months that followed, the United States and the United Kingdom insisted that Hussein still was not fully cooperating with the UN. President Bush, in his State of the Union address in January 2003, asserted that evidence existed that Iraq was attempting to buy uranium in West Africa for use in an Iraqi nuclear arms program. He then informed the Congress that while the United States continued to seek the support of its allies in the UN, he would not wait for their consent to confront Iraq. He did, however, ask the UN Security Council to pass a resolution authorizing war against Iraq on the grounds that Iraq had failed to disarm itself of illegal weapons.

The member nations on the UN Security Council strongly disagreed on whether to take military action against Iraq. Arguing for more time to seek a diplomatic solution, France, Germany, and Russia refused to support the resolution, and it was never voted upon. The governments of the United States and the United Kingdom decided to go forward with the war despite having failed to receive UN authorization.

The war begins

On March 19, President Bush ordered U.S. armed forces already deployed in Kuwait and the Persian Gulf—more than 250,000 in number—to launch an attack on Iraq. U.S. forces were joined by some 50,000 British troops as well as relatively small numbers of soldiers from other countries, including Australia and Poland. President Bush announced that the war had begun minutes after U.S. Tomahawk missiles and bombs from "stealth" aircraft struck Baghdad, the Iraqi capital. The president noted in his declaration that his purpose was to "disarm Iraq, to free its people, and defend the world from grave danger."

In the days that followed, the coalition carried out intense bombing aimed at key targets in Baghdad and elsewhere. On March 20, a barrage of Tomahawk cruise missiles and guided bombs launched from U.S. Navy ships in the Red Sea and Persian Gulf rocked the capital in what U.S. officials described as a "decapitation attack" aimed directly at Saddam Hussein. The

The author:
Scott Thomas is the managing editor of *The Year Book.*

following day, an intense air assault on Baghdad triggered a series of explosions, sending columns of smoke and fire into the skies over the city. Officials with the U.S. Department of Defense announced that the assault was the opening of a promised "shock and awe" campaign that targeted Baghdad and other Iraqi cities with massive and widespread bombing. The U.S. Air Force subsequently dropped "bunker busters"—enormous bombs, weighing 4,700 pounds (2,100 kilograms)—on limited targets in Baghdad. Coalition warplanes also bombed the city of Al Basrah (also known as Basra) in the south and areas of northern Iraq controlled by Ansar al Islam, an Islamic militant group that U.S. and British officials identified as having links to the al-Qa'ida terrorist network.

A Tomahawk Land Attack Missile is launched against a target in Iraq on March 23 from the U.S.S. *Cape St. George*. The guided missile cruiser operated in the eastern Mediterranean Sea during the combat phase of the war in Iraq.

The First Marine Expeditionary Force met heavy Iraqi fire on March 20 as U.S. troops, under the cover of intense allied artillery and aircraft bombardment, moved into Iraq from its southeastern border with Kuwait. The U.S. and British invasion forces seized strategically important airfields in southwest Iraq and the key port of Umm Qasr on the Faw Peninsula in southern Iraq. Umm Qasr is Iraq's only outlet to the Persian Gulf. By March 23, U.S. forces reached An Najaf, an Islamic holy city, 100 miles (160 kilometers) south of Baghdad. However, a number of U.S. units further south remained engaged in fierce combat in and around the city of An Nasiriyah. U.S. Army General John Abizaid confirmed that Iraqi forces had ambushed a supply convoy and that U.S. military personnel, both men and women, were missing in action.

U.S. military commander General Tommy Franks confirmed on March 24 that coalition troops were within 60 miles (100 kilometers) of Baghdad, but he acknowledged that both U.S. and British forces were meeting stiff resistance and casualties were increasing. Franks announced that outlying units of Hussein's elite Republican Guard were under fire by the U.S. 3rd Infantry Division, which was backed by a fleet of helicopter gunships. Republican Guard units stationed on the southern outskirts of Baghdad were also under aerial attack. In the south, British units shelled Al Basrah, Iraq's second largest city, in response to attacks by Iraqi forces. At the same time, U.S. Marines battled their way through the streets of An Nasiriyah in southern Iraq in the kind of urban battle that U.S. military commanders had hoped to avoid. U.S. forces in the city reported that armed Iraqi men were jumping from buses and rooftops to shoot at them. The Marines were ordered into the city to secure two bridges over the

Euphrates River that were needed to move troops north to Baghdad.

Large numbers of U.S. troops began crossing the Euphrates over the An Nasiriyah bridges on March 25 despite a desert sandstorm. U.S. and British forces were now positioned in a heavily armed column that stretched from Umm Qasr on the Persian Gulf to the city of Karbala just 50 miles (80 kilometers) southwest of Baghdad, severely stretching coalition supply lines. Iraqi troops ambushed the U.S. 7th Cavalry between An Najaf and Karbala. In the fierce ensuing battle, U.S. troops, hunkered down in the blinding sandstorm, fought off hundreds of regular Iraqi soldiers and Fedayeen Saddam militiamen. The Fedayeen was a paramilitary group that answered directly to Saddam Hussein's eldest son, Uday. At Karbala, coalition troops faced the Republican Guard's Medina Division. U.S. General Richard Meyers, chairman of the Joint Chiefs of Staff, characterized the division as the best

equipped, best trained, and most loyal of Saddam Hussein's forces.

Continuing fighting between Iraqi forces and coalition troops at An Nasiriyah and Karbala as well as on the road between the two cities forced allied military leaders to shift the focus of the land campaign in Iraq. The attack on the Republican Guard around Baghdad was delayed while U.S. and British forces fought Iraqi militia groups that were repeatedly attacking advancing allied troops from the rear.

The British offensive

In Al Basrah to the southeast, British forces continued to battle an estimated 1,000 Saddam Hussein loyalists for control of the city, where a rebellion against the ruling Ba'ath Party had broken out. According to British military officials, Ba'ath members attempted to put down the rebellion by firing mortars at the civilian population. The British responded by shelling the mortar positions and bombing Ba'ath head-

Key to map:

* Major battle
✗ Airfields
→ Coalition campaign
American forces
British forces

0 ——— 100 Miles
0 ——— 100 Kilometers

Map labels:
Turkey
Caspian Sea
Syria
Harir Air Base
Coalition forces open northern front in Kurdish-controlled Iraq.
Mosul
Arbil
Kirkuk
Chamchamal
Halabjah
Iran
Tikrit
Tigris River
Euphrates River
Sunni Triangle
Balad
I R A Q
Baghdad — Coalition forces gain control of central Baghdad.
Ar Ramadi
Al Fallujah
Jordan
Ar Rutbah
Coalition forces gain control of airfields in western Iraq.
Karbala
Al Musayyib
Al Kut
An Najaf
Ad Diwaniyah
As Samawah
An Nasiriyah
Al Basrah
Abu al-Qassib
Umm Qasr
Shatt al Arab
Coalition forces move north from Kuwait into the towns of Umm Qasr and Al Basrah.
Kuwait
Persian Gulf
Saudi Arabia

Two major columns of U.S. ground forces, which had been amassing in Kuwait, invaded Iraq from the south in March. They were joined by a British division, which marched toward Al Basrah. Later, a reinforced airborne infantry brigade attacked from the north, while special operations forces secured Iraqi airfields in the west. Ground forces were accompanied by a massive air campaign featuring B-1, B-2, and B-52 heavy bombers and hundreds of air force and navy carrier-based attack aircraft.

A U.S. Marine convoy slows to a walking pace as it spreads out across the Euphrates River Valley on March 27 on its way north to the town of An Nasiriyah. Repeated Iraqi harassment of U.S. convoys strung out across 350 miles (560 kilometers) of desert slowed down what U.S. military planners had hoped would be a lightning fast push on the Iraqi capital, Baghdad.

quarters. A force of 1,000 Royal Marines next launched a massive offensive to take the town of Abu al-Qassib just outside Al Basrah. The capture of Abu al-Qassib completed the British encirclement of Al Basrah.

A second front

U.S. forces opened a second front, in the north, on March 27. More than 1,000 members of the 173rd Airborne Brigade parachuted into Kurdish-held territory about 30 miles (48 kilometers) northeast of Arbil, the main Kurdish city. Upon landing, the paratroopers were joined by Kurdish guerrilla fighters. U.S. military leaders noted that the second front would keep the Iraqi military from concentrating all its defenses against coalition forces in the south. After four days of allied air strikes in northern Iraq, the Iraqi Army abandoned Chamchamal. The town, located northeast of the major oil center Kirkuk, had been a stronghold of Ansar al-Islam militants. Kurdish guerrillas immediately moved into Chamchamal, providing coalition forces with a strategically important forward position from which to drive on to Kirkuk.

Resistance to U.S. forces advancing northward into Baghdad began to crumble. U.S. Marines easily overcame the Baghdad Division of Iraq's Republican Guard after capturing a bridge over the Tigris River on April 2. The Guards were defending Al Kut, a city approximately 100 miles (160 kilometers) southeast of the capital. Soldiers with the U.S. Infantry, advancing north from An Najaf, seized a bridge over the Euphrates River at Al Musayyib, a city some 30 miles (48 kilometers) due south of the capital. Near Karbala, 50 miles (80 kilometers) southwest of Baghdad, an estimated 15,000 U.S. troops routed two other Republican Guard divisions and began moving toward the nearby Euphrates River.

The U.S. Army's 3rd Infantry Division, closing in from the southwest, pushed forward to Saddam International Airport, approximately 12 miles (20 kilometers) outside central Baghdad, and secured it on April 3 with little opposition. Other Army units moved forward to within 6 miles (10 kilometers) of the capital. U.S. Marines, driving toward the city from the southeast, met only scattered resistance from the Republican Guards and managed to cover 20 miles (32 kilometers) in a few hours. Allied aircraft made about 1,000 bombing runs over Baghdad, most of them aimed at Republican Guard divisions stationed around the capital.

The U.S. forces advancing in three columns from the southwest, south,

> A U.S. Army infantry soldier searches the ruins of Saddam Hussein's main Baghdad palace on April 7 for Iraqi forces. American forces seized the compound after pushing into the heart of the capital with more than 70 tanks and 60 Bradley fighting vehicles.

and southeast placed Baghdad in a powerful vise that led thousands of Iraqis to flee the city. On April 4, bumper-to-bumper traffic choked roads leading north and northeast as U.S. ground forces sealed off key highways to the south. U.S. Marines halted their advance from the southeast at the city limits 10 miles (16 kilometers) from downtown Baghdad. The Marines had raced behind the Republican Guard's Nida Division, which put up little resistance after being bombarded through the night. West of the city, U.S. infantry completed their takeover of Saddam International Airport, which commanders renamed Baghdad International.

Some 2,500 Republican Guard soldiers surrendered to coalition forces between Al Kut and Baghdad. The surrender took place after the Iraqi division clashed with the U.S. Marine Expeditionary Force.

British forces in southern Iraq launched a major assault on Al Basrah on April 4. The 7th Armoured Brigade, known as the Desert Rats, stormed into the center of the city with several thousand troops and hundreds of tanks. They were greeted by hundreds of cheering and waving civilians.

U.S. forces occupied the center of the Shiite Muslim holy city of Karbala on April 6. A crowd of some 10,000 people, yelling "Saddam is no more," pulled down a statue of Hussein in the city's public square. The event marked the end of a five-day battle in which coalition forces routed several hundred Fedayeen Saddam fighters.

U.S. troops move into Baghdad

U.S. troops pressed into the center of Baghdad on April 7 and took control of a major presidential palace and other key buildings. The 3rd Infantry Division, backed by air support, met with only scattered pockets of resistance as it rumbled into the heart of the capital with more than 70 tanks and 60 Bradley fighting vehicles. The troops seized Iraqi President Saddam Hussein's main palace on the west bank of the Tigris River and secured a second palace, which had been abandoned by the Republican Guard. Late in the day, a U.S. Air Force B-1 bomber dropped four bombs, each weighing 2,000 pounds (900 kilograms), on a house in an affluent Baghdad neighborhood. U.S. military officials had ordered the bombardment minutes after intelligence agents reported that they believed that Hussein, his sons, and other Iraqi leaders were meeting there. Hussein and his sons escaped the assault.

The following day, more than 20 buses and trucks filled with an estimated 500 Republican Guard soldiers and Fedayeen Saddam militia fighters crossed the Tigris River in Baghdad to stage a counterattack. According to U.S. military commanders, the Iraqis intended to retake control of the U.S.-held west bank of the river. The Iraqis fired assault rifles and rocket-propelled grenades at U.S. tanks blocking an intersection beyond the bridge. The U.S. infantry responded with artillery and mortar fire, and A-10 attack planes strafed the Iraqis, driving them back across the river.

A British Marine fires a wire-guided missile at an Iraqi position in the Fao region of southern Iraq on March 21. After encircling Al Basrah, Iraq's second largest city, the 7th Armoured Brigade secured the city's center on April 6.

Much of Baghdad had fallen to U.S. forces by April 9, and the government of Iraqi President Saddam Hussein had collapsed. Allied tanks and armored vehicles met no resistance as they swept across the Tigris River into Baghdad's eastern sector. As in Karbala days earlier, U.S. soldiers were met by cheering crowds of Iraqis attempting to topple an enormous statue of Hussein that dominated one of the city's public squares. In Baghdad's heavily populated southeastern neighborhoods, throngs of Shiite Muslims, long oppressed by the Hussein regime, cheered U.S. Marines as they pushed toward the center of the city. Hussein's government was dominated by members of the Sunni branch of Islam, a minority in Iraq compared with the Shiite branch.

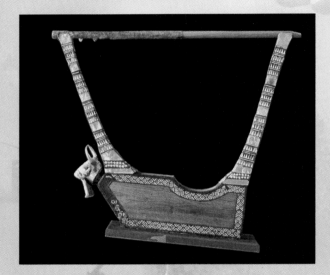

A lyre, or harp, dating from about 2450 B.C. and discovered in the grave of a king of the ancient city of Ur (in southeastern Iraq), was one of the antiquities looted from the National Museum of Iraq. Most of the important looted pieces were eventually returned.

during the actual combat. And car bombings left dozens of people dead, including 23 officials with the United Nations mission in Iraq. By August, Defense Department officials had labeled the continuing hostilities in Iraq a classic guerrilla war.

The collapse of civil authority

The collapse of the Hussein government and the pullout of the Iraqi Army left much of Iraq without civil authority, and looting became widespread. In Baghdad, looters stripped most of the public buildings, including hospitals, of supplies. Looters also ransacked the National Museum of Iraq. Thieves made off with about 12,000 items, including 32 ancient objects that archaeologists described as "of extreme importance." (Most of the important pieces eventually turned up or were quietly returned to the museum.)

By mid-April, coalition forces held all of Iraq's major cities. Several hundred Kurdish fighters under the command of U.S. special forces occupied Kirkuk on April 10. On April 11, U.S. special forces and Kurdish fighters entered the northern city of Mosul without a fight. U.S. Marines entered Tikrit, the last remaining Iraqi city not under allied control, on April 13. U.S. commanders had expected the Republican Guard and the Fedayeen Saddam militia to make a last stand at Tikrit, because it was Saddam Hussein's birthplace. However, the Marines met only sporadic resistance. A spokesperson for the U.S. Department of Defense announced on April 14 that major combat operations in Iraq were over.

After the fall of the Hussein regime, coalition forces in Iraq focused largely on restoring order and helping the Iraqi people establish a new government. However, the pacification and reconstruction of Iraq proved to be much more difficult than anticipated by some officials at the U.S. Defense Department. Massive postwar looting and the breakdown of Iraqi Army and security forces left a good deal of Iraq's infrastructure in shambles. Guerrilla attacks on coalition soldiers resulted in more U.S. casualties after May 1 than

Looting combined with sabotage at oil wells, refineries, and along pipelines brought much of Iraq's oil industry to a standstill. In May, Iraq, a country with the world's second largest oil reserves, was forced to import gasoline—at U.S. expense—from neighbors in the Middle East. A spokesperson for the Bush administration conceded in September that oil revenues from Iraq had proven to be a major disappointment. Prior to the war, the administration had claimed that Iraqi oil fields would quickly yield $100 billion a year, which could be used to fund the country's reconstruction. According to the latest estimates, Iraqi oil revenues may climb to $12 billion by the end of 2004.

Looting also crippled Iraq's electric power system, already damaged by coalition bombing. Copper and other salable metals were repeatedly stripped from power plants and electric wires, which made it difficult to get the system up and keep it running. The resulting loss of power to run air conditioners, refrigerators, and water pumping stations made life for many Iraqis nearly unbearable, particularly at the height of the summer of 2003, when temperatures climbed as high as 130 °F (55 °C). The failure of the U.S.-led coalition, with its vaunted technological know-how, to keep the lights on and the water running was a public relations disaster. Many Iraqis ended up blaming their misery on the Americans, rather than on the looters among them.

International observers who visited Iraq during this period blamed the widespread civil disorder on three factors—too many Iraqi criminals; too few U.S. soldiers; and the premature disbanding of the Iraqi Army. Saddam Hussein emptied Iraq's prisons in October 2002. His mass pardon released the country's entire criminal element into the general population just months before the beginning of the war. It is likely that Iraq's criminals took every advantage of the breakdown of civil authority that came with the collapse of Hussein's regime.

Critics of the Bush administration's handling of the war and its aftermath claimed that U.S. Secretary of Defense Donald Rumsfeld's determination to keep the U.S. force in Iraq as small as possible resulted in too few troops to maintain

security in the cities. They argued that coalition forces—which were reduced to about 160,000 after May 1, 2003—were stretched too thin to hunt down members of Hussein's regime, round up emerging guerrilla fighters and terrorists, and safeguard Iraqi national assets and the general population. The Army was also reluctant to take responsibility for day-to-day security. In May, U.S. Brigadier General Vincent Brooks, a spokesperson for the U.S. Central Command in the Persian Gulf, told reporters that the military was involved in rebuilding Iraq's civil administration and had no intention of becoming a police force.

Experts also questioned the wisdom of a decision made in May by L. Paul Bre-

> **Looters wheel their plunder up al-Rashid Street in Baghdad on April 11 as buildings burn with no one to fight the fires. After the collapse of the Hussein government, the capital and other Iraqi cities descended into near anarchy, the streets controlled by thieves and murderers.**

mer III, the civilian head of the U.S.-led occupation, to disband the Iraqi Army. They noted that this resulted in thousands of armed men, many of them Hussein loyalists, on the streets with no pay and few ways to legally support themselves. The experts suggested that many members of the former Iraqi Army ended up becoming looters or joining guerrilla forces to the north.

The war that was fought in Iraq, the swift march north to Baghdad, was not the war that Defense Department officials originally had planned. Defense Secretary Rumsfeld wanted to fight on two fronts. In the south, coalition forces were to drive north from Kuwait; in the north, U.S. troops were to advance south to Baghdad from Turkey. However, the Turkish parliament, dominated by an Islamist party— that is, a political party rooted in Islamic theology and law—defied its own government leaders and refused to grant the United States permission to move troops across Turkish soil. As a result, very few U.S. troops were stationed north of Baghdad when the war ended. This allowed Hussein loyalists to freely move north. Experts on Iraq believe that the remnants of the Republican Guard and the Fedayeen Saddam militia, motivated by tribal loyalties and nationalism, regrouped in and around Tikrit, an area of anti-American resistance that became known as the "Sunni Triangle." The area was so named because it was home to many of the Sunni Muslims who continued to support Hussein.

A guerrilla war

From the Sunni Triangle, insurgents launched near daily attacks on coalition forces, usually U.S. soldiers, resulting in mounting casualties. Guerrillas generally ambushed convoys on roads in the countryside and quickly disappeared. Typically, they possessed a variety of arms, including such sophisticated weapons as rocket-propelled grenades, which they apparently freely picked up from Hussein's weapon depots (places where military supplies are stored). Lacking the personnel, coalition forces did not, for the most part, guard these depots. According to the U.S. Central Intelligence Agency, Iraq's store of conventional weapons at the start of the war was enormous—an estimated 1 million tons (907,000 metric tons).

A new U.S. commander in Iraq, General John P. Abizaid, announced shortly after his arrival there in August that the United States was involved in a classic guerrilla war. Deputy U.S. Secretary of Defense Paul Wolfowitz subsequently confirmed Abizaid's assessment and told reporters that U.S. war planners were most surprised by the fact that Saddam Hussein loyalists would continue to fight a guerrilla war after the collapse of the regular Army. Lieutenant General Ricardo Sanchez, commander of U.S. ground forces in Iraq, later disclosed that U.S. military officials were convinced that fighters other than Saddam Hussein loyalists were taking part in attacks on allied forces in Iraq. According to U.S. intelligence sources, Islamic militants were crossing into Iraq in ever greater numbers from Syria and northern Iran to join forces with Hussein loyalists.

On October 28, two U.S. soldiers were killed when their tank hit an "unidentified explosive device" during a late-night patrol near Balad, 45 miles (72 kilometers) north of Baghdad. The deaths of the two soldiers brought to 116 the number of U.S. soldiers to die in hostile action since the war was declared over on May 1, higher than the 115 U.S. soldiers who died in combat during the actual offensive. Just days before, Lieutenant General Sanchez had noted that attacks on U.S. troops had escalated, to an average of 25 a day.

The insurgents eventually began to employ terrorist tactics on civilians, both foreign and Iraqi. A huge explosion outside the Jordanian embassy in Baghdad on August 7 killed at least 17 people. The explosion was so powerful it reduced the front of the building to rubble, threw shrapnel as far away as 3,000 feet (900 meters), and sent a car onto the roof of a nearby building some 60 feet (18 meters) above ground. Less than two weeks later, another very powerful bomb exploded outside the offices of the United Nations in Baghdad, killing 22 people, including the top UN envoy to Iraq, Sergio Vieira de Mello. A suicide bomber detonated a second device near the same complex on September 22, killing himself and an Iraqi policeman. Three days later, UN officials announced that the organization was "downsizing" in Iraq because of the "deteriorating

security situation." Late in October, a suicide bomber hidden inside an ambulance hit the Baghdad headquarters of the International Committee of the Red Cross.

Iraqi civilians who cooperated with the coalition forces also became targets. Gunmen killed an Iraqi politician, Akila al-Hashemi, outside her house in Baghdad in September. She had been appointed to a board entrusted with creating a new Iraqi government. The repeated bombing of Baghdad police stations, which left 18 police officers dead during August, September, and October, served as warnings of what could happen to Iraqis who worked with the coalition.

During the same period, violence spread to the south, where the Shiite branch of Islam is dominant and where Hussein and his Sunni-dominated government was despised. In late August, a car bomb exploded outside a mosque in An Najaf, killing Ayatollah Mohammed Baqr al-Hakim, one of Iraq's most prominent Shiite clerics. The attack also resulted in the deaths of more than 80 bystanders. In mid-October, three U.S. soldiers and two Iraqi police officers were killed in a 12-hour gunfight with Islamic militants in Karbala. U.S. forces, joined by members of the Iraqi Civil Defense Corps, later raided the city's al-Mukhayam Mosque and arrested followers of a Shiite cleric who was attempting to generate public support for an Islamic republic in Iraq. U.S.

> A U.S. Army ammunition truck is hit by a rocket-propelled grenade in a guerrilla ambush in Al Fallujah in October. Attacks on U.S. convoys in the so-called Sunni Triangle, an area of strong anti-American resistance north of Baghdad, left dozens of U.S. soldiers dead and many more wounded.

officials in Iraq attributed the violence in the south to a power struggle between rival Shiite factions.

U.S. weapons inspector David Kay reported to Congressional intelligence committees on October 3 that the Iraq Survey Group, which he headed, had yet to find weapons of mass destruction in Iraq. He testified that his team had found "a large body of continuing activities and equipment that were not declared to the UN inspectors," and he informed the joint committee that it would take probably another six to nine months to give a firm indication of the state of the Iraqi weapons program.

Politics at home

The rationale that the Bush administration and Tony Blair's Cabinet had used for going to war—that Iraqi weapons of mass destruction threatened the security of the West—quickly came under intense public scrutiny. Political experts noted that the coalition's inability to uncover poison gas, chemical weapons, or evidence of a nuclear program had hurt both leaders politically. Blair in particular faced very blunt questioning by senior members of Parliament during the regular Prime Minister's Question Time. A journalist with the British Broadcasting Company even accused Blair and members of his Cabinet of having altered intelligence reports on Iraq's weapons programs in order to justify going to war.

In the United States, the lack of evidence of weapons of mass destruction forced the Bush administration into two embarrassing admissions. In August, a spokesperson acknowledged that the president had relied on incomplete information when he had declared, in his State of the Union speech, that Saddam Hussein was buying uranium for a nuclear weapons program. One month later, the president himself declared that he knew of no evidence linking Iraq and Saddam Hussein to the terrorist attacks on the United States in 2001.

The president's troubles in Iraq also were compounded by the mounting costs associated with the war. In early September, Bush asked Congress to allocate an additional $87 billion in fiscal year 2004 (Oct. 1, 2003 to Sept. 30, 2004) to cover security and rebuilding costs in Iraq. The size of the request met with criticism from Democrats in Congress as well as from members of the president's own Republican Party.

The Bush administration responded to the mounting criticism with a concerted public relations campaign, which included an attack on the national media. The president accused the media of reporting negative rather than positive developments in Iraq. He and members of the administration toured the country pointing out that considerable progress had been made in Iraq. Coalition forces had toppled Saddam Hussein's government in a very short period of

Firefighters attempt to put out a blaze ignited by a car bombing in August in the city of An Najaf. The bombing, which killed a prominent Shiah cleric and some 100 other Iraqis, signaled the beginning of a wave of insurgent attacks on civilians, both Iraqi and foreign.

The United Nations Security Council votes unanimously on October 16 to endorse a resolution designed to attract international aid to help stabilize Iraq and to push the country toward independence from the U.S.-led occupation.

time with relatively little loss of life. Many of the top leaders in Hussein's government, including his sons, Uday and Qusay, had either been killed or captured. Administration officials noted that the electrical grid in Iraq was up and running and at higher capacity than before the war. Most Iraqi schools and hospitals had reopened. The U.S.-led coalition had established a new border patrol, police network, and Iraqi Army, and these organizations already had enlisted about 85,500 Iraqis in various security positions, freeing coalition soldiers for other responsibilities. On December 13, U.S. forces captured the greatest prize of all, Saddam Hussein.

Rebuilding Iraq

In July, U.S. Envoy Paul Bremer appointed 25 prominent Iraqis to an interim government council. The Governing Council, which consisted of Iraqi men and women of various ethnic and religious backgrounds, was charged with setting Iraq on a course that would lead to the estab-

lishment of a democracy. Officials with the Bush administration pointed out that a viable democracy in Iraq would serve as a shining example to other countries in the Middle East.

In October, the UN Security Council passed a resolution that endorsed the U.S.-led occupation of Iraq. The resolution charged the Iraqi Governing Council with completing a timetable for the creation of a constitution and the scheduling of national elections as a preamble to a timely return of sovereignty to the Iraqi people. In response to the UN resolution, several nations and international organizations joined the United States in offering about $33 billion for the pacification and physical and economic rebuilding of Iraq.

Critics argued the continuing violence in Iraq belied Bush administration claims of material and political progress. The critics noted that the daily attacks on U.S. soldiers and the spiraling numbers of casualties among coalition forces proved one thing—that the war in Iraq was not over. In October, U.S. Defense Secretary Donald Rumsfeld fueled the critics' fire with a memo circulated to his top four advisers before being "leaked" to the press. He wrote that U.S.-led coalitions in Iraq, as well as Afghanistan, faced a "long, hard slog."

SHIFTING ALLIANCES ON THE WORLD STAGE

By Mary-Jane Deeb

Relations between the United States and many countries around the world changed considerably as a result of the decision of the U.S. government to go to war against Iraq in March 2003. That decision grew out of a new foreign policy announced by U.S. President George W. Bush in 2002. The Bush administration's "policy of preemption" is based on the idea that the United States will, if necessary, act "preemptively," that is, ahead of another nation, "to forestall or prevent" hostile acts by adversaries. The adoption of this policy and the subsequent war in Iraq brought about significant changes in relations between the United States and two of its strongest European allies—France and Germany.

President Jacques Chirac of France and Chancellor Gerhard Schroeder of Germany strongly disagreed with the United States about the imminent danger to global security posed by Iraq. That disagreement altered relationships that had endured for more than half a century, from the end of World War II (1939-1945) through the intense rivalry between Communist and non-Communist nations that became known as the Cold War. Arguing against a United Nations (UN) resolution authorizing a war in Iraq, the French and German leaders maintained that no military action should be launched until inspectors from the UN Monitoring, Verification and Inspection Commission (UNMOVIC) and the International Atomic Energy Agency (IAEA) completed their investigations into Iraqi weapons of mass destruction (WMD), that is, chemical, biological, and/or nuclear arms. The French and German stand-off against the United States was supported by many other countries around the world, particularly Arab and other Islamic nations.

United Nations weapons inspections

UNMOVIC was created in December 1999 to monitor Iraq's weapons of mass destruction. The Iraqi government, however, rejected the resolution and refused to let the inspectors' team into Iraq. The Security Council passed Resolution 1441 in November 2002, offering Iraq a final chance to comply with the disarmament obligations specified in previous resolutions. Resolution 1441 demanded that inspectors be allowed unrestricted access to any sites they chose and threatened consequences if these obligations were not met.

An estimated 600,000 protesters demonstrate against the possibility of a war in Iraq at a February rally at the foot of the Colosseum in Rome. European leaders who committed their countries to the U.S.-led coalition in Iraq, such as Italian Prime Minister Silvio Berlusconi, generally did so in defiance of public opinion in their countries.

Iraq accepted the resolution, and UNMOVIC and the IAEA began inspections on Nov. 27, 2002. On December 7, Iraq produced a 12,000-page report on the state of its weapons programs, which the two agencies judged to be incomplete. At the end of January 2003, UNMOVIC Chairman Hans Blix, and IAEA Chief Muhammad al-Baradei reported that no evidence had been uncovered that Iraq had resumed its nuclear program but that outstanding issues regarding Iraqi WMD programs remained unanswered. On March 6, UNMOVIC and the IAEA released "Unresolved Disarmament Issues: Iraq's Proscribed Weapons Programs," in which the agencies maintained that inspections had to continue. Although Iraq was cooperating, it had not provided all the information that had been requested.

The government of the United States responded that it would wait no longer. When the Bush administration could not rally enough votes in the UN Security Council for authorization to go to war against Iraq, the United States withdrew the resolution. Instead, President Bush argued that the United States had the "sovereign authority to use force in assuring its own national security" and cited UN Resolutions 678 and 687, which he maintained authorized the use of force against Iraq. The two decisions—to go to war against Iraq and to do so without UN authorization—antagonized many European powers and other nations worldwide.

Hours before the start of hostilities, U.S. Secretary of State Colin Powell announced that 30 nations had joined a coalition of forces against Iraqi President Saddam Hussein. The coalition consisted of Afghanistan, Albania, Australia, Azerbaijan, Colombia, the Czech Republic, Denmark, El Salvador, Eritrea, Estonia, Ethiopia, Georgia, Hungary, Iceland, Italy, Japan, Latvia, Lithuania, Macedonia, the Netherlands, Nicaragua, the Philippines, Poland, Romania, Slovakia, South Korea, Spain, Turkey, the United Kingdom, and Uzbekistan. On March 20 (March 19 in the United States), the United States and the United Kingdom, with the support of the rest of the coalition, launched a war against Iraq.

A divided Europe

The nations of Europe were sharply divided in their stands on the war. The United Kingdom remained the staunchest U.S. ally and sent the second largest contingent of troops to Iraq—nearly 41,000. The United States sent around 250,000 troops. Spain sided with the United States and offered to send a small contingent of soldiers. The position taken by President of the Government Jose Maria Aznar of Spain, however, was in direct opposition to his constituency. According to some polls, as many as 90 percent of Spaniards opposed the war. Italy's Prime Minister Silvio Berlusconi also defied public opinion to support the U.S.-led coalition. Most polls showed that about 80 percent of Italians were against the war.

The Netherlands had a parliamentary election in January 2003 in which the Christian Democrats, who publicly supported a U.S.-led war on Iraq, won with a slim majority. The main opposition, the Labour Party, campaigned against the war. The same scenario was played out in Denmark, where Prime Minister Anders Fogh Rasmussen, head of a liberal-conservative coalition, supported the United States and sent a submarine and troops to help in the war effort.

Leaders of Denmark's Socialist and Radical parties complained that their representatives in parliament had been given no say in the government's decision to support the war effort. As in the case of the other European countries, the Dutch and the Danish people were divided over their governments' decision to support the United States, especially without a UN mandate.

The support the United States received from the former Communist countries of central and eastern Europe—Albania, the Czech Republic, Hungary, Macedonia, Poland, Romania, and Slovakia, and the Baltic states of Estonia, Latvia, and Lithuania—surprised many experts on international affairs. They suggested that the former Communist nations, motivated by their own interests, endorsed U.S. action in Iraq in order to foster closer ties with the United States—the world's only superpower—rather than out of any particular fear of Iraqi aggression. Romania and Bulgaria, which were scheduled to join the North Atlantic Treaty Organization (NATO) in 2004, may have wanted to show the United States what reliable allies they were on both the war on Iraq and terrorism. However, support was expressed primarily in political statements issued by heads of state, rather than in terms of military participation or monetary contributions. Of the former Communist countries, only Poland offered to send troops.

The support voiced by these countries angered some European powers. French President Chirac publicly warned leaders of these countries to keep their opinions regarding a U.S.-led war on Iraq to themselves or risk losing their chance to join the European Union (EU). (Cyprus, the Czech Republic, Estonia, Hungary, Latvia, Lithuania, Malta, Poland, Slovakia, and Slovenia were set to become EU members in 2004. Romania was scheduled to join the EU in 2007.) The French position, in turn, increased tensions within the European Union, already split by the defection of the United Kingdom, Spain, Italy, the Netherlands, and Denmark.

Russia, after giving hesitant support to the United States as it sought to go to war with Iraq, decided to side with France and Germany and take a stand against the war. A month before the war began, representatives of France, Germany, and Russia met in Paris and issued a joint declaration. While reaffirming their wish to disarm Iraq in accordance with a series of UN resolutions, they stated that they wished to continue a discussion with the United States about how to achieve this disarmament. According to the three countries, UN Resolution 1441 provided a framework for different possible means to achieve the same goal.

Traditional allies take sides

Canada, another traditional U.S. ally and its most important trading partner, took a similar position to that of France and Germany. On March 13, Canadian Prime Minister Jean Chretien stated in the House of Commons, the lower house of Canada's Parliament, that his government would not support a war on Iraq without the approval of the UN Security Council.

Another long-term U.S. ally, Australia, not only supported President Bush's decision to go to war, but sent 2,000 troops to Iraq to fight alongside U.S. and British troops. Polls indicated, however, that the majority of Australians did not back their government's decision.

The war complicated U.S. relations with India. U.S. officials viewed India as being of enormous strategic importance. The U.S. Navy needed a relatively neutral country fairly close to the Middle East to provide ports and logistic support for the war. India's coast on the Arabian Sea made it ideal for U.S. operations in the area. International affairs experts noted that India would become of even greater importance if the United States one day could no longer rely on its traditional allies in the Middle East, Saudi Arabia and the Gulf emirates. The strategic importance of this U.S.-India alliance initially emerged during the Persian Gulf War, when India provided refueling facilities for U.S. warplanes, and Indian naval ships provided escorts for commercial vessels sailing in the North Arabian Sea. India did not, however, join the coalition against Iraq in 2003. When the United States asked the Indian government to send about 17,000 troops to join a stabilization force in Iraq after the end of hostilities, Indian Prime Minister Atal Behari Vajpayee refused. He offered aid for the

The author:
Mary-Jane Deeb is the Arab World Area Specialist at the Library of Congress.

U.S. President George W. Bush and French President Jacques Chirac appear friendly at the start of a Group of Eight summit in Evian, France, in June despite strained relations between the two leaders. Chirac led European opposition to the war in Iraq.

sanctions imposed on Pakistan in 1998 for initiating a nuclear test program. The United States also resumed major U.S. military and humanitarian assistance that had been cut in 1990 in an attempt to stop Pakistan from developing a nuclear weapon.

The war in Iraq also placed Turkey, another Islamic country, in an ambiguous relationship with the United States. While Turkey was named as one of the coalition partners, its parliament, the Turkish Grand National Assembly, failed to muster the necessary votes to allow 62,000 U.S. combat troops to launch an attack on Iraq from Turkish territory. Turkey also refused to permit the United States to use U.S. bombers stationed at Incirlik, a U.S.-Turkish airbase in Turkey, to fly missions against Iraq. This lack of cooperation was due, in large measure, to strong opposition to the war by the Turkish people, who staged huge antiwar demonstrations in Istanbul and Ankara, the capital, in the weeks preceding the war.

Despite the tension in the relations between the two countries, the United States continued to view Turkey as a critical ally in the Middle East. In a June 2003 speech at the Brookings Institution, an independent organization for research and education in economics, government, and foreign policy, U.S. Undersecretary of State Alan Larson admitted to being disappointed in Turkey's lack of cooperation during the Iraq war. He maintained, however, that "the United States will be working with our Turkish friends to build a mature economic partnership far into the 21st century."

reconstruction of Iraq but stated that Indian troops could be deployed only in accordance with a UN mandate. The Indian public had been strongly against the war, and Prime Minister Vajpayee was not ready to risk voter displeasure, particularly when key state and national elections were scheduled to take place in 2004.

Response of Islamic nations

The war in Iraq also divided Islamic countries. While the president of Pakistan, Pervez Musharraf, supported the United States, the Pakistani people largely opposed the war and staged enormous antiwar demonstrations to vent their displeasure. To prevent the political situation in Pakistan from unraveling and to reward Musharraf for his support, President Bush in July 2003 announced a five-year, $3-billion development and defense aid package for Pakistan. Musharraf's military government also enjoyed U.S. support for its assistance in the war against terrorism. Musharraf had proved very helpful to the U.S. government in the capture of high-level members of the al-Qa'ida terrorist network, including the apprehension of Khalid Sheikh Muhammad, the alleged commander of the 2001 terrorist attacks on the United States. In response to Musharraf's support, the United States lifted

Indonesia, another U.S. ally and the country with the world's largest Muslim population, condemned the war in Iraq as illegal, because the United States had failed in its attempt to receive a UN mandate. International affairs experts suggested that the attitude of the Indonesian government was in part a reaction to the country's radical Muslims, who had become very active in recent years. Indonesia's radical Muslims have been blamed for attacks against Western tourists, including a nightclub bombing in Bali in October

2002—which killed over 200 people—and an attack on a tourist hotel in Jakarta in August 2003—which left 14 people dead. Anti-American sentiment, expressed in large antiwar demonstrations, increased after the war, and the arrival of President Bush in Indonesia in October sparked protests in several cities.

Malaysia's former prime minister, Mahathir bin Mohammad, also was critical of the U.S. decision to go to war against Iraq. The Malaysian government expressed its disapproval by refusing an invitation to participate in 2003 in the annual Cobra military exercises with the United States, Singapore, and Thailand.

Reactions to the war by leaders of the Arab nations of the Middle East were highly ambiguous. At the Arab League summit in Cairo in March, the member nations officially condemned the war and passed a resolution declaring it "a violation of the United Nations charter" and "a threat to world peace." However, a number of Arab countries allowed U.S. troops, weapons, and combat equipment to be based on their territory. King Hamad bin Khalifa al-Thani allowed the United States to locate its Central Command Headquarters in Qatar. Bahrain, where the U.S. Navy's Fifth Fleet was headquartered, provided its port facilities to the U.S. forces fighting in Iraq. Kuwait provided a launching pad for the U.S. and British invasion of Iraq and remained a major base for coalition forces in the Gulf. The Saudi Prince Sultan Base, located northeast of Riyadh, the Saudi capital, was used as the airfield from which the air war against Iraq was run, despite the fact that Saudi Arabia publicly opposed the conflict.

The "Arab street," that is, the majority of the people of these countries, was, however, clearly against the war and the policies of their governments. In early April, there were major riots in Bahrain's capital, Manama, during which thousands of people stormed the U.S. embassy compound, hurled firebombs, broke windows, and torched embassy vehicles. U.S. Marines eventually drove the mob away with tear gas. Anti-American demonstrations throughout the Arab and Muslim world were massive despite the efforts of government security services and the police to control the "street." The governments were worried about possible acts of terrorism against U.S.

and Western individuals and organizations. However, they also worried about political instability within their own countries, as Arabs blamed their government for their inaction and contradictory policies toward the U.S.-led war on Iraq.

Long term effects

The war strained U.S. relations with countries around the world but also strengthened relations with some nations. Whether these changes will be long-lasting remains in question. Relations between the United States and Britain reached a high point in 2003 reminiscent of their cooperation during World War II. However, the U.S.-UK connection placed the British government in a bind that might ultimately undermine the special relationship between the two countries. British Prime Minister Tony Blair came under mounting attack at home in 2003, both from members of Parliament and from the British press, for his unquestioning support of the United States. International affairs experts noted that Blair's stand on Iraq might even lead to his eventual downfall.

British participation in the U.S.-led coalition also created tension with other members of the European Union. A founding member of the EU, the United Kingdom in 2003 remained very much engaged in strengthening the organization. Experts in international affairs have suggested that if Britain's long-term relationship with the United States continues to place it at odds with fellow EU members—for example, over such issues as national sovereignty versus the global role of the United Nations—then U.S.-UK relations may become strained over time.

U.S. relations with France, Germany, and Russia could remain difficult for the foreseeable future. France has taken the lead in opposing U.S. positions on a number of issues—U.S. rejection of the Kyoto Treaty on emission of greenhouse gases; U.S. refusal to be a party to the International Criminal Court at The Hague; and the war against Iraq. In recent years, the leaders of France, Germany, and Russia preferred international matters to be addressed multilaterally—that is, in consultation with the major European powers, and generally within the framework of the United Nations. Under the Bush administration, the government of the United States saw no reason, as the world's only superpower, to consult the major European powers in every situation. The Bush administration, in its first years in office, preferred to deal bilaterally with other nations—that is, in a one-on-one, reciprocal relationship. The war in Iraq highlighted the differences between the European approach to

British Prime Minister Tony Blair plays host to U.S. President George W. Bush at a summit in April near Belfast in Northern Ireland to discuss plans for postwar Iraq. The United Kingdom, the strongest of U.S. allies, sent nearly 41,000 troops to Iraq.

international affairs and the approach adopted by the United States.

Unilateralism vs. multilateralism

France, Germany, Russia, and the United States, nevertheless, continued to have a great number of common economic and political interests, which none was willing to sacrifice. Their economies remained interlocked and interdependent in 2003, and the four nations all belonged to a number of international organizations created to ensure the protection of the wealth, security, and well-being of their citizens. Furthermore, the people of Europe and the United States may face a common threat—the international terrorist movement. The threat is likely to bring them closer together as they assume shared responsibilities and adopt similar strategies to combat it. Experts also predict that cooperation between these countries will increase as critical issues affecting the world community—for example, instability in developing countries and the AIDS epidemic—become more serious. Finally, European countries and the United States share common values and beliefs in democracy, the rule of law, and human rights, which have fostered close ties.

The war in Iraq left the Arab world with a very negative public image of the United States. The media throughout the region continuously criticized the United States during and after the war, depicting it as a force of occupation not liberation. Since weapons of mass destruction were not found in 2003, Arabs claimed that the war was unjustified. Furthermore, the deterioration of Israeli-Palestinian relations and the failure of the U.S.-sponsored "Road Map to Peace" to produce a Palestinian nation increased Arab antagonism toward the United States. U.S. attempts at public diplomacy before and after the war failed to "capture the minds and hearts of the Arabs and Muslims."

The long-term relationship between the United States and Saudi Arabia, perhaps its most important Arab ally, also shifted in 2003. The Saudis asked the United States to pull all U.S. military forces out of Saudi territory. The presence of U.S. troops there, which began with the Persian Gulf War of 1991, had caused major discord among the Saudi people. The forces also had become likely targets of such terrorist organizations as the al-Qa'ida network. Tension between the two governments also grew in 2003 as the result of a U.S. congressional report. Twenty eight pages of the report that were purported to refer to Saudi Arabia's role in the terrorist attacks on the United States in 2001 remained classified, and the Bush administration refused the Saudi foreign minister's request to make them public. Experts suggested that this small U.S.-Saudi rift may foreshadow more tense relations between the United States and the Arab world in the years to come.

The loss of the U.S. military base in Saudi Arabia made the United States more dependent on bases outside the Persian Gulf, specifically in India. U.S. policymakers view India as being of enormous strategic importance to U.S. interests worldwide—an importance that is likely to grow since the war on Iraq. How India responds to U.S. overtures remains unclear.

Pakistan, now one of the closest allies to the United States in the region, proved to be invaluable in the war against terrorism. However, this policy turned out to be highly unpopular with the Pakistani people, and Musharraf's military government may have to curtail support for the United States if it wants to survive.

Relations with other countries that have large Muslim populations, for example, Indonesia and Malaysia, are likely to deteriorate further before they get better. A successful transition to an Iraqi-led government, and the pullout of U.S. forces from Iraq may be the only way to defuse the growing political resentment against the United States in the Islamic world.

U.S. policy is tested

The first big test of the long-term effects of the U.S. policy of preemption and the war on Iraq came in autumn 2003. U.S. troops in Iraq were under daily attack from guerrilla fighters, and American casualties mounted alarmingly. In September, President Bush instructed U.S. Secretary of State Colin Powell to propose a resolution to the UN Security Council calling for a UN-sponsored multinational force in Iraq. According to many experts on international affairs, the Bush administration hoped that the resolution would pave the way for member nations to provide troops and money for the pacification and rebuilding of Iraq.

On October 16, the Security Council unanimously passed the resolution, which confirmed that the U.S.-led coalition would remain in power in Iraq for an unspecified period. However, the resolution had gone through a number of revisions. France and Russia, both permanent members of the Security Council with veto power, demanded that the resolution specify that sovereignty was to be transferred to a government representing the Iraqi people as soon as practicable. They also demanded a timetable and a program for the drafting of a new constitution for Iraq; the establishment of Iraqi police and security forces; and assistance in economic development and reconstruction, including financial aid. While the unanimity of the Security Council vote appeared to be a diplomatic coup for the United States, the appeal for troops and money for the pacification of Iraq proved to be less of a success.

In late October, representatives of 77 nations, meeting in Madrid, pledged in excess of $13 billion for the reconstruction of Iraq. However, the $13 billion combined with the $20 billion pledged by the United States fell short of the $56 billion that the World Bank, a UN affiliate, estimated was needed to rebuild the country. In addition, much of the money from countries other than the United States was pledged in the form of loans, not outright grants. Experts noted that Iraq was already overburdened with some $120 billion in debt and, in fact, had no one in authority to guarantee the repayment of such loans. France and Russia donated nothing toward the reconstruction. Germany gave only $100 million, half of which was its share of the EU contribution.

Bangladesh, Portugal, South Korea, and Turkey agreed to send troops. In the face of escalating violence in Iraq, Bangladesh and Portugal backed out of their agreement. South Korea announced it would delay sending troops "pending further study." Turkey reversed its commitment after members of the Iraqi Council protested allowing Turkish soldiers on Iraqi soil.

Relations between the United States and its traditional allies appeared to improve toward the end of 2003. On December 13, U.S. forces captured Saddam Hussein. Foreign affairs experts speculated that Hussein's capture might improve relations between the United States and countries that had opposed the war, and French foreign minister Dominique de Villepin appeared to confirm that view when he announced that it encouraged "the international community to be united again." Then, on December 16, France and Germany agreed to work with the United States toward reducing Iraq's substantial foreign debt by forgiving all or part of billions of dollars in Iraqi loans. International affairs experts described the cooperation of the two countries that had most strongly opposed the war in Iraq as both a significant step forward in the U.S. effort to rebuild Iraq and major progress in mending strained relations.

More than 1,000 farmers protest economic problems in rural Ireland by parking their tractors around the office of the prime minister in Dublin in January.

Ireland. The popularity of *Taioseach* (prime minister) Bertie Ahern and his coalition government, made up of the Fianna Fail and Progressive Democrat parties, fell to a record low in 2003. In September, a poll conducted by the *Irish Times* showed that 58 percent of respondents were dissatisfied with the performance of Ahern and his center-right coalition, which had been reelected in 2002. The dissatisfaction stemmed, in part, from the fact that the Irish economy had slowed. Ahern was also criticized for his government's handling of a national child abuse scandal and for failing to present an accurate picture of the economic situation. The same poll showed that support for Fianna Fail had fallen to 30 percent, from 41 percent during the May 2002 election. However, opposition parties also failed to make gains. Fine Gael enjoyed only 22 percent of support, while the Labour Party earned 19 percent.

Economy. The Irish economy grew modestly in 2003. The Central Statistics Office reported that the country's *gross national product* (the total value of all goods and services produced in a year) grew by only 3.1 percent in the second quarter (the latest figure available). The rate stood in sharp contrast to the growth rates of the late 1990's, which reached as high as 10 percent. The modest growth was attributed to a drop in exports and industrial production because of the poor international economic climate and reduced consumer spending. Unemployment rose to 4.6 percent in mid-2003, the highest since 2000. Nevertheless, Prime Minister Ahern pointed out that unemployment in Ireland was well below the European Union average of 8.9 percent in July 2003. Declining tax revenues posed a problem for Finance Minister Charlie McGreevy, raising the possibility that he might be forced to cut expenditures for public services.

Child abuse. In October, Ireland's *auditor general* (a parliamentary watchdog) revealed that the government could face a bill of up to 1 billion euros ($1.19 billion) as part of its agreement with the Roman Catholic Church in Ireland over compensation for people who had been victims of sexual abuse. The abuse occurred from the 1930's to the 1970's in children's homes run by the church. The church agreed to pay 128 million euros ($152 million), and the government was to make up the remainder.

Smoking. The government's ban on smoking in all workplaces, which was to go into effect Jan. 1, 2004, was postponed until spring 2004. Health ministry officials cited concerns about possible legal challenges to the law, which was expected to have a serious effect on pub, restaurant, and hotel revenues. ■ Rohan McWilliam

See also **Europe; Northern Ireland.**

Thousands of Shiah Muslims gather in the holy city of Karbala in central Iraq on April 22, 2003, to honor the Prophet Muhammad's grandson, Imam al-Husayn, who was beheaded on this site in A.D. 684 in a battle over control of Islam. Former Iraqi President Saddam Hussein, who had long repressed Iraq's Shiite majority, had banned the annual pilgrimage for more than 30 years.

Islam. The "clash of civilizations" sharpened in 2003 with the United States-led war in Iraq; European campaigns against Islamic dress; and Islamic terrorist attacks on European, U.S., and Middle Eastern targets.

The war in Iraq. The U.S.-led war in Iraq had multiple consequences for Islam in 2003. The destruction of Saddam Hussein's Ba'athist regime meant the liberation of Shiah Islam in Iraq. Sunni Muslims, who had been in power in Iraq for more than 80 years, controlled the Ba'ath Party, which was Hussein's secular political party. For the last 20 years, the Ba'athist government persecuted the Shiites and forbade them from practicing their religious rituals.

During and after the war in 2003, many senior religious figures who had fled Iraq returned; many religious groups came out of hiding, and new groups were established; and the senior religious leaders known as the Hawzah became important political players in post-war Iraq. Their new role made them targets for the insurgents, and one senior figure, Ayatollah Baqr al-Hakim, was assassinated in An Najaf in August 2003.

Religious symbols. In Europe, several incidents heightened a culture conflict as indigenous Europeans and immigrant Muslims continued to come to terms with one another. In France, a special commission recommended in December that Islamic headscarves, large crosses, and Jewish skullcaps are religious symbols and should be banned under the 1905 law mandating secularism in public institutions. By the end of 2003, French President Jacques Chirac announced that he would support legislation to make the ban law by autumn 2004.

Italian Muslim activist Adel Smith filed a complaint that a religious symbol, a crucifix, was displayed prominently in the classrooms of his children. A judge ruled in October that state schools may not display crucifixes in public schools. Outraged Leftists, Roman Catholics, and even some Muslims and Jews protested that the crucifix was a cultural symbol, not a religious one, and should not offend Muslim schoolchildren.

Terrorism. In Iraq, Morocco, Saudi Arabia, and Turkey, Islamic terrorists bombed sites identified with foreigners, Judaism, or the governments. In all cases, the local Muslim leadership deplored these activities and denounced their perpetrators as enemies of Islam. In Indonesia, religious authorities denounced Islamist violence and applauded the conviction and death sentence in August of the Islamist bombers Amrozi bin Nurhasym and Imam Samudra, who claimed responsibility for the October 2002 bombing in Bali that killed 202 people. ■ A. Kevin Reinhart

See also **Iraq: A Special Report; Judaism; Terrorism.**

Israel. The failure in 2003 of the implementation of the "road map" for peace between the Israelis and the Palestinians led to the resignation of the Palestinian prime minister, Mahmoud Abbas, who was replaced by Ahmad Quray, the former speaker of the Palestinian Legislature. The road map was devised by representatives of the United States, Russia, the United Nations (UN), and the European Union (EU), an organization of 15 western European countries. Political experts suggested that because Prime Minister Quray and Israeli Prime Minister Ariel Sharon had known each other for many years, there may be a better chance that the two can broker a cease-fire between Israeli forces and the militant Palestinian groups Hamas and Islamic Jihad.

Sharon's policies criticized. More than three years of Israeli-Palestinian violence that resulted in the deaths of an estimated 2,500 Palestinians and 900 Israelis eroded Prime Minister Sharon's popularity as prime minister. Four former heads of Shin Bet, the Israeli counterintelligence and internal security service—Ami Ayalon, Carmi Gilon, Yaakov Perry, and Avraham Shalom—strongly denounced various actions taken by Sharon in 2003. Shalom stated on November 14 that, "We must once and for all admit that there is another side, that it has feelings and that it is suffering, and that we are behaving disgracefully." The former Shin Bet chiefs also condemned the fence that Prime Minister Sharon ordered to be constructed around areas of the West Bank in an effort to prevent terrorists

from infiltrating Israel. Shalom argued that the fence was producing the opposite of the prime minister's intention: "It creates hatred, it expropriates land, and annexes hundreds of thousands of Palestinians to the state of Israel."

Virtual peace treaty. On October 12, after several years of negotiations in Switzerland, Yossi Beilin, a former Israeli minister of justice, and Yasir Abd Rabbuh, a former Palestinian minister of information, signed what they called the Geneva Accord—a virtual peace treaty between the Israelis and the Palestinians. Hebrew and Arabic copies of the accord were mailed in November to every household in Israel, the West Bank, and Gaza Strip. The Geneva Accord calls for the establishment in the West Bank and Gaza of a nonmilitarized Palestinian nation coexisting in peace with Israel. The accord specified that the Palestinians had sovereignty over the Arab neighborhoods of East Jerusalem and the Temple Mount, an area that Muslims refer to as *Haram al-Sharif* (Noble Sanctuary) and that is sacred to both Jews and Muslims. The accord places the Temple Mount under a permanent international security force, which is to provide Jews with complete access. In exchange for keeping some densely populated Jewish settle-

Israeli workers construct a fence that, in conjunction with sections of concrete walls, was to separate much of Israel from the West Bank. Israeli Prime Minister Sharon ordered the construction of the highly controversial "defense wall" to prevent terrorists from infiltrating Israel.

ments in the West Bank, the Palestinians were to be given equivalent land from Israel proper. Another provision specified that almost all new Jewish neighborhoods in Arab East Jerusalem are to be evacuated and returned intact to the Palestinians. A limited number of the Palestinian refugees—approximately 30,000—were to be allowed to return to Israel.

Official visits. Israeli President Moshe Katzav made an official visit to Turkey on July 8 to meet with President Ahmet Necdet Sezer. Sezer emphasized the common bonds that tie Turkey and Israel as the two Middle Eastern countries that are democracies with free-market economies. President Katzav stressed that Israel appreciated Turkey's European identity and, therefore, supported Turkey's application to join the EU. In an interview prior to his visit, Katzav spoke of Turkey's "strategic value" to the region and its good relations with Arab countries, the United States, and the EU.

Prime Minister Sharon visited Russia in November to meet with President Vladimir Putin. Sharon informed Putin that Israeli intelligence agents had proof that Iran possessed "a serious threat to world security." Sharon previously had tried to dissuade Russia from selling Iran nuclear technology. ■ Marius Deeb

See also **Judaism; Middle East; Terrorism.**

Italy. Prime Minister Silvio Berlusconi generated a series of controversies that dominated Italian politics in 2003. The first arose out of his position as Italy's richest businessman and owner of the country's largest media empire. On May 5, Berlusconi appeared in a Milan court to deny charges of bribery, the first time an Italian prime minister had testified at his own trial while holding office. He was accused of having bribed judges in an attempt to gain control of a state-owned food company, SME, during a privatization auction in 1985. Berlusconi denied the charges and claimed he was the victim of a politically motivated attack by left-wing judges.

The prime minister's trial was suspended in June, after Berlusconi's government won parliamentary approval for a law granting immunity to the prime minister and four other top government officials while in office. Opposition parties criticized the law for putting the prime minister beyond the reach of justice and noted that the bribery case would expire under Italian law by the time Berlusconi reaches the end of his five-year term in 2006. The government justified the law as being in line with those of several other European countries and in line with Italian practice before 1993. Immunity was revoked in 1993 because of a scandal called "Clean Hands" in which hundreds of politicians were jailed on cor-

ruption charges. In December 2003, parliament passed a law relaxing limits on media ownership. The government drafted the law in response to an earlier court ruling that ordered Berlusconi's company Mediaset to sell one of its three television stations. In a rare move, President Carlo Azeglio Ciampi refused to sign the law and urged parliament to change it. Berlusconi said he would consider "intelligent" changes to the law.

EU presidency. While Italy held the presidency of the 15-nation European Union (EU) during the second half of 2003, comments by Berlusconi sparked a diplomatic incident with Germany. In an appearance before the European Parliament to announce plans for the EU presidency, a German parliamentarian criticized Berlusconi for an alleged conflict of interest for owning a media company while serving as prime minister. Berlusconi responded by comparing the man to a Nazi concentration camp guard. German politicians protested the comments, only to have Italy's tourism minister, Stefano Stefani, call German tourists "hypernationalistic blondes." The incident prompted Gerhard Schroeder, the German chancellor, to cancel his planned summer vacation in Italy.

During the remainder of the EU presidency, Berlusconi chaired difficult negotiations aimed at drafting the EU's first formal constitution. It included a charter of fundamental rights similar to the U.S. Bill of Rights, the creation of an EU foreign minister, and greater EU powers in such areas as immigration and asylum. The negotiations broke down, however, when Poland and Spain objected to changes that would give greater influence to the EU's largest countries, such as Germany and France.

Economy. Italy slipped into a recession in 2003 as a Europe-wide slowdown depressed the economy. Economists generally define a recession as at least two quarters in which a country's *gross domestic product* (GDP, the value of goods and services produced in a year) declines. Italy's GDP declined in the first and second quarters of 2003 but grew in the third quarter. EU economists forecast that the country's annual GDP would grow by 0.3 percent in 2003, compared with 0.4 percent in 2002. Unemployment remained high at 8.8 percent of the labor force.

Pension reform. In August 2003, Berlusconi outlined plans to reform Italy's state-run retirement system by raising the retirement age by five years. In 2003, the retirement age was 60, but Italians retired at about 57 after working for 35 years. Berlusconi argued that the changes were necessary to contain the cost of retirement pensions as Italian society ages.

Corporate troubles. Both Fiat, the automaker and Italy's largest manufacturing company, and Parmalat, an international dairy giant and Italy's largest food company, underwent wrenching changes in 2003. On January 24, Fiat's honorary chairman, Giovanni Agnelli, who had dominated Italian business, politics, and society for half a century, died, and his brother, Umberto Agnelli, took over as chairman. Umberto installed a new management team to deal with the company's loss of $4.6 billion for 2002, reported In March 2003. Under a restructuring, Fiat sold its main nonautomotive subsidiaries for more than $4 billion and raised $2 billion from its shareholders. The company also planned to eliminate some 20,000 jobs worldwide.

On December 27, an Italian court declared Parmalat officially insolvent in a scandal the government referred to as "Europe's Enron." Parmalat's founder, Calisto Tanzi, admitted to defrauding the company of $627 million, while government investigators put the shortfall at closer to $13 billion.

A major power failure on September 28 left more than 50 million Italians—about 95 percent of the population—without power for as long as 18 hours. The blackout began when a storm blew trees onto two power lines in Switzerland that carry electricity from France to Italy. The disruption overloaded the rest of Italy's power grid until it shut down. ■ Tom Buerkle

See also **Europe; Iraq: A Special Report.**

Ivory Coast. See Cote d'Ivoire in **Africa.**

Jamaica. See **West Indies.**

Thousands of mourners gather outside the Victor Emanuel monument in Rome on November 17 to pay their respects to 19 Italians killed in Iraq. A suicide bombing at An Nasiriyah caused the deaths of the 17 servicemen and 2 civilians in Italy's worst single military loss since World War II (1939-1945). Although Italy had not contributed troops to the war in Iraq, the nation did send security officers to help pacify Iraq.

Japan. The Japanese parliament approved legislation in July 2003 that paved the way to sending as many as 1,000 troops to help a United States-led coalition to stabilize Iraq. The legislation, which was narrowly approved after much bitter debate, would allow deployment of Japanese troops to a combat zone for the first time since World War II (1939-1945). The vote was a major victory for Prime Minister Junichiro Koizumi, who overcame a no-confidence vote and a filibuster to pass the measure.

Under the law, troops would be limited to noncombat areas in Iraq. However, opponents of the action said the law violated Japan's Constitution, which banned the use of Japan's military to settle international conflicts. The Constitution was drawn in 1946 by the United States following the Allied victory over Japan in World War II. The United States vowed to protect Japan from aggressors and helped Japan build a so-called Self-Defense Force. In 2003, the Self-Defense Force had 240,000 troops armed with modern weaponry and one of the five largest military budgets in the world.

Since the early 1990's, the Japanese government attempted to expand the military's role in international affairs and sent small forces to take part in peacekeeping operations in Cambodia and East Timor. In 1991, Japan provided logistical help and $13 billion in financial support for the Persian Gulf War. In 2001, Japanese ships patrolled the Indian Ocean during the U.S.-led campaign in Afghanistan.

Liberal members of the Japanese government and the majority of the public opposed the decision to send troops to Iraq in 2003. Polls showed that only 28 percent of the public backed the legislation. Opponents said the action would set a precedent for sending troops on other dangerous missions. Koizumi's governing Liberal Democratic Party (LDP) argued that Japan needed to play a larger role in world affairs in order to protect its status as a world power. On December 9, Koizumi announced he would send a ground force of 600 soldiers to southeastern Iraq for six months to one year.

North Korea. Some critics said that Koizumi's government was exploiting the public's growing concern about North Korea to build a case for a more aggressive military force. In 2003, North Korean officials announced that the country planned to test an atomic bomb to prove to the world that it had nuclear weapons. A nationwide poll showed that 92 percent of the Japanese public felt very anxious or somewhat anxious about North Korea's nuclear ambitions.

In March, Japan launched two spy satellites to monitor activities in North Korea. Japan and the United States, which also used satellites to spy on North Korea, streamlined intelligence sharing to crack down on North Korea's illegal weapons and drug trafficking. A U.S. State Department official said in 2003 that North Korea relied on money from illegal activities to fund its nuclear program. In June, North Korea suspended its lone passenger ferry link with Japan in response to a new Japanese policy that subjected all North Korean shipping to intensive inspections.

Relations between the neighboring countries were further strained in 2003 over North Korea's refusal to release families of Japanese citizens abducted by North Korea in the 1970's and 1980's. In 2002, North Korean officials admitted that the government kidnapped Japanese citizens so that North Korean spies could be tutored in the Japanese language and culture. North Korea allowed five abductees to visit Japan in 2002. The abductees decided to stay in Japan, but North Korea refused their demands to let their families travel to Japan.

Politics. Koizumi struggled against sagging approval ratings in 2003 and battled with critics who claimed he was doing little to speed Japan's economic recovery. Some observers questioned whether the LDP would retain its hold on the government, which it had ruled since 1955.

The two largest opposition parties, the Democratic Party of Japan (DPJ) and the Liberal Party, joined forces in July 2003 under the DPJ name to challenge Koizumi's government. DPJ officials released a campaign document that detailed the party's positions on various issues. The action was a watershed moment for a national political campaign. Traditionally, candidates refused to take stands on specific issues. As a result, voters were not able to measure the government's success in implementing campaign promises.

In response, Koizumi returned to the pledges he made when he was elected prime minister in 2001. He vowed in mid-2003 to reform Japan's corrupt political system, to cut public spending, and to reform the bank industry. His own party members resisted political reforms, which would disallow appointed government jobs that have been traditionally used to reward party faithful.

Koizumi's renewed commitment to reform won him public and political support. In September, he was reelected leader of the LDP in a decisive victory. Koizumi beat out three challengers and received 60 percent of the vote. His easy victory led him to call general elections in November, six months before elections were scheduled to take place.

Koizumi led the LDP to victory in the election, but the LDP coalition lost 12 seats. The DPJ made a strong showing, gaining 40 seats. Analysts said the success of the DPJ could lead to a two-party system in Japan.

Bank reform. In September, Koizumi reappointed Heizo Takenaka as Japan's economy minister. Takenaka had angered many conservative members of the LDP in 2002 when he unveiled a plan to revive the nation's ailing financial system by calling on banks, which were staggering under the weight of bad loans estimated at $423 billion, to purge half of their bad loans by 2005. Bankers and their political allies opposed the plan because it would push several major banks and hundreds of debtor companies into insolvency.

Criticism of Takenaka's policies eased in 2003 after economists noted that bank reforms were starting to pay off. Banks began to cut costs and wrote off nonperforming loans. Takenaka reassured economists that he would not allow major banks to fail when he engineered a $17-million bailout of Japan's fifth-largest bank in May.

Other economic reforms did little to improve Japan's economy in 2003. Japan continued to struggle with *deflation* (decline in prices) and high unemployment, and its ratio of government debt to the *gross domestic product* (GDP, the value of all goods and services produced in a given year) was at 150 percent, the highest of any major world economy. Personal savings also continued to decline. In 1975, Japanese citizens saved 23 percent of their income. By 2003, the figure had dropped to 2 percent.

Certain indicators brightened, which led some economists to suggest that the Japanese economy, the second-largest in the world, was showing signs of pulling out of a 13-year slump. The GDP expanded at a rate of nearly 4 percent, which eased concerns that the economy would slip back into *recession* (a decline of overall business activity for two consecutive quarters).

The Tokyo Electric Power Company shut down the last of its 17 nuclear reactors in April for safety checks. The other plants were taken out of service in 2002 after company officials admitted covering up structural problems and obstructing inspections in the 1990's. Japan, which in 2003 relied on nuclear reactors for approximately 30 percent of its energy, suffered power outages as a result of the shutdowns.

Crime. The National Police Agency reported in August that murders, robberies, and other serious crimes had increased by nearly 17 percent in the first half of 2003. Crime experts said the increase in crime was caused by the prolonged economic slump.

Shintaro Ishihara was reelected governor of Tokyo in April 2003. Polls showed that he was the most popular politician in Japan.

◼ Henry S. Bradsher

See also **Asia; Iraq: A Special Report; North Korea.**

Jordan. King Abdullah II of Jordan opened the World Economic Forum (WEF) in 2003, which convened in June on the shores of the Dead Sea. Over 1,200 economic, political, academic, and religious leaders from 65 countries attended the conference. The speakers discussed issues of peace and political development as well as economic and social problems. According to the president of the WEF, Klaus Schwab, the conference was a "global reconciliation summit, bringing in all the stakeholders of the global community . . . to reestablish mutual trust."

Peace summit. Abdullah actively pursued reviving the peace process between the Israelis and the Palestinians in 2003. In June, he hosted a summit in Al Aqabah attended by Israeli Prime Minister Ariel Sharon, Palestinian Prime Minister Mahmoud Abbas, and United States President George W. Bush. The summit constituted the first attempt by the Israelis and Palestinians to discuss implementation of the "road map," an internationally sponsored peace plan.

Elections. In an election in early May, *Islamists* (Muslim hardliners) in alliance with *Pan-Arabists* (supporters of a movement to politically unite all Arab people) won control of the prestigious Jordan Engineers Association (JEA), which has 55,000 active members. Despite the professional nature of the JEA, its leaders have been at loggerheads with the Jordanian government by promoting a movement that supports anti-normalization of relations with Israel.

In June, 1.3 million Jordanians—58.8 percent of the total registered voters—participated in the parliamentary elections. Tribal or independent candidates won 85 of the 110 available seats. The remaining seats were won by candidates from political parties. The Islamic Action Front (IAF), the political arm of the fundamentalist Muslim Brothers Movement, won 17 seats, making it the leading political opposition bloc in parliament.

On October 25, King Abdullah II swore in a cabinet headed by the new prime minister, Faisal al-Fayez. The number of ministers in the new cabinet was reduced from 28 to 20 and included, for the first time, 3 women. The new cabinet announced that its goal was to find remedies for Jordan's major social and economic problems, such as poverty and unemployment.

Jordan and Iraq. Jordanian authorities announced in July that two daughters of former Iraqi President Saddam Hussein, Rana and Raghad, along with their nine children, were allowed to enter Jordan and were given protection by the Jordanian government.

A bomb detonated outside the Jordanian Embassy in Baghdad in August, killing 17 persons and wounding over 50 others. Iraqis subsequently looted the embassy compound. ◼ Marius Deeb

Judaism. In 2003, Jews continued to experience the uncertainties and insecurities that have dominated Jewish life in recent years. In Israel, the troubles between Israelis and Palestinians continued for a third year; the Jewish population declined in the United States; and anti-Semitism appeared to be on the increase.

Israel. The administration of U.S. President George W. Bush sponsored a "road map for peace" for the Middle East in 2003 that specified creation of a Palestinian nation alongside Israel by 2005. President Bush met Israeli Prime Minister Ariel Sharon and the new Palestinian prime minister, Mahmoud Abbas, in Aqaba, Jordan, in June 2003 to encourage implementation of the plan. The evacuation of some Israeli settlements on the West Bank and a cease-fire declared by Palestinian militants suggested the possibility of a resolution in the Israeli-Palestinian conflict. However, hopes were subsequently dashed by a series of terrorist attacks in cafes and restaurants in Israel's major cities. In September, Mahmoud Abbas resigned, and Ahmad Quray became the Palestinian prime minister, but the violence continued. Controversy swirled around Israel's construction of a security fence to defend its citizens. Critics charged that the fence intruded into Arab lands and represented an attempt to set future borders without negotiation.

The conflict hurt Israel's economy, which continued to deteriorate through much of 2003. The finance minister, Benjamin Netanyahu, tried to institute a series of cost-cutting measures, but these policies were met with strikes and protests, including a well-publicized 120-mile (193-kilometer) walk by single mother Vicky Knafo to protest the cuts in monthly assistance to single mothers.

North America. Results of the National Jewish Population Study 2000-2001, commissioned by United Jewish Communities (UJC), were released in September 2003. The UJC is an organization that represents local Jewish federations and communities in North America. The controversial report suggested that the North American Jewish community had declined by 300,000 persons since 1990, and it projected low fertility among Jews in their childbearing years. While pointing to impressive gains in Jewish education nationwide, the survey revealed a slight rise in Jewish poverty, due primarily to the aging of the population.

Anti-Semitism. Heightened anti-Semitism made many Jews feel less secure in 2003. A report published in April by Tel Aviv University noted that the number of violent anti-Semitic incidents worldwide increased from 228 in 2001 to 311 in 2002. In Europe, Jewish institutions were threatened and some were burned to the ground. In May 2003, car bombs exploded in Casablanca, Morocco, outside a Jewish cultural center. In June, the Organization for Security and Cooperation in Europe (OSCE) held a conference in Vienna considering ways to combat anti-Semitism. The OSCE is a regional security organization of 55 participating countries active in conflict prevention and crisis management. In October, Malaysia's outgoing Prime Minister Mahathir bin Mohamad, in a public address to world leaders, alleged that Jews controlled international finance and exercised undue influence on world affairs. Arab television stations broadcast several programs in October and November on Zionism and Jewish life that critics considered anti-Semitic. In November, just outside Paris, a Jewish school was set on fire. Also in November, car bombs exploded simultaneously outside two synagogues in Istanbul, Turkey, killing at least 25 people and wounding more than 250 others.

During a November visit to Italy, Prime Minister Sharon said the world was experiencing a "great wave of anti-Semitism" and encouraged Jews who wanted to escape persecution to come to Israel. A spokesperson for the Anti-Defamation League of B'nai B'rith compared world anti-Semitism to the situation Jews faced in the 1930's with the rise of Adolf Hitler.

■ Jonathan D. Sarna and Jonathan J. Golden

See also **Israel; Middle East; Terrorism.**

Kampuchea. See Cambodia.

Kansas. See **State government.**

Kazakhstan. Prime Minister Imangali Tasmagambetov resigned on June 11, 2003, claiming a vote of confidence in the Kazakh parliament had been falsified. The vote on May 18 ended a stalemate over land reform, paving the way for the introduction of private land ownership in Kazakhstan. Despite winning the vote, Tasmagambetov declared his willingness to resign rather than cover up the voting irregularities. President Nursultan Nazarbayev chose Daniel Akmetov as the new prime minister.

The government turnover was expected to have little impact on Kazakh politics, which were dominated in 2003 by President Nazarbayev. That domination became more absolute in April, when the Kazakh Justice Ministry denied registration to 12 of the 19 political parties active in Kazakhstan. Of the seven parties permitted to reregister, all except the Communists supported Nazarbayev's government.

In February, the European Parliament condemned the convictions in 2002 of Kazakhstan opposition politicians Mukhtar Abliyazov and Ghalymzhan Zhaqiyanov. On May 13, 2003, Nazarbayev pardoned Abliyazov, but Zhaqiyanov refused to request clemency and remained in prison.

■ Steven L. Solnick

See also **Asia.**

Kentucky. See **State government.**

Kenyan government officials stack rifles and handguns for burning near Nairobi, the capital, in May 2003. The government of President Mwai Kibaki ordered the confiscation and destruction of the weapons in an effort to stop the proliferation of small arms.

Kenya. President Mwai Kibaki began addressing the problem of Kenya's deeply rooted corruption from the first days of his new administration in January 2003. He quickly appointed John Githongo, former head of Kenya's branch of Transparency International (TI), to oversee the anticorruption campaign. TI is an organization based in Berlin, Germany, that surveys corruption in countries around the world. In 2002, TI ranked Kenya the world's sixth most corrupt nation.

Kibaki's party, the National Alliance of Kenya, swept to power in partnership with the National Rainbow Coalition in a December 2002 presidential election. Kibaki had campaigned on a promise to purge Kenya of the corruption and human rights abuses that he said characterized the 24-year rule of his predecessor, Daniel arap Moi.

Kibaki proposed a series of anticorruption laws and started a clean-up of government agencies, initially targeting procurement officers, officials who buy goods and services for the government. The officials were alleged to have pocketed funds while failing to deliver goods and services.

Economy. In a May 29, 2003, report, Planning and National Development Minister Peter Anyang Nyong'o said Kenya had lost nearly $1 billion yearly to corruption during the Moi era. The report underlined the weakness of the economy, noting a growth rate of only 1.1 percent in 2002 and an unemployment rate of nearly 50 percent.

Economists said that restoring the flow of international aid was crucial to Kenya's economic revival. In the last years of Moi's administration, many international donors, citing widespread corruption, suspended aid to Kenya. In 2000, the International Monetary Fund (IMF), a United Nations affiliate, cut off all loans to Kenya. In late November 2003, more than $250 million in new IMF loans were approved, but other donor agencies refused to immediately release an additional $225 million tied to the renewal of IMF aid.

Terrorism. Kenya went on high security alert on May 15, when authorities warned that a suspected member of the al-Qa'ida terrorist network was planning new attacks in Kenya. The alert led to temporary closures of embassies in Nairobi, the capital, and suspension of international flights.

Terrorism experts hold al-Qa'ida responsible for the August 1998 bombings of U.S. embassies in Kenya and Tanzania, which killed at least 220 people, and the November 2002 attacks in Mombasa, Kenya. In those attacks, operatives tried to shoot down an Israeli airliner, and suicide bombers smashed into a coastal hotel, killing 13 people and themselves. On June 24, 2003, prosecutors in a Nairobi court charged four Kenyans with 13 counts of murder in connection with the Mombasa hotel bombing. ■ Simon Baynham

See also **Africa; Terrorism.**

North Koreans gather in Pyongyang in January to support the decision of Kim Chong-Il, North Korea's leader, to withdraw from the international nuclear nonproliferation treaty. The action preceded the announcement that North Korea had developed nuclear weapons.

Korea, North. Officials in North Korea announced in 2003 that the country had developed nuclear weapons and had stockpiled enough material to build several more bombs. Foreign governments struggled to convince North Korea to give up its nuclear ambitions.

North Korean officials had admitted in 2002 that the country had been conducting a secret nuclear weapons program. The program was a violation of a pact North Korea had signed in 1994 to freeze its nuclear weapons development. In April 2003, North Korea became the first country to withdraw from the 187-nation nuclear nonproliferation treaty. In June, United States intelligence reports claimed that North Korea had developed the technology to mount nuclear warheads on its arsenal of missiles.

North Korea's nuclear program alarmed neighboring countries and the United States. International observers feared that North Korea might sell nuclear materials to rogue countries and international terrorists.

China—North Korea's closest ally and leading aid donor—exerted pressure on North Korea to hold talks with diplomats from China, the United States, South Korea, Russia, and Japan. Representatives from those countries met in Beijing, China's capital, in August.

At the meeting, North Korean officials con-

tended that the country needed nuclear weapons to protect it from the United States. North Korea demanded a nonaggression treaty with the United States and economic aid for its bankrupt economy. Korean officials also warned that North Korea planned to test an atomic bomb to prove to the world that it had nuclear weapons. United States negotiators said they would not consider North Korea's demands until the country admitted nuclear inspectors and dismantled its nuclear program.

In September, however, the United States softened its position. U.S. President George W. Bush said that the United States was prepared to ease economic sanctions on North Korea and would work toward a peace treaty if North Korea agreed to begin destroying its nuclear arsenal.

Poverty. Aid agencies reported widespread malnutrition in North Korea in 2003. In addition, Chinese officials said that North Koreans were slipping over the border in increasing numbers to escape poverty, famine, and political repression.

The Supreme People's Assembly unanimously reelected Kim Chong-Il to his primary job, chairman of the National Defense Commission. Kim became leader of North Korea after his father, Kim Il Sung, died in 1994.

■ Henry S. Bradsher
See also **Asia; Japan; South Korea.**

Korea, South. President Roh Moo-hyun of South Korea was inaugurated in February 2003. He enjoyed the support of more than 75 percent of the public early in the year. However, his approval rating plunged to less than 25 percent later in 2003, as the public grew weary of the scandals and political missteps that plagued his administration. In May, he accused political and business factions of paralyzing his administration and said, "I feel incompetent as president and a sense of crisis that I will not be able to perform my presidential duties."

Roh, a member of the ruling Millennium Democratic Party (MDP), was narrowly elected in December 2002. In October 2003, he resigned from MDP after facing mounting public and political criticism about his ability to lead the government.

The public blamed Roh for South Korea's economic problems. After strong growth in 2002, the economy slipped into a recession in 2003—South Korea's first since 1998. Roh, a former labor mediator, also was criticized for his government's handling of a series of strikes in mid-2003.

North Korea. Roh pledged to continue South Korea's "sunshine policy" of reconciliation with North Korea, even after North Korean officials announced that their country had developed nuclear weapons. Some South Korean officials said aid should be withheld until North Korea gave up its nuclear program. However, Roh approved shipments of food, fertilizer, and other aid to North Korea.

In May, Roh met with United States President George W. Bush to coordinate an international policy on North Korea. Roh, who once called for the withdrawal of U.S. troops from South Korea, told Bush that he now supported a U.S. presence in South Korea.

Scandal. In June, a South Korean special prosecutor said that the government and a South Korean company gave $500 million to the North Korean government shortly before a historic summit meeting in 2000 between the leaders of North and South Korea. The prosecutor charged in 2003 that the government of former South Korean President Kim Dae-jung paid North Korea $100 million to convince officials to attend the summit. The prosecutor charged that Hyundai Asan, one of South Korea's most powerful companies, contributed an additional $400 million as a bribe to establish businesses in North Korea. Chung Mong Hun, the head of Hyundai, committed suicide in August while awaiting trial. Seven other people were convicted in September.

Typhoon. More than 115 people died in a typhoon that struck southeast South Korea in September. ■ Henry S. Bradsher

See also **Asia; North Korea.**

Kyrgyzstan. On Feb. 2, 2003, Kyrgyz voters approved a constitutional referendum that replaced the country's two-chamber parliament with a single-chamber body. They also overwhelmingly voted yes to a ballot question asking whether President Askar Akayev should stay in office until the end of his term in December 2005. The referendum represented an important victory for Akayev, who had been embattled since the March 2002 shootings of five peaceful protesters by police in the city of Aksy. Officials in the United States and from the Organization for Security and Cooperation in Europe complained that the referendum was too hastily organized. Opposition politicians were more critical, claiming that the vote results were invalid and even illegal and that the turnout had fallen below the legal requirement of 50 percent. Kyrgyz officials said that 86 percent of registered voters cast their ballots.

In October 2003, Russian President Vladimir Putin visited Kyrgyzstan to open a Russian air force base in the city of Kant. The new base represented a resurgence of Russian military interest in Kyrgyzstan, which had opened its own military bases to U.S. troops in 2002. The U.S. forces in Kyrgyzstan conducted antiterrorist operations in nearby Afghanistan.

■ Steven L. Solnick

See also **Asia; Russia.**

Labor and employment. Job growth

in the United States finally improved in August, September, and October 2003 for the first time since the nation's brief recession ended in the fourth quarter of 2001. Nevertheless, labor market analysts agreed that job growth would have to be much stronger to reduce unemployment rates. During 2003, the jobless rate stuck at about 6 percent.

Adult men have for decades had the lowest unemployment rates in the United States. However, the 2001 recession reversed this trend, giving adult women the lowest rates. In 2003, the jobless rate for adult women (20 years old and over) averaged 5.2 percent, compared with 5.6 percent for adult men. The reversal developed because the jobless rates for white women fell below those of white men. (The jobless rates of black women had been lower than those for black men for some time. Rates by gender are not published for Hispanic and Asian workers.)

Unemployment rates for other major groups were 5.1 percent for white workers; 11.5 percent for black workers; 7.2 percent for Hispanics or Latinos; and 6.1 percent for Asians. Teen-agers of all groups had the highest rate—over 17 percent.

Bargaining climate. Although the output of goods and services in the United States had been growing since late 2001, jobs continued to be lost each month—a cumulative total of 2.7 million—before the number of jobs started to grow in late 2003. Analysts estimated that at least 200,000 additional jobs were needed each month to absorb the monthly increase in the number of job seekers. By the end of 2003, job growth had not reached that level.

Partly because jobs were scarce, workers found it difficult to negotiate for improvements in wages, pensions, and health benefits, both in the general economy and in collective bargaining situations. However, consumer price increases remained low in 2003 (2.2 percent on an annual basis), so there was no strong impetus for workers or unions to recoup inflationary losses. In addition, *total compensation* (wages and benefits) of all workers was 3.9 percent higher in the third quarter of 2003 than it had been a year earlier, according to the U.S. Bureau of Labor Statistics.

Airlines. In 2003, bargaining between airlines based in the United States and labor organizations centered mostly on cuts in wages and benefits and on restructuring to save the companies from bankruptcy or to emerge from bankruptcy. The airline industry had been severely buffeted by the 2001 recession and by the terrorist attacks on the United States in 2001.

In mid-January 2003, U.S. Airways, as part of its bankruptcy reorganization, reached agreement with the Association of Flight Attendants, the Communications Workers of America, the International Association of Machinists, the Transport Workers Union, and the Airline Pilots Association on a final round of labor cost savings. In all, the airline achieved about $1 billion in annual savings through wage and job cuts and the replacement of the pilots' pension plan.

Also in January, members of the International Association of Machinists ratified an agreement with Dallas-based Southwest Airlines that provided an increase in hourly wages from $19.50 to $24.35. The contract acknowledged that the success of the airline made the increases possible.

In April, American Airlines of Dallas threatened to file for bankruptcy unless labor agreed to collective reductions that would save about $1.6 billion annually. The unions, which included the Allied Pilots Association, the Association for Professional Flight Attendants, and the Transport Workers Union, agreed to the reductions.

Illinois-based United Airlines, which had filed for bankruptcy in 2002, agreed in April 2003 with the International Association of Machinists, the Association of Flight Attendants, and the unions of its pilots, flight controllers, and meteorologists on concessions that were estimated to save the airline $2.7 billion annually.

Trucking industry. At the end of March, members of the International Brotherhood of Teamsters overwhelmingly approved a contract with the major trucking companies. The five-year agreement, which covered 65,000 workers, raised hourly wages by a total of $2.35. The pact also included a provision for additional wage increases if the Consumer Price Index rose more than 3 percent in any year. Employers agreed to fund employee health benefits without employee contribution—in contrast with other industries, where employers sought new or increased co-payments from employees.

Longshore. A difficult bargaining session that began in 2002 between the Pacific Maritime Association and the International Longshore and Warehouse Union finally ended in late January 2003 when union members approved a six-year contract. Under the agreement, pensions were to rise by 60 percent and average salaries were to reach $90,000. The bargaining included a lockout in which 29 ports were closed for 10 days in 2002.

Steel industry. Battered by steel imports that had prompted U.S. President George W. Bush to impose tariffs on imported steel in 2002, American steel producers and the United Steelworkers union cooperated in restructuring and other moves to make the companies more competitive internationally. In February 2003, Bethlehem Steel of Bethlehem, Pennsylvania, agreed to sell its assets to the International Steel Group of Cleveland, Ohio. As part of the sale, Bethlehem agreed to continue health benefits for retirees for six months after a March 31 termination date set by a bankruptcy court. The company and union also sought to qualify Bethlehem for a 65-percent subsidy of health benefit costs under provisions of the federal Trade Adjustment Assistance program. In June, union members overwhelmingly approved a 64-month contract covering 8,500 workers from six former Bethlehem Steel plants. The contract included hourly wages of $15 to $20.50 per hour and profit sharing but also called for some jobs to be lost in the restructuring.

In mid-May, U.S. Steel Group of Pittsburgh, Pennsylvania, and the United Steelworkers agreed on a five-year pact covering some 20,000 workers at U.S. Steel and at the National Steel Group, which had been purchased by U.S. Steel in April. The pact featured the same increases as the International Steel Group contract. In addition, under the agreement, U.S. Steel was required to terminate contract workers before members of the union could be terminated.

Communications. In mid-June, both the Communications Workers of America and the International Brotherhood of Electrical Workers extended their contracts with AT&T Corp. of New York City for two years. Collectively, the contracts covered 22,000 workers and provided a 5.75-percent increase in wages over the contract's life, a 5-

percent boost in defined pensions, and other improvements.

In early August, members of the Communications Workers ratified a two-year agreement with Qwest Communications International, Inc., of Denver, Colorado. The contract, covering 27,000 workers, froze wages but provided for bonuses if the company met its earnings targets. The union members also approved a three-year contract with Avaya, Inc., of Basking Ridge, New Jersey, covering 5,000 members. The contract provided 3-percent increases in each year of the contract. The International Brotherhood of Electrical Workers approved contracts covering about 1,500 workers with the same two companies, with similar terms.

In October, Verizon Communications of New York City concluded agreements with the International Brotherhood of Electrical Workers and the Communications Workers of America, covering 80,000 workers. The contract provided that all employees on the East Coast would receive lump-sum payments equal to 3 percent of wages. It also stipulated annual 2-percent increases in wages over the term of the five-year contract. The company agreed to continue to pay the full premium costs for employees' health care.

Motor vehicle manufacturing. Bargaining in the U.S. motor vehicle manufacturing industry was shadowed by a competitive international industry. Industry analysts suggested that the sagging U.S. economy, price pressures that resulted in widespread rebates to consumers, and declining market shares for domestic producers dictated the moderate settlements. The 2003 contracts between the United Automobile Workers union (UAW) and the "Big Three" U.S. manufacturers— General Motors Corporation of Detroit; Ford Motor Company of Dearborn, Michigan; and the Chrysler Group of Germany's Daimler-Benz—were marked by quick settlements, as unions sought to make the U.S. auto industry more competitive.

The first agreement was reached between DaimlerChrysler and the UAW in late September and became the basis for agreements at Ford and at General Motors. All of the agreements, which covered a four-year term, included modest pay increases and full employer-paid health care provisions. The UAW agreed to cuts of as many as 50,000 jobs by 2007 and to the closing of plants for the first time in almost 20 years.

Rubber. In September 2003, United Steelworkers members ratified a contract with Goodyear Tire and Rubber Co. of Akron, Ohio. The agreement froze wages but added a profit sharing arrangement. It also provided some job security guarantees for 16,000 workers. Goodyear promised that 12 of 14 plants would not be shut down and that employment would be maintained at 85 percent of Aug. 1, 2002, levels.

CHANGES IN THE UNITED STATES LABOR FORCE

	2002	2003*
Civilian labor force	144,875,000	146,351,000
Total employment	136,485,000	137,589,000
Unemployment	8,378,000	8,805,000
Unemployment rate	5.8%	6.0%
Change in real weekly earnings of production and nonsupervisory workers (nonfarm business sector)†	+1.3%	+0.2%
Change in output per employee hour (nonfarm business sector)	+5.4%	+5.0%

*All 2003 data are through the third quarter of 2003 (preliminary data).
†Real weekly earnings are adjusted for inflation by using constant 1982 dollars.
Source: U.S. Bureau of Labor Statistics.

Unions. The proportion of U.S. workers in labor unions declined from 13.4 percent to 13.2 percent in 2002, according to a February 2003 U.S. Bureau of Labor Statistics report. There were 13,181,283 members of unions affiliated with the AFL-CIO in 2002, a decrease of 72,788 workers. This slight decline continued to reflect the loss of manufacturing jobs, where unions were strongest, and the growth of white-collar and service employment, where unions were weakest.

In March, the International Brotherhood of Teamsters ended its three-year representation battle with the Overnite Transportation Company of Richmond, Virginia. Former members at 21 of 26 locations then voted to decertify the union.

The Screen Actors Guild again declined to affiliate with the larger American Federation of Television and Radio Artists. However, the two unions cooperated in signing a contract with the entertainment industry in October.

International unemployment. Unemployment rates in 27 nations of the Organization for Economic Cooperation and Development (OECD) rose slightly between the end of 2002 and October 2003. The average rate of unemployment in the 27 countries increased to 7.1 percent in October 2003 from 7 percent in 2002. In the 15 nations of the European Union, rates rose to 8 percent from 7.7 percent in 2002. In the seven major OECD countries (Canada, France, Germany, Italy, Japan, United Kingdom, and the United States), the rate rose to 6.6 percent from 6.5 percent in 2002. Continuing past trends, Japan (at 5.2 percent) and the United States (at 6 percent) had the lowest jobless rates among the major OECD countries. ■ Robert W. Fisher

See also **Automobile.**

LATIN AMERICA

The new leaders of South America's two most populous countries, Brazil and Argentina, quickly proved themselves skillful players on the world stage in 2003. Brazilian President Luiz Inacio Lula da Silva, drawing on the experience he developed during his lengthy career as a labor leader, worked passionately to forge solidarity among the continent's nations to work for a fairer system of international trade. Among his goals was a reduction in the subsidies that wealthy nations were providing their farmers to grow crops, such as cotton, sugar, and citrus fruits. These subsidies placed Latin America at a competitive disadvantage in competing for world markets, according to many economists.

In Argentina, President Nestor Kirchner completed an accord with the International Monetary Fund (IMF), an affiliate of the United Nations that provides credit to member nations. In a move that was applauded throughout Latin America, the IMF did not impose a rigid timetable on Argentina for repaying its debts as it emerged from the worst recession in its history. Instead, the IMF allowed the nation to maintain essential social welfare spending and invest in job creation, while making repayments on its debts as the national economy improved.

The accord placed the needs of the Argentine people before the demands of banks holding Argentina's debt, according to economists. This change was welcome, they noted, as in many previous IMF agreements poor people shouldered the burden of absorbing the impact of IMF-mandated measures such as higher prices for such necessities as food and fuel.

Solidarity. At their first official meeting in Brazil's capital, Brasilia, in June, da Silva and Kirchner pledged to revitalize the South American common market (Mercosur). Later in June, the two presidents met in Paraguay's capital, Asun-

cion, with the leaders of other Mercosur member-nations—Bolivia, Chile, Paraguay, and Uruguay—as well as with the president of Venezuela. The leaders agreed on a strategy for achieving, as early as 2004, a continental common market with a combined population of 370 million people and an annual *gross domestic product* (GDP, the value of all goods and services produced in a country in a given year) of $1.2 trillion.

Da Silva worked to strengthen Mercosur, traveling abroad more in his first months in office than his predecessor had during his entire four-year term. In August 2003, da Silva visited Lima, Peru, where Peruvian President Alejandro Toledo signed documents making Peru an associate Mercosur member. Da Silva then went to Caracas where he announced that Brazil's national bank

ers. More than half the members of the group also felt that hemisphere free trade would benefit the United States more than their region.

This view was heartily endorsed throughout Latin America, particularly in nations that still depended on agricultural commodities for a large part of their export earnings. Moreover, as economists pointed out, the subsidies not only reduced the access of Latin America's agricultural products to wealthy nations, but had also resulted in the flooding of the region's own markets with crops produced at an unfair advantage.

Economists cited the North American Free Trade Agreement (NAFTA) as an example of what can happen when agricultural products from a poor country vie in the same market with products from a country that subsidizes its farmers. NAFTA is a free trade pact between the United States, Canada, and Mexico that went into effect in 1994. According to Oxfam International, an Oxford, England-based relief organization, NAFTA resulted in some 15 million subsistence farmers in Mexico los-

Thousands of demonstrators march on Bolivia's capital, La Paz, in October, protesting the government's controversial plan to export natural gas to the United States. Two weeks of demonstrations in the capital left more than 80 people dead and brought down the government of President Gonzalo Sanchez de Lozada.

would grant Venezuela a $1-billion line of credit toward the purchase of Brazilian-made goods. President Hugo Chavez Frias then announced that Venezuela was joining Mercosur.

Agricultural subsidies. During 2003, da Silva repeatedly demanded that governments in the world's wealthy nations phase out the nearly $300 billion in annual subsidies that they were paying their farmers, which many economists said constituted an unfair advantage. Latin Americans rallied to da Silva's support on this issue, according to an October poll by Zogby International, a U.S.-based market research firm, and the University of Miami Business School in Miami, Florida. The poll, a survey of the region's opinion makers, government officials, and prominent business people, found that da Silva enjoyed the highest approval rating—69 percent—among Latin America's lead-

ing their livelihoods when cheap U.S. corn flooded their markets, driving down the price of local corn by 70 percent.

According to political experts, the perceived inequities in world commerce fueled protest and violence across Latin America in 2003, a year in which the regional GDP decreased. In Colombia, farmers, unable to make a living raising other crops, continued to grow coca and poppies, sources of drugs, for illegal markets in wealthy nations. The farmers were protected by rebel groups financed by drug-trafficking. Despite U.S. claims that an aerial spraying campaign in Colombia cut coca production in half in 2003, the rebel armies continued to profit enough from drug-trafficking to see little need in negotiating a settlement with the Colombian government to end that country's long civil war.

FACTS IN BRIEF ON LATIN AMERICA

Country	Population	Government	Monetary unit*	Foreign trade (million U.S.$) Exports†	Imports†
Antigua and Barbuda	78,000	Governor General James B. Carlisle; Prime Minister Lester Bird	dollar (2.67 = $1)	40	357
Argentina	37,533,000	President Nestor Kirchner	peso (2.88 = $1)	26,655	20,312
Bahamas	320,000	Governor General Ivy Dumont; Prime Minister Perry Christie	dollar (1.00 = $1)	561	1,860
Barbados	271,000	Governor General Sir Clifford Husbands; Prime Minister Owen Arthur	dollar (1.99 = $1)	227	987
Belize	259,000	Governor General Sir Colville Young; Prime Minister Said Wilbert Musa	dollar (1.97 = $1)	290	430
Bolivia	9,069,000	Interim President Carlos Mesa	boliviano (7.76 = $1)	1,300	1,600
Brazil	177,971,000	President Luiz Inacio Lula da Silva	real (2.89 = $1)	59,400	46,200
Chile	15,942,000	President Ricardo Lagos Escobar	peso (660.07= $1)	17,800	15,600
Colombia	44,847,000	President Alvaro Uribe Velez	peso (2,880.00 = $1)	12,900	12,500
Costa Rica	4,129,000	President Abel Pacheco de la Espriella	colon (409.23 = $1)	5,100	6,400
Cuba	11,334,000	President Fidel Castro	peso (1.00 = $1)	1,800	4,800
Dominica	72,000	President Vernon Shaw; Prime Minister Pierre Charles	dollar (2.67 = $1)	50	135
Dominican Republic	8,887,000	President Rafael Hipolito Mejia Dominguez	peso (31.40 = $1)	5,300	8,700
Ecuador	13,549,000	President Lucio Edwin Gutierrez	U.S. dollar	4,900	6,000
El Salvador	6,748,000	President Francisco Flores Perez	colon (8.75 = $1)	3,000	4,900
Grenada	102,000	Governor General Daniel Williams; Prime Minister Keith Mitchell	dollar (2.67 = $1)	78	270
Guatemala	12,606,000	President Oscar Berger	quetzal (8.11 = $1)	2,700	5,600
Guyana	767,000	President Bharrat Jagdeo	dollar (179.00 = $1)	500	575
Haiti	7,636,000	President Jean-Bertrand Aristide; Prime Minister Yvon Neptune	gourde (38.25 = $1)	298	1,140
Honduras	7,028,000	President Ricardo Maduro	lempira (17.56 = $1)	1,300	2,700
Jamaica	2,669,000	Governor General Sir Howard Cooke; Prime Minister P. J. Patterson	dollar (59.00= $1)	1,400	3,100
Mexico	103,011,000	President Vicente Fox Quesada	new peso (11.25 = $1)	158,400	168,400
Nicaragua	5,617,000	President Enrique Bolanos Geyer	gold cordoba (15.24 = $1)	637	1,700
Panama	3,005,000	President Mireya Elisa Moscoso	balboa (1.00 = $1)	5,800	6,700
Paraguay	6,057,000	President Nicanor Duarte Frutos	guarani (6,250.00 = $1)	2,000	2,400
Peru	27,344,000	President Alejandro Toledo; Prime Minister Carlos Ferrero	new sol (3.48 = $1)	7,600	7,300
Puerto Rico	3,944,000	Governor Sila Maria Calderon	U.S. dollar	46,900	29,100
St. Kitts and Nevis	37,000	Governor General Cuthbert Montraville Sebastian; Prime Minister Denzil Douglas	dollar (2.67 = $1)	47	152
St. Lucia	163,000	Governor General Perlette Louisy; Prime Minister Kenny Anthony	dollar (2.67 = $1)	68	319
St. Vincent and the Grenadines	116,000	Governor General Sir Frederick Nathaniel Ballantyne; Prime Minister Ralph Gonsalves	dollar (2.67 = $1)	54	186
Suriname	424,000	President Runaldo Ronald Venetiaan	guilder (2,515.00 = $1)	445	300
Trinidad and Tobago	1,317,000	President George Maxwell Richards; Prime Minister Patrick Manning	dollar (6.15 = $1)	4,200	3,800
Uruguay	3,431,000	President Jorge Batlle	peso (28.01 = $1)	2,100	1,870
Venezuela	23,950,000	President Hugo Chavez Frias	bolivar (1,597.00 = $1)	28,600	18,800

*Exchange rates as of Oct. 3, 2003, or latest available data.   †Latest available data.

Coffee slump. The continued stagnation of international prices for coffee reduced Colombia's coffee revenues by 50 percent in the decade ending in 2003. In Brazil, an estimated 90 percent of the 3 million people who had earned a living in the coffee industry were out of work in 2003. Brazilian growers, unable to afford machinery to mechanize their coffee production, were on the brink of bankruptcy.

The World Bank, headquartered in Washington, D.C., estimated that 600,000 Central Americans lost their jobs in the coffee industry over the past few years. Among the unemployed were peasants living in the region of Matagalpa, Nicaragua, who planned to march in July 2003 to protest their plight. They demanded cheap credit and uncultivated lands in order to grow subsistence crops to feed their families. Peasants in northern Nicaragua organized sit-ins and other protests as a result of the economic collapse.

Stagnation in rural areas. The stagnation of the rural economy in much of Latin America led to a decrease in the area's GDP in 2003. The stalling also fueled the migration of peasants into already overcrowded city slums and was a major factor behind illegal immigration into the United States. In 2003, displaced Salvadorans in the United States sent home more than $1 billion, according to the central bank of El Salvador. This money offset 80 percent of that country's *trade deficit* (an unfavorable balance of trade).

Failure at Cancun. Brazil led the developing nations in walking out when the world's wealthy nations refused to discuss reductions in their agricultural subsidies at a September meeting of the World Trade Organization (WTO), an international body that promotes free trade, in Cancun, Mexico. In October, da Silva joined Kirchner of Argentina in issuing a statement called the Buenos Aires Consensus, which called for the creation of jobs in addition to profit, and fair, not just free, global trade.

In November, 34 trade ministers met in Miami to discuss steps toward achieving a "Latin American Free Trade Area." However, owing to the continued differences over the issue of agricultural subsidies, the meeting produced few results, and the United States decided to negotiate individually with Latin American nations in working out future free trade agreements.

Bolivian president resigns. Bowler-hatted Indian women dressed in traditional, many-layered skirts stood with Bolivia's trade unionists at the forefront of antiglobalization protests in Bolivia in 2003. They demanded that the government of President Gonzalo Sanchez de Lozada stop a plan to allow an international consortium to build a 400-mile (640-kilometer) pipeline to tap natural gas reserves from Bolivia's eastern low-

lands. The protesters claimed that exporting natural resources enriched a small minority at the expense of Bolivia's largely impoverished native people. "Globalization is just another name for submission and domination," said Nicanor Apaza, an unemployed miner, who joined the protest. "We've had to live with that here for 500 years, and now we want to be our own masters." The protests grew into weeks of demonstrations that left some 80 people dead and paralyzed the government and the economy.

Finally, on October 17, President de Lozada stepped down, and Vice President Carlos Mesa was sworn in as Bolivia's interim president. Mesa promised to oversee a national referendum on the natural gas deal that had sparked the protests. Sanchez de Lozada was the fourth South American president forced out of office by massive popular protests between 2000 and 2003.

Pervasive government corruption. Experts in 2003 pointed out that rampant government corruption continued to drain scarce resources from Latin American nations, particularly the Dominican Republic, Guatemala, Nicaragua, Panama, and Paraguay. In Mexico, Francisco Barrio, the anticorruption czar, estimated in April that *graft* (the payment of unlawful bribes in connection with government business) was so widespread that it accounted for 9.5 percent of Mexico's total GDP—twice what the government spent on education in 2003.

The U.S. government established a new Miami-based multiagency task force in 2003 to help Latin American countries fight corruption. The task force could seize illegal assets, including laundered drug money in U.S. banks, under a provision of the USA PATRIOT Act, an antiterrorism bill passed shortly after the terrorist attacks on the United States on Sept. 11, 2001. Federal agents targeted Arnoldo Aleman Lacayo, the former president of Nicaragua, with nine different investigations, seizing $5 million in cash and real estate that Aleman held in Florida. Officials estimated that Aleman stole some $100 million while president of Nicaragua.

Crackdown on smuggling. Nicanor Duarte Frutos of the Colorado Party was sworn in as president of Paraguay in August 2003. His election followed six years of steady economic decline in which the average Paraguayan's annual income fell from $1,700 to $900. During the same period, unemployment climbed to an estimated 35 percent. A former journalist and education minister, Duarte pledged to crack down on corruption and smuggling, which was so rampant in 2003 that it accounted for one-fifth of Paraguay's GDP.

Street gangs. Honduras' Congress passed a tough law in August that imposed jail terms of up to 12 years for members of street gangs. The law was welcomed by residents of Tegucigalpa, the capital, where, despite repeated crackdowns on crime, people lived in fear of particularly violent gangs among the more than 400 groups that operated in the country. In El Salvador, police estimated that about 30,000 youngsters belonged to gangs and that, on average, three gang members were killed daily in 2003. In Guatemala, where authorities put the number of gang members at about 500,000, there were 2,582 arrests of youngsters in the first eight months of 2003 on charges ranging from drug dealing to murder.

Military aid. The administration of U.S. President George W. Bush, emphasizing the global war on terrorism, provided more military assistance to Latin America in 2003 than economic aid. Beginning in October, the United States increased military assistance to several countries in Latin America—including Mexico, Ecuador, and Panama—as part of the U.S. wars on terrorism and drug-trafficking. The shift was most marked in Colombia. In 2003, Colombia received $605 million in U.S. military assistance, compared with $137 million in economic aid.

■ Nathan A. Haverstock
See also the various Latin American countries.

Latvia. See Europe.

Law. See Courts; Supreme Court of the United States; United States, Government of the.

Lebanon. In August 2003, Muhammad Mughraby was arrested in Beirut, Lebanon's capital. Political experts suggested that he was arrested because he planned to run for the presidency of the Beirut Bar Association, a body that Mughraby had criticized for years. Because Syria controlled Lebanon through a puppet government, Mughraby, who defended victims of the Syrian occupation of Lebanon, was arrested by the Lebanese authorities under Syrian pressure. Mughraby wrote a report entitled "An Alliance Beyond Law" for Human Rights Watch, a New York City-based nongovernmental organization that investigates human rights violations. In the report, he recorded the disappearance and incarceration of Lebanese citizens in Syria. Mughraby, with activist Kamal Batal, founded the Multi-Initiative on Rights: Search, Assist and Defend, a human rights watchdog group.

Hezbollah. The continued presence of the Hezbollah, a militant Islamic group, in southern Lebanon remained a major problem in 2003. The Syrian pretext for allowing Hezbollah to operate across the Lebanese-Israeli line was the claim that Israel still occupied the border area called Shebaa Farms. The United Nations, however, asserted that Israel had completely withdrawn from Lebanon on May 24, 2000, and that Shebaa Farms was part of Syrian Golan Heights, not Lebanon.

Since 2000, Hezbollah has initiated some 125 cross-border incidents. Experts have suggested that the group has links with the militant Palestinian organizations Hamas and Islamic Jihad. In August 2003, a leading Hezbollah security official who dealt with these organizations was killed in a car bombing in Beirut. Believing Israel to have masterminded the attack, Hezbollah retaliated by shelling Israeli settlements, killing one person and wounding four others on Israel's border. Some local leaders in southern Lebanon called for the deployment of the Lebanese Army along the border. The leaders contended that the southern Lebanese had suffered enough at the hands of Syrian-controlled militias.

New law. Lebanese opposition to Syrian occupation won a major victory when the United States Congress passed the Syria Accountability and Lebanese Sovereignty Restoration Act of 2003. The act called for Syria to withdraw its troops from Lebanon and stop supporting terrorist groups or suffer sanctions. The exiled Lebanese leader General Michel Awn had urged the passage of the act because the Syrian occupation had deprived the Lebanese people of freedom and democracy, devastated the economy, and turned Lebanon into a hotbed for Syrian-sponsored terrorist organizations.   ■ Marius Deeb
See also **Middle East; Terrorism.**

Library. Libraries in the United States grappled with three major issues in 2003: a sluggish economy; the effects of the U.S. Supreme Court's ruling on the Children's Internet Protection Act (CIPA); and a U.S. Department of Justice that many librarians believed was increasingly hostile to long-held standards of patron privacy in its application of the USA PATRIOT Act. The act was signed into law in response to the terrorist attacks on the United States in 2001.

Economic woes. A sluggish U.S. economy continued to take a toll on the nation's libraries in 2003. Budget shortfalls in most of the 50 state governments as well as in many municipal governments endangered library funding through much of the country. Library boards and directors resorted to cutting hours, closing branches, and laying off staff in order to keep libraries open.

California's massive budget crisis caused the state to slash $30 million from library support funds in 2003, threatening many smaller libraries with extinction. The Minneapolis Public Library cut 80 staff positions, leading to a reduction in open hours systemwide. The Anchorage, Alaska, public library system cut its staff by 20 percent.

Some library systems fared better in 2003. In New York state, the legislature overrode a veto by Governor George Pataki to restore $13.3 million in library support funds. In Jacksonville,

Seymour Lubetzky: Library Legend

Seymour Lubetzky, cataloging theorist, librarian, and teacher, died of heart failure on April 5, 2003, at the age of 104. He was a leader in the field of descriptive cataloging and introduced a system of rules for organizing bibliographic information that is used in most libraries around the world today.

Lubetzky was born Shmaryahu Lubetzky in Zelva, Poland, on April 28, 1898, and came to the United States in 1927. He attended the University of California at Los Angeles (UCLA), received his library degree in 1932, and went on to earn a master's degree in German at the University of California at Berkeley, where he also studied at the library school. He worked as a cataloger and classifier at UCLA from 1936 to 1942. During this time, Lubetzky wrote extensively about library practices, presented his ideas for improvement to library professionals, and earned a national reputation for his cataloging work.

The Library of Congress hired Lubetzky as its chief cataloger in 1943. He found the catalog disorganized, inconsistent, and cluttered with unnecessary details. He developed a code of rules to describe a book, refer to other editions of the book, and relate it to other books in the library in a way that would make it easy to understand for the majority of readers. During his 17 years at the Library of Congress, he wrote *Rules for Descriptive Cataloging* and *Cataloging Rules and Principles*.

Lubetzky's career in the field of cataloging culminated at the International Conference on Cataloging Principles in Paris in 1961, at which Lubetzky read a paper presenting the ideas he developed while creating the Library of Congress's new catalog code and writing his books. These principles became standard practice, not only in the Library of Congress, but in most libraries worldwide. They are used for card catalogs, print catalogs, and in computer catalogs as well.

Lubetzky returned to UCLA in 1960 as a professor at the School of Library Service. He wrote *Code of Cataloging Rules* in 1960 and *Principles of Cataloging* in 1969. He received the 1955 Margaret Mann Citation, the highest honor in cataloging bestowed by the American Library Association, and in 2002 he was awarded Honorary Membership in the American Library Association. "He was the greatest cataloging theorist of the 20th century," said Maurice J. Freeman, president of the American Library Association. "He represents the culmination of the development of the Anglo-American cataloging ideology that began with [scholars] in the 19th century."

■ Carol Yehling

Florida, revenue from a sales tax increase allowed the Jacksonville Public Library to fill 142 new librarian and support staff positions and fund library expansion projects.

CIPA. In June 2003, the U.S. Supreme Court upheld the Children's Internet Protection Act (CIPA), overturning a lower federal court's 2002 decision that the act unconstitutionally blocked access to protected speech on the Internet. The law, passed by Congress in late 2000, requires public libraries to use software filters on public-access computers to prevent people from viewing Web sites offering pornography or other content considered objectionable. Libraries that do not comply risk losing their e-rate funding.

Congress set up the e-rate program in 1996 to help schools and libraries pay for Internet connections for their computers. Money for the fund comes from a tax on phone companies. In 2003, the fund was expected to provide subsidies of up to $2.25 billion.

In the wake of the Supreme Court decision, federal officials set a July 2004 deadline for compliance with CIPA requirements. Officials at public libraries will choose whether to forego e-funding or incur the expense of installing filtering software. Officials of the Chicago Public Library reported in June 2003 that the library would have to invest $200,000 in such software to retain $500,000 in annual e-funding and that the money would come out of budgets for book purchases or salaries.

USA PATRIOT Act. Librarians, led by the American Library Association (ALA), have protested the library investigative provisions (Section 215) of the USA PATRIOT Act since the act became law in 2001. Prior to passage of the act, all 50 states had enacted laws protecting the privacy of library patron information. Section 215 allowed government agents to inspect library patron records in secrecy and barred librarians from revealing such requests to the public.

In a September 2003 speech supporting the USA PATRIOT Act, U.S. Attorney General John Ashcroft characterized librarians' concerns about Section 215 as "hysteria." In response, ALA President Carla Hayden, director of the Enoch Pratt Free Public Library in Baltimore, Maryland, issued a statement challenging Ashcroft to release information on the use of Section 215 by the Federal Bureau of Investigation (FBI). Ashcroft then released a report stating that FBI agents had never used the USA PATRIOT Act to request library circulation records. A subsequent survey of California librarians, however, indicated that FBI agents had made requests for information from at least 16 libraries in the state.   ■ Rob Carlson

See also **Civil rights; Internet; Supreme Court of the United States.**

Libya. Libyan leader Muammar Muhammad al-Qadhafi agreed on Dec. 19, 2003, to abandon Libya's program of *weapons of mass destruction* (biological, chemical, and nuclear weapons) and open weapons facilities to inspections by the International Atomic Energy Agency (IAEA), a Vienna, Austria-based organization, founded by the United Nations, that promotes safe and peaceful uses of nuclear energy throughout the world. Libya, which is already a signatory of the nuclear nonproliferation treaty, will sign on to the IAEA's inspections protocol, which allows inspectors to visit nuclear sites on short notice. The agreement came after nine months of secret negotiations between the governments of Libya, the United States, and the United Kingdom. Libyan Prime Minister Shukri Ghanim also announced that his government intended to participate in the international fight against terrorism.

Politics and economics. Certain sectors of the Libyan economy did not fare well in 2003, despite an expected gross domestic product (GDP) increase of 2.1 percent. The GDP is the value of all goods and services produced in a country in a given year. In June, al-Qadhafi announced that Libya's public sector had failed economically and should be abolished. He called for privatization in several areas, including the oil industry. Later in June, Prime Minister Ghanim, a U.S.-educated proponent of privatization and the former trade and economy minister, was elected prime minister.

Claiming responsibility. In August 2003, Libya accepted responsibility for the 1988 Lockerbie, Scotland, bombing of Pan Am flight 103 and agreed to pay $2.7 billion in compensation to the families of the victims. In September 2003, the United Nations Security Council members voted on Resolution 1506—which involved lifting sanctions against Libya—and approved it.

The Security Council had suspended but not permanently lifted these sanctions in April 1999 after the Libyan government turned over the two main suspects in the bombing to a Scottish court in The Hague, Netherlands. France agreed to the principle of the lifting of the sanctions but urged a delay so that it could negotiate an increase in the indemnity payments to French families of the victims of a 1989 bombing of a French airliner over Niger.

The United States, however, did not lift its own unilateral sanctions on Libya, claiming to remain deeply concerned about other actions by Libya's government, including its human rights record and its role in perpetuating regional conflicts in Africa. The U.S. sanctions include a ban on direct trade.   ■ Mary-Jane Deeb

See also **Middle East; Terrorism; United Nations.**

Literature, American. Many well-established writers in the United States published strong new literary works in 2003, providing tough competition in the major prize categories. American literature continued to defy marketing tactics, however, as shown in the closure of *Book* magazine, a bimonthly that featured stories about authors and book reviews. The magazine, co-owned by Barnes & Noble, Inc. and West Egg Communications, both of New York City, ceased publication with its November/December issue in 2003 after Barnes & Noble announced it would make no further investment in the venture.

Other attempts to market books seemed to be foundering as well, as several book columnists writing for major newspapers discussed the dwindling importance of bookstore readings. These readings given by authors had in the past been a way to capture sales and new readers. The sparse attendance at readings and the large number of these events being held by bookstores meant smaller sales. Publishers searched for new ways to market lesser known or first-time writers.

Oprah Winfrey, the television personality who helped sell millions of copies of contemporary fiction during the seven years she had a book club, reformed her club in 2003 after a nearly year-long hiatus. Her new club, however, will mostly recommend classic literary works, as evidenced by her first two choices—*East of Eden* by John Steinbeck and *Cry the Beloved Country* by Alan Paton (first published in 1952 and 1948, respectively).

Despite these marketing difficulties, several prominent writers were able to make healthy sales while offering critically acclaimed books to readers, and a number of first-time authors had tremendous success with their offerings as well.

Best sellers. As if to make his own theme a reality, Garrison Keillor, famous for his "Prairie Home Companion" radio show and several literary works also featuring the imaginary Lake Wobegon, penned *Love Me*, the story of a writer whose first novel becomes a huge bestseller. Dan Brown's blockbuster, *The DaVinci Code*, was a thriller featuring secret religious societies, a quest for the Holy Grail, and a compelling murder mystery. Larry McMurtry, best known for his westerns, offered readers the second installment in his "Berrybender Narratives," *The Wandering Hill*. (The third novel in the series, *By Sorrow's River*, was published in November.) *Fight Club* author Chuck Palahniuk published *Diary*.

Pulitzer Prizes. Jeffrey Eugenides's *Middlesex* won the Pulitzer Prize for fiction in 2003. Eugenides, author of *The Virgin Suicides*, had readers wait for nearly a decade before his second entry. However, *Middlesex*, the story of a Greek-American hermaphrodite—a person with both male and female characteristics—showed the author was able to write intimately about a single character while spanning three generations of a family as well.

Other top contenders for the Pulitzer Prize in fiction included *Servants of the Map*, a collection of stories by Andrea Barrett. Barrett has written extensively about historical figures, both famous and ordinary, living in the 1800's and witnessing the radical new discoveries and theories of natural history and exploration. Adam Haslett penned *You Are Not a Stranger Here*, a collection of short stories nominated in 2002 for a National Book Award.

National Book Awards. Nearly all of the nominees for the National Book Award were historical novels. The winner of the award in the fiction category was Shirley Hazzard's *The Great Fire*. The book was about a U.S. military hero who comes to Japan at the close of World War II (1939–1945) to write about that war's effects on Japanese culture. He ends up falling in love with a young Australian girl. Other nominees in this category included *Drop City*, a novel by the prolific and inventive T. Corraghessan Boyle. In *Drop City*, the members of a commune make a collective decision to move from northern California to rural Alaska. The book focuses on the harsh conditions, interpersonal strife, and unsympathetic local people that threaten the group's commitment to peace and love. *The Known World* by Edward P. Jones is another historical novel. Against the background of the looming Civil War (1861-1865), a black former slave purchases a plantation and becomes a slave owner himself. Scott Spencer, author of *Ship Made of Paper*, tells the story of a New York City lawyer who returns to his hometown to face a family crisis, race and class issues, and romantic obsession. Marianne Wiggins wrote *Evidence of Things Unseen* about a veteran of World War I (1914–1918) whose artistic and scientific interests lead him to a fatal radiation poisoning.

Other notable fiction. Many other established American authors offered new novels in 2003. Jane Smiley published *Good Faith*, Robert Stone produced *Bay of Souls*, and Charles Baxter fashioned his well-loved stories about an urban couple relocating to small-town Michigan into a novel, *Saul and Patsy*. Other prominent volumes included *The Time of Our Singing* by Richard Powers, *The Tattooed Girl* by Joyce Carol Oates, *The King in the Tree* by Steven Millhauser, *Old School* by Tobias Wolff, *Cosmopolis* by Don DeLillo, *The Fortress of Solitude* by Jonathan Lethem, Louise Erdrich's *The Master Butchers Singing Club*, *The Namesake* by Jhumpa Lahiri, *L'Affaire* by Diane Johnson, and *The Rabbit Factory* by Larry Brown. Nobel laureate Toni Morrison published *Love* in 2003, a eulogy for a lady's man as remembered by the people in a dying beach community.

Like Hazzard, several prominent nonfiction writers tried their hands at fiction. Memoirist Maxine Hong Kingston, known for her volumes *China Men* and *The Woman Warrior,* broke a long hiatus with her book *The Fifth Book of Peace.* Pico Iyer, known for his travel narratives and essays, published the novel *Abandon,* concerning a graduate student's worldwide pursuit of a beautiful woman and a lost manuscript by an Islamic Sufi poet. Sherman Alexie, a Native American memoirist and essayist, published *Ten Little Indians.*

Debut works. Important debuts included short-story writer ZZ Packer's *Drinking Coffee Elsewhere,* with many of the tales centered around young African American women and men confronted by race issues at such places as a Girl Scout camp and in Tokyo. Audrey Niffenegger wrote *The Time Traveler's Wife,* about a librarian who moves about in time from his otherwise ordinary life in present-day Chicago. Carolyn Parkhurst offered an affecting work, *The Dogs of Babel,* about a man who tries to teach his dog to talk because it was the only witness to the death of his beloved wife.

Nonfiction. The National Book Award for nonfiction was awarded to *Waiting for Snow in Havana: Confessions of a Cuban Boy.* Cuban-born Yale historian Carlos Eire wrote this memoir about his eccentric family and escape, as a child, from his island homeland. Other nominees included *Gulag: A History* by Anne Applebaum, a comprehensive examination of life in the Soviet labor camps; *The Big House: A Century in the Life of an American Summer Home,* by George Howe Colt, depicting a summer home as the emotional center for several generations of the author's own family; *Lost Prophet: The Life and Times of Bayard Rustin,* John D'Emilio's biography of the little-known and openly gay civil rights leader who organized the 1963 March on Washington, D.C.; and, finally, *The Devil in the White City,* Erik Larson's account of a serial killer at large in Chicago during the 1893 World's Fair and of the fair's supervising architect, Daniel Burnham.

Other important nonfiction works published in 2003 included Phillip Lopate's *Getting Personal.* A truly strong entry was *A Problem from Hell: America and the Age of Genocide* by Samantha Power, which won the 2003 Pulitzer Prize and the National Book Critics Circle Award for nonfiction. Finally, Richard Rodriguez's essay *Brown: The Last Discovery of America,* was well received.

■ Brian Bouldrey

See also **Literature for children; Literature, World; Poetry; Pulitzer Prizes.**

Literature, World. South African novelist and essayist John Maxwell (J. M.) Coetzee won the 2003 Nobel Prize for literature in October. He was born in Cape Town, South Africa, in 1940, and is of both English and *Boer* descent (Africans of Dutch descent who speak Afrikaans, a dialect of Dutch), but his parents sent him to school in England, so that his first language is English. He has studied and taught literature in the United States and Australia. Since 2002, he has been Distinguished Service Professor in the Committee on Social Thought at the University of Chicago. He described his childhood in schools and the South African countryside in his memoirs *Boyhood* (1997) and *Youth* (2002).

In Coetzee's first novel, *Dusklands,* a man working for the U.S. government during the Vietnam War (1957-1975) dreams of devising an unbeatable system of psychological warfare. The novel was published in South Africa in 1974. Coetzee followed *Dusklands* with *In the Heart of the Country* (1977), about a remote South African farm. The short novel *Waiting for the Barbarians* (1982), an allegorical story of a man attempting to navigate a repressive regime, was the first novel to earn him international attention.

Coetzee is the only author to receive the Booker Prize, the most prestigious British literary award, twice. He received the prize in 1983 for *Life and Times of Michael K.* He earned his second Booker Prize in 1999 for *Disgrace,* another novel that takes place on an isolated farm in South Africa, but after the abolition of *apartheid* (racial segregation) in that country.

South Africa's apartheid system is a fundamental theme in Coetzee's novels. In his view, apartheid could arise anywhere, and his novels shuttle between specific historical and geographical places and imagined locations. The Nobel Prize Committee stated, "J. M. Coetzee's novels are characterized by their well-crafted composition, pregnant dialogue, and analytical brilliance, but at the same time he is a scrupulous doubter, ruthless in his criticism of the cruel rationalism and cosmetic morality of Western civilization. His intellectual honesty erodes all basis of consolation and distances itself from the tawdry drama of remorse and confession. Even when his own convictions emerge to view, as in his defense of the rights of animals, he elucidates the premises on which they are based rather than arguing for them."

Coetzee has written nine novels and several volumes of essays, as well as two volumes of memoirs. In 2003, Coetzee published *Elizabeth Costello,* a hybrid work that mixes both essays and fiction.

Other South African writers. Coetzee's Nobel Prize helped spotlight the rich tradition of literature in South Africa. Three other distinguished authors from that country produced new works in 2003. Norman Rush, best known for his novel *Mating* (1992), wrote *Mortals,* a deeply rendered depiction of the end of a marriage. Andre Brink published *The Other Side of Silence,* a historical novel about importing German women to South Africa at the turn of the last century. Nadine Gordimer produced *Loot & Other Stories,* in which she investigates the new post-apartheid era of her country.

Whitbread Prize. The Whitbread Prizes are given annually to citizens of the United Kingdom for best first novel, best novel, best poetry, best biography, and best new book of the year. In 2003, the best new book prize was given to Claire Tomalin for *Samuel Pepys: The Unequalled Self,* which also was named the best biography.

Tomalin won the best new book prize in a competition against her husband, novelist Michael Frayn, who was nominated for *Spies.* Frayn's novel, about a man recalling his childhood in England during World War II (1939-1945), did however, win the Whitbread Prize for best novel.

The prize for best first novel was given to Norman Lebrecht for *The Song of Names,* the first work of fiction by an established music critic, dealing with the British Jewish community and the Holocaust, the mass destruction or extermination of European Jews and others by the Nazis during World War II.

The Whitbread Prize for best first novel is often used as a barometer for future literary success. The three other contenders for the best first novel prize were *The End of My Tether* by Neil Astley, *Homage to a Firing Squad* by Tariq Goddard, and *The Impressionist* by Hari Kunzru.

Notable entries on the shortlist for best novel included *The Story of Lucy Gault* by William Trevor, *Rumours of a Hurricane* by Tim Lott, and *White Lightning* by Justin Cartwright.

Man Booker Prize. The jury for the Booker Prize, sponsored until 2007 by the Man Group, a British securities fund, considers only books published by writers of the British Commonwealth or the Republic of Ireland. The top six nominees for the Booker Prize in 2003 were *Brick Lane,* a novel set in the Asian community of London's East End, by Bangladeshi emigre Monica Ali; distinguished Canadian writer Margaret Atwood's *Oryx and Crake,* set in a futuristic *dystopia* (a bad or imperfect place, the opposite of utopia); *The Good Doctor* by Damon Galgut, a story of a physician sent to a rural post; *What Was She Thinking?: Notes on a Scandal* by Zoe Heller, about a teacher's defense of a friend involved in an affair with an underage student; *Astonishing Splashes of Color* by Clare Morrall, about a woman recovering from the loss of an unborn child; and *Vernon God Little* by Australian DBC Pierre.

In October, the prize was awarded to Pierre, an Australian cartoonist who grew up in Mexico and moved to Ireland. The protagonist of his novel is Vernon, a 15-year-old boy who is accused of a high school massacre. An unforgettable innocent, the boy is surrounded by a cast of grotesque adults, all of whom are determined to see him as a scapegoat for their own failings. A critic described Pierre's novel as "like Flannery O'Connor on an overdose of amphetamines and cable television." Another critic likened Pierre to *Catcher in the Rye* author J. D. Salinger.

Prix Goncourt. France's 2003 Prix Goncourt, named for two French brothers who were literary collaborators, is given annually to the best novel written in French. In October, the prize was awarded to novelist and playwright Jacques-Pierre Amette for *La Maitresse de Brecht* (Brecht's Mistress). It tells the story of the German poet, playwright, and devout Marxist Bertolt Brecht, who returns to postwar East Berlin after years in exile and begins an affair with an actress who influences his work. The prize, usually given in November, was announced early in order to surprise the author, an arts critic for *Le Point,* a French news magazine.

Other new works. Previous Nobel Prize winners in the field of literature continued to produce new works in 2003. German Nobel laureate Gunter Grass offered his new volume, *Crabwalk,* about the sinking of a Nazi cruise ship in World War II. Japanese winner Kenzaburo Oe wrote the lengthy *Somersault,* a departure from his slim memoirs. This novel depicts a fictional religious cult intent on taking over a nuclear power plant.

An English translation of Chinese Nobel laureate Gao Xingjian's *One Man's Bible,* a fictionalized depiction of the writer's youth, appeared in 2003. Other important newly translated literature by international writers included Italian Antonio Tabucchi's *The Missing Head of Damasceno Monteiro; Repetition* by Frenchman Alain Robbe-Grillet; *On the Natural History of Destruction,* the final work of the late German writer W. G. Sebald; and *Platform* by Frenchman Michel Houellebecq.

Translations of classics. Two notable translations of classic novels were published in 2003. U.S. novelist Lydia Davis finished the monumental task of a new translation of *Swann's Way,* the first volume of Marcel Proust's *Remembrance of Things Past.* Edith Grossman translated the first volume of Nobel laureate Gabriel Garcia Marquez's memoirs *Vivir para contarla* (*Living to Tell the Tale*). Grossman also completed a translation of *Don Quixote* by Miguel de Cervantes.

■ Brian Bouldrey

See also **Literature, American; Literature for children; Nobel Prizes; Poetry.**

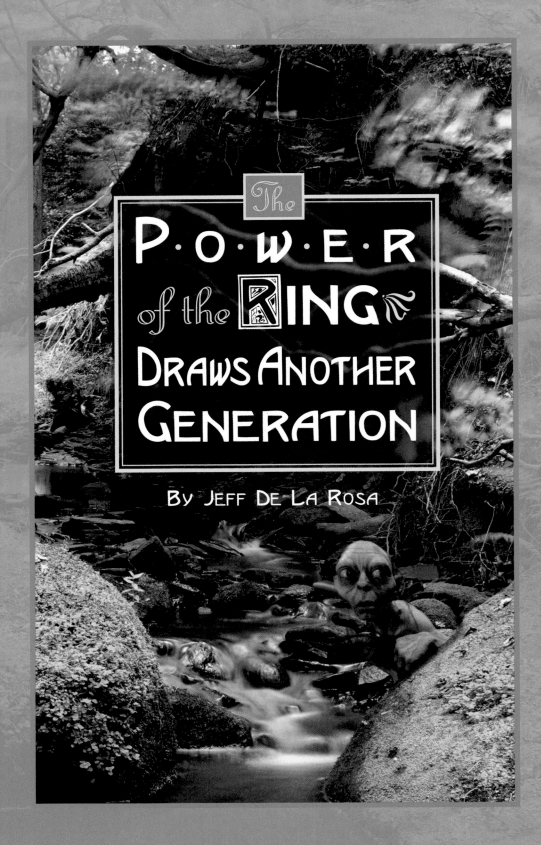

The POWER of the RING DRAWS ANOTHER GENERATION

By Jeff De La Rosa

Tens of millions of moviegoers around the world crowded into theaters in December 2003 to see *The Lord of the Rings: The Return of the King.* Audiences flocked to the movie's premiere filled with anticipation but not necessarily suspense—the story's ending had been published nearly 50 years earlier. Many felt the wait had been worthwhile, allowing moviemaking technology to mature enough to capture the epic grandeur and breathtaking scope of J. R. R. Tolkien's novel *The Lord of the Rings.*

The Lord of the Rings is the masterwork of English author J. R. R. Tolkien, a scholar and storyteller whose love of ancient languages and myths led him to create an entire fantasy world complete with its own geography, history, and culture. Tolkien began writing *The Lord of the Rings* as a sequel to *The Hobbit* (1937), his popular novel about imaginary creatures called hobbits. *The Lord of the Rings* ultimately grew until it took on a life of its own, consuming more than 12 years of Tolkien's writing career. When the work was finally published as a three-volume set—consisting of *The Fellowship of the Ring, The Two Towers,* and *The Return of the King*—in the mid-1950's, neither Tolkien nor his publisher thought they would profit from it. However, the story's classical themes and rich detail found a dedicated following among readers, and its popularity grew with each successive generation.

THREE MOTION PICTURES LEAD LEGIONS OF NEW FANS TO TOLKIEN'S LORD OF THE RINGS TRILOGY.

The Lord of the Rings takes place in Middle-earth, a fictional world that human beings share with strange and fantastic creatures and peoples. The immortal elves, Middle-earth's fairest and wisest people, endure in sadness while the world decays around them. They share their world with humans, dwarfs, and wizards. The free peoples of Middle-earth struggle against the *orcs,* savage goblins bred for violence and cruelty.

At the center of Tolkien's story are hobbits, a short people whose feet are covered in thick, curly hair. As a rule, hobbits avoid adventure. They prefer to live quiet lives filled with food, drink, and merriment in the Shire, their peaceful rural homeland. The hero of *The Lord of the Rings,* a hobbit named Frodo Baggins, must leave the Shire after he inherits a magic ring. A powerful wizard named Gandalf informs Frodo that it is the One Ring, which was forged by the evil Dark Lord Sauron. The ring would give Sauron the power he needs to enslave all the peoples of Middle-earth.

Frodo sets out with a small band of companions to take the Ring to the only place where it can be destroyed, Mount Doom, located in the heart of Sauron's land. Along the way, the so-called "Fellowship of the Ring" must avoid capture by Sauron's many servants and struggle to resist the One Ring's dark power. Tolkien sets the tale of their quest against the backdrop of the War of the Ring, a final assault by the armies of Sauron and his allies on the free peoples of Middle-earth.

The troubled creature Gollum (far left) snatches a fish from a wooded stream. Tortured by his lust for the One Ring, Gollum ranks among the most memorable characters in J. R. R. Tolkien's *The Lord of the Rings.*

The Lord of the Rings (below) was first published in the mid-1950's and continues to be published as a three-volume set consisting of The Fellowship of the Ring, The Two Towers, and The Return of the King.

Although Tolkien did not complete *The Lord of the Rings* until he was in his late 50's, its roots lie in the author's early life. John Ronald Reuel Tolkien was born on Jan. 3, 1892, in Bloemfontein, South Africa, to English parents. Tolkien, his mother Mabel, and his younger brother Hilary, returned to England in 1895. His father, Arthur, died in 1896 while still in South Africa, leaving little money for the care of his wife and sons. The Tolkien family moved throughout England quite often in search of a suitable living. In 1904, Mabel Tolkien died while her sons were still young.

Although Tolkien's childhood was seemingly difficult, he apparently had happy memories of one brief period when the family lived in the English countryside and he and his younger brother passed the time exploring the nearby fields and forests. The two developed imaginative stories and games that populated the area with ogres, wizards, and other magical creatures. As a child, Tolkien also enjoyed reading fantasy stories by such authors as Andrew Lang, Lord Dunsany, and Sir Walter Scott.

In 1911, Tolkien began his studies at Oxford University in Oxford, England, where he eventually enrolled in the Honour School for English Language and Literature. His education was interrupted briefly in 1916 when he joined the British Army and fought in World War I (1914-1918). Tolkien later claimed that it was there, in the trenches, that the early history of Middle-earth began to take shape in his mind. After falling ill while in France, Tolkien was sent home.

He took a series of teaching positions throughout England before returning to Oxford University in 1925. He taught at Oxford from 1925 to 1959, specializing in early English language and literature. Tolkien also wrote several scholarly works during this period.

Tolkien continued to develop his tales of Middle-earth as he and his wife, Edith, whom he married in 1916, raised their four children. He formed several of his ideas through bedtime stories that he told his children. Then, while grading papers late one night, he scribbled a sentence: "In a hole in the ground, there lived a hobbit." At the time, Tolkien had no idea what a hobbit was. As he worked on the answer, he developed the story that would be published as *The Hobbit*.

The Hobbit sold well following its publication in 1937, and the book's publishers, George Allen and Unwin of London, asked Tolkien to write a sequel. Later that year, Tolkien began laboring on a follow-up adventure. As the story progressed, Tolkien found his characters inevitably drawn into the deeper history of the world he had created.

The author:
Jeff De La Rosa is a free-lance writer and a former staff editor of *The Year Book*.

By 1949, Tolkien's simple sequel had expanded to become *The Lord of the Rings.* He later wrote in a foreword to the story, "This tale grew in the telling, until it became a history of the Great War of the Ring and included many glimpses of the yet more ancient history that preceded it." Tolkien's publishers worried that the resulting epic was too long, too complicated, and too dark to find a wide readership, but they opted to publish it in the hope that it would bring their company critical acclaim. Allen and Unwin published the first installment of *The Lord of the Rings,* titled *The Fellowship of the Ring,* in 1954. They published the next volume, *The Two Towers,* later that year, followed by *The Return of the King* in 1955.

The Lord of the Rings drew sharply divided critical opinion. During the 1950's, modernism was the dominant literary movement. Modernism favored work that reflected real life and emphasized style over plot. To many modernist reviewers, Tolkien's work was hopelessly old-fashioned. Some critics dismissed the book as a simple children's story, while others attacked it as immature, irrelevant, and overly nostalgic. Some reviewers, however, viewed Tolkien's work as one that drew upon ancient traditions and could not, therefore, be judged by dictates of contemporary taste. These critics, including British author C. S. Lewis and poet W. H. Auden, praised the book as a work of unique imagination, splendor, and complexity.

For his part, Tolkien did his best to avoid the critical debate. He insisted that *The Lord of the Rings* had been written to entertain and engage readers and often bristled when critics speculated his writing had deeper motives or meanings. In spite of attacks by reviewers, the books sold better than the publishers had predicted and found a small but dedicated audience. Soon Tolkien was spending much of his free time answering letters from a growing number of fans who wanted to know more about Middle-earth and its inhabitants.

English author J. R. R. Tolkien spent 12 years writing *The Lord of the Rings,* incorporating classic themes found in early English literature and mythology.

In the 1960's, a small publishing company in the United States tried to capitalize on Tolkien's steadily increasing popularity by publishing an unauthorized paperback edition of *The Lord of the Rings.* A court decision shut down sales of the unauthorized edition, but the resulting publicity stirred interest in the book among American readers, and sales of a newly authorized paperback edition skyrocketed. In the late 1960's, the epic tale found a new generation of readers among the growing counterculture movement on college campuses across the United States. Youth disillusioned with modern society and interested in exploring alternate realities were drawn to Tolkien's strong respect for nature and distrust of modern technology.

The trilogy's success initially delighted Tolkien. He enjoyed discussing the work with fans. But over the years he grew bewildered as to why people would be interested in the author and his private life and by attempts to turn him into a cult figure. Tolkien increasingly retreated from public life.

Public interest in Tolkien eventually faded, but interest in the book continued to spread, passing largely from reader to reader by word of mouth. Dedicated fans started Tolkien societies to meet and discuss the author's work. The development of the Internet in the 1990's enabled Tolkien fans scattered around the world to communicate with one another.

Even so, Tolkien's steadily growing readership went largely unnoticed in mainstream society. Many literary critics were stunned in the late 1990's when several prominent reader polls in the United Kingdom and the United States named *The Lord of the Rings* the best book of the 20th century and even the millennium. The heated critical debate that followed recalled the controversy that had surrounded the book's publication.

Observers credit the survival of *The Lord of the Rings* to its incorporation of classical myths and themes. Tolkien was a respected scholar of early English myths, studying works such as the epic poem *Beowulf,* written in the 700's, and the medieval romance *Sir Gawain and the Green Knight,* written in the late 1300's. He also enjoyed Norse works, including the Finnish poem *The Kalevala* (1835) and *Edda,* two separate works of medieval Icelandic literature composed in the 1000's and 1100's. Tolkien expressed disappointment that English literature had nothing that compared with such epics.

From mythology, Tolkien drew enduring themes such as the struggle between good and evil, the corrupting influence of power, and the virtue of heroism. Tolkien, however, added a twist. Many myths deal with strong and brave adventurers who set out to retrieve objects of great power. Tolkien's hobbits set out on a quest to destroy an item of power.

The virtue of heroism and the corrupting influence of power probably held particular appeal for Tolkien, who conceived of Middle-earth in the midst of World War I and wrote much of *The Lord of the Rings* during World War II (1939-1945). In fact, some reviewers theorized that the book was an *allegory* (symbolic story), in which characters and places represented the events of World War II. Tolkien despised the suggestion that his heroic tale was in any way connected with the ugly realities of world politics. He preferred to believe that people saw these connections because the simple themes in the book made the story applicable to many real-life situations. The universal nature of these themes allowed each reader to connect to the work in a different way, and their timelessness anchored the book amid shifting literary and social trends.

Heroic deeds and the struggle of good against evil are elements common to nearly all fantasy novels. Many literary experts, however, agree that the detail that Tolkien invested in his fantasy world remains unmatched. As a youth, Tolkien had read and enjoyed the popular fantasy writers of his day, but as he grew older he grew frustrated with what he perceived as sloppiness on the part of many authors. Names and details often struck Tolkien as having been invented at the authors' whim. He felt that the stories, though enjoyable on the surface, lacked substance. Tolkien understood the deeper connections between language, history, and culture that give myths their power. Tolkien would later claim that the early history of Middle-earth evolved as a supporting framework for a family of elven languages that he was creating.

Tolkien spent much of his adult life expanding the history of Middle-earth, and he kept detailed notes connecting its various elements. Once the foundation was laid, the work seemed to take on a life of its own. He began to refer to Middle-earth as his "sub-creation," a separate world that operated according to an internal logic. Many of his writings took on the tone of historical scholarship rather than that of fiction, including the *Silmarillion*, a sweeping history of elves in the early days of Middle-earth that Tolkien began in 1917. He periodically worked on the story until his death in 1973. His son, Christopher Tolkien, organized much of his notes for publication in the *Silmarillion* (1977) and *Unfinished Tales* (1980). Many readers feel this background material gives the people and places in Tolkien's sub-creation an unequaled sense of depth and solidity.

The detail in which Tolkien described Middle-earth also proved invaluable to New Zealand director Peter Jackson when he set out to capture Tolkien's vision on film. Jackson, an avid Tolkien fan, spent years developing a screenplay for three films based on the trilogy and hired or consulted with numerous Tolkien scholars and illustrators. Executives at the trilogy's production company, New Line Cinema, headquartered in Los Angeles, reportedly budgeted $150 million on a story that many motion-picture critics considered too long and complex to be translated into film. Reports and rumors about the films once again brought public attention to *The Lord of the Rings,* and sales of the books spiked as the premiere of *The Lord of the Rings: The Fellowship of the Ring* (2001) approached.

Despite the reservations of Tolkien fans and film industry experts, the film was well received. Even audience members who were unfamiliar with Tolkien's work applauded the multi-Oscar-nominated film. *The Lord of the Rings: The Two Towers* (2002) and *The Lord of the Rings: The Return of the King* (2003), also won praise from audiences and critics. Many viewers left theaters wanting to know more about Middle-earth. The dark lure of Sauron's One Ring had drawn yet another generation of readers to *The Lord of the Rings.*

Critics heralded the film adaptations of *The Lord of the Rings* trilogy. The first two films were later released on video and DVD.

Literature for children.
Fantasy, picture books, and historical fiction were especially popular in 2003. Some of the outstanding books of 2003 included the following:

Picture books. *The Shape Game* by Anthony Browne (Farrar Straus Giroux). A family visits an art museum and, with some gentle prodding from Mom, discovers stories and pieces of their own lives in the paintings. Ages 4 to 8.

Next, Please by Ernst Jandl, illustrated by Norman Junge (Putnam). Five broken toys wait to see the toy doctor. Each comes out happy and whole, and finally it is the last toy's turn. Bologna International Book Fair prize-winner. Ages 4 to 7.

The Day the Babies Crawled Away by Peggy Rathmann (Putnam). When the babies crawl away from the fair, a toddler follows and brings them safely back again. Ages 3 to 8.

Bruh Rabbit and the Tar Baby Girl by Virginia Hamilton, illustrated by James E. Ransome (Blue Sky/Scholastic). The familiar humorous folktale takes on a new flavor in this retelling. Ages 4 to 8.

One Winter's Night by John Herman, illustrated by Leo and Diane Dillon (Philomel). Martha, a pregnant cow, follows a star on a cold and snowy night and finds shelter in a hut with a human couple. Both the cow and the woman give birth that night in an unusual nativity tale. Ages 4 to 8.

Otto, The Story of a Mirror by Ali Bahrampour (Farrar Straus Giroux). When Otto tires of reflecting customers' hats and wants to see the world, he makes fun of customers and runs away, finding a lady mirror and a grand adventure. Ages 5 to 8.

Poetry. *I Hear America Singing! Folk Songs for American Families,* collected and arranged by Kathleen Krull, illustrated by Allen Garns (Knopf). This collection, with an introduction by folk singer Arlo Guthrie, includes 62 American folk songs, piano and guitar music, a compact disc, and informative notes about the songs. Ages 7 and up.

Cartwheel to the Moon: My Sicilian Childhood by Emanuel di Pasquale, illustrated by K. Dyble Thompson (Cricket). The poet brings to life the simple pleasures of growing up in a village on an island in the 1940's and 1950's. Ages 8 to 12.

Pio Peep! Traditional Spanish Nursery Rhymes selected by Alma Flor Ada and Isabel Campoy, adapted by Alice Schertle, illustrated by Vivi Escriva (HarperCollins). Beloved nursery rhymes, songs, and finger plays from Latin America and the southwestern United States are presented in both Spanish and English. Ages 1 to 6.

Fiction. *The Beast* by Walter Dean Myers (Scholastic). While Spoon leaves Harlem to attend a prep school, his girlfriend, Gabi, becomes a drug addict. He tries to help, but the "Beast" is ferocious. Ages 12 and up.

Maggie's Door by Patricia Reilly Giff (Wendy Lamb/Random House). In a sequel to *Nory Ryan's Song,* Nory follows her family to the United States during the Irish potato famine of the mid-1800's, enduring harsh shipboard conditions before she reaches the home of her sister, Maggie, in Brooklyn, New York. Ages 8 to 12.

A Cool Moonlight by Angela Johnson (Dial). Lila, almost nine, is dangerously sensitive to the sun and goes outside only in the evenings, joined by two fantasy friends. She dreams of feeling sunshine on her ninth birthday. Ages 8 to 11.

Milkweed by Jerry Spinelli (Knopf). An orphan in Nazi-occupied Warsaw, Poland, in 1939, becomes part of a group of Jewish boys who hide and steal to survive. The Holocaust is depicted through his young, uncomprehending eyes. Ages 12 and up.

Locomotion by Jacqueline Woodson (Putnam). A series of poems reveals the loneliness and heartache of orphaned fifth-grader Lonnie Collins Motion, as well as the kindness of a special teacher and the boy's foster mother. Ages 8 to 11.

The Silent Boy by Lois Lowry (Houghton Mifflin). Katy Thatcher, the daughter of a physician in a small New England town in the early 1900's, befriends a silent, mentally retarded boy and is the only one to see the truth in the tragedy that befalls him. Ages 8 to 12.

Circle of Doom by Tim Kennemore (Farrar Straus Giroux). Lizzie makes a magic potion that rids her family of their hated neighbors. When she tries making others, she and her brothers become entangled in a web of secrets and misunderstandings. Ages 10 to 13.

The River Between Us by Richard Peck (Dial). Two mysterious women arrive by riverboat just before the Civil War (1861-1865), changing the lives of a family who takes them in. Ages 12 and up.

Fantasy. *The Heroic Adventures of Hercules Amsterdam* by Melissa Glenn Haber (Dutton). Hercules, only 3 inches (8 centimeters) in length at birth, discovers a city of friendly mice behind his bedroom wall. He learns of dangers and, with help, tries to avert tragedy. Ages 8 to 12.

Harry Potter and the Order of the Phoenix by J. K. Rowling (Scholastic). In his fifth year at Hogwarts School of Witchcraft and Wizardry, Harry struggles with adolescence and with lies that have been spread about him. More importantly, no one believes his warning that the evil Lord Voldemort is preparing to strike again. All ages.

Loamhedge by Brian Jacques (Philomel). In the 16th novel of the epic saga of the woodland creatures whose lives center on the abbey, Redwall comes under attack by vermin. New and old warriors rush to save it. Ages 10 and up.

The Tears of the Salamander by Peter Dickinson (Wendy Lamb/Random House). In Italy in the 1700's, Alfredo's family dies in a fire, and he is taken to live in Sicily, where he learns that his uncle, Georgio, is an evil sorcerer who can control the eruption of volcanoes. Ages 12 and up.

Guardians of Ga'hoole: The Capture by Kathryn Lasky (Scholastic). Soren, a barn owl chick, is snatched by evil owls and carried to St. Aegolius Academy. But things are not as they seem, and Soren must learn to fly to escape the place of brainwashed, mindless owls. Ages 8 to 12.

Informational books. *An American Plague: The True and Terrifying Story of the Yellow Fever Epidemic of 1793* by Jim Murphy (Clarion). Historical documents, first-hand accounts, and period art dramatically bring to life the story of the plague that swept Philadelphia. Ages 10 and up.

Jack: The Early Years of John F. Kennedy by Ilene Cooper (Dutton). Cooper provides a detailed study of the late president's childhood, plagued with illnesses and rivalry with older brother Joe, Jr. Ages 8 to 12.

King of the Mild Frontier: An Ill-Advised Autobiography by Chris Crutcher (Greenwillow). Crutcher, the author of such popular young adult books as *Stotan!, Whale Talk,* and *Iron Man,* candidly recounts both the troubling—and the hilarious—moments of his childhood and describes his later work as a therapist specializing in abused children and their families. Ages 12 and up.

My Tour of Europe By Teddy Roosevelt, Age 10 edited by Ellen Jackson, illustrated by Catherine Brighton (Millbrook). Entries from a journal written by the future president of the United States during a trip with his family depict his many adventures. Ages 5 to 8.

MATH-terpieces: The Art of Problem-Solving by Greg Tang, illustrated by Greg Paprocki (Scholastic). Tang uses paintings by such famous artists as Degas, Dali, and Picasso to pose math problems and teach problem-solving skills. Ages 5 to 10.

Dinosaurs A to Z: The Ultimate Dinosaur Encyclopedia by Don Lessem, illustrated by Jan Sovak (Scholastic). More than 700 entries cover every known dinosaur. Other sections are filled with all kinds of information and loaded with nearly 400 illustrations. Ages 10 and up.

Awards. The 2003 Newbery Medal was awarded to Avi for *Crispin: The Cross of Lead.* The award is given by the American Library Association (ALA) for "the most distinguished contribution to children's literature" published the previous year. The ALA's Caldecott Medal for "the most distinguished American picture book" was awarded to Eric Rohmann for *My Friend Rabbit.*

■ Marilyn Fain Apseloff

Lithuania. See Europe.

J. K. Rowling's latest book, *Harry Potter and the Order of the Phoenix,* broke records in both the United Kingdom and the United States. The combined sales of the British edition (above) and the U.S. edition (right) exceeded 6 million copies on the first day of release, June 21.

The Walt Disney Concert Hall, the new home of the Los Angeles Symphony Orchestra, opened in downtown Los Angeles on Oct. 26, 2003. Critics hailed architect Frank Gehry for the unique design of the highly sculptural, stainless steel-clad structure.

Los Angeles, like other cities in the United States, faced a budget crunch in 2003. Wrangling over scarce resources led to a battle between the Los Angeles City Council and Mayor James K. Hahn. At the core of the controversy was the mayor's proposal to add 300 new police officers to the Los Angeles Police Department. Financial analysts warned that the plan would put the city's finances deeply into a deficit.

The city council on May 28 passed a $5.1-billion budget for fiscal year 2003 (July 1, 2003–June 30, 2004) that excluded the request for additional police. Mayor Hahn vetoed the budget on June 4, 2004, but the city council, for the first time in Hahn's term, overrode his veto.

Los Angeles County officials approved a $16.5-billion budget on June 30. The budget decreased hospital, library, and law enforcement funding in order to reduce an $800-million budget gap.

Economy. Unemployment in Los Angeles County stood at 6.8 percent in August 2003, compared with 6.9 percent in August 2002, despite earlier predictions by economists that the jobless rate would decline to 6.4 percent in 2003. Southern California's economic picture conformed to what some economists described as the "jobless recovery" of the economy from a 2002 recession.

Health care. A federal court intervened on May 8, 2003, to prevent budget cutbacks and closures of the County-USC Medical Center in Los Angeles and Rancho Los Amigos National Rehabilitation Center in Downey. Many of the estimated 800,000 uninsured residents of the county received treatment at these facilities in 2003.

The Gold Line. In July, the Los Angeles Metropolitan Transit Authority opened the Gold Line, a 14-mile (22-kilometer) light-rail commuter system between downtown Los Angeles and Pasadena. Designed to carry 30,000 passengers per day, the line received 20,000 to 25,000 daily fares during its first month of operation.

The Walt Disney Concert Hall officially opened on October 26 in downtown Los Angeles as the new home of the Los Angeles Symphony Orchestra. The genesis of the $274-million building, designed by renowned architect Frank Gehry, was a $50-million gift in 1987 from Lillian Disney, the now-late widow of Walt Disney.

Plans for infamous hotel. In June 2003, Superintendent Roy Romer of the Los Angeles Unified School District announced five alternate plans for development of the site of the Ambassador Hotel, which the district bought in 2001. Once a gathering spot for the rich and famous, the hotel, which closed in 1989, is most widely remembered as the site of Robert F. Kennedy's assassination in June 1968. The development options, which all included plans for three new schools, ranged from the complete demolition of the hotel to its preservation. Preservationists, led by Ken Bernstein of the Los Angeles Conservancy, an organization devoted to historic preservation, insisted that the Ambassador merited preservation as a historically significant site. Others in the Los Angeles community responded that preservation would be too expensive and that the rambling structure should be razed to make room for the campus of the desperately needed schools.

Dodgers sale. News Corp., a United States-based corporation controlled by media mogul Rupert Murdoch, agreed in October 2003 to sell the Los Angeles Dodgers baseball team to Boston real estate developer Frank H. McCourt for an estimated $430 million. Conclusion of the sale awaited approval by a majority of Major League baseball team owners.

Tragedy. On July 16, a speeding automobile hurtled through nearly four blocks of a popular farmers' market in the oceanside community of Santa Monica, killing 10 people and injuring more than 50 others. The driver, an 86-year-old man with a valid driver's license, apparently mistook the car's gas pedal for the brake.

◼ Margaret A. Kilgore

See also **City.**

Louisiana. See State government.
Luxembourg. See Europe.

Macedonia in September 2003 faced a serious security challenge to the 2001 peace agreement between ethnic Albanian rebels and Macedonian government forces. That agreement had ended months of fighting between rebels from the country's Albanian minority—about 23 percent of the population—and government troops, mainly from the country's Slavic majority.

The fighting in September 2003 broke out in a mountainous area in northern Macedonia that borders Kosovo. Government security patrols came under attack from Albanian militants and responded by calling in reinforcements and counterattacking. The government forces occupied two villages, killing a number of rebels.

Diplomatic sources speculated that an extremist ethnic Albanian armed band, the Albanian National Army (ANA), was behind the attacks on the government security patrols. The United Nations mission in neighboring Kosovo has labeled the ANA a terrorist group.

Peacekeeping forces. In April, the European Union (EU) deployed a force of 450 EU soldiers in Macedonia to take over peacekeeping duties from the NATO mission that had been in the country since the end of the 2001 rebellion. In late 2003, the EU force was replaced by a smaller EU unit that was to help with training and border patrols.

Interethnic cooperation. The multiethnic coalition government of Prime Minister Branko Crvenkovski, leader of the largely Slavic Social Democratic Union, held onto power through 2003. The coalition included the ethnic Albanian Democratic Union for Integration of Ali Ahmeti, a former rebel who after the 2001 peace agreement became the leader of Macedonia's largest Albanian ethnic political party.

In February 2003, Crvenkovski and Ahmeti held their first official meeting, pledging to work together on a number of issues. In November, the coalition government launched a six-week amnesty campaign to urge citizens to turn in illegal arms. Although the campaign brought in only a tiny fraction of the estimated 100,000 to 500,000 illegal weapons in Macedonia, it demonstrated that majority Slavic and minority Albanian parties could work together on a sensitive issue, political analysts said.

Economic performance, bolstered by political stability, improved in 2003. Macedonia's gross domestic product—the value of all the goods and services produced in a year—grew by 2.8 percent in 2003, compared with nearly flat growth in 2002. Unemployment remained high, however, at more than 40 percent of the workforce.

◼ Sharon L. Wolchik

See also **Europe; Iraq: A Special Report.**

Magazine. The two types of magazines that grew the fastest in 2003, ironically, were those that chronicled celebrity gossip and those that focused on serious ideas. *Us Weekly*, with its Hollywood romances, increased its newsstand sales 24.8 percent in the first half of 2003, according to the Audit Bureau of Circulations (ABC), an independent auditing firm in Schaumburg, Illinois. Over the same period, literary and political magazines experienced substantial revenue increases, with *The New Yorker* up 33 percent, *The Atlantic Monthly* up 28 percent, and *Harper's* up 18 percent, according to industry publication *Folio.*

Overall, magazine advertising revenues increased in 2003 after two consecutive years of decline. Magazine Publishers of America, a trade group headquartered in New York City, reported that total revenues for the first half of 2003 were $8.59 billion, a 9.9-percent increase over the same period in 2002. However, magazine circulation continued to decline, with 54 percent of all titles reporting decreases for the first half of 2003, according to ABC.

Girls' and women's magazines. In April, Primedia Inc. of New York City agreed to sell *Seventeen* magazine, the most popular magazine for teen-age girls, to Hearst Magazines of New York City for about $180 million. Conde Nast Publications of New York City, which publishes the fashion magazine *Vogue*, launched *Teen Vogue* in January. Two of the oldest magazines for women, *Ladies Home Journal* and *Woman's Day*, were redesigned in March to attract youthful readers and new advertisers while retaining their traditional homemaker audience.

In April, Hearst Magazines launched *Lifetime*, which was intended to reach the same female audience attracted to the cable television channel Lifetime. Analysts said Hearst was trying to duplicate the success of *O: The Oprah Magazine*, which had a circulation of 2.2 million in 2003.

Job cuts. *Reader's Digest*, which publishes 48 editions in 19 languages around the world, in April announced plans to cut 580 jobs, most of them overseas. The magazine's net income decreased from $91.2 million in fiscal year 2002 to $61.3 million in fiscal year 2003.

Rosie vs. *Rosie*. In November, a New York City judge ruled that neither publisher Gruner & Jahr nor former TV talk-show host Rosie O'Donnell would collect damages in a highly public court battle. The publisher had sued O'Donnell, alleging breach of contract when she quit her magazine in September 2002. O'Donnell countersued, claiming that Gruner & Jahr left her out of key editorial decisions.   ■ Mark Fitzgerald

Maine. See State government.

Malawi. See Africa.

Malaysia. Mahathir bin Mohamad stepped down as prime minister of Malaysia on Oct. 31, 2003, and handed over power to Abdullah Ahmad Badawi, the deputy prime minister. Mahathir, who became prime minister in 1981, was Asia's longest serving elected leader.

Mahathir oversaw Malaysia's rapid economic growth and worked to improve the economic condition of Malays, the largest ethnic group in Malaysia. He emphasized a policy that enabled the Malay to own more of the nation's wealth, reducing economic dominance by ethnic Chinese and Indian citizens. In 2003, however, the government relaxed rules that required Malays to own a minimal share of companies on the stock exchange. Mahathir said that it limited foreign investment needed for economic growth.

Mahathir, who earned a reputation for making controversial statements, told an Islamic conference in October that "Jews rule the world by proxy. They get others to fight and die for them." He also attacked leaders of Muslim religious organizations, accusing them of failing to bring their people into the modern world.

Malaysia's economy grew at a rate of 5 percent in 2003. Oil exports helped fuel growth.

■ Henry S. Bradsher

See also Asia.

Manitoba. See Canadian provinces.

Manufacturing. Production of goods by United States factories declined in the first half of 2003, in part because of fears about the Iraq War and because of an uncertain recovery from a recession that began in 2001. The manufacturing sector, however, began growing during the summer and showed significant strength in autumn. Even so, factory employment continued to decrease through much of 2003 as businesses trimmed inventories instead of rebuilding stocks.

As U.S. forces in the Persian Gulf prepared for war against Iraq in March 2003, manufacturers' customers were reluctant to commit to new orders until the impact of the war on the U.S. economy became clear. Also, fears concerning the war pushed the price of crude oil up sharply, further crimping demand by stripping consumers of cash and adding to production costs. West Texas Intermediate crude oil averaged $35.90 per barrel in February, up 9 percent from January and 73 percent from the same period in 2002.

Trends. The Institute for Supply Management (ISM), a professional group based in Tempe, Arizona, for purchasing managers from U.S. manufacturing companies, reported that its index of overall factory activity slid from 53.9 in January 2003 to 50.5 in February. The ISM's overall index for factory activity tracks manufacturing trends, signaling a manufacturing contraction when the index falls below 50 and an expansion above that point. Harsh winter weather as well as war-related factors helped curb demand for new goods early in the year, and the index fell to 46.2 in March as the war began and 45.4 in April.

With the stimulus from low interest rates and tax cuts, and the major uncertainties of the Iraq War behind it, the U.S. economy finally began to strengthen and generate growth in manufacturing later in 2003. After four months of decline, the ISM index moved into positive territory with readings of 51.8 in July, 54.7 in August, and 53.7 in September. In November, ISM reported that factory activity surged in October as the group's index reached 57.0, its strongest reading since January 2000 and a sign the factory sector was picking up speed as the fourth quarter began.

Once the U.S.-led coalition enjoyed quick success against the Iraqi military and captured Iraq's oil fields with little of the damage feared by fuel markets, fuel prices began a long decline, and manufacturing orders picked up. ISM spokesman Norbert Ore said in May that April brought "a significant softening in pricing pressures" on raw materials because purchasing managers felt that "the war resulted in few, if any, consequences to supply chains."

Ore also said that manufacturers were looking to measures of consumer and business confidence to signal how factory output might grow again.

The U.S. Federal Reserve (the Fed), the nation's central bank, reported in July that, with mild gains in May and June, the manufacturing sector enjoyed its first consecutive months of improved output since July and August 2002. The ISM index, however, which also considers factors such as employment and order backlog, remained in contraction with ratings of 49.4 for May 2003 and 49.8 for June.

The Fed's policymakers stood ready in 2003 to cut short-term interest rates from already low levels in case the economy weakened further. Before the Iraq War started in March, the Fed expressed concern about the negative effects of high oil prices and geopolitical uncertainty. After major combat ended in April, the Fed said that production and employment levels continued to be low, but it avoided cutting rates through the spring to see how the economy would fare after the war. In June, the Fed decided to expand the money supply enough to reduce the federal funds rate—the interest rate that banks charge other banks on overnight loans—to 1 percent. The Fed reaffirmed the federal funds rate at 1 percent in October.

Low U.S. interest rates, compared with yields offered by key foreign economies, helped devalue the U.S. dollar against major foreign currencies in a policy development long sought by the National Association of Manufacturers (NAM), a Washington, D.C.-based lobbying group. The dollar's slide was aided by a perception in the currency market that the administration of U.S. President George W. Bush had wanted a lower-valued dollar to make U.S. goods cheaper to foreign buyers and to help head off the risk that prices at home might fall into a dangerous deflationary spiral.

In October, the U.S. government stated in a preliminary report that the overall economy had grown at a very strong 7.2-percent annual rate in the third quarter of 2003 and revised a month later to 8.2 percent—the fastest pace in nearly 20 years and a rate well beyond economists' expectations. NAM Chief Economist David Huether said that the growth report, which included broad-based business equipment spending and a surge in U.S. exports, "shows that the tax cuts passed earlier this year, combined with the ongoing correction of the U.S. dollar and low interest rates, are now shifting economic growth into high gear." Although some economists believed that 2003 would end on a high note, the report also showed that U.S. firms were still cutting inventory and factory employment.

As a reflection of the sudden growth in the economy, ISM stated in December that its factory activity index for November had soared to 62.8 percent, the highest in almost 20 years, with manufacturing employment expanding for the first time after 37 months of decline.

Regulations and rulings. Toward the end of 2003, U.S. factories prepared for tighter workday regulations on truck drivers, set to take effect in January 2004. The regulations forced trucking firms to add drivers and trucks, increasing transportation costs for manufacturers.

For most of 2003, the steel sector was protected by measures that the Bush administration imposed in early 2002 on foreign steel imports. The measures took the form of more tariffs ranging from 8 to 30 percent for a three-year period. The European Union, together with Japan, South Korea, China, Switzerland, Norway, New Zealand, and Brazil, initiated a dispute settlement procedure against these measures. A panel of the World Trade Organization (WTO), an international group that promotes trade in goods and services among nations, ruled in July 2003 that the U.S. fees violated WTO rules. In November, a WTO appellate board reaffirmed the ruling. Facing the threat of a trade war, President Bush scrapped the steel tariffs in December.

■ John D. Boyd

See also **Economics**.

Maryland. See **State government**.
Massachusetts. See **State government**.
Mauritania. See **Africa**.

Mauritius experienced a major shift of leadership in September 2003, when Sir Aneerood Jugnauth stepped down as prime minister to become the country's head of state and president. Incumbent Deputy Prime Minister Paul Berenger succeeded Jugnauth as prime minister. Pravind Jugnauth, son of Sir Aneerood, was appointed deputy prime minister in recognition of the fact that he had taken over leadership of the majority party, the Militant Socialist Movement (MSM), from his father in early April.

These political shifts came as a result of a coalition agreement between Sir Aneerood's MSM and Berenger's Militant Mauritian Movement (MMM) prior to the September 2000 national elections. In those elections, the MSM-MMM coalition had won a landslide victory over the Labor Party-dominated government of then-Prime Minister Navinchandra Ramgoolam. Under the terms of the pact, Sir Aneerood and Berenger had agreed that the former should rule for three years and the latter for two years until their mandate expired in September 2005.

Constitutional change. In August 2003, Parliament passed an amendment to the Mauritian Constitution that expanded presidential power. The amendment permitted the president to appoint members of the electoral commission and to play a greater role in the creation of a new government when the government loses a vote of confidence in Parliament.

The economy of Mauritius. The gross domestic product (GDP) grew by more than 5 percent in 2003, continuing a 20-year trend. GDP is the value of all goods and services produced in a country in a year. Despite the nation's long run of economic growth, economists warned that corruption in government and business was taking an economic toll.

In January, Housing and Lands Minister Mookhesswur Choonee was charged with secretly selling state land. In April, the manager of the Mauritius Commercial Bank, the nation's largest bank, was charged with the theft of millions of dollars of state pension funds on deposit in the bank. The pension fund case was later investigated by the country's Independent Commission against Corruption.

Chagos ruling. On October 9, the High Court of London ruled that several thousand displaced islanders from the British Indian Ocean Territory, also known as the Chagos Islands, were not entitled to compensation for unlawful exile. British officials had moved the Chagossians mainly to Mauritius in the late 1960's and early 1970's to make way for a military base on the largest island, Diego Garcia.   ■ Simon Baynham

See also **Africa.**

Medicine. Diabetes, already one of the most common chronic diseases in the United States, will reach epidemic levels among Americans born in the early 2000's, according to a study released in June 2003 by the Centers for Disease Control and Prevention (CDC) in Atlanta, Georgia. CDC researchers found that one in three Americans born in 2000 will likely develop the disease sometime during his or her lifetime. The researchers linked the findings to rising levels of obesity.

The study—the first to calculate Americans' lifetime risk of developing diabetes—drew on U.S. census data and the health records of about 360,000 people collected between 1984 and 2000. The researchers found that Hispanics had the highest risk of all groups, with 52.5 percent of girls and 45.4 percent of boys born in 2000 likely to develop diabetes during their lifetimes. Among African Americans, 49 percent of girls and 41.4 percent of boys ran the risk of developing the disease, compared with 31.2 percent of white girls and 26.7 percent of white boys. These figures were three times as high as current estimates from the American Diabetes Association.

The study also predicted a significantly shorter life span and significantly higher risk of serious health problems for those who develop diabetes at a relatively young age. For example, it estimated that a woman born in 2000 who is diag-

nosed with diabetes at age 40 will die about 14 years earlier than expected. Diabetes will shorten the life of a man born in 2000 by 12 years, the study's researchers said.

Hormone replacement therapy. Studies reported in 2003 added to recent findings on the dangers of hormone replacement therapy (HRT) for postmenopausal women. Several studies in 2002 produced evidence that taking estrogen and progesterone may actually increase a woman's risk of breast cancer, coronary heart disease, stroke, and blood clots in the lungs.

The first study, reported in May 2003, contradicted earlier research suggesting that HRT could significantly reduce the risk of dementia. The study, led by Sally A. Shumaker, a public health sciences professor at Wake Forest University Baptist Medical Center in Winston-Salem, North Carolina, found that sex hormones offer no protection against dementia and may actually increase the risk of developing the disorder.

The second study, reported in October, indicated that HRT does not lower the risk of developing ovarian cancer, as many researchers had believed. Instead, taking sex hormones may increase a woman's chances of developing this relatively rare but deadly form of cancer.

Rise in autism. The number of children in California diagnosed with autism nearly doubled from 1998 to 2000, according to a report issued in May 2003. The report, by California's Department of Developmental Services, said that caseworkers had identified 20,377 children with autism in 2002, compared with 10,360 in 1998. The increase in the disorder, characterized by a limited ability to communicate and interact with others, occurred among all ethnic groups. Researchers had no explanation for the rise but ruled out population growth or misdiagnoses.

Breast cancer drug. In October 2003, researchers found that the drug letrozole reduced by 43 percent the risk of the recurrence of the disease or the development of new breast cancers linked to estrogen. The drug, which stops the production of estrogen, was so effective that researchers halted the study two years early and offered letrozole to women in the study who had been taking a *placebo* (inactive substance). Letrozole is sold under the brand name Femara.

The study, which involved more than 5,000 women, investigated the use of Femara as a follow-up to tamoxifen, an estrogen-blocking drug that significantly lowers the risk of new breast cancers. However, tamoxifen, which is commonly prescribed after treatment for estrogen-fueled breast cancer, loses its effectiveness after five years, leaving women vulnerable to a recurrence of the disease.   ■ Barbara A. Mayes

See also **Health care issues; Public health.**

Mental health. The mental health care system in the United States is "a patchwork relic . . . of disjointed reforms and policies" that requires a "fundamental transformation," a presidential commission reported in July 2003. The President's New Freedom Commission on Mental Health, convened to study problems and gaps in the system, concluded that the system is not oriented to recovery, "the single most important goal of the people it serves." Instead, the report contended, the system is unintentionally focused on managing the disabilities associated with mental illness.

According to the report, in any given year, from 5 percent to 7 percent of adults and from 5 percent to 9 percent of children have a serious mental illness. Mental illnesses have an annual indirect cost of $79 billion, mostly in lost productivity from the illnesses and from family care and premature death, the commission said. Although the United States spent almost $71 billion treating mental illness in 1997 (the last year for which data were available), millions of people with mental disorders got no treatment at all. The report also noted that many of the 30,000 U.S. residents who commit suicide each year have undiagnosed or untreated mental illness.

The commission strongly urged government agencies and health care providers to treat mental illness with the same urgency given to physical problems. It recommended that services and treatment should be consumer- and family-oriented, with consumers given meaningful choices about treatment options and providers.

Children with mental illness. Parents in the United States surrendered custody of at least 12,700 children with mental illness to child welfare agencies or juvenile justice authorities in 2001 in a drastic effort to obtain mental health services for those children, the General Accounting Office (GAO) reported in April 2003. The GAO is the investigative arm of the U.S. Congress. About 3,700 of the children entered the child welfare system. The rest ended up in the juvenile justice system. The number of surrendered children is probably much higher than that given in the report, the GAO said, because the survey covered only 19 states and 30 counties.

The GAO found that some families traded custody for treatment because they could not obtain services to help them cope with their mentally ill children at home. Others lacked the financial resources, including adequate health insurance, for treatment or were hampered by a shortage of mental health services in their community. The families represented all income levels. Adolescent boys, often affected by multiple problems, were surrendered more often than any other group, the report said.

According to the GAO, the children were inappropriately placed in foster homes, state mental hospitals, juvenile detention facilities, and other public facilities. These facilities, said the report, were designed to serve children who are abused or neglected or who have committed a delinquent act, not children with mental illness.

Mental illness in prisoners. Three times as many people with mental illness in the United States are confined in prisons or jails as are in mental hospitals, according to a study by Human Rights Watch released in October. Human Rights Watch is an international organization dedicated to promoting and protecting human rights and freedoms. The two-year study found that from 200,000 to 300,000 prison inmates suffer from mental disorders, including such serious illnesses as schizophrenia, bipolar disorder, and major depression.

The prison system, marked by "woefully deficient" mental health services, has become "a warehouse for the mentally ill" that is "acting as an incubator for worse illness and psychiatric breakdowns," according to the study. Prisoners with mental illness, the report said, are often victimized by other prisoners and punished by staff for behaviors associated with their illness.

■ Barbara A. Mayes

See also **Supreme Court of the United States.**

Mexico. President Vicente Fox Quesada, in his State of the Union address to the Mexican Congress in September 2003, acknowledged his disappointment with his administration's economic record during his first three years in office. He cited various causes for the economic shortcomings, including a sluggish economy in the United States, which absorbed approximately 90 percent of Mexico's exports in 2003.

Mid-term elections. Mexican voters handed Fox a stinging defeat in July when his National Action Party (PAN) lost nearly a quarter of its strength in the Chamber of Deputies. PAN was able to hold onto only 151 of 500 seats in the chamber, while its chief political opponent, the Institutional Revolutionary Party (PRI), won 222.

With both houses controlled by his political opponents, Fox's ambitious legislative agenda, which included the reform of Mexico's tax system, was stalled. Progress toward encouraging the estimated $5 billion needed to modernize Mexico's overloaded electric transmission network was made more difficult by constitutional provisions that required a two-thirds majority vote by the legislature to override. These provisions severely limited the private ownership of power utilities.

Female power broker. Following her July election as head of the PRI's congressional delegation, Elba Esther Gordillo played an important role in convincing the primary parties to accommodate Fox's political agenda. Gordillo, who represented Chiapas, one of Mexico's poorest states, was the first woman to hold this position. Her removal from that post in December placed the chances of Fox advancing his political agenda in jeopardy and signaled a split within the PRI over future strategy.

Corruption. Despite the Fox administration's efforts to curb bribes, corruption continued to be widespread in 2003. Francisco Barrio, who served as Mexico's anticorruption czar until April, estimated that *graft* (the unlawful solicitation of bribes in connection with government business) annually cost Mexico the equivalent of 9.5 percent of its *gross national product* (the value of all goods and services produced in a country in a given year).

Unemployment. Because of the loss of more than 800,000 jobs since 2000, when Fox took office, experts estimated that more than 40 percent of Mexico's population lived below the poverty line in 2003. During the year, more than 1,000 Mexicans continued to illegally cross the U.S. border daily in search of opportunity.

In a report released in October, the Inter-American Development Bank, a regional financial agency, stated that Mexicans working in the United States sent home the money that enabled one Mexican in five to survive. Moreover, the bank stated that these remittances would soar to a record $14.5 billion in 2003.

Misery along the border. In May, 17 illegal immigrants from Mexico, El Salvador, and Guatemala were found dead inside a hot trailer truck by the side of the road on the outskirts of Victoria, Texas. An additional immigrant from the truck died a short time later at a local hospital.

To cut down on illegal immigration, 600 Mexican police and intelligence agents shut down rundown hostels along the U.S-Mexico border in June. The raids targeted Mexican criminals, who made an estimated $1 billion in 2003 from smuggling Mexicans into the United States.

Opposition to war with Iraq. Polls taken before the start of the war in Iraq in March indicated that between 70 and 83 percent of Mexicans opposed the war. Anti-U.S. feeling in Mexico also was fueled by the failure of U.S. President George W. Bush to work out an immigration accord, as he had promised in February 2001. The proposed accord would grant legal status to some 4.5 million undocumented Mexicans working in the United States.

■ Nathan A. Haverstock

See also **Immigration; Iraq: A Special Report; Latin America; United States, Government of the.**

Michigan. See Detroit; State government.

MIDDLE EAST

Three important events or movements dominated the Middle East in 2003—the decision made by President George W. Bush of the United States to wage a war against the regime of President Saddam Hussein of Iraq, the course of the war, and its aftermath; the U.S.-led war on terrorism versus the wave of terrorist operations around the world; and the series of unsuccessful attempts to revive the peace process between the Israelis and the Palestinians.

The war and its consequences. The war in Iraq began on March 20 (March 19 in the United States). President Bush argued that the war was justified because Hussein had *weapons of mass destruction* (chemical, biological, or nuclear weapons). President Bush also claimed that Hussein was linked to the terrorists responsible for the attacks on the United States on Sept. 11, 2001. Baghdad, the Iraqi capital, fell to U.S.-led coalition forces on April 9, 2003. On May 1, Bush declared that with coalition forces occupying the whole of Iraq, the war was effectively over. Weapons inspectors subsequently searched Iraq without success for weapons of mass destruction. In September, President Bush noted that he knew of no evidence linking Hussein to the terrorists responsible for the September 11 attacks.

The conflict in Iraq, however, was not over. Attacks on coalition soldiers began soon after Bush's May 1 declaration, and the security situation deteriorated through 2003, as the number of attacks increased from 12 a day in July, to 33 a day in late October, to 55 a day by mid-November. Attacks on civilians began in early August with the bombing in Baghdad of the Jordanian Embassy, which killed at least 17 people and wounded more than 50 others. On August 19, a truck bomb exploded outside the United Nations (UN) headquarters in Baghdad, killing 22 people and wounding at least 100 others.

In late October, insurgents launched an audacious rocket attack on the al-Rashid Hotel, which is in Baghdad's "green zone," a heavily guarded area where a large number of high-ranking CPA (Coalition Provisional Authority) officials resided. The attack, which killed a U.S. military officer, coincided with the visit to Baghdad of a major architect of the war, U.S. Deputy Secretary of

Palestinians in Nablus in the West Bank inspect shops destroyed in an Israeli raid on February 20. Describing Nablus as the center for terrorism on the West Bank, Israeli officials ordered raids on all of the city's shops that employed chemicals that could be used in the making of bombs.

Defense Paul Wolfowitz, who was staying at the hotel. Experts on the Iraqi situation suggested the attack was made in response to the optimistic claims made by Wolfowitz, while he traveled around Iraq, that the security situation was better than the media portrayed. The following day, five coordinated attacks in Baghdad, targeting four police stations and the headquarters of the International Red Cross, left 35 people dead and more than 230 others wounded in one 45-minute period.

Insurgents killed two U.S. soldiers on October 29 (October 28 in the United States). Their deaths brought to 116 the number of U.S. soldiers killed in hostile conflict since President Bush had declared on May 1 that "major combat operations in Iraq have ended"—more than had died in the combat phase of the war.

The death toll climbed higher when insurgents began firing on U.S. helicopters. In November, a total of 39 U.S. soldiers were killed in three such incidents involving four helicopters. By

November 30, the number of U.S. soldiers killed in hostile action in Iraq since May 1 reached 190.

Insurgent attacks on coalition partners also escalated. On November 12, the explosion of a truck bomb at the headquarters of the Italian military police in the southern city of An Nasiriyah killed 19 Italians and 9 Iraqis and wounded more than 100 others. On November 29, insurgents ambushed and killed 7 Spanish intelligence officers near Al Mahmudiyah. On the same day, guerrillas killed two Japanese diplomats near the northern city of Tikrit.

The commander of U.S. forces in the Middle East, General John P. Abizaid, estimated that as few as 5,000 guerrillas were attacking coalition forces in Iraq, but they were well organized and financed. According to U.S. intelligence sources, foreign terrorists were infiltrating Iraq from Syria and Iran, but they were playing a less significant role than native Iraqis in the insurgency. A classified Central Intelligence Agency report dated November 10, which was subsequently leaked to the press,

| Country | Population | Government | Monetary unit* | Foreign trade (million U.S.$) | |
				Exports[†]	Imports[†]
Bahrain	673,000	King Hamad bin Isa Al Khalifa; Prime Minister Khalifa bin Salman Al Khalifa	dinar (0.38 = $1)	5,800	4,200
Cyprus	773,000	President Tassos Papadopoulos; (Turkish Republic of Northern Cyprus: President Rauf R. Denktash)	pound (0.51 = $1)	1,490	4,201
Egypt	72,534,000	President Hosni Mubarak; Prime Minister Atef Mohammed Obeid	pound (6.15 = $1)	7,000	15,200
Iran	74,293,000	Supreme Leader Ayatollah Ali Hoseini-Khamenei; President Mohammed Khatami-Ardakani	rial (8,335.00 = $1)	24,800	21,800
Iraq	25,576,000	Interim Governing Council	new dinar (0.31= $1)**	[††]	[††]
Israel	6,543,000	President Moshe Katzav; Prime Minister Ariel Sharon	shekel (4.41 = $1)	28,100	30,800
Jordan	5,506,000	King Abdullah II; Prime Minister Faisal al-Fayez	dinar (0.71 = $1)	2,500	4,400
Kuwait	2,118,000	Amir Jabir al-Ahmad al-Jabir Al Sabah; Prime Minister Sabah al-Ahmad al-Jabir Al Sabah	dinar (0.29 = $1)	16,000	7,300
Lebanon	3,718,000	President Emile Lahoud; Prime Minister Rafiq Hariri	pound (1,511.00 = $1)	1,000	6,000
Oman	2,887,000	Sultan Qaboos bin Said Al Said	rial (0.39 = $1)	10,600	5,500
Qatar	600,000	Amir Hamad bin Khalifa Al Thani; Prime Minister Abdallah bin Khalifa Al Thani	riyal (3.64 = $1)	10,900	3,900
Saudi Arabia	22,998,000	King & Prime Minister Fahd bin Abd al-Aziz Al Saud	riyal (3.75 = $1)	71,000	39,500
Sudan	34,056,000	President Umar Hasan Ahmad al-Bashir	dinar (261.35 = $1) pound (2,610.00 = $1)	1,800	1,500
Syria	17,905,000	President Bashar al-Assad; Prime Minister Muhammad al-Utri	pound (46.00 = $1)	6,200	4,900
Turkey	71,455,000	President Ahmet Necdet Sezer; Prime Minister Recep Tayyip Erdogan	lira (1,388,889.00 = $1)	35,100	50,800
United Arab Emirates	2,790,000	President Zayid bin Sultan Al Nuhayyan; Prime Minister Maktum bin Rashid al-Maktum	dirham (3.67 = $1)	44,900	30,800
Yemen	21,524,000	President Ali Abdallah Salih; Prime Minister Abd al-Qadir Ba Jamal	rial (178.01 = $1)	3,400	2,900

*Exchange rates as of Oct. 3, 2003, or latest available data.
[†]Latest available data.

**New Iraqi dinar was issued on Oct. 15, 2003.
[††]Figure unavailable.

maintained that Iraqis were losing faith in the United States and that the insurgency was gaining strength.

The war on terrorism. The ousting of the Taliban regime in Afghanistan in 2001, which pushed Osama bin Laden, the leader of the al-Qa'ida terrorism network, underground, did not result in the pacification of that country. Incursions of Taliban fighters into Afghanistan from its eastern and southern boundaries with Pakistan continued in 2003. Skirmishes between the Taliban and U.S. forces in Afghanistan left 11 U.S. soldiers dead between August and December.

Al-Qa'ida continued to threaten the United States and other Western powers involved in the war against terrorism. On May 12, terrorists shot their way into three residential compounds in Riyadh, Saudi Arabia, and detonated car bombs that killed 35 people, including 9 Americans. On May 16, the simultaneous explosion of five car bombs outside Spanish, Belgian, and Jewish establishments in Casablanca, Morocco, killed 43 persons. Terrorists killed another 17 people on November 8 when they again struck a housing complex in Riyadh. Four major terrorist operations in Istanbul, Turkey, killed a total of 57 persons in coordinated attacks on two synagogues on November 15 and on the British Consulate and the British Bank HSBC on November 20. The attacks on British facilities in Istanbul coincided with President Bush's state visit to the United Kingdom. Terrorism experts attributed all of the attacks to al-Qa'ida, suggesting that some operations were directed from Iran, where some leading al-Qa'ida figures may have taken refuge.

The stalled peace process. World leaders had little success in reviving the stalled peace process between Israelis and Palestinians in 2003. Experts pointed out various roadblocks, including the hardline Cabinet formed by Ariel Sharon after his reelection as Israeli prime minister on Jan. 26, 2003; and the unwillingness of the militant Palestinian organizations Hamas, Islamic Jihad, and al-Aqsa Brigades to declare a cease-fire to the second *Intifadah* (the renewal of Israeli-Palestinian violence that began in September 2000).

Palestinian leader Yasir Arafat's appointment of Mahmoud Abbas as the Palestinian prime minister on March 19, 2003, offered a glimmer of hope. President Bush tried to revive the peace process by meeting with prime ministers Sharon and Abbas on June 1 in al-Aqabah, Jordan, at a summit hosted by the Jordanian king. Abbas, however, had no power to guarantee a Palestinian cease-fire as Arafat refused to yield control over Palestinian security forces. The chief of staff of the Israeli armed forces, Lieutenant General Moshe Yaalon, accused Sharon of doing nothing substantive to support Abbas, who resigned on September 6. He was replaced by Ahmad Quray. Sharon proved more conciliatory towards Quray whom Sharon had known for years.

Sharon was also criticized in 2003 by four former heads of Shin Bet, Israel's Internal Security Service. They argued that the fence Sharon ordered built as a security barrier against terrorists increased the hostility of the Palestinian people who felt that they were losing land to the barrier. The former Shin Bet leaders also maintained that Sharon's policies increased, rather than prevented, terrorist attacks.

The most interesting peace initiative between Israelis and Palestinians in 2003 was unofficial. On October 12, Yossi Beilin, a prominent member of Israel's Labor Party, and Yasir Abd Rabbuh, a long-time Arafat associate, signed the Geneva Accord, which calls for the establishment in the West Bank and Gaza of a Palestinian nation. The nonbinding accord specifies that the Palestinians have sovereignty over the Temple Mount, or *Haram al-Sharif* (Noble Sanctuary), an area of East Jerusalem that is sacred to both Jews and Muslims. It also specifies that the Palestinians would effectively give up the "right of return" to Israel.   ■ Marius Deeb

See also **Iraq: A Special Report; People in the news** (Paul Wolfowitz); **Terrorism;** various Middle East country articles.

Montreal. One of Canada's biggest murder trials came to an end on Sept. 11, 2003, when 9 of 12 Hells Angels bikers charged with first-degree murder pleaded guilty to lesser counts of conspiracy to commit murder, gangsterism, and drug trafficking. Two weeks later, they were sentenced to between 15 and 20 years imprisonment for their involvement in a drug war that has claimed 164 lives in Montreal since it broke out in 1996.

Museum news. The renovated and expanded Montreal Holocaust Memorial Museum reopened on June 30, 2003. (The Holocaust was the systematic killing during World War II [1939-1945] of millions of Jews, Gypsies, and homosexuals by Germany's Nazi government.) An estimated 8,000 Holocaust survivors lived in Montreal in 2003. The facility has more than 400 Holocaust-related artifacts, most donated by local survivors or their families.

The Montreal Museum of Archaeology and History in 2003 exhibited portions of three Dead Sea Scrolls discovered in 1947 in a cave in what is now Israel. The exhibit, which ran from June 17 to November 2, 2003, coincided with a September conference on Christianity, Judaism, and other Greco-Roman religions in antiquity.

Air Canada. Montreal-based Air Canada, the country's largest airline, filed for bankruptcy on April 1 to buy time for restructuring its $12-billion debt and lease obligations. A last-minute deal reached on June 1 with the Air Canada Pilots Association and its nine unions resulted in annual labor cost savings of $1.1 billion. The company planned to choose an equity investor to provide $700 million as part of its reorganization plan.

Layoffs and Closings. Several Montreal-based companies moved or shut down operations in 2003, affecting hundreds of workers. Avon Canada announced in January that it would transfer its manufacturing unit from Montreal to Illinois and Ohio. About 150 workers were laid off by the end of 2003.

About 120 employees at the research laboratory of Shire Pharmaceuticals PLC of the United Kingdom received layoff notices at the beginning of August. Shire shut down the lab in the Montreal suburb of Laval and ceased its early-stage drug-research projects.

Nearly 600 plant and head office workers at Imperial Tobacco, Canada's leading cigarette maker, lost their jobs on June 18, when the company moved its manufacturing plant from Montreal to Guelph, Ontario.

Sports news. In August, race promoters announced that the Canadian Grand Prix in Montreal would be canceled for the 2004 season because of Ottawa's ban on tobacco advertising, which went into effect in October 2003. Half of the F1 teams have tobacco ads on their cars and uniforms. Federal and provincial governments revealed on November 18 that they will jointly contribute $12 million to keep the race in Montreal until 2006.

Former Montreal Expos catcher Gary Carter on July 27, 2003, became the team's first player inducted into the National Baseball Hall of Fame.

Airport renamed. On September 9, one of Montreal's two international airports (Dorval) was officially rechristened Pierre Elliott Trudeau Airport in honor of Canada's 15th prime minister. The new name went into effect Jan. 1, 2004.

Deaths. Charlie Biddle, the Philadelphia bass player who moved to Quebec in 1948 to escape segregation in the United States and became an icon in Canadian jazz history, died of cancer on Feb. 4, 2003, at age 76. He is credited with helping create the Montreal International Jazz Festival.

Quebec separatist Pierre Bourgault died on June 16 at age 69 from a chronic pulmonary infection. He was a pivotal figure in Quebec's sovereignty movement and devoted his life to fighting for a unilingual French province. Bourgault worked for 40 years in journalism and communications at several Montreal newspapers and magazines. He also was a political commentator and university professor in Montreal. ■ Mike King

See also **Canada; Canadian provinces; City.**

Morocco. See Africa.

Motion pictures. From an artistic perspective, 2003 was another erratic year for filmmakers in the United States. The public seemed tired of hotly hyped sequels and was more willing to embrace literary adaptations. As is often the case, filmgoers had to wait until October, November, and December to see most of the highly anticipated motion pictures of the year.

High praise. One of the most widely praised films of 2003 was Clint Eastwood's adaptation of Dennis Lehane's novel *Mystic River.* It won Eastwood, who directed the film, some of the strongest reviews of his career. The film also earned praise for members of its prestigious cast, including Kevin Bacon, Laurence Fishburne, Marcia Gay Harden, Laura Linney, Sean Penn, and Tim Robbins.

Mystic River is an intense and often moody film that weighs the relativity of guilt and innocence and of actions and consequences. The film tells the story of a case of child abuse that, 25 years later, haunts both the victim and his friends in the wake of a brutal murder. *Mystic River* also became one of the most heavily analyzed films of 2003, with some critics interpreting it as an apology for the vigilante films, such as *Dirty Harry* (1971), that made Eastwood an action hero.

Other literary adaptations that gained attention in 2003 included *The Human Stain,* based on

ACADEMY AWARD WINNERS IN 2003

The following winners of the 2002 Academy Awards were announced in March 2003:

Best Picture, *Chicago*
Best Actor, Adrien Brody, *The Pianist*
Best Actress, Nicole Kidman, *The Hours*
Best Supporting Actor, Chris Cooper, *Adaptation*
Best Supporting Actress, Catherine Zeta-Jones, *Chicago*
Best Director, Roman Polanski, *The Pianist*
Best Original Screenplay, Pedro Almodovar, *Talk to Her*
Best Screenplay Adaptation, Ronald Harwood, *The Pianist*
Best Animated Feature, Hayao Miyazaki, *Spirited Away*
Best Cinematography, Conrad L. Hall, *Road to Perdition*
Best Film Editing, Martin Walsh, *Chicago*
Best Original Score, Elliot Goldenthal, *Frida*
Best Original Song, Eminem, Jeff Bass, and Luis Resto, "Lose Yourself" from *8 Mile*
Best Foreign-Language Film, *Nowhere In Africa* (Germany)
Best Art Direction, John Myhre and Gordon Sim, *Chicago*
Best Costume Design, Colleen Atwood, *Chicago*
Best Sound, Michael Minkler, Dominick Tavella, and David Lee, *Chicago*
Best Sound Editing, Ethan Van der Ryn and Michael Hopkins, *The Lord of the Rings: The Two Towers*
Best Makeup, John Jackson and Beatrice De Alba, *Frida*
Best Visual Effects, *The Lord of the Rings: The Two Towers*
Best Animated Short Film, *The Chubbchubbs!*
Best Live-Action Short Film, *This Charming Man*
Best Feature Documentary, *Bowling for Columbine*
Best Short Subject Documentary, *Twin Towers*

Philip Roth's novel of a disgraced college professor who invented his own identity. Director Robert Benton controversially cast Anthony Hopkins as the light-skinned African American professor and Nicole Kidman as the cleaning woman with whom he has an affair.

Seabiscuit proved to be a sincere version of Laura Hillenbrand's best-selling book. Some fans of Hillenbrand's work claimed that the film oversimplified the story of the champion horse that became a beacon of hope during the Great Depression (a worldwide economic slump of the 1930's).

Director Quentin Tarantino, who became a celebrity with *Pulp Fiction* in 1994, released *Kill Bill: Vol. 1* in 2003, his first film since *Jackie Brown* (1997). A wildly controversial martial-arts celebration, *Kill Bill: Vol. 1* was both praised and attacked for its comic book view of extreme violence. The film was the first of two installments, and some critics and audience members found that it did not stand on its own as a coherent example of filmmaking.

Sofia Coppola, the daughter of legendary motion-picture director Francis Ford Coppola, won rave reviews in 2003 for her gentle romantic film, *Lost in Translation,* which also garnered praise for Bill Murray. Often seen in broad comedies, such as *Ghostbusters* (1984), Murray gave a wry, understated performance as a bored actor who is filming a whiskey commercial in Japan. While overseas, he meets and forms a tender relationship with a young woman who is a fellow insomniac, played by Scarlett Johansson.

Thirteen, a film that examined the life of a 13-year-old girl as she succumbs to peer pressure, won praise for its realistic portrayal of teen-age life. The film starred Evan Rachel Wood and Nikki Reed. Reed cowrote the screenplay, when she was 13, with director Catherine Hardwicke. Reed told reviewers that the film's graphic depiction of drugs, violence, and sexuality was meant to give audiences a glimpse of what many teen-agers face on a daily basis.

Johnny Depp emerged from his long-time cult film status to become a mainstream star in 2003 with his outrageous portrayal of a buccaneer in the box-office hit *Pirates of the Caribbean: The Curse of the Black Pearl.*

The delightful computer-animated motion picture *Finding Nemo* proved to be one of the biggest successes of 2003. The film, which featured the voices of Albert Brooks and Ellen DeGeneres, told of the adventures of a young clownfish who is stolen away from his father. His travels take him from the ocean floor to a dentist's aquarium and back again. In August, the film became the top-grossing animated feature film of all time, surpassing *The Lion King* (1994). The success of *Finding Nemo,* created by Pixar Animation Studios Inc., led some critics to wonder whether filmmakers would soon abandon traditional, hand-drawn animation in favor of computer animation.

Flops. A highly publicized film featuring two of Hollywood's highly publicized stars proved to be the biggest flop of 2003. *Gigli,* an offbeat comedy starring real-life celebrity couple Jennifer Lopez and Ben Affleck, grossed approximately $6 million in the United States. The motion picture cost approximately $54 million to produce, with an advertising budget estimated at $20 million.

Other disappointments in 2003 included such sequels as *Legally Blonde 2: Red, White and Blonde; Charlie's Angels 2: Full Throttle;* and *Lara Croft Tomb Raider: The Cradle of Life.*

The Matrix Reloaded, the eagerly anticipated sequel to *The Matrix* (1999), was one of the few sequels in 2003 that did attract large audiences following its release in May. However, another sequel, *The Matrix Revolutions,* released in November, did not live up to the advertising blitz preceding it. Critics said that *The Matrix Revolutions* was released too soon after the first sequel.

Film receipts for the summer box-office season in the United States, which ran from Memorial Day to Labor Day, totaled $3.8 billion, an increase of almost $200 million from the same period in 2002. However, studio executives noted that with slightly higher ticket prices, the total number of tickets actually sold decreased when compared with the summer of 2002. In fact, researchers said that summer attendance decreased about 2 percent in 2003 from the same period in 2002.

Year-end surprises. A number of films were released at the end of 2003 that promised to yield both strong reviews and popular acclaim. *The Last Samurai* featured Tom Cruise as a disillusioned U.S. Civil War (1861-1865) veteran who travels to Japan to train the Japanese army in methods of modern warfare. While staying in Japan, his character becomes fascinated with the samurai way of life. *Something's Gotta Give* starred Jack Nicholson as an aging ladies' man who surprises himself by falling in love with his girlfriend's mother, played by Diane Keaton. Julia Roberts portrayed a progressive teacher at a conservative woman's college during the 1950's in *Mona Lisa Smile.*

Three films released in late 2003 were based on highly acclaimed novels. The Civil War epic *Cold Mountain,* based on the novel by Charles Frazier, starred Jude Law as a wounded soldier struggling to return to his North Carolina home to be reunited with his girlfriend, played by Nicole Kidman. The film, directed by Anthony Minghella, also starred Renee Zellweger.

Director Peter Weir won high praise from audiences and critics for his version of Patrick O'Brian's historical novel *Master and Commander: The Far Side of the World.* The film starred Russell Crowe as a British naval captain whose vessel stalks a much larger French warship during the Napoleonic Wars of the early 1800's. The movie, however, did not produce the box office revenue that its producers had predicted.

Andre Dubus III's novel, *House of Sand and Fog,* received what many critics considered an excellent film treatment. Jennifer Connelly and Ben Kingsley portrayed tragic competitors for a home that represents their American Dream.

Fans of J. R. R. Tolkien eagerly awaited the December 2003 release of *The Lord of the Rings: The Return of the King,* the final installment of Tolkien's trilogy. The film's cast included Sean Astin, Cate Blanchett, Sir Ian McKellen, Viggo Mortensen, and Elijah Wood. Many fans thought that producer Peter Jackson's adaptation of *The Return of the King* was the best of his film trilogy.

Among the best feature-length documentaries was *Capturing the Friedmans,* a strong but disturbing film tracing what takes place within a respected family in Long Island, New York, when accusations of child molestation surface.

Catherine Zeta-Jones (right) won the Academy Award for best supporting actress for her role in *Chicago* in 2003. The film, based on a Broadway musical, also won the Oscar for best picture.

Nicole Kidman (left) and Stephen Dillane star in *The Hours,* a psychological drama about three women in three eras whose lives are intertwined by the Virginia Woolf novel *Mrs. Dalloway.* Kidman received the Academy Award for best actress for her portrayal of Woolf.

Several dramas about characters struggling to survive dominated the Academy Awards in 2003.

Adrien Brody portrays the Polish pianist Wladyslaw Szpilman in *The Pianist,* for which he won the Oscar for best actor. Roman Polanski won the Academy Award for best director for the film, the true story of a Polish Jew who escapes deportation and eludes capture by the Germans by living in the ruins of Warsaw during World War II (1939-1945).

Cannes. *Dogville,* by writer and director Lars von Trier, was the controversial winner of the 2003 Cannes International Film Festival's Golden Palm Award. The festival, one of the oldest and most prestigious film festivals in the world, is an annual motion-picture exhibition and competition held in the resort city of Cannes, on the French Riviera.

Set in the 1930's, *Dogville* featured Nicole Kidman as a woman escaping from gangsters. The citizens of a small town in the Rocky Mountains offer her shelter and then horribly abuse her. Some critics saw *Dogville* as a strongly anti-American film, a metaphor for U.S. relations with third-world nations.

On the international scene, Chinese director Zhang Yimou enjoyed one of his most personal successes in 2003 with *Hero,* the story of a man who slays the most feared enemies of the emperor. *Hero* was the most expensive film ever made in China.

In Hong Kong, directors Johnny To and Ka-Fai Wai found success with the romantic comedy *Turn Left, Turn Right.* Derived from Jimmy Liao's novel of romance among lonely apartment dwellers, the film proved to be such a success that other directors in Hong Kong looked to novels for their next motion pictures.

Egyptian moviegoers turned to a number of highly successful comedies in 2003, including the slapstick capers *Thieves in Thailand* and *Mido Problems,* as well as the romantic farce *How to Let Girls Fall in Love With You.* Egyptian films customarily represent a small percentage of worldwide grosses, but these entries also did well in other Arab countries, such as Lebanon and the United Arab Emirates.

Dramatic films also proved to be popular in Egypt. The controversial adult drama *Sleepless Nights* drew viewers despite its mature themes and graphic sexual scenes. The film was considered an intense study of relationships and marital life.

In France, the freewheeling *La Beuze* and the sophisticated *Chouchou* received positive reviews and drew large numbers of audiences to theaters.

In Brazil, Hector Babenco's stark prison drama *Carandiru* was one of the best-received films of 2003. Critics applauded the true-life tale of a physician's experiences inside a penitentiary in Sao Paulo, Brazil.

Korea was the site of a politically auspicious opening that turned into a fast flop. *Arirang* opened in both North Korea and South Korea in May. It marked the first time that a film made in either country opened simultaneously in both. *Arirang* was a remake of a 1926 Korean film about a student who kills a rural landowner for attempting to rape his sister. Critics viewed the original film as a criticism of Japan's control over Korea in the early 1900's. Despite the publicity, the 2003 remake of *Arirang* was a box-office disappointment.

■ Philip Wuntch

See also **Literature, World: A Special Report; People in the news** (Adrien Brody, Nicole Kidman).

Mozambique. See Africa.

Music. See Classical music; Popular music.

Katharine Hepburn:

An Independent Woman

By Philip Wuntch

The death of Katharine Hepburn on June 29, 2003, brought an end to a 60-year screen reign that left an indelible impression on the public's consciousness.

No other motion-picture star stayed in the public's eye for such a long period of time. Her public image ran the gamut from haughty individualist to good-sport comedienne, and from staunch feminist to no-nonsense geriatric. The public virtually always viewed her with affection.

Katharine Houghton Hepburn was born on May 12, 1907, in Hartford, Connecticut. Her mother, Katharine Houghton, crusaded for women's rights. Her father, Thomas Norval Hepburn, was a surgeon and a pioneer in the fight against sexually transmitted disease. They taught their children to form strong personal opinions, a habit Hepburn retained throughout her life.

Hepburn made her Broadway stage debut in 1928 and first won notice for her role in the 1932 play *The Warrior's Husband.* From the start, she earned a reputation

for being outspoken and argumentative. She made her film debut as John Barrymore's compassionate daughter in *A Bill of Divorcement* (1932). Being a newcomer to motion pictures, she was billed among the supporting players, but hers was actually a starring role. Unlike most actresses, Hepburn never had to work her way through the ranks of small parts.

Hepburn quickly rose to stardom following her first role, but neither filmmakers nor movie audiences knew what to make of her. In the 1930's, movie stars were pigeonholed into types. Hepburn was not exotic along the lines of Greta Garbo and Marlene Dietrich. Nor was she sensual and dynamic like Jean Harlow and Joan Crawford. Always an individualist, Hepburn defied being slotted into a category in both her professional and personal life.

In 1928, Hepburn married Ludlow Ogden Smith, a member of a wealthy Pennsylvania family. She later convinced him to change his name to S. Ogden Ludlow because she refused to be known as "the second Kate Smith," referring to the popular singer of that era. But she was more interested in her career than in domesticity. The couple remained on friendly terms, however, even after their divorce in 1934.

Hepburn's other romantic attachments of that era included directors John Ford and George Stevens, agent Leland Hayward, and businessman, aviator, and motion-picture producer Howard Hughes. Even during such high-profile relationships, she shunned the publicity spotlight and refused to cooperate with Hollywood columnists who thrived in the tabloid journalism of the era.

Hepburn stars with (left to right) Cary Grant, Mary Nash, John Halliday, James Stewart, and Ruth Hussey in *The Philadelphia Story*. The 1940 motion picture reestablished her popularity as a film actress, which never again waned.

Spencer Tracy and Katharine Hepburn star in *Woman of the Year* (1942), the first of nine films they made together. A chemistry between the two actors, apparent in the film, changed the direction of both their professional and private lives.

The author:
Philip Wuntch is the film critic for *The Dallas Morning News.*

Hepburn continued to find success in her early motion-picture career with such films as *Little Women* (1933), which proved to be one of the most popular movies of the 1930's. However, many of her later films of the 1930's were box-office disappointments, including *Bringing Up Baby* (1938), in which she starred with Cary Grant. Although the motion picture was later considered a classic, it was a box-office flop following its release. In 1938, her name was among those whom film exhibitors labeled "box-office poison."

Reinventing herself

The label forced Hepburn to retreat from Hollywood and take inventory of her career. She decided to take charge of her career in a way that few other actresses of the era ever attempted. Her friend dramatist Philip Barry crafted the character of a judgmental socialite, Tracy Lord, in the 1939 play *The Philadelphia Story* specifically for Hepburn. The romantic comedy was a smash hit on the Broadway stage, and Hollywood studios were anxious to purchase the screen rights to the production.

Always an astute businesswoman, Hepburn had optioned the screen rights for the play herself. She eventually sold the rights to Hollywood film studio Metro-Goldwyn-Mayer with the provision that she would star in the film. The 1940 motion picture version of *The Philadelphia Story* restored her popularity.

Hepburn's next film, *Woman of the Year* (1942), provided one of the most important moments of her long life—meeting Spencer Tracy, who became an integral part of her personal and professional life. *Woman of the Year* co-starred Tracy, an actor whom she had long admired but never met. Their onscreen chemistry was obvious to moviegoers, and their off-screen chemistry became equally apparent to their friends. Tracy, however, was married and refused to seek a divorce. Even so, the couple began a 25-year relationship that was known within the industry but rarely written about until after Tracy's death in 1967 and the release of their ninth and final film together, *Guess Who's Coming to Dinner?* (1967). The relationship remains a somewhat contradictory part of the actress's life. Always professionally ambitious, she remained offscreen from 1962 to 1967, caring for Tracy, who was in ill health.

Much of Hepburn's life seemed a harbinger of the sexual and cultural revolutions of the 1960's. Her outspokenness on political and social issues, her penchant for playing strong, intelligent, and independent women, and her habit of wearing slacks in public planted seeds of feminism among American women. She often said that she was a woman who never needed marriage to consider her life complete.

Hepburn was also outspoken in her political beliefs. She strongly and vocally opposed *McCarthyism* (the widespread accusations and investigations of suspected Communist activities in the United States during the 1950's), which led some studios to *blacklist* (refuse to hire) people suspected of having Communist ties. Her support of Henry Wallace, Progressive Party presidential nominee in 1948, led some to question her political beliefs and made her a target of the United States House of Representatives Un-American Activities Committee. Members of the committee, which investigated the threat of subversion, questioned her politics. Rather than be silenced, Hepburn counterattacked, calling the innuendos a "smear campaign."

Unlike such contemporaries as Bette Davis, Joan Crawford, Tallulah Bankhead, and Barbara Stanwyck, Hepburn always held herself and her reputation in high regard. She never appeared in horror films to sustain her movie-star profile or took a role she considered to be beneath her. In her later years, many fans admired her ability to age both gracefully and energetically.

Hepburn's final motion picture was in a minor but emotional role in *Love Affair* (1994), in which she offered sage advice to a woman portrayed by Annette Bening. That same year she appeared in the made-for-television movie *One Christmas*. In her role as a wise old aunt, Hepburn's character said, "I've always lived my life exactly as I wanted. I wouldn't change a single thing. No regrets." The line perfectly fit Katharine Hepburn's view of her own life as well.

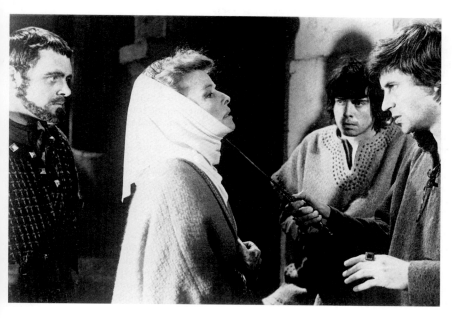

Anthony Hopkins (far left) appears with Hepburn, Nigel Terry, and John Castle in a scene from *The Lion in Winter* (1968), for which Hepburn received an Academy Award for her portrayal of Eleanor of Aquitaine. It was one of four Academy Awards for best actress that Hepburn captured in her career.

Myanmar. General Khin Nyunt, the head of military intelligence, became prime minister of Myanmar in August 2003. He succeeded General Than Shwe, who remained chairman of the ruling military junta and the military's commander-in-chief. Lieutenant General Soe Win, a hard-line protege of Than Shwe, replaced Khin Nyunt in the powerful position of junta first secretary.

Reform plans. Political observers considered Khin Nyunt to be among the more moderate members of the junta. Observers agreed, however, that he would fail to carry out a seven-stage plan designed to help the country make the transition from military rule to democracy. The first stage of the so-called "road map to democracy" included the writing of a new constitution that would guarantee free and fair elections. In September, the junta appointed a committee to draft a constitution but invited no representatives of the National League for Democracy (NLD), the leading opposition party, to take part.

The junta first announced plans to rewrite the constitution in 1990, after the NLD won a landslide victory in parliamentary elections. The junta announced it would not allow a transfer of power to the NLD until a new constitution was written and approved. In 1996, NLD delegates walked out of a constitutional convention, claiming that the military wanted too much power. They also protested the treatment of their leader, Aung San Suu Kyi, and of many other NLD members who had been arrested by the junta.

Aung San Suu Kyi was first placed under house arrest in 1989. She was released in 1995 but was arrested again in 2000. In 2002, the junta released her and said they would allow her to pursue political activities. In May 2003, Aung San Suu Kyi and her supporters were attacked by a gang wielding rocks and nail-studded clubs. Between 70 and 100 people were killed in the attack. Announcing that Aung San Suu Kyi would be put into protective custody, the military again imprisoned her for a period of several months.

International response. The United States demanded that the junta release Aung San Suu Kyi and imposed tough sanctions on the impoverished country. Some members of the Association of Southeast Asian Nations suggested that Myanmar be expelled for human rights violations. In response, Than Shwe said that Aung San Suu Kyi, who won the 1991 Nobel Peace Prize for her nonviolent struggle for democracy, was encouraging people to stage violent uprisings against the government. In July 2003, military officials arrested 12 people on charges they were plotting to assassinate junta leaders. ■ Henry S. Bradsher

See also **Asia; Human rights.**

Namibia. See **Africa.**

Nebraska. See **State government.**

Netherlands. Prime Minister Jan Peter Balkenende's Christian Democratic Party won re-election in 2003 and sought to end a year of political and economic instability. Balkenende's previous government, elected in 2002, fell apart after a few months because of infighting within the List Pim Fortuyn, a new party whose leader, Pim Fortuyn, was murdered days before that election. The Christian Democrats won 44 parliamentary seats in the Jan. 22, 2003, election, slightly ahead of the Labour Party, which won 42 seats.

New government. Balkenende first sought to form a government with Labour, but differences proved too great. Balkenende supported the United States-led war in Iraq, while Labour opposed it. The parties also disagreed about the need for cuts in government spending to reduce the budget deficit. After four months of negotiations, Balkenende formed a center-right coalition with the Liberal Party and the centrist Democracy 66 and took office on May 27. The coalition controlled 78 seats in the 150-seat parliament.

The Dutch economy, which boomed during the 1990's, suffered its worst recession in 20 years in 2003. High wage increases at the start of the 1990's hurt the country's competitiveness, while weakness in Germany and France depressed exports. The European Commission, the executive agency of the European Union, forecast that the Netherlands' economic output would decline by 0.9 percent in 2003. Unemployment rose to 4.4 percent from 2.7 percent in 2002. The recession caused the budget deficit to grow significantly and forced Balkenende's government to cut spending. The government agreed to limit pay increases for civil service workers and to cut costs of the state-run health care system by requiring individuals to pay a greater share of the costs of treatment.

Airline merger. KLM Royal Dutch Airlines agreed in September 2003 to be acquired by Air France in a $900-million deal that would create Europe's biggest airline. The merger was the first between major European airlines and was intended to help both companies face competitive pressures in the industry.

Pim Fortuyn killer Volkert van der Graaf was sentenced to 18 years in prison in April, despite demands by Fortuyn supporters for the maximum life sentence. Van der Graaf said he killed Fortuyn because of his anti-immigrant views.

■ Tom Buerkle

See also **Aviation; Europe.**

Nevada. See **State government.**

New Brunswick. See **Canadian provinces.**

New Hampshire. See **State government.**

New Jersey. See **State government.**

New Mexico. See **State government.**

New York. See **State government.**

Throngs of New Yorkers cross the Brooklyn Bridge on August 14, as the worst power outage in the history of North America paralyzes the city. Human error and computer failure at an Ohio utility company caused the outage, which cut power to 50 million people in an area that stretched from Toronto south to New York City and as far west as Detroit.

New York City. The worst blackout ever to strike North America paralyzed New York City, the northeastern United States, and southern Ontario, Canada, on August 14 and 15, 2003. The power outage affected some 50 million people and cost New York City an estimated $700 million to $1 billion in economic activity.

The 24-hour blackout brought the city to a halt. ATM machines, air conditioners, refrigerators, elevators, street lights, and cell phones (because transmission towers were rendered useless) all lost power. Airports closed down, stranding thousands of travelers. Buses ran for free, but subways did not run at all. Tens of thousands of passengers were evacuated from aboard trains that had been forced to a stop in tunnels.

In November, U.S. and Canadian energy officials released a report of their investigation into the cause of the blackout. According to the report, a series of computer malfunctions, compounded by the inaction of inadequately trained control room workers at an Ohio utility company, contributed to the power outage.

Ferry disaster. Ten passengers died and dozens of others were injured on October 15, when a Staten Island ferry crashed at almost full speed into a concrete pier. The ferry, called the *Andrew J. Barberi,* was one of several that carry 65,000 commuters and visitors a day between Staten Island and Lower Manhattan. The ferries' 5.2-mile (8.4-kilometer) trip has long been regarded as the city's safest form of mass transit.

The pilot of the *Barberi,* who claimed he had blacked out as the boat made its approach, fled the scene and attempted suicide. The ferry, with a capacity of 6,000 passengers, was carrying about 1,500 people when the accident occurred.

Councilman murdered. New Yorkers were stunned on July 23 when City Councilman James Davis, a Brooklyn Democrat and former police officer who preached against violence, was gunned down in City Hall by a former political foe, Othniel Askew. A City Hall security guard then shot and killed Askew. On July 28, Davis became the first elected official in 85 years to lie in state in the majestic rotunda of City Hall as more than 7,000 mourners filed past.

Askew had been able to bring a concealed handgun into the chambers because, as Davis's guest, he was exempt from screening by a metal detector. After the lawmaker's death, Mayor Michael R. Bloomberg and Council leaders agreed that all people—including legislators and their guests—would be required to submit to security checks. The shooting was the first assassination attempt of a city official since Mayor William Gaynor was wounded in 1910 by a city worker.

New York Stock Exchange. Richard Grasso, the chairman of the New York Stock Exchange, was forced to resign Sept. 18, 2003. The heads of the nation's two biggest public employee retirement systems, along with a number of state treasurers and stock exchange members, had demanded his resignation after learning of Grasso's $140-million salary and pension package.

The compensation of Grasso, who began working at the exchange in 1968 as a clerk, became an issue when even supporters agreed his high pay and benefits sent the wrong message at a time of corporate scandals and loss of investor confidence. He was replaced by former Citicorp chairman John Reed, who promised to end the Stock Exchange's secrecy and vowed more regulation for the world's largest market.

Hispanic communities. Demographers in October 2003 predicted that Dominicans would become New York City's largest Hispanic ethnic group by 2010. Census figures showed that the Dominican population reached 554,638 in 2000, while the city's once-dominant Puerto Rican population fell 13 percent to 789,172.

Governors Island in Upper New York Bay was turned over to the city and state of New York on Jan. 31, 2003, after 203 years of use as a U.S. Army and Coast Guard base. Part of the island, which guarded the city's harbor during the 1800's, was to become a national monument, while the remainder was to be used as a state park and for other educational and public purposes. ■ Owen Moritz

See also **Canada; City; Toronto.**

New Zealand. On Oct. 14, 2003, New Zealand's Parliament voted to abolish the right of legal appeal to the Privy Council in London, breaking one of New Zealand's last ties to its colonial past. Appointed by the king or queen of the United Kingdom (U.K.), the Privy Council traditionally served as a court of appeal for British colonies and dominions. The parliamentary vote was part of a legal reform package establishing a new supreme court in New Zealand that would begin hearing cases in July 2004.

Members of New Zealand's 120-seat House of Representatives engaged in heated debate over the reforms. Some opposition members called for the reform proposals to be put to voters in a referendum. In the end, the Labour-led government of Prime Minister Helen Clark passed the reforms by a six-vote margin.

Economy. New Zealand experienced solid economic growth in 2003. The *gross domestic product* (the value of all goods and services produced in a country in a given year) grew by 2.6 percent, according to economists, who forecast 2.8-percent growth for 2004. Unemployment, at 4.4 percent, reached a 16-year low in 2003.

However, the strength of the New Zealand dollar, which in 2003 reached a six-year high against the U.S. dollar, began to suppress export income. When a nation's currency becomes too highly valued, its exported goods sold in foreign currency—such as U.S. dollars—return a lower amount in local currency. In September, New Zealand posted a $721-million (New Zealand dollars) *trade deficit* (unfavorable balance between imports and exports)—the worst on record.

Foreign relations. New Zealand did not take part in the U.S.-led war in Iraq in March but later sent a team of army engineers to participate in reconstruction projects in Iraq. In May, Prime Minister Clark criticized U.S. President George W. Bush's Iraq policy, voicing her view that the United States would not have gone to war in Iraq if Al Gore, Bush's opponent in 2000, had been elected president.

Although Clark publicly apologized to President Bush, opposition members in New Zealand's Parliament accused her of jeopardizing the nation's chances of getting a free trade agreement (FTA) with the United States. The FTA remained on hold through 2003.

Politics. National Party politicians in October chose Don Brash as the new party leader, replacing Bill English, who in July 2002 had led the National Party to its worst-ever electoral defeat. The National Party is the largest opposition party in New Zealand. ■ Gavin Ellis

See also **Iraq: A Special Report; Pacific Islands.**

Newfoundland. See **Canadian provinces.**

NEWS BYTES

Selected news from 2003:

Bill of Rights reclaimed. Agents with the Federal Bureau of Investigation (FBI) recovered a rare copy of the Bill of Rights in 2003 after two antique dealers tried to sell the document to a museum. A Union soldier had stolen the copy from the North Carolina Statehouse during the Civil War (1861-1865). The document was one of at least 14 commissioned by President George Washington in the late 1700's.

The soldier who took the document reportedly sold it to an Indiana businessman. The man's descendants sold it to the antique dealers, who had it authenticated as North Carolina's missing copy. FBI agents, posing as potential customers, seized the document in March 2003. The U.S. Attorney's Office in Raleigh, North Carolina, sued the owners of the document, the antique dealers, claiming that it was stolen property and should be returned to the state. In September, one of the dealers withdrew his claim. The state later dropped its lawsuit and took possession.

Watergate papers. Officials at the University of Texas at Austin announced in April 2003 that the university had purchased the Watergate documents of Carl Bernstein and Bob Woodward, two newspaper reporters. Woodward and Bernstein investigated the infamous Watergate political scandal of the 1970's that led to President Richard M. Nixon's resignation in 1974.

University of Texas officials said that the school had paid $5 million for the records, which filled about 75 file boxes and included carbon drafts of newspaper articles, book manuscripts, more than 250 spiral notepads and loose notes, typed office memos, correspondence, clippings, several audio cassette tapes, and photographs. The material was slated to be kept at the university's Harry Ransom Humanities Research Center and made available for study in 2004.

Cypress Gardens, Florida's oldest theme park, closed on April 13, 2003. Cypress Gardens, which opened in Winter Haven, Florida, in 1936, featured elaborate gardens punctuated with young women in *antebellum* (pre-Civil War) costumes. The park also featured water-skiing, canal rides, education shows, children's rides, and games. The once-famous theme park had served as the backdrop for several films starring Esther Williams, including *On an Island with You* (1948) and *Easy to Love* (1953), and the Betty Grable movie *Moon Over Miami* (1941).

In 1963, Cypress Gardens boasted an attendance of 1.5 million visitors, but competition

Members of the Cypress Gardens ski show demonstrate a pyramid on skis during the historic theme park's last day of operation. Years of dwindling attendance forced Florida's oldest theme park to close on April 13, 2003.

A "flash mob" of nearly 100 people bang their shoes on a city street in Sao Paulo, Brazil, in April. The scene was part of the Mob Project, a worldwide phenomenon involving thousands of people that developed in 2003. Participants, who signed on on Internet sites, followed anonymous instructions, given via e-mail or cellular phone text-messaging systems, to gather in public places to perform harmless, if eccentric, acts.

from other entertainment venues, such as Walt Disney World, which opened in nearby Orlando, Florida, in 1971, slowly began to draw crowds away from the old park. Cypress Gardens officials noted that the park never recovered from the sharp drop in tourism that followed the terrorism attack on the United States in 2001.

In September 2003, officials at the Trust for Public Land (TPL), a national nonprofit land conservation organization, announced that it would purchase Cypress Gardens with the goal of long-term protection of the historic attraction. TPL agreed to pay $22 million for 142 acres (57 hectares) of the original 176-acre (71-hectare) site. The land included botanical gardens, a water ski arena, a butterfly conservatory, and other historic structures. TPL officials planned to sell a portion of the property to the state of Florida and the remainder of the site to another owner.

Polar history. In 2003, Pen Hadow of the United Kingdom became the first person to walk unassisted from Canada to the geographic North Pole. Hadow began his trek on March 17 from the northern coast of Canada. He walked alone for 478 miles (769 kilometers), hauling a 330-pound (148-kilogram) supply sled over constantly moving, cracking, sea ice. He arrived at the North Pole on May 19. Hadow reported that he saw nothing during his two-month trek except for polar bear prints in the ice and a small bird.

Feud over. One of the most infamous family feuds in U.S. history officially ended in June 2003, some 100 years after it had begun. More than 60 descendants of the Hatfield and McCoy families gathered in Pikeville, Kentucky, and signed a truce marking an official end to the bloody conflict. At least 20 people died in the battles between the Hatfields of West Virginia and the McCoys of Kentucky. The feud began in the 1860's and remained active for some 30 years. United States historians believe that the original dispute centered on a pig and escalated during a court battle over timber rights in the 1870's. The conflict

The Old Man of the Mountain, a natural rock formation in New Hampshire, is shown in photographs before (right) and after (far right) erosion caused it to crumble in May 2003. The formation, which resembled the profile of a man, had been one of New Hampshire's best-known and most-visited sites.

became a part of U.S. folk history as well as the subject of many local stories and songs. Family members said that the truce was a symbolic message of peace at a time when national security is at risk.

No more e-mail. The French Culture Ministry announced in July 2003 that the use of the term "e-mail" was banned in all government documents, publications, or Web sites. French officials said that the only acceptable term would be "courriel," a fusion of the French words "courrier electronique" (electronic mail). The move was part of an effort by French officials to rid the French language of English-inspired terms and phrases.

Enola Gay. An exhibit featuring a reassembled *Enola Gay*, the B-29 from which the first atomic bomb was dropped on the Japanese city of Hiroshima during World War II (1939-1945), was unveiled in December 2003 at the National Air and Space Museum's Steven F. Udvar-Hazy Center in Chantilly, Virginia. Restoration work

The *Enola Gay,* a B-29 used to drop the atomic bomb on Hiroshima, Japan, on Aug. 6, 1945, is displayed at the Steven F. Udvar-Hazy Center in Virginia. The aircraft was part of an exhibit of vintage war planes that opened to the public in December 2003.

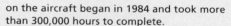

on the aircraft began in 1984 and took more than 300,000 hours to complete.

The *Enola Gay,* which has a wingspan of 141 feet (43 meters) and weighs approximately 137,500 pounds (62,370 kilograms), was too large and heavy to be housed intact in the National Air and Space Museum's main building in Washington, D.C. Museum officials opted to place it on display at the Udvar-Hazy Center.

The *Enola Gay* exhibit drew sharp criticism before it opened from a group of scholars, writers, and antiwar activists. More than 100 people signed a petition in October 2003 arguing that the exhibit, as planned, described the aircraft as "the largest and most technologically advanced airplane for its time," but failed to mention its role in delivering the first atomic bomb on Aug. 6, 1945. When the museum formally opened in December 2003, visitors were informed that the *Enola Gay* was the plane from which the first atomic bomb had been dropped, but the consequences of the bombing were not provided, as critics had asked.

Recapturing the past. Three pieces of historic and popular culture memorabilia were sold to private collectors in 2003.

A navigational notebook carried to the surface of the moon during the first lunar landing on July 20, 1969, sold for $222,500 in April 2003. The notebook was autographed by astronaut Buzz Aldrin, the second person to set foot on the moon. A Pennsylvania autograph dealer purchased the flight document, which had been kept by Aldrin. The notebook contained smudges of moon dust.

In June 2003, Todd McFarlane, a comic book illustrator and writer who created the *Spawn* comic book, paid $450,000 for the baseball that Barry Bonds of the San Francisco Giants hit for his 73rd home run—the most in a season—in 2000. McFarlane had paid $3.2 million for St. Louis Cardinals' Mark McGwire's 70th home-run ball from the 1998 season. Two men had claimed ownership of the Bonds baseball, which was hit into the stands at Pac Bell Park in San Francisco. In 2002, a judge determined that the men would split the proceeds of a sale. Sports memorabilia experts said that the delay in offering the ball for sale resulted in a lower-than-expected sale price.

A one-of-a-kind prototype of the G. I. Joe action figure, which was made in 1963, sold to a private collector for $200,000 in August 2003. The handmade figure, which measured 11.5 inches (29 centimeters) tall, had failed to meet a minimum bid of $250,000 at an auction in July.
■ Tim Frystak

A collector paid $200,000 for a G.I. Joe figure made in 1963. Experts claimed the toy revolutionized the toy industry in the United States when it was introduced to the public in the late 1960's.

Newspaper. Editors at *The New York Times* revealed in May 2003 that the newspaper had published articles containing material that a reporter had falsified, *plagiarized* (presented another person's work as his own) from other news organizations, or written while he was far from the events he had claimed to be covering. *New York Times* officials said that an investigation of the reporter, Jayson Blair, found 36 errors in 73 articles written between October 2002 and April 2003. Blair left *The New York Times* on May 1.

In the wake of the scandal, *The Times* Executive Editor Howell Raines and Managing Editor Gerald Boyd resigned on June 5. They had been criticized for the way they had handled complaints about Blair's reporting. Bill Keller, a columnist and former managing editor at the newspaper, was named executive editor on July 14.

On May 23, *The Times* suspended another reporter, Rick Bragg, for two weeks because of a 2002 story that was published under his name but had been largely reported by a free-lance journalist. Bragg, who won the 1996 Pulitzer Prize for feature writing while at the newspaper, resigned on May 28, 2003.

Ownership rules. The Federal Communications Commission (FCC), the agency charged with regulating communication through radio, wire, and cable, voted 3 to 2 on June 2 to change several media-ownership rules. One change involved an FCC rule that prevented a company from owning both a daily newspaper and a radio or television station in the same market. The change allowed newspaper and broadcast corporations to expand into new markets and extend their operations where they already had a presence. Before the new rules took effect, the United States Court of Appeals for the Third Circuit Court of Appeals in Philadelphia issued an order on September 3 temporarily blocking all new FCC ownership rules.

Circulation figures released in May by the Audit Bureau of Circulations (ABC), an industry trade group in Schaumburg, Illinois, revealed that most major newspapers essentially maintained weekday circulation. Some newspaper owners reported minor declines in readership. The average daily circulation for 814 newspapers reporting to the ABC fell 0.1 percent to 49.9 million for the six-month period ending in March 2003, compared with the same period in 2002. Sunday circulation through March 2003 fell 0.1 percent to 54.3 million copies.

The ABC reported that among large newspaper chains, daily circulation increased 1.7 percent at *USA Today*; declined 5.3 percent at *The New York Times;* and declined 10.2 percent at *The Boston Globe.*   ■ Mark Fitzgerald

See also **Radio; Telecommunications; United States, Government of the.**

Nicaragua. In July and August 2003, over 5,000 peasant families participated in the "March of the Hungry," a 75-mile (121-kilometer) protest that originated in the coffee-growing region of Matagalpa. The protesters, bent on marching to Managua, the capital, demanded land and government aid for workers hard hit by the global drop in coffee prices. After a week of negotiations, the administration agreed to distribute land to 2,500 peasant farmers, who are to pay for the land over a period of 30 years. The authorities also announced school lunch programs and temporary jobs for 4,000 rural workers.

Destroying missiles. United States Secretary of State Colin Powell traveled to Nicaragua in November to study advances made in the Central American disarmament initiative proposed in October by Nicaraguan President Enrique Bolanos Geyer. Nicaragua agreed to destroy 2,000 surface-to-air missiles that its government bought in the 1980's to use against rebels.

Former president jailed. Former President Arnoldo Aleman Lacayo was jailed in Managua in August 2003 on charges of fraud and money laundering. Prosecutors asked a judge in Miami to freeze and confiscate Aleman's bank accounts in the United States. ■ Nathan A. Haverstock

See also **Latin America.**

Niger. See Africa.

Nigeria. President Olusegun Obasanjo of Nigeria was sworn in for a second four-year term on May 29, 2003, after being reelected in April. Obasanjo's party, the People's Democratic Party (PDP), also swept parliamentary and state elections in April and May. Obasanjo first won election to the presidency in 1999, ending 15 years of military dictatorship.

Elections. In parliamentary elections on April 12, 2003, Obasanjo's PDP won large majorities in both houses of Nigeria's federal parliament. About 80 percent of those elected were newcomers, prompting some critics to charge that Obasanjo had pressured veteran legislators not to run in order to tighten his control over parliament.

In the presidential election, held on April 19, Obasanjo outpolled his nearest rival, General Muhammadu Buhari of the All Nigeria People's Party (ANPP), by 62 percent to Buhari's 32 percent. Opposition leaders condemned the election as fraudulent, and international monitors logged numerous irregularities. However, the Commonwealth Observer Group, election monitors sponsored by the Commonwealth of Nations, an association of countries that have lived under British law and government, declared that the April elections marked an "important step in the consolidation of democracy" in Nigeria, and international leaders largely accepted the results.

Delta disturbances. On May 2, striking workers released 100 westerners and a larger number of Nigerians from oil rigs off Nigeria's Niger Delta after holding them hostage for 13 days. The crisis ended after labor unions struck a deal with the company operating the rigs, Houston-based Transocean, Inc. The strike was one in a series of setbacks to Nigeria's oil industry. In March, ethnic conflict between the Ijaw and Itsekiri communities in the Delta resulted in a 40-percent reduction of daily oil output.

Pipeline carnage. At least 125 villagers scavenging gasoline gushing from a vandalized pipeline in southeastern Nigeria died on June 19, when the fuel exploded. Area residents alleged that officials of the Nigerian National Petroleum Corporation, the owner of the pipeline, had known about the pipeline break but did nothing to repair it.

Riots. At least 12 protesters died in Abuja, the capital, and in Nigeria's largest city, Lagos, in July riots associated with a general strike. Labor unions had called the strike to protest a government hike of fuel prices. The disturbances, which preceded the arrival of U.S. President George W. Bush in Abuja on July 12, prompted Nigerian officials to tighten security in the capital.

■ Simon Baynham

See also **Africa; Energy supply.**

Nobel prizes in literature, peace, the sciences, and economics were awarded in October 2003 by the Norwegian Storting (parliament) in Oslo and by the Royal Swedish Academy of Sciences, the Karolinska Institute, and the Swedish Academy of Literature in Stockholm. Each prize was worth about $1.3 million.

The 2003 Nobel Prize for literature went to South African novelist J. M. Coetzee. Writing in spare, brutally honest prose, Coetzee often uses the South African system of *apartheid* (segregation) to symbolize the injustices and moral dilemmas individuals face in their personal lives. The Nobel Committee praised Coetzee, who immigrated to Australia in 2002, for his "well-crafted composition, pregnant dialogue, and analytical brilliance." Coetzee's best-known novels include *The Life and Times of Michael K* (1983) and *Disgrace* (1999), both of which won the Booker Prize, the United Kingdom's highest literary award. His other works include *Dusklands* (1974), *Waiting for the Barbarians* (1980), and *Elizabeth Costello* (2003).

The 2003 Nobel Peace Prize was awarded to Shirin Ebadi, an Iranian lawyer, writer, and human rights activist. Ebadi, the first Muslim woman to win the peace prize, was honored for her efforts to advance the rights of women and children and to promote democracy.

One of Iran's first female judges, Ebadi was forced from the court after Islamic revolutionaries, who took control of the government in 1979, severely restricted women's rights. Her efforts to defend prodemocracy activists have led to her own imprisonment on several occasions. Ebadi, however, has argued against any contradiction between Islam and human rights.

The 2003 Nobel Prize for physiology or medicine went to physical chemist Paul C. Lauterbur of the University of Illinois at Urbana-Champaign and British physicist Sir Peter Mansfield of the University of Nottingham in the United Kingdom. The scientists were honored for discoveries leading to the development of modern magnetic resonance imaging (MRI). MRI, a technique used to produce highly detailed cross-sectional images of tissues inside the body, has revolutionized medical diagnoses and research. MRI involves exposing tissue to a magnetic field and radio waves. By recording differences in radio waves emitted by different molecules in a substance, researchers can determine the properties of the tissue being imaged.

The Nobel Committee credited Lauterbur with discovering how to use variations in a magnetic field to determine the location of energy-emitting molecules in body tissues. Mansfield was recognized for showing how MRI signals could be analyzed mathematically to create a two-dimensional image of the body's internal structures.

The 2003 Nobel Prize for economics went to Robert F. Engle of New York University in New York City and British-born Clive W. J. Granger of the University of California at San Diego. The two economists won for developing groundbreaking statistical methods for studying *economic time series,* that is, sets of economic observations recorded over time. Time series generally track such economic variables as interest rates, gross domestic products, and stock prices. The Nobel Committee praised Engle's and Granger's work for improving economists' ability to predict economic conditions.

Engle was honored for devising methods for predicting the rate at which economic variables change over time. These methods have influenced the ways in which economists and investors evaluate risks in the stock market. The Nobel Committee recognized Granger for developing a method to analyze two variables that have a long-term trend as well as an element of randomness.

The 2003 Nobel Prize for chemistry went to Roderick MacKinnon of Rockefeller University in New York City and Peter C. Agre of Johns Hopkins University in Baltimore. The two scientists were honored for findings describing how water and *ions* (electrically charged atoms) pass in and out of living cells through tiny pores called channels. The channels are actually proteins that form tunnels through the cell membrane.

Agre, a biochemist, won his share of the prize for discovering the first known *aquaporin,* a channel for water molecules. MacKinnon, a biophysicist, discovered the structure of ion channels and the way in which they filter the material attempting to pass through them. The work of both scientists has improved researchers' understanding of diseases that may be caused by defects in these channels.

The 2003 Nobel Prize for physics was awarded to Russian physicist Vitaly L. Ginzburg of the P. N. Lebedev Physical Institute in Moscow; Soviet-born American physicist Alexei A. Abrikosov of Argonne National Laboratory in Illinois; and British and American physicist Anthony J. Leggett of the University of Illinois at Urbana-Champaign. Abrikosov and Ginzburg were recognized for their research on *superconductivity,* the ability of some substances to conduct electric current without resistance at temperatures near absolute zero. Ginzburg made his discoveries with Soviet physicist Lev Landau, who died in 1968. Leggett was honored for research on *superfluids,* liquids that flow without friction at extremely low temperatures.   ■ Barbara A. Mayes

See also **Iran; Literature, World.**

Northern Ireland.

Northern Ireland. The peace process between Roman Catholics and Protestants in the United Kingdom's province of Northern Ireland remained fragile in 2003. Hostilities between the two groups, which had reignited in 1969, had been officially halted by the Good Friday agreement of 1998. The agreement, which had been negotiated by the British and Irish governments, led to the creation of an assembly representing all sides. This included Sinn Fein, the nationalist movement made up primarily of Northern Ireland's Catholic minority, which had entered the government for the first time.

Historically, the primary objective of Sinn Fein and its paramilitary wing, the Irish Republican Army (IRA), had been to force the province to withdraw from the United Kingdom and join the Republic of Ireland. Some members of the Ulster Unionist Party, made up primarily of the Protestant majority who want the province to remain part of the United Kingdom, were suspicious that the IRA had not abandoned using violence to gain its objectives, despite the decommissioning of some of its weapons. This suspicion and continued violence led to the suspension of the Northern Ireland Assembly in 2002. The United Kingdom resumed direct rule from London.

Peace talks. British Prime Minister Tony Blair and Irish Prime Minister Bertie Ahern held talks in early 2003 in an effort to restore the Assembly and hold elections. Nevertheless, elections were pushed back to November 26. David Trimble, leader of the Unionist Party, demanded a clear repudiation of violence by Sinn Fein in order for negotiations to move forward. However, he was not satisfied by Sinn Fein's response. Trimble was under pressure from his own party, which was losing ground to the more extreme Democratic Unionist Party, led by Ian Paisley. In June, Trimble survived a challenge from the leading critic in his party, Jeffrey Donaldson, who opposed the Good Friday agreement and urged supporters to resist calls for the restoration of the Assembly. In July, Trimble survived a motion of no-confidence in his own constituency, though about 40 percent of the people voted against him.

Talks centering on restoring the Northern Ireland Assembly broke down on October 21. Trimble declared that he was not satisfied with assurances by former Canadian General John de Chastelain, who led the independent body that oversaw the IRA's abandonment of weapons. De Chastelain witnessed the decommissioning of weapons at a secret location. However, as part of his agreement with the IRA, he refused to divulge the exact number of weapons put beyond use. Gerry Adams, head of Sinn Fein, insisted that his party was still committed to the peace pro-

cess. Prime Ministers Blair and Ahern remained committed to holding elections in 2003.

Election. In the election for the Assembly on November 26, Ian Paisley's Democratic Unionist Party won the most seats (30), beating Trimble's Ulster Unionists (27). Sinn Fein won 24 seats, while the more moderate Social Democratic and Labour Party won only 18. The results posed a threat to the Good Friday agreement, as Paisley refused to serve with Sinn Fein in government. Direct rule from Britain therefore continued.

The Ulster Defence Association (UDA), Northern Ireland's main Protestant paramilitary group, was divided by internal feuds in 2003 revolving around its former member Johnny "Mad Dog" Adair. Adair had been expelled in September 2002 and arrested in January 2003 for terrorist activities. In February, conflict erupted between Adair's supporters and their rivals over the murder of John Gregg, a member of the UDA's Council who had voted to expel Adair. Adair's family was forced to flee to Scotland. On February 19, the UDA handed over some of its weapons to the police as a way of restoring a cease-fire and cooling its dispute with the Adair faction.

■ Rohan McWilliam

See also **Ireland; United Kingdom.**

Northwest Territories. See Canadian Territories.

Friends and family bear the coffin of Roy Green, a member of the Ulster Defence Association (UDA), Northern Ireland's main Protestant paramilitary group, to his funeral in south Belfast in January. According to authorities, expelled UDA compatriots murdered Green, along with other members, in an internal feud that police helped settle in February.

Norway experienced weak economic growth and rising unemployment during 2003. The slow-down was the result of high interest rates during 2002 and weak economies across much of Europe. Government economists forecast that Norway's economy would grow by only 0.5 per-cent during 2003, down from 1.0 percent in 2002. Unemployment rose to 4.5 percent in 2003, from 4 percent in 2002.

The government of Prime Minister Kjell Magne Bondevik increased deficit spending and made a small tax cut in a bid to stimulate the economy. The rise in the deficit forced the gov-ernment to dip into the country's Petroleum Fund in order to balance its books. The fund, which invests a portion of the earnings from Nor-way's offshore oil and gas industry as savings for future generations, held around $120 billion at the end of 2003.

Bank merger. Den norske Bank (DnB) and Union Bank of Norway merged in 2003 in an effort to remain competitive with larger banks elsewhere in Scandinavia. The merger, announc-ed in March and approved by regulators in No-vember, created the country's largest banking and insurance firm, with a stock market value of $7.8 billion.

Gas pipeline. The governments of Norway and the United Kingdom (U.K.) signed an agree-ment in October 2003 for the construction of a major gas pipeline between the two countries. The project, called Britpipe, would be one of the largest pipelines in the North Sea and would sup-ply 20 percent of the U.K.'s gas needs from large gas fields off the coast of Norway. Britpipe was expected to enter into service in 2007.

Oil drilling. Proposals to allow oil drilling near the Lofoten Islands, in the Barents Sea off the northwest coast of Norway, stirred contro-versy in 2003. Environmental groups urged the government to ban drilling in the area because of the risk of damage to coral reefs, whales, and sea birds as well as to cod and herring stocks, which are vital to Norway's fishing industry. Oil companies contended that drilling could be done without harming the environment. The govern-ment decided in December to allow drilling in the Barents Sea but banned it near the islands.

Smoking ban. The Norwegian parliament passed a law to ban smoking in all indoor places, including bars and restaurants, in April. The mea-sure, which was to take effect on June 1, 2004, became the strictest smoking law in Europe. The law was passed to protect workers from the effects of secondhand smoke.   ■ Tom Buerkle

See also **Europe.**

Nova Scotia. See **Canadian provinces.**
Nuclear energy. See **Energy supply.**
Nutrition. See **Food.**

Ocean. Industrial fishing fleets have emptied oceans of 90 percent of the largest fish, including tuna, swordfish, marlin, and cod, since the 1950's, according to a study published in May 2003. Ran-som Myers, a biologist at Dalhousie University in Halifax, Nova Scotia, Canada, and Boris Worm, a marine ecologist at the Institute for Marine Sci-ence in Kiel, Germany, reviewed 47 years of survey data collected by research vessels and commercial fishing fleets before reaching their conclusion.

The researchers said that due to the global scope of depletions, rebuilding stocks would be difficult and the extinction of some fish species in certain areas of the world is possible. With satellite positioning systems and sonar to seek fish, indus-trial fishing fleets can reduce a *fishery* (an area where fish are caught commercially or recreation-ally) by 80 percent in 15 years.

Gulf Stream all hot air. In February, climate researcher Richard Seager of Columbia University's Lamont-Doherty Earth Observatory in Palisades, New York, and atmospheric scientist David Battisti of the University of Washington in Seattle reported that the Gulf Stream may not cause the contrast in winter temperatures between Europe and eastern North America that scientists had believed. The Gulf Stream is an ocean current carrying water from the Caribbean Sea to the North Atlantic Sea.

Seager, Battisti, and their colleagues analyzed meteorological data dating to the 1950's and dis-covered that the prevailing westerlies, winds that blow westward across North America and Europe, transport a greater amount of heat to Europe than the Gulf Stream. Furthermore, they believe that much of the warming effect of the ocean comes from heat stored in the ocean's thin surface layer, not from the Gulf Stream.

Climate *models* (computer simulations) showed the Gulf Stream had little effect on winter temper-atures. Models that assumed the ocean current carried no heat still predicted that Europe's winters would be about 15 degrees warmer than in the eastern United States. About half of the tempera-ture difference was traced to the presence in North America of the Rocky Mountains, the mountain chain that extends more than 3,000 miles (4,800 kilometers) through the western United States and Canada. The chain steers the westerlies, causing them to move in a snakelike pattern instead of blowing west to east. In the United States, the westerlies blow out of the northwest, pushing cold winter air from Canada and the Arctic into the continental United States. In Europe, the westerlies blow out of the southwest, bringing heat from lower latitudes.

Pygmy sea horse. In May 2003, researchers led by Sara Lourie, a biologist at McGill University in Montreal, Canada, discovered a new species of sea horse. The pygmy sea horse, which averages about

.64 inches (6 millimeters) long, is native to the western Pacific Ocean, where it lives among corals. The species was the smallest ever found. Researchers knew of its existence but mistook it for an immature sea horse of another species.

Sonar system scaled back. In October, the U.S. Navy agreed to limit the use of a sonar system that environmentalists and some scientists said could harm whales and other marine animals. The Navy agreed to use the Surveillance Towed Array Sensor System-Low Frequency Active (SURTASS-LFA) only off the eastern coast of Asia. The Navy agreed not to use the system when marine mammals are migrating through the area.

SURTASS-LFA emits powerful low-frequency soundwaves to detect enemy submarines. Scientists believe that the blasts also interfere with whale communication and navigation and can cause fatal brain damage in the animals.

Oceanic census. Scientists involved in the Census of Marine Life (CoML) reported the first findings from their $1-billion census of animal life in the world's oceans in October. Scientists have cataloged more than 15,000 species of fish and 200,000 species of animals and plants since the study began in 2000. ■ Christina S. Johnson

Ohio. See **State government.**

Oklahoma. See **State government.**

Old age. See **Social Security.**

Olympic Games. On July 2, 2003, the International Olympic Committee (IOC) awarded the 2010 Winter Olympic Games to Vancouver, Canada, in a surprisingly close vote. In the first round of voting, Pyeongchang, South Korea, received 51 votes, 11 more than were cast for Vancouver, but four short of the required majority for victory. Vancouver prevailed in the second round of voting, 56 to 53.

Scandal trial. On Dec. 5, 2003, a federal judge dismissed all charges against two Salt Lake City executives accused of bribing IOC delegates in the early 1990's to bring the Winter Games to that city. Tom Welch, president of the Salt Lake City bid and organizing committees, and Dave Johnson, senior vice president, had faced 15 felony charges of bribery, fraud, and conspiracy.

Medals changed. Organizers of the 2004 Summer Olympic Games in Athens made major changes to the Olympic medals for the first time since 1928. The new design featured Nike, the Greek goddess of victory, and an image of the Panathenaic Stadium in Athens, which had been the site of the first modern Olympic Games in 1896. ■ Michael Kates

Oman. See **Middle East.**

Ontario. See **Canadian provinces.**

Opera. See **Classical music.**

Oregon. See **State government.**

Steve O'Shea, senior research fellow at Auckland University of Technology in New Zealand, examines the remains of a colossal squid (Mesonychoteuthis hamiltoni). Scientists said it was an immature female weighing 330 pounds (150 kilograms), with a body 8 feet (2.5 meters) long and with tentacles spreading out to a length of 16 to 20 feet (5 to 6 meters). Fishermen working off Antarctica caught the very rare marine mollusk in April 2003.

Country	Population	Government	Monetary unit*	Foreign trade (million U.S.$) Exports†	Imports†
Fiji	881,000	President Josefa Iloilo; Prime Minister Laisenia Qarase	dollar (1.82 = $1)	442	642
Kiribati	88,000	President Anote Tong	Australian dollar (1.35 = $1)	6	44
Marshall Islands	54,000	President Kessai Note	U.S. dollar	9	54
Micronesia, Federated States of	135,000	President Joseph J. Urusemal	U.S. dollar	22	149
Nauru	13,000	President Rene Harris	Australian dollar	27	33
New Zealand	3,890,000	Governor General Dame Silvia Cartwright; Prime Minister Helen Clark	dollar (1.69 = $1)	15,000	12,500
Palau	21,000	President Tommy Remengesau, Jr.	U.S. dollar	18	99
Papua New Guinea	5,606,000	Governor General Sir Silas Atopare; Prime Minister Sir Michael Somare	kina (3.32 = $1)	1,800	1,100
Samoa	176,000	Head of State Malietoa Tanumafili II; Prime Minister Tuila'epa Sailele Malielegaoi	tala (2.86 = $1)	16	130
Solomon Islands	509,000	Governor General Sir John Lapli; Prime Minister Sir Allan Kemakeza	dollar (7.52 = $1)	47	82
Tonga	100,000	King Taufa'ahau Tupou IV; Prime Minister Lavaka ata Ulukalala	pa'anga (2.12 = $1)	9	70
Tuvalu	11,000	Governor General Sir Tomasi Puapua; Prime Minister Koloa Talake	Australian dollar	1	7
Vanuatu	211,000	President Father John Bani; Prime Minister Edward Natapei	vatu (118.33 = $1)	22	93

*Exchange rates as of Oct. 3, 2003, or latest available data.
†Latest available data.

Pacific Islands.

Political events rocked the Pacific Islands in 2003. An international armed force stepped in to help police on the Solomon Islands. An election that had been delayed for a year in the Southern Highlands of Papua New Guinea was finally settled. Confusion marked government transitions in Kiribati and Nauru, while the Micronesian Congress chose a new president from among its members.

Solomon Islands. On July 24, Australia led a multinational force of 2,000 soldiers and 300 police to restore order in the Solomon Islands. The force also included soldiers from New Zealand, Fiji, Papua New Guinea, and Tonga. The military operation was the largest in the region since World War II (1939-1945).

A four-year civil war between groups from the Guadalcanal and Malaita islands caused the breakdown of law and order in Honiara, the capital of the Solomons. The troubled citizens welcomed the force, which collected large numbers of weapons. Officers with the multinational force announced in July 2003 that the naval patrols had been boosted to cut the flow of weapons into the Solomons.

Australia lifted travel warnings for its citizens planning trips to the Solomons in September. When New Zealand Prime Minister Helen Clark visited the islands in September, she announced that her country would contribute $1 million to restore regular power to Honiara.

Papua New Guinea. Special parliamentary elections were conducted in the Southern Highlands Province between April and May. In June 2002, the regular election had been called off because of record levels of fraud and intimidation. In June 2003, the six successful candidates began their terms in the capital, Port Moresby.

Australia, which provides millions of dollars in aid to Papua New Guinea, took a more active role in 2003 in supervising how the funds were spent. An agreement, reached in September, allowed Australian officials to work with Papua New Guinea officials regarding financial management as well as law and order.

In a separate aid package, Japan's government committed $819,500 in September to Papua New Guinea's Bougainville province, which continued to suffer from years of armed conflict. About 10 percent of the aid would go to educational institutions and 20 percent to the health sector. The remainder would be used to construct roads, bridges, and harbors.

Kiribati. In February, Teburoro Tito was elected to his third and final term as president of Kiribati, but his political foes voted him out just days into his term. In July, Anote Tong defeated his brother, Harry Tong, for the presidency.

Nauru. President Bernard Dowiyogo of Nauru died suddenly on March 9 in Washington, D.C. He was there to consult with United States officials who claimed that Nauru allowed criminals to launder money through the country's international finance center. In May, Ludwig Scotty was elected to replace Dowiyogo. However, Scotty was ousted in August by political foes and replaced with former president Rene Harris.

Federated States of Micronesia (FSM). The FSM Congress in May chose Joseph J. Urusemal from among its ranks to be president. He was then sworn in at the opening session of the 13th Congress. Political experts noted that one of his primary challenges was to create a Cabinet that represented all four states—Yap, Chuuk, Kosrae, and Pohnpei—in the federation.

Fiji. Fiji hosted the 12th South Pacific Games, held in the capital of Suva, from June 28 to July 12. Over 20 Pacific nations and territories participated. The athletes of New Caledonia won 242 medals, the largest number.

Marshall Islands. In July, a measles epidemic broke out on Majuro Atoll in the Republic of the Marshall Islands. By September, more than 700 people had been affected and 3 people died. Officials at the U.S. Centers for Disease Control and Prevention in Atlanta, Georgia, which provides health services to the Marshalls, announced that it was the worst outbreak since 1992, when 1,100 people developed the disease in Texas. Officials blamed low immunization rates for the outbreak. ■ Eugene Ogan

See also **Australia; New Zealand.**

Painting. See Art.

Pakistan. Violence between Islamic religious sects in Pakistan increased markedly in 2003. In addition, evidence suggested that members of the Taliban, a radical Islamic group that once controlled much of Afghanistan, and al-Qa'ida, a global terrorist organization, were operating in Pakistan along its border with Afghanistan.

Mosque massacre. A suicide attack on a Shiah Muslim mosque in the western city of Quetta in July killed 53 people. Police said that two of the attackers were members of a militant Sunni Muslim group that was linked to the kidnapping and murder of *The Wall Street Journal* reporter Daniel Pearl in 2002. The 2003 attack was the worst act of violence between Shiah and Sunni Muslims in Pakistan in several years.

Shiites form the smaller of the two divisions of Islam, with less than 20 percent of the believers. More than 80 percent of Muslims are Sunnis. The level of violence escalated between the groups in 2003 after a lull in 2002. In June 2003, 4 men ambushed and killed 12 police trainees, most of whom were Shiites, in Quetta. Authorities suspected that the gunmen were Sunni. In October, the murder of a radical Sunni member of parliament touched off riots nationwide.

War on terror. Pakistani President Pervez Musharraf attempted to ease international concerns that his government was secretly aiding the Taliban and al-Qa'ida. Many Taliban and al-Qa'ida members fled to Pakistan after United States-led forces overthrew the Taliban regime in Afghanistan in 2001. Pakistan officials denied claims by U.S. military officers in 2003 that the government was training Taliban guerrillas to sabotage peacekeeping efforts in Afghanistan.

U.S. President George W. Bush praised Pakistan's efforts to crack down on terrorism in June. Bush cited Pakistan's cooperation in the arrest of several terrorist suspects, including Khalid Shaikh Mohammed, who was suspected of planning the terrorist attacks on the United States in 2001.

In April 2003, a Pakistani court convicted four men of a bombing outside the U.S. consulate in the Karachi. Two men were sentenced to death and the two others received life terms. In June, three members of a militant Islamic sect were sentenced to death for a bombing that killed 11 French engineers in Karachi in 2002.

Suicide bombers attempted to assassinate Musharraf twice in December 2003 by driving vehicles loaded with explosives into his motorcade in Rawalpindi, the headquarters of Pakistan's Army. At least 15 people were killed in the second attack, which took place on December 25.

U.S. sanctions. In March 2003, the United States imposed limited economic sanctions on Pakistan for buying missiles from North Korea. In May, the United States offered Musharraf a

$3 billion in aid if Pakistan stopped its reported aid to the North Korean nuclear program.

Kashmir. Indian and Pakistani diplomats attempted to revive stalled efforts to normalize relations between the neighboring countries. However, violence in the Himalayan state of Jammu and Kashmir, which both countries claimed, threatened to derail peace efforts.

Islamic guerrillas killed hundreds of Indian troops in 2003 in Jammu and Kashmir. India accused Pakistan of supporting the guerrillas and refused to negotiate while violence continued. Indian and Pakistani military commanders agreed in November to a cease-fire in the region.

Bhutto conviction. A Swiss court convicted Benazir Bhutto, a former prime minister of Pakistan, and her husband, Asif Ali Zardari, on money-laundering charges in July 2003. An investigation found that two Swiss companies bribed Bhutto in 1994. The court ordered Bhutto to pay the Pakistani government nearly $12 million in restitution. Bhutto, who lived in exile in 2003, and Zardari, who resided in a Pakistani prison on other charges, won an appeal.

Economy. The Asian Development Bank, a United Nations affiliate, reported in August that Pakistan's economy had grown 5.1 percent in the first half of 2003. ■ Henry S. Bradsher

See also **Afghanistan; Asia; India; Islam.**

Paleontology. Fossils of the oldest known

large soft-bodied animals—dating from about 575 million years ago—were discovered in Newfoundland, Canada, according to a January 2003 report by paleontologists Guy Narbonne of Queens University in Ontario and James Gehling of the South Australian Museum in Adelaide. Previously, the oldest known impressions of large soft-bodied organisms dated from about 560 million years ago. The newly found fossils show soft, leaflike animals that may be related to modern sea pens and corals. They are among the largest such fossils ever found, at more than 7 feet (2 meters) long.

These life forms appear in the fossil record only about 10 million years after a possible massive ice age that some scientists think may have led to a global freezing that killed off almost all life. The new fossils indicate that either there was no severe mass extinction or these large animals evolved very rapidly. Narbonne suggests that the animals had evolved earlier and that the global freezing about 585 million years ago was not as severe as once thought.

Oldest vertebrate? Tadpolelike fossils found by a farmer in a mountainous area about 310 miles (500 kilometers) north of Adelaide, Australia, could represent the oldest known *vertebrates* (animals with backbones). Gehling and his colleagues, who reported the find in October, said the fossils were at least 550 million years old. This pushed the record of known vertebrates back at least 25 million years to the Ediacaran Period. Gehling said the torpedo-shaped impressions in sandstone are about 3 inches (6 centimeters) long and show evidence of a tail, a *dorsal* (back) fin, and V-shaped bands of muscles. If these specimens are vertebrates, it would be a significant finding. Because large multicelled animals first appeared during the Ediacaran Period, these ancient fossils indicate that vertebrates—which also include human ancestors—had their roots among the most ancient animal life on earth.

Earliest land plants. Newly discovered fragments of organic matter may push back the date of the origin of land plants by 50 million years. These tiny fossils, each less than .04 inch (1 millimeter) in diameter, were described in September 2003 by paleontologist Charles H. Wellman of the University of Sheffield in England.

The fossils are parts of sporangia, or spore capsules. They were found in rocks about 450 million years old from Oman. Spores had previously been found in rocks of this age in several places around the world, but some paleobotanists suggested that the spores were merely those of marine algae. The scientists noted that the newly discovered sporangia definitely indicate that these spores came from a land plant, probably similar to modern liverworts. These earliest plants would have formed a very thin layer of green, filmy growth along the shores of lakes and ponds.

Ancestral sauropods. A new dinosaur fossil, named *Antetonitrus ingenipes,* was described in July 2003 by paleontologists Adam Yates and James Kitching at the University of the Witwatersrand in Johannesburg, South Africa. These fossils represent the oldest member of the *Sauropoda,* a group of enormous *herbivorous* (plant-eating) dinosaurs that includes *Brontosaurus (Apatosaurus), Brachiosaurus,* and *Diplodocus.* The fossils were found in South African rocks that are about 215 million years old. The age of the rocks makes the remains nearly 65 million years older than *Brontosaurus.*

The skeleton of the South African fossil represents a *quadrupedal* (four legged) dinosaur about 33 to 39 feet (10 to 12 meters) long and probably weighing about 2 tons (1.8 metric tons). As such, this fossil represents one of the largest known animals from the Late Triassic Period.

The huge animal appears to be a transitional form between the prosauropods, smaller, *bipedal* (walking on two legs) dinosaurs, and the true sauropods. Like prosauropods, *Antetonitrus* was capable of manipulating food with its front limbs, or "hands."

Paleontologist Paul Sereno of the University of Chicago in August shows off a model of a meat-eating dinosaur that he and other paleontologists identified from fossils collected by scientists in India. The dinosaur's name, *Rajasaurus narmadensis,* means "regal reptile from the region of the Narmada River."

Birdlike dinosaurs from China. The discovery in China of a new species of four-winged, feathered dinosaur was reported in January 2003 by paleontologist Xu Xing and his colleagues at the Institute of Vertebrate Paleontology and Paleoanthropology in Beijing. A number of fossils, including birds and dinosaurs that may have had feathers, have emerged from deposits dating from about 128 million to 124 million years ago in China's Liaoning Province. The scientists found six new, well-preserved fossils of a dinosaur that was 3-feet (1-meter) long bearing clear impressions of feathers. The new dinosaur, named *Microraptor gui,* is a small *carnivore* (meat-eater), or theropod, related to such species as *Velociraptor.* Its existence con-

firms that there was a close relationship between these species and birds.

Microraptor did not have fully developed wings, but it had feathers, like those of birds, on the forearms and legs and along the tail. *Microraptor* was not capable of flapping its wings to fly but could spread out its limbs to form a large surface for gliding, rather like a "flying" squirrel.

Microraptor forms yet another link between dinosaurs and birds. Although *Microraptor* is some 25 million years too young to have been a direct ancestor of *Archaeopteryx,* the oldest true bird, it provides insights into what the direct ancestor must have been like. It also indicates that birds may have come from tree-climbing and gliding, not running, ancestors. ■ Carlton E. Brett

Pan American Games. Athletes from the United States won the highest number of medals at the 2003 Pan American Games, held from August 1 through 17, in Santo Domingo, Dominican Republic. Cuba captured its ninth consecutive Pan Am Games baseball championship and finished second in the medal standings.

The United States won 271 medals, 115 of which were gold, but the team won silver medals in both baseball and women's basketball and failed to capture a medal in men's basketball for the first time since 1971. Cuba finished with 152 medals, 72 of which were gold, and captured the baseball title with a 3-1 victory over the U.S. team, which did not include professional players. The U.S. men's basketball team lost 76-70 to Puerto Rico in the bronze-medal game.

Drug tests. Three athletes had to forfeit medals after failing drug tests. Argentina forfeited two medals when one of its rowers, Ulf Lienhard, tested positive for cocaine. The U.S. team forfeited its gold in the 400-meter relay when Mickey Grimes tested positive for ephedrine. Grimes also forfeited the gold he had won in the 100-meter sprint. Letitia Vriesde, of Suriname, was stripped of the gold medal she had won in the 800-meter sprint after officials found excessive caffeine in her blood. ■ Michael Kates

See also **Sports.**

Panama. Panama President Mireya Elisa Moscoso faced rising popular resentment throughout 2003 over her administration's failure to provide jobs and stamp out corruption. The breaking point occurred when Moscoso fired Juan Jovane, director of Panama's social security institute (CSS), in September after Jovane rejected a budget cut.

Jovane's dismissal prompted a nationwide wave of protests by workers who were concerned that his removal was a step toward privatization of the social security system. Critics have charged that privatization would mean the loss of tax revenues that pay the benefits of current retirees.

CSS employees went on strike for two weeks in September. They ended the strike when the CSS promised not to punish the workers.

Labor unions organized a 24-hour general protest in late September. Thousands of union members, students, private businessmen, and even government workers supported the action by marching through the streets of Panama City and Colon. ■ Nathan A. Haverstock

See also **Latin America.**

Papua New Guinea. See Asia; Pacific Islands.

Paraguay. See Latin America.

Pennsylvania. See Philadelphia; State government.

PEOPLE IN THE NEWS

in 2003 included those listed below, who were all from the United States unless otherwise indicated.

Beckham, David (1975-), the United Kingdom's most famous soccer player, and one of that country's hottest celebrities, in June 2003 was traded by his long-time team, Manchester United, to Real Madrid of Spain in a deal worth $41 million. English soccer fans idolized Beckham for his legendary ability to "bend" a shot—that is, arc the ball over the heads of opposing players. His popularity and interest in fashion have led to a highly lucrative sideline endorsing consumer products ranging from athletic gear to soda pop. In 1999, Beckham married Victoria Adams, once a member of the pop singing group Spice Girls.

David Robert Joseph Beckham was born on May 2, 1975, in London. He joined Manchester United as a trainee in 1991. Two years later, Beckham signed a professional contract with the team, making his league debut in 1995. Within two years, he had become an international superstar. Playing midfield, Beckham led Manchester United to several championships starting in 1996 and was named Young Player of the Year in 1997.

David Beckham

Beckham won a place on the English national team for the 1998 World Cup. However, his foul against an opposing player, which led to his ejection from the game, caused many fans to blame him for England's loss in that tournament. However, fans forgave Beckham in 1999 as he led United to an unprecedented "treble," winning the English League Championship, the English Cup, and the European Champions League. In 2000, he was appointed captain of the English national team.

See also **Soccer.**

Bremer, L. Paul, III (1941-), a veteran of the United States Foreign Service and a noted expert on counterterrorism, was appointed presidential envoy to Iraq on May 6, 2003, by President George W. Bush. Bremer, who strongly supported the U.S.-led attack on Iraq in March, was charged with overseeing the establishment of a new Iraqi government. His responsibilities also included supervising U.S. efforts to rebuild Iraq. In appointing Bremer, the Bush administration attempted to meet the demands of diplomats and other groups for a larger civilian role in the reconstruction process.

Lewis Paul Bremer III was born on Sept. 30, 1941, in Hartford, Connecticut. He graduated from Yale University in New Haven, Connecticut, in 1963, then studied for a year at the Institut d'Etudes Politiques in Paris. In 1966, he earned a master's degree in business administration from Harvard University in Cambridge, Massachusetts.

Bremer joined the Foreign Service in 1966, serving in Afghanistan and Malawi. From 1971 to 1976, he worked in several positions in the U.S. Department of State, one of the federal agencies that administers the Foreign Service, in Washington, D.C. In 1976, he became deputy mission chief at the U.S. embassy in Oslo, Norway, returning to the State Department in 1979. In 1983, President Ronald Reagan appointed him ambassador to the Netherlands.

From 1986 until his retirement from government in 1989, Bremer served as the State Department's ambassador at large for counter-terrorism. On leaving government, he joined Kissinger Associates, Inc., a Washington-based consulting firm, as managing director. In 1999, Bremer became chair of the National Commission on Terrorism, a congressional panel that reviewed government laws and policies on terrorism.

In 2000, Bremer joined Marsh Inc., a consulting firm in Washington. In 2003, Bush appointed him to the President's Homeland Security Advisory Council, established to recommend strategies for protecting the United States from terrorism.

See also **Iraq: A Special Report.**

Brin, Sergey (1973-) and **Larry Page** (1972-) founded Google, which, by 2003, had become the Internet's dominant search engine. A search engine is a computer program that allows a user to locate information on the Internet by typing in key words or phrases.

Page and Brin named their company, based in Palo Alto, California, after the mathematical term googol, which refers to the number represented by 1 followed by 100 zeros. The name is intended to reflect the company's mission to organize the seemingly infinite amount of information available on the World Wide Web and make it universally accessible and useful.

Sergey Brin, Google's "president, technology," was born in Moscow in August 1973. He and his parents, both scientists, moved to the United States in 1979 and settled in Maryland. He earned a bachelor's degree in mathematics and computer science from the University of Maryland at College Park in 1993.

Larry Page, Google's "president, products," was born in December 1972 in Michigan. After graduating from the University of Michigan in Ann Arbor with a degree in engineering in 1995, he worked for software companies in Washington, D.C., and Evanston, Illinois.

Brin and Page met in 1995 at Stanford University in Stanford, California, where they were enrolled in the doctoral program in computer science. By early 1996, they had begun collaborating on a search engine called BackRub. For the next 18 months, they worked to perfect their search technology. This technology involves determining the relevance or importance of a Web page by measuring the number and popularity of other sites linked to it as well as by how prominently the search terms figure in the page.

After raising start-up money, Page and Brin opened Google Inc. in September 1998 in a garage in Menlo Park, California. By December, Google was answering 10,000 queries per day. By 2003, Google's fifth anniversary, the company reported handling more than 200 million queries a day from more than 100 countries. According to Google, the search engine indexes at least 3 billion Web pages.

See also **Internet.**

Brody, Adrien (1968-), received the Academy Award for best actor on March 23, 2003, for his portrayal of a gifted Jewish pianist struggling to survive in Nazi-occupied Warsaw, Poland, during World War II (1939-1945) in the film *The Pianist.* Only 29, Brody became the youngest winner of the best-actor award.

Brody was born on April 14, 1973, in New York City. While a child, he accompanied his mother, photojournalist Sylvia Platchy, on assignment, an activity that he reported helped him feel comfortable in front of a camera. At age 12, he began performing as a magician at children's parties. Encouraged by his mother, Brody attended the prestigious American Academy of Dramatic Arts and the High School for the Performing Arts, both in New York City.

Brody made his acting debut in 1988 in the short-lived television series *Annie McGuire*. He made his movie debut the following year in *New York Stories* (1989). In 1993, his portrayal of a juvenile delinquent in the drama *King of the Hill* brought him favorable reviews from critics and wider public notice. It also led to a steady stream of roles in such films as *Angels in the Outfield* (1994), *The Last Time I Committed Suicide* (1997), and *The Undertaker's Wedding* (1997).

Strong performances in *The Thin Red Line* (1998) and *Summer of Sam* (1999) placed Brody on the brink of stardom. After roles in a number

Howard Dean, presidential candidate

of well-reviewed but only moderately successful films from 1999 to 2002, *The Pianist* gave him worldwide recognition.

See also **Motion pictures.**

Clark, Wesley (1944-), a retired U.S. Army

general, in September 2003 launched his campaign for the Democratic nomination for U.S. president in the 2004 election. He quickly leaped ahead of other Democratic candidates in public opinion polls, despite charges that he had supported the Republican Party for most of his life.

Clark was born Wesley Kanne on Dec. 23, 1944, in Chicago. After his father died, his mother moved the family to Little Rock, Arkansas. She later married Victor Clark, who adopted Wesley. Clark graduated first in his class from the U.S. Military Academy at West Point, New York, in 1966. He attended Oxford University in the United Kingdom as a Rhodes scholar, receiving a master's degree in philosophy, poli-

tics, and economics in 1968. In 1975, he earned a master's degree in miliary science from the U.S. Army Command and General Staff College in Fort Leavenworth, Kansas.

Clark was wounded in action four times in 1969, while serving as an infantry commander during the Vietnam War (1957-1975). After the war, Clark rapidly moved up through Army ranks, earning his first general's star at age 43.

In the mid-1990's, Clark led military negotiations for the peace plan that ended Bosnia's war for independence from the former Yugoslavia. In 1996, he was promoted to the rank of four-star general. From then until he retired from the military in 2000, Clark led the U.S. European Command, which coordinates all U.S. armed forces in Europe, and served as supreme allied commander of the North Atlantic Treaty Organization. Clark is the author of several books, including *Winning Modern Wars: Iraq, Terrorism, and the American Empire* (2003).

See also **Democratic Party.**

Dean, Howard III (1948-), a

physician and long-time governor of Vermont, in 2003 attracted significant voter attention to his campaign to win the Democratic nomination for United States president in the 2004 election. Dean's combative style and his mix of traditionally liberal and conservative political positions set him apart from other candidates in the race.

Dean also achieved amazing success at raising campaign funds through his Web site on the Internet. Hundreds of thousands of donors, offering contributions that averaged less than $100, poured at least $25 million into his campaign coffers. As a result, Dean declined the use of public funds available to presidential candidates, which would have subjected him to a $45-million spending limit.

Howard Brush Dean III was born on Nov. 17, 1948, in New York City. He received a bachelor's degree from Yale University in New Haven, Connecticut, in 1971 and a medical degree from Albert Einstein College of Medicine in New York City in 1978. In 1982, he opened a medical practice in Vermont with his wife, also a physician.

From 1982 to 1986, Dean served in the Vermont House of Representatives. In 1986, he was elected lieutenant governor for the first of three two-year terms. While in political life, he also continued working as a physician.

Dean became governor of Vermont after the sudden death of Governor Richard A. Snelling in August 1991. Dean won election to a full term as governor in 1992 and reelection in 1994, 1996,

1998, and 2000. As governor, he expanded health care for children, revamped Vermont's funding system for education to increase revenues for poorer schools, and signed legislation legalizing civil unions for same-sex couples.

See also **Democratic Party.**

Frist, Bill (1952-), a conservative Republican from Tennessee, became his party's leader in the U.S. Senate on Jan. 7, 2003. Frist was elected Senate majority leader for the 108th Congress in December 2002, following the forced resignation of former leader Senator Trent Lott (R., Mississippi). Lott resigned amid widespread criticism for remarks praising the 1948 presidential campaign of retiring Senator Strom Thurmond (R., South Carolina), whose platform had favored racial segregation.

Political experts noted that Frist, who had first won election to the Senate in 1994, had relatively little legislative experience. However, as chair of the Senate Republican campaign committee for the November 2002 elections, he had directed his party's successful efforts to regain control of the Senate.

William Harrison Frist was born in Nashville, Tennessee, on Feb. 22, 1952. He earned a bachelor's degree from Princeton University in Princeton, New Jersey, in 1974. He received a medical degree from Harvard Medical School in Cambridge, Massachusetts, in 1978. In 1984, after completing residencies at several medical centers, he joined the faculty at Vanderbilt University in Nashville as a heart and lung surgeon. In 1989, Frist consolidated the transplant clinics at Vanderbilt into the Vanderbilt Transplant Center. He is the author of numerous publications, including *When Every Moment Counts: What You Need to Know About Bioterrorism from the Senate's Only Doctor* (2002).

See also **Congress of the United States; Republican Party.**

Hu Jintao *hoo jihn tow* (1942-), vice president of China since 1998, became president of that country on March 15, 2003. In November 2002, Hu had succeeded retiring President Jiang Zemin as general secretary of the Chinese Communist Party in the first orderly transition of power in China's modern history. Hu pledged to follow the policies of economic reform and international cooperation established by Jiang, who remained China's most powerful leader despite his official retirement.

Hu was born in December 1942 in Jixi, Anhui province, and grew up in Taizhou, Jiangsu province, and in Shanghai. In 1965, he graduated from Tsinghua University in Beijing, where he studied hydraulic engineering.

Hu joined the Communist Party in 1964, rising through party ranks during the 1970's. In 1982, he was named as an alternate member to the Communist Party's Central Committee, becoming a full member in 1987. Hu served as party chief in Guizhou province from 1985 to 1988. For the next four years, he headed the Communist Party in Tibet, presiding over China's 1989 imposition

Bill Frist (center), Senate majority leader

of martial law to quell unrest in that region. In 1992, Hu won election to the Communist Party's powerful Politburo Standing Committee. In 1998, he became the youngest person ever chosen as vice president by the Chinese parliament.

See also **China.**

Jones, Norah (1979-), a 23-year-old singer, pianist, and composer, dominated the Grammy Awards in February 2003, winning five Grammys, including awards for best new artist and best female pop vocal performance. She also won awards for record of the year for "Don't Know Why" as well as album of the year and best pop vocal album for *Come Away With Me*, which sold millions of copies worldwide.

Jones, the daughter of legendary Indian musician Ravi Shankar, was born in New York City on March 30, 1979. She grew up in Grapevine, Texas, with her mother, singing in church choirs and studying the piano. Jones earned several awards while a student at Booker T. Washington School for the Performing and Visual Arts in Dallas. After graduation, she attended the University of North Texas in Denton, majoring in jazz piano.

In 1999, she returned to New York City for the summer, but enthralled by the music scene, decided to stay. She first performed in small clubs with the funk-fusion band Wax Poetic, then formed her own group. In 2001, she signed a recording contract that resulted in *Come Away with Me*, her first full-length album.

See also **Popular music.**

Kidman, Nicole (1967-), won the Academy Award for best actress on March 23, 2003, for her performance as British writer Virginia Woolf in the 2002 film *The Hours*. The film, a multilayered psychological drama, explores the lives of Woolf and two other women, all of whom are confronting death, disease, or loss.

Nicole Mary Kidman was born on June 20, 1967, in Honolulu, Hawaii. At age 4, she moved with her family to Longueville, Australia, a suburb of Sydney, and soon discovered a love of performing. A student of dance and drama throughout her teens, Kidman trained at St. Martins Youth Arts Centre near Melbourne and the Philip Street Theatre in Sydney. She made her television debut in 1983 in *Bush Christmas*, which became an Australian holiday movie classic. In 1988, the

Nicole Kidman and Adrien Brody, Academy Award winners

Australian Film Institute honored her performance in the television miniseries *Vietnam* (1986) with an award for best performance by an actress in a leading role in a television drama.

Kidman's favorable reviews for her American film debut in *Dead Calm* (1989) earned her a leading role in *Days of Thunder* (1990), which also starred American actor Tom Cruise. The two married in December 1990 but divorced in 2001.

During the early 1990's, Kidman's acting reputation grew steadily. Her performance as a murderous TV reporter in *To Die For* (1995) brought her the 1996 Golden Globe Award for best actress in a motion-picture comedy or musical and established her as a major box-office draw. In 1999, she and Cruise starred in the sexual thriller *Eyes Wide Shut*. Kidman won critical

recognition for her work in the highly successful suspense film *The Others* (2001). In 2002, she was nominated for an Oscar for best actress for her performance as a glamorous singer and prostitute in the lavish musical *Moulin Rouge* (2001).

See also **Australia; Motion pictures.**

Kirchner, Nestor (1950-), the former governor of a sparsely populated province in southern Argentina, took office as president of that country on May 25, 2003. He won the presidency after former President Carlos Saul Menem withdrew from a two-man runoff election in the face of almost certain defeat.

During the campaign, Kirchner had pledged stronger government involvement in Argentina's economy, which underwent the worst crisis in Argentine history in 2001 through 2002. However, political observers expected Kirchner's weak electoral mandate and his lack of a national political base to hamper his ability to make significant changes.

As governor, Kirchner expanded medical and housing programs and reduced unemployment. He also came under attack for significantly increasing the number of government employees, investing provincial oil revenues abroad, and amending the Constitution so that he could run for governor indefinitely.

Nestor Carlos Kirchner was born on Feb. 25, 1950, in Rio Gallegos, the capital of Santa Cruz, Argentina's southernmost mainland province. In 1987, Kirchner won election as mayor of Rio Gallegos. In 1991, he narrowly captured the governor's office, winning reelection in 1995 and 1999.

See also **Argentina.**

Page, Larry. See **Sergey Brin** (page 307).

Parks, Suzan-Lori (1964-), a Pulitzer Prize-winning playwright, published her much-anticipated first novel in 2003, *Getting Mother's Body*. The novel tells the story of a family struggling over a decision to open a woman's coffin to retrieve valuable jewelry. Like many of Parks's other works, *Getting Mother's Body* explores themes of family, race, and history. In 2002, Parks became the first African American woman to win the Pulitzer Prize for drama, for *Topdog/Underdog* (2001).

Suzan-Lori Parks was born in Fort Knox, Kentucky, in 1964. The daughter of a career Army officer, she and her family moved frequently during her childhood. After graduating from high school in Germany, she earned a bachelor's degree from Mount Holyoke College in South Hadley, Massachusetts, in 1985. At Mount Holyoke, she studied with the eminent American

Roh Moo-hyun (right),
president of South Korea

novelist and playwright James Baldwin, who
urged her to pursue a career in theater.

In 1990, Parks won an Obie (off-Broadway
theater) Award for best new American play for
Imperceptible Mutabilities in the Third Kingdom
(1989). She won a second Obie in 1996 for *Venus*.
Her other works include *The Sinner's Place* (1984),
*The Death of the Last Black Man in the Whole
Entire World* (1990), and *In the Blood* (1999). In
2001, Parks won a MacArthur Foundation Fellowship (genius award).

See also **Literature, American; Theater.**

Robinson, V. Gene (1947-), was conse-
crated as the first openly gay bishop in the Episcopal Church, USA, on Nov. 2, 2003. On June 7,
Robinson had been elected head of the Diocese
of New Hampshire, where he had served since
1988. The ratification of Robinson's election by
the church's governing General Convention on
Aug. 5, 2003, created turmoil within the worldwide Anglican Communion, to which the Episcopal Church, USA, belongs. Other member
churches in Africa, Asia, and Australia, as well as
some United States parishes and clergy, condemned the ratification as a rejection of Biblical
teachings.

V. Gene Robinson was born on May 29, 1947,
in Lexington, Kentucky. He graduated from the
University of the South in Sewanee, Tennessee, in
1969 and then earned a master of divinity degree
at the General Theological Seminary of the Epis-

copal Church in New York City in 1973. After his
ordination that same year, he served as an assistant at Christ Church in Ridgewood, New Jersey.

In 1975, Robinson moved to New Hampshire,
where he co-owned and directed a girls' summer
camp. From 1978 to 1985, he served as youth
ministries coordinator for the Episcopal Church's
New England region. In 1988, he became an assistant to the bishop of New Hampshire. In this
position, he won praise for his efforts to help
congregations and clergy in conflict and for the
creation of a mentoring program for clergy.

See also **Protestantism.**

Roh Moo-hyun (1946-), a lawyer and for-
mer human rights activist, was sworn in as president of South Korea on Feb. 25, 2003. Roh, the
candidate of the governing liberal Millennium
Democratic Party (MDP), narrowly won the presidency in elections held in December 2002.

During the campaign, Roh pledged to reduce
the power of the family-run business conglomerates that dominate South Korea's economy. He
also promised to continue the MDP's policy of
seeking reconciliation with North Korea without
conditions, which had come under criticism in the
United States.

Roh was born on Aug. 6, 1946, to farmers in
Kimhae, a village in what is now southeastern
South Korea. Because of his family's poverty, Roh
attended a vocational high school, graduating in
1966. After serving in the Army, he began studying law on his own and in 1975 passed South
Korea's rigorous national bar examination.

In 1981, Roh became involved with South
Korea's prodemocracy movement, defending a
student who was jailed and tortured for studying
leftist political theories. In 1987, Roh was jailed
briefly on charges of aiding striking workers.

In 1988, Roh won election to parliament as a
member of a prodemocracy party. He quickly
established a reputation as a reformer at parliamentary hearings on government corruption and
human rights abuses. Roh lost his seat in the 1992
elections, then mounted two other unsuccessful
political campaigns. In 1998, he regained a seat in
parliament but lost again in 2000.

See also **South Korea.**

Snow, John W. (1939-), was sworn in as
United States secretary of the treasury on Feb. 3,
2003, after winning confirmation by the U.S. Senate on January 30. When nominated for the post
by President George W. Bush in December 2002,
Snow was chairman, president, and chief executive officer of CSX Corporation, a rail freight
company based in Richmond, Virginia.

As chairman of the Business Roundtable, an
influential lobbying group, in 1995 and 1996,

Snow had argued strongly against tax cuts and in favor of balancing the federal budget. However, at a press conference announcing his nomination to the Treasury Department, Snow stressed the importance of promoting economic growth and lowering taxes for business, even at the risk of increasing the budget deficit.

John William Snow was born on Aug. 2, 1939, in Toledo, Ohio. After graduating from the University of Toledo in 1962, he earned a doctorate in economics from the University of Virginia in Charlottesville and a law degree from George Washington University in Washington, D.C. From 1974 to 1977, Snow served in several positions at the Department of Transportation, including administrator of the National Highway Safety Administration from 1976 to 1977.

After leaving the government, Snow joined CSX, rising through the company's management ranks. From 1996 to 1998, Snow oversaw a takeover of Conrail, Inc., a major U.S. rail freight carrier, in a $10.2-billion deal with Norfolk Southern Corporation of Norfolk, Virginia.

See also **Cabinet, U.S.**

Sorenstam, Annika (1970-), a Swedish golfer, in 2003 became the first woman golfer since American Babe Didrikson Zaharias in 1945 to play in a tournament on the men's professional tour in the United States. Sorenstam played the first two rounds of the Bank of America Colonial tournament but did not qualify to play in the final two rounds, tying for 145th out of a field of 154. With her victory in the 2003 Weetabix Women's British Open in August, Sorenstam also became only the sixth woman to complete a

career Grand Slam, winning all four major tournaments in women's professional golf. Sorenstam won the Kraft Nabisco Championship in 2001 and 2002, the U.S. Women's Open in 1995 and 1996, and the McDonald's Ladies Professional Golf Association (LPGA) Championship in 2003.

Annika Sorenstam was born on Oct. 9, 1970, in Stockholm, Sweden. Determined at first to play professional tennis, she began focusing on golf at age 16 after experiencing difficulties with her backhand stroke. In 1991, while a student at the University of Arizona in Tucson, she won the National Collegiate Athletic Association championship. She became world amateur golf champion in 1992.

Sorenstam turned professional in 1992 and competed on the Women Professional Golfers' European Tour, where she was Rookie of the Year in 1993. She joined the LPGA in 1994 and again was named Rookie of the Year. She was the LPGA Player of the Year in 1995, 1997, and 1998. In 2001, Sorenstam shot an 18-hole score of 59, the lowest ever by a woman in professional competition. In 2002, she won 11 tournaments, the most in a single year by a professional woman golfer since 1964.

See also **Golf; Sports.**

Spitzer, Eliot (1959-), attorney general of New York state, spearheaded an investigation into fraudulent practices in the securities industry that resulted in a $1.4-billion settlement with 10 top investment firms in April 2003. Spitzer's office and the United States Securities and Exchange Commission had charged the firms with giving customers falsely favorable stock recommendations about financially troubled companies in order to win those companies as clients.

As attorney general, Spitzer developed a reputation as an aggressive reformer who used the law in creative ways to curb wrongdoing. He also launched attacks against electric-power producers, Internet companies, organized crime, and gun manufacturers.

Eliot Spitzer was born on June 10, 1959, in New York City, where he spent his childhood. He graduated from Princeton University in New Jersey in 1981. While a student, he spent one summer working at menial jobs "to see the world from a different perspective" than his upper-middle-class life, he said.

After graduating from Harvard Law School in Cambridge, Massachusetts, in 1984, he joined a private law firm. Dissatisfied with the work, he joined the Manhattan district attorney's office in

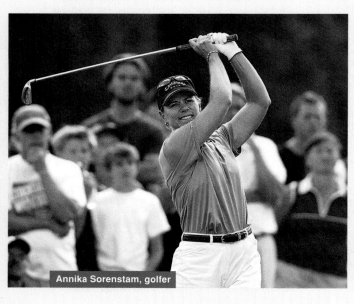
Annika Sorenstam, golfer

Eliot Spitzer, New York state attorney general

Serena Williams, tennis star

and Venus also won a gold medal in women's doubles at the 2000 Summer Olympic Games.

See also **Deaths** (Althea Gibson); **Tennis**.

Wolfowitz, Paul

(1943-), United States deputy secretary of defense, was a major architect of the U.S.-led war on Iraq in 2003. Wolfowitz ranks among leading U.S. neoconservatives—that is, conservatives who advocate the unilateral use of American power, including preemptive military strikes, to counter terrorism and other serious threats to the United States.

Paul Wolfowitz was born in New York City on Dec. 22, 1943, and raised in Ithaca, New York, where he attended Cornell University. After graduating in 1965, he earned a master's degree and doctorate in political science from the University of Chicago.

From 1970 to 1973, Wolfowitz taught at Yale University in New Haven, Connecticut. In 1981, he taught at the Paul H. Nitze School of Advanced International Studies at Johns Hopkins University in Baltimore, Maryland. He served as dean of the school from 1994 to 2001.

Wolfowitz began working in government in 1973 as special assistant in the federal Arms Control and Disarmament Agency. In 1977, he was named deputy assistant secretary of defense for regional planning. In 1981, he joined the U.S. Department of State as director of policy and planning, becoming assistant secretary of state for East Asian and Pacific Affairs in 1982. From 1986 to 1989, he served as U.S. ambassador to Indonesia. He then became undersecretary of defense for policy, a post he held until 1993.

See also **Iraq**.

1986. Four years later, he returned to private practice. In 1994, he ran unsuccessfully for the Democratic nomination for New York attorney general. In 1998, however, he captured that office by a narrow margin.

See also **Courts**.

Williams, Serena

(1981-), the world's top-ranked women's tennis player, in 2003 became only the fifth woman to win tennis's Grand Slam. In January, Williams defeated her older sister Venus, also a top player, to capture the women's singles title at the Australian Open, one of the four competitions that make up the Grand Slam. The others are the French Open, the All-England Tennis Championship at Wimbledon, and the United States Open, all of which Williams won in 2002.

In July 2003, Williams also captured her second straight women's singles title at Wimbledon, also by defeating Venus. Both sisters are known for their powerful serves and groundstrokes as well as for their complete all-around games.

Williams was born in Saginaw, Michigan, on Sept. 26, 1981, and grew up in Compton, California. She began playing tennis at age 5 under the guidance of her father, Richard Williams. She turned professional in 1995 and joined the Women's Tennis Association Tour in 1997.

At age 17, Williams won the 1999 U.S. Open, becoming the first African American woman to win a Grand Slam title since Althea Gibson of the United States won what is now the U.S. Open in 1958. In addition, Williams became the second African American, after Arthur Ashe, to win a Grand Slam singles event.

With Venus, Williams has won numerous doubles titles, including the Australian Open in 2001 and 2003 and Wimbledon in 2000 and 2002. She

Yao Ming

(1980-), a Chinese-born basketball player for the Houston Rockets, ranked as one of the outstanding rookies of the National Basketball Association (NBA) during the 2002-2003 season. In 2003, Yao earned spots on the NBA All-Rookie team and the West team in the NBA All-Star game.

Yao, who stands 7 feet 6 inches (2.3 meters) tall and weighs 310 pounds (140 kilograms), had been a star center in China before joining the Rockets in 2002. His skill and pleasing personality made him one of the most popular young players in the league. He attracted large crowds on the road, especially in cities with large Chinese American populations.

Some sports commentators questioned whether Yao would succeed in the highly physical NBA. Yao, however, quickly became a consistent scorer and rebounder. With his height and delicate shooting touch, he averaged almost 50 percent on field goal attempts. During his first year with Houston, Yao averaged 13.5 points, 8.2 rebounds, and 1.74 blocked shots per game. He was the only rookie to rank in the NBA top 20 in all three categories.

Yao was born in Shanghai, China, on Sept. 12, 1980. Both his parents played basketball for Chinese national teams. At age 18, Yao won his own place on the Chinese national team. He also played for China in the 2000 Olympic Games and the 2002 World Championship Games. He played for five seasons with the Shanghai Sharks of the Chinese Basketball Association before entering the NBA. Yao was the first choice of the Houston Rockets in the 2002 NBA player draft.

See also **Basketball**.

■ Barbara A. Mayes

Yao Ming, outstanding rookie

Peru. President Alejandro Toledo, Peru's first elected leader of Indian ancestry, faced intense public dissatisfaction in 2003 over his administration's failure to provide the 400,000 new jobs he had promised at his 2001 inauguration.

Teachers' strike. The 280,000 members of the Peruvian Education Workers Union went on strike in May 2003, demanding that their monthly salaries of $190 be raised by $60. Many Peruvians found the teachers' demand reasonable, and students, health workers, court employees, and farmers soon joined their strike.

Toledo declared a state of emergency on May 27. Civil liberties normally guaranteed by the Peruvian Constitution were suspended for a month, and police and military units used force to restore order.

These actions led to immediate clashes between protesters and police and army units across the country. In the southeastern city of Puno, troops fired upon students, killing one and wounding dozens of others. Over 30,000 people marched through the streets of Lima, the capital, in June to defy the state of emergency. The Toledo administration caved into the teachers' demand on May 30, agreeing to provide an immediate monthly raise of $29 and a similar increase within three years.

First woman premier. After President Toledo's approval rating dropped to 11 percent in June, he reshuffled his Cabinet and Beatriz Merino, the former head of Peru's tax agency, became Peru's first woman premier. However, Toledo replaced Merino in December with Carlos Ferrero, a veteran lawmaker, amid allegations regarding Merino's personal life.

Resurgence of violence. On June 9, terrorists reputedly belonging to Shining Path abducted 71 workers involved in building a natural gas pipeline for Techint, an Argentine conglomerate, in an area of southeastern Peru. Shining Path is a militant group founded in the 1960's whose stated goal is to destroy existing Peruvian institutions and replace them with a Communist peasant revolutionary regime. The workers were released the following day, allegedly after Techint officials paid a large ransom.

Authorities captured a key member of Shining Path, Florentino Cerron Cardoso, in July 2003. Known as "Comrade Marcelo," he was allegedly linked to 122 killings and many rebel attacks.

Shining Path guerrillas responded to Cardoso's arrest by killing five Peruvian marines and two civilian guides in an ambush in south-central Peru. The attack on Peruvian government forces was the deadliest in four years and occurred amid credible reports that terrorists and drug traffickers had joined forces.

Commission report. The Truth and Reconciliation Commission, a body appointed by the government to investigate and hear testimony on Peru's civil war, issued a report in August that more than 69,000 Peruvians were killed or "disappeared" during revolutionary violence between 1980 and 2000—more than twice as many as previously estimated. The report was based on testimony taken from nearly 17,000 people in the course of a two-year investigation.

According to the report, about 85 percent of the killings occurred within five provinces, including Ayacucho. Three-quarters of the victims were Quechua-speaking Indian peasants.

Corruption trials. Vladimiro Montesinos, the former head of Peru's intelligence service, was convicted in March 2003 in the first of more than 60 public trials. He faced charges of corruption during the 10-year rule of former President Alberto Fujimori, who fled Peru in 2000.

While exiled in Japan, Fujimori claimed innocence of any wrongdoing in the matter and of charges that his administration had brutally suppressed dissension. To clear his name, Fujimori launched an hour-long, weekly radio broadcast, which aired in Peru starting in September 2003 and was paid for by his supporters.

◼ Nathan A. Haverstock

See also **Latin America; Terrorism.**

Petroleum and gas. See Energy supply.

Philadelphia. Major events in Philadelphia in 2003 revolved around a hotly contested mayoral election as well as the restructuring of schools and buildings. Democrat John Street was elected to a second term as mayor on November 4 after a bitter campaign against Republican businessman Sam Katz, who had run unsuccessfully against Street in the previous mayoral race.

In October, investigators assigned by the Philadelphia police discovered a listening device with multiple microphones hidden in the ceiling of the mayor's office in City Hall. Federal Bureau of Investigation (FBI) officials confirmed that the bug was theirs but also said that the mayor was not the target of an investigation. Even so, FBI officials raided city offices and politically connected firms for files.

The federal agents made no charges during the campaign but indicated that they were conducting a wide-ranging investigation of local government. The discovery of the bug galvanized the city's black community to rally for the African American mayor.

Street positioned himself in the campaign as the city's "neighborhood mayor" because of his program to raze blighted housing and an expensive crime prevention initiative. Katz based much of his campaign on bold tax proposals. Street ran on his 20 years of government experience and

criticized Katz for putting the city at risk with his tax proposals.

School reform. Paul Vallas, who became the chief executive of the School District of Philadelphia in July 2002, instituted various programs in 2003, including a strict disciplinary policy; a project to elevate academic standards in the city's high schools; new after-school and summer school programs; and a teacher recruitment program. He also planned to build 5 schools and renovate 22 others.

The new discipline policy mandated that all violent incidents be reported and addressed by authorities. It also ordered disciplinary action for students who committed crimes away from school grounds.

Educators labeled the after-school project, called the Extended Day program, a success. Citing the program, officials announced in November 2003 that almost 17,000 fewer students in the school district tested in the bottom quartile of the TerraNova national standardized exam in 2003 than in 2002.

The teacher recruitment program garnered 700 new educators for the 2003-2004 academic year. The Campaign for Human Capital, which led the effort to develop effective recruitment and retention strategies, provided many of the recommendations that resulted in over 4,000 teaching applications.

National Constitution Center. The new, privately-funded National Constitution Center opened on July 4, 2003, in Independence National Historical Park in Philadelphia's Center City. The park is the site of Independence Hall, the Liberty Bell, and other historic symbols.

As part of a general reconstruction of the national park that includes the new center, the Liberty Bell was installed in a new facility, called the Liberty Bell Center. The structure replaced a smaller pavilion where the bell had been displayed since 1976.

New football stadium. The Philadelphia Eagles football team played its first home game of the season in September 2003 in Lincoln Financial Field, the new stadium on the city's south side. The $512-million stadium was the most expensive to date among National Football League teams. The stadium features 69,030 seats, 2 giant video screens, and 172 luxury suites.

Archbishop named. Justin Rigali was installed as archbishop of Philadelphia, the sixth-largest diocese in the United States, and spiritual leader of 1.5 million Roman Catholics in October. He succeeded Cardinal Anthony J. Bevilacqua, who retired. Rigali was elevated to cardinal by Pope John Paul II in Rome later in October.

◼ Howard S. Shapiro

See also **City; Education; Elections; Football.**

Philippines. A group of approximately 320 military officers and soldiers barricaded themselves inside an apartment building in Manila, the Philippine capital, on July 27, 2003. The mutineers, who rigged the building with explosives, demanded the resignations of Philippine President Gloria Macapagal-Arroyo and Defense Secretary Angelo Reyes. They also asked for better pay and living conditions. Shortly after the siege began, Arroyo declared that the country was under a state of rebellion and demanded on national television that the mutineers surrender.

The mutineers accused the government of selling weapons to Muslim and Communist rebels and of staging bombings to justify more aid from the United States. They charged that the government staged bombings in Davao City in March and April that killed dozens of people.

The mutineers surrendered on July 28 after military commanders agreed to investigate the mutineers' grievances and allowed the rebels to return to their military posts. In her state of the union address on July 28, Macapagal-Arroyo pledged that she would establish three independent commissions to investigate the origins of the uprising and the charges made by the mutineers. On August 11, Macapagal-Arroyo lifted the state of rebellion.

The mutiny concerned many Filipinos, who have seen two presidents toppled by *coups* (overthrows) since the mid-1980's. Widespread public protests against President Ferdinand Marcos, who was elected in 1965, forced him to leave office in 1986. Macapagal-Arroyo, who was elected vice president in 1998, assumed the presidency in 2001, when her predecessor, Joseph Estrada, was forced out of office by a combination of public protest and military opposition. Political observers speculated that the 2003 mutiny was meant to overthrow Macapagal-Arroyo and return the government to Estrada, who was in prison on corruption charges.

Some government officials said that the 2003 mutiny was organized by Philippine Senator Gregorio Honasan, a former Army colonel who mounted three unsuccessful coup attempts against Corazon Aquino, Philippine president from 1986 to 1992. Honasan, who declared his candidacy for president in the 2004 election, denied involvement in the mutiny.

Aftermath. In August 2003, Reyes resigned as defense secretary. He warned of a "well-organized and well-funded effort by certain forces to bring down our democracy through massive disinformation and political agitation." Victor Corpus, the chief of military intelligence, also resigned in August.

Macapagal-Arroyo won popular support for her handling of the mutiny. In October, she announced that she would run for reelection in 2004, reversing her decision in December 2002 that she would not seek another term. The Philippine Constitution limits presidents to a single, six-year term, but Macapagal-Arroyo was eligible to run because she became president halfway through Estrada's term.

Rebel violence. The Philippine military battled rebellions by Islamic separatists and Communist guerrillas in 2003. It also continued to work with the United States to crack down on international terrorist groups that were taking root in the country.

Islamic rebel groups had been fighting for independence in the Philippines since the 1970's. The Moro Islamic Liberation Front (MILF), the largest of the rebel groups, signed a peace agreement with the government in 2002, but neither side honored terms of the accord, and violence continued in 2003. Investigators said that the MILF—and not the government—masterminded the deadly March and April bombings in Davao City. Officials also suspected the involvement of Jamaah Islamiyah, an Asian terrorist group with ties to al-Qa'ida, an international network of Muslim extremists.

Prison escape. In July, Fathur Rohman al-Ghozi, an Indonesian fugitive and a member of Jemaah Islamiyah, escaped from jail with two other cellmates. The three men opened the door of their cell and walked out of the maximum-security prison located on the grounds of the national police headquarters. The two cellmates were members of Abu Sayyaf, an Islamic separatist group responsible for much of the terrorist activity in the Philippines in the 2000's. Philippine authorities found and killed al-Ghozi in October.

The escape raised questions about corruption and incompetence among police. The head of the prison resigned following the escape, and four guards were fired and held on criminal charges.

The United States announced in 2003 that 1,700 U.S. soldiers would go to the southern Philippines, an area known to be a training ground of Jamaah Islamiyah. In June, the United States canceled its plans because it would have violated a Philippine constitutional ban on foreign troops fighting on Philippine territory.

Economy. The Philippine economy, which grew approximately 4.4 percent in 2003, benefited from the government's efforts to improve tax collection. New methods to control tax evasion helped the government trim its enormous budget deficit for the first time since 1998.

The Philippine Supreme Court ruled in July 2003 that the government was entitled to $658 million that was stolen by Marcos when he was president. ■ Henry S. Bradsher

See also **Asia; Terrorism.**

Physics. Scientists searching for "gravity waves" were handed a new and powerful tool in July 2003 in the form of a super-sensitive antenna designed to detect tiny ripples in the fabric of space-time. German-born physicist and Nobel prize winner Albert Einstein had predicted the existence of gravity waves in 1916. More recently, researchers concluded that strong gravity waves should arise from some of the most violent events in the universe, such as collisions between heavy objects such as black holes or neutron stars. Despite these violent origins, by the time they reach Earth, gravity waves would be very feeble and hard to detect.

The new tool, called VIRGO, was located near Cascina, Italy, and completed by a team of Italian and French physicists. Two similar antennas of the Laser Interferometer Gravitational-Wave Observatory (LIGO), located in the states of Louisiana and Washington, neared completion in 2003.

Measuring gravity waves. A passing gravity wave makes the distance between two objects alternately grow and shrink. It simultaneously stretches space in one direction and squeezes it in a perpendicular direction. But the expected changes in distance are extremely small. Two objects many miles apart will change their separation by less than the diameter of an atomic nucleus. To detect an effect this minute, the VIRGO and LIGO scientists use very fine rulers—waves of laser light. Each detecting antenna is an interferometer, a device in which two beams of light bounce back and forth between widely separated mirrors. After hundreds of round trips between the mirrors, the light beams are combined to see whether they are in step.

Light waves in step will reinforce one another, producing a brighter wave. If they are one-half wavelength out of step, they will cancel each other out. Einstein predicted that a gravity wave that makes one path longer will make the perpendicular path shorter, adding to the effect. A small change in the distance either beam traveled would make a noticeable change in the brightness of the combined beam.

VIRGO's beams bounce between mirrors located 1.9 miles (3.0 kilometers) apart. Scientists expected months or even years of fine-tuning before these antennas reach full sensitivity.

Antineutrinos have mass, too. Just as 2002 brought conclusive proof that neutrinos have mass, 2003 began with the first indications that the same is true for their antimatter counterparts, antineutrinos. In January, a team of physicists from Japan and the United States, reported that they had observed antineutrinos produced by nuclear power plants in Japan and South Korea. The team used a 990-ton (900-metric-ton) device called KamLAND, located in Japan.

Neutrinos and antineutrinos both interact so feebly with matter that they can pass freely through the Earth. Scientists must use tons of sensitive material to intercept just a few of the trillions of neutrinos that pass through a detector. Detectors must be located deep underground to avoid being swamped by the normal background radiation at the Earth's surface.

Everything on Earth is bathed in an intense stream of neutrinos that come from nuclear reactions that power the sun. Antineutrinos are much rarer, but nuclear reactors produce large numbers of them. There are 22 reactors close enough to KamLAND to provide detectable antineutrinos. The sun and nuclear reactors both produce electron neutrinos and electron antineutrinos. There are two other types of neutrinos and antineutrinos, and if electron neutrinos and antineutrinos have mass they convert themselves into the other types while in flight. KamLAND can detect only electron antineutrinos, so if they are changing into other types, it will see fewer particles than expected, which was what happened.

The experiment gave a rough estimate of the antineutrino's mass—about 100 million times smaller than the electron's mass. This result is obtained with neutrinos from the sun. So, the symmetry (balance) between matter and antimatter remains on firm ground. ■ Robert H. March

Poetry. The 2003 Pulitzer Prize for poetry was awarded to Paul Muldoon for his collection, *Moy Sand and Gravel*. (The noun *moy* means a measure for salt, or a bushel. As an adjective, it means mild or demure.) Muldoon, a native of Ireland, came to the United States in 1987.

Muldoon writes poems that incorporate the poetic traditions of both Ireland and the United States. In his new collection, he explored the often mundane subject of life in modern suburbia with traditional strict poetic forms, such as *sestinas* (poems with six, six-line stanzas and a three-line concluding stanza), *terza rima* (poems in three-line groupings with the rhyme scheme aba bcb cdc, . . .) and *haiku* (three-line poems with 17 syllables). Muldoon also invented his own forms and used word play and cliche in writing about serious issues, such as Ireland's relationship with the United Kingdom. In the poem "At the Sign of the Black Horse, September 1999," he addresses Irish, Jewish, and U.S. history, formalism and invention, and seriousness and comedy. He writes of himself as "I, the so-called Goy from the Moy." The other nominees for the 2003 Pulitzer Prize were J. D. McClatchy's *Hazmat* and *Music Like Dirt* by Frank Bidart, winner of the 2002 Wallace Stevens Award.

Wallace Stevens Award. The Academy of American Poets honored Richard Wilbur with the

2003 Wallace Stevens Award, a prize given for a body of substantial work created over the course of a career. Wilbur was born in New York City. He has won numerous awards, including the Pulitzer Prize, the National Book Award, and the Frost Medal. He was the 1987-1988 poet laureate of the United States.

National Book Awards. Four volumes of poetry were nominated for the National Book Awards in 2003. The award went to C. K. Williams for his collection *The Singing.* Williams also was a National Book Award finalist in 1999 for his work *Repair.* The collection *The Singing* was a departure from his usual style of writing in very long lines. In a poem about Rembrandt's self-portrait, Williams reflected on the pleasures of living and how pleasure must always end: "whatever it is beyond/ dying and fear of dying/. . . eludes me,/ yet no longer eludes me."

The finalists for the 2003 award included Carol Muske-Dukes, who was nominated for *Sparrow.* Her poems, dedicated to her late husband, are meditations on grief and longing. Charles Simic received a nomination for his collection *The Voice at 3:00 A.M.,* poems of manic emotional states, wit, and foreboding. In *Jelly Roll: A Blues,* Kevin Young plays with the blues form and other kinds of music, with titles such as "Dixieland," "Ragtime," "Scherzo," and "Nocturne."

National Poetry Slam. The 2003 National Poetry Slam was held in Chicago from August 6 to 9. A poetry slam is a cross between a poetry reading and a sporting event. Competitors are as interested in the delivery and performance of a poem as they are in the words and subject matter. Individual competitors and four-person teams compete in fast-paced, rehearsed, and intense performances. Audiences loudly cheer or jeer slam competitors.

Mike McGee, a slam poet from San Jose, California, was the individual winner of the 2003 National Poetry Slam. McGee calls himself a "standup poet," referring to the form of comedy in which a single comedian entertains an audience. Team Los Angeles was the winner out of the 63 teams from the United States and Canada that participated.

Poet laureate. James H. Billington of the U.S. Library of Congress announced on August 28 the appointment of Louise Gluck as the library's 12th Poet Laureate Consultant in Poetry. She began her duties in October with a reading of her work. Gluck has written nine books of poetry, including *Vita Nova* (1999), which won *The New Yorker* magazine's Book Award in Poetry and *The Wild Iris* (1992), which received the Pulitzer Prize.

■ Brian Bouldrey

See also **Pulitzer Prizes.**

Poland. In March 2003, Prime Minister Leszek Miller expelled the Peasant Party from the ruling coalition headed by his party, the Democratic Left Alliance, reducing the coalition's voting strength in parliament to a minority. Later in March, two of Miller's key ministers resigned. In June, Miller's minority government survived a vote of no-confidence.

Miller's political difficulties were tied to his government's performance on the economy, political analysts noted. According to a report by the European Commission, Poland's unemployment rate hovered around 20 percent in mid-2003, the highest level among European Union (EU) member or candidate member nations.

In a June referendum, Polish voters approved their nation's entry into the EU by a three-to-one margin. The poll drew 60 percent of registered voters. Poland was among 10 candidate nations slated to join the EU in May 2004.

Poland's government supported the United States-led war in Iraq in early 2003. In May, Polish authorities agreed to send more than 2,000 troops to administer one of the stabilization zones in postwar Iraq, at the request of U.S. officials. By early August, the troops were on the ground in Iraq. ■ Sharon L. Wolchik

See also **Europe; Iraq: A Special Report.**

Pollution. See Environmental pollution.

Popular music. The Recording Industry Association of America (RIAA) took legal action in September 2003 against more than 200 people whom the organization accused of illegally exchanging copyrighted music downloaded from the Internet. The RIAA is a Washington, D.C.-based organization that represents the recording industry's intellectual property rights. A number of Web sites allowed millions of people to trade copyrighted music on the Internet for no charge. RIAA attorneys claimed that the process, called file sharing, was to blame for a 31 percent decrease in compact disc (CD) sales since mid-2000.

On Sept. 8, 2003, the RIAA, acting on behalf of five major record companies, sued 261 people whom the organization accused of downloading "substantial amounts" of copyrighted songs. Federal copyright law allows penalties ranging from between $750 and $150,000 for each violation. The RIAA also instituted an amnesty program for file sharers who had not already been sued. To qualify, file sharers had to identify themselves and remove all illegal music files from their computers.

Subscription services offered consumers an authorized alternative to illegal file sharing and CD *burning* (copying) in April 2003, when Apple Computer, Inc., of Cupertino, California, launched a new service called the iTunes Music Store for Macs. The service sold digital music over the Inter-

Norah Jones performs during the 45th Annual Grammy Awards in New York City on Feb. 23, 2003. Jones won five Grammy Awards, including Album of the Year, for *Come Away With Me.*

GRAMMY AWARD WINNERS IN 2003

Record of the Year, "Don't Know Why," Norah Jones

Album of the Year, "Come Away With Me," Norah Jones

Song of the Year, "Don't Know Why," Norah Jones

New Artist, Norah Jones

Pop Vocal Performance, Female, "Don't Know Why," Norah Jones

Pop Vocal Performance, Male, "Your Body Is a Wonderland," John Mayer

Pop Performance by a Duo or Group, "Hey Baby," No Doubt

Traditional Pop Vocal Album, "Playin' with My Friends:

Bennett Sings the Blues," Tony Bennett

Rock Vocal Performance, Female, "Steve McQueen," Sheryl Crow

Rock Vocal Performance, Male, "The Rising," Bruce Springsteen

Rock Performance by a Duo or Group with Vocal, "In My Place," Coldplay

Hard Rock Performance, "All My Life," Foo Fighters

Metal Performance, "Here To Stay," Korn

Rock Song, "The Rising," Bruce Springsteen

Rock Album, "The Rising," Bruce Springsteen

Alternative Music Album, "A Rush of Blood to the Head," Coldplay

Rhythm-and-Blues Vocal Performance, Female, "He Think I Don't Know," Mary J. Blige

Rhythm-and-Blues Vocal Performance, Male, "U Don't Have To Call," Usher

Rhythm-and-Blues Performance by a Duo or Group with Vocal, "Love's In Need Of Love Today," Stevie Wonder & Take 6

Rhythm-and-Blues Song, "Love Of My Life (An Ode to Hip-Hop)," Erykah Badu, Madukwu Chinwah, Rashid Lonnie Lynn, Robert Ozuna, James Poyser, Raphael Saadiq, and Glen Standridge

Rhythm-and-Blues Album, "Voyage to India," India.Arie

Rap Solo Performance, Female "Scream a.k.a. Itchin'," Missy Elliott

Rap Solo Performance, Male "Hot in Herre," Nelly

Rap Performance by a Duo or Group, "The Whole World," OutKast featuring Killer Mike

Rap Album, "The Eminem Show," Eminem

Contemporary Jazz Album, "Speaking of Now," Pat Metheny Group

Jazz Vocal Album, "Live in Paris," Diana Krall

Jazz Instrumental, Solo, "My Ship," Herbie Hancock

Jazz Instrumental Album, Individual or Group, "Directions in Music," Herbie Hancock, Michael Brecker, and Roy Hargrove

Large Jazz Ensemble Album, "What Goes Around," Dave Holland Big Band

Country Album, "Home," Dixie Chicks

Country Song, "Where Were You (When the World Stopped Turning)," Alan Jackson

Country Vocal Performance, Female, "Cry," Faith Hill

Country Vocal Performance, Male, "Give My Love to Rose," Johnny Cash

Country Performance by a Duo or Group with Vocal, "Long Time Gone," Dixie Chicks

Country Vocal Collaboration, "Mendocino County Line," Willie Nelson with Lee Ann Womack

Country Instrumental Performance, "Lil' Jack Slade," Dixie Chicks

net. It charged users 99 cents to download each song. In the first two weeks, users downloaded approximately 2 million songs. A version for personal computers (PC's) was introduced in October. Several other companies introduced similar download services in 2003, including Napster, which was reintroduced in October. In 2000, the music industry sued Napster, then a free Internet file-sharing service, for its role in the unauthorized copying of sound recordings.

Album sales in the United States declined 8.1 percent in the first six months of 2003, according to Nielsen SoundScan, a White Plains, New York, company that tracks the sales of music and music video products throughout the United States and Canada. To spur sales, officials at Universal Music Group, a recording company headquartered in Santa Monica, California, announced in September that they would reduce the suggested retail price of new CD's.

Top sellers. *Get Rich or Die Trying* by rap artist 50 Cent, whose real name is Curtis Jackson, was the best-selling album of 2003, according to Nielsen SoundScan. The album sold 6.2 million copies and featured the hit song "In Da Club."

Other best-selling CD's of 2003, according to Nielsen SoundScan, included *Meteora* by Linkin Park, *Fallen* by Evanescence, and *Chocolate Factory* by R. Kelly.

Change of pace. Several female singers released albums in 2003 that were departures from their previous efforts. In June, Jewel released *0304,* an album that mined rap, pop, and dance genres in an attempt to distance herself from such lighter releases as her 1995 album *Pieces of You.*

Liz Phair, whose 1993 album *Exile in Guyville* was considered by critics to be one of the most influential albums of the 1990's, released *Liz Phair* in June 2003. The album was an attempt by Phair to be more of a commercial success and less of a feminist icon. Both albums, though well-received by critics, received mixed reviews by fans who preferred the earlier releases to the new endeavors.

In an attempt to mature beyond her mainly adolescent audience, Britney Spears released *In the Zone* in November. The album, which received lukewarm reviews, contained songs of a more provocative nature.

Hip-hop. *Speakerboxxx/The Love Below* by OutKast, released in September, was the most critically acclaimed hip-hop album of 2003. The album was actually comprised of two solo albums by Andre "Andre 3000" Benjamin and Antwan "Big Boi" Patton. The album included the song "Hey Ya!," which received strong reviews from both hip-hop and rock music fans.

Country music. The Dixie Chicks, one of country music's most critically acclaimed and commercially successful acts, were the center of controversy in 2003 over remarks many people perceived to be unpatriotic. In March, before the start of the U.S.-led war on Iraq, singer Natalie Maines told a London concert audience, "Just so you know, we're ashamed the president of the United States is from Texas." Both the group and President George W. Bush have roots in Texas. Maines later apologized and said though the group disagreed with the policies of the Bush administration, they meant no disrespect to U.S. armed forces.

The Dixie Chicks also feuded publicly with fellow country singer Toby Keith, who found success in 2002 with his prowar song, "Courtesy of the Red, White & Blue (The Angry American)." Keith maintained that Maines's comment was anti-American.

In the days following Maines's comment, many country and top 40 radio stations stopped playing the Dixie Chicks' music, which affected the sales of their Grammy Award-winning 2002 album, *Home.* Protesters also publicly destroyed copies of their CD's.

Patriotic songs and albums enjoyed a resurgence in 2003 in country music following President Bush's declaration of war in Iraq. These included Darryl Worley's album *Have You Forgotten,* released in April, and Toby Keith's "The Taliban Song" from *Shock'n Y'all,* which Keith released in November.

Lost Elvis song. Fans of entertainer Elvis Presley, who died in 1977, awaited the release of a forgotten song originally recorded for the motion picture *Roustabout* (1964). "I'm a Roustabout" was included on the compilation disc *Elvis 2nd To None,* released in October 2003. The song did not appear in the movie, and the only known recording was forgotten among boxes of records and tapes belonging to Winfield Scott, who co-wrote the song. Scott said he remembered the song during an interview about his career that he gave in 2002.

Veteran artists. *Elvis 2nd To None* was just one of several "greatest hits" albums and concert tours in 2003 that were marketed to adults over age 40. The Eagles, one of the most successful U.S. rock bands of the 1970's, released *The Very Best of the Eagles* in October 2003. The two-disc CD contained previously released material. Paul Simon and Art Garfunkel, who formed the pop duo Simon & Garfunkel, reunited in 2003 and performed several sold-out concerts across the United States. The duo was a success in the 1960's but separated in 1970. They briefly reunited in the early 1980's for a concert in New York City's Central Park and a subsequent tour.

Renewed success. Several former pop music, rhythm-and-blues, and rock stars enjoyed renewed success in 2003 by recording albums of jazz and popular standards. Among the releases were *Here*

Johnny Cash: The Man In Black

Johnny Cash, one of popular music's most enduring and influential figures, died on Sept. 12, 2003, at age 71. Although he was known as a country singer, Cash's music spanned several genres, including folk, gospel, blues, and rock 'n' roll. His songs about the hard lives of the rural poor, gamblers, and convicts endeared him to generations of fans. He was one of the few musicians ever inducted into the Country Music Hall of Fame, the Rock & Roll Hall of Fame, and the Songwriter's Hall of Fame.

John R. Cash was born in Kingsland, Arkansas, on Feb. 26, 1932, one of seven children born to sharecroppers Ray and Carrie Cash. While growing up, Cash found escape from his harsh surroundings in music. In 1950, after graduating from high school, he enlisted in the United States Air Force and taught himself to play guitar while stationed in Germany.

In 1955, Cash began recording for Sun Records in Memphis, the label that launched the careers of Elvis Presley, Carl Perkins, Roy Orbison, and Jerry Lee Lewis. Cash's first success was the song "Cry, Cry, Cry" (1955) followed by "I Walk the Line" (1956). Like many artists who recorded with Sun Records, Cash's songs broke through regional, musical, and racial barriers.

Cash was known for his unique rumbling baritone and the gritty originality of his empathetic songs. In most of the 1,500 songs Cash wrote, subjects such as love, God, and murder were handled with passion and sung from the flawed perspective of a common man.

The 1969 live album *At San Quentin* contained Cash's biggest hit, "A Boy Named Sue." Another success, the love song "Ring of Fire," was co-written by June Carter, a member of the famous Carter family of country musicians. Carter became Cash's wife in 1968. Her death on May 15, 2003, preceded his by almost exactly four months.

Though in ill health, Cash recorded some of his most critically acclaimed music in his final years. In 1994, he released the first of four *American Recordings* albums. On these albums, Cash revisited his older works and interpreted newer songs by contemporary songwriters.

His final musical testament, "Hurt," was a rendition of a Nine Inch Nails song about drug addiction. A music video for the song depicted a ravaged Cash seemingly reflecting on his wilder, younger days. Much of Cash's career was marked by wild behavior and substance abuse, which he chronicled in his autobiography, *Man in Black* (1975). The title was based on Cash's nickname, which came from his fondness for dressing entirely in black.

Cash refused to compromise in his music. He once said that country music legend Ernest Tubb had told him, "You sound different, you act different, you look different; if that's the way you honestly feel it, then that's the way you want to do it, and don't let anybody change you."

Cash never did.　■ Donald Liebenson

I Am: Isley Meets Bacharach by Ronald Isley and Burt Bacharach; *Bette Midler Sings the Rosemary Clooney Songbook* by Bette Midler; *But Beautiful, Standards: Volume 1* by Boz Scaggs; and *As Time Goes By ... The Great American Songbook: Volume II* by Rod Stewart.

Independent efforts. Veteran artists who felt ignored by major record labels independently released albums in 2003. *Just an American Boy: An Audio Documentary* by Steve Earle; *Beneath This Gruff Exterior* by John Hiatt, and *Population Me* by Dwight Yoakam were among the releases. Independent albums allowed artists more creative freedom. Artists were also under less pressure to sell millions of copies. An independent release might sell tens of thousands of copies.

Let It Be...Naked, a remixed version of the Beatles' 1970 album *Let It Be,* was released in November 2003. The original album was intended to be a spontaneous, back-to-basics recording, but after the group disbanded, producer Phil Spector released the album with lavish production. The new version presents songs such as "The Long and Winding Road" as the band recorded them—without such elements as strings, choir, and horns.

■ Donald Liebenson

See also **Computer; Deaths; Internet; People in the news** (Norah Jones); **Supreme Court of the United States.**

Population. According to the United Nations (UN), the world's population climbed to more than 6.3 billion people in 2003. During the year, UN Secretary General Kofi Annan urged world leaders to focus more attention on two groups, adolescents and the urban poor.

Youth. From June 30 to July 1, the UN, the International Labour Organization (ILO), and the World Bank cosponsored a meeting of the Youth Employment Network (YEN) in Geneva. The ILO is a UN agency that promotes the welfare of workers. The World Bank is an international organization that provides loans for development. YEN was established in 2000 to help provide the world's young people with opportunities for meaningful and productive work. At the meeting in Geneva, YEN representatives reported that an estimated 1.2 billion young people aged 15 to 24 will reach working age in the next 10 years. In 2003, according to the ILO, about 74 million 15- to 24-year-olds were unemployed. An additional 59 million youths aged 15 to 17 were engaged in hazardous forms of work. The organizations urged governments to provide the education and training young people need to start a career.

On World Population Day, July 11, the UN Population Fund (UNFPA), which is responsible for family planning programs, reported that youths aged 10 to 19 numbered more than 1 bil-

lion in 2003, the largest youth generation in history. UNFPA representatives said that more than 70,000 teen-age girls marry and nearly 40,000 give birth each day. These teen-agers have an incomplete education, limited opportunities for a professional career, and serious health risks. The Fund called for assisting girls to complete high school and to delay marriage and childbirth, in order to break the cycle of poor health, illiteracy, and poverty in many developing countries.

The State of World Population 2003 report, released by the UNFPA in October, expressed further concern about adolescents. According to the report, half of all new HIV infections each year occur in young people aged 15 to 24. The UNFPA called on governments to increase their efforts for youth-friendly reproductive health services.

The urban poor. The UN Human Settlement Programme (UN-Habitat) reported in October that one-sixth of the world's population—about 1 billion people—live in substandard living conditions. Because of rapid urbanization, by 2030, the number of people throughout the world living in slums is expected to double. UN-Habitat officials called for governments to aid the urban poor by providing help with employment, shelter, food, health, education, and access to public services. ■ J. Tuyet Nguyen

Portugal suffered through a devastating series of forest fires in 2003. The fires broke out across the country in August after a period of heat and drought, which also affected many other parts of Europe. The fires claimed at least 18 lives and burned more than 530,000 acres (214,500 hectares) of woodland. Timber, cork, and other forest products are a major industry in the country, and the government estimated that the fires caused around $1.1 billion in damage.

The damage affected the country's economy, which was struggling to recover from a budgetary crisis. In 2002, Portugal became the first country using the euro to report a budget deficit that exceeded the allowable limit of 3 percent of *gross domestic product* (GDP, the total value of goods and services produced in a country in a year.)

The government of Prime Minister Jose Manuel Durao Barroso had increased some taxes and frozen government spending to reduce the deficit. Those measures pushed the economy into recession in 2002, but they did succeed in reducing the deficit. The European Commission, the agency that enforces the rules for euro members, announced in March 2003 that Portugal's deficit had declined to 2.7 percent of the GDP in 2002 from 4.1 percent in 2001. The 2003 fires, however, threatened to worsen the deficit and deepen the recession. In November, the commission forecast that the Portuguese economy would decline by 0.8 percent in 2003. It also forecast that the budget deficit would be 2.9 percent of the GDP for the year.

Child abuse scandal. Allegations of child abuse at state-run orphanages shocked the people of Portugal in 2003. The allegations first surfaced in late 2002, with the arrest of an employee at the Casa Pia orphanage. He was accused of helping wealthy pedophiles sexually abuse boys at the orphanage. The affair erupted into a national scandal in May 2003, when police arrested the spokesman of the opposition Socialist Party, a former Portuguese ambassador, two of the country's leading television personalities, and other prominent figures. In December 2003, prosecutors formally charged 10 of the individuals arrested. The revelations shook the faith of many Portuguese in state institutions, as the investigation into the affair disclosed that former government ministers and the police were aware of allegations of abuse at the orphanage in the early 1980's but failed to act.   ■ Tom Buerkle

See also **Europe; Weather.**

President of the United States.
See **United States, President of the.**

Prince Edward Island. See **Canadian provinces.**

Prisons. The United States Department of Justice reported in July 2003 that 1,440,655 prisoners were detained under federal or state authority as of Dec. 31, 2002, with 1,361,258 in federal or state prisons and the remaining 79,397 in local jails. The total federal and state incarceration of 1,440,655 represented a 2.6-percent increase over the 2001 total, down from the 3.6-percent rate of growth during the mid-1990's but sharply up from the 1.1-percent increase between 2000 and 2001.

The federal prison system and the states of California and Texas were nearly on par, with 163,528 men and women in federal prisons and about 162,000 prisoners in each of the two state prison systems. Each state has its own justice and prison system. The federal system is a separate entity.

The overall U.S. prison population in 2002, including local jails and military and juvenile facilities, totaled 2,166,260. Women comprised 6.8 percent of the adult prison population.

Overcrowding. According to a survey conducted by the Department of Justice in 2003, state prisons operated at between 1 and 17 percent above capacity in 2002. The survey revealed that federal prisons operated at 33 percent above capacity during 2002.

Personnel change. In April 2003, U.S. Attor-

ney General John Ashcroft appointed Harley G. Lappin director of the Federal Bureau of Prisons to replace outgoing director Kathleen Hawk Sawyer, who retired. Lappin, the former director of the bureau's Mid-Atlantic region, had been warden of the U.S. penitentiary in Terre Haute, Indiana, in 2001 when Oklahoma City bomber Timothy McVeigh was put to death in the first federal execution in nearly 40 years.

Death row. As of July 15, 2003, a total of 3,517 prison inmates awaited execution in federal and state prisons, down from 3,718 in July 2002. The decline was due in part to actions by Illinois Governor George Ryan before he left office on Jan. 13, 2003. Explaining that revelations of flawed convictions on death row rendered the death penalty unenforceable, Ryan cleared the state's death row of 171 prisoners by issuing 167 *commutations* (reduction to specific prison terms) and 4 pardons. In September, the Ninth U.S. District Court of Appeals overturned death sentences of more than 100 inmates on death row in Arizona, Montana, and Idaho.

Between January and mid-October, 2003, state and federal authorities executed 57 people. Texas and Oklahoma together accounted for more than half of the total.   ■ Brian Bouldrey

See also **Courts; Crime; State government.**

Prizes. See **Nobel Prizes; Pulitzer Prizes.**

Protestantism. Two issues dominated Protestantism in 2003—the war in Iraq and the place of homosexuals in the church.

The war in Iraq. Most of the leaders of the mainline Protestant churches in the United States opposed the war in Iraq. In autumn 2002, leaders in the National Council of Churches and representatives from mainline Protestant faiths joined with non-Protestant clergy to compose a letter to U.S. President George W. Bush outlining their disagreement with his plan for Iraq.

Mainline Protestant leaders continued their criticism of U.S. policy in Iraq after the war began in March 2003. Most of these religious leaders had advocated the United States take military action only if supported by the United Nations.

While many Protestant leaders opposed the war in Iraq, polls revealed that support for the war among the U.S. Protestant laity was slightly stronger than that within the general population. Some 62 percent of mainline Protestants backed the war in Iraq, compared with 59 percent of the general U.S. public. By contrast, 77 percent of the white Evangelical Protestant laity in the United States supported the war, as did much of their leadership.

Interfaith controversy. In September, the president and the pastor of Valparaiso University, a Lutheran school in Valparaiso, Indiana, officially "repented" to the Lutheran Church-Missouri Synod (LCMS). Valparaiso's president, Alan Harre, and pastor, Joseph Cunningham, had hosted a service on the first anniversary of the Sept. 11, 2001, terrorist attacks on the United States. Muslim and Jewish clerics also led prayers at this memorial. Because of this service Harre and Cunningham were charged with participating in an event featuring *syncretism* (an attempt to combine differing beliefs into one system of religion) by conservative congregations within the LCMS. Both men were then requested to ask forgiveness. David Benke, president of the Atlantic district of the LCMS, had been suspended under similar circumstances surrounding a service in 2001, but was reinstated in 2003.

Enthronement. In an elaborate ceremony held in February 2003, noted theologian Rowan Williams was enthroned in historic Canterbury Cathedral in Canterbury, England, as the spiritual head of the Anglican Communion. Williams had studied and taught at both Cambridge and Oxford, England's most prestigious universities. Canterbury was a Roman Catholic *see* (district under a bishop's authority) before the English branch of the Roman Catholic Church broke away to form the Anglican Church in the 1500's. Thus, the see of Canterbury is older than the Anglican Church, and Williams is the first Welshman in at least 1,000 years to become its archbishop.

Openly gay bishop elected. In June 2003, the New Hampshire diocese of the U.S. Episcopal Church (ECUSA) elected V. Gene Robinson as its bishop. Robinson, a gay man in a long-term committed relationship, had served as a canon in the Episcopal Church since 1988.

Conservative Episcopalians in the United States were vocal in their criticism of Robinson's election and bishops from Africa threatened to break ties with the American church. The ECUSA was committed to maintaining close ties with the African church, but the majority of U.S. bishops meeting in August at the ECUSA General Convention in Milwaukee, Wisconsin, could not in conscience refuse to confirm Robinson.

Leaders—called primates—of the Anglican Communion (the worldwide body of Anglicans) subsequntly were convened in London by Rowan Williams, who hoped to prevent a *schism* (a split that divides a church into two or more sects). Nevertheless, 13 Episcopal bishops announced in December that they had formed a rival U.S. network of dioceses and parishes called the Network of Anglican Communion Dioceses and Parishes. The group insisted it was not seceding from the ECUSA, but rather hoped for world recognition as the true Episcopal Church in the United States.
◼ Martin E. Marty

Psychology. See **Mental health.**

Rowan Williams is enthroned as the 104th Archbishop of Canterbury on Feb. 27, 2003. Only months after the enthronement, the issue of gay clergy threatened to create a schism in the worldwide Anglican Communion led by Williams.

Public health and safety. A mysterious disease never before identified in human beings killed more than 700 people and infected at least 8,000 others in 30 countries in 2003. The disease, which became known as severe acute respiratory syndrome (SARS), apparently originated in southeastern China in November 2002, though health officials did not recognize it as a new disease until February 2003.

SARS produces a high fever and one or more symptoms of respiratory illness, such as a cough, sore throat, chills, or muscle aches. Some cases, particularly in people over age 65, progress to pneumonia and respiratory failure. Scientists believe SARS spreads chiefly through fluid ejected in the coughs or sneezes of an infected person.

The spread of SARS triggered serious concern among public health officials worldwide because it is highly contagious and does not respond to standard medications used to treat respiratory infections or pneumonia. To combat the spread of the disease, health officials relied mainly on isolation—separating SARS patients from healthy people—and quarantine—restricting the movements of people who had been exposed to the virus but had not developed symptoms of the disease.

On April 2, 2003, the World Health Organization (WHO), an agency of the United Nations, issued the first of several warnings advising travelers to avoid areas seriously affected by SARS. The warnings were the first ever issued by WHO over an infectious disease.

Also in April, researchers at Erasmus University in Rotterdam, the Netherlands, confirmed theories identifying a new strain of the coronavirus as the cause of SARS. Coronaviruses are highly contagious microbes that cause some cases of the common cold in humans, as well as serious or fatal diseases in livestock and some other animals.

Monkeypox, a viral disease normally found in central and western Africa, infected at least 37 people in Illinois, Indiana, Kansas, Missouri, Ohio, and Wisconsin from May to July, according to the U.S. Centers for Disease Control and Prevention (CDC) in Atlanta, Georgia. The disease, which usually lasts for two to four weeks, produces a rash similar to but milder than that of smallpox. The outbreak did not cause any deaths.

The CDC said most victims had handled infected prairie dogs purchased from a pet distributor near Chicago. The prairie dogs had contracted the virus from monkeypox-infected Gambian giant pouched rats and other animals imported from Africa for sale as pets. On June 11, the CDC and the Food and Drug Administration banned the importation into the United States of all rodents from Africa.

West Nile virus continued to pose a health threat to Americans in 2003. As of November 19, 8,470 people throughout the United States had contracted the virus and 189 had died, according to the CDC. In 2002, the CDC reported, the virus infected 4,156 people and caused 284 deaths in 39 states and the District of Columbia.

West Nile virus usually spreads from infected birds to human beings and other animals by mosquito bite. Although most people exposed to the virus experience only mild, flulike symptoms or no symptoms, about 1 in 150 infected people develop a life-threatening brain inflammation.

The geographic focus of the virus moved westward in 2003. Several states only mildly affected by West Nile in 2002—including Colorado, North Dakota, and South Dakota—became hot spots in 2003. In contrast, Illinois, which led the nation with 884 cases and 64 deaths in 2002, reported 50 cases and 1 death as of November 2003.

Hepatitis outbreak. Health authorities in Pennsylvania in November identified 530 cases of hepatitis linked to a chain Mexican restaurant at a shopping mall northwest of Pittsburgh. At least three people believed to have been infected with hepatitis at the site died of the disease. Health screenings revealed that nearly 10,000 patrons were exposed to the virus before the restaurant was shut down. ■ Barbara A. Mayes

See also **Aviation; Canada; China; Medicine; Toronto.**

Puerto Rico. Governor Sila Calderon arrived on the island of Vieques, off Puerto Rico's east coast, to the sounds of cheering crowds on April 30, 2003. Her visit preceded four days of festivities launched after the United States Navy, after more than 60 years, formally stopped using a portion of the island for target practice.

"Together we achieved the end of the bombing," announced Governor Calderon, alluding to the group of protesters that included prominent luminaries from the United States. The coalition had pressured U.S. President George W. Bush's administration to stop the target practice in the wake of a 1999 accident in which a civilian security guard was killed and four people injured by two bombs that were mistakenly detonated.

Departing Vieques, the U.S. Navy transferred 15,000 of the 27,000 acres (6,070 of 10,926 hectares) to the U.S. Department of the Interior, which will turn the land into a private wildlife refuge. The Interior Department, meantime, earmarked $2.3 million in 2003 to clean up the transferred land, where there were still toxins and unexploded bombs.

Tourism development of Vieques. Calderon's administration pledged $50 million in May for public works improvements on Vieques, which became a matchless site for future Caribbean tourism development once the U.S.

Navy departed. Environmentalists and the island's 9,000 residents urged a gradual approach to prevent the realization of projects that might destroy natural habitats. They also urged special care for the delicate ecology of the 1,200-acre (486-hectare) Bio-Bay Nature Reserve and the nearby Bioluminescent Bay, an area filled with microorganisms that glow in the dark.

No second term. Calderon stunned her supporters within the ruling Popular Democratic Party in May by announcing that she would not seek reelection in 2004. While Calderon, Puerto Rico's first woman governor, cited the desire to devote more time to her family as her reason for withdrawal, critics pointed to her inability to eradicate drug-trafficking and jump-start the commonwealth's economy.

Death penalty. Jurors in a San Juan court acquitted Joel Rivero Alejandro and Hector Oscar Acosta Martinez in July of all charges in connection with the February 1998 kidnapping and murder of a grocery store owner. The verdict averted a possible showdown between Puerto Rico, a U.S. commonwealth that lawfully abolished capital punishment in 1929, and the U.S. Department of Justice, which sought the death penalty under federal law.   ■ Nathan A. Haverstock

See also **Latin America; United States, Government of the.**

Pulitzer Prizes

Pulitzer Prizes in journalism, letters, drama, and music were awarded on April 7, 2003, by Columbia University in New York City on the recommendation of the Pulitzer Prize board.

Journalism. *The Boston Globe* won the prize for public service journalism for its series of articles exposing sexual abuse in the Boston archdiocese of the Roman Catholic Church. The investigative reporting prize went to Clifford J. Levy of *The New York Times*, who exposed abuse of the mentally ill in state-regulated residences. *The Wall Street Journal* won the explanatory reporting prize for a series about corporate scandals.

Diana K. Sugg of *The Baltimore Sun* was awarded the prize for beat reporting for stories on medical challenges faced by patients. The staff of the *Eagle-Tribune* (Lawrence, Massachusetts) won the breaking news prize for stories on the drownings of four boys in a local river.

Kevin Sullivan and Mary Jordan of *The Washington Post* won the international reporting prize for their examination of Mexico's criminal justice system. *Post* writer Colbert I. King received the commentary prize for his column focusing on Washington, D.C., residents. Film critic Stephen Hunter, also of the *Post,* won the criticism prize.

Los Angeles Times writers Alan Miller and Kevin Sack received the national reporting prize for their investigation of a military aircraft linked

to the deaths of 45 pilots. Sonia Nazario, also of the *Times,* won the feature writing prize with a story on a Honduran boy's search for his mother.

Cornelia Grumman of the *Chicago Tribune,* writing against the death penalty, was awarded the editorial writing prize. The editorial cartooning prize went to David Horsey of the *Seattle Post-Intelligencer.* The *Rocky Mountain News* staff took the prize for breaking news photography for its coverage of forest fires. *Los Angeles Times* photographer Don Bartletti won the prize for feature photography for his portrayal of young, illegal Central American immigrants.

Letters, drama, and music. Jeffrey Eugenides won the fiction prize for his second novel, *Middlesex.* The drama prize went to Nilo Cruz for *Anna in the Tropics.* Rick Atkinson won the history prize for *An Army at Dawn: The War in North Africa, 1942-1943.* Robert A. Caro's *Master of the Senate,* volume three of the life of Lyndon B. Johnson, took the biography prize. Paul Muldoon won the poetry prize for his collection *Moy Sand and Gravel.* The general nonfiction prize went to Samantha Power for *A Problem from Hell: America and the Age of Genocide.* John Adams won the music prize for his symphonic work *On the Transmigration of Souls.*

■ Brian Bouldrey

Quebec. See **Canadian provinces.**

Radio

Radio. The radio industry found itself in turmoil during much of 2003 following Federal Communications Commission (FCC) efforts to change regulations governing the ownership of radio and television stations and newspapers. The FCC is the agency charged with regulating communication through radio, wire, and cable.

The FCC voted 3 to 2 on June 2 to change federal guidelines regarding media ownership. Under the ruling, corporations would be allowed to own both a radio or television station and a daily newspaper in the same market. Such ownership had been prohibited since the mid-1970's. The new regulations allowed a single company in cities in which there are nine or more television stations to own eight radio stations, as many as three television stations, and an unspecified number of newspapers. A single company could own eight radio stations if there were at least 45 stations broadcasting in that market. The FCC upheld a ban on the cross-ownership of radio stations, TV stations, and newspapers in smaller cities where there are three or fewer TV stations.

FCC members claimed "neither the newspaper-broadcast prohibition nor the TV-radio cross-ownership prohibition could be justified for larger markets, in light of the abundance of sources that people rely upon for news." The comment was a reference to cable and satellite television stations.

The FCC also redefined the way in which radio markets are determined. The definition of a radio market had been based on broadcast engineering calculations on how far a radio signal could reach. The FCC redefined a radio market based on ratings used by the radio industry that reflect which stations compete in a geographic area. The new definition led to smaller radio markets.

Opponents of the FCC guidelines argued that allowing one company to own multiple news outlets would lead to a narrow perspective on local, national, and world events. Opponents also said the rules would make it more difficult to get diverse viewpoints on the airwaves.

The guidelines faced strong opposition. In September 2003, the U.S. Senate voted 55 to 40 to approve a "resolution of disapproval," a tactic that allows Congress to overturn decisions by federal regulators. Supporters claimed the measure did not have enough votes to override a veto by President George W. Bush. Before the new rules took effect in September, the United States Court of Appeals for the Third District Court in Philadelphia temporarily blocked them.

Howard Stern ruling. The FCC ruled in September that "The Howard Stern Show," a radio and television show hosted by radio personality Howard Stern, is a news interview program and exempt from the FCC's equal-time provisions covering interviews of political candidates. Infinity Broadcasting Operations Inc., a New York City-based company that syndicates Stern's program, sought a ruling so Stern could interview California gubernatorial candidate Arnold Schwarzenegger before a recall election held in October. Station officials feared that they might have to grant equal time to all 135 candidates if Stern interviewed the actor or any other candidate on the program.

National Public Radio. Officials at National Public Radio (NPR) announced in September 2003 that its listenership had increased by 56 percent since 1998. NPR is a public radio system that acquires or produces news, cultural, and information programming and distributes it to more than 600 radio stations in the United States, Puerto Rico, and Guam. NPR officials said that weekly listenership increased from 13 million to 21 million people between 1998 and 2003.

In November, officials announced Joan Kroc, widow of the founder of the McDonald's restaurant chain, had bequeathed $200 million to NPR. The bequest was more than twice NPR's annual budget. ■ Greg Paeth

See also **Newspaper; State government; Telecommunications; Television.**

Railroad. See Transportation.

Religion. See Islam; Judaism; Protestantism; Roman Catholic Church.

Republican Party. The Republican Party in 2003 celebrated three victories in races for governor in off-year elections. The victories included a highly unusual win in California resulting from a recall vote.

On October 7, California voters selected motion-picture actor Arnold Schwarzenegger, a Republican, to replace Governor Gray Davis, a Democrat, in the first gubernatorial recall election in California state history. The recall election came less than one year after Davis's election to a second term in office. Fifty-five percent of voters cast ballots to recall Davis. Political experts suggested that many California voters disapproved of the way Davis handled the state's finances.

Schwarzenegger triumphed over 134 other candidates in his first bid for public office. The experts noted that his victory provided the GOP (for Grand Old Party) with a boost going into the 2004 presidential election. Schwarzenegger's high profile and popularity could improve President George W. Bush's chance of taking California, the most populous state with the largest number of votes in the Electoral College.

Other Republican victories. In gubernatorial elections held on Nov. 4, 2003, Republican Haley Barbour defeated Democratic incumbent Governor Ronnie Musgrove in Mississippi. Barbour was a former chairman of the Republican National Committee and a lobbyist.

United States Representative Ernie Fletcher (R., Kentucky) defeated Kentucky Attorney General Ben Chandler, a Democrat, in the race to succeed Kentucky Governor Paul Patton. Term limits prevented Patton, a Democrat, from running for reelection.

The Republican Party failed to capture the only other gubernatorial race held in 2003. On November 15, Bobby Jindal lost to Lieutenant Governor Kathleen Babineaux Blanco in the race to succeed Louisiana Governor Mike Foster. Term limits also prohibited Foster, a Democrat, from seeking reelection.

Fundraising. Republicans outpaced Democrats in fundraising in 2003. The Federal Election Commission (FEC), a U.S. government agency that enforces campaign financing regulations, reported on August 28 that through June 2003, federally registered Republican Party committees raised $139.1 million and spent $106.8 million. The contributions were an increase over the nearly $95 million the party raised during the same period in 2002. Federally registered Democratic Party committees, by comparison, raised $56.4 million and spent $39.3 million.

Republicans received $129.1 million from individual contributions and $6.7 million from political action committees (PAC's), the FEC reported. PAC's are groups set up by a labor union, corporation, or other organization to contribute money to candidates for federal and state offices in the United States.

Soft money surge. The Republican National Committee raised $250.3 million in "soft money" contributions in 2002, prior to changes in campaign finance law. That finding was reported in January 2003 by Common Cause, a citizens advocacy group headquartered in Washington, D.C. Soft money contributions are individual contributions to political parties that are not subject to the same restrictions placed on contributions to candidates. The new campaign finance law that went into effect in November 2002 barred political parties from raising and spending soft money.

The Democratic National Committee raised approximately $220 million in soft money contributions between January and November 2002, Common Cause reported.

Filibuster protest. Senate Republicans in mid-November 2003 tried to break a filibuster carried out by Senate Democrats to prevent a vote on three of President Bush's nominees to federal appellate courts. Filibustering is the practice by which a minority in a legislature uses extended debate to block or delay action on a proposed bill.

In response to the tactic, GOP senators made certain that the Senate remained in session, forcing Democrats to stay on the floor at all times to keep the filibuster going. The marathon session began on November 12 and lasted until the early morning of November 14. Cots were brought into the Senate chambers to allow senators to rest. The Republicans, who hold a slim majority in the Senate with 51 votes, were unable to muster the 60 votes necessary to break the filibuster and vote on the nominees.

Reagan miniseries. The Republican Party and several conservative groups opposed a planned broadcast of "The Reagans," a miniseries about former President Ronald Reagan and First Lady Nancy Reagan that CBS had scheduled to air in November. Critics alleged that the miniseries was historically inaccurate. CBS executives agreed to move the series to Showtime, a subscription-only cable network channel. Republican National Committee Chairman Ed Gillespie noted that Showtime executives should allow historians to review the program for accuracy before airing it.

Strom Thurmond, the former U.S. senator from South Carolina, died on June 26 at the age of 100. Thurmond had served in the Senate from 1955 to 2003, longer than any other person.

■ Geoffrey A. Campbell

See also **Congress of the United States; Deaths; Democratic Party; Elections; People in the news** (Bill Frist, John Snow)**; State government; Television; United States, Government of the.**

Roman Catholic Church.
Pope John Paul II and Vatican representatives took a strong stand on major social and political world issues in 2003, including the war in Iraq, the New Age movement, the sex-abuse scandal in the United States, and same-sex marriages.

Pope John Paul II and Iraq war. Pope John Paul II was among the most vocal peace petitioners in the months leading up to the war in Iraq, which began on March 19 (March 20 in Iraq). Beginning with an impassioned plea in early January, the pope repeatedly stated that he opposed military force in Iraq. He called on both U.S. President George W. Bush and Iraqi President Saddam Hussein to work with the United Nations to bring about disarmament and peace to the region.

In February, the pope sent papal envoy Cardinal Roger Etchegaray, along with Monsignor Franco Coppola of the Vatican Secretariat of State, to Iraq for direct talks with Hussein. Etchegaray carried a personal letter from the pope urging Hussein to cooperate with weapons inspectors and all United Nations resolutions. After the Hussein meeting on February 15, Etchegaray said, "I'm convinced that today Saddam Hussein wants to avoid war."

New Age spirituality. The Vatican released an 88-page "reflection" on the New Age movement in February, offering cautions about New Age spirituality while avoiding outright condemnations or prohibitions. The New Age movement is a network of people who share similar spiritual beliefs and practices but have no central organization, creed, or formal clergy. New Age followers often combine such practices as astrology, meditation, paganism, and many other beliefs, with the doctrines of a more formal, organized religion.

The authors of the paper wrote that New Age spirituality is "difficult to reconcile with Christian doctrine and spirituality." The document pointed out, for example, that for New Age followers, God is often an impersonal force, but for Christians, God is a being with whom believers have a personal relationship. The document also noted that in New Age thinking, Jesus Christ is one god among many, while for Christians, He is the one Savior of the world.

Capuchin to lead Boston. Pope John Paul II in July named Bishop Sean Patrick O'Malley of Palm Beach, Florida, as the new archbishop of Boston. He replaced Cardinal Bernard F. Law, who resigned in December 2002 amid accusations that he had failed to remove from ministry priests who had sexually abused children.

O'Malley came to Boston with a record for successfully cleaning up dioceses troubled by sex-abuse scandals. After his installation, O'Malley's first priority was the sex-abuse issue, and he negotiated a settlement by early September 2003. The

Bishop Sean O'Malley blesses the altar during his installation as arch-bishop of Boston at the city's Cathedral of the Holy Cross on July 30, 2003. Vatican observers suggested that he was named to the post because of his experience dealing with sex-abuse scandals in the Church.

552 plaintiffs who accused 140 priests and brothers of sexual abuse over the past 60 years were to receive between $80,000 and $300,000 each. The archdiocese also promised to pay for lifetime counseling for victims who want it.

Gay marriage immoral. In July, the Vatican issued a 12-page paper entitled "Considerations Regarding Proposals to Give Legal Recognition to Unions Between Homosexual Persons." The document appealed to Roman Catholic lawmakers to block legislation granting legal gay unions in Europe and North America. "To vote in favor of a law so harmful to the common good is gravely immoral," stated the author of the paper, which also denounced the adoption of children by gay couples.

New cardinals named. Pope John Paul II in September 2003 selected 31 new cardinals. He has appointed more cardinals than any other pope. With the new cardinals, 135 are under age 80 and, therefore, eligible to vote for the next pope. All but five were elevated by John Paul II.

Anniversary celebration. John Paul II marked his 25th year as pope on October 16. The longest serving popes were Pius IX, who was pope for 32 years, and Leo XIII, who served 25 years. ■ Thomas C. Fox

See also **Eastern Orthodox Churches; Canada; Iraq; Protestantism.**

Romania. Romania's parliament passed constitutional amendments in 2003 emphasizing democratic rights and private ownership. One amendment, however, designated Romania as a "nation-state," raising fears among minorities that minority language rights would be repealed and that the Romanian language would become required in government business. The Hungarian Democratic Federation, representing Romania's Hungarian minority and a partner in Prime Minister Adrian Nastase's coalition, initially blocked passage of the amendments. To break the deadlock, legislators crafted a compromise extending language rights to the Hungarian minority. Voters approved the amendments in October.

In January, Romania's parliament approved prospective NATO membership for 2004. As a part of Romania's campaign to gain entry into the European Union (EU) by 2007, Nastase's government in 2003 passed budget-tightening measures endorsed by the EU.

In March, Romania joined the United States-led coalition in the war in Iraq. Romanian officials opened a Black Sea military base for coalition troops to use as a staging point. In September, Romania sent 500 peacekeeping troops to Iraq. ■ Sharon L. Wolchik

See also **Europe; Iraq: A Special Report.**
Rowing. See Sports.

Russia. A period of economic growth and political stability in Russia yielded by the end of the summer of 2003 to political struggles over the fate of the nation's largest oil company and the composition of the new parliament.

Economy. Russia enjoyed its fourth consecutive year of strong economic growth in 2003. Inflation was also moderate, averaging about 13 percent. High world prices for oil remained the primary engine pulling the economy, since Russia remained the world's largest producer of oil and natural gas. Foreign currency reserves grew to over $60 billion by the end of 2003, and the Russian ruble increased in strength by about 10 percent, compared with the U.S. dollar, since 2002.

The Yukos affair. In July 2003, Russian prosecutors arrested Platon Lebedev, a major shareholder in Russia's largest oil company, Yukos. Lebedev was charged with embezzlement for his role in the purchase of a state-run fertilizer manufacturer by a Yukos-affiliated company in 1994.

During the summer of 2003, federal prosecutors questioned several of the top executives at Yukos, raided the company's headquarters and archives in central Moscow, and even seized computers at an orphanage supported by the company's charity arm. On October 25, a team of officers from the Federal Security Service arrested Yukos Chief Executive Officer Mikhail Khodorkovsky at gunpoint when his chartered plane stopped to refuel in Siberia. They returned him to Moscow where he was imprisoned on seven charges of massive fraud and tax evasion.

Khodorkovsky's arrest marked a new stage in the running struggle between the Russian government and the so-called oligarchs—business leaders who became wealthy through insider deals and Kremlin connections during the first decade after the collapse of Communism in 1991. Khodorkovsky was by far the richest man in Russia and the 26th richest man in the world, according to *Forbes.* The U.S. business magazine estimated that his fortune exceeded $8 billion. After acquiring Yukos in 1995 for $350 million through an allegedly rigged state auction, Khodorkovsky built Yukos into one of the most profitable and financially straightforward companies in Russia. At the time of his arrest, Khodorkovsky had agreed to acquire rival Russian oil firm Sibneft to create the fourth-largest private oil company in the world. On Dec. 15, 2003, however, the two companies signed a letter of intent to reverse the merger. Negotiations of the separation terms were likely to take months.

The arrest created chaos in the company, the Russian stock market, and the Russian government. Khodorkovsky, jailed pending trial but with no prospect of parole, resigned on November 3 as head of Yukos. He passed voting control of his Yukos shares to the second-largest share-holder, Leonid Nevzlin, who fled to Israel and was granted Israeli citizenship in November. A third billionaire shareholder, Vasily Shakhnovsky, was charged with tax evasion and fraud. On November 28, the merger with Sibneft was postponed just hours before it was to be finalized. On December 2, the Russian tax authorities claimed that Yukos had underpaid taxes by $5 billion (150 billion Russian rubles) since 1998, possibly setting the stage for the state to seize the oil company.

Investors struggled to understand whether the attack on Yukos might lead to the unraveling of the privatization deals of the Yeltsin era and a widespread redistribution of property. Russian President Vladimir Putin voiced his support for the prosecutors but assured investors that the Yukos affair should not be seen as the first step in a campaign of renationalizations. Putin's statements halted a sharp drop in the Russian stock market, but there were other causes for concern. Deputy Prosecutor General Vladimir Kolesnikov in November 2003 warned that "those who are not yet jailed" should not rest easy, and he called the Yukos case just "one part of a chain" of similar cases.

The Yukos affair also shook the administration of President Putin. Presidential chief of staff Aleksandr Voloshin resigned in October 2003, after Khodorkovsky's arrest, apparently in protest. Voloshin was the most powerful remaining link between Putin's staff and the preceding Yeltsin administration. His departure seemed to signal the consolidation of power by a group of conservative bureaucrats drawn largely from the military and security services, many with ties to Putin's days in St. Petersburg. As if to underline the open split within the government, several Cabinet officials were openly critical of prosecutors' handling of the Yukos affair, including Prime Minister Mikhail Kasyanov.

At the end of 2003, the factors triggering the arrest of Khodorkovsky were still unclear. Some politicians speculated that he had angered the Kremlin political machine by openly supporting opposition political parties. Others saw the roots in Yukos's growing dominance of the oil sector, a vital source of state tax revenue. Still others felt that Khodorkovsky had offended Putin by speculating about leaving Yukos by 2007 and entering politics, just as Putin's second term would be drawing to a close. Regardless of the precise trigger, most business leaders in Russia saw Khodorkovsky's fate as a sign that despite the end of formal state control over the economy in the 1990's, the state would remain the dominant force in Russian society for many years to come.

Duma elections. On Dec. 7, 2003, Russian voters went to the polls to elect a new *Duma* (parliament). Opposition party leaders, such as Grigory Yavlinsky of Yabloko and Anatoly Chubais of the Union of Right Forces, attempted to use the Yukos affair to prove that Putin was becoming an authoritarian leader, but voters with an average wage of a few hundred dollars a month showed little sympathy for jailed billionaires.

The United Russia Party won a landslide victory in both party-list and individual district voting, capturing 222 of the 450 seats in the Duma. Two national-patriotic parties considered supportive of the Kremlin—the Liberal Democratic Party and Motherland—captured 75 seats. With these three parties, combined with a group of independent deputies likely to vote with the government, the Kremlin seemed assured of the 300 votes it would need to amend constitutional laws, possibly to extend Putin's presidential term after his expected reelection in March 2004.

The 2003 vote also heralded the collapse of the opposition parties that had defined the Duma's structure during the Yeltsin era. The Communist Party dropped from 88 deputies to 53, while the pro-Western liberal parties led by Yavlinsky and Chubais fared even worse, dropping from 51 seats to just 7. The electoral setback, combined with the loss of Khodorkovsky's financing, seemed to push these parties to the brink of extinction.

United Russia's victory had seemed preordained after Putin, whose popularity level has remained over 70 percent, announced publicly that he supported the party. Most local politicians dutifully joined it, and the state-controlled television channels gave it uniformly positive coverage throughout the campaign.

Terrorism. Suicide bombers believed to be from Chechnya struck on several occasions in 2003. After a 1994-1996 war left separatists in charge, Russian forces withdrew from Chechnya, but they returned in 1999 when Chechnya-based militants invaded a neighboring region.

On July 5, 2003, two suicide bombers at a rock concert in Moscow killed 16 people and wounded 59 others. The following week, a police bomb expert was killed defusing a bomb left at a cafe in central Moscow. Chechen rebels were also suspected in the August suicide truck bomb that killed at least 50 people at a hospital in the city of Mozdok, close to the Russia-Chechnya border. On December 5, a suicide bomb attack aboard a crowded commuter train in southern Russia killed at least 40 people and wounded over 170 others. On December 9, another suicide bomb attack in Moscow, just 300 feet (91 meters) from the Kremlin, killed 6 pedestrians. These acts of terrorism were reminders of the extensive violence that continued in and around the breakaway region of Chechnya, largely shielded from the eyes of Western observers. Russian military installations and transport aircraft in the area were regular targets of Chechen guerrillas throughout 2003.

Putin moved to impose a political solution on Chechnya in 2003, in a bid to stem the violence and extract the Russian Army. On March 23, a Kremlin-authored constitution for Chechnya was approved in a referendum that most international observers dismissed as a sham. On October 5, the Kremlin's hand-picked candidate, Akhmed Kadyrov, was elected president of Chechnya, after all of his serious rivals either withdrew or were removed from the ballot on technicalities. Kadyrov received 80 percent of the vote and claimed a large turnout, but observers claimed his large militia intimidated many voters into supporting him.

Foreign policy. Despite supporting the war on terrorism mounted by the United States immediately after the terrorist attacks on the United States in 2001, Russia joined France and Germany in opposing the U.S.-led war in Iraq in 2003. Since Russia holds a permanent veto on the United Nations (UN) Security Council, its opposition to the war put a brief strain on U.S.-Russian relations and helped doom the U.S. bid to gain UN legitimacy for its Iraq campaign.

Kyoto Protocol. In December, Andrei Illarionov, a presidential aide and economic adviser, announced that Russia would not ratify the Kyoto Protocol. The protocol was an international agreement among industrialized nations, reached in 1997 in Kyoto, Japan, to reduce emissions of six greenhouse gases. A day after the announcement, Mukhamed Tsikhanov, a deputy minister, said no decision had been made, and Russia was still moving toward ratification. The decision was likely to be delayed until after the March 2004 presidential elections.

St. Petersburg. Forty-six heads of state converged on President Putin's hometown of St. Petersburg at the end of May to help Russia's second city celebrate its 300th anniversary. Putin hosted a Russia-European Union summit during the jubilee, which included a series of galas and arts festivals during the celebrated White Nights. The White Nights occur for a three-week period in June, when the sky is never completely dark because of the city's northern location. Putin also met in St. Petersburg with U.S. President George W. Bush—one of three meetings between the presidents during the course of 2003.

■ Steven L Solnick

See also **Belarus; Europe; Georgia; Iraq: A Special Report; Russia: A Special Report; Terrorism; Ukraine; United States, Government of the.**

Sailing. See Boating.

Saskatchewan. See Canadian provinces.

Celebrating the

By Carol Yehling

Russia and its president, Vladimir Putin, hosted many of the world's most powerful leaders at an elaborate party in May 2003. The event was a celebration of the 300th anniversary of St. Petersburg, Russia's "second city" and Putin's home town. During the nine-day anniversary jubilee, Putin showed off the city to nearly 50 heads of state and heads of government—including Italian Prime Minister Silvio Berlusconi, British Prime Minister Tony Blair, U.S. President George W. Bush, French President Jacques Chirac, Chinese Leader Hu Jintao, Japanese Prime Minister Junichiro Koizumi, and German Chancellor Gerhard Schroeder. The leaders and their entourages watched fireworks displays and light shows, attended concerts and a water parade, and gaped at the wonders of an imperial city reborn after nearly a century of decline.

St. Petersburg began as a fortress in a swamp but quickly grew, through the will of one man—Czar Peter I (1672-1725), called Peter the Great—into the political, social, and cultural capital of one of the world's largest empires. For two centuries, St. Petersburg's palaces, gardens, and

A water and light show is staged at the Peterhof Palace outside St. Petersburg to entertain guests at the city's birthday festivities in May 2003. Russian President Vladimir Putin, a native of the city, hosted the jubilee, which was attended by nearly 50 foreign dignitaries.

Heads of state and heads of nations from three continents gather in St. Isaac's Cathedral on May 30. The cathedral's lavish interior is decorated with semiprecious stones and amazingly colorful mosaics.

CITY OF THE CZARS

St. Petersburg, Russia, unveils its restored architectural wonders at a lavish party to honor the city's 300th year.

museums were the residences and playgrounds of Russia's all-powerful czars and the country's immensely privileged aristocracy. When the old system collapsed in 1917, much of St. Petersburg's glory collapsed with it. The new Communist government moved the capital back to Moscow in 1918 and gave St. Petersburg the name Leningrad for Communist leader V. I. Lenin (1870-1924) upon his death. During World War II (1938-1945), the city suffered through the longest and most brutal siege of the 20th century. The siege left more than half of the city's residents dead and many of its extraordinary buildings, monuments, and art collections damaged or destroyed.

St. Petersburg's rebirth as a city of international significance began with the rise of Vladimir Putin, who became president of Russia on Dec. 31, 1999. Putin made no secret of the fact that he intended to reestablish his city as an international center of diplomacy, and he used his influence to push the pace of the city's restoration. The occasion of St. Petersburg's 300th anniversary provided further impetus for tackling major restoration projects. While not all the work was completed

The golden dome of St. Isaac's Cathedral dominates the skyline above the English Embankment (above), which is lined with palaces dating from when St. Petersburg was the capital of czarist Russia. Peter the Great's plan turned a marsh into a series of islands and canals (map at right) that earned his new city the title "Venice of the north."

The author:
Carol Yehling is a staff editor on *The Year Book.*

by May 2003, the city of Peter I and other czars of yesterday nevertheless dazzled the visiting world leaders.

Peter I assumed full power as czar of Russia in 1689. An autocrat, or absolute monarch, Peter literally held the power of life and death over his subjects. He ruled over a feudal system in which nearly all the land was held by his nobles. They in turn ruled over their serfs—that is, the people who worked the land and were little better off than slaves. Most Europeans considered Russia an isolated and backward country that was more Asian than European.

As a youth, Peter had been interested in military matters and had enjoyed spending time with foreign military officers who lived in Moscow. From them, he learned much about European culture and technology. In 1697 and 1698, Peter toured Western Europe, primarily England and the Netherlands, where he studied ship building and other construction methods. While in Europe, he recruited Western experts to bring modern techniques of engineering, architecture, art, and science to Russia.

In 1700, Peter led Russia in a war against Sweden, which was then a leading European power. With the help of his Western advisers, he improved his army and created a navy. By 1703, Peter had gained control over important territory along the eastern shores of the Baltic Sea. This land gave Russia a direct approach by water to the rest of Europe. The

ambitious czar needed a fortress to protect his newly conquered lands, and he began construction of what was to become the Peter and Paul Fortress on May 16 (May 27 on a contemporary calendar), 1703—the official birthday of the new city of St. Petersburg. Peter's goal was to build his new city on Western models and use it to encourage his country and his subjects to adopt Western ways.

Peter chose the marshy Neva River delta as the site for his fortress, hardly a desirable location for a city, much less the grand capital he envisioned. The site was little more than desolate mudflats that flooded frequently. No stone, wood, clay, or any other kind of building material could be found in the area.

Peter the Great (to the left of map) supervises every detail of the construction of his new city in this engraving from the 1700's. The czar initially lived in a small wooden house, still standing today, from which he directed all building activity, frequently altering plans at whim.

Exercising his absolute power, Peter issued a decree banning construction of stone structures anywhere in Russia to prevent materials he needed for his city from being used up elsewhere. People who ignored his orders were exiled to Siberia. Siberia—a vast, thinly populated, and extremely cold region in northern Russia—was where criminal and political prisoners were sent. Peter also commanded that every ship that entered the St. Petersburg harbor carry a quantity of uncut stone for his building projects.

The czar lacked the labor he needed to build his city so he *conscripted* (drafted) hundreds of thousands of his subjects—even criminals bound for Siberia. The laborers initially had no tools, so they dug the mud from the marsh with their bare hands and carried it away in the long shirts that Russian peasants wore at the time. Tens of thousands, if not hundreds of thousands, of men died—from injury, disease, exhaustion, the freezing temperatures, or starvation—in order to bring the ruthless czar's dream of an imperial city to life. For himself, Peter had a small, wooden house built—which still stands—from which he directed the construction of his new city's major buildings and streets. He frequently changed his mind about these projects, abandoning structures that did not please him and altering the direction and lengths of the streets to suit his tastes.

After the first buildings were completed, Peter addressed his next problem, a lack of residents. Important, influential Russians lived in Moscow at least part of the year and had no desire to relocate to what they considered to be a cold, isolated northern wasteland. Czar Peter simply ordered merchants, nobles, and artisans to take up permanent residence in his growing metropolis or face punishment. So they came, and by 1712, St. Petersburg had become the fully functioning capital of Russia.

Through the rest of Peter's reign, the city's growth mushroomed, particularly around the Winter and Summer palaces—the czar's primary residences; the Summer Garden—the first planned garden in Russia; the Menshikov Palace—the city's first governor general's residence and headquarters; and Trinity Square—the hub of the city's commercial and social activity. Peter also built a country seat for himself, later to be called the Konstantin Palace, a short distance outside the city. The palace was to be Peter's version of Versailles, the elaborate country residence of French kings built outside of Paris in the second half of the 1600's. However, Peter lost interest in the structure before it was finished and turned his attention to the design and construction of another palace, the Peterhof, a country estate that did eventually rival Versailles in grandeur.

St. Petersburg achieves capital status

Peter's penchant for changing his mind set an example that lasted for two centuries as subsequent monarchs constantly changed palaces and gardens and reconstructed St. Petersburg's streets to suit their tastes, needs, and the fashion of the day. Peter's daughter, Elizabeth (1709-1762), who became empress of Russia in 1741, picked up where her father left off. She hired famous European architects, painters, and craftsmen of the time to design and build what would become one of Europe's most magnificent and luxurious residences. She remodeled the Winter Palace and her father's estate, the Peterhof. She turned her mother's residence, the Catherine Palace in the suburb of Tsarskoye Selo (the Czar's Village), into yet another royal residence. Under her reign, St. Petersburg became a prestigious European capital renowned for its art, architecture, and music.

In the late 1700's, Elizabeth's niece by marriage, Empress Catherine II (1729-1796), called Catherine the Great, continued to expand and rebuild the royal city. Catherine, who was born a German princess, was devoted to art, literature, science, and politics. Early in her reign, she became interested in the liberal ideas of her time, which came to be called the Age of Reason because European intellectuals of the period emphasized the use of reason to learn truths. At Catherine's invitation, scientists, writers, artists, and actors from other countries moved to St. Petersburg, which became one of the intellectual capitals of Europe. She established the Hermitage Theater, the Russian Academy of Sciences, the Academy of Fine Arts, and the city's first public library. Her greatest and most lasting achievement was the establishment of a royal art collection, which became the Hermitage Museum. Catherine's collection grew with each subsequent czar until the Hermitage became one of the world's great museums of art and St. Petersburg's cultural crown jewel.

A woman pulls a sled carrying a corpse down Nevski Prospect, the city's main avenue, during the Siege of Leningrad, which lasted from September 1941 to January 1944. An estimated 1.7 million of the city's residents died of starvation and cold during the siege.

The 1800's—Cultural growth and social oppression

St. Petersburg's era of enlightenment essentially ended with Catherine's death, and the czars that followed faced the ever-greater challenges to their rule with ever-greater repression. St. Petersburg in its second century came to be dominated by a military presence necessary to guarantee the existence of the dynasty. Nevertheless, revolutionaries managed to murder three czars between 1801 and 1917. Somehow, the city's renowned cultural life thrived in spite of the escalating oppression.

Nineteenth-century St. Petersburg was a city of poets and novelists—Pushkin, Gogle, Turgenev, and Tolstoy—and musicians and composers—Glinka, Mussorgsky, Rimsky-Korsakov, and Tchaikovsky. And the czars continued to lavish their capital with monuments and architectural works of art. In 1816, Czar Alexander I (1777-1825) began construction on a new cathedral designed to rival St. Peter's in Rome. St. Isaac's Cathedral features *monolithic* (a single block of stone) red granite columns 56 feet (17 meters) in height; the world's fourth highest dome, entirely covered in gold; and an

New paving stones are piled before St. Petersburg's Winter Palace, once the primary residence of Russia's czars. The granite blocks were used for the restoration in 2003 of the enormous square.

interior decorated with semiprecious stones and mosaics in more than 12,000 shades of color.

Czar Nicholas I (1796-1855) honored his brother Alexander, whose army had driven Napoleon and his French army out of Russia in 1814, with a column that was an extraordinary feat of both engineering and architecture. The Alexander Column, erected in 1832, is topped by an angel that stands 155 feet (47 meters) above the Winter Palace Square. The column itself is a single monolith of red granite soaring nearly 84 feet (26 meters) high, stretching 12 feet (4 meters) in diameter, and weighing 600 tons (544 metric tons). No attachment mechanism connects the column to its pedestal, which consists of granite blocks supported by 1,250 pine piles driven into the marshy earth underlying the city. When the column was initially raised, the people of St. Petersburg avoided Palace Square, for fear the monolith would topple over and crush them.

A railroad connected St. Petersburg with Moscow in 1851, marking the beginning of the Industrial Revolution, or the development of industry, in Russia. Rapid industrialization transformed St. Petersburg from a city of palaces into a city of banks, apartment flats, and factories—the city of extreme wealth and desperate poverty portrayed in Fyodor Dostoevsky's novels. As St. Petersburg moved into its third century, reconstruction and rebuilding no longer took place to suit the whims of a particular czar, but to repair the damage and destruction resulting from revolutions, wars, political upheaval, and economic crises.

The 1900's—Destruction and decline

In January 1905, thousands of unarmed workers marched to the Winter Palace Square to petition Czar Nicholas II (1868-1918) for reforms. Government troops responded by firing into the crowd, killing and wounding hundreds of marchers. After the Bloody Sunday slaughter, the revolutionary movement, led mainly by the liberal constitutionalists, gained strength, and by February, Nicholas was forced to establish a *Duma* (parliament). This would prove to be the beginning of the end of the czar's autocratic rule.

The end came during World War I (1914-1918), which Russia entered after Germany declared war on August 1. Soon after, the German-sounding St. Petersburg was renamed Petrograd, and Nicholas II left the city to lead his troops at the front in Germany and Austria-Hungary. He turned over the reins of government to his wife, Alexandra, a German princess before her marriage. Many historians consider Nicholas's absence from Russia a disastrous mistake. The czarina was ineffective as a governor and was widely disliked, even reviled by the people. Political and social tensions surrounding her behavior, and the czar's absence, tied with significant food shortages in the capital and elsewhere in Russia, led to the February Revolution in 1917. Nicholas II, the last czar of Russia, abdicated, and he and his family were imprisoned and eventually murdered.

When Communists took root in the city in the fall of 1917, civil war broke out. To survive, many of Petrograd's 2.3 million people fled into the countryside to find food and work. The city's population dwindled to less than 750,000. When German troops threatened Russia's border in 1918, Lenin moved the capital away from the front lines, to Moscow. Petrograd was renamed for Lenin in 1924. The city then slowly regained its prewar population as the Communists revived the city's industries.

The city suffered its next onslaught during World War II. Nazi Germany invaded in June 1941, and by September 8, the Germans had outflanked the Red Army and encircled Leningrad, which was strategically important as a center of weapons production. Food and fuel stocks were limited from the start,

Workers repair the pavement in central St. Petersburg in preparation for the city's 300th jubilee in May. Because the restorations of both the Peter and Paul Fortress and the Admiralty, in the background, could not be completed in time, the surrounding scaffolding was taken down for the celebration and then reassembled.

and by winter, the people of Leningrad had no heat, no running water, almost no electricity, and very little food.

Bread was the only food that was regularly available, and the daily ration was about 41.5 ounces (125 grams), the equivalent of one thick slice. During the winter of 1941-1942, temperatures dropped as low as –40 °F (-18 °C). For warmth, the residents burned books and furniture. For food, they consumed animals from the city zoo and eventually their household pets. They cooked grass and weeds and resorted to scraping wallpaper paste made from potatoes off the walls. They boiled leather to make an edible jelly. The Leningrad police formed a special division to combat cannibalism, when people began consuming the dead and even murdered people for their flesh. Historians estimate that 1.7 million of the city's 2.9 million people died during the 900 days of the siege, mostly from starvation and *hypothermia* (subnormal body temperature caused by exposure to cold).

The siege left much of the city in ruins, and the rebuilding was slow and haphazard. The country's Communist leaders, always suspicious of the city's long history of individual artistic expression, imposed strict government-mandated parameters for the arts. The Communists did restore the palaces and other important buildings, but many historic structures were destroyed in order to build the utilitarian communal housing and factories favored by the Soviet bureaucrats of the period.

Sculptures by Italian master Antonio Canova (1757-1822) grace a hallway at the Hermitage Museum in downtown St. Petersburg. The museum's enormous holdings—more than 3 million items—encompass the development of art and world culture from the Stone Age through present day.

A city reborn

In 1991, St. Petersburg regained its original name after the collapse of the Soviet Union. With that change, the people of St. Petersburg seemed to acquire a confidence in their own and their city's future. Despite several years of high unemployment and economic recession in the 1990's, St. Petersburg made a concerted effort to find the funds needed to begin to uncover the city's intrinsic beauty and restore its former glory. The initiative gained momentum when a St. Petersburg native became president of Russia.

Vladimir Putin seemed to have absorbed something of Peter's drive and vision. Putin entered office intent on breaking down the polit-

ical, cultural, and social walls erected by Communism, and like Peter before him, he planned to refocus Russia toward the West. His program included restoring St. Petersburg, Russia's most European city, as an important center of international diplomacy and culture.

Putin poured nearly $1.3 billion in federal funds into the city's restoration and the preparations for the nine-day jubilee celebration. The buildings and grounds of the Hermitage Museum, which include the Winter Palace and six other structures along the Neva River, underwent extensive and long needed improvements. A new grand entrance was created that connects the Winter Palace Courtyard directly to the museum structures outside the Winter Palace complex. The project also included the restoration of gardens, palace gates, and the Alexander Column, as well as rebuilding the palace courtyard itself, which covers 118,000 square feet (11,000 square meters). Other renovations were undertaken to protect the Hermitage's fabulous collection of art. Roofs and skylights were repaired to stop leaks, and heating and cooling systems added to improve air circulation, temperature, and humidity control in exhibition rooms.

Private businesses contributed $290 million for the restoration of some 1,000 rooms at the Konstantin Palace, which President Putin announced he would use as his official St. Petersburg residence. The renovations included the repair and construction of guest houses on the palace grounds, which were used by the heads of state and government during the 300th anniversary celebration. Beyond serving as a presidential residence, the Konstantin is to be utilized for high-level conferences and diplomatic functions that Putin hopes will elevate the city to international importance.

The Marble Hall in the extensively renovated Konstantin Palace, now called the "Palace of Congresses," has a new decor as well as the lastest communications technology to provide the necessary services for summit meetings with world dignitaries. President Putin hopes to make the Palace of Congresses, just outside St. Petersburg, an international diplomatic center.

German Chancellor Gerhard Schroeder (far left), Russian President Vladimir Putin, Doris Schroeder Koepf, and Lyudmila Putin admire the newly restored Amber Room in the Catherine Palace. The original carved amber panels covering the 32-foot (10-meter) square, 26 feet (7.8 meters) high room were stolen by Nazis during World War II and never recovered. The reconstruction of the room took 24 years.

Putin unveils a restored Amber Room

The ceremonial reopening of the Amber Room proved to be Putin's crowning moment during the 300th anniversary celebration. The room is an exact reconstruction of the fabled Amber Room in the Catherine Palace in Tsarskoye Selo. A 32-foot (10-meter) square that is 26 feet (7.8 meters) in height, the room is decorated with several tons of carved amber—a semiprecious gem formed from petrified golden tree resin. The panels are framed by mirrors and mosaics made of semiprecious stones, including quartz, jasmine, jade, and onyx.

In 1716, Frederick I of Prussia presented the amber panels, which were considered a masterpiece of Baroque art, to Peter the Great after Peter had admired them in Frederick's palace in Berlin. The czar's return gift was no less original—55 of his tallest soldiers. (Frederick admired tall soldiers.) Catherine the Great later had the amber panels installed in the Catherine Palace and commissioned craftsmen to embellish them with additional carved amber and the mirror and mosaics. "When the work was finished, in 1770, the room was dazzling," wrote art historians Konstantin Akinsha and Grigorii Kozlov. "It was illuminated by 565 candles whose light was reflected in the warm gold surface of the amber and sparkled in the mirrors, gilt, and mosaics."

Many of St. Petersburg's great treasures were moved to safety during World War II, but the Amber Room was deemed too fragile and heavy to

A detail of one of the Amber Room's reconstructed panels shows an intricate mosaic of the Romanov family crest. Part of the room's original panels were a gift to Czar Peter the Great from Frederick I of Prussia in 1716.

be moved. The Nazis had fewer qualms about the fragility of the amber and stripped the walls bare. The panels are known to have been sent west to Koenigsburg (now Kaliningrad) on the Baltic Sea, where they disappeared into history. In the more than half century since the war, the Amber Room inspired countless legends and the imaginations of treasure hunters worldwide. Some historians speculate that the Amber Room panels were destroyed when Koenigsburg was bombed by the British or were lost in the Baltic with the last German ship to be sunk in the war. Others theorize that the Germans stored the panels in an abandoned mine or well or shipped them to Argentina.

The re-creation of the Amber Room was initiated by the Soviet government and took approximately 24 years to be completed. Nearly all the work was done by three master artists, the youngest of whom was over 70 years old when the job was completed. All they had to go on were a few photographs, some amber fragments that may have broken off in the German plunder, and the eyewitness accounts of people who worked at the palace before the war. Restorers, jewelers, and stonemasons also were hired so that they would learn the refined techniques of the lost art of amber carving from the older men. Six tons (6 metric tons) of honey-colored amber was harvested from the sea around Kaliningrad and treated with a chemical process to change its color to match the rich, dark color the aged amber had before the war.

Overcoming the financial problems of reconstruction proved to be as difficult as tackling the physical and artistic challenges, but funding help came from the German energy company Ruhrgas. At the unveiling, President Putin praised the Russian-German collaboration, and German Chancellor Schroeder was obviously impressed by Russian craftsmanship. President Jacques Chirac of France reportedly became so absorbed by the masterpiece that he was late for a luncheon speech by Putin in a nearby hall.

...A century—and that city young,
Gem of the Northern world, amazing,
From gloomy wood and swamp upsprung,
Had risen, in pride and splendor blazing.

~From "The Bronze Horseman" (1833)
by Alexander Pushkin

A crowd gathers to watch the unveiling of the restored Alexander Column in St. Petersburg's Winter Palace Square on May 24, 2003. The column, a wonder of architecture and engineering originally erected in 1832, is a single piece of red granite weighing 600 tons (544 metric tons). Gravity alone holds it in place on its pedestal.

St. Petersburg today

Not all Putin's ambitions for rebuilding the city were realized in time for the celebration. Many projects were dropped because of construction violations and ineffective use of funds. An inspection team in mid-January 2003 estimated that only 30 of the 59 federally funded restorations would be completed by the jubilee. The Admiralty and the Peter and Paul Fortress are among the buildings that remain unrestored. Scaffolding around the fortress, the burial place of the czars, was dismantled for the anniversary, then reassembled after the festivities were over.

A number of cosmetic makeovers also were completed to impress visiting dignitaries. Abandoned buildings were given a coat of paint, and only roads to be used by visitors were paved. Plans to move residents out of com-

munal apartments were never begun, and a tall wooden fence was built to hide rundown houses near the Konstantin Palace. Nearly 60 unsightly sheds and huts across the street from the palace were burned.

Historians, restoration experts, city planners, and President Putin pushed for the renovations to continue. Among the future projects planned is the construction of a new Marinsky Theater building across the canal from the original theater built in 1860. A competition was held, in which five Russian and six foreign teams presented their building designs to be judged by an international jury. It was the highest-profile architectural event in Russia in 70 years. The winning design by French architect Dominique Perrault is a black marble and glass structure covered by a canopy of gold glass. The government has allocated $100 million for the project, scheduled to be completed by 2006. Restoration on the old Marinsky Theater is expected to be finished by 2008.

Moscow may be the political and economic capital of Russia, but St. Petersburg has reclaimed its identity as the nation's creative and cultural center. Artists throughout its history have been drawn to the city, and in the past 10 years, it has experienced a cultural revival. The number of theaters and concert halls has more than doubled. Jazz clubs, cafes, and nightclubs provide a variety of venues for art and entertainment. The city has become the country's rock music capital and is home to the bands DDT, Aquarium, and the critically acclaimed ska-punk group, Leningrad.

The Hermitage Museum has undertaken an ambitious expansion program, and the city's Russian Museum, Russia's most important museum for domestic art, has tripled its space for the display of treasures that have been hidden in basements and storage rooms since the 1930's. The city has some 200 museums that range from the magnificent Hermitage to the quirky Museum of Hygienics, the Bread Museum, and the Visiting Cards Museum.

The museums and city's beautifully restored architecture are attracting tourists in big numbers, as many as 3.3 million in 2003. UNESCO, the United Nations special agency, describes St. Petersburg as one of the world's top-10 tourist destinations and the capital of Russian culture. Peter the Great would no doubt be pleased that the city he raised out of mud is again flourishing after surviving nearly a century of revolution, war, and bureaucratic indifference.

Saudi Arabia. On May 12, 2003, militants believed to be linked to the al-Qa'ida terrorist network bombed three residential complexes in Riyadh, the capital, killing 35 people, including 8 citizens of the United States. Two weeks later, three men were arrested at an Internet cafe in the city of Medina, including Abd al-Rahman al-Faqasi al-Ghamdi, believed to be the mastermind behind the bombings and to have direct links to Osama bin Laden, the leader of the al-Qa'ida network. Following the attack, Saudi officials organized a major crackdown on Islamic hardliners and detained more than 200 people for questioning.

Terrorist report. The United States Joint Intelligence Committee, a coalition based in Washington, D.C., that follows U.S. government intelligence activities, released a 900-page report in July that assessed the U.S. intelligence situation before the terrorist attacks on the United States in 2001. Twenty-eight pages of the report that purported to discuss the involvement of foreign governments in the bombings were classified, and the administration of U.S. President George W. Bush refused to make the pages public. Leaks from the report linked the Saudi government to the attacks, suggesting that the Saudis had not cooperated fully with the U.S. authorities on matters related to bin Laden.

According to foreign affairs experts, the Saudis were incensed and sent their foreign minister, Prince Saud al-Faisal, to Washington, D.C., to protest against what they called "spurious charges." They also demanded that the pages be made public.

Troop withdrawal. On April 30, 2003, a day before President Bush declared the end of combat in Iraq, the United States and Saudi Arabia reached an agreement to withdraw U.S. forces from Saudi territory. By September, the last U.S. combat troops had left the Prince Sultan Air Base and the 363rd Air Expeditionary Wing that operated there had been deactivated. Some of these forces were then sent to the Al-Udayd air base in neighboring Qatar.

The U.S. military buildup in Saudi Arabia began during the Gulf War of 1991. The U.S. Air Force used the Prince Sultan Air Base to launch more than 286,000 flying missions over Iraq between 1991 and 2003 to enforce the no-flight zone. However, Saudi Arabia refused to join the coalition forces in the war against Iraq in 2003 and did not allow U.S. air strikes on Iraq to originate from Saudi territory.   ■ Mary-Jane Deeb

See also **Iraq: A Special Report; Middle East; Terrorism.**

School. See Education.
Senegal. See Africa.

Saudi civil defense personnel search for bodies in debris following the May 2003 bombing of the Al-Hamra compound. Attackers shot their way into the housing compound and set off suicide car bombs, killing 20 people.

Hundreds of thousands of Serbians march silently in the funeral procession of Prime Minister Zoran Djindjic in Belgrade, the capital, on March 15, 2003. An assassin shot Djindjic outside of a government building in Belgrade on March 12.

Serbia and Montenegro. The political entity known as Yugoslavia ceased to exist in 2003 and was replaced by a loose union known as Serbia and Montenegro. An assassination in Serbia, however, threatened the political stability of the new nation days after it was established. By the end of the year, Serbia's moderate coalition government had lost its hold on power.

Birth of a new nation. In January, the parliaments of Serbia and Montenegro approved the constitution for the new union of their republics, and on February 4, Yugoslavia's parliament dissolved the Yugoslav federation and officially created Serbia and Montenegro. Each republic kept its own parliament and governmental institutions but also participated in a joint government. The new joint parliament convened in early March and elected Svetozar Marovic, a Montenegrin, president of Serbia and Montenegro.

Assassination. Days after the founding of Serbia and Montenegro, the assassination of Serbian Prime Minister Zoran Djindjic disrupted political life in the new country. On March 12, a gunman shot and killed Djindjic in Belgrade, the capital. In response, Serbia's government declared a state of emergency for one month and launched a crackdown on organized crime figures and Serb nationalist extremists, both suspected of involvement in the crime.

The government of Djindjic, who was widely regarded as a pro-Western reformer, had embraced policies designed to end Serbia and Montenegro's isolation from the international community. In 2001, Djindjic had handed over Slobodan Milosevic, Serbia's former president, to the War Crimes Tribunal in The Hague, Netherlands, for prosecution as a war criminal. In early 2003, Djindjic appointed a special prosecutor to pursue organized crime cases. Both actions earned enemies for the prime minister.

On August 21, the office of the special prosecutor announced the indictment of 44 people allegedly involved in the conspiracy to kill Djindjic. Most were either nationalist extremists or figures known to be involved in Serbia's criminal underground.

Stambolic body discovered. On March 28, Serbian detectives, while pursuing leads in the Djindjic investigation, discovered the remains of Ivan Stambolic, a former president of Serbia. Stambolic, an ally-turned-opponent of Slobodan Milosevic, disappeared in September 2000.

Officials in April 2003 charged Milosevic and eight others with Stambolic's murder. Prosecutors alleged that Milosevic had arranged the killing to remove a critic during an election campaign. Authorities also issued arrest warrants for Milosevic's wife and son, believed to be in hiding.

Kosovo talks. Officials of Serbia and Montenegro met with Albanian Kosovar leaders in Vienna, Austria, beginning Oct. 14, 2003, for direct talks. The talks were convened by the United Nations (UN) to ease tensions between the Albanian majority and the Serb minority in Kosovo. Sporadic fighting broke out between the two groups in 2003. Kosovo, officially a part of Serbia and Montenegro, has been administered by UN officials and policed by a UN force since the 1999 NATO police action against then-Yugoslav forces occupying the province.

Political developments. Serbia on Nov. 15, 2003, held a presidential election, which was the third to be invalidated in 14 months. None of the three elections met the 50-percent voter turnout threshold required by the Constitution.

Serbia's ultranationalist Serbian Radical Party (SRS) won approximately 28 percent of the popular vote in parliamentary elections on December 28, making it the biggest single political force in Serbia. However, the party, whose leader Vojislav Seselj was held as a war crimes suspect by the United Nations war crimes tribunal in The Hague, Netherlands, was not strong enough to form a government. Political experts predicted that four pro-reform groups would likely form a governing coalition.   ■ Sharon L. Wolchik

See also **Europe.**

Sierra Leone.
Rebels from neighboring Liberia launched cross-border raids into Sierra Leone in 2003, threatening the country's fragile peace after years of civil war. The 10-year civil war had ended in a treaty in 2001 between the democratically elected government of President Ahmad Tejan Kabbah and the rebel group the Revolutionary United Front (RUF). Amid concerns that the violence in war-torn Liberia could spread, the United Kingdom dispatched 300 troops to Sierra Leone in March 2003.

Since the 2001 cease-fire, Sierra Leone held democratic elections and, with the help of a large United Nations (UN) peacekeeping force, remained essentially peaceful until the incursions of the Liberians in 2003. Some 10,000 UN peacekeeping troops remained in Sierra Leone at the end of 2003.

Rebel deaths. The deaths in 2003 of three key rebels implicated in massacres and mass mutilations during the civil war reduced the list of rebels to be tried for war crimes by a UN-backed Special Court in Freetown, the capital. Liberian soldiers killed Sam Bockarie, a senior RUF commander, in May. Another rebel leader on the run, Johnny Paul Koroma, was killed in June in Liberia. He had seized power in 1997 from President Kabbah, but a Nigerian-led force ousted Koroma in 1998 and restored Kabbah to power.

Both Bockarie and Koroma died in mysterious circumstances, leading international affairs experts to speculate that the two men had been killed on orders of Charles Taylor, then Liberia's president and another of the Special Court's indictees. Observers theorized that Taylor may have acted to stop the two men from giving testimony implicating him in various crimes.

On July 30, 2003, Foday Sankoh, the founder of the RUF, died in UN custody in a Freetown hospital. He had been incapacitated since suffering a massive stroke in August 2002. Sankoh was under indictment by the Special Court for a long list of charges, including crimes against humanity.

Truth commission. In April 2003, Sierra Leone's Truth and Reconciliation Commission (TRC) opened public hearings in Freetown to probe atrocities in the civil war. The commission began to hear testimony from hundreds of victims, perpetrators, and witnesses.

President Kabbah set up the seven-member panel in December 2002, modeling it on South Africa's TRC. Between 1995 and 1998, the South African commission investigated human rights abuses that had occurred during apartheid, the era of rigid racial separation in South Africa that ended in 1994.   ■ Simon Baynham

See also **Africa.**

Singapore
underwent its sharpest economic decline on record between April and June 2003. Economists said the 11.4-percent contraction was caused mainly by a loss of tourism due to severe acute respiratory syndrome (SARS). More than 30 people in Singapore died from SARS, which killed more than 700 people worldwide.

In August, Prime Minister Chok Tong Goh lowered the government forecast for economic expansion for 2003 from 0.5 to 2.5 percent to 0 to 1 percent. The government, which had experienced two recessions since the Asian financial crisis in 1997 and 1998, ran a budget deficit for an unprecedented third consecutive year in 2003.

Goh announced in August that he would step down when the economy recovered from the downturn. He named as his successor Deputy Prime Minister Lee Hsien Loong, son of Singapore's founding leader, Lee Kuan Yew.

The United States Congress approved a free-trade agreement with Singapore in July 2003. The deal with Singapore was the first such pact between the United States and an Asian country.

Singapore relaxed several strict laws on public behavior in 2003. The government eased laws that prohibited bungee jumping, gum chewing unless medically prescribed, and spitting in public.
                              ■ Henry S. Bradsher

See also **Asia; China; Public health and safety.**

Bode Miller of the United States begins his run in the combined event at the World Alpine Ski Championships in St. Moritz, Switzerland, in February 2003. Miller won the gold medal, making him the first American man ever to win two golds at the World Championships.

Skiing. The United States Alpine team turned in its best performance in history at the World Alpine Ski Championships in February 2003, winning six medals at the competition in St. Moritz, Switzerland. Bode Miller became the first U.S. man to win two gold medals. He also won a silver. The women's team also put on a show, taking two medals in the Super Giant Slalom (Super-G).

Miller had the best season of his career. On January 4 in Kranjska Gora, Slovenia, he captured his second straight World Cup giant slalom. Miller's victory put him briefly into first place in the world overall points standings, making him the first American to lead the standings since Phil Mahre in 1983. On Jan. 25, 2003, Daron Rahlves became the first American since Buddy Werner in 1959 to win the downhill at Kitzbuhel, Austria.

However, Stephan Eberharter of Austria surged past Miller to capture his second straight overall title with 1,333 points, 233 ahead of second-place Miller. Eberharter clinched the overall, Super-G, and downhill titles. Kalle Palander of Finland won the slalom title, becoming the first Finn to win a World Cup alpine discipline. Michael von Gruenigen of Switzerland won the giant slalom title. Bode Miller won the combined title.

In women's alpine skiing, Janica Kostelic of Croatia captured the overall title with 1,570 points to 1,100 for Karen Putzer of Italy. Kostelic also cap-

tured the slalom and combined titles. Carole Montillet of France won the women's Super-G title. Anja Paerson of Sweden won the giant slalom title, and Michaela Dorfmeister of Austria won the downhill title.

World Alpine Ski Championships. U.S. skiers captured six medals at the World Alpine Ski Championships in February in St. Moritz, Switzerland. Miller took home two gold medals and one silver.

Miller started his run on February 2 by winning the silver in the giant slalom. On February 6, in the combined competition, Miller turned in two spectacular slalom runs after finishing in 17th place in the downhill portion. The performances earned him a gold medal. On February 12, Miller took gold in the giant slalom.

Maier returns. Hermann Maier, the Austrian star who nearly lost a leg in a motorcycle accident in August 2001, continued his comeback in 2003, winning the Super-G in a World Cup event in Kitzbuehel, Austria, on January 27.

Nordic skiing. On February 28, Johnny Spillane became the first U.S. skier to win a gold medal in the Nordic World Ski Championships by capturing the Nordic combined sprint in Val di Fiemme, Italy.

Germany's Ronny Ackermann won his second straight overall Nordic combined title when he won his fourth World Cup event of the season March 14 in Lahti, Finland. ■ Michael Kates

Slovakia. The coalition government of Prime Minister Mikulas Dzurinda narrowly held onto power in 2003, holding the allegiance of 75 of the 150 deputies in parliament. In April, Slovak and European Union (EU) officials signed a treaty approving Slovakia's entry into the EU, scheduled for May 2004, and Slovak voters approved the treaty in a May 2003 referendum.

Shaky coalition. During 2003, issues involving religion strained the ruling coalition. In July, opposition members of parliament, joined by members of New Citizens' Alliance (ANO), one of four parties in Dzurinda's governing coalition, passed a bill intended to perpetuate abortion rights for women. Another coalition party, the conservative Christian Democratic Movement (KDH), responded by threatening to quit the government. In a 2001 survey, a majority of Slovaks identified themselves as Roman Catholics, and Catholic leaders consistently opposed abortion.

Abortion was legal in Slovakia in 2003, but the old law, passed in 1986 under the former Communist government, was under review in a legal challenge brought before Slovakia's constitutional court. On July 23, 2003, President Rudolf Schuster vetoed the abortion bill. Proabortion forces in parliament lacked strength to override the veto, so they simply awaited the court's review of the old law.

Also in July, the government approved a treaty with the Vatican, the Roman Catholic Church's central administration, endorsing Catholic religious courses in Slovak schools. The treaty confirmed the existing situation in Slovak schools, where such courses were already being offered. ANO ministers in the coalition cabinet rejected the pact, prompting their KDH counterparts to demand dismissal of the ANO ministers.

Slovakia's economy continued to experience strong growth in 2003. *Gross domestic product* (the value of all goods and services produced in a year) grew by 4.1 percent in 2003, compared with 4.4 percent in 2002. However, inflation edged up in 2003, reaching 9.2 percent in August. Unemployment fell from 18 percent in 2002 to 14.3 percent in August 2003.

A plan to introduce a uniform income tax in 2004, part of the government's economic reform program, sparked protest in 2003. On September 26, labor unions sponsored a one-hour general strike that thousands of workers supported.

Foreign policy. Slovak leaders supported the United States-led war in Iraq in early 2003, opening Slovakia's territory to overflights and troop transit. On April 9, Prime Minister Dzurinda met in Washington, D.C., with U.S. President George W. Bush, affirming his government's support.

■ Sharon L. Wolchik

See also **Europe; Iraq: A Special Report.**

Soccer. Germany defeated Sweden 2-1 to win the Women's World Cup on Oct. 12, 2003. The competition was originally scheduled to be played in China, but was moved to the United States due to the spread of severe acute respiratory syndrome (SARS), a viral disease sweeping through Asia. In Major League Soccer (MLS), the San Jose Earthquakes defeated the Chicago Fire 4-2 to win their second title in three years.

International soccer. France won the Federation Internationale de Football Association (FIFA) Confederations Cup, defeating Cameroon 1-0 with a golden goal by striker Thierry Henry in the seventh minute of extra time of the final in Saint-Denis, France, on June 29. Three days earlier, Cameroon lost its star player, Marc-Vivien Foe, who had collapsed in the semifinal against Colombia and later died. The United States finished last in its group, losing by a single goal to both Brazil and Turkey before drawing 0-0 with eventual finalist Cameroon.

Mexico won the 2003 Confederation of North, Central American, and Caribbean Association Football (CONCACAF) Gold Cup, held in Mexico and the United States in July. Mexico defeated Brazil 1-0 in the final, which was played in front of 80,000 fans at the Azteca Stadium in Mexico City on July 27. Mexico's substitute, Daniel Osorno, scored the winner, a golden goal in the seventh minute of extra time. The United States took third place, coming from behind twice to defeat Costa Rica 3-2 on July 26 at the Orange Bowl in Miami, Florida.

In the semifinals, the United States had led Brazil 1-0 until conceding a goal in the final minute of regulation time and losing to a golden-goal penalty kick in the 100th minute. In the quarterfinals, Landon Donovan scored four goals in the U.S. team's 5-0 victory over Cuba. Canada was eliminated at the group stage on goal difference after all three teams in its group finished with 3 points.

As of mid-December, Brazil topped the FIFA/Coca-Cola World Rankings with 848 points, followed by France (827) and Spain (798). The United States (732) was ranked 11th, one place above Germany.

Under-17. Brazil defeated Spain 1-0 in the final of the FIFA Under-17 World Championships on August 30 at Toolo Stadium in Helsinki, Finland, to claim a record third world title out of the last four. Brazilian defender Leonardo scored in the seventh minute. Spanish midfielder Cesc scored five goals and won both the Adidas Golden Ball as top goalscorer and the Golden Shoe as best player of the tournament.

U.S. striker Freddy Adu also made a name for himself in the tournament. The 14-year-old Ghana-born prodigy, the youngest player in the tournament, scored a *hat-trick* (three goals in a game) to lead the U.S. team in its first match, a 6-1 drubbing of South Korea. The United States won through to the quarterfinals, but was shut out 3-0 by Brazil.

Artificial turf made its debut at the tournament, with 10 out of 32 matches being played on an artificial surface. Players and fans reported that the experiment was a success.

Under-20. Brazil won the FIFA World Youth (Under-20) Championship, defeating Spain 1-0 in the final on December 19 at the Zayed City Sports Stadium in Abu Dhabi, United Arab Emirates. The United States was eliminated in the quarterfinals, but Ed Johnson won the Golden Boot with four goals and an assist.

International club competition. Milan won the European Champions League (also known as the European Cup) on May 28 by defeating another Italian team, Juventus (Turin), 3-2 on penalties. The match, played at Old Trafford (Manchester), England, was tied 0-0 after extra time, but Milan won it in a penalty shoot-out.

Boca Juniors (Argentina) defeated Santos (Brazil) 5-1 on aggregate in the two-legged final of the Copa Libertadores, South America's club championship. Boca won its home leg 2-0 on June 25 at La Bombonera, Buenos Aires, and took the return 3-1 in Sao Paulo, Brazil, on July 2.

Boca Juniors defeated Milan 3-1 on penalties in the match for the World Club Cup, played between the club champions of Europe and South America, in Yokohama, Japan, on December 14. The score after 90 minutes and extra time was 1-1.

Major League Soccer (MLS). The San Jose Earthquakes defeated the Chicago Fire 4-2 in the MLS Cup Championship match at the Home Depot Center in Carson, California, on November 23. San Jose took a 2-0 half-time lead in front of the capacity crowd of about 27,000. The Fire fought hard, coming back to within a goal of San Jose in the second period, but Landon Donovan finished them off with his second goal of the game in the 71st minute. Donovan later received the Honda Most Valuable Player award.

Chicago lost an opportunity when striker Ante Razov failed to convert a penalty in the 56th minute with Chicago down 3-2. San Jose goalkeeper Pat Onstad made a diving stop to deny Razov and the Fire.

San Jose and Chicago had easily won their respective conferences in the regular season. San Jose won the Western Conference by nine points over Kansas City, and Chicago won the Eastern Conference by eight points over New England. In the play-offs, San Jose staged a remarkable comeback in the semifinal against the Los Angeles Galaxy. After losing the first leg 2-0 in Los Angeles, San Jose was quickly down 4-0 on aggregate in the return game. But the Earthquakes scored four

times and tied the game in the 90th minute. Substitute Rodrigo Faria capped off San Jose's unlikely victory with a golden goal in the sixth minute of extra time.

Both conference finals went to sudden death, with Landon Donovan's goal in the 27th minute of extra time giving San Jose the edge over Kansas City. In the Eastern Conference final between Chicago and New England, Chris Armas of Chicago hit the only goal of the game in the 11th minute of the first extra period.

Women's soccer. Germany won the FIFA Women's World Cup, defeating Sweden 2-1 with a golden-goal winner at the Home Depot Center in Carson on October 12 in front of more than 26,000 fans. The tournament was moved from the scheduled host country, China, because of a health scare caused by the deadly SARS virus. Officials hurriedly planned the tournament in four months as opposed to the normal six years of planning. The defending champion U.S. team breezed to victory in its three group matches, defeating opponents by a combined 11 goals to 1, including a 3-1 defeat of eventual finalist Sweden. The U.S. team went on to defeat Norway 1-0 in the quarterfinals before losing to Germany in the semifinals.

Germany defeated the United States in a semifinal match on October 5 in Portland, Oregon, that many observers, including U.S. coach April Heinrichs, later claimed was among the finest women's matches of all time. In the other semifinal, Canada, enjoying its most successful World Cup, took the lead against Sweden, but allowed two late goals to lose 2-1.

In the championship match, Sweden's Hanna Ljungberg scored first near the end of the first half. But Maren Meinert leveled the score for Germany soon after the interval. The game went into extra time, and German substitute defender Nia Kuenzer scored the winner when she headed in a free kick after eight minutes to give the German team their first title.

Germany's Birgit Prinz scored seven goals and won the Adidas Golden Shoe for top scorer and the Golden Ball for the tournament's top player. The U.S. team defeated Canada 3-1 for third place to continue their streak of finishing in the top three of every Women's World Cup.

Germany's World Cup triumph put the team atop the FIFA women's world rankings, bumping the U.S. team to the second spot in the rankings, which were first compiled in July.

Awards. Zinedine Zidane of France and Real Madrid (Spain) was named World Player of the Year for the third time at the FIFA World Gala in Basel, Switzerland, on December 15. The women's award went to Birgit Prinz of Germany and FFC Frankfurt.

■ Norman Barrett

Social Security. Officials with the Social Security Administration (SSA) reported on March 17, 2003, that revenue surpluses for the Social Security program would continue until 2018 and that the program would have adequate revenues until 2042. Both dates are one year later than administration officials had projected in their 2002 report. The 2003 report disclosed that Social Security paid approximately $453.8 billion in benefits in 2002 and ran a surplus of $165 billion. However, SSA officials reported in 2003 that the surplus was being used to support tax cuts approved by the administration of President George W. Bush and to pay for other government expenses. The Social Security program is funded by taxes on employees, which help pay for the benefits of retirees.

Military benefits spared. SSA officials announced on April 11, 2003, that military families that received supplemental security income (SSI) would not see a decrease in their benefits if a mother, father, or spouse received special combat-related increases in military pay. Ordinarily, SSI benefits are reduced when family income increases. The question arose after some members of the U.S. armed forces were assigned to combat duty overseas in 2003 during the war in Iraq. ■ Geoffrey A. Campbell

See also **United States, Government of the.**

South Africa. Corruption trials involving senior members of the ruling African National Congress (ANC) and political maneuvers to tighten ANC control over parliament dominated South Africa's political life in 2003. In the international arena, President Thabo Mbeki's criticism of the United States-led war in Iraq and the subsequent occupation of Iraq by U.S. and allied troops complicated South Africa's relations with the United States and its chief ally, the United Kingdom (U.K.).

Parliamentary realignment. In April, a controversial "floor-crossing" plan in the National Assembly (parliament) secured for the ANC a threshold two-thirds majority that would enable the party to rewrite the constitution and effectively rule unopposed. The plan prescribed a 15-day period for members of parliament (MP's) to "cross the floor" (switch parties) without losing their seats. Typically, in a parliamentary system, such as South Africa's, a change of party affiliation requires an MP to resign and run again for election. During the "window," nine opposition MP's defected to the ANC. Opposition political leaders accused the party of attempting to establish one-party rule in South Africa.

Fraud trials. In March 2003, a South African court convicted senior ANC member Tony Yengeni for fraud and sentenced him to four years in jail. Yengeni admitted that while overseeing defense contracts in 1998, he had received a luxury automobile at a large discount from a bidder in a multibillion-dollar arms deal. Political observers regarded the trial as a test of President Mbeki's anticorruption drive, a cornerstone of his administration since it began in 1999.

In April 2003, a court convicted ANC leader Winnie Madikizela-Mandela on charges of fraud and theft and sentenced her to five years in prison with one year suspended. During the trial, government prosecutors presented evidence that Madikizela-Mandela had used her position as a high-ranking ANC official to obtain bank loans for nonexistent applicants and had pocketed the funds.

After being sentenced, Madikizela-Mandela gave up her seat in South Africa's National Assembly, quit her post as president of the ANC Women's League, and resigned from the ruling ANC's powerful executive committee. Madikizela-Mandela, former wife of former South African President Nelson Mandela, remained a popular figure among some South Africans who regarded her as a hero of the movement that ended apartheid, the system of racial separation brutally enforced in South Africa prior to 1994.

Right-wing plot. South Africa's first treason trial since the end of apartheid in 1994 began in Pretoria in May 2003, though the trial was repeatedly postponed due to legal maneuvering by the defense. Government prosecutors charged that 22 alleged members of a white extremist group called Boeremag (Farmers' Force) had plotted in 2002 to overthrow South Africa's black majority government and reinstate white rule.

The extremists had allegedly planned a series of attacks and an assassination plot targeting Nelson Mandela. According to testimony given during the trial, the Boeremag also had developed plans to drive black South Africans and South Africans of Asian background out of the country. Legal experts said the trial could last several years.

AIDS policy change. President Mbeki's Cabinet announced in November 2003 that government health clinics would make HIV antiviral drugs available to South Africans infected with HIV, the virus that causes AIDS. Previously, Mbeki had opposed distribution of the drugs, asserting that they were toxic and too expensive.

According to the United Nations, South Africa in 2003 had one of the world's highest HIV infection rates. Some 25 percent of adults—about 5 million South Africans in all—were infected with the virus. About 600 people died of AIDS daily in South Africa in 2003, reported health experts.

International relations. President Mbeki refrained in 2003 from condemning Robert

Mugabe and his ruling Zimbabwe African National Union-Patriotic Front in Zimbabwe, South Africa's neighbor to the north. Mugabe, who has held power in Zimbabwe since the establishment of black majority rule in 1980, drew widespread international condemnation in recent years for alleged corruption, election fraud, and widely reported human rights abuses. Some political observers said that Mbeki's silence on the abuses of the Mugabe regime damaged his own international standing.

President Mbeki sharply criticized the U.S.-led war in Iraq and subsequent occupation in 2003, straining South Africa's relations with the United States and its main ally, the U.K. However, when U.S. President George W. Bush visited President Mbeki in July in Pretoria, the two leaders publicly sidestepped their policy differences on Iraq and Zimbabwe.

Death. Walter Max Sisulu, a founding leader of South Africa's antiapartheid movement, as well as a close friend and mentor of former President Nelson Mandela, died on May 5 at age 90. Sisulu held the post of ANC vice president in the early 1990's. ■ Simon Baynham

See also **Africa; Iraq: A Special Report.**

South America. See **Latin America.**
South Carolina. See **State government.**
South Dakota. See **State government.**

Space exploration.

In 2003, a fatal space flight accident dealt a psychological blow to the United States space program, while China's first manned flight in October gave the world's most populous country a big boost in national pride and technological confidence.

Columbia tragedy. The space shuttle Columbia, returning from a mission on Feb. 1, 2003, broke apart minutes before it was to land in Florida, killing all seven astronauts on board. The accident grounded the three remaining shuttles used to haul into orbit most components for construction of the International Space Station. The accident also led some Americans to question the National Aeronautics and Space Administration's (NASA) vision for human space flight.

The loss of the Columbia was also a national tragedy in Israel and India. Among the crew were Israel's first space traveler, Ilan Ramon, a fighter pilot in the nation's air force; and shuttle mission specialist, NASA astronaut, and aeronautical engineer Kalpana Chawla, who was born in India and became that country's first woman in space. The other members of the crew included NASA astronauts Rick D. Husband, the commander; William C. McCool, the copilot; Michael P. Anderson, the payload commander; and David M. Brown and Laurel B. Clark, mission specialists.

Columbia, first launched on April 12, 1981,

had been the first shuttle orbiter to fly in space. The only previous fatal in-flight accident NASA had sustained was the explosion of the shuttle Challenger in 1986, as it launched with a crew of seven, including a teacher who was to have been the first "citizen in space."

NASA appointed a board to investigate the Columbia accident. During the weeks after the tragedy, thousands of people scoured the landscape across Texas and several other states and gathered pieces of wreckage that helped investigators understand what had happened to the shuttle. The board determined that as the Columbia was launched on Jan. 16, 2003, a piece of insulating foam broke off of the large, orange external fuel tank and struck the orbiter, probably on the *leading* (front) edge of its left wing. Two weeks later, as the Columbia descended from space and encountered the thickening air of the atmosphere, the normal heat build-up of reentry began on the spaceship. But temperatures climbed particularly rapidly at various spots in the left wing and left landing gear area.

After a dramatic test designed to simulate the foam impact on launch, the investigating board concluded that the foam had blasted a hole in Columbia's left wing, letting in hot gases that doomed the shuttle. The board and NASA were disturbed by the realization after the accident that pieces of external fuel tank foam had broken off during previous shuttle launchings. Before the crash, the agency believed that the flying foam was not a serious problem.

The effect on the station. An immediate concern after the Columbia accident was how to support the International Space Station. The shuttle carried many station crew members to and from the outpost and hauled most of the cargo and almost all of the new components for the station, which was still under construction. The crew on board the station, however, was not at risk, as Russian Soyuz spacecraft were always docked to the station for use in an emergency.

Engineers determined that supplying the station with enough water for three crew members was the biggest problem, so the international partners temporarily reduced the crew to two. Russia's Soyuz manned vehicles and Progress cargo spacecraft could then support the station until the shuttle flew again. While each Soyuz usually carries three people, only two are required to fly the spacecraft.

On April 26, Russian cosmonaut Yuri Malenchenko and NASA astronaut Edward Lu flew on a Soyuz to the space station to replace the existing station crew. U.S. astronauts Kenneth Bowersox and Donald Pettit and Russian commander Nikolai Budarin then returned to Earth on the same Soyuz. Another crew replaced Malenchenko and

Streaks (above) appear in the sky over Tyler, in central Texas, as the space shuttle Columbia disintegrates minutes before it was to land in Florida on Feb. 1, 2003. Columbia, which was returning from a science mission, carried seven astronauts (right), all of whom perished in the accident: Commander Rick D. Husband and Pilot William C. McCool (front row); Mission Specialists Kalpana Chawla and Laurel B. Clark (second row); and Israeli astronaut Ilan Ramon, Payload Commander Michael P. Anderson, and Mission Specialist David M. Brown (third row).

The Loss of the Space Shuttle Columbia

Debris from the space shuttle Columbia (above), collected from across several states by thousands of volunteers immediately after the accident, is assembled at a hangar at the Kennedy Space Center in Florida as investigators try to determine the cause of the accident.

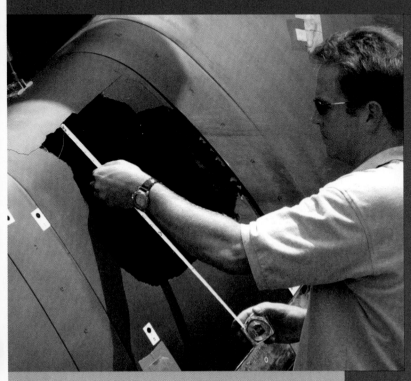

An investigator with the National Aeronautics and Space Administration measures a hole that developed in a shuttle wing panel during an experiment into the cause of the Columbia disaster. Investigators fired insulating foam from the shuttle's external fuel tank into the wing panel to see whether the foam that fell from Columbia's fuel tank during the launch on January 16 could have made a hole that damaged the wing. The simulation dramatically proved that the foam could have made such a hole. Investigators concluded that extremely hot gases entered the wing through a hole during Columbia's reentry into Earth's atmosphere and contributed to the shuttle's breaking apart.

Lu six months later. On October 18, U.S. astronaut
Michael Foale and cosmonaut Alexander Kaleri of
Latvia flew aboard a Soyuz to the station. They were
accompanied by Pedro Duque of Spain, a European
Space Agency astronaut. Ten days later, Duque, Lu,
and Malenchenko returned to Earth.

China in space. In October, China became only
the third nation (after Russia and the United States)
to launch a human being into space. *Taikonaut* (the
Chinese counterpart for *astronaut* and *cosmonaut*)
Yang Liwei lifted off in a Shenzhou spacecraft atop

China's first *taikonaut,* or astronaut, Yang
Liwei, steps from his space capsule on October 16 (left) after successfully completing 14
orbits around Earth and landing in Inner
Mongolia. Liwei's flight began with the
launching of his Shenzhou spacecraft atop a
Long March 2F rocket from the Jiuquan
launch site in the Gobi Desert (above). The
flight represented a technological triumph
for China, which became only the third
nation—after Russia and the United
States—to launch a human being into space.

a Long March 2F booster on October 15 from the Jiuquan launch complex in the Gobi desert of northwest China. The Shenzhou—which means *divine ship* or *magic vessel*—closely resembles the Soyuz spacecraft but is somewhat larger. Liwei spent 21 hours in space, orbiting Earth 14 times before landing in Inner Mongolia. Chinese officials said they planned other flights for Shenzhou and hoped to send a spacecraft to the moon.

Missions to Mars. Both NASA and the European Space Agency (ESA) launched missions to Mars in 2003. The U.S. spacecraft carried a pair of surface rovers named Spirit and Opportunity and were launched from Cape Canaveral, Florida, on June 10 and July 7, respectively. They were to arrive on the red planet in January 2004, each with a parachute and air-bag landing system similar to that used by the Mars Pathfinder rover in 1997. However, Spirit and Opportunity were much larger, more power-ful, and able to roam farther.

On June 2, 2003, ESA's Mars Ex-press was launched on a Soyuz/Fregat booster from the Baikonur Cosmo-drome in Kazakhstan. Mars Express was to look for evidence of life on the planet, both by studying the atmo-sphere from orbit and by dropping a lander, called Beagle 2 after naturalist Charles Darwin's ship, to collect rock and soil samples. Mars Express reached the red planet in December and released the Beagle 2, which was to have dropped to the surface on December 25. However, at the end of 2003, no signals from the lander had been received by scientists on Earth.

On December 9, Japan's space agency abandoned its Nozomi orbiter, launched to Mars in 1998, after it mal-functioned and veered off course.

Death of Galileo. Scientists oper-ating the Galileo spacecraft, in orbit around Jupiter and its moons since 1995, deliberately crashed the robot-ic explorer into the planet on Sept. 21, 2003. As it fell through Jupiter's atmosphere, Galileo continued to send data back to Earth, as part of one of NASA's most successful missions. ■ James R. Asker

See also **Astronomy: A Special Report; Space Telescopes; Astronomy.**

Spain. The government of Prime Minister Jose Maria Aznar supported the United States-led war in Iraq in 2003, despite strong opposition from most Spaniards. Polls conducted in February indi-cated that as many as 90 percent of the Spanish public opposed the war. Nevertheless, Aznar sought to strengthen relations between Spain and the United States and supported U.S. Presi-dent George W. Bush's campaign largely because of Spain's experience with terrorism in its north-ern Basque region.

Aznar endorsed the decision to attack Iraq at a meeting with Bush and British Prime Minister Tony Blair in the Azores Islands on March 16, days before the war began. Aznar declined to commit Spanish troops to the war, but he did send 1,300 troops after the war to help with peacekeeping. Spain also hosted an international donors' con-ference for Iraq in October and pledged $300 million for reconstruction efforts.

Local elections. Aznar's Popular Party did better than expected in local and regional elec-tions on May 25, despite an attempt by the main opposition group, the Socialist Party, to turn the election into a referendum on the war. The Popu-lar Party won 33.9 percent of the vote, narrowly behind the Socialists' 34.7 percent. The party also won control of assemblies in 9 of the country's 13 regions and a majority of its cities.

Aznar succession. On August 30, Aznar announced his selection of Mariano Rajoy, his deputy prime minister, to succeed him as head of the Popular Party. The choice made Rajoy the party's candidate for prime minister in national elections to be held in 2004. Aznar, who came to power in 1996 and won reelection in 2000, had promised to step down after two terms.

Independence controversies. A plan to give greater autonomy to the Basque region in northern Spain generated controversy in 2003. Juan Jose Ibarretxe, prime minister of the Basque regional parliament, unveiled a proposal in Sep-tember that would introduce dual Basque and Spanish citizenship and allow the region to represent itself directly in the European Union. Ibarretxe claimed the plan would reduce violence by Basque separatists, but Aznar's government rejected the plan as a step toward secession. The government asked the Constitutional Court to prevent Ibarretxe from holding a referendum on the plan in 2004.

A party seeking independence for Catalonia, the region around Barcelona in northeast Spain, made big gains in local elections on Nov. 16, 2003. The Republican Left doubled its number of seats in the regional parliament from 12 in 1999 to 23 in 2003, increasing its power as a coalition partner. ■ Tom Buerkle

See also **Europe; Iraq: A Special Report.**

Sports. Spectacular individual performances dominated the sporting world in 2003. Americans Lance Armstrong and Michael Phelps made the biggest waves. Armstrong battled against tough competition and personal challenges to become only the second cyclist in history to win the Tour de France five consecutive times. Michael Phelps broke five individual world swimming records in a six-day span in July and established himself as the dominant male swimmer in the world.

However, amid these accomplishments, a major drug scandal struck the sports world in October. The scandal involved a performance-enhancing drug that could not be detected by traditional drug tests.

In professional golf, Annika Sorenstam of Sweden became the first Ladies Professional Golf Association (LPGA) member to play in a men's event in 58 years. Sorenstam failed to play well enough to qualify to finish at The Colonial, in

Fort Worth, Texas, in May. She rebounded to later capture two major LPGA championships. In men's professional golf, all four major championships of the Professional Golfers' Association (PGA) were won by men who had never won a PGA major.

In professional team sports, the San Antonio Spurs won the National Basketball Association (NBA) title in June; the New Jersey Devils captured the Stanley Cup in the National Hockey League in June; Tampa Bay captured Super Bowl XXXVII in the National Football League in Jan-

Lance Armstrong of the United States races toward his record-tying fifth consecutive Tour de France title in July 2003. During the race, Armstrong overcame some of the toughest obstacles—including two falls—since his winning streak began in 1999.

uary; and the Florida Marlins captured Major League Baseball's World Series in October.

In college sports, fans experienced a turbulent year in which several football and basketball coaches resigned or were fired for ethical lapses or rules violations. College sports fans in 2003 also witnessed the beginning of what could be a realignment of its major conferences.

Drug scandal. In October, revelations that high-profile athletes in several disciplines may have knowingly taken a performance-enhancing drug that could not previously be detected by drug tests began to make waves in the sports world. The controversy centered on a drug called tetrahydrogestrinone (THG), a steroid that had allegedly been altered so it would not be detectable by usual drug test methods. Forty athletes, including such stars as Barry Bonds, Jason Giambi, and Marion Jones, were questioned by a grand jury in connection with an investigation of BALCO Laboratories, Inc., of Burlingame, California, for allegedly supplying the drug.

In October, the Food and Drug Administration ruled that THG was an illegal drug and that anyone found making or selling it would be prosecuted. Several athletes tested positive for THG, and officials of several sports bodies announced they would attempt to test urine samples from competitions going as far back as the Winter Olympics to determine if any athletes used THG.

Tour de France. On July 27, Lance Armstrong captured his record-tying fifth Tour de France victory. Armstrong won the 2,129-mile (3,427-kilometer) 20-stage race by 61 seconds, the slimmest margin of victory by far of all his Tour wins. Germany's Jan Ullrich, who had won in 1997, finished in second place behind Armstrong for the fifth time. With his win, Armstrong joined Eddy Merckx of Belgium; Jacques Anquetil and Bernard Hinault of France; and Miguel Indurain of Spain as the only racers to win the Tour five times. Only Armstrong and Indurain have won the race five consecutive times.

Phelps flies. Michael Phelps of the United States had a record-breaking season in 2003. In July, he became the first swimmer to set five individual records in a single meet with a dominating performance at the World Swimming Championships in Barcelona, Spain. In a six-day span, Phelps became the first man to break two individual records in one day and just the third to hold four records simultaneously. Mark Spitz of the United States and Michael Gross of Germany also held four world records at once.

On July 22, Phelps broke his own record in the 200-meter butterfly with a time of 1 minute, 53.93 seconds. Two days later, he broke the mark he had set a month earlier in the 200-meter individual medley with a time of 1

minute, 57.52 seconds. The next day, Phelps set records in the 200-meter individual medley (1:56.04) and the 100-meter butterfly (51.47). On July 27, Phelps broke his own record in the 400-meter individual medley with a time of 4 minutes, 09.09 seconds.

Phelps continued to dominate at the U.S. National Championships in College Park, Maryland. On August 9, he lowered his 200-meter individual medley mark to 1 minute, 55.94 seconds.

College realignment. On May 13, 2003, officials with college sports' Atlantic Coast Conference (ACC) voted to expand for the first time since 1991. In a controversial move, the ACC expressed interest in adding three schools from the Big East Conference—the University of Miami, Syracuse University, and either Boston College or Virginia Tech University. The expansion would have given the ACC 12 schools, allowing the ACC to split into two divisions and host a lucrative conference championship in football.

The move sparked a lawsuit by five Big East schools, which sued Miami, Boston College, and the ACC to block the expansion. The schools feared that the ACC's move would doom the Big East Conference, which would have had just five schools left that played football. In a surprise move on June 25, 2003, ACC officials voted to add just two schools—Virginia Tech and Miami. ACC officials later added Boston College.

Land speed record. Engineers with the U.S. Department of Defense's 846th Test Squadron and the Missile Defense Agency broke the land speed record for rail vehicles on April 30 at Holloman Air Force Base in New Mexico. The group built a rocket-powered sled that reached 6,453 miles (10,385 kilometers) per hour, or Mach 8.6, nearly nine times the speed of sound. The sled broke the old record of Mach 8, or 6,122 miles (9,852 kilometers) per hour, set in 1982.

Crime. Baylor University basketball player Patrick Dennehy was found dead on July 25, 2003, in a field near the Waco, Texas, school, about six weeks after he was reported missing. Dennehy died of gunshot wounds to the head. On July 21, Carlton Dotson, a former teammate and roommate of Dennehy, was arrested and charged with the murder. Dotson reportedly told agents with the Federal Bureau of Investigation that he had shot Dennehy in self-defense and then hid the body.

On August 8, one day after a memorial service for Dennehy, Baylor officials accepted the resignations of head coach Dave Bliss and athletic director Tom Stanton, after an internal investigation disclosed major violations of National Collegiate Athletic Association (NCAA) rules. Baylor coaches allegedly had provided money to players, and Baylor players allegedly had taken drugs. Bliss came under additional fire when it was later revealed that he had tried to cover up the violations by telling coaching assistants and players to tell authorities that Dennehy sold drugs to pay his tuition. Bliss later admitted to having given Dennehy money to pay bills.

Kobe Bryant, a star for the NBA's Los Angeles Lakers and a key member of three championship teams, was charged in 2003 with felony sexual assault in Eagle County, Colorado. In October, a judge ruled that Bryant's case would go to trial. A five-time NBA All-Star, Bryant admitted having sexual relations with a 19-year-old resort employee on June 30 at a Colorado resort but denied assaulting her. Bryant was arrested on July 4 and charged with assault on July 18. He had been staying at the resort while he recovered from knee surgery. If convicted, Bryant faced a sentence of four years to life in prison, or 20 years to life on probation, and a $750,000 fine.

Awards. Lance Armstrong received the International Amateur Athletic Association's American-International Athlete Trophy in February. Armstrong, who had won the award in 2000 when it was known as the Jesse Owens International Trophy, won again for capturing his fourth consecutive Tour de France in 2002.

In March 2003, figure skater Sarah Hughes won the 2002 James E. Sullivan Memorial Award, which is presented to the best U.S. amateur athlete. Hughes, a gold medalist in the 2002 Winter Olympic Games, is the second consecutive skater to capture the award. Michelle Kwan won the 2001 award. Skater Dick Button won it in 1949.

Among the winners in 2003 were–

Gymnastics. The United States captured its first gold medal in the 2003 World Gymnastics Championships on August 20 in Anaheim, California. The U.S. women's team defeated the Romanian women's team by 1.74 points. Svetlana Khorkina of Russia captured the women's all-around title. In men's competition, China won its fifth team gold metal in the past six world championships, narrowly topping the United States by 0.875 point. Paul Hamm became the first American man to medal in the all-around.

Luge. Armin Zoeggeler of Italy won the luge singles title at the World Championships held in Sigulda, Latvia, in February. Germany's Sylke Otto won the women's singles title. Andreas and Wolfgang Linger, brothers from Austria, won the men's doubles title. Germany won the team title.

Rodeo. Trevor Brazile of Decatur, Texas, won the All-Around World Champion Cowboy title in the National Finals Rodeo on December 14.

Rowing. Victoria City Rowing Club of Canada captured the Grand Challenge Cup on July 6 at the Henley Royal Regatta in Henley-on-the-Thames, England, beating a U.S. team from the Princeton Training Center in Princeton, New Jersey, by 2 3/4 lengths. The University of Washington's team beat a squad from Rutgers University to capture the Ladies' Challenge Plate.

Sled-dog racing. Robert Sorlie of Norway won the Iditarod Trail Sled Dog Race on March 12, finishing the 1,100-mile (1,770-kilometer) trip across Alaska from Anchorage to Nome in 9 days, 15 hours, 47 minutes, and 36 seconds. Sorlie became the second non-Alaskan to win the race, joining Doug Swingley of Lincoln, Montana.

Soap Box Derby. Anthony Marulli of Rochester, New York, won the Masters Division of the All-American Soap Box Derby in Akron, Ohio, on July 26.

Speed skating. Hyun-Soo Ahn of South Korea won the men's overall title, and Eun-Kyung Choi of South Korea won the women's overall title at the World Sprint Championships, held in Warsaw, Poland, in March. Ahn finished first in the 1,500-meter and 3,000-meter events, second in the 1,000-meter race, and was on the winning 5,000-meter relay team. Choi won the 1,500-meter race and was second in both the 1,000- and 3,000-meter events, unseating six-time champion Yang Yang of China. Canada won the men's title and South Korea captured the women's title at the short-track World Team Championships held in March in Sofia, Bulgaria.

Triathlon. Peter Robertson of Australia won the men's title at the World Triathlon Championships in Queenstown, Australia, on December 8. Emma Snowsill of Australia won the women's title.

Weightlifting. Hossein Reza Zadeh of Iran won the men's gold medal at the World Weightlifting Championships in Vancouver on November 22. Ding Meiyuan of China won the women's gold medal.

Wrestling. At the World Freestyle Championships in New York City in September, the nation of Georgia captured the men's team title with 33 points. The United States was second, followed by Iran, which was tied with the U.S. team but had fewer silver medals. In women's team competition, the United States did well, capturing seven medals and tying Japan with 62 points. However, the Japanese team won the title because they had more gold medals.

Other champions:

Archery. World Target Champions: men's compound, Clint Freeman, Australia; women's compound, Mary Zorn, United States; men's recurve, Michele Frangilli, Italy; women's recurve, Mi-Jin Yun, South Korea; men's compound team, United States; women's compound team, United

States; men's recurve team, South Korea; women's recurve team, South Korea.

Bobsledding. Susi Erdmann of Germany, with Annegret Dietrich pushing, won the women's world championship on February 2 in Winterberg, Germany.

Canoe-kayak. Hungary led the medal count at the Sprint World Championships, held in September in Gainesville, Georgia, with 13, followed by Germany's 11 and Poland's 10.

Curling. Men's world champion: Canada; Women's world champion: United States.

Equestrian. World Cup Final individual show jumping champion: Marcus Ehning, Germany; dressage champion: Ulla Salzgeber, Germany.

Fencing. Men's world champions: Peter Joppich, Germany (foil); Fabrice Jeannet, France (epee); and Vladimir Lukachenko, Ukraine (sabre). Women's world champions: Valentina Vezzali, Italy (foil); Natalia Conrad, Ukraine (epee); Dorina Mihai, Romania (sabre).

Field hockey. Champions Trophy gold medal (men): Netherlands; 4-Nations Cup gold medal (women): Australia.

Lacrosse. Men's NCAA champion: University of Virginia. Women's NCAA champion: Princeton University. ■ Michael Kates

See also **Baseball; Basketball; Football; Golf; Hockey; Ice skating; Swimming; Tennis.**

Sri Lanka.
A power struggle in Sri Lanka between President Chandrika Kumaratunga and Prime Minister Ranil Wickremesinghe in late 2003 stalled efforts to end a 20-year rebellion by the Liberation Tigers of Tamil Eelam (LTTE). The two officials were members of opposing political parties and they shared power under an awkward constitutional arrangement.

The LTTE and the Sri Lankan government began peace talks in 2002. The LTTE had been fighting since 1983 for a separate nation for 3.2 million ethnic Tamil Hindus in northeast Sri Lanka. LTTE guerrillas battled troops controlled by the majority Sinhalese, who are Buddhists. The conflict resulted in the deaths of some 64,000 people and damaged the country's economy.

The two sides agreed to a cease-fire in 2002 and began work on a governing plan that would allow Tamil-dominated regions to govern themselves. Negotiations continued until April 2003, when the LTTE suspended talks after expressing anger about being named a terrorist organization by Western nations. As a terrorist group, the LTTE had difficulty raising money from Tamils living abroad.

In November, the LTTE proposed the establishment of an LTTE-controlled interim authority in Tamil areas. Officials in Wickremesinghe's government said that the proposal could lead to a resumption of peace talks. Kumaratunga, who had repeatedly accused Wickremesinghe of being too soft on peace terms, blocked new peace talks by firing three of Wickremesinghe's cabinet ministers. Political observers called Kumaratunga's action a "constitutional coup." The deadlock between Kumaratunga and Wickremesinghe continued through the end of 2003.

Despite the setbacks in peace talks, both sides continued to honor a cease-fire agreement. However, there were isolated outbreaks of fighting. In March, the Sri Lankan Navy sank a boat that it claimed was smuggling weapons to the LTTE, and the LTTE sank a Chinese fishing boat, killing 17 people. In June, a sniper killed a former leader of the Tamil independence struggle who had been working with the government.

The economy grew strongly in 2003. Increases in agriculture and manufacturing helped spark growth. In addition, the country experienced a sharp increase in tourism, which reached its highest level since 1983.

More than 30 countries raised $4.5 billion in aid to Sri Lanka at a donor conference in Tokyo in June 2003. The funds would be provided over three years. Sri Lanka would not receive the aid if the government discontinued negotiations with the LTTE. ■ Henry S. Bradsher

See also **Asia.**

State government.
Worldwide attention focused on the historic 2003 California recall election that ousted the Democratic governor and replaced him with a motion-picture star. Two of the three other states that chose governors in off-season elections in 2003 also selected Republicans. According to political experts, California voters were upset over the Democratic governor's ineffectiveness in the face of an enormous budget deficit. Nevertheless, the leaders of most other states were besieged by fiscal woes with less drastic results.

California recall. The people of California on October 7 voted to remove from office Governor Gray Davis, a Democrat in the first year of his second term, and replace him with film actor Arnold Schwarzenegger, a Republican. More than 1 million Californians had signed recall petitions, paving the way for the election. Voters were asked two questions on the ballot: whether Davis should be recalled, and if so, who would be his successor.

Schwarzenegger defeated 134 other candidates crowding the ballot, including California Lieutenant Governor Cruz Bustamante, a Democrat who, political experts said, had failed to ignite the Hispanic vote in the state.

Schwarzenegger took the oath of office on November 17. He promised to reverse a car-tax increase that had been sponsored by Davis and passed by the California state legislature.

Schwarzenegger, an immigrant from Austria, had parlayed success as a body builder in the 1970's into fame as an action-adventure actor. He was married to Maria Shriver. Shriver, a Democrat, was an NBC news reporter and the niece of former U.S. President John F. Kennedy.

The California recall election was just the second in history among the 18 states that permit them. The only other occurred in North Dakota in 1921, when voters recalled Governor Lynn Frazier.

Elections and transitions. Republicans held 28 of the 50 governor offices in the United States following their victory in California and two wins in Kentucky and Mississippi during elections held on Nov. 4, 2003.

In Mississippi, Republican Haley Barbour, a former chairman of the Republican National Committee and Washington, D.C., lobbyist, defeated incumbent Democratic Governor Ronnie Musgrove, to become the state's second Republican governor since *Reconstruction* (the period following the Civil War [1861-1865]).

In Kentucky, U.S. Representative Ernie Fletcher (R., Kentucky) easily defeated the state's attorney general, Ben Chandler, a Democrat and the grandson of former governor and baseball commissioner A. B. "Happy" Chandler. Fletcher became the first Republican to win the governorship since 1967. His victory ended the longest control of the governor's office by one party in the state's history.

Prior to the 2003 election, Kentucky Governor Paul Patton, a Democrat who was barred by term limits from seeking reelection, had admitted to an extramarital affair. On November 16, Patton settled ethics charges in which he acknowledged two instances of using his power and influence to benefit the woman with whom he had a relationship. Patton admitted to the charges before the Executive Branch Ethics Commission. He agreed to pay a $5,000 fine and admitted to unknowingly violating portions of the state ethics law.

In a runoff election on November 15, Louisiana gained its first female governor when Lieutenant Governor Kathleen Babineaux Blanco, a Democrat, captured the office held by Republican Governor Mike Foster, who was prevented from running for reelection by term limits. Blanco defeated Bobby Jindal, a Republican whose parents immigrated to the United States from India. Jindal had held various political positions under Foster and U.S. President George W. Bush.

New governors also took office in Indiana and Utah in 2003. Indiana Lieutenant Governor Joe Kernan succeeded Governor Frank O'Bannon, who died on September 13. Both were Democrats. Utah Governor Mike Leavitt, a Republican,

resigned on November 5 to become administrator of the U.S. Environmental Protection Agency. Lieutenant Governor Olene S. Walker, a Republican, was sworn in as Utah's first female governor.

Legislative elections. Democratic candidates fared better in the few legislative elections on November 4, gaining control of the New Jersey Senate and widening their margin in the Assembly. The party also kept their majority in the Mississippi legislature. Republicans retained their majorities in the Virginia House and Senate.

In ballot referenda, Maine voters rejected the proposed construction of a large casino but approved slot machines at horse racing tracks. On September 9, Alabama voters soundly defeated Governor Bob Riley's $1.2-billion tax package, designed to fund schools and college scholarships.

State budgets. Most states faced another year of budget problems in 2003, as state lawmakers and governors cut programs, including higher education and social services, more often than they raised taxes. That finding was reported in July by the National Conference of State Legislatures (NCSL), a nonprofit organization headquartered in Denver, Colorado. The NCSL report revealed that of 43 surveyed states, 31 states cut programs and 17 states raised taxes. Some states used a combination of measures.

State legislatures were forced to employ a variety of measures to deal with their fiscal shortfalls. The state legislature in Illinois raised taxes on riverboat casinos and liquor license fees to generate approximately $207 million. In Connecticut, the state legislature passed its budget 31 days past its June 30 deadline and balanced it by cutting spending on social services and raising taxes.

Some economists predicted in late 2003 that the state fiscal crises would be nearing an end. With the exception of a $38-billion shortfall in California, state and local governments had nearly erased spending deficits in the fiscal quarter ending September 30, according to a study by the U.S. Department of Commerce's Bureau of Economic Analysis.

Education. President Bush announced on June 10 that all state legislatures had approved plans to meet requirements of the federal No Child Left Behind program. Sponsors of the legislation, which went into effect in 2002, envisioned all children being proficient at reading and math within 12 years.

By December 2003, at least 19 states required high school seniors to take exit exams to graduate. School districts had denied thousands of students diplomas as a result of failing the exams, according to a report released in October by the Center on Education Policy, a Washington, D.C.-based organization that advocates for public education.

Death row decision. Illinois Governor George

SELECTED STATISTICS ON STATE GOVERNMENTS

State	Resident population*	Governor†	House (D)	House (R)	Senate (D)	Senate (R)	State tax revenue‡	Tax revenue per capita‡	Public school expenditure per pupil§
Alabama	4,486,508	Bob Riley (R)	63	42	25	10	$ 6,879,000,000	$ 1,530	$ 5,420
Alaska	643,786	Frank Murkowski (R)	13	27	#8	11	1,090,000,000	1,690	9,560
Arizona	5,456,453	Janet Napolitano (D)	21	39	13	17	8,477,000,000	1,550	5,200
Arkansas	2,710,079	Mike Huckabee (R)	70	30	27	8	5,034,000,000	1,860	5,790
California	35,116,033	Arnold Schwarzenegger (R)	48	32	25	15	77,755,000,000	2,210	7,240
Colorado	4,506,542	Bill F. Owens (R)	28	37	17	18	6,923,000,000	1,540	7,430
Connecticut	3,460,503	John G. Rowland (R)	94	57	21	15	9,033,000,000	2,610	11,380
Delaware	807,385	Ruth Ann Minner (D)	12	29	13	8	2,174,000,000	2,690	10,270
Florida	16,713,149	Jeb Bush (R)	39	81	14	26	24,816,000,000	1,480	6,410
Georgia	8,560,310	Sonny Perdue (R)	**106	73	26	30	13,772,000,000	1,610	8,240
Hawaii	1,244,898	Linda Lingle (R)	36	15	20	5	3,421,000,000	2,750	7,460
Idaho	1,341,131	Dirk Kempthorne (R)	16	54	7	28	2,271,000,000	1,690	6,380
Illinois	12,600,620	Rod Blagojevich (D)	66	52	32	27	22,460,000,000	1,780	9,380
Indiana	6,159,068	Joe Kernan (D)	51	49	18	32	9,995,000,000	1,620	8,310
Iowa	2,936,760	Tom Vilsack (D)	46	54	21	29	5,006,000,000	1,700	6,970
Kansas	2,715,884	Kathleen Sebelius (D)	45	80	10	30	4,808,000,000	1,770	7,620
Kentucky	4,092,891	Ernie Fletcher (R)	65	35	16	22	7,975,000,000	1,950	7,270
Louisiana	4,482,646	Kathleen Blanco (D)	**68	36	26	13	7,346,000,000	1,640	6,700
Maine	1,294,464	John Baldacci (D)	††80	67	18	17	2,627,000,000	2,030	9,290
Maryland	5,458,137	Robert Erlich (R)	98	43	33	14	10,821,000,000	1,980	8,120
Massachusetts	6,427,801	Mitt Romney (R)	**136	23	34	6	14,820,000,000	2,310	10,690
Michigan	10,050,446	Jennifer Granholm (D)	47	63	16	22	21,864,000,000	2,180	8,170
Minnesota	5,019,720	Tim Pawlenty (R)	52	82	**35	31	12,936,000,000	2,580	8,630
Mississippi	2,871,782	Haley Barbour (R)	‡‡74	45	29	22	4,729,000,000	1,650	5,820
Missouri	5,672,579	Bob Holden (D)	73	90	14	20	8,679,000,000	1,530	6,820
Montana	909,453	Judy Martz (R)	47	53	21	29	1,443,000,000	1,590	7,370
Nebraska	1,729,180	Mike Johanns (R)	unicameral (49 nonpartisan)				2,993,000,000	1,730	7,200
Nevada	2,173,491	Kenny Guinn (R)	23	19	8	13	3,945,000,000	1,820	6,130
New Hampshire	1,275,056	Craig Benson (R)	119	281	6	18	1,884,000,000	1,480	8,150
New Jersey	8,590,300	James E. McGreevey (D)	47	33	22	18	18,329,000,000	2,130	11,100
New Mexico	1,855,059	Bill Richardson (D)	43	27	24	18	3,628,000,000	1,960	6,860
New York	19,157,532	George E. Pataki (R)	103	47	25	37	43,262,000,000	2,260	11,520
North Carolina	8,320,146	Mike Easley (D)	59	61	28	22	15,535,000,000	1,870	6,550
North Dakota	634,110	John Hoeven (R)	28	66	16	31	1,117,000,000	1,760	4,770
Ohio	11,421,267	Robert Taft (R)	37	62	11	22	19,617,000,000	1,720	7,520
Oklahoma	3,493,714	Brad Henry (D)	53	48	28	20	6,053,000,000	1,730	6,830
Oregon	3,521,515	Ted Kulongoski (D)	25	35	15	15	5,139,000,000	1,460	7,240
Pennsylvania	12,335,091	Ed Rendell (D)	94	109	21	29	22,136,000,000	1,790	8,330
Rhode Island	1,069,725	Don Carcieri (R)	**63	11	32	6	2,128,000,000	1,990	9,890
South Carolina	4,107,183	Mark Sanford (R)	51	73	21	25	5,749,000,000	1,400	7,400
South Dakota	761,063	Mike Rounds (R)	21	49	9	26	977,000,000	1,280	6,920
Tennessee	5,797,289	Phil Bredesen (D)	54	45	18	15	7,798,000,000	1,350	6,050
Texas	21,779,893	Rick Perry (R)	62	88	12	19	28,662,000,000	1,320	7,150
Utah	2,316,256	Olene S. Walker (R)	19	56	7	22	3,925,000,000	1,690	4,910
Vermont	616,592	James Douglas (R)	§§69	74	19	11	1,534,000,000	2,490	9,940
Virginia	7,293,542	Mark Warner (D)	‡‡37	61	16	24	12,781,000,000	1,750	6,320
Washington	6,068,996	Gary Locke (D)	52	46	24	25	12,629,000,000	2,080	7,520
West Virginia	1,801,873	Bob Wise (D)	68	32	24	10	3,552,000,000	1,970	8,720
Wisconsin	5,441,196	Jim Doyle (D)	41	58	15	18	11,814,000,000	2,170	9,020
Wyoming	498,703	Dave Freudenthal (D)	14	46	10	20	1,094,000,000	2,190	9,230

*July 1, 2002 estimates. Source: U.S. Census Bureau.
†As of December 2003. Source: National Governors' Association;
 National Conference of State Legislatures; state government officials
‡2002 figures.
§2002-2003 estimates for elementary and secondary students in fall enrollment
Source: National Education Association.

#One Republican moderate.
**One independent.
††One Green independent, three independents.
‡‡Two independents.
§§Three independents, four progressives.

Ryan commuted the death sentences of 167 inmates two days before his term expired in January. The decision affected 156 inmates on death row in Illinois and 11 other inmates who were sentenced to death but were awaiting resentencing or trials in other cases. Ryan, a Republican who did not seek reelection in 2002, said the state's death penalty process was "arbitrary and capri-

cious." Rod Blagojevich, a Democrat who succeeded Ryan, announced in November 2003 that he would continue the hold on executions.

Ryan charged. Federal authorities indicted Ryan on December 17 on multiple counts of racketeering conspiracy, mail fraud, making false statements, and income tax violations while he was Illinois secretary of state in the 1990's and governor between 1999 and 2003.

Redistricting. The Texas legislature in October 2003 approved a congressional redistricting map, which Democrats argued favored Republicans. Democrats held a 17 to 15 majority in the state's congressional delegation, but Republicans held a majority in the state legislature, giving them the power to redraw congressional districts. More than 50 Democrats from the state House of Representatives twice had fled Texas in 2003 to prevent a quorum in the state legislature in order to avoid a vote on the measure passed in October.

■ Elaine Stuart

See also **Democratic Party; Education: A Special Report; Elections; Republican Party; United States, Government of the**.

California Governor Gray Davis (above) concedes defeat as his wife, Sharon, looks on following a recall election on October 7. Davis's sucessor, Arnold Schwarzenegger, with his wife, Maria Shriver, celebrates his victory in the special election.

Stocks and bonds. The stock market in the United States avoided a fourth straight yearly decline in 2003, as investors anticipated an economic rebound and stronger corporate profits. Major stock indexes, including the Dow Jones Industrial Average and the Standard & Poor's 500 (S&P 500) index, remained well below their all-time highs reached in early 2000, though a market rally that began in March 2003 remained strong through December. The Dow is a composite of the stock prices of 30 major companies. The S&P 500 is a set of large-company stocks that are used to measure the level of the U.S. stock market.

The Dow was up 17 percent to 9,782.46 through November 2003. The S&P 500 index was up 20 percent to 1,058.20 during the same period. The Nasdaq composite index, a composite of the more than 3,000 stocks that traded electronically on the system operated by the Nasdaq Stock Market, was up 47 percent, to 1,960.26. Technology stocks, which dominate the Nasdaq market, rallied throughout 2003 after suffering major declines that began in early 2000.

Business scandals shook investor confidence in 2003. Officials of the nation's $7-trillion mutual fund industry were accused of allowing a handful of influential investors to trade mutual fund shares in ways that created losses for ordinary fund shareholders.

The scandal erupted in early September, when Eliot Spitzer, attorney general of New York State, accused several major fund organizations, including Denver, Colorado-based Janus Capital Group and Charlotte, North Carolina-based Bank of America, of permitting improper trading. In November, Lawrence Lasser, chief executive of mutual fund giant Putnam Investments in Boston, was fired for permitting improper trading. In December, Richard Strong resigned as chairman, chief executive officer, and chief investment officer of Strong Financial Corporation, a mutual fund company headquartered in Menomonee Falls, Wisconsin, amid charges that he had engaged in improper fund trading. Strong, who had founded the company in 1974, also left his positions on the boards of directors at Strong Financial and Strong Mutual Funds.

In other scandals, Richard Grasso resigned as chairman of the New York Stock Exchange in September 2003 amid public outcry over his $188-million pay package. In November, Richard Scrushy, former chief executive officer of Health-South Corp., a Birmingham, Alabama-based operator of rehabilitation and outpatient surgery centers, was charged with accounting fraud in an 85-count criminal indictment.

Bond rally stalls. As the economy gathered

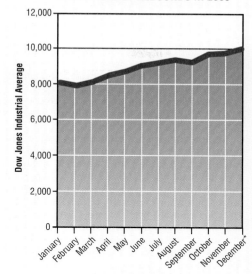

STOCK MARKET REBOUNDS IN 2003

Dow Jones Industrial Average

Closing month averages for 2003
* December figure is as of the 11th.

The stock market in the United States in 2003 broke free of three years of decline and, in mid-December, the Dow Jones Industrial Average climbed back to above 10,000 for the first time in 18 months.

steam in 2003, interest rates rose, eroding the value of most bond market investments. By November, the yield on 10-year U.S. Treasury bonds, which reflect changes in price to accommodate current market rates, rose slowly to 4.33 percent from 3.82 percent in 2002.

Interest rates. The Federal Reserve (the Fed), the central bank of the United States, helped the stock and bond markets in June 2003 when it cut a key short-term interest rate by a quarter percentage point. The Fed reduced the federal funds rate—the interest rate on overnight loans between banks—from 1.25 percent to 1 percent, the lowest level since 1958. Low short-term rates meant that investors in money-market mutual funds, which invest in short-term debt securities, made only about a half percentage point on their money after the funds deducted their expenses.

Winners and losers. Nearly all categories of stock market investing posted gains in 2003. The only mutual fund category showing a loss for the year was "bear market" fund category, which bet against a rising stock market.

Among S&P 500 stocks, companies reporting gains through November included Tulsa, Oklahoma-based energy producer Williams Cos Inc., which reported stocks rose 313 percent; Internet software developer Novell Inc. of Provo, Utah, reporting increases of 200 percent; and department store retailer Sears, Roebuck & Co., of Hoffman Estates, Illinois, which reported a 132-percent increase.

Companies reporting losses included Eastman Kodak Co., of Rochester, New York, whose stock declined 31 percent through November; pharmaceuticals maker Merck & Co., of Whitehouse Station, New Jersey, whose stock fell 24 percent; and AT&T Corp., of Bedminister, New Jersey, which reported a 20-percent decrease.

Several categories of commodities posted substantial gains. The price of gold, as measured by futures trading at the Comex exchange in New York City, rose nearly $50 an ounce, or 14 percent through November, to $396.80. Wheat rose 69.25 cents a bushel, or 21 percent, to $3.94 at the Chicago Board of Trade. Oil prices were flat for the year, ending November at $30.41 a barrel at the New York Mercantile Exchange.

International stock markets. Signs of economic recovery in several parts of the world, including Europe and Japan, boosted stock prices overseas. The Dow Jones STOXX 50 index of 50 major companies in Europe was up more than 6 percent through November. The Nikkei 225 index of 225 major Japanese stocks rose 19 percent in the same period.   ■ Bill Barnhart

See also **Economics; People in the news** (Eliot Spitzer).

Sudan. Peace talks between the government of President Umar Hasan Ahmad al-Bashir and John Garang, leader of the rebel group Sudan People's Liberation Movement/Army (SPLM/A), resumed in January 2003. In March, the two sides extended their cease-fire of the civil war to June to reach a final peace agreement. The war was primarily between government forces in the Muslim-dominated north and Christians and *animists* (those believing that souls are present in all parts of nature) in the south. The talks stalled in April when the Sudan Liberation Army (SLA), a smaller rebel faction, and government forces clashed in the western region of Darfur. By October, over 400,000 people were forced to move within Darfur and another 70,000 people had fled to Chad, according to the United Nations (UN).

Further agreements. In May, the government and the SPLM/A signed a partnership agreement that outlined specific measures necessary to meet the needs of southern Sudan. The sides agreed to yet another cease-fire in September. This agreement was designated to last 45 days to release prisoners of war and to implement economic and social measures. Following this agreement, the UN submitted a plan to both the government and the SPLM/A that would provide $140 million in immediate aid to the country if they reached a permanent peace agreement. The

money would be spent on 37 projects, including the reintegration of displaced persons and refugees as well as the rehabilitation of services such as health care. United States Secretary of State Colin Powell won a commitment from Sudanese negotiators to reach an agreement by the end of December.

Slave raids. The Center for Religious Freedom, a Washington, D.C.-based organization that reports on worldwide religious persecution, announced in March that slave raids in Sudan's Bahr al-Ghazal region had stopped. Experts attributed the end of the raids to publicity and U.S. pressure.

Oil exploration. Officials at OMV, an Austrian oil company that is part of a consortium that includes Sudapet of the Sudan and Petronas of Malaysia, announced in March 2003 that the companies would resume petroleum exploration in the Sudan. Explorations had stopped in January 2002 due to security concerns. However, OMV sold its exploration areas to India's ONGC Videsh Ltd. in September 2003.

Plane crash. A Sudanese airliner crashed in July after taking off from Port Sudan Airport. The crash killed 115 people, including 105 passengers and 10 crew members. Only a child survived.
     ■ Mary-Jane Deeb

See also **Disasters; Middle East.**

Supreme Court of the United States.

In 2003, the Supreme Court of the United States issued rulings on affirmative action, free speech, pornography regulation, laws regarding sodomy, and other areas.

Affirmative action. On June 23, the court ruled that universities can take an applicant's race into account in order to achieve a diverse student body. By a 5-to-4 vote, the justices upheld admissions procedures for the law school at the University of Michigan at Ann Arbor. However, in a 6-to-3 vote, the court determined that schools could not use admissions formulas that awarded bonus points for a student's race.

The second decision struck down the University of Michigan's method of factoring race into undergraduate admissions. The ruling affirmed a 1978 decision, *Regents of the University of California v. Allan Bakke,* which was the court's last guidance on affirmative action in higher education. In *Bakke,* the court struck down the use of minority admissions quotas but determined that race, among other factors, could be considered because a diverse student body enhances the educational climate.

In January 2003, U.S. President George W. Bush announced that his administration would file a brief with the Supreme Court asking that the University of Michigan's admission policies be

Attorneys Bill Hohengarten (left), Ruth Harlow, and Paul Smith celebrate after the U.S. Supreme Court struck down a Texas law that made it illegal for persons of the same gender to have sexual relations. Supporters called the decision a victory for advocates of gay rights.

declared unconstitutional. President Bush had described policies used by the school as "flawed" because they rewarded or penalized prospective students based solely on their race.

Privacy rights. On June 26, the court voted 6 to 3 to strike down a Texas law that had made private sexual acts between two people of the same gender, a crime. The court said that the U.S. Constitution guarantees protection to gay men and women from government intrusion into private sexual conduct between consenting adults. Legal experts described the court's decision as having profound legal and political implications, including invalidating laws in 13 states that criminalized private sexual acts, either between members of the same or opposite sex, that do not result in *procreation* (reproduction).

Megan's Law. The court on March 5 upheld two "Megan's Laws," which required convicted sex offenders to register with state authorities upon release from incarceration. In a case from Connecticut, the court unanimously ruled that convicted sex offenders are not entitled to individual hearings on whether they should still be considered dangerous before the state can include their names in an online registry. The justices also voted 6 to 3 that Alaska's law does not amount to a second punishment for offenders who served their sentences before the law was passed.

"Three strikes" law upheld. In a 5-to-4 decision on March 5, the court upheld California's "three-strikes-you're-out" law. The law imposes a prison term of no less than 25 years without parole for any person found guilty of committing a third felony offense, no matter how minor the crime. The court rejected two challenges based on the Eighth Amendment's ban on cruel and unusual punishment.

Abortion protests. On February 26, the court overturned lower court rulings that had required antiabortion groups to pay $258,000 in damages for violence that disrupted operations at two abortion clinics in the 1980's. The court, voting 8 to 1, determined that the federal Racketeer Influenced and Corrupt Organizations (RICO) Act did not apply because the protesters' actions did not amount to *extortion* (the act of obtaining another's property by threat or force). The groups had been sued under the RICO Act.

Internet filters. In a decision handed down on June 23, 2003, the court ruled 6 to 3 that the U.S. Congress can require public libraries and schools to install Internet filters on all computers in order to qualify for federal technology funding and discounts. The Children's Internet Protection Act was designed to protect library patrons, especially children, from viewing online pornography or other material deemed unsuitable. The American Library Association and other groups argued that the law prevented adult patrons from accessing material that was not illegal. The court ruled that the law does not violate the First Amendment right of free speech because adults can ask librarians to bypass the filters for specific research needs.

Cross-burning verdict. The court ruled on April 7 that states can make the burning of a cross a crime as long as prosecutors target actions designed as a threat and not as a form of expression. By a 6-to-3 decision, the court ruled that given its association with racist organizations, cross-burning could be treated differently than the burning of another shape such as a circle or a square.

Copyright Act. On January 15, the court upheld Congress's authority to extend copyrights by 20 years. Copyright gives the author of a creative work the exclusive right to use the product for a specific amount of time to enable artists to make a profit from their efforts. Other people may use copyrighted works with the author's permission for a fee or under limited circumstances. When a copyright expires, the work moves into the public domain, where anyone can use it for free. By a vote of 7 to 2, the court determined that the Sonny Bono Copyright Term Extension Act of 1998 did not violate the constitutional restriction on copyrights running for "limited times" or impede the free exchange of ideas by extending copyrights to the length of an author's life plus 70 years.

Medicating defendants. On June 16, 2003, the court restricted the government's ability to medicate mentally ill defendants in an attempt to make them competent to stand trial. In the 6-to-3 decision, the court ruled that antipsychotic drugs can be administered, but only if they are in the best medical interest of the defendant. The court also ruled that the risk of any side effects of the medication must be "substantially unlikely" if the medication is prescribed against the will of a patient.

Medical marijuana. In a 6-to-3 decision on October 14, the court let stand a ruling by the U.S. Court of Appeals for the Ninth District in San Francisco on the use of marijuana for medical purposes. Federal officials may not investigate, threaten, or punish physicians who recommend marijuana as a medical treatment in states where such treatments are legal. The U.S. Department of Justice had warned that physicians who recommend the medical use of marijuana could lead the Drug Enforcement Administration to revoke a physician's registration.

Family and Medical Leave Act. In a decision handed down on May 27, the court voted 6 to 3 to allow state employees to sue state gov-

ernments for violating the 1993 Family and Medical Leave Act. The legislation allows men and women to take up to 12 weeks of unpaid leave from their jobs to take care of ill family members or other emergencies. The state of Nevada had challenged Congress's authority to pass the law after the state Human Resources Department was sued by an employee who was dismissed because he wanted to take a leave of absence to help his wife recover from a car accident.

Ten Commandments appeal. The court rejected appeals on November 3 from suspended Alabama Chief Justice Roy Moore over the removal of a granite monument inscribed with the Ten Commandments in the lobby of the Alabama Supreme Court. The court on August 20 also had refused an emergency stay of a 2002 federal district court ruling requiring the monument's removal on the grounds that it was an unconstitutional endorsement of religion. Alabama's judicial ethics panel removed Moore, who had the monument installed in the courthouse rotunda, from the bench in November 2003 for failing to obey orders to remove the display.

◾ Geoffrey A. Campbell

See also **Courts; Library; Medicine.**

Surgery. See Medicine.

Suriname. See Latin America.

Swaziland. See Africa.

Sweden experienced a turbulent year in 2003, as the country's foreign minister, Anna Lindh, was murdered during a heated referendum campaign. Lindh's death stunned Swedes and sparked a debate about Sweden's informal style of politics. Like most Swedish politicians, Lindh mixed frequently with ordinary citizens and had no bodyguard when she was attacked.

Lindh, an advocate for human rights, was one of the country's most popular politicians. She played a leading role in a government-backed referendum campaign to persuade Swedes to vote in favor of replacing the Swedish currency, the krona, with the euro, the single European currency. On September 10, four days before the actual vote, Lindh was stabbed by an unknown assailant while shopping in a department store in Stockholm, the capital. She died the next day.

Police arrested a man in the case but provided no explanation for the murder. The killing evoked painful memories for Swedes of the still-unexplained murder of then-Prime Minister Olof Palme. Palme was shot in 1986 on a Stockholm street while walking with his wife. A suspect was arrested in 1988 but was acquitted.

Euro rejected. Swedish voters rejected the euro in the Sept. 14, 2003, referendum by a margin of 56 percent to 42 percent. The result was a setback for Prime Minister Goran Persson, who claimed that adopting the euro would help the economy and enhance Sweden's influence in the European Union (EU). Most major political parties and business leaders also supported the euro. However, opponents argued that Sweden would lose economic and political control to the EU by abandoning its own currency. They also pointed to the slow growth rates in Germany and France—and the inability of those countries to respect the EU's limits on budget deficits —as evidence that the euro posed risks as well as potential advantages. After the vote, Persson promised to consider new economic measures, including cuts in corporate and capital gains tax rates, to maintain Sweden's attractiveness to investors and international businesses.

Blackout. Southern Sweden and eastern Denmark were hit by an electrical blackout on September 23. The outage cut power to 5 million customers for several hours and forced the temporary shutdown of two nuclear power plants. The blackout was triggered by a fault in a transmission line between Sweden and Denmark.

Merger. OM AB, the company that operates the Stockholm Stock Exchange, agreed to acquire the Helsinki Stock Exchange, creating a single market for Swedish and Finnish stocks. The $270-million deal, completed in October, created a new company, OM HEX, which controlled 80 percent of equity trading in Scandinavia.   ■ Tom Buerkle

See also **Europe.**

hamnar vi på efterkälken.

Mourners in Stockholm comfort each other before a billboard featuring Swedish Foreign Minister Anna Lindh. An unknown assailant stabbed Lindh while she was shopping at a department store in downtown Stockholm on September 10. She died the following day.

Michael Phelps of the United States starts the men's 400-meter individual medley at the World Swimming Championships in Barcelona, Spain, in July. Phelps set a world record in the event, in addition to setting four other world records during the meet.

Swimming. Michael Phelps of the United States established himself in 2003 as the dominant swimmer in the world. Phelps became only the third man to hold four individual world records at the same time. He set five records in a single competition at the World Swimming Championships in Barcelona, Spain, in July. Phelps's performance topped swimmers Mark Spitz of the United States and Michael Gross of Germany, the only other two swimmers to hold four records at once.

World Swimming Championships. Phelps's performances helped propel the United States to victory with 31 medals, 12 of which were gold. In all, 13 world records were broken at the meet and 1 was equaled.

Phelps began his burst of record-breaking on July 22, beating his own record in the 200-meter butterfly with a time of 1 minute, 53.93 seconds. On July 24, Phelps broke the mark he had set a month earlier in the 200-meter individual medley with a time of 1 minute, 57.52 seconds. The next day Phelps set records in the 200-meter individual medley (1:56.04) and the 100-meter butterfly (51.47), making him the first man to break two individual world records in one day.

Phelps was not the only swimmer who achieved success. His record in the 100-meter butterfly lasted only one day. Phelps's teammate, Ian Crocker, posted a new record time of 50.98 seconds, taking the gold medal ahead of Phelps, who finished in 51.10 seconds. On July 27, Phelps bettered the mark he had set in April in the 400-meter individual medley, finishing in 4 minutes, 9.09 seconds.

Other world records. Several other swimmers broke world records at the meet, including Australian Matt Welsh in the 50-meter butterfly (23.43); Germany's Thomas Rupprath in the 50-meter backstroke (24.80); Japan's Kosuke Kitajima in the 100-meter breaststroke (59.78) and 200-meter breaststroke (2:09.42); and the U.S. team of Aaron Peirsol, Brendan Hansen, Ian Crocker, and Jason Lezak in the 400-meter medley relay (3:31.54). Australia's Leisel Jones set a new women's mark in the 100-meter breaststroke (1:06.37) and American Amanda Beard equaled the 200-meter breaststroke mark of China's Qi Hui (2:22.99).

Phelps was the only swimmer to capture three individual gold medals, for the 200-meter individual medley, the 200-meter butterfly, and the 400-meter individual medley. He took silver in the 100-meter butterfly and the 800-meter free-style relay. Alexander Popov of Russia, the world record-holder in the 50-meter free-style, failed to set new marks but took gold in both the 50-meter and 100-meter freestyle events. He also swam on Russia's gold-medal-winning, 400-meter free-style relay.

■ Michael Kates

See also **Sports.**

Switzerland. National elections in 2003 reflected an increasing polarization of the Swiss electorate. The change posed a challenge to the country's tradition of governing by consensus among major parties and led to a shifting of political alignment to the right for the first time since World War II (1939-1945).

The big winner in the Oct. 19, 2003, election was the conservative Swiss People's Party, which had grown during the 1990's by promising to restrict immigration. During the campaign, People's Party candidates blamed immigrants for crime and welfare abuse. The party also campaigned against the judiciary's role in citizenship applications. The stand came after a Swiss court in July 2003 overturned a decision by residents in the town of Emmen to deny citizenship to 48 Eastern European and Turkish immigrants, many of whom had lived in the country for decades. Critics charged the party with whipping up racism by featuring the faces of black immigrants in its advertisements.

The People's Party won 55 seats in the 200-seat parliament, up from 44 seats in the previous election in 1999. Switzerland's main left-wing party, the Social Democrats, won 52 seats, up from 51 seats previously. The country's two main centrist parties, the Radical Democratic Party and the Christian Democratic Party, won a total of 64 seats, down from 78 previously. Under the so-called magic formula that had prevailed since 1959, the Social Democrats, the Radicals, and the Christian Democrats were each allotted two seats in the seven-member government cabinet, while the People's Party took one seat. However, Christoph Blocher, a wealthy business executive and leader of the People's Party, demanded that his party be allowed two seats because of the party's strong showing. In December 2003, the Swiss parliament elected Blocher as one of two People's Party members to the cabinet. The move limited the Christian Democratic Party to one seat and averted a bitter confrontation.

The economy remained weak in 2003, because of sluggish growth in neighboring European countries and the strength of the Swiss franc, which made Swiss exports more expensive on global markets. European Union economists expected output to grow by 0.6 percent in 2003, up from 0.1 percent in 2002. Unemployment hit a four-year high of 3.9 percent early in 2003.

Swiss International Air Lines, which succeeded Swissair after its bankruptcy in 2001, formed an alliance with British Airways in October 2003. Swiss had posted a net loss of $95.8 million in the first half of 2003. In June, the company announced plans to cut its fleet by one-third and lay off 3,000 workers. ■ Tom Buerkle

See also **Europe.**

Syria. The Syrian government dealt with three major issues in 2003—the war in Iraq; the pressure from the United States to close down offices of hostile Palestinian organizations; and the ramifications of the Syria Accountability Act, which the U.S. House of Representatives passed in October and the U.S. Senate passed in November. The act called on Syria to withdraw its forces from Lebanon and to stop supporting terrorism.

Syria condemned the U.S.-led war in Iraq, a stand that was popular among the masses of people in the Arab world. The Syrian media branded the conflict as "flagrant aggression [that targeted] the steadfast Iraqi people." Teachers, denouncing the aggression, staged sit-ins and other antiwar demonstrations in major cities and university campuses throughout Syria in April.

United States and British intelligence agents claimed during the combat in Iraq in March and April that they had evidence that Syria was helping Arab volunteers move into Iraq to fight U.S. and British forces. According to intelligence sources, such weapons as night-vision equipment were being moved from Syria to Iraq during the early stages of the war. U.S. Secretary of Defense Donald Rumsfeld criticized Syria in September for failing to stop terrorist fighters from infiltrating Iraq from Syria.

In 2003, U.S. Secretary of State Colin Powell asked Syrian President Bashar al-Assad to break off relations with and close down the Syrian offices of militant Palestinian groups, such as Hamas, Islamic Jihad, and the Popular Front for the Liberation of Palestine (PFLP-GC). The Syrian response did not satisfy U.S. officials. Ahmad Jibril, the leader of PFLP-GC, claimed that no Syrian officials asked him to stop his activities in Syria.

Mixed messages. The administration of U.S. President George W. Bush sent mixed messages to Syria in 2003. On one hand, the Syria Accountability Act called for the withdrawal of the Syrian army from Lebanon and the adoption of sanctions against Syria. On the other hand, the Bush administration did not oppose U.S. companies Devon Energy and Gulfsands Petroleum signing a contract with the Syrian government in May to explore for gas and oil in a region of northeastern Syria.

Resignations. Syrian Prime Minister Mohammed Mustafa Miro and his Cabinet resigned in September. The resignations came after Syrian President al-Assad said the country needed a government geared toward reform. President al-Assad designated Muhammad al-Ultri, a former regional administrator, as the new prime minister later in September. The new Cabinet was not expected to affect Syria's foreign policy, which President al-Assad controlled. ■ Marius Deeb

See also **Iraq: A Special Report; Middle East.**

Taiwan in 2003 added the name "Taiwan" to its official Republic of China passports for the first time. The Taiwan parliament also passed a law that would allow for a national referendum on independence if China prepared to attack the island state.

Taiwan separated from China politically in 1949, when Communists conquered mainland China. China, however, continued to regard Taiwan as a province. The Chinese government threatened to attack Taiwan if its government refused to accept the "one China" principle, which maintained that Taiwan was part of China. In 2000, China warned President Chen Shui-bian, leader of Taiwan's Democratic Progressive Party (DPP), that any move toward independence would provoke war. In 2002, Chen backed passage of a law allowing a referendum on the question of independence.

On Nov. 27, 2003, Taiwan's parliament passed a law that gave the president limited powers to call a national referendum on independence. However, the law specified that such a referendum may be used only in case of an imminent attack on the island from China. The measure was far more restrictive than Chen had wanted. The DPP was unable to rally support in the parliament for referendums on changes to the constitution, flag, and the official name of the island, changes Chinese leaders might have interpreted as provocative.

SARS. Hostility against the mainland government mounted in 2003 following reports that China suppressed information about severe acute respiratory syndrome (SARS), which spread to Taiwan, where 45 people died of the disease. International observers claimed that China blocked officials from the World Health Organization, a United Nations (UN) affiliate, from taking immediate action in Taiwan to stop the spread of the disease. China denied the charges, but officials admitted that they had long opposed any UN involvement in Taiwan.

In September, thousands of activists marched in Taipei, the capital, demanding that the island's official name be changed from the Republic of China to Taiwan. In October, Chen accused China of "hostile intent" toward Taiwan.

Politics. Taiwan's two main opposition parties—the Kuomintang (KMT) and the People First Party (PFP)—forged an alliance in April when KMT Chairman Lein Chan named his longtime rival James Soong, head of the PFP, as his running mate in the 2004 presidential elections. Chan and Soong split the vote in the 2000 elections, which allowed Chen to become president, ending 51 years of KMT rule on the island.

■ Henry S. Bradsher

See also **Asia; China; Public health and safety.**

Taxation. United States President George W. Bush in January 2003 proposed legislation to cut taxes for individuals and small businesses in an attempt to spur the U.S. economy. The legislation provided $330 billion in tax cuts and $20 billion in federal aid to states. Among other provisions, the legislation accelerated some tax cuts approved in 2001, including the child tax credit.

Both the U.S. House of Representatives and the U.S. Senate voted to approve the legislation on May 23, 2003. President Bush signed the tax-cuts package—the third largest in U.S. history—on May 28. Provisions in the new law included an increase in the tax credit from $600 to $1,000 per child in 2003 and 2004; an acceleration of provisions from earlier tax law intended to eliminate the so-called "marriage penalty," anomalies in the tax structure that resulted in married couples paying higher taxes than single taxpayers; and a tax reduction on dividends and *capital gains* (income from the sale of capital assets, which include stocks, bonds, real estate, and partnerships). The legislation also authorized the Internal Revenue Service (IRS) to make advance refund payments to the estimated 25 million middle-income families in the United States with an annual income between $27,000 and $110,000.

Supporters said the measure would help stimulate the economy by giving individuals and families additional money to spend on goods. Critics claimed the measure was unfair because it assisted middle- and upper-income families but excluded low-income families earning less than $27,000.

Internet taxes. The House of Representatives in September voted to prohibit the states from taxing Internet access or imposing taxes on electronic commerce, often called e-commerce. The legislation was approved by voice vote in the House on Sept. 17, 2003, after which it was referred to the Senate. The Senate had not acted on the legislation by December. The legislation was created to foster the continued growth of the Internet. Many state leaders, however, contended that the states, facing serious budget deficits, needed the additional source of revenue.

Taxpayer protection. The House of Representatives approved legislation in June designed to protect taxpayers and reform the IRS. Representatives approved the Taxpayer Protection and IRS Accountability Act by a vote of 252 to 170. The legislation was designed to give the IRS greater flexibility in dealing with people who attempt to avoid paying taxes but also to provide greater protection for taxpayers when dealing with the IRS. The Senate had not voted on the legislation by the end of 2003.

■ Geoffrey A. Campbell

See also **Economics; United States, Government of the.**

Telecommunications.

With the exception of wireless and broadband, the long telecommunications decline that followed the bursting of the dot-com bubble in 2000 continued to hold back the industry throughout 2003. The number of *wireline* (land-based phone) customers served by phone companies diminished, and the companies responded by cutting the amount they spent on network upgrades. This, in turn, prolonged the downturn for Lucent Technologies of Murray Hill, New Jersey, and other equipment suppliers.

The wireless phone industry continued to grow in 2003. The number of wireless customers increased to about 150 million as many carriers introduced new features, such as camera phones, to entice consumers. A survey by TNS Telecoms in Jenkintown, Pennsylvania, released in October, predicted that spending for wireless phone service would overtake spending for traditional wireline phone calls by the end of the year. "If you just look at local phone service, wireless is already beating wireline," said TNS Telecoms vice president Charles White. "When you combine local and long-distance, wireline spending is still ahead, but it's falling, and wireless is rising."

The FCC gave cell phone customers the option of keeping their phone numbers when changing carriers after Nov. 24, 2003. Wireless companies braced for anticipated increases in the movement of customers from one cell phone company to another as soon as number portability went into effect.

Wi-Fi bandwagon. Wireless and wireline phone carriers alike in 2003 jumped on the bandwagon supporting Wi-Fi (wireless fidelity), a wireless broadband technology that delivers high-speed Internet service to laptop computers and personal digital assistants. Wi-Fi antennas were installed at many public places, such as airports and coffee shops, during 2003. Verizon Communications, Inc., of New York City used pay phone outlets in New York City as Wi-Fi antennas, and Texas-based SBC Communications Inc. planned to install thousands of Wi-Fi "hot spots" throughout its service territory.

Wi-Fi works best when computers are less than 100 yards (91 meters) from the antenna.

Motorola Inc., of Schaumburg, Illinois; Nokia of Finland; and other wireless phone makers said they would design cell phones that could receive Wi-Fi signals in addition to signals transmitted over cell phone networks. SBC and Verizon executives said they would package Wi-Fi as a wireless extension of their wired digital subscriber line (DSL) service.

DSL service grew during 2003, but it continued to lag behind the cable modem high-speed Internet connections offered by cable television operators. The cable operators maintained a two-to-one advantage over DSL service. Recognizing their competitive disadvantage, three local phone service providers—Atlanta-based BellSouth Corp., SBC, and Verizon—made plans to extend fiber optic network service to residences and businesses of their customers.

The handheld Garmin's iQue (above) receives signals from Earth-orbiting satellites in the Global Positioning System (GPS) to help hikers, bikers, boaters, and drivers find their way. A number of such devices became available to consumers in mid-2003.

Local and long-distance service. Most local phone carriers were granted the right to sell long-distance service during 2003. To compete, companies offered many flat-rate wireline deals. Some plans enabled customers to make unlimited local and long-distance calls for around $50 a month.

The growing level of competition brought growing acrimony among rivals. AT&T joined Verizon and SBC in complaining that WorldCom, of Clinton, Mississippi, which changed its name to MCI, had illegally rerouted telephone calls to avoid paying charges for using rival company networks to complete calls.

MCI bankruptch. A federal bankruptcy court on October 31 approved a plan that would allow MCI to emerge from bankruptcy. MCI had filed for bankruptcy in July 2002, following a scandal over a multibillion dollar accounting fraud. AT&T, SBC, Verizon, and other telecommunications companies expressed fears that a reorganized MCI, freed of massive debt, would be able to offer extremely low rates to customers and put other telecommunications companies at a competitive disadvantage. MCI's rivals feared that this kind of pricing competition could further damage the already struggling telecommunications industry. ■ Jon Van

Television. Deception, practical jokes, and faded celebrity defined reality television in 2003, a year in which five gay men and a popular female singer became surprising new stars. Post-season major league baseball also hit a home run in the ratings, but its popularity negatively impacted the start of the new fall season, as new shows struggled to find audiences.

Reality TV continued to draw large audiences during the 2002-2003 television season. "Joe Millionaire," which aired on Fox, was the top-rated reality television series in 2003, according to Nielsen Media Research, a New York City-based research agency. The program's premise involved a group of female contestants vying to be chosen by Evan Marriott, whom they were told was worth $50 million. Marriott was actually a construction worker who earned $19,000 a year. Approximately 40 million viewers tuned in to the final episode in February, in which Marriott revealed his secret and selected a winner.

Television networks tried to duplicate the success of "The Osbournes," which was a ratings success in 2002, with several celebrity-based series in 2003. The most successful, "The Newlyweds," aired on the cable television channel MTV and starred pop singers Nick Lachey and Jessica Simpson. Simpson's seemingly clueless and ditzy behavior captivated some viewers.

Other hits featured former entertainment stars whose fame had long since dimmed. On the WB, seven celebrities, including former child star Emmanuel Lewis and former "Baywatch" star Brande Roderick, shared a house on "The Surreal Life." The ABC series "I'm a Celebrity...Get Me Out of Here!" featured 10 stars, including former talk-show host Alana Stewart and Olympic champion Bruce Jenner, living in an Australian rainforest.

"Queer Eye for the Straight Guy" became a popular culture phenomenon in 2003. The makeover series, which debuted in July on the fine-arts cable network Bravo, featured the "Fab Five"—Ted Allen, Kyan Douglas, Thom Filicia, Carson Kressley, and Jai Rodriguez—gay men who in each episode gave a heterosexual man tips on culture, fashion, food and wine, grooming, and home design. Episodes were rerun on NBC, which owns Bravo.

Some TV critics noted that the series and other gay-themed programs—including the Bravo series "Boy Meets Boy," in which a gay bachelor chose a partner from a field of 15 men—made the topic of homosexuality more commonplace on prime-time television.

Two other series offered twists on the reality formula. On the cable channel Spike TV series "The Joe Schmo Show," Matt Kennedy Gould believed he was a contestant on a reality show. In fact, the entire show around him was staged and everyone else in the cast was an actor. In "Average Joe," which debuted in November on NBC, former beauty pageant contestant and National Football League cheerleader Melana Scantlin looked for love amongst average-looking men.

Milestones. "The Simpsons," the longest-running animated series in television history, broadcast its 300th episode on Fox in February. "Buffy the Vampire Slayer," a critically acclaimed comedy-horror series that aired on the WB, broadcast its final episode in May. The series premiered in 1997.

The war. For the first time since the Vietnam War (1957-1975), journalists were embedded with U.S. troops in combat during the war in Iraq in 2003. During the combat phase of the war, two high-profile reporters generated controversy. In March, NBC officials fired Pulitzer Prize-winner journalist Peter Arnett after he gave an interview on Iraqi television in which he criticized the U.S. war plan. Military officials ordered Fox News Channel reporter Geraldo Rivera expelled from Iraq after he revealed a troop's location and operations during a live report in March. On April 1, executives at Fox News Channel and the U.S. Department of Defense reached an agreement in which Rivera voluntarily left Iraq.

A Sad Day in
Mr. Rogers' Neighborhood

Fred Rogers, a soft-spoken Presbyterian minister and puppeteer who became a friendly neighbor called Mister Rogers to a generation of American children, died on Feb. 27, 2003, at age 74. As the host of the television series "Mister Rogers' Neighborhood," Rogers, with his gentle and courteous manner, was a welcome sight in his sneakers and zippered cardigan sweater. He also was a calming influence in the often turbulent world in which children find themselves. He used television—a traditionally fast-paced medium—to teach children to be true to themselves and to love, not hate. Above all else, Rogers showed his young viewers that they were not the first persons to be sad, afraid, or lonely. This genuinely "nice guy" persona turned Rogers into a cultural icon whose goal was to provide young viewers a foundation for a good life.

Fred McFeely Rogers was born in Latrobe, Pennsylvania, on March 20, 1928, the only son of James and Nancy Rogers. As a young boy, Rogers toyed with puppets and used them as an outlet to deal with his own feelings and struggles. The outlet ultimately became a teaching tool.

Rogers earned a degree in music composition at Rollins College in Winter Park, Florida, in 1951. After graduation, he worked as an assistant producer and director for a television station in New York City. In 1953, executives at WQED in Pittsburgh, Pennsylvania, the first community-sponsored educational television station in the United States, hired Rogers to develop the station's program schedule. One of the first programs he created was "The Children's Corner," a daily, hour-long, live show featuring music and puppets. Several characters on the show would later find new life on "Mister Rogers' Neighborhood," including Daniel Striped Tiger, X the Owl, King Friday XIII, and Henrietta Pussycat.

While working on the children's series, Rogers attended Pittsburgh Theological Seminary and the University of Pittsburgh's Graduate School of Child Development. He graduated from the seminary and was ordained in 1963.

Later in 1963, the Canadian Broadcasting Company (CBC) hired Rogers to create a program titled "Misterogers." Rogers hosted the series before returning to Pittsburgh in 1966. He melded parts of the CBC series into a local program called "MisteRogers' Neighborhood." A retitled "Mister Rogers' Neighborhood" debuted in national distribution on the Public Broadcasting System in 1968.

"Mister Rogers' Neighborhood" produced its last original episode in 2001, but remained on PBS in reruns, allowing Rogers to become a role model for an entire generation of American children. He calmly talked to his young audience about disease, divorce, death, and war because he knew that the real life neighborhoods of some viewers were far from pleasant. Mister Rogers' neighborhood was, therefore, a safe haven. He constantly assured viewers that although the world was not always a kind place, things would get better.

"I always thought I was a neighbor who came in for a visit," Rogers once said in an interview. Children welcomed Fred Rogers—their neighbor in the land of make-believe—because they saw him as a person that they could trust. That is all anyone could ever ask for.   ■ Tim Frystak

Contestants on the Fox television series "American Idol" perform during the show's grand finale on May 21. The series—a talent contest with performers competing for a recording contract—was one of the highest-rated television programs in 2003.

Spike TV. Motion picture director Spike Lee filed a lawsuit that postponed the June debut of Spike TV, which was advertised as "the first network for men." Lee objected to the use of the name "Spike," which he contended would mislead people into believing he was associated with the network. After an out-of-court settlement, Spike TV, formerly TNN, premiered in August. The network featured programming primarily designed to attract young male viewers.

Ritter dies. The *sitcom* (situation comedy) "8 Simple Rules for Dating My Teenage Daugh-

TOP-RATED U.S. TELEVISION SERIES

The following were among the most-watched television series for the 2002-2003 regular season, which ran from Sept. 23, 2002, to May 25, 2003.

1. "C.S.I." (CBS)
2. "Friends" (NBC)
3. "Joe Millionaire" (FOX)
4. "E.R." (NBC)
5. "American Idol" (Tuesday) (FOX)
6. "American Idol" (Wednesday) (FOX)
7. "Survivor: Thailand" (CBS)
8. "Everybody Loves Raymond" (CBS)
9. (tie) "Survivor: Amazon" (CBS)
    "Law and Order" (NBC)
11. NFL Monday Night Football (ABC)
12. "C.S.I.: Miami" (CBS)
13. "Will & Grace" (NBC)
14. "The Bachelorette" (ABC)
15. "Scrubs" (NBC)
16. (tie) "Law and Order: SVU" (NBC)
    "Without a Trace" (CBS)
18. "The Bachelor" (ABC)
19. (tie) "60 Minutes" (CBS)
    "Judging Amy" (CBS)

By permission of Nielsen Media Research, Inc.

ter" lost its star when actor John Ritter died on September 11. ABC executives decided to continue production of the popular sitcom. After broadcasting three episodes completed before Ritter's death, the series went on a brief hiatus. It returned on November 3 with a critically acclaimed one-hour episode that dealt with the death of Ritter's character, an over-protective father, and its impact on the grieving family.

Post-season baseball proved a ratings success in 2003 for Fox. Fox, which owned exclusive broadcast rights to Major League Baseball (MLB) play-offs and the World Series, enjoyed its highest ratings for the entire post-season since 1995.

The participation of the Chicago Cubs in the National League and the Boston Red Sox in the American League, two teams that had not won a World Series since the early 1900's, added to the drama during the 2003 season. Both teams suffered dramatic losses during post-season play. Despite the high ratings for the play-offs, Nielsen Media Research reported that the World Series between the Florida Marlins and the New York Yankees was the third-lowest ratings series since the games have been televised.

The fall television season got off to a slow start in September 2003. Only Fox, aided by its baseball coverage, enjoyed an increase over ratings for the same period in 2002. ABC, NBC, and CBS substituted reruns, instead of new episodes, of its most popular series to avoid competing with baseball.

Some network executives in 2003 blamed the quality of several new series for audience disinterest. Fox promoted "Skin" and "The Next Joe Millionaire" heavily during its baseball broadcasts, but both debuted to low ratings. Fox canceled "Skin," a modern-day tale of *Romeo and Juliet,* after three episodes.

NBC canceled "Coupling," an adaptation of a popular sitcom in the United Kingdom, after four episodes. The network had promoted "Coupling" as a successor to the popular sitcom "Friends." The network also put "The Lyon's Den," a drama starring former "West Wing" star Rob Lowe, on hiatus during the crucial November ratings period. Many critics viewed the move as spelling doom for the series.

Among the most popular new series was "The O.C.," a Fox drama about a troubled teenager who enters the affluent world of Orange County, California. Fox debuted the series in the summer of 2003.

Two CBS series also were well received. The quirky "Joan of Arcadia" starred Amber Tamblyn as a teen-age girl who receives weekly visits from God in various identities. "Two and a Half Men" featured Charlie Sheen as a playboy whose divorced brother and young son move in with him.

"Arrested Development," an unconventional Fox series about a wealthy but dysfunctional family that loses its fortune, was among the best-reviewed shows of the fall season. The series starred Jeffrey Tambor and Jason Bateman and was co-produced by director Ron Howard. Howard also served as the series' narrator.

"The Reagans," a miniseries starring James Brolin as U.S. President Ronald Reagan and Judy Davis as First Lady Nancy Reagan, ignited controversy before it was broadcast. Supporters of the Reagan family demanded that CBS not air the program because of what they perceived to be historical inaccuracies and an unflattering portrayal of the former president, who in 2003 suffered from Alzheimer's disease. In November, CBS officials pulled the miniseries from the schedule because, they said, it did not present "a balanced portrayal" of the Reagans. CBS sold the program to its sister network, the subscriber cable network, Showtime. When it aired in late November, most viewers failed to understand the reasons behind the various criticisms.

■ Donald Liebenson

See also **Baseball; Deaths; Newspaper; Radio; Republican Party.**

EMMY AWARD WINNERS IN 2003

COMEDY

Best Series: "Everybody Loves Raymond"
Lead Actress: Debra Messing, "Will & Grace"
Lead Actor: Tony Shalhoub, "Monk"
Supporting Actress: Doris Roberts, "Everybody Loves Raymond"
Supporting Actor: Brad Garrett, "Everybody Loves Raymond"

DRAMA

Best Series: "The West Wing"
Lead Actress: Edie Falco, "The Sopranos"
Lead Actor: James Gandolfini, "The Sopranos"
Supporting Actress: Tyne Daly, "Judging Amy"
Supporting Actor: Joe Pantoliano, "The Sopranos"

OTHER AWARDS

Miniseries: *Steven Spielberg Presents 'Taken'*
Variety, Music, or Comedy Series: "The Daily Show with Jon Stewart"
Made for Television Movie: *Door to Door*
Lead Actress in a Miniseries or Movie: Maggie Smith, *My House in Umbria*
Lead Actor in a Miniseries or Movie: William H. Macy, *Door to Door*
Supporting Actress in a Miniseries or Movie: Gena Rowlings, *Hysterical Blindness*
Supporting Actor in a Miniseries or Movie: Ben Gazzara, *Hysterical Blindness*

Tennis. Serena Williams continued her domination of women's tennis in 2003, capturing two of the four Grand Slam events—the Australian Open and Wimbledon—before undergoing knee surgery in August. In men's tennis, eight different players won the last eight Grand Slam tournaments, tying a record.

Australian Open. On January 26, Andre Agassi crushed Rainer Schuettler 6-2, 6-2, 6-1 for his fourth Australian Open title and eighth Grand Slam title overall. Agassi, at 32, became the oldest man to win a Grand Slam title since Ken Rosewall did so in the 1972 Australian Open at 37.

Serena Williams outlasted her sister, Venus, 7-6 (4), 3-6, 6-4, on Jan. 25, 2003, to capture her fourth consecutive Grand Slam title. Williams is only the fifth woman to win four Grand Slam titles in a row. Her victory also meant she was the first woman since Steffi Graf in 1988 to hold all four Grand Slam titles at once.

Fabrice Santoro and Michael Llorda won the men's doubles title in 2003, Martina Navratilova and Leander Paes won the mixed doubles title, and Serena and Venus Williams won the women's doubles title.

French Open. Justine Henin-Hardenne of Belgium won her first Grand Slam title on June 7, beating countrywoman Kim Clijsters 6-0, 6-4 in the final. Henin-Hardenne had ousted Serena Williams in the semifinal round, ending Williams's streak of consecutive Grand Slam match wins at 33.

Spain's Juan Carlos Ferrero won his first Grand Slam title on June 8, routing unseeded Martin Verkerk 6-1, 6-3, 6-2. Twin brothers Bob and Mike Bryan of the United States won the men's doubles title; Clijsters and Ai Sugiyama won the women's doubles title; and Lisa Raymond and Mike Bryan won the mixed doubles crown.

Wimbledon. Lleyton Hewitt of Australia became the first defending men's champion to lose in the first round in modern professional tennis and only the second since the Wimbledon tournament began in 1877. Ivo Karlovic of Croatia ousted Hewitt in four sets on June 23, 2003. On July, Roger Federer became the first Swiss man to win a major title, edging Mark Philippoussis of Australia 7-6 (5), 6-2, 7-6 (3).

On July 5, Serena Williams rallied from one set down to beat her sister Venus 4-6, 6-4, 6-2 to defend her Wimbledon title. Todd Woodbridge of Australia and Jonas Bjorkman of Sweden won the men's doubles title, Clijsters and Sugiyama won the women's doubles title, and Paes and Navratilova won the mixed doubles title.

U.S. Open. The women's field at the U.S. Open in Flushing Meadows, New York, in September was wide open after Venus Williams withdrew from the tournament with a strained abdominal muscle. Henin-Hardenne toppled Clijsters in a rematch of the French Open final 7-5, 6-1. Clijsters had climbed to the top position in the world rankings during the summer, unseating

Roger Federer of Switzerland wins the first Grand Slam title of his career at Wimbledon on July 6, 2003. Federer defeated Australian Mark Philippoussis to become the first Swiss player ever to win a Grand Slam event.

Serena Williams, who fell to third in the rankings behind Henin-Hardenne after completion of the U.S. Open. That ranking was Williams's lowest in 16 months.

American Andy Roddick rode his blistering serve to his first Grand Slam title, throttling Juan Carlos Ferrero of Spain in the final 6-3, 7-6 (2), 6-3. Woodbridge and Bjorkman won the men's doubles title, Virginia Ruano Pascal of Spain and Paola Suarez of Argentina won the women's doubles title, and Katarina Srebotnik of Slovenia and Bob Bryan won the mixed doubles title.

Milestones. Two U.S. champions—Pete Sampras and Michael Chang—retired in 2003. Sampras won a record 14 Grand Slam titles in his career. Chang won the French Open in 1989 at the age of 17, becoming the first U.S. player to win there since 1955.

On July 6, 2003, Navratilova tied Billie Jean King's record of winning 20 Wimbledon titles with her mixed doubles title with Paes. The pair defeated Andy Ram of Israel and Anastassia Rodionova of Russia 6-3, 6-3. King had won her 20th title in 1979, while paired with Navratilova for the doubles event. Navratilova's Wimbledon triumph was her 58th Grand Slam title. She is second only to Australia's Margaret Court, who won 62. ■ Michael Kates

See also **Sports**.

Terrorism. Terrorist attacks in 2003 killed more than 500 people and wounded several thousand others, not including those killed and injured in the ongoing struggles in Iraq and Afghanistan. The main battleground was the Middle East, but terrorism also afflicted Russia and countries in South Asia and Southeast Asia.

Middle East and North Africa. Palestinian terrorists associated with the militant groups Hamas, Islamic Jihad, and al-Aqsa Martyrs Brigade launched more than a dozen attacks against Israeli targets in 2003. The most destructive of these were a double suicide bombing in Tel Aviv that killed 23 people and wounded more than 100 on January 5; the March 5 bombing of a bus in Haifa that killed 14 Israelis and 1 American; the August 19 suicide bombing of a bus in Jerusalem that took 22 lives and wounded 136 others; suicide bombings in Jerusalem and Rishon Le Zion, a Tel Aviv suburb, that killed 15 people and wounded dozens more on September 9; and a suicide attack on a restaurant in Haifa that killed 19 people and injured 24 others on October 4.

Saudi Arabia suffered two major attacks, both blamed on al-Qa'ida, the network led by Osama bin Laden. On May 12, a suicide bomber struck three housing complexes in the city of Riyadh, killing 35 people. On November 9, at least 17 people were killed in Riyadh, and 122 others

were wounded when a car bomb exploded at another housing compound for foreigners. In May, bomb attacks in Casablanca, Morocco, allegedly linked to al-Qa'ida, took at least 43 lives and injured more than 100 people. The targets included a Jewish cultural center and cemetary, a Spanish restaurant, and the Belgian consulate.

Turkey. In November, two truck bombers killed 25 people and injured over 300 others in attacks on two Jewish synagogues in Istanbul, Turkey. A group called the Abu Hafs al-Masri Brigades, said to be connected to al-Qa'ida, claimed responsibility. Six days later, two more truck bombs struck the British consulate and a British bank in Istanbul, killing at least 25 people and wounding more than 400 others. Al-Qa'ida and the Islamic Great Eastern Raiders Front claimed responsibility.

Russia. In May, two suicide bombings in Chechnya attributed to Chechen separatist rebels took 75 lives and injured more than 200 others. Two suicide bombers killed 16 people and injured 40 others in an attack in July at a popular music festival near Moscow. In August, a truck bomb destroyed a military hospital in southern Russia, killing at least 50 people. In December, a suicide bomb attack aboard a train in southern Russia killed at least 40 people and wounded 170 others, and another suicide bomb attack in Moscow killed 6 pedestrians.

South Asia. In August, two car bombs killed at least 50 people and injured 150 others in Mumbai, India. The Indian government blamed the Students Islamic Movement of India, which it said was acting with the support of the Pakistan-based group Lashkar-e-Taiba.

In Pakistan, a group called the Muslim United Army claimed responsibility for bombing 21 gasoline stations. In July, 32 people were killed and 52 others injured in a suicide bomb attack on a Shiah Muslim mosque in the city of Quetta. Militant Sunni Muslims were blamed.

Southeast Asia. On March 4, a bomb at the Davao International Airport in the Philippines killed at least 21 people and injured more than 150 others. The government blamed the Moro Islamic Liberation Front, the country's largest separatist group. In May, another separatist group, the Abu Sayyaf, claimed responsibility for a bombing that killed nine people in a market in the city of Koronadal.

A car bomb exploded outside a Marriott Hotel in Jakarta, Indonesia, in August, killing 12 people and injuring about 150 others. Jemaah Islamiyah, a group allegedly linked to al-Qa'ida, claimed responsibility. ■ Richard E. Rubenstein

See also **Asia; Europe; Iraq: A Special Report; Middle East; Russia**.

Texas. See Dallas; Houston; State government.

Thailand. Prime Minister Thaksin Chinnawat declared a war on drugs in 2003 that resulted in the deaths of more than 2,500 people and the arrests of nearly 50,000 other people. Police said that most people killed during the three-month campaign were murdered by drug dealers trying to silence informers. However, international observers said that Thai police carried out many executions of suspected drug dealers.

Most people in Thailand supported the campaign when it began in February, but some media groups began to criticize the campaign when reports surfaced that innocent people had been murdered in the crackdown. The campaign also sparked outrage from human rights groups.

Thailand experienced an epidemic of methamphetamine abuse in 2003. Officials alleged that 5 percent of the country's population used the drug, which made Thailand the world's largest per capita consumer of methamphetamines.

In August, Thaksin decreed two antiterrorism laws that allowed Thai authorities to arrest terror suspects instead of deporting them and provided a penalty of life imprisonment for terrorist acts. Human rights groups criticized Thaksin's decision to enact the law without first seeking parliamentary approval. ■ Henry S. Bradsher

See also **Asia**.

Theater. Despite the continued popularity of plays imported from the United Kingdom, including Peter Nichols's tragic farce *A Day in the Death of Joe Egg* on Broadway, theater in the United States in 2003 took on a distinctly American quality. New works by celebrated playwrights Arthur Miller and August Wilson, as well as revivals of works by Wilson, Miller, and Edward Albee, were performed on stages around the country. Also, revivals of works by American masters Eugene O'Neill and Tennessee Williams underscored the audiences' ongoing enthusiasm for the tradition of great playwriting.

Philadelphia's Wilma Theater staged the East Coast premiere of Arthur Miller's satire *Resurrection Blues*, directed by Jiri Zizka, in September. The play, which was first performed at Minneapolis's Guthrie Theater in 2002, depicted a fictional South American country in which guns and drugs were as common as the contaminated drinking water. Mingling Miller's traditional engagement with political and social commentary, the action centered on a Christ-like figure whose crucifixion at the hands of the state was to be broadcast by a U.S. television network.

Other regional productions of Miller's work included a revival of his family drama *All My Sons* at the Westport Country Playhouse in Westport, Connecticut, in August 2003. The drama starred Richard Dreyfuss. Joanne Woodward, an accomplished actress and wife of actor Paul Newman, was the artistic director.

Miller's *Finishing the Picture* received a workshop reading in New York City in July. Among the all-star cast were actors Harris Yulin, Brian Dennehy, Frank Langella, and Tovah Feldshuh. Kitty, the central character in Miller's unfinished play, was loosely based on Miller's ex-wife Marilyn Monroe as she struggled to complete her last film project, *The Misfits*. *Finishing the Picture* was Miller's second play about Monroe, after 1964's *After the Fall*.

August Wilson's America. One of America's greatest living playwrights, Wilson was handsomely represented in 2003 by numerous productions, including a Broadway revival and two new works. Wilson, whose plays document African American life in the 20th century, typically combined traditional well-made play structures and soaring poetic dialogue. His landmark drama from 1984, *Ma Rainey's Black Bottom*, portrayed a recording session in Chicago at the height of the jazz age. The play was revived at the Royale Theater in New York City in February 2003 with Whoopi Goldberg and Charles Dutton in the cast.

Wilson's latest play, *Gem of the Ocean*, premiered at the Goodman Theatre in Chicago in April under the direction of Marion McClinton. The ninth in a projected 10-play cycle, *Gem of the Ocean* is set in Pittsburgh in 1904. The play focuses on the relationship between Aunt Ester, born 287 years earlier, and a young man named Citizen Barlow. Barlow is convinced that he has committed a mortal sin and wants Ester to wash his soul clean.

Perhaps the most provocative work by Wilson in 2003 was his one-man show at the Seattle Repertory Theater, which ran from May to June. Titled *How I Learned What I Learned*, the play was a 100-minute monologue performed by the playwright. His pointed diatribe on race in the United States included a series of stories about his own life, punctuated by indictments of racism.

Edward Albee in Chicago. Chicago's Goodman Theatre showcased a six-week retrospective celebrating the career of playwright Edward Albee between September and November 2003. The plays included in the festival ranged from his earliest, *The Zoo Story* (1959), to his most recent, *The Goat or Who Is Sylvia?*, which received the Tony Award for best play in 2002. *The Zoo Story*, a two-character play in one act, takes the audience from Peter's innocuous opening line—"I've been to the zoo"—to his murder at the hands of Jerry, a normally mild-mannered man whom Peter bullies into stabbing him. Albee is planning a one-act prequel to *The Zoo Story*, called *Home Life*, in which Peter is seen at home with his wife prior to

Vanessa Redgrave and Brian Dennehy portray Mary and James Tyrone in the 2003 Broadway revival of Eugene O'Neill's *Long Day's Journey into Night*. Both actors won rave reviews as well as Tony Awards for their performances.

his fateful meeting with Jerry.

While *Who's Afraid of Virginia Woolf?*, Albee's most famous play, was absent from the line-up, other plays depicting marital discord included *The Marriage Play* and *The Play About the Baby*. Other events in the retrospective included a panel titled *Acting Albee*, in which performers discussed the particular challenges and pleasures of bringing Albee's work to the stage.

U.S. classics revived. Two noteworthy revivals of classic American plays were staged on Broadway in 2003. Eugene O'Neill's autobiographical saga of the troubled Tyrone family, *Long Day's Journey into Night*, which ran from May to August, benefitted from a sterling production and received the Tony Award for best play revival. The powerhouse cast included Brian Dennehy as the stingy father James, Vanessa Redgrave as the morphine-addicted mother Mary, Philip Seymour Hoffman as Jamie, the loutish older brother, and Robert Sean Leonard as the consumptive brother Edmund. Stars were also plentiful in the revival

TONY AWARD WINNERS IN 2003

Best Play, *Take Me Out*
Best Musical, *Hairspray*
Best Play Revival, *Long Day's Journey into Night*
Best Musical Revival, *Nine The Musical*
Leading Actor in a Play, Brian Dennehy, *Long Day's Journey into Night*
Leading Actress in a Play, Vanessa Redgrave, *Long Day's Journey into Night*
Leading Actor in a Musical, Harvey Fierstein, *Hairspray*
Leading Actress in a Musical, Marissa Jaret Winokur, *Hairspray*
Featured Actor in a Play, Denis O'Hare, *Take Me Out*
Featured Actress in a Play, Michele Pawk, *Hollywood Arms*
Featured Actor in a Musical, Dick Latessa, *Hairspray*
Featured Actress in a Musical, Jane Krakowski, *Nine The Musical*
Direction of a Play, Joe Mantello, *Take Me Out*
Direction of a Musical, Jack O'Brien, *Hairspray*
Book of a Musical, Thomas Meehan and Mark O'Donnell, *Hairspray*
Original Musical Score, Scott Whittman and Marc Shaiman, *Hairspray*
Orchestration, Stuart Malina and Billy Joel, *Movin' Out*
Scenic Design, Catherine Martin, *La Boheme*
Costume Design, William Ivey Long, *Hairspray*
Lighting Design, Nigel Levings, *La Boheme*
Choreography, Twyla Tharp, *Movin' Out*
Regional Theater, The Children's Theatre Company
Special Theatrical Event, *Russell Simmons' Def Poetry Jam on Broadway*
Lifetime Achievement, Cy Feuer, music director and composer
Honors for Excellence in Theater, The principal ensemble of *La Boheme*, Paul Huntley, Johnson-Liff Casting Associates, and The Acting Company

Al Hirschfeld:
Enchanted with Line

Al Hirschfeld, an American artist who used a graceful scroll of thin, black lines to capture the essence of Broadway theater personalities and events for more than 75 years, died on Jan. 20, 2003, at age 99 in New York City. Hirschfeld was best known for his *caricatures* (pictures that exaggerate the physical features or peculiarities of a person or object). The black-and-white drawings of theater and film stars were a fixture of the New York City theater scene through much of the 20th century and transformed Hirschfeld into a celebrity in his own right.

Albert Hirschfeld was born on June 21, 1903, in St. Louis, Missouri, one of three children of Isaac and Rebecca Hirschfeld. His mother moved the family to New York City when Hirschfeld was a young boy so he could hone his seemingly innate artistic ability. He attended public school and studied at the Art Students League in New York City. By age 18, he had already worked for two motion-picture studios, including a stint as an art director. During the mid-1920's, Hirschfeld moved to Paris with the goal of becoming a painter and sculptor.

During a return visit to New York in 1926, Hirschfeld attended a theater performance and sketched the star of the show on a theater program. A friend convinced Hirschfeld to redraw the image on a clean sheet of paper and submit it for publication to the *New York Herald Tribune*. Hirschfeld's artwork continued to appear in the *Herald Tribune* until 1927, when he began a working relationship with *The New York Times*, a relationship that lasted until his death.

Although Hirschfeld was an accomplished artist by the 1920's, he had not yet developed the technique for which he would become famous. During a trip to the South Pacific in the early 1930's, Hirschfeld noted how the bright sunlight bleached out all color and reduced people to what he called "walking line drawings." He later recalled how he had become "enchanted with line" and began developing his unique style of using simple, flowing lines to capture a personality or a performance.

Hirschfeld inadvertently launched another of his trademark styles following the birth of his daughter, Nina, in 1945. He wove her name into the lines of a drawing as a personal celebration of her birth. He hid her name in a few more drawings before stopping, believing that the novelty had worn thin. Once he stopped, however, newspaper readers began writing letters asking why. Public response, thus,

of Tennessee Williams's grim family portrait *Cat on a Hot Tin Roof*, with Ashley Judd as Maggie, Jason Patric as the hard-drinking Brick, and Ned Beatty as Big Daddy. In Connecticut, the Hartford Stage presented a two-evening cycle of Williams's one-acts titled "8 by Tennessee."

Home-grown Shakespeare. New star-studded productions and a national initiative to present William Shakespeare in the United States proved that Shakespeare, without question, is the most enduring playwright in the English language. Actor Kevin Kline portrayed Falstaff in *Henry IV*, a production that combined both parts of Shakespeare's great history play into a single evening at Lincoln Center's Vivian Beaumont Theatre in New York City. Also in the cast of the

November 2003 production were Richard Easton, who played British poet A. E. Housman in the New York City production of *The Invention of Love*, and Billy Crudup, who played the title role in the 2002 revival of *The Elephant Man*.

Fans did not, however, need to travel to New York City to see a Shakespeare play in 2003. In addition to annual productions at the Alabama and Oregon Shakespeare Festivals, the National Endowment for the Arts (NEA) inaugurated a new program designed to bring touring companies of Shakespeare to cities around the country. The NEA, which the U.S. Congress established in 1965, helps to foster, preserve, and promote excellence in the arts; brings art to U.S. citizens; and provides leadership in arts education. NEA

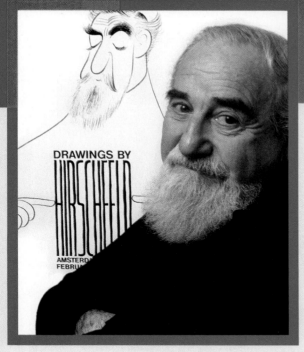

led Hirschfeld to embed "Nina"—often several times—into each caricature. The name popped up in the fold of a dress, a curl of the hair, or the crook of an arm. Readers of *The New York Times* ultimately requested that Hirschfeld give them some hint as to how many Nina's were embedded in each Hirschfeld drawing, which led the artist to add a number next to his signature indicating how many "Ninas" appear in the drawing. Readers made a game out of finding the hidden tributes woven into each caricature.

Hirschfeld produced more than 7,000 caricatures, featuring most of Broadway's elite, during his long career. He won an honorary Tony Award in 1975 and was the subject of a documentary film titled *The Line King* (1996). His drawings were also published in several volumes, including *The American Theatre As Seen by Hirschfeld* (1961), *Hirschfeld* (1979), *Hirschfeld: Art and Recollections from Eight Decades* (1991), and *Hirschfeld On Line* (1999). During the 1990's, the United States Postal Service hired Hirschfeld to design a series of first-class postage stamps honoring comedians and silent-film stars. The commission was the first in which the postal service allowed a hidden message— Hirschfeld's "Nina"—to appear on a stamp. The artist's work also found its way into the collections of several museums, including New York City's Metropolitan Museum of Art and the Museum of Modern Art.

Marquee lights across Broadway dimmed in memory of Hirschfeld after word spread that he had died in his sleep, and in June 2003, the Martin Beck Theatre, located on 45th Street in New York City, was renamed the Al Hirschfeld Theatre. The theater's marquee includes a self-portrait of the artist outlined in white lights, a lasting and highly appropriate tribute to a person who helped define the magic and glamour of Broadway in the 20th century. ■ Tim Frystak

chairperson Dana Gioia created "Shakespeare in American Communities," to reinstate the tradition of touring companies that brought theater to a wide audience in the 1800's.

Participating companies included The Acting Company of New York City performing *Richard III*, the Chicago Shakespeare Theater's production of *Romeo and Juliet*, and the Guthrie Theater's staging of *Othello*. The project was supported by The Players' Guild, which includes such theatrical luminaries as actors Jane Alexander, James Earl Jones, Angela Lansbury, and Michael York; directors Michael Kahn and Julie Taymor; and Shakespeare critic Harold Bloom.

Standouts. The musical *Hairspray*, based on John Waters's film of the same name, was a big winner at the 2003 Tony Awards. The play won eight prizes, including best musical. Richard Greenberg's play *Take Me Out*, about a gay baseball player, was chosen best play. Greenberg's latest play, *The Violet Hour*, opened at the refurbished Biltmore Theatre in November 2003.

Broadway productions that were critically and commercially successful in 2003 included *Avenue Q*, a ribald comedy performed by uncensored puppets, and *Nine*, the revival of a musical based on Federico Fellini's classic film *8 1/2*. *Nine* opened in April with Antonio Banderas, who, after a successful run that culminated in a Tony nomination, was replaced by John Stamos in October. ■ David Yezzi

Togo. See **Africa**.

A crowd of 450,000 people gathers at Downsview Park in Toronto on July 30, 2003, for a SARS relief concert. The Rolling Stones headlined the show, and 15 bands performed during the 11-hour production, nicknamed SARStock, the biggest concert in Canadian history.

Toronto. In the spring of 2003, the Toronto area suffered a devastating outbreak of severe acute respiratory syndrome (SARS). The summer was marked by record heat waves and an electrical blackout. The year ended with a change in the provincial government and an upset mayoral election.

SARS—a disease with symptoms similar to influenza, but difficult to treat and much more likely to be fatal than flu—was first detected in a suburban Toronto hospital in March. The patient had recently visited China, where the SARS epidemic began. The disease spread to a hospital in the York Region north of Toronto and by March 26, SARS was so widespread that the provincial government declared an emergency, restricting most hospitals in the area to critically ill patients and necessary staff. Physicians, nurses, and public health officials set up hotlines around the city to consult with anyone who was afraid he or she might have come in contact with a carrier of SARS. Those who faced potential risk were warned to put themselves into voluntary quarantine.

On April 23, the World Health Organization (WHO), the United Nations agency for health based in Geneva, Switzerland, issued a travel advisory for Toronto but stopped short of telling people to avoid the city altogether. A week later, WHO lifted its travel warning, and the province

lifted its emergency on May 17. However, on May 27, WHO reinstated its advisory when a second outbreak of SARS began at a convalescent home and quickly spread.

The second outbreak was contained more quickly than the first, and no new cases of SARS were reported in Toronto after June 12. WHO lifted its second advisory on July 3. A total of 375 people suffered serious illness, with 44 deaths. Almost 30,000 people were required to isolate themselves for 10-day periods. Canada was the only country outside Asia where people died of SARS, all of them in and around Toronto.

Heat wave. In August, a brutal heat wave drove temperatures in Toronto to 100.2 °F (37.9 °C). Toronto residents' discomfort increased on August 14, when in most parts of the city, electrical systems—and air-conditioning units —shut down for 23 hours during the power outage that afflicted much of northeastern North America, including Ontario.

Elections. In provincial elections on October 3, the Liberal Party ousted the Progressive Conservative Party (PCP), which had been in power since 1995. The Liberals carried almost every *riding* (administrative division) in the Toronto area, where voters were particularly unhappy with the PCP government's cutbacks in funding for municipalities. Toronto politicians claimed provincial cutbacks were largely responsible for a municipal budget shortfall that had grown to $300 million by some estimates.

In municipal elections, incumbent Mayor Mel Lastman announced that he was retiring after 34 years in local politics. Four candidates competed to succeed Lastman, among them David Miller, a city councillor and member of the left-wing New Democratic Party, who was not well-known outside his own west-end ward. On November 10, Miller was elected by over 30,000 votes.

Miller's administration was expected to push for more federal money for cities, with strong support from the Toronto City Summit Alliance, a group of prominent businessmen, union executives, and community activists. This broadly based lobby group was something new to Toronto politics. The alliance was particularly concerned with increasing federal funding for Toronto's public transportation system.

Theater collapse. Toronto's landmark Uptown Theatre collapsed on Dec. 9, 2003, killing 1 person and injuring 14 others. Demolition work on the theater caused bricks and masonry to fall on a neighboring building, ripping a 50-foot by 20-foot (15-meter by 6-meter) hole in the roof.

■ David Lewis Stein

See also **Canada; Canadian provinces; City; Public health and safety.**

Toys and games. The toy industry in the United States bounced back in 2003 with a 4 percent increase in sales after a flat year in 2002. Buoyed by a strengthening of the U.S. economy late in the third quarter, a strong wave of consumer confidence helped push toy sales (excluding video hardware and games) to an estimated $21 billion in 2003.

Still, toy manufacturers and retailers continued to struggle with obstacles such as age compression—that is, the fact that children seemed to be "getting older younger." Traditionally, toys had been marketed to children ages birth to 14 years. However, the late 1990's brought a new age category called tweens, 8 to 12 year olds who were "graduating" earlier from toys and developing interests in other activities and products, such as music, fashion, sports, and the Internet.

Blasts from the past. One of the biggest trends in the toy industry in 2003 was the "retro" effect. A number of top-selling playthings from earlier eras were reintroduced and repeated their success with a whole new audience. Bandai America Incorporated of Cypress, California, had a "berry" good year with the new-edition Strawberry Shortcake, the fruit-scented mini-doll from the early 1980's that found a new generation of fans in 2003. Saddled up to ride again, another

A boy demonstrates his skill with Astrojax, a "free-dimensional orbiter," which Active People of Zurich, Switzerland, introduced in the United States in 2003. The toy consists of three foam balls with weighted metal cores. Two balls are attached by a string while a third ball slides freely. By holding one of the end balls and jerking the string, players can make the balls jump, spin, and bounce in an endless variety of tricks.

1980's favorite, My Little Pony, returned to charm little girls who loved to brush the figures' long manes. Collecting the pastel-colored ponies, manufactured by Hasbro Incorporated of Pawtucket, Rhode Island, became a passion once again for the 3-year-old-and-over set. And wearing their hearts (and flowers and rainbows), not on their sleeves but on their tummies, the Care Bears stuffed toys returned to offer warmth, fun, and hugs to kids of all ages. Cheer Bear, Funshine Bear, Tenderheart Bear, and Wish Bear were just some of the warm and fuzzy characters rolled out in 2003 by Play Along Incorporated of Deerfield Beach, Florida.

Still playing after all these years. Crayola crayons—not a retro version, but the originals—celebrated 100 years of creativity and fun in 2003. The familiar eight-pack of crayons, which sold for a nickel when first introduced in 1903, remained a familiar sight in kindergartners' pencil boxes 10 decades later. Three billion crayons per year continued to roll off the assembly line in the Easton, Pennsylvania, factory of the manufacturer, Binney & Smith, Incorporated. According to a study conducted by Yale University of New Haven, Connecticut, Crayola crayons were ranked number 18 on the list of the most recognizable scents to American adults. (Coffee and peanut butter were rated first and second, respectively.)

Another favorite plaything also reached a milestone in 2003. Still blasting out of the park at the half-century mark were the signature perforated plastic playthings made by Wiffle Ball Incorporated of Shelton, Connecticut.

Undersea and Down Under wonders. Two of the biggest-selling licensed toys in 2003 were based on a popular animated movie and a top-rated children's television show from Australia—namely, a fish named Nemo and four young Aussies called The Wiggles. Released in the summer of 2003, the film *Finding Nemo* was an immediate blockbuster, spawning sales of stuffed toys, made by Hasbro, Inc., based on the film's aquatic heroes and villains.

The singing and dancing Wiggles charmed their way into the hearts of preschoolers with their television series that offered a combination of live-action and animation. Each episode featured a theme relevant to the world of a young child, such as the body, food, friendship, and family. The Wiggles themselves were an actual touring band of musicians with backgrounds in preschool education. Sales of Wiggles videotapes, CD's and DVD's soared, along with a line of musical toys, such as the Wiggles guitar, made by Spin Master of Toronto, Ontario, Canada.

■ Diane P. Cardinale

See also **United States, History of: A Special Report**.

Track and field. Athletes from the United States enjoyed moments of glory as well as moments of great embarrassment at the 2003 World Championships in Paris, August 23-31. U.S. athletes won 20 medals, more than any other country. One U.S. athlete failed a drug test and stood to lose two gold medals. Another withdrew from the meet after showing poor sportsmanship by lying on the track to protest a referee's decision.

Steroids. In October, an investigation into the possible widespread use among track and field athletes of an illegal performance-enhancing drug threatened the reputation of the sport. The investigation involved tetrahydrogestrinone (THG), a steroid that had allegedly been altered so it could not be detected. Urine samples from several U.S. track and field athletes taken during the World Championships in June tested positive for THG. Officials expected the investigation to continue into 2004.

World Championships. U.S. athletes won 10 gold medals in 2003, including two by Kelli White in the women's 100-meter and 200-meter sprint events. However, White later tested positive for moda-finil—a mild stimulant not specifically banned by the International Association of Athletics Federation (IAAF), the ruling body of international track and field. However, the IAAF considers the drug to be a "related substance" and punishes athletes for its use. White had a prescription for the drug, which she said she was taking for a sleep disorder. She admitted taking the drug on the morning of the 100-meter event, but she said she did not seek an exemption to use the drug because it was not specifically banned.

IAAF officials did not suspend White, but they did reject her assertion that the stimulant did not enhance her performance. The IAAF ruled that White should be stripped of her two gold medals and the $120,000 prize money she won. In September, White's case was sent to the U.S. Anti-Doping Agency, the body that oversees drug tests for Olympic sports in the United States, for hearings and further appeals.

On August 24, U.S. sprinter Jon Drummond put on an embarrassing display at the World Championships, lying on his back on the track for more than a half-hour to protest a referee calling him for a false start in the 100-meter quarterfinals. Drummond's tantrum caused delays that affected hundreds of athletes preparing to compete. IAAF officials told officials with USA Track and Field, the national governing body for track and field, that if they did not punish Drummond, the IAAF would do it for them. Drummond withdrew from the meet voluntarily on August 26.

In other highlights at the event, Ana Guevara became the first Mexican runner to capture the gold with her victory in the 400-meter sprint on

Tyree Washington celebrates his victory in the 400-meter sprint at the U.S. Track and Field Championships in Palo Alto, California, in June 2003. Washington's time of 44.33 seconds was the fastest in the 400-meter event at the competition since 2001.

WORLD TRACK AND FIELD RECORDS ESTABLISHED IN 2003

Event	Holder	Country	Where set	Date	Record
WOMEN INDOOR					
Pole vault	Svetlana Feofanova	Russia	Birmingham, U.K.	March 16	15' 9" 4.8 m
1,500 meters	Regina Jacobs	U.S.	Boston	February 1	3:59.98
3,000 meters walk	Gillian O'Sullivan	Ireland	Belfast, Ireland	February 15	*11:35.34
MEN OUTDOOR					
50-kilometer race	Robert Korzeniowski	Poland	Paris	August 27	3:36:03
30-kilometer road race	Takayuki Matsumiya	Japan	Kumamoto, Japan	February 16	1:28:36
Marathon	Paul Tergat	Kenya	Berlin	September 28	2:04.55**
WOMEN OUTDOOR					
3,000-meter steeplechase	Gulnara Samitova	Russia	Tula, Russia	August 10	9:08.33
30,000-meter	Tegla Loroupe	Kenya	Warstein, Germany	June 6	1:45.50
400-meter hurdles	Yuliya Pechonkina	Russia	Tula, Russia,	August 8	52.34
Pole vault	Yelena Isinbayeva	Russia	Gateshead, U.K.	July 13	*4.82
10-kilometer road race	Paula Radcliffe	U.K.	San Juan, Puerto Rico	February 23	30:21.00**
Marathon	Paula Radcliffe	U.K.	London	April 13	*2:15:25**

m = meters   ** = not recognized as a world record, but world best performance.
* = not yet ratified.   Source: International Association of Athletics Federation (IAAF).

August 27. The U.S. women's 4-x-400-meter relay team won the gold.

Gold rush. On September 5, Maria Mutola of Mozambique became the only athlete to win all six Golden League races in 2003, taking the final race in Brussels. Mutola won $1 million for her efforts.

Marathon marks. Paul Tergat of Kenya shattered the world's best time in the marathon on September 28, in Berlin, finishing in 2 hours, 4 minutes, and 55 seconds. England's Paula Radcliffe broke her own world mark in the marathon with a time of 2 hours, 15 minutes, and 25 seconds at the London Marathon on April 13.

Other world records. Regina Jacobs of the United States broke a world record when she became the first woman to run the 1,500-meter sprint in less than 4 minutes, clocking in at 3 minutes, 59.98 seconds on February 1 in Boston.

Svetlana Feofanova of Russia recaptured the record for the indoor pole vault at the world indoor championships in Birmingham, England, on March 16 with a vault of 15 feet, 9 inches (4.8 meters). Feofanova topped the record of 15 feet, 8-1/4 inches (4.78 meters) set two weeks earlier by Stacy Dragila of the United States.

Russia's Gulnara Samitova set a world record in the women's 3,000-meter steeplechase on August 10 with a time of 9:08.33. ■ Michael Kates

See also **Sports.**

Transportation.

Drivers in London, England, began paying 5 pounds ($8) a day in 2003 to drive into the center of the city. The charges were introduced in February to reduce the congestion that had slowed average speeds to less than 10 miles (16 kilometers) per hour. The charges applied to an 8-square-mile (20.7-square-kilometer) area of the British capital from 7 a.m. to 6:30 p.m. during weekdays. Drivers who failed to pay the fees had their license plates photographed by cameras mounted at entry points and were sent penalty notices in the mail. The revenue raised was used to pay for improvements to public transportation. Early results revealed that traffic levels within the zone fell 16 percent while the average traffic speed rose 37 percent.

Container security. Concerns about terrorists hiding bombs in shipping containers continued during 2003. The newly formed United States Department of Homeland Security announced a $300-million program in June to increase security at U.S. ports. The plan included expanding the Container Security Initiative, where U.S. agents inspect containers at foreign ports before they are loaded onto ships bound for the United States. Under the Port Security Grant Program, most of the money—$170 million—was divided among 199 state and local governments as well as private companies.

Tugboats escort the Queen Mary 2 (QM2) from the French port of Saint-Nazaire for a test run in September. The newly completed QM2 is the longest, tallest, and most expensive passenger ship ever built. Its maiden voyage was scheduled for January 2004.

S.S. *United States.* Representatives of Norwegian Cruise Lines in Miami, Florida, announced in April that the company was buying the S.S. *United States* and intended to refit it as a cruise ship. One of the world's most famous ocean liners, the ship had been out of service for more than 30 years and had been docked in Philadelphia since 1996. The 990-foot (301.8-meter) vessel's maiden voyage, in 1952, set a transatlantic speed record of 3 days, 10 hours, and 42 minutes, which was not broken until 1990.

Maglev. In March 2003, magnetic levitation technology, or Maglev, allowed more than 80,000 visitors to float from China's Longyang Road Station to Pudong Airport and back. Maglev uses magnets to levitate the train off its tracks. The reduced friction allows speeds of up to 260 miles (418 kilometers) per hour. Once the technology is fully implemented, trains will cover the 19 miles (30.6 kilometers) between the center of Shanghai and its airport in less than eight minutes. Following additional testing, the line was expected to open for regular use at the end of 2003.

A token gesture. After 50 years, New York City subway turnstiles stopped accepting tokens when the fare was raised to $2 on May 4. Tokens were introduced in 1953 when the fare was just 15 cents. Passengers placed the tokens in slots that activated the turnstiles as the people entered stations. The tokens were replaced with magnetically imprinted cards.

Federal funding. In May 2003, the U.S. Congress passed a six-year, $247-billion reauthorization of surface transportation funding. The Safe, Accountable, Flexible and Efficient Transportation Equity Act of 2003 (SAFETEA) followed two previous acts that, since the early 1990's, encouraged state transportation departments to

implement programs that integrate driving, transit, and other methods of transportation.

Trucking merger. Officials at two large U.S. trucking firms announced in July that they would merge. Yellow Corporation of Overland Park, Kansas, purchased Roadway Corporation of Akron, Ohio, in a $966-million deal. Both firms provided service where goods from various shippers were consolidated at stations into larger trucks for long-distance moves. The enterprise, known as Yellow-Roadway Corporation, became one of the largest transportation service providers in the world. However, the third-largest firm in this section of the industry, Consolidated Freightways of Vancouver, Washington, liquidated its assets in 2003 after declaring bankruptcy and ceasing operations in September 2002.

Testing the waters. The *Queen Mary 2*, the largest passenger ship ever built, left the French port of Saint-Nazaire on a test run in September 2003. The $800-million-dollar liner is as long as four football fields and is as high as a 23-story building. The ship is slated to make a January 2004 trip from Southampton, England, to Fort Lauderdale, Florida.

Railroad privatization. The policy of privatizing railroad operations around the world, popular in the 1990's, was reexamined in 2003. In the United Kingdom, the Strategic Rail Authority (SRA) ended its contract with Connex, a private company that operated commuter trains. The SRA terminated the contract three years early. Connex was the first company ever to lose an operating franchise with the SRA. The government took exception to the many late and canceled trains as well as Connex's inability to stay within budget.

Asian disasters. India's railways, which daily move more than 11 million people to and from 7,000 stations, suffered a series of derailments, collisions, and fires that claimed more than 100 lives in 2003. In Bangladesh, over 600 people died in ferry disasters in 2003. Lastly, almost 200 people perished in a subway train fire in February in the South Korean city of Daegu when a man, apparently attempting suicide, lit a canister of gasoline. ■ Ian Savage

See also **Automobile; Aviation.**

Trinidad and Tobago. See Latin America.

Tunisia. See Middle East.

A U.S. ship lies at anchor off the port of Iskenderun in Turkey in February, awaiting Turkish permission to unload military supplies intended for the war in Iraq. The Turkish parliament's refusal in early March to grant permission for U.S. troops to launch an attack against Iraq from Turkish soil essentially closed down U.S. plans for opening a full-scale second front north of Baghdad.

Turkey. In March 2003, the Turkish Parliament narrowly rejected a proposal to allow more than 60,000 United States troops to use Turkish bases to launch attacks on Iraq in the event of war, thus forfeiting an offer of $15 billion made by the United States. The reason for the parliament's refusal was that public opinion polls revealed that 90 percent of the Turkish population opposed a war in Iraq. The Turkish people also showed disapproval through massive rallies and demonstrations in the weeks and months before the launch of the U.S.-led war on Iraq.

In September, U.S. Treasury Secretary John Snow, at an International Monetary Fund (IMF) meeting in Dubai, United Arab Emirates, announced that the United States was granting Turkey a loan of up to $8.5 billion to assist in its economic recovery and to soften the effect the Iraq war had on Turkey's economy. The loan carried the conditions that Turkey activate strong economic policies and cooperate with the United States in Iraq. The International Monetary Fund, a United Nations-affiliated group that provides credit to member nations, praised the Turkish government for targeting the manageable goals of 5-percent economic growth and a 20-percent inflation rate.

The Turkish parliament approved a motion in October to send peacekeeping troops to Iraq. The move, requested by the United States, would have led to the first contingent of Muslim peacekeepers in Iraq. However, in November, Turkey reversed course and dropped plans to send troops amid opposition from members of the Iraqi Council, a 25-member multiethnic group formed after the war to restore operations.

Pipeline shutdown. In April, Turkey shut down Russia's new Blue Stream natural gas pipeline, a $3.2-billion project built across the Black Sea by Italy's ENI oil company and Russia's gas monopoly Gazprom. Experts speculated that the pipeline shutdown seemed to be motivated by the need for cheaper energy sources and by the need to end Turkey's dependence on Russian gas. Instead, Turkey planned to obtain gas from Iran, with which it already had a supply deal, and from Azerbaijan.

Bombings. Two Istanbul synagogues were bombed in November, killing as many as 25 people and injuring more than 300 others. Authorities concluded that Turkish militants possibly connected with the al-Qa'ida terrorists were behind the blasts. In another attack later in November, at least 25 people were killed and more than 400 others injured when two explosions rocked the British consulate and a British bank in Istanbul. Al-Qa'ida and a local militant group claimed responsibility. ■ Mary-Jane Deeb

See also **Iraq: A Special Report; Terrorism.**

Turkmenistan. See Asia.

Uganda. In March 2003, Uganda's constitutional court ruled that the Political Organizations and Parties Act was unconstitutional. The law, sponsored by President Yoweri Koguta Museveni's National Resistance Movement (NRM) and passed by Uganda's parliament in May 2002, restricted parties from sponsoring political activities of any kind outside Kampala, the capital.

President Museveni and the NRM seized power in Uganda in 1986. In 1995, Museveni's government imposed a "no-party" political system that restricted activities of independent parties, claiming that the policy was necessary to restrain religious and tribal conflict. The 2002 law was an extension of the "no-party" policy.

In response to the court ruling, President Museveni proposed putting the question of a return to multiparty politics to the voters in a national referendum. Museveni's government had conducted just such a referendum in 2000, when voters had upheld the "no-party" status quo, but opposition politicians boycotted the poll and voter turnout was low. Some opposition leaders charged that Museveni's new referendum proposal was part of a campaign to retain power beyond his presidential term, set to expire in 2006. Uganda's Constitution bars Museveni from seeking a third term in office.

Regional relations. In May 2003, Uganda withdrew its troops from Congo (Kinshasa), the last of seven African nations to pull out of the country under the terms of a peace agreement to end Congo's civil war. However, on May 14 senior United Nations officials accused Uganda of continuing to supply weapons to two ethnic militias battling each other for control of the Ituri region in the northeastern part of Congo (Kinshasa).

Child abductions. On June 24, members of the Ugandan rebel group called the Lord's Resistance Army (LRA) kidnapped about 100 schoolgirls from a village school in northeastern Uganda. Most of the children were subsequently released by their captors or rescued by Ugandan soldiers. Officially, the LRA advocates imposition of "Christian rule" in Uganda but, in fact, carries out a campaign of terror against civilians, especially children. Human rights groups estimated that LRA units had kidnapped as many as 12,000 children during 17 years of armed rebellion.

Former dictator dies. Idi Amin, military dictator of Uganda during the 1970's, died in exile in Saudi Arabia on Aug. 15, 2003. Amin's rule, marked by torture, the murder of perhaps 250,000 people, and the expulsion of as many as 50,000 Asians living in Uganda, came to an end in 1979 when Ugandan opponents aided by Tanzanian troops ousted him.   ■ Simon Baynham

See also **Africa; Congo (Kinshasa).**

Ukraine. A showdown in October 2003 between Russia and Ukraine over their maritime border threatened to sour relations between the two countries. The crisis began when construction workers in the Russian province of Krasnodar Krai began work on a dam that was intended to reunite Ukraine's Tuzla Island at the mouth of the Kerch Strait with mainland Russia. Ukrainian officials claimed the dam construction violated Ukrainian sovereignty in the Kerch Strait and viewed the construction as an attempt by Russia to annex the island. Ukrainian President Leonid Kuchma interrupted a trip to Latin America to fly to the region and inspect the readiness of his country's border guards. A military clash was averted when President Kuchma spoke with President Vladimir Putin of Russia by telephone, and the two agreed that the dam construction would halt to allow the dispute to be resolved through diplomatic channels.

The crisis appeared linked to a more significant disagreement over the border between the two countries in the Azov Sea. In January, Russia and Ukraine finally signed a treaty demarcating their mutual land border, but the treaty left open the question of competing claims on the Sea of Azov. The sea lies mostly within Ukrainian territory, but the Russian government has been insisting on joint sovereignty over the sea shelf and water and the potentially rich resources underlying them. Political analysts noted that the confrontation over the Ukrainian border in the Kerch Strait may have been intended to set a precedent that would apply to the Azov Sea as well.

Economic commonwealth. Russia and Ukraine appeared to move closer in 2003 to creating an economic commonwealth. On September 19 in Yalta, Crimea, the presidents of Russia, Ukraine, Belarus, and Kazakhstan signed a pact to create a "single economic zone" across all four countries. The agreement was controversial in Ukraine, and three cabinet ministers denounced it publicly, including Foreign Minister Kostyantyn Hryshchenko. The plan would create a supranational body to regulate customs, tariffs, and transportation across the zone, to which all four nations would yield some degree of sovereignty.

As the union's largest member, Russia would receive a majority of votes in this new body, and many critics in Ukraine complained that the scheme would surrender some of the country's independence and place Ukraine back under Russian imperial control. Some European analysts observed that the alliance might hurt Ukraine's chances of joining the European Union or the World Trade Organization.   ■ Steven L. Solnick

See also **Europe; Russia.**

Unemployment. See Economics; Labor.

United Arab Emirates. See Middle East.

UNITED KINGDOM

The United Kingdom's (U.K.) involvement in the Iraq War and its aftermath dominated events in the country during 2003. The Labour Party, which had been elected to govern in 1997 and reelected in 2001, remained the ruling party in 2003. However, the government, led by Prime Minister Tony Blair, faced fierce criticism over the way it had informed the public about its reasons for supporting the war, and the cabinet underwent frequent changes. The opposition party, the Conservatives, failed to make progress in implementing its goals and replaced its leader in late 2003.

War In Iraq. In early 2003, Blair made clear that he would provide the United States with military support in the event of a war in Iraq. Nevertheless, the Labour government also repeatedly sought to obtain a United Nations (UN) resolution giving consent for the war.

On February 15, an estimated 1 million people gathered in Hyde Park in central London to protest against the idea of going to war in Iraq. The demonstration was the largest in British history, an indication of the extent of public unease at the prospect of war. On February 26, Blair suffered the biggest rebellion among his party members since he took office; 122 Labour Members of Parliament (MP's) voted against a government motion expressing support for continuing efforts to disarm Iraqi President Saddam Hussein. The MP's backed an amendment that argued that the case for military action was unproven. Nevertheless, the government's motion carried. Public opinion polls showed a shift in favor of the war as the time for military action neared.

On March 18, Blair secured a majority in favor of war in the House of Commons. The Leader of the Commons, Robin Cook (a former Labour foreign secretary), resigned from the government in protest over the war, as did two junior ministers. British troops took part in the invasion of Iraq on March 19 (March 20 in Iraq) and assisted in the defeat of Hussein's regime. Blair's international secretary, Clare Short, resigned in May, in protest over the failure to involve the UN in the reconstruction of Iraq.

The Hutton inquiry. A major part of the government's case for the Iraq war was the claim that Hussein possessed *weapons of mass destruction* (WMD, biological, chemical, or nuclear

weapons). Such an allegation had been made in a government document published in September 2002. The failure to uncover such weapons in the wake of the Iraq war led to criticism that the public had been misled. On May 29, 2003, a report on BBC (British Broadcasting Company) radio by defense correspondent Andrew Gilligan alleged that Blair's director of communications, Alastair Campbell, had "sexed up," or exaggerated, facts in the document. According to Gilligan, Campbell had included a dubious claim that Hussein could deploy weapons of mass destruction within 45 minutes. Gilligan stated that his source, whom he would not name, was a British intelligence official who had helped to prepare the document.

On July 9, the Ministry of Defense named the official as one of its advisers, scientist and weapons expert David Kelly. Kelly was called to testify before the House of Commons Foreign Affairs committee investigating the allegations. Although Kelly admitted he had spoken to Gilligan, he claimed that he could not have been Gilligan's only source. Kelly was reprimanded by the Ministry of Defense for talking to the BBC. On July 17, Kelly took his own life. The BBC then revealed that Kelly had been Gilligan's sole source. Blair reacted to the scandal surrounding Kelly's death by appointing Lord Hutton, a *law lord* (member of the U.K.'s highest court of appeal) to chair an inquiry into the affair.

The Hutton inquiry conducted hearings throughout August and September. Blair testified, denying the BBC's allegation that his office had falsely inserted claims about the speed with which Iraq could deploy WMD's, and he suggested that if it were true, the charge would merit his resignation. (Blair's testimony represented only the second time that a British prime minister had appeared before a public inquiry.) The defense secretary, Geoff Hoon, denied any involvement in naming Kelly to the press, insisting that responsibility lay with the prime minister's office. Gilligan admitted his original report had exaggerated the evidence available to him. After the hearings, Lord Hutton prepared a final report, which was to be presented in 2004. In August 2003, Campbell resigned as director of communications. He was replaced by David Hill, though the position was redefined in reaction to criticism that Campbell had wielded too much power.

Budget. Chancellor of the Exchequer (finance minister) Gordon Brown presented his budget to the House of Commons on April 9. Brown estimated that the economy would grow by 2 to 2.5 percent during 2003, which was down slightly from previous forecasts because of the poor eco-

nomic climate. Brown also estimated that the economy would grow by 3 to 3.5 percent in 2004 and 2005. In the first and second quarters of 2003, the economy grew by 0.7 and 2.4 percent, respectively. Although economists were optimistic about achieving the forecasted 2003 growth, they remained concerned that the budget would produce insufficient revenue to pay for Brown's ambitious spending plans.

Brown also announced a "baby bond" program, in which all children born in September 2002 and after would receive an endowment from the government of 250 to 500 pounds ($426 to $852), depending on parental income. The funds would mature in an account that could be added to. The money was to be used after the child reached 18 years of age, for education or a similar investment in the child's future.

Euro. The question of whether the U.K. would adopt the single European currency, the euro, remained unsettled in 2003. Polls continued to show that the majority of Britons were against the change. Brown had made U.K.'s entry dependent on a series of economic tests, based on such issues as flexibility in economic policy and the impact of the change on long-term investment. In June, Brown reported to the Commons that he had come to a positive assessment on only one of his tests, the impact on financial services. Although the Labour government remained in favor of adopting the euro, analysts predicted that a referendum on the question was unlikely to be held before the next general election.

Traffic congestion. The mayor of London, Ken Livingstone, introduced a controversial program in February to reduce traffic in central London, where traffic jams frequently brought the capital to a standstill. All motorists entering central London were required to pay 5 pounds ($8) a day. Surveillance cameras monitored all cars as they entered the city's central zone, and any drivers who did not pay the fee were fined 80 pounds ($136). Livingstone also introduced more buses to persuade people to use public transportation. By mid-year, traffic in central London had been reduced by 16 percent.

Anglican Church. Rowan Williams was formally enthroned as archbishop of Canterbury and head of the Church of England in

February. He immediately encountered problems that threatened to divide the worldwide Anglican Communion. In June, Jeffrey John, who made no secret of his homosexuality or his male partner of 27 years, was nominated to become bishop of Reading. The nomination generated widespread criticism, particularly from leaders of the Anglican Church in Africa—the Anglican Communion's largest branch—despite John's insistence that he had been celibate for a long time. To prevent further discord, John withdrew his name from the nomination. Williams also faced conflict over the consecration in November of openly gay V. Gene Robinson as bishop of New Hampshire in the United States, a move that led to further divisions within the Communion.

Asylum. The issue of *asylum seekers* (applicants from foreign countries claiming political asylum in the U.K.) continued to cause controversy in 2003. The numbers of such immigrants had set a new record in 2002. In February 2003,

Members of the Charter 88 group, which advocates a "fair and modern democracy" in the U.K., demonstrate, dressed as Parliamentary lords, outside the Houses of Parliament in February. The group demanded that members of the House of Lords be elected, not appointed, as Prime Minister Tony Blair advocated. On February 4, Parliament rejected Blair's proposal.

HOUSE OF COMMONS

Queen Elizabeth II opened the 2003-2004 session of Parliament on Nov. 26, 2003. As of October 24, the House of Commons was made up of the following:

408	Labour Party
163	Conservative Party
54	Liberal Democrats
3	Ulster Unionists
5	Scottish National Party
4	Plaid Cymru
3	Social Democratic and Labour Party
5	Ulster Democratic Unionist Party
4	Sinn Fein
1	Independent
1	Independent Labour
1	Independent Conservative
3	Independent Union

In addition, the unaffiliated speaker and 3 deputies attend sessions but do not vote.

Blair promised to halve the number of people seeking asylum by September. Far-right organizations such as the British National Party used the issue to capture some seats in local government. In May, the government announced that the goal of halving the number of applicants was already being met, though critics claimed that the U.K. remained the "asylum capital of the world." Blair, in his speech to the Labour Party conference in September, insisted that the U.K. should remain open to refugees but conceded that immigration reforms were needed.

Cabinet changes. Tony Blair was forced to reshuffle his Cabinet throughout 2003. Robin Cook's resignation as leader of the House of

THE CABINET OF THE UNITED KINGDOM*

Tony Blair—prime minister; first lord of the treasury; minister for the civil service

John Prescott—deputy prime minister; first secretary of state

Gordon Brown—chancellor of the exchequer

Peter Hain—leader of the House of Commons, lord privy seal, and secretary of state for Wales

Lord Falconer of Thoroton—secretary of state for constitutional affairs

Jack Straw—secretary of state for foreign and Commonwealth affairs

David Blunkett—secretary of state for the home department

Margaret Beckett—secretary of state for environment, food, and rural affairs

Hilary Benn—secretary of state for international development

Andrew Smith—secretary of state for work and pensions

Alistair Darling—secretary of state for transport and Scotland

John Reid—secretary of state for health

Paul Murphy—secretary of state for Northern Ireland

Geoff Hoon—secretary of state for defense

Paul Boateng—chief secretary to the treasury

Baroness Amos—leader of the House of Lords, lord president of the council

Patricia Hewitt—secretary of state for trade and industry

Charles Clarke—secretary of state for education and skills

Tessa Jowell—secretary of state for culture, media, and sport

Hilary Armstrong—parliamentary secretary to the treasury, chief whip of the House of Commons

Ian McCartney—minister without portfolio, chairman of the Labour Party

*As of Dec. 2, 2003.

became the new secretary of state for constitutional affairs and interim lord chancellor until the post could be formally abolished. Falconer's office also took over Scottish and Welsh affairs. Since the introduction of *devolved government* (partial self-government), it was deemed unnecessary to have separate Scottish and Welsh secretaries. Blair was criticized for introducing major constitutional reforms without prior consultation with the House of Commons.

A further change took place in September following the death of Lord Williams, the Labour Party leader in the House of Lords. He was replaced by Baroness Amos, whose role as international development secretary was taken in October by Hilary Benn, who entered the Cabinet for the first time. Benn was the son of former Conservative Cabinet Minister Tony Benn, who had served in Labour governments during the 1960's and 1970's.

Commons over the Iraq War of 2003 led to his replacement in April by John Reid, whose post as chairman of the Labour Party was then taken by Ian McCartney. Blair favored Reid for his ability to deliver party support on policy issues. When International Development Secretary Clare Short resigned in May, she was replaced by Baroness Valerie Amos, a member of the House of Lords who became the first black woman, and the second black person, to be part of a British Cabinet.

Blair's planned Cabinet reshuffle in June became more far-reaching than expected when Health Secretary Alan Milburn, one of Blair's leading supporters, resigned, citing family reasons. Political analysts had expected Milburn to one day rise to a top government position. He was replaced by John Reid, while Welsh Secretary Peter Hain took on additional responsibilities as leader of the Commons.

Blair also decided, as part of the reshuffle, to abolish the ancient position of lord chancellor, a post that controlled the legal profession, selected judges, and presided as speaker of the House of Lords. The post, occupied at the time by Blair's mentor, Lord Irvine, was judged to be outdated. Blair announced that an independent judicial appointments commission would oversee the selection of judges. The law lords would become an independent supreme court, and the House of Lords would select its own speaker. Lord Falconer

Local elections. In May 2003, the Conservatives became the dominant party in local government. The Conservatives won 4,400 of the seats in local government contested in 2003. Labour suffered a loss of more than 800 seats nationwide and lost control of Birmingham, the second-largest city in the country. However, Labour remained dominant in elections for the Scottish Parliament and the Welsh Assembly.

Conservatives. The Conservatives, led by Iain Duncan Smith, failed to make much of an impression in 2003, despite their good showing in the local elections. Dissatisfaction with Duncan Smith, who had been elected by the party membership following the 2001 election defeat, continued to increase in 2003. In October, Duncan Smith faced allegations that he had improperly paid money to his wife for work she did not do as a secretary in his office.

Duncan Smith used that month's party conference to urge his critics to back down and unite under his leadership. However, on October 29 he failed to win a vote of confidence and resigned. Conservative Party leaders quickly chose as his successor former Cabinet Minister Michael Howard, who had served as home secretary in the last Conservative government. As there was no other candidate, Howard was appointed leader. Many Conservative MP's believed that Howard had the authority that Duncan Smith lacked to oppose Blair and put himself forward as a future prime minister.

Royal family. Prince William, son of Prince Charles and second in line to the throne, celebrated his twenty-first birthday on June 21. A costume party held in his honor at Windsor Castle was disrupted by comedian Aaron Barschak, who obtained access to the event dressed as terrorist Osama bin Laden. Barschak was apprehended by the police but the serious breach of security embarrassed Home Secretary David Blunkett.

The monarchy was plagued by scandal in the latter part of the year when Paul Burrell, former butler to Princess Diana (1961-1997), published a book that included the allegation that the princess believed she would be killed in a car accident so that Prince Charles could marry Camilla Parker-Bowles. In November 2003, the royal family was forced to deny allegations by a former valet about a sexual incident involving Prince Charles.

Sophie, Countess of Wessex and wife of Prince Edward, the Queen's youngest son, gave birth to a daughter in November. The child was named Lady Louise Alice Elizabeth Mary Mountbatten-Windsor. ■ Rohan McWilliam

See also **Europe; Iraq: A Special Report; Protestantism.**

United Kingdom, Prime Minister of.

In 2003, Tony Blair experienced his most difficult year in office since becoming prime minister in 1997. He led the United Kingdom into the Iraq War of 2003, as part of a United States-led coalition, a decision that divided the country and his own Labour Party. His plans to increase tuition fees for students and to introduce more private enterprise in the National Health Service were also unpopular. Blair's ratings in the polls declined during 2003, amid criticism that he spent too much time on international affairs and neglected domestic issues.

Blair confronted his critics in a speech to the Labour Party conference in September, insisting that he would not change his policies. Although the speech was well-received, party members rose to their feet in response to remarks by Chancellor of the Exchequer Gordon Brown, a former partner of Blair who had become Blair's rival. Brown appeared to chart a left-wing political course more in tune with the mood of the Labour Party than Blair's often centrist position.

Concerns about Blair's health surfaced on October 19, when he was briefly admitted to a hospital with chest pains and an abnormal heart rhythm. He was discharged after a few hours and advised to rest for a day. ■ Rohan McWilliam

See also **Iraq: A Special Report; United Kingdom.**

United Nations.
The war in Iraq dominated United Nations (UN) concerns during 2003, with the Security Council holding an unprecedented number of meetings. During the first such meeting, on January 9, chief arms inspector Hans Blix told the council that inspectors had yet to find evidence that Iraq has possession of—or the capability to make—*weapons of mass destruction* (chemical, biological, or nuclear weapons).

A preliminary report was formally presented on January 27. Both Blix and the director of the International Atomic Energy Agency, Muhammad El Baradei, agreed that the Iraqi government had failed to cooperate fully with inspections and showed no "genuine acceptance" of the 1991 UN resolution that Iraq divest itself of weapons of mass destruction. In meetings on February 5 and Feb. 14, 2003, U.S. Secretary of State Colin L. Powell presented satellite images and intelligence reports that he stated were evidence of Iraq's possession of weapons of mass destruction.

Nevertheless, council members were deeply divided on whether Iraq still possessed those weapons. The United States and the United Kingdom maintained that the banned weapons existed in Iraq and claimed that their presence justified the use of force to topple the regime of Iraqi President Saddam Hussein. Many UN members—particularly France, Germany, Russia, and China—opposed using force against Iraq.

In mid-March, the UN withdrew its arms inspectors and humanitarian workers. On March 19, the Security Council met in an unsuccessful effort to prevent a war. That same day (March 20 in Iraq), the U.S.-led coalition, which included the United Kingdom and Australia, launched an air strike against Iraq. UN Secretary-General Kofi Annan on March 25 questioned the legitimacy of the war and stressed the right of the Iraqi people to govern themselves.

By May 1, the government of Saddam Hussein had been *deposed* (removed from power), and U.S. President George W. Bush declared that major fighting in Iraq had ended. On May 22, the Security Council adopted a resolution lifting the economic sanctions imposed on Iraq in 1990. The resolution gave the UN a role in the political and economic reconstruction of Iraq, and Annan appointed Sergio Vieira de Mello, the UN High Commissioner for Human Rights, as the UN special envoy for the war-torn country.

On Aug. 19, 2003, a truck bomb exploded at the UN headquarters in Baghdad, killing Vieira de Mello and 21 other people. More than 100 other workers were injured. The attack was a major blow to the UN's humanitarian mission.

In September, the United States called upon the UN to authorize a multinational force under U.S. command to be deployed in Iraq and asked countries to contribute funds and troops to assist with reconstruction. On October 16, the Security Council approved a compromise resolution. The document pledged an expanded role for the UN in Iraq, provided a timetable for the transfer of power to the Iraqi people, and opened the possibility that other nations would send troops to relieve U.S. forces. Although they agreed to the resolution, France, Germany, and Russia maintained that they would not send troops to Iraq.

The International Criminal Court (ICC), established in 2002 to try war crimes, crimes against humanity, and genocide, moved toward becoming permanent in 2003 with an official inauguration on March 11 at The Hague, Netherlands. Member nations elected 18 judges and a prosecutor, Argentine lawyer Luis Moreno Ocampo, who was sworn in on June 16. One week later, Bruno Cathala was elected registrar, with the responsibility of forming a defense team.

By mid-2003, the ICC had been recognized by 92 countries, though the United States continued to oppose the court. United States representatives maintained that the country's troops and diplomats could be targeted in politically motivated indictments. In July, the United States obtained from the Security Council a renewed one-year exemption for U.S. diplomats and military personnel from prosecution under the ICC.

In August, the council split the responsibility of the ICC into two courts. One court was to continue investigating war crimes in the former Yugoslavia during the Balkan wars of the 1990's. The other court was to concentrate on Rwanda, the site of genocide by the Hutu majority of a Tutsi minority in 1994.

General Assembly. The 58th annual session of the UN General Assembly opened on Sept. 16, 2003. The new president of the Assembly, Saint Lucia's Foreign Minister Julian Robert Hunte, called on delegates to act more quickly, decisively, and cooperatively in responding to the serious problems of the world. In an opening address on September 23, Kofi Annan urged the Assembly to reform and expand the 15-nation Security Council, as its five permanent members currently decide virtually all of the world's conflicts. President Bush defended his decision to launch war against Iraq and called on the UN to support his efforts to make Iraq a democracy.

On September 29, the United States rejoined the UN Educational, Scientific and Cultural Organization after boycotting the group for 19 years to protest what it called anti-U.S. propaganda. First Lady Laura Bush raised the U.S. flag at the organization's headquarters in Paris. ■ J. Tuyet Nguyen

See also **Iraq: A Special Report; United States, Government of the.**

United States Secretary of State Colin Powell presents satellite images and intelligence reports to the United Nations Security Council on Feb. 5, 2003, that he characterizes as evidence of Iraq's weapons of mass destruction. Deeply divided over Iraq's weapons program, the Security Council did not pass a resolution authorizing a U.S.-led war in Iraq.

United States, Government of the.

A war in Iraq dominated much of the federal government's attention in 2003, but federal agencies also tackled issues ranging from the fight against terrorism to the struggling U.S. economy.

War. In January, U.S. President George W. Bush vowed to remove Iraqi President Saddam Hussein from power as part of an effort to bolster security in the Middle East as well as in the United States. In his State of the Union address on January 28, President Bush began building a case for war with Iraq by claiming that Iraq had attempted to purchase significant amounts of uranium from Niger. The president claimed that it was a move by Iraq to build nuclear armaments. In addition, President Bush claimed that Iraq had failed to account to the United Nations weapons inspectors for significant amounts of *weapons of mass destruction* (biological, chemical, or nuclear weapons).

On March 17, the president announced that unless Hussein relinquished the presidency and left Iraq within 48 hours, the United States would launch a military campaign to force him from power. When Hussein did not comply, President Bush on March 20 (March 19 in the United States) announced that U.S. forces had begun to move against Iraq.

On April 9, coalition forces took control of Baghdad, the Iraqi capital, and U.S. officials declared that Hussein and his government had been removed from power. On May 1, President Bush, aboard the U.S.S. *Abraham Lincoln,* declared that major combat operations in Iraq had ended.

On December 13, U.S. troops captured Hussein, ending a nearly nine-month search. Troops discovered the former dictator hiding in a hole on a farm near Tikrit. Military authorities described Hussein as "tired" and "resigned" and said he surrendered without putting up a fight. In a televised address on December 14, President Bush said that Hussein's capture meant that "a dark and painful era is over."

Homeland security. The U.S. Senate on January 22 voted 94 to 0 to confirm Tom Ridge as the secretary of the U.S. Department of Homeland Security. The new Cabinet position oversees domestic defense, specifically coordinating efforts to protect the United States from terrorist attack. The 170,000-employee department incorporated the Office of Homeland Security, a government agency consisting of all or parts of 22 federal agencies that had been created in response to the terrorist attacks on the United States on Sept. 11, 2001.

On Sept. 2, 2003, Ridge announced a reorganization of the department as part of an effort to improve national security. Among other things,

The Bureau of Engraving and Printing and the Federal Reserve System introduced a redesigned $20 bill in October. It included new colors and various other features designed to deter counterfeiters.

SELECTED AGENCIES AND BUREAUS OF THE U.S. GOVERNMENT*

Executive Office of the President
President, George W. Bush
 Vice President, Richard B. Cheney
 White House Chief of Staff, Andrew H. Card, Jr.
 Presidential Press Secretary, Scott McClellan
 Assistant to the President for Domestic Policy,
  Margaret Spellings
 Assistant to the President for National Security Affairs,
  Condoleezza Rice
 Director, Office of Science and Technology Policy,
  John H. Marburger III
 Council of Economic Advisers—Nicholas Gregory Mankin,
  Chairperson
 Office of Management and Budget—
  Josh B. Bolten, Director
 Office of National Drug Control Policy—
  John P. Walters, Director
 U.S. Trade Representative, Robert B. Zoellick

Department of Agriculture
Secretary of Agriculture, Ann M. Veneman

Department of Commerce
Secretary of Commerce, Donald L. Evans
 Bureau of Economic Analysis—J. Steven Landefeld, Director
 Bureau of the Census—Charles Louis Kincannon, Director

Department of Defense
Secretary of Defense, Donald H. Rumsfeld
 Secretary of the Air Force, James G. Roche
 Acting Secretary of the Army, Les Brownlee
 Secretary of the Navy, Gordon R. England
 Joint Chiefs of Staff—
  General Richard B. Myers, Chairperson
  General John P. Jumper, Chief of Staff, Air Force
  General Peter J. Schoomaker, Chief of Staff, Army
  Admiral Vern Clark, Chief of Naval Operations
  General Michael W. Hagee, Commandant, Marine Corps

Department of Education
Secretary of Education, Roderick R. Paige

Department of Energy
Secretary of Energy, Spencer Abraham

Department of Health and Human Services
Secretary of Health and Human Services, Tommy G. Thompson
 Office of Public Health and Science—Cristina Beato,
  Acting Assistant Secretary
 Centers for Disease Control and Prevention—
  Julie Louise Gerberding, Director
 Food and Drug Administration—Mark B. McClellan,
  Commissioner
 National Institutes of Health—Elias A. Zerhouni, Director
 Surgeon General of the United States, Richard H. Carmona

Department of Homeland Security
Secretary of Homeland Security, Thomas J. Ridge
 Bureau of Citizenship and Immigration Services—
  Eduardo Aguirri, Jr., Director
 U.S. Coast Guard—Admiral Thomas H. Collins, Commandant
 U.S. Secret Service—W. Ralph Basham, Director
 Federal Emergency Management Agency—Michael D. Brown,
  Undersecretary

Department of Housing and Urban Development
Secretary of Housing and Urban Development,
 Mel Martinez

Department of the Interior
Secretary of the Interior, Gale A. Norton

Department of Justice
Attorney General, John Ashcroft
 Bureau of Prisons—Harley G. Lappin, Director
 Drug Enforcement Administration—
  Karen P. Tandy, Administrator
 Federal Bureau of Investigation—
  Robert S. Mueller III, Director
 Solicitor General, Theodore B. Olson

Department of Labor
Secretary of Labor, Elaine L. Chao

Department of State
Secretary of State, Colin L. Powell
 U.S. Ambassador to the United Nations, John D. Negroponte

Department of Transportation
Secretary of Transportation, Norman Y. Mineta
 Federal Aviation Administration—
  Marion C. Blakey, Administrator

Department of the Treasury
Secretary of the Treasury, John W. Snow
 Internal Revenue Service—Mark W. Everson, Commissioner
 Treasurer of the United States, Vacant
 Office of Thrift Supervision—James E. Gilleran, Director

Department of Veterans Affairs
Secretary of Veterans Affairs, Anthony J. Principi

Supreme Court of the United States
Chief Justice of the United States, William H. Rehnquist
 Associate Justices—
  John Paul Stevens   David H. Souter
  Sandra Day O'Connor   Clarence Thomas
  Antonin Scalia   Ruth Bader Ginsburg
  Anthony M. Kennedy   Stephen G. Breyer

Congressional officials
President of the Senate pro tempore, Ted Stevens
 Senate Majority Leader, William H. Frist
 Senate Minority Leader, Tom Daschle
 Speaker of the House, J. Dennis Hastert
 House Majority Leader, Thomas DeLay
 House Minority Leader, Nancy Pelosi
 Congressional Budget Office—Douglas Holtz-Eakin, Director
 General Accounting Office—David M. Walker, Comptroller
  General of the United States
 Library of Congress—James H. Billington, Librarian of Congress

Independent agencies
Central Intelligence Agency—George J. Tenet, Director
Commission on Civil Rights—Mary Frances Berry, Chairperson
Commission of Fine Arts—David M. Childs, Chairperson
Consumer Product Safety Commission—
 Harold D. Stratton, Jr., Chairperson
Corporation for National and Community Service—
 Stephen Goldsmith, Chairperson
Environmental Protection Agency—Michael O. Leavitt, Administrator
Equal Employment Opportunity Commission—
 Cari M. Dominguez, Chairperson
Federal Communications Commission—Michael K. Powell, Chairperson
Federal Deposit Insurance Corporation—
 Donald E. Powell, Chairperson
Federal Election Commission—Ellen L. Weintraub, Chairperson
Federal Reserve System Board of Governors—
 Alan Greenspan, Chairperson
Federal Trade Commission—Timothy J. Muris, Chairperson
General Services Administration—Stephen A. Perry, Administrator
National Aeronautics and Space Administration—Sean O'Keefe,
 Administrator
National Endowment for the Arts—Dana Gioia, Chairperson
National Endowment for the Humanities—Bruce Cole, Chairperson
National Labor Relations Board—Robert J. Battista, Chairperson
National Railroad Passenger Corporation (Amtrak)—
 David Gunn, President & CEO
National Science Foundation—Rita R. Colwell, Director
National Transportation Safety Board—
 Ellen G. Engleman, Chairperson
Nuclear Regulatory Commission—Nils J. Diaz, Chairperson
Peace Corps—Gaddi H. Vasquez, Director
Securities and Exchange Commission—
 William H. Donaldson, Chairperson
Selective Service System—Lewis C. Brodsky, Acting Director
Small Business Administration—Hector V. Barreto, Jr., Administrator
Smithsonian Institution—Lawrence M. Small, Secretary
Social Security Administration—Jo Anne Barnhart, Commissioner
U.S. Postal Service—John E. Potter, Postmaster General

*As of Dec. 31, 2003.

FEDERAL SPENDING
United States budget for fiscal 2003*

Billions of dollars

National defense	404.2
International affairs	20.6
General science, space, technology	22.6
Energy	–0.8
Natural resources and environment	27.6
Agriculture	24.1
Commerce and housing credit	–1.6
Transportation	65.2
Community and regional development	17.7
Education, training, employment, and social services	82.1
Health	219.2
Social security	474.7
Medicare	249.4
Income security	336.1
Veterans' benefits and services	57.0
Administration of justice	36.3
General government	23.5
Interest	153.0
Undistributed offsetting receipts	–54.4
Total budget outlays	**2,156.5**

*Oct. 1, 2002, to Sept. 30, 2003.
  Source: U.S. Department of the Treasury.

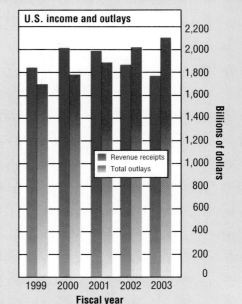

U.S. income and outlays

Revenue receipts
Total outlays

Billions of dollars

Fiscal year
Source: U.S. Department of the Treasury.

Ridge ordered the Federal Air Marshal Service, which had been a part of the Transportation Security Administration, moved to the department's U.S. Immigration and Customs Enforcement unit. According to Ridge, the move provided better coordination and information sharing between federal agencies.

On October 1, President Bush signed a $31-billion appropriations bill for the Homeland Security Department. Provisions of the appropriations package were targeted at securing the U.S. borders, while at the same time allowing for a free flow of legitimate international commerce.

USA PATRIOT Act debate. The USA PATRIOT Act, passed following the terrorist attacks on the United States in 2001, came under increasing criticism in 2003. Many civil rights organizations argued that the increased government powers the law provided to identify and arrest terrorism suspects had significantly eroded civil liberties.

The U.S. House of Representatives in July approved legislation to roll back some provisions of the act. The new legislation would prevent the federal government from funding secret government searches of terrorism suspects. Under the USA PATRIOT Act, the government was empowered to search the property of suspects secretly before notifying

them that a warrant had been issued.

By December, more than 150 municipalities across the United States also had approved resolutions critical of the act.

Growing criticism led the Bush administration to launch an unusual public relations campaign on the law's behalf. In August, Attorney General John Ashcroft began a multistate speaking swing in defense of the USA PATRIOT Act. Ashcroft argued that enhanced powers were essential to prevent future terrorist attacks and had been instrumental in the arrests of a number of terrorism suspects.

In addition to Ashcroft's campaign-style speaking tour, the Justice Department in August launched a Web site—www.lifeandliberty.gov—that provides information on key elements of the law.

Columbia disaster. The space shuttle Columbia disintegrated over Texas and Louisiana prior to its scheduled landing on February 1. All seven astronauts aboard died.

After the disaster, the National Aeronautics and Space Administration (NASA) halted shuttle flights and appointed an independent commission to investigate the accident. Investigators collected thousands of pieces of shuttle debris that had fallen to Earth after the accident. They also studied communications, sensor readings, video recordings, and other records from the mission. The team of investigators also interviewed NASA employees.

In August, the commission concluded that a piece of insulating foam that broke loose on takeoff and struck and punctured a wing had caused the accident. During reentry into Earth's atmosphere, superheated gases entered the hole and caused the shuttle to disintegrate. Investigators also cited a lax safety culture at NASA and other management problems as contributing factors.

Taxation. President Bush on May 28 signed legislation that accelerated some earlier enacted tax cuts. Congress voted to approve the legislation on May 23. Provisions in the law included an increase in the tax credit from $600 to $1,000 per child in 2003 and 2004; an acceleration of provisions from earlier tax law intended to eliminate the "marriage penalty," anomalies in the tax structure that resulted in married couples paying higher taxes than single taxpayers; and a tax reduction on dividends and *capital gains* (income from the sale of capital assets, which include stocks, bonds, real estate, and partnerships). The law also authorized the Internal Revenue Service (IRS) to make advance refund payments to an estimated 25 million families in the United States earning between $27,000 and $110,000 annually. During the summer, the IRS mailed out refund checks valued at $400 per child to these families, providing them the difference between the old child tax credit and the new credit.

Economic issues. The Bush administration reported on Oct. 20, 2003, that the federal deficit had increased to $374.2 billion, more than double the $158-billion deficit recorded in 2002. However, the 2003 deficit was less than the $455 billion deficit the Bush administration had predicted in July, and officials cited the lower deficit as evidence that the administration's economic policies were helping the economic recovery.

Although some political experts took aim at the assertions, the Bureau of Economic Analysis, a division of the U.S. Department of Commerce, reported in November that the U.S. gross domestic product (GDP) had increased 8.2 percent between July and September 2003. GDP is the value of all goods and services produced in a country during a given year. The increase dwarfed a 3.3-percent growth in GDP for the economic period ending in June.

New color of money. The U.S. Department of the Treasury's Bureau of Engraving and Printing and the Federal Reserve System introduced a redesigned $20 bill in October. The bill included a larger portrait of President Andrew Jackson and a faded bald eagle on the front. For the first time since 1905, the new bill featured colors other

than black and green. A peach color, which fades into the green, was added to the design. "TWENTY USA" is also printed in blue, and small 20's in faded yellow were added to the background on the back of the bill. Treasury department officials planned to redesign U.S. currency every 7 to 10 years to keep up with technological advances in counterfeiting.

Declining birth rates. Tommy Thompson, secretary of the U.S. Department of Health and Human Services, reported in June 2003 that the U.S. birth rate fell to a record low. Thompson reported that the birth rate declined to 13.9 per 1,000 persons in 2002, compared with 14.1 per 1,000 persons in 2001. The birth rate has been in decline since the early 1990's.

EPA administrator. The Senate on Oct. 28, 2003, confirmed Utah Governor Michael O. Leavitt as administrator of the Environmental Protection Agency (EPA). The EPA protects the U.S. environment from pollution. President Bush nominated Leavitt for the post in August. Leavitt replaced Christine Todd Whitman, who resigned in June. Some environmentalists criticized Leavitt's nomination and claimed that he had failed to support conservation initiatives while governor of Utah.

Racial profiling. The U.S. Department of Justice issued guidelines in June banning the use of racial profiling by federal law enforcement officers. Racial profiling uses race as the main factor in deciding whether to question or arrest a person. The ban meant that federal law enforcement officials cannot rely on generalized racial or ethnic stereotypes when investigating crimes.

Computer access in public schools had increased from 1994 to 2002, according to a study released in October 2003 by the U.S. Department of Education. The study showed that in 2003, 99 percent of all public schools in the United States had access to the Internet, compared with 35 percent of public schools in 1994. The study also revealed that minority and low-income students lack computer access outside of school.

Obesity. The U.S. Department of the Interior launched a program in October 2003 to promote the use of public lands for recreational activities. The initiative was aimed at reducing obesity among U.S. residents. Health care experts estimated that 65 percent of U.S. residents were overweight or obese in 2003.

■ Geoffrey A. Campbell

See also **Armed forces; Cabinet, U.S.; Civil rights; Congress of the United States; Courts; Economics; Immigration; Iraq: A Special Report; Labor and employment; People in the news** (Bill Frist, John Snow, Paul Wolfowitz); **Space exploration; State government; Taxation; United States, President of the.**

Moments in TIME

By Tim Frystak

LOOKING BACK THROUGH MORE THAN 200 YEARS OF U.S. HISTORY.

1783 TREATY OF PARIS SIGNED
220 YEARS AGO

Representatives from the United States and Great Britain sign the Treaty of Paris on September 3, officially ending the Revolutionary War in America (1775-1783). With the treaty, the British formally recognized the existence of the United States by ceding to the new nation control of all of North America from the Atlantic Ocean to the Mississippi River between Canada and Florida.

1793 ELI WHITNEY INVENTS COTTON GIN
210 YEARS AGO

Eli Whitney completes the first cotton gin, providing a fast and economical way to separate seeds from cotton fibers. The invention immediately made growing cotton enormously profitable and led to the widespread expansion of slavery in the United States. Before the bonanza known as "king cotton," the "peculiar institution" of slavery had become uneconomical.

1793 CAPITOL CORNERSTONE LAID
210 YEARS AGO

President George Washington lays the cornerstone for the U.S. Capitol in what would become the city of Washington, D.C.

1803 LOUISIANA PURCHASE
200 YEARS AGO

President Thomas Jefferson purchases 827,987 square miles (2,144,476 square kilometers) of land from France for about $15 million, doubling the area of the United States. The Louisiana Purchase covered a tract of land stretching from the Gulf of Mexico to the Canadian border, between the Mississippi River and the Rocky Mountains. Part or all of 15 states were eventually formed out of the region.

1803 LEWIS AND CLARK EXPEDITION BEGINS
200 YEARS AGO

United States Army officers Meriwether Lewis and William Clark on December 13 set up winter camp near St. Louis, Missouri, in preparation for an expedition that would cover 8,000 miles (12,800 kilometers) up the Missouri River, across the Rocky Mountains, down the Columbia and other rivers to the Pacific coast, and back again. The explorers returned with maps of their route and surrounding regions; descriptions of plant, animal, and mineral resources; and information about American Indians. This made possible the pioneer movement, resulting in the settling of the West. The expedition also enabled the United States to claim the Oregon region, which included what would become the states of Oregon, Washington, and Idaho.

1803 MARBURY V. MADISON
200 YEARS AGO

The Supreme Court of the United States declares a federal law unconstitutional. In *Marbury v. Madison,* the court ruled that it was the duty of the judicial branch of the federal government to determine what the law is. The decision established the power of judicial review—the court's authority to declare laws unconstitutional—making the judiciary the equal of the executive and legislative branches of the U.S. government.

1823 A VISIT FROM ST. NICK
180 YEARS AGO

The *Troy* [New York] *Sentinel* publishes "A Visit from St. Nicholas," the poem commonly called "'Twas the Night Before Christmas," on December 23. According to tradition, the author, Clement Clarke Moore, wrote it as a gift for his children. "A Visit from St. Nicholas" formed the basis for the American tradition of Santa Claus.

1853 STEINWAY'S GRAND PIANO
150 YEARS AGO

German-born piano maker Henry Engelhard Steinway founds Steinway & Sons in New York City. In 1855, Steinway introduced a piano with a cast-iron frame that allowed its strings to be stretched to new levels of tension, greatly improving the sound of the instrument. The arrangement quickly became the standard design for all pianos.

The author:
Tim Frystak is a senior editor on *The Year Book.*

1853 CENTRAL PARK
150 YEARS AGO

The state legislature of New York authorizes New York City to acquire 700 acres (283 hectares) in the center of Manhattan for a "central park." Frederick Law Olmsted and Calvert Vaux designed what would be the first landscaped public space in the United States. The park's success launched a movement that produced similar public spaces in cities across the country.

1853 THE FIRST POTATO CHIP
150 YEARS AGO

The potato chip makes its first appearance in the United States at a restaurant in Saratoga Springs, New York. The paper-thin slices of potatoes, deep fried and salted, were an instant hit.

1863 EMANCIPATION PROCLAMATION
140 YEARS AGO

United States President Abraham Lincoln on January 1 signs the Emancipation Proclamation, a historic document that led to the end of slavery in the United States. The proclamation declared freedom for slaves in all areas of the Confederacy that were still in rebellion against the Union. The Emancipation Proclamation prompted as many as 500,000 slaves to flee the South during the war to freedom behind Northern lines. Many of them joined the Union Army or worked for the armed forces as laborers, strengthening the North's war effort.

1863 GETTYSBURG ADDRESS
140 YEARS AGO

On November 19, President Abraham Lincoln delivers what comes to be known as the Gettysburg Address at the dedication of a national cemetery at the site of the Battle of Gettysburg in Pennsylvania. The address reshaped the country during the Civil War (1861-1865) by defining the United States as a nation dedicated to the principle of equality and freedom.

1883 METROPOLITAN OPERA HOUSE OPENS
120 YEARS AGO

New York City's Metropolitan Opera Company debuts at the city's new Metropolitan Opera House, on Broadway between 39th and 40th streets, with a performance of Gounod's *Faust*.

1883 BROOKLYN BRIDGE
120 YEARS AGO

Work crews complete the Brooklyn Bridge after a 14-year building campaign. The $15-million suspension bridge was at the time the longest bridge in the world. Spanning 1,595 feet (486 meters) across the East River, it connected Manhattan Island, New York City, to the then independent city of Brooklyn.

1883 BUFFALO BILL CODY
120 YEARS AGO

Buffalo Bill Cody, a frontiersman and marksman of the American West, opens "Buffalo Bill's Wild West," a traveling show touring the United States and Europe. The show included a mock battle with Indians and a demonstration of Cody's shooting skills.

1893 COLUMBIAN EXPOSITION
110 YEARS AGO

The World's Columbian Exposition opens in Chicago to celebrate the 400th anniversary of Columbus's discovery of America. The fair featured the first Ferris Wheel. The fair's carefully composed grounds and sparkling white structures sparked a revival of classical architecture that resulted in wide spacious parks and graceful public buildings in U.S. cities.

1903 EARLY AUTOMOBILES
100 YEARS AGO

Henry Ford founds the Ford Motor Company and introduces the Model A. Ford's subsequent introduction of the assembly line drove down unit cost through mass production. Mass production made the automobile affordable for the middle class, changing American life. The Buick Motor Company also manufactured the first Buick in 1903.

1903 THE FIRST FLIGHT
100 YEARS AGO

Orville and Wilbur Wright successfully test the first power-driven airplane at Kitty Hawk, North Carolina, on December 17. With Orville Wright at the controls, the plane flew 120 feet (37 meters) and was in the air for 12 seconds. The feat fulfilled mankind's greatest dream—to fly like a bird—and revolutionized human perception of space and time.

1903 CRAYOLA CRAYONS DEBUT
100 YEARS AGO

Binney & Smith Company of New York City introduces the first Crayola crayons. The five-cent box held eight wax crayons in the colors black, brown, blue, red, purple, orange, yellow, and green.

1903 HARLEY-DAVIDSON ROARS
100 YEARS AGO

Bill Harley and Arthur Davidson of Milwaukee, Wisconsin, attach an engine to a modified bicycle to produce the first motorcycle—the Harley-Davidson.

1903 THE WORLD SERIES
100 YEARS AGO

The Boston Pilgrims defeat the Pittsburgh Pirates 5 games to 3 in baseball's first World Series between American League and National League teams.

1903 BIRTH OF THE MOVIE
100 YEARS AGO

Pioneering film director Edwin S. Porter makes *The Great Train Robbery*, the first film to use modern film techniques to tell a story. Porter utilized many of the techniques that became standard—close-ups, panoramic shots, and editing many scenes into a continuous narrative. The 11-minute movie describing a train robbery and the pursuit and capture of the robbers was also the first "Western."

1923 YANKEE STADIUM OPENS
80 YEARS AGO

Yankee Stadium, located in the Bronx, New York City, opens for its inaugural game on April 18. Home of Major League Baseball's New York Yankees, the stadium became known as "the House That Ruth Built" in honor of the legendary hitter Babe Ruth.

1933 FDR LAUNCHES NEW DEAL
70 YEARS AGO

Franklin Delano Roosevelt takes the oath of office as president of the United States on March 4. During the next 100 days, the president proposed and Congress passed an economic reform program—collectively known as the New Deal—designed to restore the confidence of the American people in the face of the Great Depression. During the first of an unprecedented four terms in office, President Roosevelt and Congress created the Securities and Exchange Commission, the Tennessee Valley Authority, and Social Security, repealed prohibition, and greatly strengthened the right of workers to bargain collectively.

1943 ITALY SURRENDERS
60 YEARS AGO

Allied forces, led by the United States, invade the mainland of Italy during World War II (1939-1945), forcing Benito Mussolini's Fascist government to surrender.

1953 THE FIRST CORVETTE
50 YEARS AGO

A sleek new sports car, the Corvette, rolls off the Chevrolet assembly line on June 30 in Flint, Michigan. More than 1.2 million Corvettes were sold in the next 50 years.

1953 KOREAN WAR ENDS
50 YEARS AGO

The Korean War (1950-1953) ends when representatives from the United Nations (UN) and North Korea sign an armistice agreement. The United States provided about 90 percent of the troops, military equipment, and supplies that were sent to South Korea during the conflict.

1963 "I HAVE A DREAM"
40 YEARS AGO

More than 200,000 people descend on Washington, D.C., on August 28 and gather at the Lincoln Memorial as part of a civil rights rally. Civil rights leader Martin Luther King, Jr., in an address called "I Have a Dream," defined the moral basis of the civil rights movement in the second half of the 20th century.

1963 JFK ASSASSINATED
40 YEARS AGO

John F. Kennedy, the 35th president of the United States, is assassinated in Dallas on November 22, sending shock waves around the world. Vice President Lyndon B. Johnson was sworn in as president aboard Air Force One before he, his wife, Lady Bird Johnson, and former First Lady Jacqueline Kennedy accompanied the former president's remains back to Washington, D.C.

1963 MR. ZIP DEBUTS
40 YEARS AGO

The United States Postal Service introduces Mr. Zip, a wide-eyed caricature of a letter carrier designed to promote the use of the new Zone Improvement Plan (ZIP) Code system.

1973 NASA LAUNCHES SKYLAB
30 YEARS AGO

NASA launches Skylab, the first U.S. space station, into orbit on May 14. Skylab was actually assembled from the empty third stage of a Saturn 5 rocket, with an attached air lock module, docking port, and solar telescope.

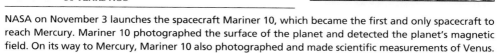

1973 MARINER 10 REACHES MERCURY
30 YEARS AGO

NASA on November 3 launches the spacecraft Mariner 10, which became the first and only spacecraft to reach Mercury. Mariner 10 photographed the surface of the planet and detected the planet's magnetic field. On its way to Mercury, Mariner 10 also photographed and made scientific measurements of Venus.

1973 SPIRO T. AGNEW RESIGNS
30 YEARS AGO

Vice President Spiro T. Agnew resigns while under criminal investigation by federal prosecutors. The first resignation of a U.S. vice president came in the middle of Watergate, the biggest political scandal in U.S. history. The term Watergate covered a variety of illegal activities designed to help President Richard M. Nixon win reelection in 1972. President Nixon resigned in July 1974 after the House Judiciary Committee recommended that he be impeached.

1983 RIDE, SALLY RIDE
20 YEARS AGO

National Aeronautics and Space Administration (NASA) astronaut Sally K. Ride, traveling aboard a six-day flight on the space shuttle Challenger, becomes the first American woman in space in June. In August, Astronaut Guion S. Bluford becomes the first African American in space when he takes part in a six-day flight aboard Challenger.

1993 WORLD TRADE CENTER BOMBED
10 YEARS AGO

A powerful car bomb explodes in an underground parking garage at the World Trade Center in New York City on February 26, killing 6 people and leaving more than 1,000 people injured. Law enforcement officials concluded that Islamic extremists were responsible.

United States President George W. Bush, wearing a Navy flight suit, steps aboard the U.S.S. *Abraham Lincoln* on May 1, 2003, from a Navy fighter jet. From the deck of the aircraft carrier, the president announced that major combat operations in the war in Iraq had ended.

ance in Iraq through the end of 2003, especially from guerrilla fighters—insurgents the U.S. military believed were connected to various terrorist organizations.

President Bush's major rationale for the war was Iraq's weapons of mass destruction (WMD) program, that is, biological, chemical, and nuclear weapons. In his State of the Union address on January 28, President Bush announced that British intelligence agents had uncovered evidence that Iraq had attempted to purchase uranium from Niger, presumably to make atomic weapons. President Bush also warned that Iraq had not accounted for thousands of gallons of biological and chemical weapons. However, weapons inspectors failed, both before and after the war, to uncover any documentation or evidence of WMD's.

Taxation. The president signed legislation in May to provide $330 billion in tax cuts. The legislation authorized the Internal Revenue Service to make advance refund payments to 25 million families in the United States earning between $27,000 and $110,000 annually.

Medicare. In December, President Bush signed Medicare legislation that added new prescription drug benefits for millions of senior U.S. citizens. The president had pushed strongly for its passage.

Clean air. Officials from 12 states and more than 20 cities filed lawsuits in October to block changes authorized by the Bush administration in 2002. The new rules, which began to go into effect in December 2003, relaxed requirements for power plants or oil refineries to install pollution controls when the facilities were modernized.

Iraq visit. President Bush made a surprise visit to Baghdad to spend Thanksgiving with U.S. troops in Iraq. It was the first visit to Iraq by a U.S. president.   ■ Geoffrey A. Campbell

See also **Armed forces; Congress of the United States; Courts; Environmental pollution; Health care issues; Iraq: A Special Report; Taxation; United States, Government of the.**

Uruguay. See Latin America.

Utah. See State government.

United States, President of the.

President George W. Bush announced in March 2003 that unless Saddam Hussein relinquished the Iraqi presidency and left Iraq, the United States would launch a military campaign to force him from power. On March 20 (March 19 in the United States), a U.S.-led coalition went to war against Iraq. In April, U.S.-led forces seized control of Baghdad, Iraq's capital, causing Hussein's government to fall.

On May 1, President Bush, aboard the U.S.S. *Abraham Lincoln,* declared that major combat operations in Iraq had ended, though the president stopped short of declaring total victory. Despite the president's declaration, coalition forces continued to face heavy pockets of resist-

Uzbekistan. The European Bank for Reconstruction and Development (EBRD) held its annual meeting in May 2003 in the Uzbek capital, Tashkent. The meeting was the EBRD's first major meeting in central Asia, but it was dominated by controversy over Uzbekistan's human rights record. After a United Nations (UN) report had documented "systematic torture" in Uzbekistan, Uzbek President Islam Karimov was urged to use his speech at the conference to publicly denounce torture. Instead, Karimov avoided any mention of torture, prompting criticism from representatives of other countries present at the meeting.

On October 15, the Uzbek currency, the som, became fully convertible into other currencies. Up to that point, the government had set multiple currency exchange rates for the som, which had allowed it to restrict imports in some sectors while promoting exports in others. President Karimov had failed to come through on his promise in 2000 to make the som convertible, despite repeated pressure from the International Monetary Fund, a UN affiliate. Economists believed that the shift to convertibility would promote direct foreign investment, since profits would be converted from soms to dollars or euros at a rate set by the market, not by the government.　■ Steven L. Solnick

See also **Asia.**

Vanuatu. See **Pacific Islands.**

Venezuela. A politically polarized Venezuela began 2003 in the middle of a crippling national strike that severely damaged the economy. Over 30,000 workers at Petroleos de Venezuela, S.A., the state-controlled oil company, had walked off the job in December 2002. During the two-month strike, Venezuela, ordinarily the world's fifth-largest oil exporter and a major supplier to the United States, exported less than 300,000 barrels a day, compared with 3 million barrels daily under normal circumstances.

The strike contributed to Venezuela's growing poverty rate. By late April 2003, the unemployment rate had climbed to nearly 20 percent and 68 percent of Venezuelans were living below the poverty line. Despite these developments, poor Venezuelans remained the most ardent supporters of Venezuela's President Hugo Chavez Frias.

Faced with continuing political unrest, the Chavez government mounted showy, well-publicized programs, including government-subsidized food markets and mobile clinics, to serve some of the poorest Venezuelans.

The strike ended because of the mediation of a host of foreign diplomats, including former U.S. President Jimmy Carter. At Carter's suggestion, Chavez and his opponents, which included a broad spectrum of business and labor union leaders, agreed to negotiate differences in a series of discussions brokered by the Organization of American States (OAS). The OAS, a regional body comprising 35 nations of the Americas, often helps settle disputes both within and between member nations.

Recall referendum. One of the leaders of the strike, Carlos Ortega, head of the Confederation of Venezuelan Workers, was granted political asylum in Costa Rica in March, following his February arrest on charges of inciting a rebellion. Another leader, Carlos Fernandez, president of Venezuela's largest business group, was released for lack of evidence by an appeals court in March. These actions temporarily eased tensions between Chavez and his political foes.

Chavez signed an accord in May that affirmed the right of his opponents to hold a recall referendum after August, the midway point in his term. Electoral authorities, however, rejected a petition with over 3 million signatures that called for the referendum. The delay of the referendum gave Chavez time to mount a $50-million adult-literacy campaign and a $100-million program to improve health facilities serving Venezuela's impoverished majority.　■ Nathan A. Haverstock

See also **Latin America.**

Vermont. See **State government.**

Vice President of the United States. See **United States, Government of the.**

Vietnam. An organized crime figure was sentenced to death in 2003 following a trial that uncovered massive corruption within Vietnam's ruling Communist Party. Truong Van Cam, who was charged with murder, bribery, and five other crimes, was tried in February in Ho Chi Minh City along with 154 other people.

The trial exposed an extensive criminal network, which reached to the upper echelons of the Communist Party. Among the defendants were 2 former members of the Communist Party's powerful Central Committee, 13 senior police officers, and 3 former prosecutors. Cam was arrested in 2001 after an investigation uncovered evidence that he had bribed government officials to allow him to continue his criminal activities.

Communist Party leaders cited the trial as evidence that the government was making efforts to eliminate corruption. Foreign observers doubted that the trial would lead to reforms in Vietnam, which political experts considered to have a highly corrupt government.

The government continued its crackdown on public dissent in 2003. In June, a physician was sentenced to 13 years in prison for posting an article titled "What is Democracy?" on the Internet. In August, the Supreme Court reduced the sentence to 5 years.　■ Henry S. Bradsher

See also **Asia.**

Washington, D.C.

Washington, D.C. The largest building in Washington, D.C., the Washington Convention Center, opened on March 29, 2003, with a formal gala in the ballroom, with 3,000 people in attendance. The building consists of 2.3 million square feet (2.1 million square meters) of floor space and covers most of six city blocks. Two million tons (1.8 million metric tons) of earth were excavated in order to build the glass and limestone structure. The project cost about $834 million.

On April 8, Federal Office Systems Expo 2003, a technology trade show for government employees, became the first convention to occupy the center. Convention center officials already had booked 110 trade shows and meetings for 2003.

The new center replaced a 1983 convention center that had about one-third the floor space of the new center and could no longer compete for convention business against new, large convention centers in other cities. The older convention center was scheduled to be torn down.

Officials at the Convention Center Authority said the new center would create 17,000 jobs and attract about 3 million visitors a year. The officials estimated that convention business would pump $1.5 billion annually into the region's economy.

School voucher plan tabled. On Sept. 30, 2003, Republicans in the United States Senate withdrew a bill that would have established the first federal school voucher program in the nation. The plan would have given children from low-income families money to attend private or church-related schools in Washington, D.C. Legis-

lators tabled the plan because they lacked the 60 votes necessary to pass the legislation over a threatened Democratic filibuster.

Congress oversees local government in the District of Columbia, including the district's school system. Under the voucher plan, 1,700 children from low-income families in the District of Columbia would have received up to $7,500 each to enroll in private schools. The voucher idea was backed by Washington, D.C., Mayor Anthony A. Williams and the board of education president Peggy Cooper Cafritz. Senate Democrats opposing the bill said that helping students opt out of public schools would weaken the public school system.

Flag revision rejected. In November, a majority of members of the District of Columbia Council rejected a redesigned district flag, even though the council in July had commissioned a new design. The revised flag was similar to the existing official flag, but the new design added the letters "DC" in red and the slogan "No Taxation Without Representation" in white.

Supporters of the new design described it as a "battle flag" to embody the movement for full

President George W. Bush speaks at a rededication ceremony in the rotunda of the National Archives in Washington, D.C., on Sept. 17, 2003. The event marked the reopening of the space to the public following a two-year, $100-million renovation. The project included archival restoration of the Constitution of the United States.

voting rights in the District of Columbia. Although district residents pay federal taxes and vote in presidential elections, they elect no voting representatives to Congress, which oversees the district's government. Many D.C. residents and citizens' groups such as D.C. Vote have long lobbied for full voting rights in the nation's capital.

Council opponents claimed that the new design turned a dignified symbol of the district into an advertising ploy. Some council members cited opinions of prominent vexillologists—experts in flag design—who sharply criticized the design for the proposed new flag.

Pennsylvania Avenue plan. First Lady Laura Bush unveiled a renovation plan for Pennsylvania Avenue at a White House ceremony on Sept. 8, 2003. The plan, developed by Cambridge, Massachusetts, architect Michael Van Valkenburgh and approved by the National Capital Planning Commission, would revitalize the part of the avenue between the White House and Lafayette Square, which face each other. That section was closed to general traffic in 1995 for security reasons. The plan detailed a parklike setting with elm trees and park benches and unobtrusive security booths. ■ Howard S. Shapiro

See also **Cities; Education: A Special Report.**

Washington. See **State government.**

Water. See **Environmental pollution.**

Weather. The year 2003 began with heavy snow that blanketed parts of the interior northeastern United States on January 3 and 4. In Albany, New York, the storm dumped 20.8 inches (44 centimeters) of snow, Albany's second greatest January snowstorm since 1885.

Winter's record chills and heat. Several episodes of record chill gripped the East in 2003. At Binghamton, New York, the temperature fell below 0 °F (-18 °C) for the first time in nearly three years on January 17. In Pittsburgh, Pennsylvania, the temperature remained at or below 32 °F (0 °C) from January 11 to 29, the city's longest stretch of subfreezing temperatures since 1989. A rare snowstorm deposited more than 12 inches (30 centimeters) of snow on the sands of North Carolina's Outer Banks on Jan. 23, 2003.

The West experienced unprecedented warmth in January, while the Southwest had the warmest January on record. Records were set in over 20 cities on January 31, including Los Angeles, where the temperature reached 91 °F (33 °C). A high of 97 °F (36 °C) at Riverside, California, that day was just a degree shy of the hottest January temperature ever recorded in the United States.

The most significant winter storm along the Northeast Seaboard since the blizzard of January 1996 took place over the long President's Day weekend, from Feb. 15 to 17, 2003. The storm dumped 1 to 3 feet (0.3 to 1 meter) of snow from the upper Ohio Valley to southern New England, paralyzing major cities from Washington, D.C., to Boston. Both Baltimore and Boston experienced their greatest single-storm snowfall totals on record, with 28.2 and 27.5 inches (72 and 70 centimeters) of snow, respectively.

Wet conditions prevailed across much of the nation in February. Charleston, West Virginia, recorded its wettest February since 1887. More snow fell in February 2003 than in any February on record at Baltimore; Boston; Indianapolis; Pittsburgh, Pennsylvania; and Tulsa, Oklahoma.

Spring roars in. Record chill gripped areas from the northern plains to the Northeast in early March. On March 3, the temperature fell to -30 °F (-35 °C) at Marquette, Michigan, the city's coldest March temperature on record. At the same time, unprecedented warmth covered south Florida. Miami experienced its warmest March on record, with 15 daily record high temperatures.

A crippling snowstorm struck eastern Colorado from March 17 to 19. Denver received 32 inches (81 centimeters) of snow, its largest March snowstorm on record. Over 6 feet (2 meters) of snow covered the foothills west of the city.

In the Middle East, a severe sandstorm swept through Iraq on March 25 and 26, hampering military operations during the U.S.-led war. Wind gusts near 50 miles (80 kilometers) per hour and large hail damaged U.S. military aircraft.

Record highs and tornadoes. Record warmth spread across the northern states in mid-April, with over 100 record high temperatures set from April 13 to 18. A high of 90 °F (32 °C) in Bismarck, North Dakota, on April 13 marked the city's earliest 90 °F (32 °C) reading on record.

The deadliest outbreak of severe weather since May 1999 spawned 84 tornadoes across eight states on May 4 and 5, 2003. The twisters killed 38 people in Kansas, Missouri, and Tennessee. Days later, another outbreak of lethal tornadoes struck on May 8 and 9, prompting officials to declare Oklahoma a federal disaster area. A total of 412 tornadoes were counted from May 1 to 10, marking the most prolific tornado outbreak since record keeping began in 1950.

Heat began to build in the Western states during mid-May. An exceptional spring heat wave peaked from May 28 to 30. Boise, Idaho (99 °F, 38 °C); Las Vegas, Nevada (109 °F, 43 °C); and Salt Lake City, Utah (99 °F, 38 °C) all measured all-time high May temperatures.

Summer storms. Severe thunderstorms in the Midwest between June 22 and 28, 2003, resulted in more than 75 tornadoes and nearly 500 reports of large hail. The largest hailstone ever measured in the United States—7 inches (17.8 centimeters) in diameter—crashed to Earth

The Heat Wave in Europe in 2003

Children cool off in the fountain of the Victoria Monument at Buckingham Palace in London during a record-breaking August heat wave. Temperatures at Gravesend-Broadness, near London, hit 100.6 °F (38.1 °C) on August 10, the first 100 °F (37.8 °C) reading in the United Kingdom since records have been kept.

A firefighter near the town of Chiva in eastern Spain prepares to flee a forest fire burning out of control on August 29. Extreme heat across Europe contributed to devastating fires in Spain and Portugal that severely affected those countries' economies.

Rows of patients at a hospital in Paris are treated for heat-related conditions on August 13. At least 15,000 people, mostly the elderly, died in France during the heat wave, as well as about 5,000 people in other countries of Europe.

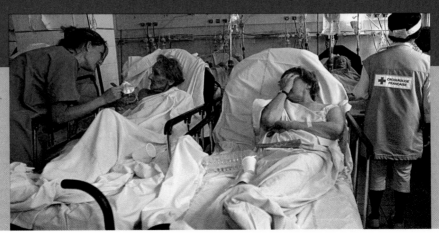

in Aurora, Nebraska, on June 22. The previous record was a 5.7-inch (14.5-centimeter) hailstone that fell in Coffeyville, Kansas, in 1970.

Tropical Storm Bill made landfall near Morgan City, Louisiana, on June 30, bringing more than 4 inches (10 centimeters) of rain to many areas near the central Gulf Coast. June 2003 was the coolest and second wettest across the Southeast since record keeping began in 1895.

Tropical Storm Claudette sprang to life in the Caribbean on July 8, 2003, then inundated the Yucatan peninsula on July 11. Claudette intensified, becoming the first hurricane of the Atlantic season. By the time it reached Port O'Connor, Texas, on July 15, the storm's windspeed had increased to 90 miles (145 kilometers) per hour.

Europe's heat wave. A severe heat wave in western Europe peaked in the first half of August. Temperatures at Gravesend-Broadness in southern England hit 100.6 °F (38.1 °C) on August 10, the first 100 °F (37.8 °C) reading on record in the United Kingdom. Throughout Europe, the heat proved deadly. In France, temperatures near or above 100 °F and a lack of air conditioning were cited by the health ministry as contributing to nearly 15,000 heat-related deaths during the summer of 2003. At least 5,000 more people died in other parts of Europe.

Heat and wildfires. A pattern of persistent heat in the western United States continued in much of July and August. Phoenix had its hottest month on record with an average temperature of

97.4 °F (36.3 °C). August was also the hottest on record in Idaho, Nevada, and Wyoming.

California experienced its hottest and seventh driest October of record. The hot, dry weather, combined with gusty Santa Ana winds, promoted a severe outbreak of wildfires across southern California in late October. The fires burned across more than 750,000 acres (306,000 hectares), including the Cedar fire in San Diego county, which became the largest single fire to burn in California since 1932. The fires killed 20 people. Nationally, 3.8 million acres (1.5 million hectares) of land had burned by November 14, close to the 10-year average.

Autumn storms. Two major hurricanes swept in from the Atlantic Ocean in September. Hurricane Fabian moved close to Bermuda on September 5 with sustained winds of 115 miles (185 kilometers) per hour. The storm, the strongest to hit the island since 1963, caused four deaths and damaged nearly 25 percent of the island's hotels and guest houses.

Hurricane Isabel became a category 5 storm, the first in the region since 1998, as it passed north of the Lesser Antilles on Sept. 7, 2003. (A category 5 storm has winds greater than 155 miles [249 kilometers] per hour.) On September 18, the storm made landfall on the Outer Banks of North Carolina with winds of 100 miles (161 kilometers) per hour. The storm brought extensive flooding to the Chesapeake Bay area as it moved inland. Hurricane Isabel was blamed for some 40 deaths, while nearly 6 million people lost power. Insurance industry officials estimated property losses at about $1 billion.

The United States experienced unusual storminess between November 12 and 14. Wind gusts of 50 to 75 miles (80 to 121 kilometers) per hour downed trees and power lines from the Midwest to the Northeast. More than 1.4 million customers lost electric power. Boat traffic was halted by 16-foot (4.8-meter) waves on lakes Erie and Ontario. An unrelated storm flooded parts of Los Angeles with over 5 inches (12.7 centimeters) of rain in two hours. Five inches (12.7 centimeters) of hail accumulated in the Watts district.

Early snow. A snowstorm pounded the Northeast between December 5 and 7, dumping more than 1 foot (30 centimeters) of snow from New York City to Maine. Fifty-two inches (132 centimeters) of snow fell in Pinkham Notch, New Hampshire, while 6-foot (2-meter) drifts were measured in metropolitan Boston. It was the largest December snowstorm of record in Providence, Rhode Island, and the largest early December snowstorm in New York City.

◼ Fred Gadomski and Todd Miner

See also **Disasters; Europe; France.**

Weightlifting. See Sports.

Welfare. The number of people in the United States receiving benefits under the Temporary Assistance for Needy Families (TANF) program declined for the sixth consecutive year, announced Tommy G. Thompson, secretary of the U.S. Department of Health and Human Services (HHS), on Feb. 13, 2003. TANF is a welfare program that provides cash assistance and helps with child care for low-income workers and the unemployed.

According to an HHS report, the number of TANF caseloads had dropped below 5 million by the end of fiscal year 2002 (Oct. 1, 2001, to Sept. 30, 2002). This amount was 6.2 percent less than in fiscal year 2001 and 59.2 percent less since 1996, when the law implementing the program went into effect. The number of families receiving TANF benefits fell 3.9 percent to about 2 million families in fiscal year 2002. Since 1996, the number of families receiving TANF has fallen by 54.1 percent, according to HHS's Administration for Children and Families.

TANF funding expired in 2002. The program continued to operate in 2003 through temporary funding approved by President George W. Bush.

Head Start faulted. HHS officials on June 9 released a sharply critical report on the Head Start program. Head Start is a federal program that provides educational, social, and health services to young children from the nation's lowest-income families. Head Start was founded on the idea that good early childhood experiences provide much of the basis for later success and well-being.

The HHS report stated that children in Head Start are not adequately prepared for school and tend to enter kindergarten with lower skills and school readiness than children who are not enrolled in the program. Consequently, the HHS reported that the children "perform significantly below their more advantaged peers in reading and mathematics once they enter school."

Energy cost assistance. On January 6, Thompson announced the availability of $545 million in grants to help low-income residents pay their heating bills. The money was provided to all 50 states, the District of Columbia, and to Native American tribes. Another $151 million in grants under the Low Income Home Energy Assistance Program, another federal program, was released on March 4.

Mentoring grants. HHS officials on May 19 provided $10 million in grants to qualified organizations to help train adult volunteers as mentors to children whose parents are in prison or jail. According to an HHS report, the number of children with a parent in a federal or state correctional facility numbered 2 million people in 1999.

◼ Geoffrey A. Campbell

See also **Education: A Special Report.**

West Indies. The fragile economies of the small nations in the West Indies were buffeted by the effects of globalization in 2003. The price of sugar fell so low on world markets that these countries found it hard to profit from the economically important crop. Moreover, the nations within the Caribbean area had to import food at a record cost of $2.7 billion in 2003.

The wages of workers in free trade zones, which were established to create jobs in manufacturing various products mainly for U.S. markets, stalled in the face of competition from countries in other areas of the world. In 2003, leaders of West Indian nations feared the complete loss of jobs in the textile industry to China, where wages were much lower.

Tourism. The tourism industry in the West Indies rebounded in the first half of 2003, despite continuing unsettled global conditions and the U.S.-led war in Iraq. Cruise ship arrivals increased 38.1 percent in Jamaica and 54.6 percent in the Dominican Republic between January and July.

Jean Holder, secretary general of the Caribbean Tourism Organization (CTO), which involves 32 governments in the region, called for the merger of the CTO with the Caribbean Hotel and Tourism Organization, a private sector group of 35 hotel associations. CTO officials estimated that the Caribbean would need 120,000 more hotel rooms by 2010 to hold its share of the lucrative tourism market.

AIDS epidemic. Officials from international health groups urged Caribbean governments to do more to battle the AIDS epidemic. By mid-2003, experts estimated that 500,000 people in the Caribbean, or 2.4 percent of the population, were infected with HIV, the virus that causes AIDS. About 80 percent of those infected with HIV in 2003 lived on the island of Hispaniola, which is shared by Haiti and the Dominican Republic.

Dominican bank scandal. Three top executives of Banco Intercontinental—the second largest bank in the Dominican Republic—were arrested in May for embezzling $2.2 billion, equivalent to 80 percent of the government's annual budget. Ramon Baez Figueroa, the bank's president and a member of one of the country's most prominent families, was allegedly involved in the scheme, which was the largest swindle in the country's history. ■ Nathan A. Haverstock

See also **Latin America.**

West Virginia. See **State government.**

Wisconsin. See **State government.**

Wyoming. See **State government.**

Yugoslavia. See **Serbia and Montenegro.**

Yukon Territory. See **Canadian territories.**

Zambia. See **Africa.**

Zimbabwe. In 2003, President Robert Mugabe's ruling Zimbabwe African National Union-Patriotic Front (ZANU-PF) faced civil turmoil as Mugabe's government attempted to repress the opposition Movement for Democratic Change (MDC) led by Morgan Tsvangirai. Zimbabwe suffered its worst economic crisis in 2003 since Mugabe came to power in 1980, as runaway inflation, massive unemployment, and acute food shortages inflicted severe hardship on the nation's population.

Analysts blamed the economic collapse on Mugabe's policy since 2000 of seizing thousands of white-owned farms for redistribution to blacks who do not own land. However, critics claimed that, in fact, the land was given to Mugabe's own family and ZANU-PF cronies. The land seizures provoked a steep decline in agricultural production, resulting in widespread famine. Even as international donors stepped up food aid to Zimbabwe, agencies accused the regime of denying its opponents access to food supplies.

Mass protests. Between March and June 2003, a series of antigovernment strikes and demonstrations further hobbled the fragile economy. Organizers of the mass actions, including the MDC and several labor unions, called on President Mugabe to resign. Human rights groups claimed that police, soldiers, and ZANU-PF youth militias known as the "Green Bombers" beat and tortured hundreds of people during the protests.

Treason charges. On June 6, Tsvangirai was arrested and held for 10 days in jail on a charge of treason relating to his role in the mass demonstrations. Government prosecutors had already leveled a charge of treason against Tsvangirai in February, alleging that he had plotted to assassinate President Mugabe prior to the 2002 elections. MDC leaders insisted that both treason charges were groundless.

International reaction. Officials of the Commonwealth, an association of 54 countries that have lived under British law and government, voted in March 2003 to extend the group's suspension of Zimbabwe for at least six months. The Commonwealth had initially suspended Zimbabwe in March 2002 to protest the Mugabe government's land seizures and alleged human rights abuses. When Commonwealth officials refused to invite Zimbabwe to a December 2003 summit in Abuja, Nigeria, President Mugabe threatened to take Zimbabwe out of the Commonwealth.

The European Union in February extended "targeted" sanctions against Mugabe and other ZANU-PF leaders originally imposed in March 2002. The United States announced similar sanctions in March 2003. ■ Simon Baynham

See also **Africa; South Africa.**

Zoology. See **Biology.**

Zoos in the United States unveiled major changes in the way they designed their exhibits in 2003. Zoos tried to immerse visitors in simulations of the natural habitats of the animals they see. New exhibits also contained elements found in nature, which encouraged the animals in captivity to display the same behavior that they would in the wild.

Walking in the wild. "Tiger Mountain," which opened in May at the Bronx Zoo in New York City, safely brings visitors up close to six Siberian tigers. Siberian tigers are considered an endangered species, that is, in danger of becoming extinct worldwide or in significant portions of the world.

"Tiger Mountain" covers 3 acres (1.2 hectares) and simulates the Siberian tiger's natural habitat in the Amur Valley, on the border between Russia and China. Visitors to the zoo are immersed in examples of the nature of the region as they walk through a trail teeming with vegetation similar to that found in the valley.

Visitors then enter a viewing area that is inset into the tigers' territory. The enclosed area is encased with very thick glass that brings audiences within a few inches (centimeters) of the tigers. The area has touch-screen monitors that show tiger behavior and how zookeepers care for the animals.

Also in May, the San Diego Zoo unveiled an exhibit that replicates a jungle in Indonesia. "Absolutely Apes" contains 40 trees that are the home of orangutans and siamangs, members of the gibbon family. Visitors view the apes from behind an enormous 110-foot (33.5-meter) long, 12-foot (3.5-meter) tall glass observation window. Zookeepers equate the exhibit as the closest thing to walking through the jungle.

The North Carolina Aquarium on Roanoke Island opened "Bite, Shock, Sting" in May. The exhibit features creatures that are interesting to see but not up close and personal. "Biters" in the exhibit include canebrake rattlesnakes and black widow spiders; "shockers" include an electric eel; and "stingers" number various jellyfish, including the lion's mane and moon jelly. The exhibit also has poison dart frogs, which have glands in their skin that they use secrete poisons to kill their prey, and a variety of sea creatures—such as stingrays and lionfish—that use venomous spines in their flesh to ward off predators.

The Columbus (Ohio) Zoo and Aquarium in May opened "Islands of Southeast Asia," which takes visitors on a boat tour or a walking tour through a re-creation of some 17,000 islands that are located between the Indian and Pacific oceans. "Islands of Southeast Asia" features orangutans and gibbons in trees; komodo dragons, which are the world's largest lizards, sunning themselves on replicas of lava rocks; and small-clawed otters romping in the water.

Clever ideas. Zoos always look for new exhibit themes. In August 2003, the Roger Williams Zoo in Providence, Rhode Island, opened "Staying Alive," an exhibit dedicated to animals that live for a very long time. The "Staying Alive" features nearly 30 amphibians and reptiles in four buildings throughout the zoo. Animals on exhibit include the brightly colored Oriental fire-bellied toad, 2-inches (5-centimeters) long, that can live for 30 years. However, the toad's lifespan is short compared with the longevity of the radiated tortoise from Madagascar, which can live for 100 years. The Mexican axolotl, an aquatic salamander, can live for up to 25 years, and the emerald tree boa, a brilliant green snake from South America, can still be going strong at 20 years of age.

Giant pandas were big news in U.S. zoos during 2003. In April, the Memphis Zoo debuted a pair of giant pandas at its 3-acre (1.2-hectare), $16-million "China" exhibit. Zoos in Beijing and Shanghai loaned the pandas, Ya Ya and Le Le, to Memphis Zoo officials as part of a 10-year program.

In August, officials at the San Diego Zoo announced that Bai Yun, a 13-year-old giant panda, had given birth to the first of twin cubs but had failed to successfully give birth to her other cub. Pandas typically give birth to a second cub within 12 hours of the first cub.

More zoo babies. The Fort Worth Zoo in Texas welcomed the birth of a white rhino in October, the first to be born at that zoo.

Three Amur tigers, which are also called Siberian tigers, were born at the Detroit Zoo in August.

The Audubon Aquarium of the Americas, in New Orleans, Louisiana, recorded the births of seven stingrays in April, including Leopaldi and Otorongo stingrays. They were the first stingrays to be born in captivity since the 1970's. The stingrays are native to rivers within the Amazon Basin of South America.

Baghdad Zoo reopens. The reopening of the Baghdad Zoo, which had been scheduled for April 7, was delayed by battles during the Iraq War of 2003. Zookeepers had closed the zoo in the Iraqi capital in 2002 as part of a renovation project. On the day it was scheduled to reopen, coalition forces led by U.S. armed forces were engaged in combat with Iraqi soldiers who had set up defensive positions within the zoo. When zookeepers returned in mid-April 2003, the zoo was in shambles and nearly all of the animals had been freed from their cages. Zoo officials finally reopened the facility in July. ■ Edward Ricciuti

See also **Conservation.**

2004 SUPPLEMENT

New encyclopedia
articles are devoted
to the following
topics:

The vast interior of Australia, often called the *outback,* consists mainly of deserts and dry grassland. Spinifex grass, *foreground,* is a common plant in the outback.

Australia

Australia is the only country that is also a continent. In area, Australia ranks as the sixth largest country and the smallest continent. It lies between the South Pacific Ocean and the Indian Ocean, about 7,000 miles (11,000 kilometers) southwest of North America and about 2,000 miles (3,200 kilometers) southeast of mainland Asia. Australia is often referred to as being "down under" because it lies entirely within the Southern Hemisphere. The name *Australia* comes from the Latin word *australis,* which means *southern.* The official name of the country is the Commonwealth of Australia.

Australia has many different kinds of environments and climates, from tropical in the north to *temperate* (with warm summers and cool winters) in the south. The huge interior of Australia, called the *outback,* is mostly desert or dry grassland and has few settlements. Kangaroos, koalas, platypuses, and wombats are only a few of

The contributors of this article are David Carter, Director of the Australian Studies Centre at the University of Queensland; Grace Karskens, Senior Lecturer in Australian History at the University of New South Wales; Clement Macintyre, Senior Lecturer, Department of Politics, University of Adelaide; and Adrian Mitchell, Associate Professor in the Department of English at the University of Sydney.

the many unusual animals that are unique to Australia. The southeastern coastal region has Australia's two largest cities—Sydney and Melbourne. Canberra, the national capital, lies a short distance inland.

Australia has a strong economy that makes it one of the world's developed countries. It has busy cities, modern factories, and highly productive farms and mines. Australia is the world's leading producer and exporter of wool and *bauxite* (the ore from which aluminum is made). Australia also produces and exports other minerals and farm goods. Income from these exports and other industries makes it possible for most Australians to have a high standard of living.

The first Australians were a people known today as Aborigines (pronounced *AB uh RIHJ uh neez*). The Aborigines had lived in Australia for about 50,000 years before the first white settlers arrived. The Torres Strait Islands are the home of Australia's other *indigenous* (native) people, known as the Torres Strait Islanders.

Great Britain (later the United Kingdom) settled Australia as a prison colony in 1788. After British settlement, the number of whites steadily increased while the Aboriginal population plummeted. The Aboriginal population slowed its decline in the early 1900's and has been increasing since the mid-1900's. Today, the majority of Australians have mixed European ancestry, although there are now also many Australians from Asian and Middle Eastern backgrounds. Australia now considers itself a multicultural nation.

Government

The Commonwealth of Australia is a federation of six states, two mainland territories, and eight additional territories. The six states, each with its own government, are New South Wales, Queensland, South Australia, Tasmania, Victoria, and Western Australia. The two self-governing territories are the Australian Capital Territory and the Northern Territory.

Australia is a constitutional monarchy like the United Kingdom. The British monarch is recognized as queen of Australia but has little power. A governor general represents the monarch at the federal level, and a state governor represents the monarch at the state level.

Australia has a *parliamentary* system of government. Under this system, the national government is controlled by the political party or the *coalition* (alliance) of parties with a majority of seats in the lower house of Parliament. The leader of the majority party or coalition heads the government as prime minister.

The federal government of Australia is officially headed by the governor general. The monarch appoints the governor general on the recommendation of the Australian prime minister. The governor general's role is mainly symbolic. In 1975, however, the governor general used his power to remove the prime minister from office. See the *History* section of this article for details.

The prime minister. The governor general appoints as prime minister the leader of the majority party or coalition in the House of Representatives. Prime ministers remain in office as long as their party has a majority in the House of Representatives, unless they retire, are replaced as party leader, or leave office. The prime minister is the chief spokesperson of the government. He or she leads the federal Cabinet, a group of senior ministers who make major decisions on government policy.

The federal Parliament has an upper house, called the Senate, and a lower house, called the House of Representatives. Most bills are introduced in the House, but both houses must approve a bill before it becomes law. *Money bills* (bills authorizing taxation and spending) must be introduced in the House. The Senate may reject, but not amend, money bills. The Senate's main work is revising rather than initiating legislation.

The House of Representatives has 150 members. Membership in the House is divided among the states and mainland territories according to population. The representatives are elected every three years unless Parliament is dissolved before its three-year term is over.

The Senate has 76 members. Each state elects 12 senators, and each mainland territory elects 2. Elections to the Senate are held every three years, at the same time as general elections to the House. Voters elect half of the senators at each election.

All Australian citizens over the age of 18 who are eligible to vote are required to cast their ballots in federal and state elections. In every state except South Australia, those who do not vote may be fined.

The federal courts. The High Court of Australia decides constitutional questions. It also serves as the nation's court of final appeals. Other federal courts deal with bankruptcy cases, family law, industrial disputes, and violations of federal law.

State government. Each state has its own parliament, court system, head of government, and governor. The heads of state government are called *premiers.* The states' governors represent the monarch.

The federal Parliament has power to make laws on particular topics, including defense and foreign affairs, overseas trade, and finance. Each state government has the power to pass laws on most matters that apply to that state, such as police and legal services, road mainte-

© Creatas

Sydney is the largest city in Australia. Founded in 1788, it is also the country's oldest city. The sail-like Sydney Opera House, *center,* is a city landmark. Sydney lies on a huge, deep harbor, officially called Port Jackson but commonly known as Sydney Harbour.

Australia in brief

General information

Capital: Canberra.
Official language: English.
Official name: Commonwealth of Australia.
Anthems: "Advance Australia Fair" (national); "God Save the Queen" (royal).
Largest cities: (2001 census)
Sydney (3,997,321)
Melbourne (3,366,542)
Brisbane (1,627,535)
Perth (1,339,993)
Adelaide (1,072,585)

Australia's flag has a British Union flag, five stars that represent the constellation Southern Cross, and a large star for the country's states and territories.

Australia's coat of arms features a kangaroo and an emu; golden wattle blossoms (the national floral emblem); a shield with the coats of arms of the six states of Australia; and a star for the states and territories.

Land and climate

Land: Australia is the only country that is also a continent. It lies between the South Pacific and Indian oceans. Australia is mostly flat, except for the Great Dividing Range in the east and several smaller mountainous regions. The major rivers include the Murray and the Darling.

Area: 2,978,147 mi² (7,713,364 km²), including 26,000 mi² (67,800 km²) for Tasmania. *Greatest distances* (mainland)—east-west 2,475 mi (3,983 km); north-south—1,950 mi (3,138 km). *Coastline*—37,118 mi (59,736 km), including 1,760 mi (2,833 km) for Tasmania and 14,825 mi (23,859 km) for offshore islands.
Elevation: *Highest*—Mt. Kosciuszko, 7,310 ft (2,228 m) above sea level. *Lowest*—Lake Eyre, 52 ft (16 m) below sea level.
Climate: The northern third of Australia lies in the tropics and is warm the year around. The rest of the country has warm summers and cool winters. About a third of the country is desert. Australia lies south of the equator, and so its seasons are opposite those in the Northern Hemisphere.

Government

Form of government: Constitutional monarchy; in practice, a parliamentary democracy.
Head of state: Queen of the United Kingdom, who is also queen of Australia. In practice, governor general performs functions in queen's absence.
Head of government: Prime minister, the leader of the party or coalition of parties holding a majority in the House of Representatives.
Parliament: *Senate*—76 members; *House of Representatives*—150 members.
Executive: Prime minister and Cabinet.
Political subdivisions: Six states, two mainland territories, and eight external territories.

People

Population: *2004 estimate*—19,541,000. *2001 census*—18,972,350.
Population density: 7 per mi² (3 per km²).
Distribution: 85 percent urban, 15 percent rural.
Major ethnic/national groups: More than 80 percent of European descent, chiefly British and Irish, but also Italian, German, Greek, Dutch, and others. About 10 percent Asian. About 2 percent Aborigine (native Australian peoples).
Religion: About 25 percent Roman Catholic, 20 percent Anglican, and 7 percent *Uniting Church,* which consists of Methodist, Congregationalist, and some Presbyterian churches.

Population trend

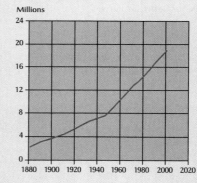

Year	Population
1881	2,250,194
1891	3,177,823
1901	3,373,801
1911	4,455,005
1921	5,435,734
1933	6,629,839
1947	7,579,358
1954	8,986,530
1961	10,508,186
1966	11,599,498
1971	12,755,638
1976	13,548,472
1981	14,574,488
1986	15,602,156
1991	16,850,540
1996	17,892,423
2001	18,972,350

Economy

Chief products: *Agriculture*—apples, barley, beef cattle, chickens and eggs, grapes, milk, oats, oranges, potatoes, rice, sheep and lambs, sugar cane, wheat, wool. *Fishing*—lobsters, oysters, shrimp. *Forestry*—eucalyptus and pine timber, wood pulp. *Manufacturing*—automobiles and other transportation equipment; chemicals; household appliances; iron, steel, and other metals; paper; processed foods; textiles, clothing, and shoes. *Mining*—bauxite, coal, copper, diamonds, gold, iron ore, lead, manganese, natural gas, nickel, opals, petroleum, silver, tin, titanium, uranium, zinc, zircon.
Money: *Basic unit*—Australian dollar.
International trade: *Major exports*—alumina, beef, coal, iron ore, petroleum products, wheat, wool. *Major imports*—electrical appliances, industrial machinery, office equipment, petroleum products, telecommunications equipment, yarns and fabrics. *Major trading partners*—Germany, Japan, New Zealand, United Kingdom, United States.

nance, and industrial and agricultural production. If a federal law conflicts with a state law, the federal law prevails, but only over the specific area of conflict.

Because the federal Parliament can impose forms of taxation that the states cannot, it has financial power over the states. The federal government collects nearly all the nation's taxes and raises more than 70 percent of the total revenue. Each state receives a share of the federal tax income, and the states depend on such federal grants for the majority of their annual revenue.

Local government. Victoria, Tasmania, and the more densely settled areas of the other states are divided into local government areas. *Shire* (county), city, and town councils are responsible for such services as street building, public works, and garbage collection.

Vast areas of outback Australia are thinly populated and have no local government. Community councils govern the small Aboriginal groups living in the sparsely populated interior areas of the Northern Territory.

Political parties. Australia has three main political parties—the Australian Labor Party (ALP), the Liberal Party of Australia, and the National Party of Australia. The ALP promotes government action in economic and social affairs, especially to improve working conditions.

National Capitol Development Commission

Parliament House in Canberra is the meeting place of the Australian Parliament. The unusual structure is set into a hill overlooking the city. The building was dedicated in 1988.

Australia map index

(Map appears on following pages.)

States and mainland territories

Map key	Name	Area In mi²	In km²	Population
I 13	**Australian Capital Territory (Canberra)**	930	2,400	311,947
H 12	**New South Wales**	309,500	801,600	6,371,745
D 9	**Northern Territory**	519,800	1,346,200	210,664
E 12	**Queensland**	666,900	1,727,200	3,655,139
G 9	**South Australia**	380,000	984,000	1,467,261
K 12	**Tasmania**	26,200	67,800	456,652
I 11	**Victoria**	87,900	227,600	4,644,950
F 5	**Western Australia**	975,100	2,525,500	1,851,252

External territories*

Name	Area In mi²	In km²	Population
Ashmore and Cartier Islands	77	199	0
Australian Antarctic Territory†	2,362,875	6,119,818	0
Christmas Island	52	135	1,906
Cocos (Keeling) Islands	5	13	655
Coral Sea Islands	‡	‡	0
Heard and McDonald Islands	183	474	0
Norfolk Island	14	36	§1,800

*Not shown on map.
†Claimed by Australia.
‡400,000 square miles (1,035,995 square kilometers), including about 1 square mile (3 square kilometers) of land.
§*World Book* estimate.

Cities and towns*

Adelaide .....1,072,585 .H 10
Albany ....I 5
Albury ....49,822 .I 12
Alice
  Springs ....E 9
Ararat ....I 11
Armidale ....G 13
Bacchus
  Marsh† ....I 11
Bairnsdale† ....J 12
Ballarat ....80,045 .I 11
Ballina ....G 14
Bathurst
  [-Orange] ....73,199 .H 13
Benalla† ....I 12
Bendigo ....75,839 .I 11
Berwick† ....J 11
Blue Moun-
  tains† ....H 13
Bourke ....G 12
Bowen ....D 13
Brisbane ...1,627,535 .G 14
Broken
  Hill ....H 12
Bunbury ....46,913 .H 4
Bunda-
  berg ....55,998 .F 14
Burdekin† ....D 13
Burnie [-Devon-
  port] ....73,682 .K 12
Busselton ....H 4
Cairns ....126,364 .C 12
Caloundra ....F 14
Camden† ....H 13
Campbell-
  town ....H 13
Canberra .....311,518 .I 13

Carnarvon ....F 3
Casino ....G 14
Cessnock ....H 13
Charters
  Towers ....D 12
Clarence† ....44,175 .K 12
Cobar ....H 12
Coffs
  Harbour ....46,338 .G 14
Colac† ....J 11
Collie ....H 4
Cooma† ....I 13
Coota-
  mundra ....I 12
Cowra ....H 13
Cran-
  bourne† ....J 12
Dalby ....F 14
Darwin ......109,419 .A 8
Deniliquin ....J 12
Dubbo ....34,232 .H 13
Echuca ....I 11
Elizabeth ....H 10
Emerald ....E 13
Esperance ....H 6
Forbes ....H 12
Fremantle ....H 4
Gawler ....H 10
Geelong ......151,851 .J 11
George
  Town ....K 12
Geraldton .....29,996 .G 3
Gladstone .....39,003 .E 14
Glen Innes ....G 14
Gold Coast ...396,588 .G 14
Gosford
  [-Wyong] ....285,508 .H 13

Goulburn ......186,950 .I 13
Grafton ....G 14
Griffith ....G 13
Gunnedah ....G 13
Gympie ....F 14
Hamilton ....I 11
Hervey
  Bay ....41,890 .F 14
Hobart ......191,169 .K 12
Horsham ....I 11
Inverell ....G 13
Ipswich ......112,104 .G 14
Kalgoorlie ....28,573 .G 5
Kempsey ....H 14
Kiama† ....I 13
Kingaroy ....F 14
King-
  borough† ....K 12
Kingston† ....C 12
Kwinana ....H 4
Launceston ....95,604 .K 12
Leeton ....H 12
Lismore ....30,083 .G 14
Lithgow ....H 13
Mackay ....143,578 .D 13
Maitland ....H 14
Mandurah ......55,081 .H 4
Mareeba ....C 12
Maroochy-
  dore-
  Mooloo-
  laba ....F 14
Mary-
  borough ....F 14
Melbourne ..3,366,542 .I 12
Melton-
  Wyndham† ..136,999 .I 11

Mildura ....44,194 .H 11
Millicent ....I 10
Moe-
  Yallourn ....J 12
Moree ....G 13
Morning-
  ton† ....125,378 .J 11
Morwell ....J 12
Mount
  Gambier ....I 10
Mount Isa ....D 10
Mudgee ....H 13
Murray
  Bridge ....I 10
Muswell-
  brook ....H 13
Nambour ....F 14
Naracoorte ....I 10
Narrabri ....G 13
Narrogin ....H 4
Newcastle ...470,610 .H 13
Northam ....H 4
Parkes ....H 12
Penrith ....H 13
Perth ....1,339,993 .H 4
Port
  Augusta ....H 10
Port Hedland ....D 4
Port Lincoln ....H 9
Port Mac-
  quarie ....38,288 .H 14
Port Pirie ....H 10
Portland ....J 11
Quean-
  beyan† ....41,631 .I 13
Richmond
  River† ....H 13

Rock-
  hampton .....62,845 .E 14
Rockingham ....H 4
Roma ....F 13
Sale† ....J 12
Salisbury ....H 10
Shell-
  harbour† ....I 13
Shepparton ....42,749 .I 12
Singleton† ....H 14
Stawell ....I 11
Sunbury† ....I 12
Swan Hill ....I 11
Sydney .....3,997,321 .H 13
Tamworth .....40,878 .H 13
Taree ....H 14
Tewantin-
  Noosa† ....F 14
Toowoomba ...105,302 .F 14
Townsville ....91,169 .D 13
Traralgon† ....J 12
Tumut ....I 12
Wagga
  Wagga ....50,634 .I 12
Wangaratta ....I 12
Warrnam-
  bool ....28,755 .J 11
Warwick ....G 14
Wellington† ....H 13
Wentworth† ....H 14
Weston
  Creek-
  Stromlot .....22,485 .H 13
Whyalla ....21,866 .H 10
Wodonga ....43,802 .I 12
Wollongong ...257,510 .I 13
Young ....H 12

*Populations are for statistical divisions and subdivisions. The Australian government does not report the populations for individual cities and towns.
†Does not appear on map; key shows general location.
Source: 2001 census.

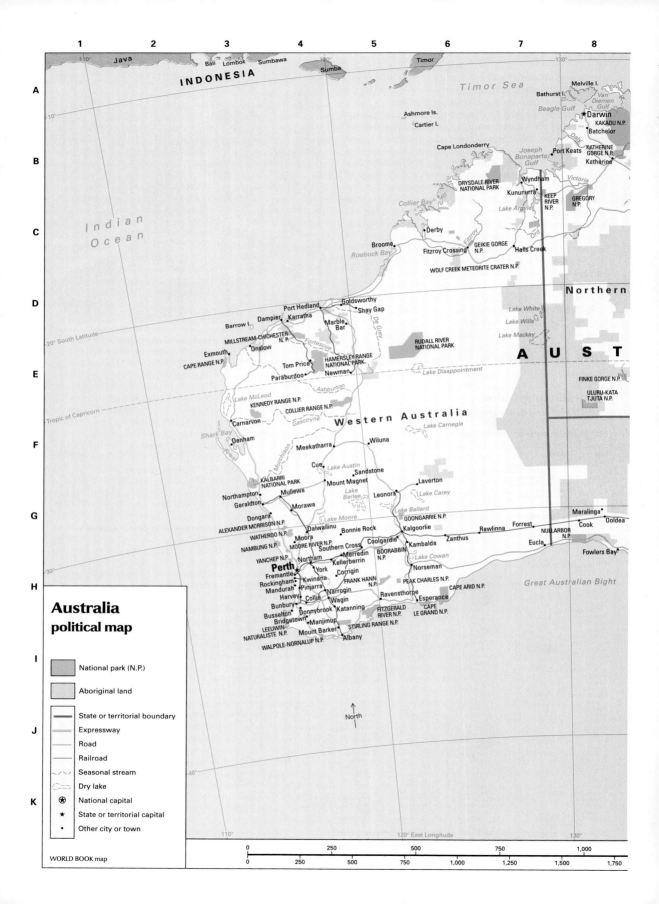

Australia
political map

Legend:
- National park (N.P.)
- Aboriginal land
- State or territorial boundary
- Expressway
- Road
- Railroad
- Seasonal stream
- Dry lake
- ⊛ National capital
- ★ State or territorial capital
- • Other city or town

WORLD BOOK map

North

| 0 | 250 | 500 | 750 | 1,000 |
| 0 | 250 | 500 | 750 | 1,000 | 1,250 | 1,500 | 1,750 |

INDONESIA
Java Bali Lombok Sumbawa Sumba Timor

Timor Sea

Indian Ocean

Melville I.
Bathurst I.
Van Diemen Gulf
Beagle Gulf
★ Darwin
KAKADU N.P.
Batchelor
Ashmore Is.
Cartier I.
Cape Londonderry
Joseph Bonaparte Gulf
Port Keats
KATHERINE GORGE N.P.
Katherine
Collier Bay
DRYSDALE RIVER NATIONAL PARK
Wyndham
Kununurra
Lake Argyle
Victoria
KEEP RIVER N.P.
GREGORY N.P.
Derby
Fitzroy
Broome
Roebuck Bay
Fitzroy Crossing
GEIKIE GORGE N.P.
Halls Creek
Ord
WOLF CREEK METEORITE CRATER N.P.

Northern

Lake White
Lake Wills
Lake Mackay

AUST

Port Hedland
Goldsworthy
Shay Gap
Barrow I.
Dampier
Karratha
Marble Bar
De Grey
MILLSTREAM-CHICHESTER N.P.
Exmouth
CAPE RANGE N.P.
Onslow
Fortescue
RUDALL RIVER NATIONAL PARK
Tom Price
HAMERSLEY RANGE NATIONAL PARK
Paraburdoo
Newman
Lake Disappointment

FINKE GORGE N.P.
ULURU-KATA TJUTA N.P.

Lake McLeod
KENNEDY RANGE N.P.
Ashburton
COLLIER RANGE N.P.
Carnarvon
Gascoyne
Western Australia
Lake Carnegie
Shark Bay
Denham
Meekatharra
Wiluna

Murchison
Cue
Lake Austin
Sandstone
Laverton
Lake Carey
Mount Magnet
KALBARRI NATIONAL PARK
Lake Barlee
Leonora
Northampton
Mullewa
Geraldton
Morawa
Lake Moore
Lake Ballard
GOONGARRIE N.P.
Maralinga
Dongara
ALEXANDER MORRISON N.P.
Dalwallinu
Bonnie Rock
Kalgoorlie
Rawlinna
Forrest
Cook
Ooldea
WATHEROO N.P.
Moora
Southern Cross
Coolgardie
Zanthus
NULLARBOR N.P.
NAMBUNG N.P.
MOORE RIVER N.P.
Kambalda
Eucla
YANCHEP N.P.
Northam
Merredin
BOORABBIN N.P.
Lake Cowan
Fowlers Bay
Perth ★
York
Kellerberrin
Fremantle
Kwinana
Corrigin
Norseman
Rockingham
FRANK HANN N.P.
PEAK CHARLES N.P.
CAPE ARID N.P.
Great Australian Bight
Mandurah
Pinjarra
Narrogin
Harvey
Collie
Wagin
Ravensthorpe
Esperance
Bunbury
Katanning
FITZGERALD RIVER N.P.
CAPE LE GRAND N.P.
Busselton
Donnybrook
Bridgetown
Manjimup
LEEUWIN-NATURALISTE N.P.
Mount Barker
STIRLING RANGE N.P.
WALPOLE-NORNALUP N.P.
Albany

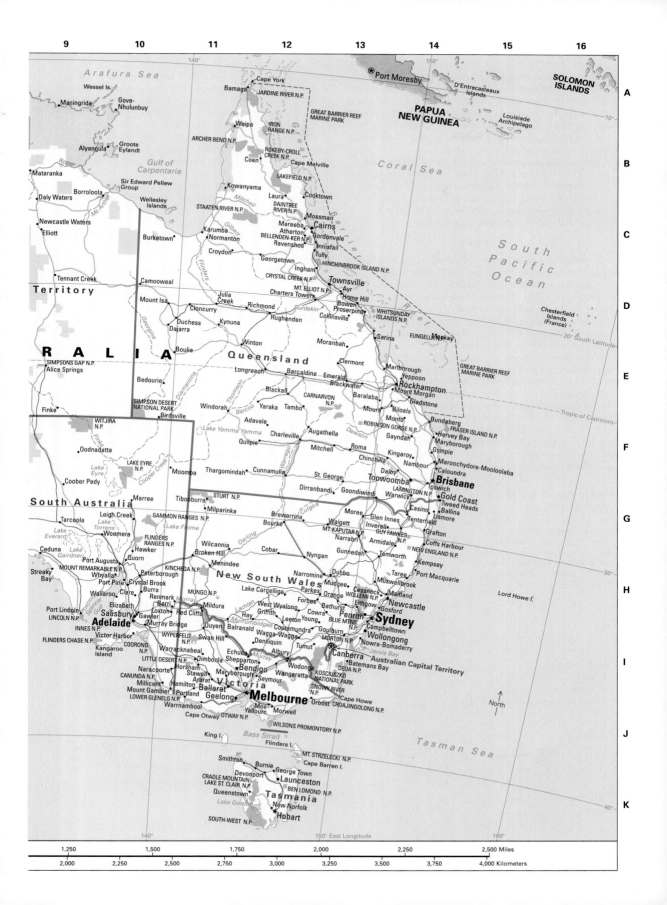

Many ALP members belong to labor unions. The Liberal Party favors the free enterprise system with little government interference. Many merchants and business executives support the Liberals. The National Party represents the interests of farmers and other rural Australians. In Parliament, the Liberal and National parties often form a coalition in opposition to the ALP.

The armed forces of Australia are called the Australian Defence Force (ADF). They consist of the Australian Army, the Royal Australian Navy, and the Royal Australian Air Force. All military service is voluntary. About 50,000 men and women serve in the ADF full-time, and about 24,000 serve as reservists.

People

Population and ancestry. Approximately 80 percent of Australia's people live in the southeastern quarter of the country, mainly in large coastal cities. Australia's three largest cities—Sydney, Melbourne, and Brisbane—lie on the east coast. Most of the rest of the people live along the northeast and extreme southwest coasts. Canberra is the largest inland city, about 80 miles (130 kilometers) from the coasts.

Most Australians are European immigrants or descendants of European immigrants. About 28 percent of all Australians were born in other countries. Australia has admitted about 6 million immigrants since the 1950's. About one-third have come from the United Kingdom and Ireland. Most of the rest of the immigrants have come from mainland Europe, especially the former Yugoslav republics and such southern European countries as Greece and Italy. Immigration from Asia has greatly increased since the 1970's, and European migration has

declined. During the late 1900's and early 2000's, the number of immigrants from New Zealand and Southeast Asia increased rapidly. Aborigines make up about 2 percent of the population.

Language. English is the official language of Australia. However, more than 15 percent of the population speak a language other than English at home. The most common languages after English are Chinese, Italian, Greek, Vietnamese, and Arabic.

Australians have an accent that is different from accents in other English-speaking countries. Australian English differs from British English in certain ways. The British who settled in Australia had to develop a vocabulary to describe the many unfamiliar animals and plants in their new environment. In some cases, the settlers used existing English words. For example, they gave the name *magpie* to a bird that resembles the British magpie but is actually unrelated to any bird in the United Kingdom. The British also borrowed words from the Aborigines. Such Aboriginal words as *kangaroo* and *koala* were thus introduced into English.

Australian English has also produced many colorful figures of speech. For example, a brave person is said to be "as game as Ned Kelly." Ned Kelly was a famous Australian outlaw of the 1870's. "Waltzing Matilda," the title of Australia's most famous song, refers neither to a dance nor to a woman. A *matilda* is a blanket roll. "To waltz matilda" means "to tramp the roads."

The Aborigines were the first inhabitants of Australia, but most were displaced after the arrival of European settlers. The majority of Aborigines now live in cities and towns. Since the late 1900's, some Aborigines in central and northern Australia have stayed on or re-

Where the people of Australia live

This map shows how Australia's population is distributed. Most of the people live along the east, southeast, and extreme southwest coasts. The vast, dry interior of the country has few settlements.

Major urban centers

● More than 3 million inhabitants

• 500,000 to 3 million inhabitants

○ Less than 500,000 inhabitants

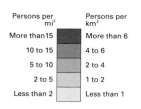

Persons per mi²	Persons per km²
More than 15	More than 6
10 to 15	4 to 6
5 to 10	2 to 4
2 to 5	1 to 2
Less than 2	Less than 1

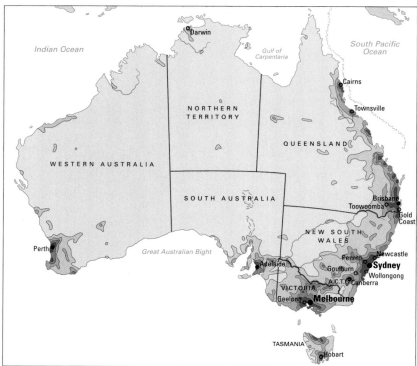

turned to their traditional lands. There they often live in community settlements. These communities preserve some traditional Aboriginal ways of life, especially languages, religious beliefs, and styles of painting and craftwork. City and outback communities also nurture new developments in Aboriginal culture. Contemporary styles of Aboriginal painting and music, such as the rock group Yothu Yindi, have flourished. Contemporary Aboriginal painting is now one of the most important and internationally recognized forms of Australian art.

Ways of life

Lifestyles in rural Australia are different from those in the cities. Many rural regions are poorer than city areas. The rural areas have higher levels of unemployment, less access to cultural and educational institutions, and fewer government or commercial services. Rural and urban voting patterns in elections differ as well. Rural voters support conservative candidates more often.

City life. About 85 percent of Australians live in cities and towns, making Australia one of the world's most urbanized countries. About 70 percent of all Australians live in cities of more than 100,000 people. These cities include the federal capital, Canberra, and the six state capitals. The state capitals, in order of size, are Sydney, New South Wales; Melbourne, Victoria; Brisbane, Queensland; Perth, Western Australia; Adelaide, South Australia; and Hobart, Tasmania. Canberra is smaller than all the state capitals except Hobart.

Each of Australia's state capitals serves as the political, commercial, industrial, and cultural hub of its state. The main business district of each state capital is its oldest section, the area nearest the waterfront. In the largest cities, modern structures, including high-rise office buildings, have replaced most of the original buildings in this section. In addition to office buildings, the city-center areas have fine shops, theaters, and restaurants.

Most city dwellers in Australia live in the suburbs, which have their own schools, shopping centers, and recreational facilities. Some suburbs, especially those around Sydney and Melbourne, also have industrial districts. Since the late 1900's, developers have built new high-rise apartment buildings in the central areas of the large cities. Older buildings, such as factories and warehouses, have been converted to modern apartments.

Most families live in single-story houses, each with its own garden. About two-thirds of families own their houses. There are differences in the older style of housing in the different cities. In Queensland, the older houses are made of wood, have *verandas* (wide porches), and are built above the ground on poles called *stumps*. In Melbourne and Sydney, many of the older houses are made of brick or stone and built in rows called *terraces*.

Australia's cities have problems common to big cities everywhere, including air pollution and rush-hour traffic jams. Before the 1950's, the *inner suburbs,* those closest to the city, were the poorest residential areas. These areas had high rates of unemployment and crime. But during the 1950's, many non-British immigrants began settling in the inner suburbs and helped to regenerate them. Now many middle-class and wealthy residents

© Bill Bachman

Aborigines are descendants of Australia's first settlers, people who migrated from Asia thousands of years ago. This school for Aboriginal children is in the Northern Territory.

© Walter Bibikow, Viesti Associates

Salamanca Place, on Hobart's waterfront, draws crowds to its outdoor market each weekend. Tasmania's scenic variety and historic sites attract many tourists.

© David R. Frazier Photolibrary

Housing in Australia varies from city to city. Most families live in single-story dwellings, such as these in Port Macquarie, New South Wales. Each house typically has its own garden.

© John Baker, Australian Picture Library

Rural communities in Australia serve mainly as marketing and shopping centers for farmers. This community, Tanunda, lies in a grape-growing and winemaking region northeast of Adelaide in South Australia.

have moved to these areas, and many poorer families live in the outer suburbs.

Country life. Only about 15 percent of Australia's people live in rural areas. Australians call the remote countryside *the bush.* The term *outback* refers to the interior. The outback consists mainly of open countryside and vast expanses of grazing land. Most of its few, widely scattered settlements are mining towns.

Nearly all farms in the outback are wheat farms or cattle and sheep *stations* (farms or ranches). Life on the stations tends to be extremely isolated. The largest stations cover over 1,000 square miles (2,600 square kilometers) and so may be 100 miles (160 kilometers) or more from the nearest town. The outback has few paved roads, and so travel by automobile is difficult or impossible. Many prosperous farm families have a light airplane, which they use for transportation to and from town. Families who do not own a plane may get to town only a few times a year. In farming regions nearer the coasts, the towns are larger and closer together. But even there, farm families may feel far from the life of the cities.

Rural Australians' sense of community is reflected in the fact that they have long had their own political party, the National Party. Many rural communities in Australia

have their own traditional *shows* (fairs), festivals, and sports competitions.

Poverty is a problem in some rural areas due to the lack of local employment. However, most farm families own their farms and live comfortably. Older farmhouses are built of wood and surrounded by a veranda. Newer farmhouses are constructed of bricks. Nearly all the houses have electric power, and a growing number of them have air conditioning.

All rural areas in Australia have such natural disasters as droughts, floods, and bushfires. Fires can even come close to the major cities in such areas as the Blue Mountains, north of Sydney, or the Dandenong Ranges, near Melbourne. In the early 2000's, fires damaged suburban neighborhoods in Sydney and Canberra.

Food and drink. Meat is plentiful in Australia and makes up a large part of the people's diet. Beef is the most popular meat, followed by poultry, pork, and lamb and mutton. British customs strongly influenced Australian food choices until the mid-1900's. Since then, European immigrants have introduced Italian, Greek, and other European styles of cooking to Australia. Australian food also shows the strong influence of Indian and Southeast Asian cooking.

Tea remains the favorite hot drink of older Australians. However, younger Australians prefer coffee. Coffee consumption has more than tripled since the mid-1900's, while tea consumption has declined. Beer is the most popular alcoholic drink. However, its consumption is declining in relation to the consumption of wine, which has increased rapidly since the 1980's. Australia is an important wine-producing country, and many Australians drink red or white wine regularly.

Recreation. Most Australians enjoy such recreation as visiting friends, going for a drive or walk, or watching television. Outdoor sports are extremely popular. Many people enjoy skin diving, surfing, swimming, or boating. Many also play golf and tennis. Team sports are a national pastime. The nation's professional sports teams have large and enthusiastic followings, and Australians often view athletes as national heroes.

The most popular team sports in Australia are cricket, Australian Rules football, Rugby League, Rugby Union, basketball, soccer, and netball. Cricket is a favorite summer sport. The Australian national cricket team regularly plays against teams from England, India, New Zealand, Pakistan, South Africa, and the West Indies.

Australian Rules football, Rugby League, Rugby Union, and soccer are mainly winter sports. Australian Rules football was invented in Australia and is played there and in Papua New Guinea, a former Australian possession. The sport is especially popular in southern Australia. Rugby League and Rugby Union are forms of football invented in England. Australia plays Rugby League and Rugby Union chiefly against France, New Zealand, South Africa, and the United Kingdom. Soccer is the fastest-growing team sport. Australia's national soccer team plays teams from many other countries.

Netball is a goal-scoring game that is played mainly by women. It is popular in the Commonwealth countries. Australia has often been the world champion. In terms of the number of people playing the sport, netball is the most popular team sport in Australia. However, it does not attract the media attention or large crowds of Australian Rules football and cricket.

Australia has produced many world-famous athletes, especially in tennis, golf, swimming, and track and field. Australians have won numerous Olympic medals in swimming, track and field, rowing, cycling, and yachting. Australians also compete successfully in the international sport of surfing.

Top Australian tennis stars include Evonne Goolagong Cawley, Margaret Smith Court, Rod Laver, John Newcombe, Ken Rosewall, Patrick Rafter, and Lleyton Hewitt. Australian golf champions include Kel Nagle, Greg Norman, Peter Thomson, and Karrie Webb. Well-known Australian swimmers include Shane Gould, Grant Hackett, Murray Rose, Dawn Fraser, Susie O'Neill, Kieren Perkins, and Ian Thorpe. Famous Australian track and field athletes include Ron Clarke, Herb Elliott, John Landy, and the Aboriginal track star Cathy Freeman.

Some of Australia's traditional sporting events receive worldwide attention. Probably the most famous event is the annual Melbourne Cup, a horse race eagerly followed by racing fans throughout the world.

Education. Each Australian state and mainland territory has its own laws concerning education. The federal government regulates education in the other territories.

© Tony Lewis, Getty Images

Australian Rules football was invented in Australia and is played mainly there and in Papua New Guinea. It is especially popular in southern Australia. This match is in Adelaide.

© Darren England, Getty Images

Cricket, an English game played with bats and a ball, is a favorite summer sport in Australia. Teams from each Australian state play each year in a championship series.

In all the states and territories except Tasmania, children must attend school from age 6 to age 15. Tasmania requires children to attend school through age 16. About 70 percent of Australian students attend state or territory schools, 20 percent go to Roman Catholic schools, and 10 percent attend other independent schools.

Each Australian state operates its own state school system. However, the state systems use some funding from the federal government to support their school system. The Roman Catholic Church owns and operates most of Australia's independent schools. Unlike the state schools, most of the independent schools in Australia

Surfing, diving, swimming, and boating are some of the many outdoor sports enjoyed in Australia. Manly Beach, north of Sydney, *shown here,* is one of Australia's most popular beaches.

charge a tuition fee. The federal government supplies funds to assist independent schools.

Australian primary schools provide six to eight years of study. Australian secondary schools offer five or six years of education. About four-fifths of the students continue beyond the required years of schooling, and about three-quarters of the students graduate from secondary school. Most graduating students go on to a university or college.

Many Australian children in remote areas of the outback receive their primary and secondary education at home by means of traveling teachers and correspondence schools, often called *schools of the air.* Each state operates a correspondence school for children in isolated areas. The students receive and turn in their assignments by mail or through the Internet.

Australia has about 40 universities or colleges. Most of Australia's universities are publicly owned. Each university offers undergraduate and graduate studies. Australia also has several publicly owned colleges or institutes that specialize in particular areas, such as the Australian Maritime College. Students at publicly owned universities and colleges pay tuition fees that cover part of the cost of their education, and the federal government pays the rest. Tuition fees at Australia's private universities are considerably higher.

Religion. The Australian Constitution forbids a state religion and guarantees religious freedom. The majority of Australians are Christians, but many do not attend church regularly. The Anglican Church and the Roman Catholic Church have the most members.

Smaller numbers of Australians belong to the Baptist, Eastern Orthodox, Lutheran, and Uniting churches. The Methodist Church of Australia joined with a majority of the country's Congregationalists and Presbyterians to form the Uniting Church in 1977. The Uniting Church is now Australia's third largest religious denomination. Australia has small Jewish and Muslim minorities. About one-quarter of the population claim no specific religion.

The religions that are growing most rapidly in Australia are Buddhism, Hinduism, and Islam. The proportion of Christians is declining.

The arts

The federal government helps fund the major opera, ballet, and theater companies; the major symphony orchestras; and the motion-picture industry. It gives financial help to writers, painters, musicians, and composers.

Literature. The Aborigines had no written record of their culture and traditions and so did not contribute to early written Australian literature. The first white settlers, explorers, and visitors wrote extensively and often beau-

Schools of the air help children in remote areas of Australia obtain an education at home. Teachers communicate with students using two-way radios, computers, and other equipment.

tifully about the new environment and society. After about the 1820's, settlers began to create poetry and literature that was uniquely Australian. This literature includes works by the poets Charles Harpur and Henry Kendall. British explorers, such as Thomas Livingston Mitchell and Charles Sturt, published their journals, which provided details of the land's interior.

The first significant novels in Australia were by British immigrants. These include *The Recollections of Geoffry Hamlyn* (1859), a romance by the novelist Henry Kingsley, and *Clara Morison* (1854), a novel by the writer, preacher, and feminist Catherine Helen Spence. One of the most important novels of the colonial period was *For the Term of His Natural Life* (1870-1872) by the novelist and journalist Marcus Clarke, based on his idea of the sufferings of convicts in Tasmania. Thomas Alexander Browne, writing under the pen name Rolf Boldrewood, wrote *Robbery Under Arms* (1882-1883), an adventure tale about a gang of *bushrangers* (outlaws in the remote countryside). The authors Ada Cambridge, Rosa Campbell Praed, and Tasma (the pen name of Jessie Couvreur) were prominent women writers of this period.

During the late 1800's, many Australian writers continued to write pieces inspired by the colorful, adventurous life in the bush. Important writers of this period include the novelists Joseph Furphy, Henry Lawson, and Steele Rudd. The bush tradition in poetry was represented by the poets Adam Lindsay, Breaker Morant, Will Ogilvie, and Banjo Paterson. Paterson's bush ballad "The Man from Snowy River" ranks as one of Australia's most famous and best-loved poems.

Novelists of the early 1900's told stories of the past and celebrated the achievements of the explorers and pioneers who opened up the land. Important writers in this period include the novelists and short-story writers Frank Dalby Davison, Miles Franklin, and Vance Palmer, and the Australian author Katharine Susannah Prichard.

In the 1930's, more complex novels began to emerge in Australian literature. Christina Stead, one of the greatest Australian novelists, wrote *Seven Poor Men of Sydney* (1934), which describes radical workers and their struggle to live in Sydney, and *The Man Who Loved Children* (1940), about a demanding, tyrannical father.

The most important literary figure of the mid-1900's in Australia was Patrick White, a novelist who received the Nobel Prize in literature in 1973. His major novels include *The Tree of Man* (1955), and *Voss* (1957). Australian drama from this period includes Ray Lawler's *Summer of the Seventeenth Doll* (1955) and Alan Seymour's *The One Day of the Year* (1961).

Recent Australian novelists have been highly successful internationally. Thomas Keneally explores themes of goodness, guilt, and sin. His most famous work is *Schindler's Ark* (1982; U.S. title *Schindler's List*). The novelist and short-story writer Thea Astley creates sharp, humorous portraits of small-town life. The Booker Prize-winning author Peter Carey's novels include *Oscar and Lucinda* (1988) and *True History of the Kelly Gang* (2001). Important women writers of the late 1900's and early 2000's include Jessica Anderson, Helen Garner, Kate Grenville, Barbara Hanrahan, and Elizabeth Jolley. Playwright David Williamson has dominated Australian drama since the early 1970's with entertaining satires of Australian life and manners. Important nonfiction authors include the feminist Germaine Greer and the Aboriginal author Sally Morgan, who tells in *My Place* (1987) of coming to terms with her Aboriginal heritage.

Painting. Aboriginal rock art is the oldest continuous art tradition in the world, dating back to at least 40,000 years ago. The Aborigines also painted on bark, using elaborate designs of human and animal figures. In the late 1930's, a group of Aboriginal artists in central Australia developed a style of water-color landscape painting. The most famous of them was Albert Namatjira.

The first white painters include artists who recorded scientific and geographical information, beginning with the voyage led by the British navigator Captain James Cook in 1768. Early artists provided colonists in Australia

Reproduced by courtesy of the artist, George Milpurrurr, and of the Aboriginal Artist Agency Ltd. (© Robert Frerck)

Aboriginal painting depicted human and animal figures on bark or rock, similar to this traditional bark painting by a modern Aboriginal artist.

Australian National Gallery

The Australian National Gallery in Canberra exhibits a variety of artworks, including Australian paintings and sculpture from the 1900's, *shown here.*

with portraits and landscapes to send to Britain.

In the 1880's, a group of Australian artists began to paint in the Impressionist style, showing the ever-changing effects of nature. They are often referred to as the Heidelberg School, after Heidelberg, a suburban village near Melbourne where they worked. Leaders of this school included Charles Conder, Frederick McCubbin, Tom Roberts, Clara Southern, and Arthur Streeton.

During the 1900's, a number of Australian painters developed unique styles. The portrait painter William Dobell became famous for his revealing character studies. Russell Drysdale became known for his haunting pictures of the outback. Sidney Nolan created fantastic, dreamlike paintings based on themes from Australian folklore. During the middle and late 1900's, paintings of the outback by Frederick Williams won admiration. Such painters as Margaret Preston and Grace Cossington Smith pioneered modern art in Australia.

The Australian National Gallery in Canberra houses the country's national art collection. The National Gallery of Victoria, in Melbourne, and the Art Gallery of New South Wales, in Sydney, also have major collections of artworks.

Music and dance. Australia has a national opera company, the Australian Opera, and a national ballet company, the Australian Ballet. Such state companies as the Sydney Dance Company and the Victoria State Opera are well known. Each state capital has a professional symphony orchestra. A number of world-famous singers and composers were born in Australia. They include opera singers Marjorie Lawrence, Nellie Melba, and Joan Sutherland and composers Percy Grainger and Peter Sculthorpe. Modern composer Richard Meale is known for his stage and instrumental works, including the opera *Voss* (1986).

Theater and motion pictures. Each of Australia's state capitals has a permanent company of professional actors and actresses. Each company offers a yearlong season of classical and modern plays.

My Brilliant Career, a 1979 film based on a 1901 novel by Miles Franklin, showed the frustrations of youth in the outback of New South Wales. It starred Judy Davis and Sam Neill, *shown here.*

Australia was one of the first countries to develop a motion-picture industry. Australian filmmakers produced their first feature film in 1901. The Australian film industry nearly died out after the late 1930's because of competition from American and British movies. But Australian filmmaking revived during the late 1960's. Today, Australian film and television production are high-profile export industries. Such motion-picture stars as Cate Blanchett, Russell Crowe, Mel Gibson, and Nicole Kidman have gained international acclaim for their work. The diverse films of directors Bruce Beresford, Baz Luhrmann, George Miller, and Peter Weir show the growing importance and creativity of the Australian filmmaking industry.

Architecture. During the 1800's, many public buildings and private houses in Australia were built in the Georgian or Victorian style of architecture. Both these styles originated in England. The Georgian style featured a simple square or rectangular design and classical ornaments, especially columns. The Australian version of the Georgian style introduced the veranda as a basic element of the country's architecture. Most Victorian buildings had an irregular shape and elaborate ornaments, such as spires and pointed domes. The railings and roof supports for Victorian verandas were made of showy iron grillwork. Australia has a state-supported movement to preserve historic buildings.

Today, Australia's architecture is international in style. The large cities have towering structures of concrete, steel, and glass similar to those in other countries. However, some modern Australian architecture is highly unusual. The Sydney Opera House, a spectacular structure with saillike roofs, has attracted worldwide attention since its completion in 1973. It was designed by the Danish architect Jorn Utzøn.

Aboriginal artists perform traditional dance and musical pieces. The seated musician is playing the *didgeridoo,* a musical instrument made from hollowed-out pieces of wood.

The Eastern Highlands extend in a narrow band along Australia's east coast. They are sometimes called the Great Dividing Range because their slopes divide the flow of rivers in the region. The highlands are the most fertile land region in Australia.

© SuperStock

The land

Australia is surrounded by water, like an island. But geographers class it as a continent rather than as an island because of its great size. It is sometimes referred to as an "island continent."

Australia covers about 5 percent of Earth's land area. The island of Tasmania, which lies about 130 miles (209 kilometers) south of the Australian mainland, is considered part of the continent. Tasmania was part of the mainland until about 12,000 years ago. It became separated because the level of the ocean rose and covered the land connection.

Most of Australia is low and flat. The highest and most mountainous land lies along the east coast. Nearly all the land west of this region—about 90 percent of the total land area—consists of level plains and plateaus.

Land regions. Australia can be divided into three major land regions. They are, from east to west: (1) the Eastern Highlands, (2) the Central Lowlands, and (3) the Western Plateau.

The Eastern Highlands include the highest elevations in Australia. The region extends from Cape York Peninsula in extreme northeastern Australia to the south coast of Tasmania. A low plain bordered by sandy beaches and rocky cliffs stretches along the Pacific coast. This coastal plain is the rainiest area in the country. The southeastern section of the plain, from Brisbane to Melbourne, is the most heavily populated part of Australia.

The Eastern Highlands are sometimes called the *Great Dividing Range* because their slopes divide the flow of the rivers in the region. Rivers that flow down the eastern slopes empty into the ocean. Rivers that run down the western slopes flow to the Central Lowlands. However, the highlands are not a single range, nor are they especially mountainous. They consist mainly of high plateaus that are broken in many places by gorges, hills, and low mountain ranges.

Many of the plateaus in the Eastern Highlands have fertile soils and are used as cropland. Grass or forests cover other plateaus. At one time, forests also covered much of the coastal plain. Except in the far north, however, people have cleared most of the coastal forests.

The Central Lowlands have the lowest elevations in Australia. The region is generally flat. Many rivers flow through the lowlands after heavy rains. Rains are infrequent, however, except along the region's north and south coasts and near the Eastern Highlands. Riverbeds farther inland are dry most of the year.

Farmers in the southern part of the Central Lowlands grow wheat. Most of the rest of the region is too dry or hot for most crops and is used to graze livestock. The west-central part of the region is a barren, sandy desert. Lake Eyre, Australia's lowest point, is 52 feet (16 meters) below sea level along the southern edge of this desert.

The region has no large cities. The two biggest cities—Mount Isa and Broken Hill—have fewer than 30,000 people each. Both cities are mining centers.

The Western Plateau covers the western two-thirds of Australia. The region has a higher average elevation than the Central Lowlands but is mostly flat.

Deserts cover the central part of the Western Plateau. Except in the south and northeast, the deserts gradually give way to land covered by grass and shrubs. Farmers use much of this land to graze livestock. Low mountain ranges rise above the plateau in the grazing areas. Rainfall is heaviest in the extreme north and southwest. These areas have most of the region's cropland. A vast, dry, treeless plateau called the Nullarbor Plain extends about 400 miles (640 kilometers) along the southern edge of the region. The name *Nullarbor* comes from the Latin words *nulla* and *arbor,* which mean *no tree.*

The Western Plateau region has two large cities, Adelaide and Perth. Both cities lie on coastal plains, Adelaide in the extreme southeastern part of the region and Perth in the extreme southwest.

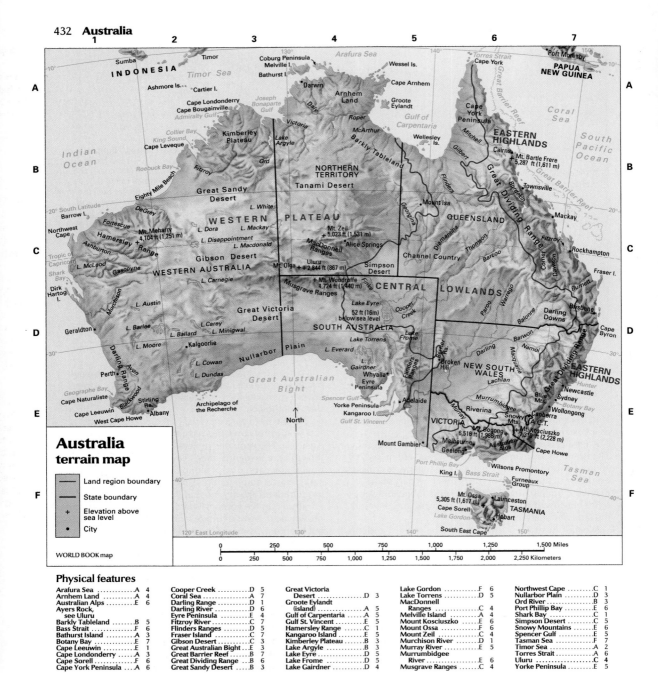

Australia terrain map

Land region boundary
State boundary
+ Elevation above sea level
• City

WORLD BOOK map

Mountains. Australia's highest mountains rise in the Australian Alps in the southern part of the Eastern Highlands. The Australian Alps consist of several ranges. The Snowy Mountains are the best known. Australia's highest peak, Mount Kosciuszko, rises 7,310 feet (2,228 meters) above sea level in the Snowy Mountains. Mount Kosciuszko and other tall peaks in the Australian Alps are snow covered in winter and attract many skiers.

The mountain ranges in the Western Plateau are lower than those in the Australian Alps. The highest peaks are in the MacDonnell and Musgrave ranges in central Australia. Uluru (also known as Ayers Rock) is a huge loaf-shaped rock formation just south of the MacDonnell Ranges in Uluru-Kata Tjuta National Park. It is a popular tourist attraction and a sacred area for Aborigines.

Deserts cover about one-third of Australia. The country has four major deserts. The Simpson Desert lies along the western edge of the Central Lowlands. The three other deserts—the Gibson, Great Sandy, and Great Victoria deserts—cover the central part of the Western Plateau. All the deserts except the Gibson consist of swirling sands that often drift into giant dunes. Some dunes measure more than 200 miles (320 kilometers) long. The Gibson Desert lies outside the path of the general wind direction and of wind-blown sands. Its surface consists of a mass of small stones and pebbles.

Rivers are one of Australia's most vital resources. Rivers provide the towns and cities with drinking water and supply farmers with much-needed water for irrigation. However, many of Australia's rivers are dry at least part of the year. They fill with water only during the rainy season. Dams and reservoirs on all the largest rivers store water for use during the dry season.

The Murray River is Australia's longest permanently flowing river. The Murray starts in the Snowy Mountains and winds west 1,609 miles (2,589 kilometers). It normally empties into the ocean southeast of Adelaide. In 2003, however, drought and irrigation demands caused the mouth of the river to dry up. During the southern dry season, the Murray is fed by the country's longest river, the Darling. The Darling River begins in the central part of the Eastern Highlands and flows southwest 1,702 miles (2,739 kilometers) to the Murray. The Darling is dry along most of its course in the winter. Its flow increases in summer, when parts of the Eastern Highlands receive most of their rain.

Australia's biggest water conservation project is the Snowy Mountains Scheme. It consists of an extensive system of dams, aqueducts, and tunnels. Some carry water from melting snows in the Snowy Mountains to nearby dams that store the water. Other aqueducts and tunnels channel water from the dams into the Murray and Murrumbidgee rivers. The increased water in these rivers is used to irrigate cropland in New South Wales and Victoria. This irrigation is crucial to agriculture in many parts of Australia. But it has also caused serious problems of *salinization* (accumulation of salt in the soil). The salts in the soil have been brought to the surface by the water, making the land unsuitable for crops.

Hydroelectric plants at the dams supply New South Wales, Victoria, and the Capital Territory with a little of their electric power. Tasmania draws almost all of its electric power from hydroelectric facilities.

Lakes. Australia's only large permanent lakes have been artificially created. They include Lake Argyle in

© Robert Frerck

Irrigation projects have greatly increased farm productivity in the southeastern part of the Central Lowlands. These irrigated orchards are in the Murrumbidgee River Irrigation Area.

© David Moore, Black Star

Dry grazing land covers much of Australia west of the Eastern Highlands. This sheep-grazing area in South Australia is part of the Western Plateau land region.

Uluru (also called Ayers Rock), a popular tourist attraction, stands in Uluru-Kata Tjuta National Park in central Australia. The rock is about $1\frac{1}{2}$ miles (2.4 kilometers) long. It rises 1,142 feet (348 meters) above the desert floor and 2,844 feet (867 meters) above sea level. It has many small caves. The walls of many caves are covered with rock paintings made long ago by Aboriginal artists.

Western Australia and Lake Gordon in Tasmania. Both are reservoirs for water conservation projects.

Most of Australia's natural lakes are dry for months or years at a time. Dry lakes called *playas* are common in South Australia and Western Australia. Most of the time, a playa is simply a dry bed of salt or clay. It fills with water only after heavy rains. The largest playas are in South Australia. They include Lake Eyre, Lake Torrens, Lake Gairdner, and Lake Frome.

Underground water. Australia has fairly plentiful underground water. But most of it is too salty for people to drink or use as irrigation water. In many areas, however, the water is not too salty for livestock to drink. On many large cattle and sheep stations, underground wells supply all the drinking water for the animals.

Much of Australia's underground water is *artesian water*. Artesian water is trapped under such great pressure that it gushes to the surface through any opening. The

water can thus be brought to the surface merely by digging a well. It does not have to be pumped.

Australia's chief source of artesian water is a vast underground rock formation called the Great Artesian Basin. The basin extends across much of eastern Australia. Other artesian basins lie near the northwest, west, and south coasts. Most of the water in the Great Artesian Basin is quite salty and so can be drunk only by livestock. In general, the water in the coastal basins has less salt. Farmers use some of this water for irrigation. Adelaide, Perth, and many small communities get some drinking water from coastal basins.

The Great Barrier Reef is the world's largest coral reef and one of Australia's most popular tourist attractions. Although its name suggests one reef, the Great Barrier Reef is a chain of more than 2,500 reefs and many small islands. The reefs and islands extend in a nearly unbroken chain for about 1,400 miles (2,300 kilometers) along Australia's northeast coast. The reefs are composed of about 400 species of corals of many shapes and colors. The waters around the Great Barrier Reef are always warm. The Great Barrier Reef is protected because of its environmental importance. It is one of Australia's 14 World Heritage areas, areas on an international registry of sites that have great natural or cultural value. Others include Kakadu National Park and Uluru-Kata Tjuta National Park in the Northern Territory.

Climate

The northern third of Australia lies in the tropics and so is warm or hot the year around. The rest of the country lies south of the tropics and has warm summers and mild or cool winters.

In winter, many parts of the south may have frosts. But the Australian Alps and the interior of Tasmania are the only areas of the country where temperatures remain below freezing for more than a day or so at a time.

Australia receives most of its moisture as rain. Snow falls in Tasmania, the Australian Alps, and occasionally in the central western part of New South Wales. About two-thirds of the country receives less than 10 inches (25 centimeters) of rain a year. Much of the rest of Australia has less than 20 inches (51 centimeters) of rainfall annually. These regions require irrigation for farming. The heaviest rainfall occurs along the north, east, southeast, and extreme southwest coasts.

The Great Barrier Reef, the world's largest coral reef, supports a fascinating variety of life, including fish and colorful water animals called *polyps*. The reef's beauty attracts many divers.

The east coast of Queensland is the wettest part of the continent. Some places along this coast receive as much as 150 inches (381 centimeters) of rain a year. Parts of the southeast coast and of Tasmania are the only areas of the continent that get uniform amounts of rainfall throughout the year. Rainfall is seasonal throughout the rest of Australia.

Australia lies south of the equator, and so its seasons are opposite those in the Northern Hemisphere. The southern part of the continent has four distinct seasons. Winter, the wettest and coolest season in Australia, lasts from June to August. Summer, the hottest and driest season, lasts from December to February.

Tropical northern Australia has only two seasons—a wet season and a dry one. The wet season corresponds with summer and lasts from November to April. The dry season corresponds with winter and lasts from May to October. The wet season brings heavy downpours and violent storms, especially on Australia's north coast. In 1974, for example, a cyclone destroyed much of the northern coastal city of Darwin. Floods plague many parts of Australia during the wet season. However, droughts are usually a far more serious problem. Nearly every section of Australia has a drought during the country's annual dry season. Water conservation prevents these droughts from doing serious harm in most cases, but they can cause severe water shortages.

Animals and plants

Native animals. At one time, all the continents were part of one huge land mass. Australia became separated from this land mass about 200 million years ago. As a result, its animals developed differently from those on oth-

er continents. Australia's most famous native animals include kangaroos, koalas, wallabies, wombats, and other *marsupials*. Marsupials are mammals that give birth to tiny, poorly developed offspring. In most species, the babies mature in a pouch on the mother's abdomen. Australia has about 200 species of marsupials.

The platypus and the echidna are among the unique Australian animals. They are the only mammals that hatch their young from eggs. Platypuses live only in Australia. Echidnas live in Australia and on the neighboring island of New Guinea.

Australia has about 700 species of native birds. They include the world's only black swans and about 60 kinds of cockatoos, parakeets, and other parrots. Two large flightless birds, the emu and the cassowary, are also native to Australia. The kookaburra, a member of the king-fisher family, is one of Australia's best-known birds. Its loud call sounds like laughter and is a familiar sound in residential areas.

Australia has about 140 species of snakes and about 500 species of lizards. The lizards are nonpoisonous. Most of the snakes are poisonous. The taipan and the tiger snake are among the deadliest snakes in the world.

Native plants. Two main kinds of native plants, acacias and eucalyptuses, dominate Australia's landscape. They are the most common shrubs in the dry lands and the most common trees in the moister areas. Acacias, which Australians call *wattles,* bear their seeds in pods. Australia has about 700 species of acacias. Many of them have brightly colored flowers. Common shrubby species include the mulga and the myall. The silver wattle and the blackwood are tall trees.

Eucalyptuses—or *eucalypts,* as they are known in Aus-

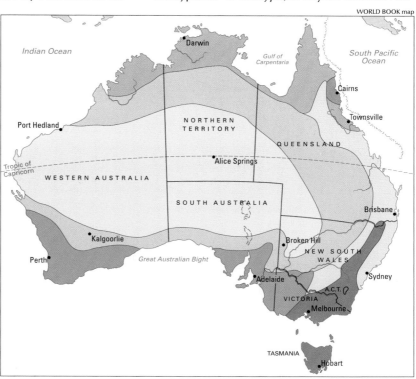

WORLD BOOK map

What Australia's climate is like

In general, Australia has a warm, dry climate. But the climate differs from one part of the country to another, as this map shows. Australia lies south of the equator, and so its seasons are opposite those in the Northern Hemisphere.

Tropical wet-Always hot and wet. Heavy precipitation well distributed throughout year.

Tropical wet and dry-Always hot, with alternate wet and dry seasons. Heavy precipitation in wet season.

Semiarid-Hot to cold. Great changes in temperature from day to night except in coastal areas. Light precipitation.

Desert-Hot to cool. Great changes in temperature from day to night except in coastal areas. Very little precipitation.

Subtropical dry summer-Hot, dry summers and mild, rainy winters. Moderate precipitation in winter.

Humid subtropical-Warm to hot summers and cool winters. Moderate precipitation in all seasons.

Humid oceanic-Moderately warm summers and generally cool winters. Moderate precipitation in all seasons.

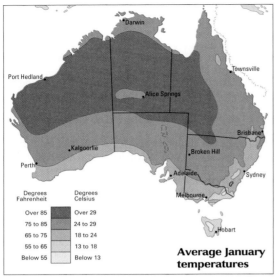

Average January temperatures

Degrees Fahrenheit	Degrees Celsius
Over 85	Over 29
75 to 85	24 to 29
65 to 75	18 to 24
55 to 65	13 to 18
Below 55	Below 13

WORLD BOOK map

This map shows the average temperatures in Australia during January, midway through the country's summer. Australia's summers are hottest in the northwest and coolest in the southeast.

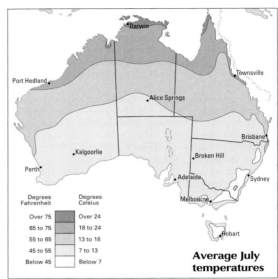

Average July temperatures

Degrees Fahrenheit	Degrees Celsius
Over 75	Over 24
65 to 75	18 to 24
55 to 65	13 to 18
45 to 55	7 to 13
Below 45	Below 7

WORLD BOOK map

July is the coolest month in every part of Australia. Light frosts are common in the south during July. But the extreme southeastern highlands are the only areas that ever have cold weather.

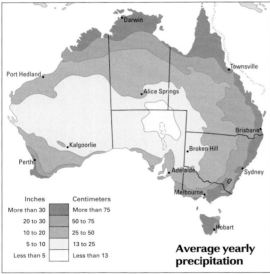

Average yearly precipitation

Inches	Centimeters
More than 30	More than 75
20 to 30	50 to 75
10 to 20	25 to 50
5 to 10	13 to 25
Less than 5	Less than 13

WORLD BOOK map

This map shows the average amounts of annual precipitation in Australia. Almost all the precipitation is in the form of rain. Snow falls only in the southeastern mountains and in Tasmania.

© David Moore, Black Star

Snow covers Mount Kosciuszko and other peaks in the Australian Alps in winter. The area attracts many skiers.

tralia—are the most widespread plants in the country. Australia has about 500 species of eucalyptuses. Most species have narrow, leathery leaves. The leaves contain a fragrant oil that gives the tree a unique smell. In bushfires, the oil can heat up and burst into flames even before the fire reaches the tree.

Scrubby eucalyptuses, which are also known as *mallee scrub,* cover large areas of the interior. Eucalyptus trees, which Australians call *gum trees* or *gums,* include the tallest hardwood trees in the world. Two species, the mountain ash and the karri, may grow to

about 280 feet (85 meters). Eucalyptuses once grew only in Australia and on a few islands to the north. However, eucalyptuses now grow in many other warm areas, including California, Hawaii, and Africa and countries bordering the Mediterranean Sea.

Palms and trees that resemble palms grow in many parts of Australia. Grass trees are palmlike trees of the western dry lands. They are related to the yucca trees of the American Southwest. Macrozamia trees grow throughout Australia. They have palmlike or fernlike leaves and bear cones, as needleleaf trees do. Australia has few native needleleaf trees, other than kauri pines and bunya pines. Shrubs called *saltbushes* are common in the dry grazing areas of southern Australia. They are so named because their leaves have a salty taste. The leaves provide excellent feed for livestock.

Australia has thousands of wildflowers. Many of them are desert species whose seeds lie buried until brought to life by a heavy rain. Then, for a few days or weeks, the

Animals of Australia   Some of the many mammals, birds, and reptiles of Australia are pictured on this map. The animals live in various other areas on the continent in addition to those indicated. For example, emus live everywhere in Australia except the rain forests.

WORLD BOOK map; illustrations by Tom Dolan

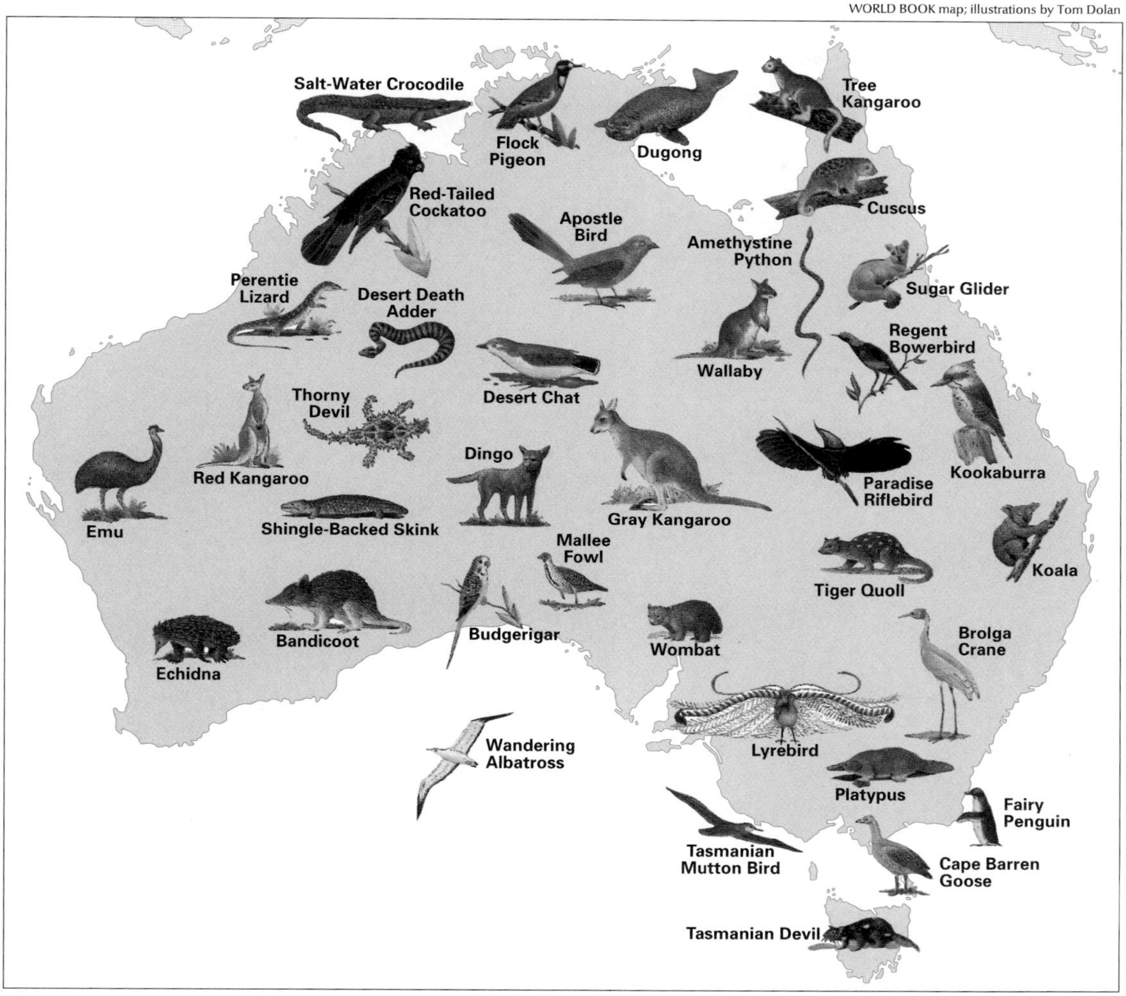

Salt-Water Crocodile
Flock Pigeon
Dugong
Tree Kangaroo
Red-Tailed Cockatoo
Cuscus
Apostle Bird
Amethystine Python
Sugar Glider
Perentie Lizard
Desert Death Adder
Regent Bowerbird
Wallaby
Thorny Devil
Desert Chat
Kookaburra
Red Kangaroo
Dingo
Paradise Riflebird
Emu
Shingle-Backed Skink
Gray Kangaroo
Koala
Mallee Fowl
Tiger Quoll
Bandicoot
Budgerigar
Wombat
Brolga Crane
Echidna
Wandering Albatross
Lyrebird
Platypus
Fairy Penguin
Tasmanian Mutton Bird
Cape Barren Goose
Tasmanian Devil

desert bursts into bloom with flowers of every color.

Introduced species. The mammals that lived in Australia before the first settlers arrived were bats, echidnas, mice, platypuses, rats, and the various kinds of marsupials. The first settlers, the Aborigines, brought along a type of dog known as a *dingo.* Some dingoes escaped into the wild. Today, their descendants are Australia's chief beasts of prey. European settlers introduced into Australia many mammals, including cats, dogs, cattle, deer, foxes, goats, hogs, horses, rabbits, and sheep. They also introduced camels, water buffaloes, various kinds of birds, and many species of plants.

Camels, cane toads, water buffaloes, and certain other introduced species have become wild and are pests. Some domestic cats have gone wild and pose a great risk to native birds and small animals. In some cases, species have had to be exterminated. Wild rabbits caused extensive damage to crops and grazing lands. In the 1950's, Australian officials attempted to wipe them

out with a deliberately introduced disease called *myxomatosis.* This policy was successful until the rabbits developed *immunity* (natural protection from the disease). In the mid-1990's, scientists released a new virus that has helped to control the number of rabbits.

Economy

Australia is one of the world's rich, developed countries. Most developed countries have become rich through the production and export of manufactured goods. Australia's wealth, however, has come chiefly from farming and mining.

The processing of farm and mineral products makes up a major part of Australia's manufacturing industry. Manufacturing was once the leading employer in Australia. But during the late 1900's, manufacturing declined in importance, while *service industries* increased in importance. Service industries are economic activities that provide services, rather than produce goods.

Plants of Australia

This map pictures some of the trees, shrubs, and other plants of Australia. Many of the plants, such as wallaby grass and golden wattles, grow in other areas of the continent in addition to those shown. However, forest trees grow only in the moist coastal regions.

WORLD BOOK map; illustrations by Tom Dolan and James Teason

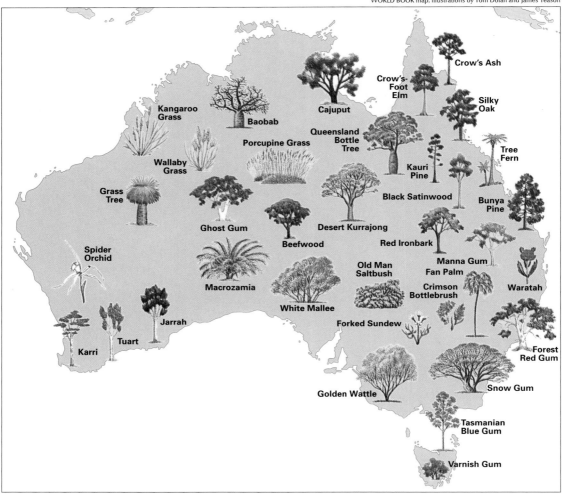

Australia relies on its farms and mines for export goods. By selling farm products and minerals abroad, Australia earns the export income that most other developed countries earn from the sale of manufactured products. Part of Australia's export income goes to the farmers and mining companies that produce the goods originally. Much of it goes to firms that process and distribute the goods. Thus, Australia's agricultural and mineral exports benefit the economy as a whole.

Australia has traditionally been limited by a lack of *capital*—that is, money to finance business and industrial development. As a result, the country has had to borrow capital from other nations and has become heavily indebted to them. American, British, Japanese, and other foreign investors own or control many mining companies, factories, and other businesses in Australia.

Service industries provide nearly three-quarters of Australia's jobs and make up more than two-thirds of Australia's *gross domestic product*—the total value of

goods and services produced within the country annually. Hospitals, schools, government agencies, stores, hotels, and restaurants are service industries. Also included in this category are banking, trade, transportation, communication, education, and tourism activities.

Manufacturing. Unlike most other developed countries, Australia imports more manufactured goods than it exports. Australian factories produce many of the consumer goods, such as processed foods and household articles, that the people require. But the nation has to import most of its *producer goods*—that is, factory machinery, construction equipment, and other goods used in production. Iron and steel are the chief exceptions. Australia's iron and steel industry produces enough of the metals to meet the needs of other industries. Australia's factories depend heavily on foreign capital.

Most of Australia's factories specialize in assembly work and light manufacturing. Many plants process farm products or minerals for export. The leading manu-

Some typical Australian plants
These pictures show three common kinds of Australian plants. Acacias, or *wattles,* have attractive flowers. Eucalyptus trees are among the world's tallest trees. Grass trees resemble palms.

© G. R. Roberts

A flowering wattle

© David R. Frazier Photolibrary

Eucalyptus trees

© Robert Frerck

Grass trees

Some typical Australian animals
These pictures show four common kinds of Australian animals. Emus are big, flightless birds. Platypuses are egg-laying mammals. Kangaroos and koalas are marsupials.

© Robert Frerck

An emu and its eggs

© Dave Watts, A.N.T. Photo Library

A platypus in water

© G. R. Roberts

A koala eating eucalyptus leaves

Australian Information Service

A red kangaroo

factured products are processed foods and beverages; metals, including iron and steel; transportation equipment, including cars; paper; chemicals; textiles and clothing; printed materials; and household appliances. New South Wales and Victoria have about two-thirds of the country's factories and about two-thirds of the factory workers. Most of the factories operate in and around Sydney and Melbourne. Manufacturing provides about 15 percent of Australia's gross domestic product.

Mining. Australia has rich mineral resources. But many of the deposits lie in the dry areas, far from major settlements. Such deposits are extremely expensive to mine. Workers must construct roads and railways to the mining sites. The miners and their families must have housing. The costs of mining development in Australia are so high that the mining industry depends heavily on foreign capital. Foreign investors own or control about half of the mining industry.

Australia began to develop its mineral resources during the 1800's. By the end of the century, it was exporting

Assembly plants, such as this automaking plant in the Melbourne suburb of Broadmeadows, account for much of Australia's industrial output. Many other plants process farm products or minerals.

© Nick Rains, Australian Picture Library

large amounts of copper, gold, lead, silver, tin, and zinc. These minerals remained the chief products of the mining industry until the mid-1900's. During the 1950's, geologists discovered huge deposits of bauxite, coal, and iron ore in Australia. They discovered manganese, natural gas, nickel, and petroleum during the 1960's.

Australia has become one of the world's major mining countries. It ranks first in the production of bauxite, diamonds, and lead, and is a leading producer of coal, copper, gold, iron ore, manganese, nickel, silver, tin, titanium, zinc, and zircon. Nearly all the world's high-quality opals are mined in Australia.

Western Australia, Queensland, and New South Wales are the leading mining states. Western Australia produces most of the nickel, iron ore, and gold and much of the bauxite. Queensland is the chief producer of bauxite, copper, and silver. New South Wales leads in the production of coal, lead, and zinc. All the manganese comes from the Northern Territory. Most of Australia's tin comes from Tasmania. Offshore fields along the northwest coast of Western Australia are Australia's main source of petroleum. Other major petroleum producers include South Australia and Victoria. Natural gas is produced in South Australia and Western Australia. The country has the world's largest undeveloped deposits of uranium. The richest uranium deposits lie in the Northern Territory and South Australia.

Agriculture in Australia is highly mechanized, requiring minimal human labor. Only about 5 percent of the workers are farmers, but they produce nearly all the food the people need. Agriculture provides only 3 percent of Australia's gross domestic product.

Farmland covers about 60 percent of Australia. However, most of this land is dry grazing land. Farmers grow crops on only about 10 percent of the farmland. They irrigate about 10 percent of the cropland.

Australia's leading farm products are cattle and calves, wheat, and wool, followed by dairy products, fruit, and sugar cane. These products are also the country's chief agricultural exports. Australia is the world's largest producer and exporter of wool and a leading producer and exporter of beef, sugar, and wheat. Another rapidly

growing industry is winemaking. All the Australian states produce wine, but New South Wales, South Australia, and Victoria produce the best vintages. Western Australia also has a developing wine industry. In regions suitable for growing grapes, winemakers are turning old farms and orchards into vineyards to produce grapes for wine. The country's other major farm products include barley, chickens and eggs, oats, rice, potatoes, sheep and lambs, vegetables, and cotton.

Farmers raise sheep and cattle in all the Australian states. New South Wales and Western Australia together raise more than half the country's sheep and produce about half its wool. Queensland and New South Wales raise more than half of Australia's beef cattle. Victoria is the leading producer of dairy products. Farmers grow wheat in all areas of the country that have adequate rainfall and climate. But production is heavily concentrated in New South Wales and Western Australia. Farms on the east coast of Queensland grow sugar cane, bananas, pineapples, and other crops that need a wet tropical cli-

Australia's gross domestic product

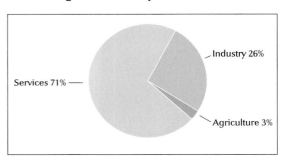

Services 71% —
Industry 26%
Agriculture 3%

Australia's gross domestic product (GDP) was $364,511,000,000 in U.S. dollars in 1998. The GDP is the total value of goods and services produced within a country in a year. *Services* include community, government, and personal services; finance, insurance, and real estate; transportation and communication; and wholesale and retail trade. *Industry* includes construction, manufacturing, mining, and utilities. *Agriculture* includes agriculture, forestry, and fishing.

Production and workers by economic activities

Economic activities	Percent of GDP produced	Employed workers	
		Number of people	Percent of total
Finance, insurance, real estate, & business services	27	1,247,400	15
Community, government, & personal services	22	2,697,500	31
Manufacturing	13	1,099,600	13
Wholesale and retail trade	12	1,776,200	21
Transportation & communication	10	545,000	6
Construction	6	620,300	7
Mining	4	83,700	1
Agriculture, forestry, & fishing	3	422,200	5
Utilities	3	64,900	1
Total	100	8,556,800	100

Figures are for 1998.
Sources: International Labour Organization; International Monetary Fund.

Mining and manufacturing in Australia

This map shows the location of Australia's chief mineral deposits and manufacturing centers. Most of the mineral deposits are mined, and so they are the centers of Australia's mining industry. Major deposits are shown in large type, and lesser ones in small type. Manufacturing centers are in red.

- ● Perth   Manufacturing center
- ● Coal   Major mineral deposit
- ● Tin   Other mineral deposit

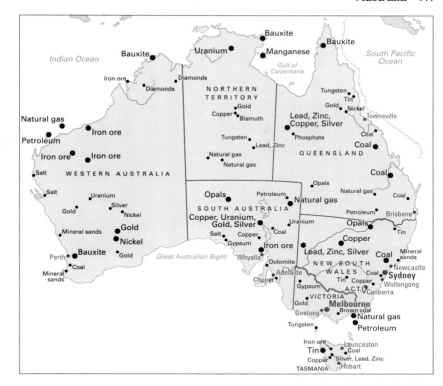

Indian Ocean

Bauxite

Uranium

Bauxite

Bauxite

Manganese

South Pacific Ocean

Gulf of Carpentaria

Iron ore

Diamonds

Diamonds

NORTHERN TERRITORY

Tungsten

Tin

Natural gas

Petroleum

Iron ore

Gold

Copper

Bismuth

Lead, Zinc, Copper, Silver

Gold

Nickel

Townsville

Iron ore

Iron ore

Tungsten

Lead, Zinc

Phosphate

Coal

Coal

Salt

WESTERN AUSTRALIA

Natural gas

Natural gas

QUEENSLAND

Salt

Uranium

Silver

Nickel

Opals

Opals

Petroleum

Natural gas

Natural gas

Coal

Coal

Gold

Mineral sands

Gold

Nickel

Opals

SOUTH AUSTRALIA

Copper, Uranium, Gold, Silver

Natural gas

Uranium

Petroleum

Brisbane

Opals

Tin

Salt

Copper

Coal

Copper

Perth

Bauxite

Gold

Coal

Great Australian Bight

Gypsum

Whyalla

Iron ore

Dolomite

Lead, Zinc, Silver

Coal

Mineral sands

Mineral sands

Coal

NEW SOUTH WALES

Newcastle

Sydney

Copper

Adelaide

Tin

Copper

Coal

Gypsum

A.C.T.

Canberra

Wollongong

VICTORIA

Gold

Melbourne

Brown coal

Geelong

Natural gas

Tungsten

Petroleum

Iron ore

Launceston

Coal

Tin

Copper

Silver, Lead, Zinc

TASMANIA

Hobart

WORLD BOOK map

Agriculture and fishing in Australia

This map shows Australia's chief agricultural and fishing regions. The most fertile cropland lies along the east, southeast, and extreme southwest coasts. Dry grasslands cover much of the interior and are used to graze livestock. Shellfish are Australia's leading fishery products.

- Crop farming
- Dairying
- Wheat and sheep farming
- Sheep grazing
- Beef cattle grazing
- Generally unproductive land
- Fishing

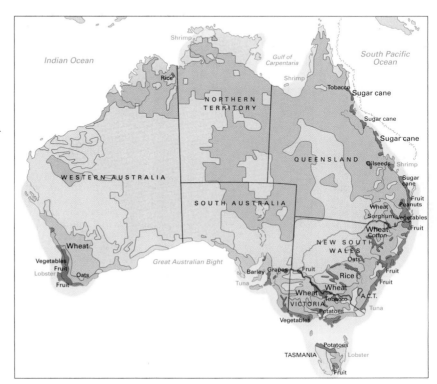

Indian Ocean

Shrimp

Gulf of Carpentaria

South Pacific Ocean

Rice

Shrimp

Tobacco

Sugar cane

NORTHERN TERRITORY

Sugar cane

Sugar cane

WESTERN AUSTRALIA

QUEENSLAND

Oilseeds

Shrimp

Sugar cane

Fruit

Peanuts

SOUTH AUSTRALIA

Wheat

Vegetables

Sorghum

Wheat

Cotton

Fruit

NEW SOUTH WALES

Wheat

Oats

Vegetables

Fruit

Lobster

Oats

Fruit

Great Australian Bight

Barley

Grapes

Fruit

Rice

Fruit

Tuna

A.C.T.

Wheat

Wheat

Tobacco

Tuna

VICTORIA

Potatoes

Vegetables

TASMANIA

Potatoes

Lobster

Fruit

WORLD BOOK map

mate. Such fruit as apples and pears are common in all the states. New South Wales and South Australia produce most of the country's oranges.

Forestry and fishing. Forests cover about 20 percent of Australia, mostly in the Eastern Highlands and moist coastal areas. The northeast coast has tropical rain forests. The vast majority of Australia's forest trees are eucalyptuses. Industries use the wood of some eucalyptus species for making paper and such items as floorboards and furniture. But eucalyptus wood is too hard for most other purposes, including most types of housing construction. Therefore, tree farms plant imported species of softwoods. Monterey pines, originally from California, have become Australia's second most important timber trees, after eucalyptuses.

Although Australia is surrounded by water, its fishing resources are limited. Thousands of species of fishes live in the coastal waters, and Australia has developed a small but profitable fishing industry. The industry earns most of its income from the catch of shellfish, especially abalones, lobsters, oysters, prawns, and scallops. The fishing fleet also brings in fairly large catches of mullet, salmon, and tuna. Australia exports much of the shellfish catch. Divers collect some pearls from oysters.

Tourism. Australia has a variety of tourist attractions. They include wildlife sanctuaries, sandy beaches, the Great Barrier Reef, the Australian Alps, Uluru, and numerous points of historical interest. More than 4 million foreign tourists visit Australia each year. Tourism aids the economy, especially the service industries, such as retail trade, restaurants, and hotels.

Distance and cost have been the major obstacles to growth of Australia's tourist industry. Australia is about twice as far from North America and Europe as North America and Europe are from each other, so travel to Australia is costly for North American and European vacationers. About half of Australia's visitors come from less distant places, especially New Zealand and other Pacific islands, Japan, and Southeast Asia. These places

© Robert Frerck

The Snowy Mountains Scheme is a vast irrigation and hydroelectric power project in Australia's southeastern highlands. Pipelines like those at the left carry water from mountain streams to a nearby series of dams and hydroelectric plants. The runoff from the dams flows into the Murray and Murrumbidgee rivers for use in irrigation.

are also the ones most visited by Australians, although many Australians also visit Europe and North America.

International trade. Farm products, minerals, and other raw materials are important to the nation's economy. They account for about half of export earnings. Manufactured goods account for about one-third of export earnings. More than three-fourths of Australia's imports are manufactured goods.

Australia exports minerals, wheat, and fruit to the United Kingdom and other western European countries, but Japan is Australia's biggest customer. It especially buys coal, iron ore, and other minerals. China, Japan, and other Asian countries are major purchasers of Australian farm products, especially wheat. Japan is by far the leading buyer of Australian wool. The United States and Japan are Australia's chief source of *producer goods*, machinery and other goods used in manufacturing. The United States, in turn, imports large amounts of Australian beef, shellfish, sugar, and *alumina*—the substance in bauxite that is used to make aluminum.

Transportation. Automobiles are the chief means of passenger transportation in Australia. Paved roads link the state capitals and the largest inland cities. Many roads in the outback are unpaved.

Brisbane, Cairns, Melbourne, Perth, and Sydney have large international airports. Air transportation is particularly important in the outback. A private, nonprofit organization called the Royal Flying Doctor Service flies emergency medical help to all areas of the outback except the Northern Territory. A publicly owned company provides this service in the Northern Territory.

Trucks, railroads, and ships haul most of Australia's intercity freight. The trucking industry is mainly privately owned. Australia's main-line railroads were all publicly owned until the late 1900's, but many are now privately owned. The Trans-Australian Railroad is the country's

© Mike James, Photo Researchers

Australia's thriving mining industry produces large amounts of bauxite, coal, copper, diamonds, iron ore, lead, opals, and zinc. This iron ore mine is near Iron Knob, South Australia.

Golden wheat fields, such as this one in New South Wales, are important to the Australian economy. Australia exports great quantities of wheat to China, Japan, and other Asian countries.

© Lance Nelson, Stock Photos

longest rail line. It extends 1,108 miles (1,783 kilometers) from Port Pirie in South Australia to Kalgoorlie in Western Australia. The main-line railroads chiefly haul farm goods and minerals from the producing areas to the coastal cities and ports. In addition to the main rail lines, Australia has several small private railroads. These lines largely haul minerals from out-of-the-way mines to the main-line railroads. Sydney and Melbourne have extensive commuter rail systems.

Ships carry large amounts of minerals between Australian coastal ports, and they haul nearly all the country's overseas freight. However, Australia has only a small merchant fleet. Foreign vessels carry most of the nation's intercoastal freight and almost all its overseas cargo. The busiest eastern ports include Gladstone, Hay Point, Melbourne, Newcastle, and Sydney. Dampier, Fremantle, Port Hedland, and Port Walcott are among the busiest ports in Western Australia.

Communication. Australia's postal, telephone, and telegraph systems are partly or fully owned by the federal government and operated by independent govern-ment agencies. The Australian Postal Corporation runs the postal system. The telephone system was fully government-owned until the 1990's. However, the telecommunications industry now operates in a fully competitive market. Except in the outback, nearly every Australian household has a telephone. In the remotest parts of the outback, many people use two-way radios in place of telephones. The Internet has also become a crucial means of communication in outback Australia.

Almost all Australian families own one or more television sets and radios. Commercial broadcasters own and operate about half the radio stations and three of the five free TV stations. Almost all the rest are owned and financed by the federal government and operated by the Australian Broadcasting Corporation (ABC), an independent government agency.

Almost all cable and satellite TV is privately owned. The federal government owns the Special Broadcasting Service (SBS), a free public broadcaster that operates radio stations and a TV station, with programs in English and other languages.

Australia has experienced rapid expansion of new electronic and telecommunications technologies, in industry, government, education, and private household use. More than 50 percent of Australian homes have at least one computer.

Australia has about 50 daily newspapers, all privately owned. The daily newspapers include *The Herald-Sun* and *The Age* in Melbourne, and the *Sydney Morning Herald* and *Daily Telegraph* in Sydney. A national daily, *The Australian,* is published in Adelaide, Brisbane, Melbourne, and Sydney. There are also many foreign-language newspapers published in Australia's cities.

History

Aboriginal settlement. The first people to discover, explore, and colonize the Australian continent were the Aborigines. Scientists believe that the Aborigines traveled to Australia and New Guinea by boat from Southeast Asia about 50,000 years ago. They soon spread throughout Australia. By 30,000 to 25,000 years ago, Aborigines had colonized most of the country.

The Aborigines were a *nomadic* (traveling) people

© Robert Frerck

Beef cattle are raised throughout Australia except the deserts. But production is greatest in New South Wales and Queensland. This cattle auction is being held in Rockhampton, Queensland.

who hunted, grew or gathered food, and fished. They made tools and weapons from stone, shell, bone, wood, fiber, and natural gums. The Aborigines were active traders of such goods as shells, stone, tools, and *pituri,* a desert plant that contains nicotine. They exchanged these goods, along with ideas and news, through extensive trading networks across Australia.

By the time of European settlement in 1788, there were about 750,000 Aborigines and at least 250 distinct languages. The Europeans often assumed that the Aborigines had a primitive society. But it was a society rich in spirituality, art, languages, and understanding of the Australian environment.

Ships from Asia reached Australia's northern shores in the 1400's. These visitors included Chinese, Arabs, and Pacific Islanders. The most important Asian visitors were fishing crews from Macassar (now Indonesia), who stayed several months each year and influenced Aboriginal society and culture.

European explorations. Some historians believe that Portuguese navigators sighted the coast of Australia in the 1500's. The first recorded date for a European sighting of Australia is 1606, when the Dutch explorer Willem Jansz and the Spanish navigator Luis Vaez de Torres explored the waters off northeastern Australia. The Torres Strait is named for the Spanish explorer.

Throughout the 1600's, the Dutch explored and roughly mapped every Australian coastline except the eastern seaboard. In 1642, the Dutch sea captain Abel Tasman sailed around the southern part of Tasmania. He named it *Van Diemen's Land,* in honor of a Dutch governor, and claimed it for the Netherlands. In 1855, the island was renamed *Tasmania* in Tasman's honor. The Dutch found Australia harsh and forbidding, with no trading possibilities. They made no settlements there.

Captain Cook. In 1768, the British Admiralty appointed the British navigator Captain James Cook to find and take possession of what it called the *southern continent.* Cook landed at Botany Bay on the southeast coast of Australia on April 29, 1770. The fertile land and comfortable climate of Botany Bay left a good impression on Cook. He did not understand the Aboriginal ways of land management and assumed the land was free for British settlement. Cook claimed the east coast of the continent for Britain, naming it *New South Wales.*

British settlement. Until the Revolutionary War in America (1775-1783), Britain regularly sent convicts to the American Colonies. This practice, called *transportation,* helped to relieve overcrowded jails in Britain. But after their independence, the American Colonies would not accept any more British convicts. British officials needed a new prison colony. They also were interested in establishing a new colony in the east as a strategic post. They selected Australia as the settlement site.

The First Fleet, under the command of Captain Arthur Phillip, left for Australia in May 1787. Of the more than 1,000 people who sailed, about 750 were convicts and their families, with more than 200 marines to guard them. The fleet reached Botany Bay in January 1788, but Phillip found the area unsuitable for settlement. He selected a cove about 7 miles (11 kilometers) north of Botany Bay as the site for the settlement, which became the city of Sydney. On Jan. 26, 1788, the First Fleet sailed into Sydney Cove and unfurled the British flag over the lands of an Aboriginal people called the Cadigal.

The convicts sent to Australia were mainly from the working classes of England and Ireland. They provided the skilled and unskilled labor to build the colony. Convicts worked on government projects, such as constructing roads, bridges, and buildings. They also labored on government farms. Although the colony was established as a kind of jail, the convicts did not live in jail conditions. In the early years, the colony operated much like a village in England. Convicts wore their own clothes, lived in their own homes, and could run their own businesses. Free husbands, wives, and children came to the colony to join convict spouses or parents.

The New South Wales Corps. Governor Phillip left the colony in 1792. The marines who had accompanied him were replaced by the New South Wales Corps, a

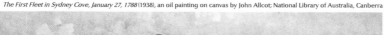
The First Fleet in Sydney Cove, January 27, 1788 (1938), an oil painting on canvas by John Allcot; National Library of Australia, Canberra

The First Fleet sailed into Sydney Cove on Jan. 26, 1788, to establish the first permanent European settlement in Australia. The fleet consisted of 11 ships carrying about 750 British convicts, their spouses, and their children, with more than 200 marines to guard them.

Important dates in Australia

50,000 years ago Ancestors of the Aborigines may have settled Australia.

A.D. 1606 Willem Jansz became the first European known to sight Australia and land there.

1642 Abel Janszoon Tasman sighted Van Diemen's Land. It was renamed Tasmania in 1855.

1770 James Cook explored Australia's east coast. He claimed the area for the United Kingdom and named it New South Wales.

1788 Great Britain (later the United Kingdom) established New South Wales as a prison colony.

1801-1803 Matthew Flinders sailed completely around Australia, proving it to be one large land mass.

1829 Charles Fremantle claimed the entire western part of the

Australian continent for the United Kingdom.

1851 Gold was discovered in New South Wales and Victoria.

1868 The United Kingdom ended the transportation of convicts to Australia.

1901 Australia became an independent nation. Melbourne was named the temporary capital.

1927 The federal capital was transferred to Canberra.

1967 The Australian Constitution was amended to permit the establishment of federal programs to aid the Aborigines.

1978 The Northern Territory became responsible for its own administration, the first step toward Australian statehood.

1999 Voters rejected a plan to make Australia a republic and chose to keep the British monarch as Australia's head of state.

Australia exploration and discovery

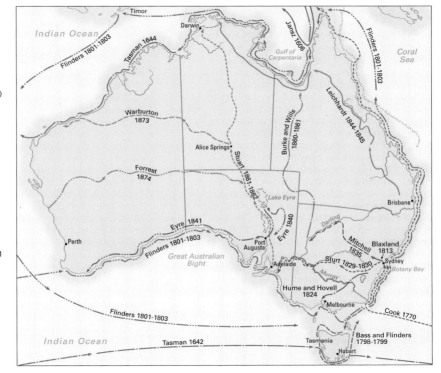

Sea Explorers

——— Jansz 1606 (Neth.)

—·—·— Tasman 1642, 1644 (Neth.)

- - - - - Cook 1770 (U.K.)

— — — Bass and Flinders 1798-1799 (U.K.)

—··—··— Flinders 1801-1803 (U.K.)

Land Explorers

——— Blaxland 1813

—·—·— Hume and Hovell 1824

- - - - - Sturt 1829-1830

——— Mitchell 1835

—··—··— Eyre 1840-1841

——— Leichhardt 1844-1845

—·—·— Burke and Wills 1860-1861

- - - - - Stuart 1861-1862

— — — Warburton 1873

—··—··— Forrest 1874

| 0 | 500 Miles |
| 0 | 500 Kilometers |

WORLD BOOK map

British infantry regiment. The corps soon gained much power in the colony. In 1806, the British sea captain William Bligh became governor. His reforms triggered conflict with the corps. On Jan. 26, 1808, the commander of the New South Wales Corps, George Johnston, arrested Bligh and took control of the colony.

In 1809, the British government appointed Lachlan Macquarie governor. Macquarie brought his own troops to replace the New South Wales Corps. He arrested Johnston and regained control of the colony.

Macquarie's administration. Macquarie had a liberal, tolerant policy toward convicts and *emancipists* (ex-convicts who had served their time or been pardoned). These policies angered wealthy free settlers, who thought they were superior to the emancipists. In 1819, British officials appointed John Thomas Bigge to lead an investigation of the colony. Bigge's report was critical of Macquarie's policies. Bigge recommended the exten-

sion of *assignment,* the practice of assigning convicts to free settlers who put them to work. He also concluded that transportation did not discourage crime and should be made more severe.

In response to Bigge's report, the British recalled Macquarie to England and increased the severity of the convict system. After the 1820's, life for convicts became much stricter and more controlled.

End of transportation. Free immigrants had been arriving in Australia since 1788, attracted by free land grants and cheap convict labor. By 1828, those born in the colony already made up almost one-fourth of the population, and free people outnumbered convicts.

Opposition to convict transportation became widespread during the 1830's. In the United Kingdom, many reformers questioned the effectiveness of transportation as a way to stop crime. In Australia, free immigrants objected to living in a prison colony. Cheap convict labor kept wages low, and restrictions on civil liberties were greater than those in the United Kingdom.

In 1838, a committee led by the British colonial official Sir William Molesworth examined transportation and the convict system. The committee, known as the Molesworth Committee, recommended that the government end transportation to New South Wales and Van Diemen's Land and abolish assignment. The British government followed the recommendations and stopped transportation to New South Wales in 1840, suspended it in Van Diemen's Land in 1846, and officially abolished it there in 1852. In Western Australia, convict transportation started in 1850 and was not abolished until 1868. There, convicts, or *exiles,* as they were called, provided labor that the struggling colony desperately needed. Altogether, more than 160,000 convicts were sent to Australia from 1788 to 1868.

The Molesworth Report was a victory for the anti-transportation movements in Australia. But it also had a harmful impact because it portrayed the colonies as deeply tainted and corrupted by convicts. This inaccurate picture of Australia disappointed and shocked the colonists. This portrayal had a lasting impact on Australian society into the 1900's. It made many Australians ashamed and sensitive about their convict origins.

Mapping the continent. Two British navigators, Matthew Flinders and George Bass, completed the exploration of Australia's coastlines in the late 1700's and early 1800's. Flinders was the first European to sail completely around the continent. He suggested the name *Australia,* and Governor Macquarie adopted it.

The settlers in New South Wales explored the area around Sydney during the early 1800's. In 1824, the Australian explorer Hamilton Hume and a British-born sea captain named William Hovell opened up an overland route from Sydney to the future site of Melbourne. In 1829 and 1830, the British explorer Charles Sturt sailed down the Murray River into the sea, near what is now Adelaide. His exploration opened the way for the establishment of the colony of South Australia in 1836. In 1829, the British sea captain Charles Fremantle landed on Australia's southwest coast and claimed the entire western part of the continent for the United Kingdom.

In 1860 and 1861, Robert O'Hara Burke, an Irish-born explorer, and William Wills, a British-born explorer, became the first white people to cross the continent from south to north. They died on the return trip south. John McDouall Stuart, a Scottish-born explorer, made the first round trip between the south and north coasts in 1861 and 1862.

Aboriginal people were great explorers and vital guides during this period. They guided the European parties, found food and water, and acted as peacemakers when they communicated with other, hostile Aboriginal groups. The Europeans rarely acknowledged these Aborigines and their contributions, however.

Expansion. In 1831, the British introduced *assisted migration* to the colonies. Under this system, officials raised money to help run the colonies and to assist migration to Australia. Only land within the colonies' settled areas could be sold. Between 1831 and 1840, more than 40,000 assisted immigrants arrived in Australia. By 1850, their total number was more than 110,000.

As the wool industry flourished, some *sheep graziers*

(farmers who graze sheep) moved out into new country and settled illegally on land beyond the legal limits of settlement. They were soon called *squatters.* By 1840, they had occupied most of Victoria and eastern New South Wales and had reached the Darling Downs in present-day Queensland. By the early 1850's, the colonies of Tasmania, Western Australia, South Australia, and Victoria had been established.

Aborigines. British officials ordered the early governors to protect and establish friendly relations with the Aborigines. Colonial authorities created land reserves and encouraged missionary activity for the Aborigines. But these policies were often ineffective.

Most of the colonists believed that the Aborigines were an inferior race who had no right to the land. The squatters claimed the right to take the Aborigines' land without compensating them. When Aborigines resisted the invasion of their land and attacked settlers, officials ordered raids that resulted in the Aborigines' deaths.

When the Europeans first arrived, the Aboriginal people usually tried to draw them into their own familial and legal systems. When it became clear that the Europeans would not respect the Aboriginal society, the Aborigines resisted their settlement. This resistance was strong but usually short-lived. Although the Aborigines were frightening and powerful warriors, and their spears and other weapons were deadly, they could not defeat troops on horseback armed with guns.

The Aborigines found themselves hungry and barred from their lands. Traditional Aboriginal societies began to crumble. Alcohol abuse became a problem. Many Aborigines died of malnutrition or diseases brought by Asian and European settlers. In 1789, smallpox brought to northern Australia by fishing crews from Macassar spread across the continent and reached the Aborigines of the Sydney region. In some groups, such as the Cadigal, all but a few died.

Some Aborigines survived these crises, however, and many of them stayed with their land for as long as they could. A small number managed to get some of their land back through land grants and reserves.

The discovery of gold in April 1851, near Bathurst, New South Wales, and soon after in Victoria, transformed Australia's economy and society. Gold stimulated the production and distribution of goods. It attracted a large, new population that supported the manufacturing industry. Miners poured into Australia. By early 1852, the first miners and their families arrived from overseas. The population soared from about 400,000 in 1850 to more than 1,100,000 in 1860.

Political changes. By 1856, the United Kingdom had granted self-government to all the colonies except Western Australia. Because of convict labor in that colony, steps to self-government were postponed there until the late 1800's.

Squatters settled in New South Wales north and west of Brisbane. In 1859, the United Kingdom created the colony of Queensland out of this area, with Brisbane as its capital. Western Australia received representative government in 1870 and a parliament in 1890.

Land reform. By 1860, thousands of disappointed gold miners wanted to buy plots of land and take up farming. But squatters held most of the best farmland. During the early 1860's, the colonial legislatures passed

Australian prime ministers

Name	Dates served	Party	Name	Dates served	Party
Edmund Barton	1901-1903	Protectionist	Robert G. Menzies	1939-1941	United
Alfred Deakin	1903-1904	Protectionist	Arthur Fadden	1941	Country
John Christian Watson	1904	Labor	John Curtin	1941-1945	Labor
George H. Reid	1904-1905	Free Trade	Francis M. Forde	1945	Labor
Alfred Deakin	1905-1908	Protectionist	Ben Chifley	1945-1949	Labor
Andrew Fisher	1908-1909	Labor	Robert G. Menzies	1949-1966	Liberal
Alfred Deakin	1909-1910	Fusion	Harold E. Holt	1966-1967	Liberal
Andrew Fisher	1910-1913	Labor	John McEwen	1967-1968	Country
Joseph Cook	1913-1914	Liberal	John G. Gorton	1968-1971	Liberal
Andrew Fisher	1914-1915	Labor	William McMahon	1971-1972	Liberal
William M. Hughes	1915-1917	Labor	Gough Whitlam	1972-1975	Labor
William M. Hughes	1917-1923	Nationalist	Malcolm Fraser	1975-1983	Liberal
Stanley M. Bruce	1923-1929	Nationalist	Robert Hawke	1983-1991	Labor
James Scullin	1929-1932	Labor	Paul Keating	1991-1996	Labor
Joseph A. Lyons	1932-1939	United	John Howard	1996-	Liberal
Earle Page	1939	Country			

laws to redistribute the squatters' land. These acts, called *selection acts,* allowed individuals to select a small block of land. Selectors had to live on their land, cultivate and fence it, and pay for it.

Selection was less successful than its supporters expected. Farms were often too small, and the environment was often unsuitable for agricultural use. Many people who took up the land knew nothing about farming. Squatters often used illegal means to keep their farms intact. However, selection succeeded where the land was suitable for crop growing and dairy farms, and in places that also had ready access to markets. In some parts of Victoria, New South Wales, and Queensland, selection boosted the agriculture industry.

By the 1880's, colonial governments had begun to set aside the drier regions for grazing use. They introduced new settlement plans in the 1890's to further divide the large landholdings into small family farms.

Economic changes. Historians have called the period from 1860 to 1890 *the long boom.* The discovery of gold during the 1850's and 1860's boosted the Australian economy. Agriculture and manufacturing industries grew. Railroad construction increased greatly. The railroads opened up new areas for settlement, lowered transport costs, and carried such bulky goods as wheat.

Despite the boom, life was hard for the working classes. Wages were low, working hours were long, and many workplaces were dangerous. Unemployment was common. Without a social security system, unemployed people relied on aid from charities. These difficult conditions contributed to a rise in the reform and labor union movements. In the late 1800's, the colonial governments passed several factory acts regulating workplace safety and hours and wages of workers.

By the late 1880's, the economic boom had begun to falter. Public and private debt rose greatly during the 1880's. Unemployment soared, reaching crisis proportions in 1893 and 1894. In 1893, the Australian banking system suffered a near collapse. Victoria was the hardest hit. Recovery from the depression was slow. Only Western Australia escaped the depression, because the discovery of gold created a boom economy.

The struggle for women's rights. Even though women played an essential role in building the new na-

tion, they were treated as second-class citizens in the early and middle 1800's. In most places, they could not vote and were excluded from most employment. Deserted or widowed women were often left in poverty. Wives married to abusive husbands had little prospect of escape, because divorce and property laws favored men. In 1870, the average number of children in a family was seven. Many women died in childbirth, so having large families was a danger for them.

The 1880's were an important turning point for Australian women. The colonial governments amended divorce laws to be fairer to women. The birth rate declined, which made family life more manageable and reduced childbirth-related deaths. Female education levels rose. Women won the right to vote in South Australia in 1894 and in Western Australia in 1899.

Federation. The 1890's saw the first steps toward the federation of the six Australian colonies as a nation. A growing number of Australians believed that the colonies would be better off as a single nation with a unified government. A new sense of Australian identity favored a united, white Australia. The works of the writers Mary Gilmore, Henry Lawson, Banjo Paterson, and Steele Rudd illustrated this distinctly Australian view.

In 1897 and 1898, a federal convention drew up a constitution for Australia. The people approved it in balloting during 1898 and 1899, and Australian leaders submitted it to the British Parliament in 1900. The United Kingdom approved it, and the Commonwealth of Australia came into being on Jan. 1, 1901. However, Australians were still British citizens, and the United Kingdom continued to control Australia's foreign policy.

Building a nation. The federal Parliament met in Melbourne until a site for a national capital could be selected. At first, Australia had three political parties—the Protectionists, the Labor Party, and the conservative Free Traders. The Protectionists wanted high *tariffs* (taxes on imports) to protect Australian industries from foreign competition. The Free Traders wanted low tariffs or none. The Labor Party represented the labor unions. Protectionist leader Edmund Barton became Australia's first prime minister. No single group held a majority in the House of Representatives between 1901 and 1910.

By 1909, Parliament agreed to adopt a national tariff. With this solution, the major issue separating the Free Traders and Protectionists had gone. The two groups joined together as the Fusion Party in 1909. The name was changed to the Liberal Party shortly afterward.

Prosperity returned to Australia during the early 1900's. Australia's *gross domestic product*—that is, the value of all goods and services produced by the country—soared. Production of wool, wheat, and other agricultural products rose. New railroads were built.

Social policies. White women won the right to vote in federal elections in 1902, and states that had not yet given women the vote were forced to grant it. But at the same time women won the vote, the federal government took the right to vote away from the Aborigines not already registered to vote. White Australians did not consider Aborigines citizens of the new nation and did not count them in the census.

Most white Australians had British ancestry and believed that non-Europeans were inferior to them. They passed the Immigration Restriction Act of 1901, which prevented non-European immigration to Australia. This act was the basis of the White Australia policy, an anti-immigration policy that lasted for more than 60 years.

Numerous women's groups campaigned actively for social reform, and Australia became known internationally for its groundbreaking social welfare policies. In 1910, the government introduced pensions for the elderly and for sick people. Some state governments introduced workers' compensation. In 1912, women's lobbying achieved the establishment of a maternity allowance for white mothers. This policy was aimed at boosting Australia's population, but it failed to do so.

The Stolen Generation. The new Constitution prohibited the federal government from making laws and policies for Aborigines. Over the first half of the 1900's, most Australians expected the Aborigines to die out. The governments of the states and territories increased policies of segregation and control. By 1912, all of the state governments except Tasmania passed legislation that allowed authorities to take Aboriginal children from their families and place them in institutions and foster homes. This led to some Aboriginal families trying to hide their Aboriginal heritage, for fear of losing their children. The children who were taken from their homes are often called the *Stolen Generation.*

World War I (1914-1918). When the United Kingdom declared war on Germany on Aug. 4, 1914, Australia was automatically at war. The government formed the Australian Imperial Force (AIF). By the end of 1914, more than 50,000 men had enlisted. They were sent with troops from New Zealand to train in Egypt, where the term *Anzac* (Australian and New Zealand Army Corps) was coined to describe them. Australian troops played important roles at battles on the Gallipoli Peninsula in present-day Turkey and on the Western front in Europe. More than 58,000 Australian soldiers died and over 152,000 were wounded, the highest casualty rate in proportion to total number of troops among the Allies.

Between the wars. Two new political parties were founded in Australia after World War I. The conservative Australian Country Party (now the National Party) was formed at the national level in 1920. The party was called the Australian Country Party until 1975 and the National Country Party from 1975 to 1982. The Communist Party of Australia formed in 1920. The capital was transferred from Melbourne to Canberra in 1927.

The period between the two world wars was initially prosperous for Australia. After 1929, however, the country fell into the grip of the Great Depression, the worldwide economic slump of the 1930's. In the worst of the Depression, nearly a third of the country's workers had no job. The Depression lasted until 1936, when a general world recovery took effect. The recovery took even longer for Australia's poorest workers.

The period between the wars was significant for Aboriginal people. In New South Wales, the government took back nearly 13,000 acres (5,260 hectares) of land given to Aborigines through official reserves and individual grants, often giving it to white farmers and returning white soldiers instead. This process started a move of Aboriginal people to the cities, and it caused Aborigines and their white supporters to form the first activist groups promoting Aboriginal rights.

World War II (1939-1945). Australia entered World War II on the side of the United Kingdom on Sept. 3, 1939. The government announced the formation of the Second AIF, but enlistment was slow. The Second AIF fought in battles in Crete, Greece, and northern Africa.

In 1829, Western Australia became the third British colony in Australia. Britain had established New South Wales in 1788 and Van Diemen's Land in 1825.

In 1836 and 1851, the United Kingdom founded two more colonies—South Australia and Victoria. The land for the colonies was taken from New South Wales.

WORLD BOOK maps

By 1911, the map of Australia looked much as it looks today. Queensland and the mainland territories were set up. Van Diemen's Land was renamed Tasmania.

On Feb. 19, 1942, the Japanese launched the first of more than 60 air raids against Darwin. In May 1942, three Japanese submarines entered Sydney Harbour. The United States Navy, with the Royal Australian Navy, defeated the Japanese in the Battle of the Coral Sea in May 1942. From then until the end of the war, Australia was the base for the Allied offensive against Japan.

Women played a significant role in the war effort. Many joined the services. Others were drafted into factory jobs, in areas such as weapons production. They also took jobs left by the men, often in areas where women had previously been excluded. These women for the first time received the same wages as men.

Postwar Australia. The war boosted Australia's manufacturing industry. The status of women increased, particularly in the work force. The ethnic composition of the country experienced substantial change with postwar immigration. In all, 853,953 assisted immigrants arrived in Australia between 1947 and 1960.

The Labor Party governed Australia from 1941 to 1949, when it was defeated in parliamentary elections. The Liberals won enough seats to form a government with the Country Party. Liberal and Country Party coalitions held power until 1972.

The 1950's and the 1960's were years of peace, prosperity, and political stability for many Australians. A mineral boom aided economic growth. Marriage and childbirth rates rose, along with home ownership levels. A generation of Australians emerged from depression and war into lives of well-being and security.

The women's movement reemerged in a new and more radical form during the late 1960's. One of its major international leaders was the Australian writer Germaine Greer. The feminists of the 1960's and 1970's believed that women should be equal in every sphere of life, and that all jobs and public positions should be open to them.

Aboriginal rights. The campaign for Aboriginal rights forced its way into the Australian public awareness during a new wave of activism and organization in the 1960's. Aboriginal workers held strikes to demand better working conditions, equal pay for black and white workers, and the right to own land.

A constitutional referendum in 1967 overwhelmingly approved proposals to grant Aborigines the right to vote and allowed the federal government to legislate on their behalf. The first Aboriginal land claims were made in the late 1960's, and Aboriginal groups petitioned the United Nations for compensation for the injustices done to them. In 1971, for the first time, the Aboriginal population was included in the national census.

The Vietnam War led many people to question both the war and their society in general. The war was fought between the Communist-led nationalists of North Vietnam and anti-Communists in South Vietnam, who were supported by the United States. In 1965, the first Australian troops went to South Vietnam. Opposition to the Vietnam War began in Australia almost immediately. By the late 1960's, opposition was widespread. Mass demonstrations against the war took place in 1970 and 1971. When the soldiers returned home in 1973, few public welcomes greeted them.

Political upheavals. In 1972, the Labor Party came to power with a majority in the House of Representatives. Gough Whitlam, the party leader, became prime minister. But no elections were held for the Senate, which remained under the control of a Liberal-Country coalition.

The Whitlam government passed important reforms but was plagued by problems, including an economic recession in Australia. In October 1975, the Liberal and National parties blocked the approval of funds needed to run the government. A constitutional crisis followed, and in November 1975, Governor General John Kerr intervened and removed Whitlam from office. Kerr named Malcolm Fraser, head of the Liberal Party, to serve as prime minister until new elections could be held.

The Liberal and National coalition won elections in December 1975 and in 1977 and 1980. Fraser remained prime minister. Don Chipp, a former Liberal minister, formed a party called the Australian Democrats, which held the balance of power in the Senate after 1980. The Labor Party, led by Bob Hawke, regained power in 1983 and won elections in 1984, 1987, and 1990.

In 1991, the Labor Party elected Paul Keating as party leader. Keating replaced Hawke as prime minister. The Labor Party won parliamentary elections held in 1993, and Keating remained prime minister.

A coalition of the National and Liberal parties won general elections in 1996, 1998, and 2001. John Howard, the leader of the Liberal Party, served as prime minister.

Aboriginal land victory. The long struggle for Aboriginal land rights won an important victory in 1992. That year, the High Court ruled in the case of *Mabo v. Queensland* that Aborigines and Torres Strait Islanders had legal title to their land before European settlers took it. The *Mabo decision,* as the ruling is often called, recognized that native title still existed where Aborigines and Torres Strait Islanders remained on their land.

In 1993, the federal government passed the Native Title Act, a law granting Aborigines ownership rights to their traditional lands. An equally important case was the 1996 High Court ruling called the *Wik decision.* The Wik people of the Cape York peninsula succeeded in their challenge to have native title recognized in areas where graziers had leases. In this case, the High Court ruled that graziers' leases had not taken the place of native title, but that the two had coexisted. However, the Liberal-National government attempted to reduce the rights established by the High Court.

Referendum on the republic. During the 1990's, many Australians called for their nation to become a republic with a president replacing the British monarch as head of state. In 1998, a constitutional convention voted in favor of making Australia a republic by Jan. 1, 2001. In a *referendum* (direct vote of the people) held in 1999, however, Australian voters rejected the convention's model for the republic, and so the British monarch remained Australia's head of state.

Persian Gulf War of 2003. In 2003, troops from the Australian Army, the Royal Australian Navy, and the Royal Australian Air Force took part in a U.S.-led war against Iraq. The allied forces quickly gained control of Iraq and ended the rule of Iraqi dictator Saddam Hussein.

David Carter, Grace Karskens, Clement Macintyre, and Adrian Mitchell

People with disabilities can lead active, fulfilling lives and contribute greatly to their communities. These men are using *prosthetic* (artificial) legs to run in a track competition. Prosthetic limbs are just one of many *assistive* (aid-giving) devices that help people with disabilities.

© Robert W. Ginn, PhotoEdit

Disability

Disability is a condition that affects a person's ability to perform the activities of everyday life. Disability was once considered a biological impairment with a specific medical cause. Today, the term is more broadly defined as any physical or mental condition that substantially limits one or more major life activities. Some people are born with disabilities, while others develop them later in life. Common disabilities include blindness, deafness, deformity, loss of limbs, mental illness, mental retardation, and muscular, nervous, and sensory disorders.

Disability has traditionally been described in medical terms. Many common disabilities are related to diseases or chronic conditions associated with aging. For example, heart disease may decrease a person's strength and endurance. Strokes may produce paralysis or loss of speech. Arthritis and many bone diseases can lead to deformity and problems with mobility. Certain nerve diseases may result in blindness, deafness, and lack of coordination. Cerebral palsy is a disorder that damages the brain before, during, or after birth. Depending on what part of the brain is damaged, cerebral palsy can cause speech problems, mental retardation, muscular weakness, or involuntary movements. In addition, accidents can cause a wide range of disabilities, including blindness, spinal damage, paralysis, and loss of limbs.

Throughout history, people have characterized those with disabilities in a variety of ways. Many people who were disabled tried to hide their condition, fearing that their disabilities would appear to be signs of weakness or inferiority. But since the mid-1900's, attitudes toward disabilities have changed significantly, largely as a result of *disability rights movements* throughout the world. Such movements promote increased acceptance, rights, and visibility for people with disabilities.

Today, many people view a person's disability as just one of many traits that define the person's unique identity. Most people are not ashamed of their disabilities. Instead, they do what activists call "claiming their disability"—that is, they actively accept their condition and integrate it into their identity. Many countries have passed laws to provide assistance and to protect the rights of people with disabilities. In addition, the development of *assistive technologies* has led to devices and products that help people with disabilities carry out a wide range of activities.

Disability is not a condition to fear or shun. Instead, it is a natural part of the human experience, and it should be respected and supported. Today, millions of people with disabilities contribute to their communities, go to school or hold jobs, marry, and have children. They live productive lives just as people without disabilities do.

The scope of disability

There are many types of disabilities, both physical and mental, and they vary greatly in their causes, degrees, and treatments.

Mobility problems and other physical disabilities. Many disabilities interfere with a person's ability to move in certain ways. Some make it difficult or impossible to use one or both hands. Others interfere with the ability to walk or run. Still other disabilities involve the loss of a limb or other body part.

Illnesses and chronic conditions—such as diabetes, arthritis, strokes, and osteoporosis—may limit a person's ability to climb stairs, walk, open doors, stand and reach, or write. But the use of *assistive* (aid-giving) devices, such as wheelchairs and walkers, can reduce many of these limitations. Other limitations can be overcome through physical assistance from other people or by the removal of architectural or structural barriers.

Hearing disabilities range from mild hearing loss to complete deafness. They can be caused by problems at birth, illness, injury to the ears, exposure to noise, or aging. Hearing disabilities affect a person's ability to communicate and receive information. However, these difficulties can be reduced or overcome through the use of hearing aids and other assistive technology devices, and the use of sign language. A system called *closed captioning* enables viewers with hearing impairments to understand dialogue on television. Printed captions appear on the screen during programs.

Speech and language disabilities also affect a person's ability to communicate. Speech disabilities include voice disorders of pitch, volume, or quality, as well as articulation and fluency problems, such as stuttering. Language disabilities affect the learning and use of words and grammar. Speech and language disabilities may be caused by strokes, brain tumors, head injuries, diseases, or other central nervous system problems. People with speech and language disabilities may have difficulty reading and writing, communicating with others, or talking on the telephone. But assistive technologies, speech therapy, and help from listeners can greatly reduce these communication problems.

Visual disabilities range from mild loss of sight to complete blindness. Visual disabilities can be present at birth due to disease, birth trauma, or genetic conditions. They can also develop later in life as a result of strokes, injury, tumors, illness, or aging. Visual impairments can limit a person's ability to get from place to place, to read and write, or to follow signs. Such disabilities can also result in difficulties using computers or other devices, such as telephones and automated teller machines. However, a number of methods can greatly reduce the limitations. For example, *braille,* a code of raised dots, enables people who are blind to read by touch. People with visual disabilities can also use a variety of adapted computers and other accommodations.

Mental illness and cognitive disabilities. A mental illness is a condition that seriously affects a person's thoughts, emotions, personality, or behavior. Common mental illnesses include schizophrenia, clinical depression, and anxiety disorders. Mental illness can affect a person's concentration, stamina, and ability to manage time. It can also interfere with personal interactions and the ability to make or carry out plans. However, with medication and counseling, people can reduce these limitations. Many people who are mentally ill go to work or school, live in the community, and enjoy their lives.

Cognitive disabilities are conditions that affect the abilities of learning, perception, and awareness. Cognitive disabilities include mental retardation, dementia, and traumatic brain injury. One of the most common causes of mental retardation is Down syndrome, a genetic disorder that is present at birth. Other causes include accidents, brain injury, and inadequate nutrition. Dementia is a disability marked by a decrease in mental activity. Alzheimer's disease, Parkinson disease, Huntington's disease, tumors, and brain infections are the most common causes of dementia.

Like other disabilities, cognitive disabilities vary greatly in the limitations they create. However, with education and rehabilitation, individualized community supports and accommodations, effective health care, and adaptive equipment, most people with cognitive disabilities can live productive lives in the community.

Chicago Transit Authority

Wheelchair accessibility ensures that people with certain physical disabilities can use public transportation and other services. This man uses a wheelchair ramp to board a bus.

Living with disabilities

A disability can affect many areas of a person's life, both because of the disability itself and because of society's attitudes and barriers toward disabilities.

Personal life. People with disabilities may encounter a variety of challenges in their personal lives. For example, a physical disability may make it difficult to perform daily activities, such as dressing, eating, and maintaining personal hygiene. However, with assistive devices, help from others, and accessible buildings and public transportation, most people with disabilities can manage their personal needs.

Family life. People with disabilities may face additional challenges in their family lives. Many challenges result not from disability itself, but from the attitudes of family members and members of the community.

Many families experience difficulty balancing the desire to protect a family member who has a disability with the need to respect that member's independence. *Siblings* (brothers or sisters) of a child with a disability may feel guilty about not having a disability. But at the same time, those siblings may be jealous of the additional attention given to the child with a disability. Additional family challenges may arise if the traditional roles of family members are changed. For instance, when a parent is deaf and has a hearing child, the child may have to handle much of the family's communication with the outside world, a role traditionally performed by parents.

People with disabilities may also experience financial difficulties that affect family life. Some family members may have to work extra hours or multiple jobs to pay expenses associated with a disability. Many countries provide family support programs to help families meet challenges related to disabilities.

Life in the community. One of the greatest challenges of living with a disability is dealing with other people's unfavorable or pitying attitudes toward disability. Such attitudes can form a social barrier and interfere with important personal relationships. For instance, a child with a disability may have difficulty developing friendships because he or she looks different from other children or cannot play the same games that others do.

© Ellen Senisi, The Image Works

Sign language and assistive listening devices help many people with hearing disabilities receive information. This child is using both methods to communicate with his teacher.

The use of touch helps people with visual disabilities receive information. This museum exhibition in Lima, Peru, provides descriptions in braille and touchable replicas of historical artifacts.

Special education classes help students with disabilities reach their full learning potential. This teacher in Sergiyev Posad, Russia, leads a language lesson for children with hearing disabilities.

Many societies view a person with a disability as a victim and someone to be pitied. Societies may also portray a well-known or successful person with a disability as "heroic" or as someone who has "overcome" disability. Such messages can contribute to psychological problems, such as low self-esteem and depression, for many people with disabilities.

The attitudes and accessibility of a community and its members greatly affect the everyday life of a person with a disability. Communities that lack accessible transportation systems, public buildings, recreational programs, health care, places of worship, and schools may isolate children and adults with disabilities. A single detail, such as a step at the entrance to a building or a lack of braille signs in a shopping mall, may lead a person to feel unwelcome. Community barriers can contribute to discrimination, social isolation, inadequate education, unemployment, and poverty for people with disabilities.

Needs, services, and supports

Like all people, people with disabilities need accessible and affordable education, health care, employment, housing, and transportation. People with disabilities often need special assistance, accommodations, or supports. This section describes some of the services and supports that are essential for people with disabilities.

Education is extremely important for all children. Civil rights laws in the United States and many Western countries guarantee students with disabilities the right to a free, appropriate public education. *Special education* services help people with disabilities use their full learning abilities. Special education usually involves instructional modifications and the use of different materials, such as recorded books instead of printed ones. It may also involve simplifying the language of instruction or allowing students more time to take a test. In addition, special education services can include the use of aides, tutors, and special therapies and assistance to help students with disabilities learn.

People often disagree over where the education of students with disabilities should take place. Many parents, people with disabilities, and advocates call for a system of *inclusive education*. They believe that students with disabil-ities should be included in regular classes, with any necessary services and aides provided there. Others believe that appropriate education for students with disabilities can best be provided in separate special education classes.

Health care and assistive devices. Accessible, effective, respectful, and affordable health care is essential for individuals with disabilities and their families. Proper health care often requires specialized services for certain disabilities. Some people may require physical, occupational, or speech therapy, or specialized equipment, such as portable breathing machines.

Assistive technology devices help many people with disabilities carry out their daily activities. For example, a wheelchair helps a person with mobility problems to move around the home, workplace, and community. Screen readers enable someone who is blind to use a computer. Assistive listening devices can help a person with a hearing disability enjoy a play. There are hundreds of assistive technology devices available. However, many people with disabilities lack the information or money to obtain the technology that would help them.

Employment. Most people—even those with significant disabilities—have the desire and the ability to work, with proper accommodations and supports. However, in many countries, including the United States, the rate of unemployment for people with disabilities is significantly higher than that for people without disabilities. Seeking to address this situation, many governments have established laws that ban employment discrimination based on disability. Governments have also established programs that help remove barriers and provide improved opportunities. Government-funded *vocational rehabilitation* programs help many people with disabilities to join the work force.

Housing and transportation must be accessible and affordable for people with disabilities. A person who uses a wheelchair, for example, needs ramps instead of stairs, wide doorways, and other structural adaptations. Many nations have established government programs to address the housing needs of people with disabilities and other groups. Nations have also passed laws that require basic transportation services to be accessible to people with disabilities. For example, many transit services must provide ramps or lifts for people in wheelchairs, and signs in braille for customers who are blind.

Attitudes toward people with disabilities

Disability has been part of the human experience since the beginning of history. But the ways communities have treated people with disabilities have varied significantly throughout the ages and across cultures.

Early beliefs. During ancient times, people with disabilities were thought to be incapable, threatening, or even evil. Communities often drove them out or left them to die. In Rome, parents could legally drown disfigured infants. During the Middle Ages, the period from about the 400's through the 1400's, people ridiculed individuals with disabilities and regarded them with suspicion. Some nobles used people with physical disabilities as court jesters. Many women with disabilities were burned as witches.

Attitudes toward disabilities began to change in the 1700's and 1800's. Many cultures began to pity people with disabilities and to treat them with special care and compassion. In Paris in 1755, the French clergyman Charles Michel de l'Epée founded the first free school for the deaf. In 1824, Louis Braille, a French student, invented the braille reading system. In 1857, the Columbia Institution for the Instruction of the Deaf and Dumb and the Blind (now Gallaudet University) opened in Washington, D.C. In the United Kingdom, the Royal National Institute for the Blind was founded in 1868 to promote the welfare of blind people. Despite these advances, many people still felt that people with disabilities brought shame on themselves and their families.

The 1900's were a time of great change for people with disabilities. Advances in medicine and science saved the lives of many people with health-related and injury-related disabilities. In addition, nonprofit organizations helped support children and adults with physical and sensory disabilities. New groups campaigned for disability rights, including the American Foundation for the Blind, founded in 1921, and the League of the Physically Handicapped, founded in 1935.

While many cultures offered increased support for people with disabilities, others continued to view disability unfavorably. Some governments even carried out *sterilization programs,* aimed at preventing people with disabilities from having children, and *euthanasia programs,* aimed at killing people with disabilities. From 1939 to 1941, the German dictator Adolf Hitler ordered the murder of nearly 100,000 Europeans with disabilities.

Following World War II (1939-1945), many veterans who had acquired disabilities in the war demanded medical and vocational rehabilitation. Military hospitals established rehabilitation centers, and many other hospitals set up facilities to help people with disabilities. In 1972, a polio survivor named Edward Roberts founded the Center for Independent Living (CIL) in Berkeley, California. The center was a community-based organization that emphasized dignity, peer support, civil rights, and equal access for people with disabilities. In the following years, hundreds of CIL's began operating throughout the United States and other countries.

During the late 1900's, the U.S. Congress passed several important laws to help people with disabilities. The Rehabilitation Act of 1973 prohibits unfair treatment of individuals with disabilities in programs or activities that receive government funds. The act also requires many federally funded businesses to make an effort to hire qualified people with

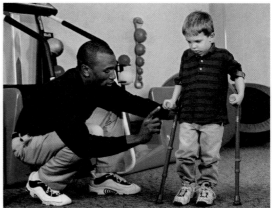
© Corbis

Physical therapy helps prevent, relieve, or correct physical conditions that interfere with a person's ability to carry out daily activities. This therapist is helping a child with a disability walk.

disabilities. The Education for All Handicapped Children Act of 1975 orders states to provide a free education for any child with a disability who is of school age. Canada has a similar law.

The Americans with Disabilities Act of 1990 (ADA) protects people with disabilities from discrimination by private employers. It requires that public buildings and transportation services be accessible to people with disabilities. The act also orders telephone companies to provide telephone relay services that allow people with speech or hearing disabilities to make and receive calls.

Many other governments throughout the world have passed similar disability rights laws. The United Kingdom's Disability Discrimination Act of 1995 prohibits employers from discriminating against people with disabilities. It also requires people providing goods and services to make suitable provisions for people with disabilities. The Education Act of 1996 requires education authorities to provide educational as well as noneducational facilities for students with special educational needs.

Australia's Disability Services Act of 1986 ensures that people with disabilities receive services that enable them to live and work independently in the community. The Disability Discrimination Act of 1992 prohibits various forms of discrimination against people with disabilities.

South Africa's Constitution, adopted in 1996, prohibits the state from discriminating against anyone on a number of grounds, including disability. These constitutional requirements led the South African government to bring in the Employment Equity Act of 1998 and the Promotion of Equality and Prevention of Unfair Discrimination Act of 2000.

Recent developments. The disability rights movement has continued to grow. In many cases, disability activists have helped reshape how buildings and facilities are arranged, and how services and supports are funded and provided. In addition, the rights movement has led to a field of university study called *disability studies.* The field focuses on the history, literature, culture, and politics of the disabled community. As a result of these and other advances, disability has become increasingly accepted as a natural part of the human experience.

Diane Nelson Bryen and Carol A. Marfisi

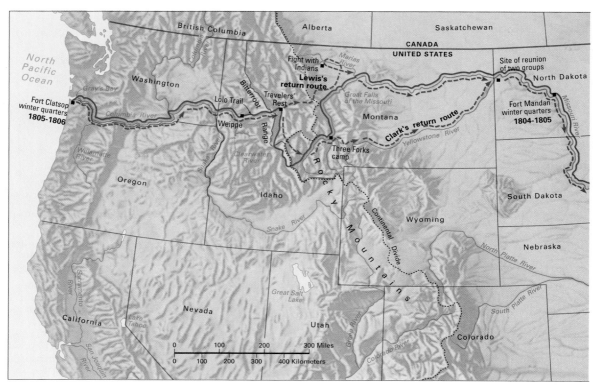

The Lewis and Clark expedition left a camp near St. Louis in 1804, journeyed up the Missouri River, and crossed the Rocky Mountains. The explorers reached the Pacific coast in 1805. They returned to St. Louis in 1806 with valuable information about the new frontier.

Lewis and Clark expedition

Lewis and Clark expedition was an early exploration of the vast wilderness of what is now the northwestern United States. The United States government sponsored the expedition, and U.S. Army officers Meriwether Lewis and William Clark served as co-leaders. The Lewis and Clark expedition began near St. Louis, Missouri, in May 1804 and returned there in September 1806. Historians often refer to the explorers as the Corps of Discovery. Lewis called them the Corps of Volunteers for North Western Discovery. In time, the group became known simply as the Lewis and Clark expedition.

The expedition traveled a total of about 8,000 miles (12,800 kilometers). Starting from a camp near St. Louis, the group journeyed up the Missouri River, across the Rocky Mountains, and down the Columbia and other rivers to the Pacific coast. The explorers returned to St. Louis with maps of their route and surrounding regions; specimens and descriptions of plant, animal, and mineral resources; and information about American Indian cultures. The expedition's success enabled the United States to claim the Oregon region, which included what are now the states of Oregon, Washington, and Idaho.

The Lewis and Clark expedition was a remarkable achievement by a band of brave, determined, and skillful explorers. The group crossed half the continent of North America, traveling through a largely unknown wilderness on foot, on horseback, and by boat. They faced scorching and freezing weather, swift river currents, rugged mountain trails, and dangerous animals. At times, they suffered from hunger and exhaustion. But the group returned safely home with a wealth of information. The expedition's journey ranks as one of the greatest adventure stories in United States history.

Planning the expedition

Jefferson's plans. Within a year after Thomas Jefferson became president of the United States in 1801, he began to plan an expedition through the Louisiana Territory and the Oregon region. The Louisiana Territory was a huge area owned by France that lay between the Mississippi River and the Rocky Mountains, stretching from the Gulf of Mexico to Canada. The Oregon region included a large area between the Rocky Mountains and the

Gary E. Moulton, the contributor of this article, is Thomas C. Sorensen Professor of American History at the University of Nebraska and editor of The Lewis and Clark Journals.

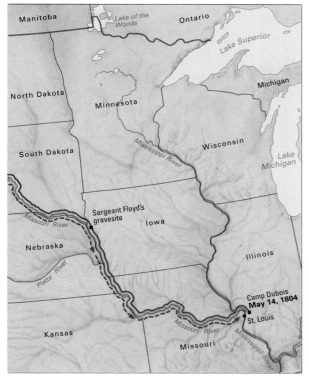

WORLD BOOK map

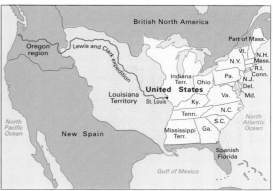

WORLD BOOK map

The size of the United States almost doubled in 1803 with the purchase of the Louisiana Territory. The Lewis and Clark expedition was sent to explore the territory and the Oregon region.

Detail of an oil portrait (1807) by Charles Willson Peale; Independence National Historical Park Collection, Philadelphia

Meriwether Lewis

Detail of an oil portrait (1807-1808) by Charles Willson Peale; Independence National Historical Park Collection, Philadelphia

William Clark

Pacific coast. Spain, Russia, and England claimed parts of the region. Jefferson believed that a route to the Pacific coast along the Missouri and Columbia rivers could form part of a land-and-water passage between the Atlantic and Pacific oceans.

The president's plan included gathering scientific information about the Louisiana Territory and the Oregon region and establishing communication with the local Indians. The plan expanded after May 2, 1803, when U.S. representatives signed a treaty with France to buy the Louisiana Territory. Then the expedition received the additional tasks of tracing the boundaries of the territory and laying U.S. claims to the Oregon region.

Jefferson chose Meriwether Lewis to lead the expedition. Lewis was a U.S. Army captain and Jefferson's private secretary. Lewis, in turn, selected William Clark, a former U.S. Army officer, to join him in leading the expedition. Lewis had served under Clark in the Army. Clark had resigned from the Army in 1796 but reenlisted in 1803 to join the expedition. When Clark reenlisted, he received the rank of lieutenant. This rank was below that of Lewis, but members of the expedition regarded Clark as a co-leader and addressed him as captain. Both Lewis and Clark had wilderness experience and had served in Army campaigns against Indians. In addition, Clark had

considerable mapmaking skills, while Lewis had some training in the study of animals and plants.

Preparation. During the summer of 1803, Lewis spent time studying in Philadelphia. He learned how to classify plants and animals and how to determine geographical position by observing the stars. He then went to Pittsburgh, Pennsylvania, and, in late August, left the city in a large flat-bottomed boat called a *keelboat.* Clark, meanwhile, began to recruit members of the expedition. The explorers chose skilled woodsmen and hunters accustomed to manual labor and military discipline. Most of the men were soldiers. The party also included York, an adult slave who belonged to Clark. The lone pet in the expedition was Seaman, a Newfoundland dog owned by Lewis.

In December 1803, the party set up winter quarters at Camp Dubois (Camp Wood), across the Mississippi River from St. Louis in present-day Illinois. There, Lewis and Clark trained their men and learned from fur traders and travelers about the regions the party would explore.

Journey to the Pacific

Up the Missouri. On May 14, 1804, the expedition set out from Camp Dubois in the keelboat and two canoes. The group numbered about 50 men. Many were French

Important dates in the Lewis and Clark expedition

1803

January 18	President Thomas Jefferson asked Congress to finance an expedition to explore the western part of North America. Congress quickly approved the request.
May 2	U.S. representatives signed a treaty with France to purchase the Louisiana Territory.
June 19	Captain Meriwether Lewis, Jefferson's choice to lead the expedition, asked William Clark to serve as co-leader.
August 31	Lewis launched the expedition's boat down the Ohio River from Pittsburgh, Pennsylvania.
October 15	Lewis and Clark met in Clarksville, Indiana, where Clark had recruited men for the trip.
December 13	The expedition established winter quarters at Camp Dubois, near St. Louis, Missouri.

1804

May 14	The expedition set out from Camp Dubois and headed up the Missouri River.
August 20	Sergeant Charles Floyd became the expedition's only member to die on the journey.
October 24	The group began to build Fort Mandan in present-day North Dakota for its winter camp.
November 4	Lewis and Clark hired the French-Canadian fur trader Toussaint Charbonneau and his Shoshone Indian wife Sacagawea to interpret Indian languages.

1805

April 7	The journey resumed up the Missouri River.
June 13	The group reached the Great Falls of the Missouri River and soon began an 18-mile (29-kilometer) overland trip around the waterfalls.
September 11	The expedition entered the Lolo Trail of the Bitterroot Range in the Rocky Mountains. The party spent 11 days crossing the mountains under severe conditions.
November 18	Members of the expedition reached the Pacific coast.
December 7	The expedition began to build Fort Clatsop in present-day Oregon for its winter quarters.

1806

March 23	The homeward journey started.
July 3	The expedition split into two groups to find a shortcut home and to explore more of the Louisiana Territory.
July 27	Lewis's group killed two Blackfeet Indians who tried to steal guns and horses in what was the only bloodshed on the entire trip.
August 12	The two groups of explorers reunited on the Missouri River near the mouth of the Yellowstone River.
September 23	The expedition arrived back in St. Louis.

boatmen temporarily hired to move the heavy keelboat and other craft against the Missouri's swift current. The men moved the keelboat by pushing poles against the river bottom or by pulling the boat with ropes from shore.

The keelboat carried a large amount of supplies, including food, medicine, scientific instruments, and weapons. Lewis and Clark also took many presents for the Indians they expected to meet. These gifts included brass kettles, brightly colored cloth, colored beads, ivory combs, knives, pipes, pocket mirrors, scissors, sewing needles and thread, silk ribbons, and tobacco.

The beauty of the land and its abundant wildlife amazed Lewis and Clark as they traveled up the Missouri. The first tragic event of the expedition occurred on August 20, when Sergeant Charles Floyd died from what may have been a burst appendix. The explorers buried Floyd near present-day Sioux City, Iowa. He was the only member of the group to die on the journey.

In September, the explorers had a tense encounter with Teton Sioux Indians. After the explorers had talked and exchanged gifts with them, the Sioux refused to allow Clark to return to the boat. The Indians let him go only after they saw that the soldiers in the party were preparing to fight. Most meetings with Indians, however, were friendly. Indians often helped the men by describing the way ahead and by providing food. Indians the explorers met early in the expedition included the Oto, Yankton Sioux, and Arikara.

When Lewis and Clark talked with Indians, they spoke about President Jefferson. One of the expedition members, Sergeant Patrick Gass, described the basic speech in his diary. He noted that the two captains told the Indians all the "Red children were now under the protection of a new father, the Great White Father at Washington. They must keep the peace. The Great White Father

would send traders to supply them with all necessities."

In October, the expedition reached the villages of the Mandan and Hidatsa Indians near what is now Bismarck, North Dakota. The group established its winter camp, Fort Mandan, near the villages. At that time, the population of the Indian villages totaled about 4,500—about three times the population of St. Louis.

During the winter, the French-Canadian trader Toussaint Charbonneau and his Shoshone Indian wife Sacagawea *(sah KAH guh WEE uh)* joined the expedition. The explorers hired the couple mainly to help interpret Indian languages. At the winter camp, Lewis and Clark brought their diaries and maps up to date and wrote about the Indians. Some of the explorers joined the Mandan on buffalo hunts.

West to the Rockies. The journey resumed on April 7, 1805. Part of the group started back to St. Louis with the keelboat, which was loaded with maps, reports, and animal, plant, and mineral specimens. The rest of the group, called the "permanent party," continued west. It had 33 people. Besides Lewis and Clark, this group consisted of 3 sergeants, 23 privates, 3 interpreters, York, and a baby, Jean Baptiste Charbonneau. Sacagawea had given birth to him in February. The party traveled in the two original canoes and six newly built canoes.

As Lewis and Clark moved west into what is now Montana, the terrain became increasingly dry, treeless, and rugged. The explorers began to see animals that were unknown to them, such as bighorn sheep and grizzly bears. The Indians had warned them of the ferocious bears. After one encounter with a grizzly, Lewis wrote in his journal: "I must confess that I do not like the gentlemen and had reather [rather] fight two Indians than one bear." Some grizzlies stood to a height of 8 feet (2.4 meters) and had to be shot several times to be killed. Great herds of buffalo also amazed the explorers. At times,

Interesting facts about the Lewis and Clark expedition

For their leadership, Meriwether Lewis and William Clark each received 1,600 acres (650 hectares) of land as rewards. The rest of the men got double pay and 320 acres (130 hectares). The interpreter Toussaint Charbonneau received an additional $533.33 for his services. His wife Sacagawea got nothing.

The explorers passed through what are now 11 states: Illinois, Missouri, Iowa, Kansas, Nebraska, South Dakota, North Dakota, Montana, Idaho, Oregon, and Washington.

Sacagawea, the only woman to make the round trip, gave birth to a boy, Jean Baptiste, on Feb. 11, 1805. After the expedition, Charbonneau and Sacagawea asked Clark to raise and educate the boy, and he agreed.

Several members of the party often teamed up to communicate with the Indians. To talk to the Shoshone, for ex-

ample, Lewis and Clark spoke in English to Private François Labiche. Labiche spoke in French to Toussaint Charbonneau. Charbonneau spoke in Hidatsa to Sacagawea, who spoke in Shoshone to members of her tribe.

York, the only black member of the expedition, had been a slave in the Clark family since boyhood. William Clark's father, John Clark, gave William rights to York in his will.

Seaman, the only pet to accompany the explorers, was a Newfoundland dog owned by Lewis. Seaman proved to be especially dependable for guard duty. Indians once kidnapped Seaman, but the explorers rescued the dog.

The journals of Lewis and Clark describe about 180 plants and 125 animals that had not been reported to scientists.

these beasts thundered across the plains in numbers ranging from 3,000 to 10,000.

The Great Falls of the Missouri River, near what is now Great Falls, Montana, presented the first major obstacle to the expedition. Lewis and a few men arrived at the majestic falls on June 13, 1805. Lewis described them as "the grandest sight I ever beheld." These falls were about 90 feet (27 meters) high and, with several other falls and rapids in the region, blocked travel by boat.

Indians had told Lewis and Clark that it would take the group about a half day to carry their boats and supplies around the falls and rapids. After arriving at the Great Falls, Lewis and Clark realized that the trip would take longer. Broken, rocky trails and steamy temperatures slowed the group. Savage hailstorms left them bleeding. In one region, sharp spines of prickly pear cactuses stung the explorers' legs and feet. In addition, rattlesnakes and grizzlies constantly menaced the group. By the time the exhausted explorers returned to the river, they had hauled their boats and supplies 18 miles (29

kilometers). The effort took about a month.

As the explorers approached the mountains, they hoped to meet friendly Indians who would provide horses and information to guide the party through the region. Luckily, in mid-August, they met a band of Shoshone Indians whose chief was Sacagawea's brother or a close relative. The explorers traded for horses and supplies, obtained an Indian guide, and began their passage through the rugged Bitterroot Range of the Rocky Mountains in present-day Montana and Idaho.

Crossing the mountains on what is now the Lolo Trail in Idaho became perhaps the most difficult part of the journey. The trail passed through mountains that rose from 5,000 to 7,000 feet (1,500 to 2,100 meters) high. The explorers entered the trail on Sept. 11, 1805. They led their horses along rocky, narrow mountain paths. Some horses lost their footing and fell to their death, and precious supplies and equipment were lost. Winter had set in, and deepening snow covered part of the trail. The men found few wild animals to kill for food and

The Huntington Library, San Marino, CA

The Great Falls of the Missouri River presented the first major obstacle to the expedition. These falls were about 90 feet (27 meters) high and, with other nearby falls and rapids, forced the explorers to take an overland route. This part of the trip took about a month.

Crossing the Bitterroot Range of the Rocky Mountains became perhaps the toughest part of the journey. Deep snow covered part of the trail. The men found few wild animals to kill for food. To avoid starvation, they ate some of their pack horses.

Lewis and Clark in the Bitterroots (1967), a water color by John Clymer; the Clymer family and the Clymer Museum of Art

grew increasingly hungry. To avoid starvation, they finally killed and ate some of their pack horses.

Clark and a few men in a hunting party came out of the mountains near present-day Weippe, Idaho, on September 20. The rest of the group arrived there two days later. The party met helpful Nez Perce Indians and traded for food and fresh supplies. The explorers camped near the site of present-day Lewiston, Idaho, on the Idaho-Washington border. There, the group built canoes, which they used to travel down the Clearwater,

Snake, and Columbia rivers. On the rivers, they faced treacherous falls and rapids. The members of the expedition became the first white people to have direct contact with the Indians in this region.

The Indians told Lewis and Clark that they were near the Pacific Ocean. On Nov. 7, 1805, Clark recorded in his journal his excitement at reaching what he thought was the Pacific coast. He wrote: "Ocian [ocean] in view! O! the joy." The explorers later discovered that Clark had seen what is now Gray's Bay, about 20 miles (32 kilometers)

Detail of a mural (1938) by Barry Faulkner and F. H. Schwartz in the Oregon State Capitol, Salem, Oregon

The explorers traveled down the Columbia River in 1805 . Lewis and Clark, *left of center,* led the group. Sacagawea, *right,* a Shoshone Indian woman, helped interpret Indian languages.

The journals of Lewis and Clark are filled with drawings of plants and animals seen along the route. The two leaders' notes describe about 180 plants and 125 animals that had not been reported to scientists. The sketches shown here, of a trout and a sage grouse, appear in one of Clark's notebooks.

Granger Collection

Granger Collection

from the ocean. After reaching the sea, the explorers built Fort Clatsop near present-day Astoria, Oregon. They named the fort for nearby Indians. They all moved into their new quarters by Dec. 25, 1805.

The group spent a rainy winter at the fort. They studied the Indians and prepared for the return trip. The new tribes they met included the Chinook, Tillamook, Walla Walla, Wanapam, and Yakima.

Return to St. Louis

The homeward journey began on March 23, 1806. In May, the expedition again reached the Nez Perce villages. Lewis describes these Indians as "the most hospitable, honest and sincere people that we have met with in our voyage."

Indians had told Lewis and Clark that the route they had followed through the mountains was not the shortest. In June, Lewis and Clark divided the expedition into two groups at a spot they called Travelers' Rest. One group, led by Lewis, would follow the shortcut from the mountains to the Missouri River that the Indians had suggested. Clark led the other group in an exploration of the Yellowstone River area.

Lewis's group reached the Missouri River by the new, shorter route and set out to explore the Marias River. Along the Marias, the party fought some Blackfeet Indians who tried to steal their guns and horses. The explorers escaped unharmed but killed two Indians.

Clark's group reached the Yellowstone River by a new route. At the Yellowstone, they built canoes and followed the river to its junction with the Missouri. On Aug. 12, 1806, the two groups reunited on the Missouri River below the mouth of the Yellowstone.

Nothing had been heard from the explorers for over a year, and most Americans feared they were all dead. As the group of explorers neared St. Louis, reports of their survival created great excitement. The expedition arrived at St. Louis on Sept. 23, 1806, to the welcoming cheers of the city's people.

Results of the expedition. The most important result of the Lewis and Clark expedition was that it enabled the United States to claim the Oregon region. This claim helped make possible the great pioneer movement that settled the West in the mid-1800's. The explorers also established peaceful contact with most of the Indian tribes they met. They collected a variety of Indian goods and gathered information on Indian languages and culture.

Lewis, Clark, and several other members of the expedition prepared journals of the trip. These journals describe the natural resources and Indian peoples of the West and contain information on many scientific matters. The journals of Lewis and Clark are the most detailed records of the expedition. They describe about 180 plants and 125 animals that had not been reported to scientists. The journals were first published in an edited version in 1814 and nearly in their entirety in 1905.

Celebrating the bicentennial

In 2003, the states that the explorers crossed, and many other states as well, began to mark the bicentennial of the Lewis and Clark expedition. Performers in costume reenacted historical events of the expedition, such as the launch up the Missouri River and the explorers' arrival at the Pacific coast. Native American tribes who met the expedition held traditional gatherings called *powwows*. Colleges and universities, museums, and state and national park sites along the route offered exhibits and activities that recalled the great exploration. Many special programs took place at the Lewis and Clark National Historic Trail Interpretive Center in Great Falls, Montana; the Nez Perce National Historical Park near Lewiston, Idaho; and the Fort Clatsop National Memorial near Astoria, Oregon.   Gary E. Moulton

Prehistoric people are the ancestors of modern human beings. This illustration is an artist's idea of how two prehistoric species may have looked about 1,500,000 years ago in eastern Africa—*Homo erectus* in the foreground and *Australopithecus boisei* in the background. The small-brained *A. boisei* died out by 1 million years ago. Cultural advantages, such as stone tools, helped *Homo erectus* survive and spread throughout much of the world.

WORLD BOOK illustration by Ian Jackson for Wildlife Art Ltd.

Prehistoric people

Prehistoric people are human beings who lived before writing was invented about 5,500 years ago. Writing enabled people to record information they wished to save, including descriptions of events in their lives. In this way, the invention of writing marked the beginning of history. The period before human beings learned to write is called prehistory, and people who lived during this period are known as prehistoric people.

Most scientists believe the first human beings lived about 2 million years ago. But early people probably arose from prehuman ancestors who first lived more than 6 million years ago. These ancestors were small, humanlike creatures who walked in an erect, upright position. This article will discuss both prehistoric people and their ancestors.

Scientists first discovered evidence of prehistoric people during the mid-1800's. Most of this evidence consisted of ancient, sharp-edged tools that prehistoric people had made of stone. The first fossilized bones of prehistoric people were also found during this time.

As scientists collected more fossils of prehistoric people, they began to form a clearer picture of what these early people looked like. For example, scientists learned from fossil evidence that early human beings had smaller brains than most modern people have. This evidence indicated to many scientists that humans had *evolved*—that is, modified their physical structure over time. Scientists developed a set of ideas about human origins called the theory of hu-

man evolution. This theory states that, as the environment of the prehistoric world changed, our prehuman ancestors went through a series of changes that resulted in the first human beings. They, in turn, evolved into modern human beings.

Today, many kinds of scientists work together to learn about prehistoric people. Physical anthropologists examine the fossilized bones and teeth of prehistoric people and their prehuman forerunners. The scientists study these objects to learn more about what our ancestors looked like, how long they lived, and what foods they ate. Archaeologists search for and examine evidence, such as pottery and tools, to help explain how prehistoric people lived. Botanists study the remains of prehistoric plants, and zoologists analyze fossils of animals that lived at the same time as prehistoric people. Geologists study the rock in which fossils are found. All these scientists are called *paleoanthropologists* if their chief concern is the study of human physical and cultural development.

Evidence of prehistoric people—such as fossils, tools, and other remains—is rare and often fragmented. Evidence of the earliest types of prehistoric people is the most difficult to find, and anthropologists must base their theories on this extremely limited evidence. As a result, scientists cannot yet present a detailed picture of early human life. Over time, new discoveries sometimes disprove theories that scientists previously held.

Prehuman ancestors

Most scientists believe that human beings and apes—such as chimpanzees and gorillas—share a common ancestor. To support this theory, scientists point out that the fossilized remains of ancient humanlike beings and apes reveal many similarities, including similar brain sizes. In addition, studies comparing the physical structure, blood, and genetic material of modern human beings with those

Alan E. Mann, the contributor of this article, is Professor of Anthropology at Princeton University and coauthor of Human Biology and Behavior.

of apes show that people are more similar to apes than to any other living animal.

The ancestor of human beings probably evolved from an apelike common ancestor of apes and human beings between about 10 million and 5 million years ago. This evolutionary split marks the beginning of the development of *hominids.* Hominids make up the scientific family that consists of human beings and early humanlike ancestors.

Scientists consider the ability to walk on two legs, called *bipedal locomotion,* a feature unique to the hominids. In human beings, bipedal locomotion has brought about several changes in anatomy, especially in the bones and muscles of the hips and legs. Anthropologists look for such changes when deciding whether or not a fossil will be classified in the hominid family.

The earliest hominids. Anthropologists believe the hominid family originated in Africa. The oldest known fossil remains of hominids are found there. The closest living relatives to human beings, the chimpanzee and gorilla, are also native to Africa. Hominid fossils are extremely rare, and most are fragmentary and incomplete. In addition, anthropologists do not agree on how many species of hominids have existed in the past. Fossil species are distinguished by features of their skeletal anatomy. However, it is often difficult to determine if differences in anatomy in a group of fossils mean that two or more different species are present. Anthropologists do know, however, that there have been times in the past when more than one species of hominid lived at the same time.

Anthropologists discovered fossils of the oldest known hominid species in 2001 in the Djurab Desert area, near Faya-Largeau, in the north central African nation of Chad. The skull of this humanlike creature, called *Sahelanthropus tchadensis (suh hehl AN throh puhs cha DEHN sihs),* looks in some ways like an early ancestor to human be-

ings. Other parts of the skull, however, are more like that of an ape. The word *Sahelanthropus* comes from the term *Sahel,* a region of northern Africa where the fossils were found, and the Greek word *anthropus,* which means *human.* The fossils are between 6 million and 7 million years old. Anthropologists are not sure exactly how this early species is related to later hominids and modern human beings because the species is so ancient and is known from only a few fossils.

Fossils of another early hominid, called *Orrorin tugenensis (aw RAWR ihn too guh NEHN sihs),* were discovered in Kenya in 2000. The fossils are about 6 million years old. Fossilized fragments of limb bones show features that indicate this species may have been bipedal—that is, it may have walked on two legs. But anthropologists know little else about the appearance of this creature because only small fragments of the skull and jaw were found. The term *Orrorin* means *original man* in the language of the people of the Tugen Hills region of Kenya where the fossils were found.

Another early hominid group was a species called *Ardipithecus ramidus (AR duh PIHTH uh kuhs RAM uh duhs).* These creatures lived in what is now Ethiopia in northeast Africa from about 5,800,000 to about 4,400,000 years ago. Like *Orrorin* and other hominids, *Ardipithecus* appears to have been bipedal. The name *Ardipithecus* comes from words in the Afar and Greek languages meaning *ground ape.*

Scientists know little about the anatomy of these earliest hominids or their relationship to later hominids. The fossil remains are incomplete and fragmentary. Anthropologists hope that future discoveries will tell them more about the appearance and lifestyle of these earliest possible ancestors to modern human beings.

The australopithecines. A much better-understood group of early hominids are the *australopithecines (aw stray loh PIHTH uh seenz).* The australopithecines are classified in the genus *Australopithecus,* a term that means *southern ape.* They first appeared about 4 million years ago in Africa. Fossil evidence suggests that these creatures became extinct between 2 million and 1 million years ago, about when the first human beings appeared. Scientists have found australopithecine fossils in eastern, southern, and north central Africa.

What they looked like. The australopithecines looked much different from modern human beings. In some ways, such as in their facial features, they may have resembled chimpanzees. But they could stand upright, they were bipedal, and their *canine teeth* (eyeteeth) were much smaller and less pointed than those of apes.

The australopithecines had large faces that jutted out in front of their foreheads compared to the relatively flat face of human beings. Their brains were about one-third the size of modern human brains. Their *molars* (back chewing teeth) were large, flat, and suitable for grinding food. Anthropologists believe from the shape of these creatures' teeth and from chemical analysis of their bones that they ate such foods as fruits, vegetables, nuts, seeds, insects, and small animals.

Types of australopithecines. Most scientists have divided the genus *Australopithecus* into six species based on differences in the creatures' overall size, in the shape and size of their jaws and teeth, and in the size of their brains. The six species are (1) *Australopithecus anamensis,*

Footprints of a prehuman ancestor were discovered in 1978 at a site called Laetoli in Tanzania. These footprints, which were fossilized in volcanic ash, are about 3,600,000 years old. They provide evidence that early hominids walked upright.

(2) *A. afarensis,* (3) *A. africanus,* (4) *A. garhi,* (5) *A. robustus,* and (6) *A. boisei.*

The earliest known species of *Australopithecus* was *A. anamensis (an uh MEHN sihs),* which appeared in eastern Africa around 4 million years ago. Another *Australopithecus* species, *A. afarensis (af uh REHN sihs),* appeared about 3,700,000 years ago. One of the most complete australopithecines that scientists have found is a partial skeleton of a female *Australopithecus afarensis.* It was found at Hadar, Ethiopia. Scientists estimate that this creature, nicknamed "Lucy," was about $3\frac{1}{2}$ feet (110 centimeters) tall and weighed about 60 pounds (27 kilograms). Scientists also have discovered the fossilized footprints of *A. afarensis* individuals at Laetoli, in Tanzania. The footprints resemble those of modern people and show, with the skeleton of "Lucy," that *A. afarensis* walked bipedally. However, these humanlike creatures may have had arms that, in proportion to their bodies, were longer than those of modern people. Australopithecine bones that may be those of *A. afarensis* have also been found in Chad, in north central Africa. *A. afarensis* had about the same size brain as a chimpanzee has.

By about 3 million years ago, another australopithecine, *A. africanus (af rih KAN uhs),* lived in southern Africa. These creatures had rounder skulls and slightly larger brains than those of *A. afarensis.* In 1998, a complete skeleton of *A. africanus* was discovered at Sterkfontein, a fossil site near Johannesburg, in South Africa.

During the time of *A. africanus,* three more australopithecine species appeared. One of them, *A. garhi (GAH ree),* lived in northeastern Africa. *A. garhi* resembled *A. afarensis* but had larger teeth. Another australopithecine, *A. boisei (BOY zee eye),* lived in eastern Africa. Still another, *A. robustus (roh BUHS tuhs),* lived in southern Africa. Scientists call *A. boisei* and *A. robustus* the *robust australopithecines.* The other four species are called *gracile* (slender) australopithecines. The robust australopithecines had much larger molars and more powerful jaws than the gracile *Australopithecus* species, and they may have had larger bodies. But their brain size was about the same as that of *A. africanus.* The robust species probably became extinct between $1\frac{1}{2}$ million and 1 million years ago.

Some scientists think that the robust australopithecine species should be classified in a separate genus, called *Paranthropus (PAR an THROH puhs).* These scientists argue that the differences in the anatomy of the robust and gracile forms are so great that they represent two different groups.

Scientists are uncertain about the precise relationships between the *Australopithecus* species. Some think the gracile species evolved one after the other, from the earliest, *A. anamensis,* to the latest, *A. garhi.* According to this theory, the robust species formed an evolutionary side branch. Other scientists think the australopithecine species were linked differently. They believe that, early in australopithecine evolution, these creatures spread to different parts of Africa, changing to adapt to the environments in which they lived. As a result, different species developed in different environments.

Some anthropologists think that *A. garhi* may be the species from which early human beings developed. However, another hominid species lived at the same time as the australopithecines and may be the ancestor of human beings. This species, called *Kenyanthropus platyops (KEHN*

© Nature-M.F.T. from Getty Images

The oldest known hominid fossil is this skull of a species called *Sahelanthropus tchadensis,* between 6 million and 7 million years old. The species, known only from this fossil skull and a few jaw fragments, shows a mix of ape and humanlike features.

yuhn THROH puhs PLAT ee ahps), is known from a fossil skull discovered in northwestern Kenya in 1999. The term *platyops* means *flat,* and refers to the relatively flat, non-projecting face of this creature. A relatively flat face is a physical feature also seen in early human beings. Most anthropologists believe the first people evolved from an australopithecine, or possibly from a creature like *Kenyanthropus,* more than 2 million years ago.

The first human beings

The first human beings lived in Africa about 2 million years ago. Anthropologists have found important fossils of these people near the shores of Lake Turkana in Kenya and in Olduvai Gorge in Tanzania. Many scientists divide these people into three species—*Homo habilis, Homo rudolfensis,* and *Homo erectus.*

Homo habilis and **Homo rudolfensis.** *Homo habilis (HOH moh HAB uh luhs)* had a brain larger than an australopithecine brain but only about half the size of a modern human brain. *Homo habilis* also had smaller molar teeth and a less protruding face than the australopithecines had. The Latin word *Homo* means *human being.* The term *habilis* means *handy* or *skillful.*

Homo rudolfensis (HOH moh roo dawl FEHN sihs) had a brain larger than that of *H. habilis.* It also had large molars,

© David L. Brill

Robust australopithecines had broad faces and large teeth, as seen in this fossil skull of *Australopithecus boisei.* A ridge of bone on top of the skull, called a *sagittal crest,* held large muscles used for chewing tough plant foods.

© National Museums of Kenya, Nairobi, photo by Fred Spoor

A possible prehuman ancestor, this fossil skull of *Kenyanthropus platyops* is 3,500,000 years old. The skull's flattened face is an anatomical feature also seen in early and modern human beings.

like those of the australopithecines. The term *rudolfensis* comes from Lake Rudolph, an old name for Lake Turkana. Fossils of *H. rudolfensis* have been discovered near the lake.

Some anthropologists are uncertain whether *H. habilis* and *H. rudolfensis* were two different species or whether they represent, respectively, the females and males of one species. A difference in size, coloring, or body structure between the sexes is known as *sexual dimorphism*. Sexual dimorphism with respect to size appears among many modern apes and was present among the australopithecines. Such dimorphism is less extreme in modern human beings.

Homo erectus. Another species of early human being, *Homo erectus (HOH moh ih REHK tuhs),* lived at the same time as *H. habilis* and *H. rudolfensis.* The term *erectus* refers to the upright posture of these creatures. Most scientists believe *H. erectus* was the species that evolved into modern people.

Homo erectus had a brain slightly larger than that of *H. rudolfensis,* but it also had smaller molars. During the course of *H. erectus* evolution, brain size increased, eventually reaching a size just slightly smaller than that of a modern human brain. *Homo erectus* individuals had thick skulls, sloping foreheads, and large, chinless jaws. Their skulls had a *browridge,* a raised strip of bone across the lower forehead. *H. erectus* also had a smaller and flatter face than *H. habilis* and *H. rudolfensis* had. Fossils indicate that the *Homo erectus* males were larger than the females.

The earliest *Homo erectus* fossils have been found in Africa. They date from more than 1,900,000 years ago. One of the best-known examples of *H. erectus* is a nearly complete fossil skeleton of a boy who was probably about 11 or 12 years old when he died. The skeleton, which is over 1,500,000 years old, was found near Lake Turkana. The boy had already reached 5 feet 3 inches (160 centimeters) in height and might have grown to 6 feet 1 inch (185 centimeters) if he had lived to adulthood.

These early people were like modern human beings in many ways. However, it is difficult for anthropologists to fully picture them. Physical remains of prehistoric people consist only of fossilized bones and teeth. Sci-

entists do not know whether, for example, early hominids had fur, like chimpanzees or gorillas, or if they were largely hairless like modern human beings. Anthropologists do not know if these hominids had ears, noses, and lips more like the features of modern people or more like those of apes. Scientists can only guess about the color of early people's skin. Such questions remain impossible for anthropologists to answer.

How the first people lived

Toolmaking. Anthropologists believe that *H. habilis, H. rudolfensis,* and *H. erectus* made and used stone tools. The earliest tools were sharp-edged stones used for cutting, scraping, and chopping. Prehistoric people made them by striking one stone with another, chipping pieces away to produce a cutting edge. The first tools were crude, but over time early human beings began to craft tools of a finer quality. Later toolmakers used mallets of wood or bone to tap away small chips of stone, producing a straight, sharp cutting edge.

Scientists believe the early human beings ate meat in addition to fruits, insects, and plants. Archaeologists have found animal bones buried with stone tools from the time of the first people. Some of the bones show scratch marks that were probably made by the cutting action of stone tools. These marks indicate that the early butchers used tools to cut up game and to scrape meat off bones. But scientists do not know whether these early people killed large animals themselves or merely ate the meat after the animals had been killed by predators.

During the time of *Homo erectus,* tools became more skillfully made, and new types of tools appeared. For example, *H. erectus* created double-edged cutting tools of stone called *hand axes*. Workers probably held these axes in their hands and used them without a handle for many tasks, such as shaping wood or bone and cutting up meat. *H. erectus* may have hunted large animals.

The use of fire. *Homo erectus* was probably the first human being to master the use of fire. These people may also have been the first to wear clothing. Scientists believe that as *H. erectus* moved into northern areas and faced cold winters, fire and clothing became necessary. Archaeologists have not found any traces of early clothing, but it was probably made from animal hides. The oldest evidence of the use of fire was found in a cave that *H. erectus* occupied between 600,000 and 400,000 years ago near what is now Beijing, in northern China. Stone tools and the remains of more than 40 *H. erectus* individuals were found in the cave, along with burnt animal bones.

Migration from Africa. *Homo erectus* was the first

Transvaal Museum, Pretoria (© David L. Brill)
Australopithecus africanus

KNM-ER 1470, National Museums of Kenya, Nairobi (© David L. Brill)
Homo habilis

Mauricio Anton © National Geographic Society

National Museums of Kenya, Nairobi (© David L. Brill)

The skull of *Homo erectus* displays a distinct shape. The species was characterized by thick skull bones; a low, sloping forehead; and a flat face. The species also had a thick ridge of bone above the eyes, called a *browridge*. The features can be seen on these fossil skulls from Dmanisi, Republic of Georgia, *facing front*, and Koobi Fora, Kenya, *in profile*. These fossils are about 1,700,000 to 1,800,000 years old.

hominid species to migrate out of Africa. Anthropologists think these early people first migrated out of Africa sometime after 1,800,000 years ago. Archaeologists believe a site called Ubeidiya *(oo buh DY uh)* lies along what may have been a main migration route from Africa. An archaeological site is any place where remains of past human activity are found. The site, near the bank of the Jordan River in what is now Israel, is about 1,600,000 years old. Stone tools discovered at the site resemble stone tools from Africa.

Archaeologists also found the fossilized bones of many African mammals at Ubeidiya. They interpret the fossils as evidence that the migration of early human beings from Africa was part of a larger migration by many species. Scientists are not certain why hominids left Africa at this time. Some believe that stone tools enabled early human beings to obtain a greater variety of foods, so they could successfully move into new lands.

Early human beings quickly migrated to Asia once they had left Africa. Anthropologists have found hominid fossils along with stone tools at a site called Dmanisi *(duh mah NYEE see)* in what is now the Republic of Georgia. The site was formed about 1,700,000 years ago. Fossils of *Homo erectus* have been found on the island of Java in present-day Indonesia. Anthropologists think the fossil remains of early human beings in Java are about 1,800,000 years old.

Some anthropologists think that what has been called *Homo erectus* was actually two species. They point to differences in the appearance of the fossil bones of *Homo erectus* from Africa and those from Asia. According to this idea, the earliest fossils, from Africa, should be called *Homo ergaster (HOH moh UR gas tuhr)*. The term *ergaster* comes from a Greek term that means *workman.* The name refers to the stone tools found in association with the fossils. These fossils have thinner skull bones and browridges compared to the Asian fossils. Once *Homo ergaster* migrated out of Africa, another species, *Homo erectus*, evolved in Asia from *Homo ergaster* ancestors. According to this theory, *Homo erectus* is a species found only in Asia and is not related to modern human beings. Other anthropologists, however, think that all the fossils represent one species, *Homo erectus,* which is a distant ancestor to human beings.

Massive glaciers repeatedly covered much of Europe during the ice ages of the Pleistocene Epoch, which lasted from about 2 million to 11,500 years ago. Scientists believe that the glaciers prevented people from migrating to the region. Anthropologists have found the oldest fossil remains of early human beings in Europe at the Atapuerca *(ah tah PWEHR kuh)* Mountains in northern Spain. The site is about 800,000 years old. The presence of early human beings in ice age Europe was closely tied to the advance and retreat of the glaciers. People could not have survived in most areas of Europe during times of maximum glacial coverage.

The origin of *Homo sapiens*

Scientists classify today's people as *Homo sapiens*, a term that means *wise human being.* Anthropologists disagree about the precise evolutionary relationships between *Homo sapiens* and earlier peoples, such as *Homo erectus*. They also disagree about where and when *H. sapiens* first appeared.

Compared with the earliest human beings, people today have a high forehead and a higher and more rounded skull. They lack the browridge of earlier people, and they have a chin and a smaller, flatter face.

Anthropologists today reject the idea that human beings can be divided into biologically defined races. Only slight differences distinguish the features of any two modern peoples who developed in neighboring regions. Thus, it is hard to draw a dividing line between them. But groups of people who have lived in certain parts of the world for many thousands of years tend to differ in appearance from groups in other parts of the world. These differences are probably adaptations to local environments. For example, people whose ancestors have lived for generations in sunny climates tend to have dark skin. Dark pigment helps protect the skin from sunburn and reduces the risk of skin cancer.

Anthropologists have developed two main theories to explain the origin of modern human beings and the development of human races—that is, the physical differences among populations in different regions. These theories may be referred to as (1) the multiple origins theory and (2) the single origin theory.

The multiple origins theory states that after *H. erectus* spread out of Africa, groups of these early human beings settled in different parts of Asia, and then, later, reached Europe. As they moved to new areas, with differing climates and plants and animals, these scattered populations developed different characteristics. In each geographical area, human groups with different appearances evolved.

Cro-Magnon skull, Musée de l'Homme, Paris (© David L. Brill)

Homo sapiens

But because of the constant movement of individuals from one region to another, they continued to form a single species. Most anthropologists who support the multiple origins theory believe that between about 700,000 and 400,000 years ago, these scattered groups of *H. erectus* evolved into *H. sapiens.*

According to these scientists, the first *Homo sapiens* differed greatly from modern people, and in many ways strongly resembled *H. erectus.* The main difference between early *H. sapiens* and *H. erectus* was that early *H. sapiens* had a higher and more rounded skull. But like *Homo erectus*, the first *H. sapiens* individuals had large faces that protruded around the mouth and nose. They also had big browridges and low, sloping foreheads. These people lacked a chin, a feature found only in later *Homo sapiens.* The brain size of early *H. sapiens* varied. Some of these people had brains that were similar in size to those of late *H. erectus.* Others had brains as large as modern human brains.

Supporters of the multiple-origins theory would classify the *Neandertals (nee AN duhr tahlz)* as an early subgroup of *H. sapiens* due to their ability to make and use complex stone tools. Neandertals are the most widely known of the early human beings, mainly because their fossils were the first traces of prehistoric people ever discovered. The term *Neandertal*, also spelled *Neanderthal*, comes from the Neander Valley near Düsseldorf, Germany. The first Neandertal fossils were found there in 1856.

Neandertals lived in Europe and Central Asia between 150,000 and 35,000 years ago. They had features typical of early *H. sapiens*, including a protruding face, large browridge, and low forehead. Most Neandertals also lacked a chin. But on the average, their brain size was larger than that of modern human beings. Neandertals were also very muscular.

Physically modern human beings. According to the multiple origins theory, today's human beings eventually developed from the Neandertals and other groups of early *H. sapiens* who lived in different parts of Europe, Africa, and Asia. In time, these groups evolved higher, more rounded skulls. Their large browridges and protruding faces gradually disappeared, and they developed a chin. But they maintained certain differences in appearance that had developed during their long evolution in different regions. These local differences now distinguish different groups of modern peoples—the human races—around the world.

Evidence for the theory. The best evidence supporting the multiple origins theory comes from a series of skulls found in Indonesia and Australia. In age, these skulls span a period that began about 1 million years ago and lasted until

the appearance of physically modern human beings approximately 100,000 years ago. All of the skulls show similar features characteristic of that part of the world. The fossils appear to represent a population that continuously evolved and, over time, resulted in modern Southeast Asian peoples.

A few anthropologists who accept the multiple origins theory believe that the earliest human beings, those who lived about 2 million years ago, did not form a separate species, such as *Homo erectus* or *Homo ergaster.* Instead, they believe that the earliest people belonged to the same species as modern people, *Homo sapiens.* According to these scientists, the key difference between the first people and their prehuman ancestors was the way they lived and obtained food, including their use of stone tools and their greater reliance on hunting. These anthropologists believe that all human beings, early and late, and including those with browridges, no chins, and small brains, should be called *Homo sapiens.*

The single origin theory, like the multiple origins theory, begins with the spread of *H. erectus* (called *Homo ergaster* by some) out of Africa—perhaps as early as 1,800,000 years ago—and into Asia and eventually Europe. According to the single origin theory, however, the scattered population groups did not maintain contact from their different continents. For this reason, some anthropologists call the early human beings in Africa *Homo ergaster*, and not *Homo erectus.* For these scientists, *Homo erectus* is a species that developed later in Asia as a result of this isolation.

Scientists who support the single origin theory believe that *Homo ergaster* in Africa gave rise to another species, called *Homo heidelbergensis (HOH moh HY dehl bur GEHN sihs).* This species spread throughout Africa and then into Europe beginning about 1 million years ago. But it did not spread into Asia.

Anthropologists think that the severe climate conditions of ice age Europe isolated populations of *Homo heidelbergensis.* Some populations evolved specialized features for life in ice age Europe. These people, usually called *Homo neanderthalensis*, or Neandertals, were physically adapted for life in a cold climate.

The spread of early human beings. According to the single origin theory, the first *Homo sapiens* appeared in Africa between 200,000 and 100,000 years ago, having developed from *H. heidelbergensis* in that region. Soon afterward, *H. sapiens* spread to other parts of Africa, as well as to Asia and Europe. In these regions, modern *H. sapiens* replaced the earlier peoples who lived there. All these earlier peoples, such as the Neandertals in Europe and *Homo erectus* in Asia, became extinct.

The single origin theory and multiple origins theory are similar in many ways. The main disagreements include differences on how far back in time human races originated and how the Neandertals are related to living people. Anthropologists who support the single origins theory believe that human races developed in the last 100,000 to 200,000 years and exclude Neandertals as ancestors to modern human beings. Anthropologists who accept the multiple origins theory believe modern human races began a very long time ago, perhaps as early as 2 million years ago. In this theory, Neandertals may be the ancestors of living people, particularly Europeans.

Evidence for the theory. Two fossil skulls from Herto,

Ethiopia, dated to about 160,000 years ago show many similarities to living *Homo sapiens.* More complete evidence supporting the single origins theory, however, comes from cave sites in Israel. At two of these sites, called Qafzeh *(KAHF zuh)* and Skhul *(skool),* archaeologists excavated fossil skeletons of modern-looking human beings that date from about 100,000 years ago. These people had a chin, a high forehead, and a smaller, less-protruding face than earlier peoples had. They also lacked the large browridge of earlier people and had a higher, more rounded skull. At another site nearby, Kebara, a Neandertal skeleton that dated from about 60,000 years ago was found. This fossil evidence shows that Neandertals lived in the Middle East after the modern type of human beings appeared. Supporters of the single origin theory point out that it is difficult to place the Neandertals as ancestors of

modern human beings if they lived after modern human beings first appeared.

Some scientists also support the single origin theory through use of genetic evidence from living people. Molecular biologists have gained a greater understanding of human evolution by studying the rate of change of human genetic material. By calculating this rate, some scientists have concluded that all living people must have evolved from a small group of human ancestors who lived in Africa about 200,000 years ago. But some molecular biologists doubt that enough is known about human heredity to draw such a conclusion.

In 1997, scientists announced that they extracted a small amount of the genetic material *DNA* (deoxyribonucleic acid) from a Neandertal fossil. The DNA of the Neandertal differs from that of modern human beings. This genetic

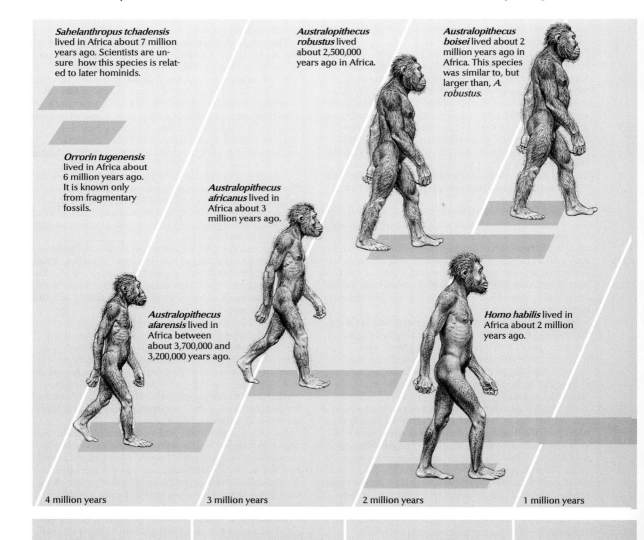

Sahelanthropus tchadensis lived in Africa about 7 million years ago. Scientists are unsure how this species is related to later hominids.

Australopithecus robustus lived about 2,500,000 years ago in Africa.

Australopithecus boisei lived about 2 million years ago in Africa. This species was similar to, but larger than, *A. robustus.*

Orrorin tugenensis lived in Africa about 6 million years ago. It is known only from fragmentary fossils.

Australopithecus africanus lived in Africa about 3 million years ago.

Australopithecus afarensis lived in Africa between about 3,700,000 and 3,200,000 years ago.

Homo habilis lived in Africa about 2 million years ago.

4 million years   3 million years   2 million years   1 million years

● Pebble tools   ● Hand axes

evidence further supports the single origin theory that the Neandertals were a separate species and not ancestral to modern human beings.

Scientists have also obtained samples of DNA from a human skeleton uncovered at a site called Lake Mungo in Australia. The skeleton is about 40,000 years old and is that of a modern human being. The DNA from this skeleton, however, also differs from that of living people. Scientists continue to debate the significance of these genetic discoveries. Most scientists agree that more fossil discoveries and genetic studies are necessary to understand the relationship between Neandertals and modern human beings.

How the Neandertals lived

The Neandertals were more skilled hunters and toolmakers than earlier people. The bones of many animals have been found at Neandertal sites. Some of the bones indicate that these people hunted such large animals as horses, reindeer, and mammoths. But they had more success in capturing hares and other small animals. The Neandertals made a variety of stone tools and used them to butcher animals, prepare vegetable foods, scrape hides, and carve wood. They also made sharp, pointed tools that may have been spearheads.

Neandertals lived in Europe between 150,000 and 35,000 years ago, during the most recent ice age, when vast sheets of ice covered many northern parts of the world. As a result, they developed qualities that enabled them to cope with harsh winter conditions. Archaeologists have found most evidence of Neandertals in the entrances of caves, where many of these people lived to escape the extreme cold. Archaeologists have also discovered sites

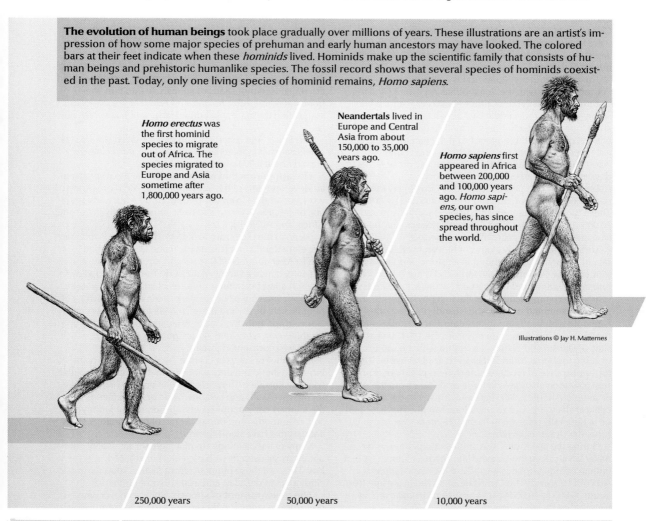

The evolution of human beings took place gradually over millions of years. These illustrations are an artist's impression of how some major species of prehuman and early human ancestors may have looked. The colored bars at their feet indicate when these *hominids* lived. Hominids make up the scientific family that consists of human beings and prehistoric humanlike species. The fossil record shows that several species of hominids coexisted in the past. Today, only one living species of hominid remains, *Homo sapiens.*

Homo erectus was the first hominid species to migrate out of Africa. The species migrated to Europe and Asia sometime after 1,800,000 years ago.

Neandertals lived in Europe and Central Asia from about 150,000 to 35,000 years ago.

Homo sapiens first appeared in Africa between 200,000 and 100,000 years ago. *Homo sapiens,* our own species, has since spread throughout the world.

Illustrations © Jay H. Matternes

250,000 years   50,000 years   10,000 years

● Burial of the dead
● Blade tools
    ● Body ornamentation
      ● Sewing
        ● Cave paintings
● Pottery
  ● Farming
● Irrigation
  ● Writing
  ● Small cities

where Neandertals camped in the open. These sites provide evidence that the Neandertals pitched large circular tents around a central hearth. The tent covering probably consisted of hides, leaves, or bark and was supported by wooden posts.

The Neandertals were the first people known to have buried their dead. In Neandertal sites in Europe and the Middle East, archaeologists have uncovered the carefully buried skeletons of women, men, and children.

The Stone Age

Most prehistoric tools that have been found are made of stone. Thus, much of the prehistoric past is often called the Stone Age. The earliest toolmakers may also have used wood and other materials, but no tools made of those materials have survived.

The oldest tools scientists have found date from about 2,600,000 years ago. They were discovered at a site called Gona in central Ethiopia. However, no hominid fossils were found with these tools, so scientists do not know whether an australopithecine or another type of early hominid made them.

The first part of the Stone Age is called the Paleolithic Period. It began with the first toolmaking over $2\frac{1}{2}$ million years ago and lasted until about 10,000 years ago, when some people in the Middle East began farming. On the basis of toolmaking techniques, scientists divide the Paleolithic Period into three parts. From the earliest to the latest, they are called the Lower, Middle, and Upper Paleolithic. Anthropologists most often use those terms to describe periods of European prehistory.

Even after some people learned to farm, many others continued to live by gathering wild plants and by hunting. These Stone Age hunters and gatherers who lived after 10,000 years ago are called *Mesolithic people*. Farmers from this period are called *Neolithic people*.

Throughout the early stages of human evolution, the rate of cultural change among prehistoric people was extremely slow. At times, stone tools and other products of human skill remained unchanged for many thousands of years. The cultural activities of the first physically modern people resembled those of the Neandertals and other early people who lived during that time. For example, the modern-looking human beings from the 100,000-year-old sites of Qafzeh and Skhul were found with the same kinds of stone tools that Neandertals used at sites nearby. Thus, the appearance of modern human beings did not represent a sudden change in lifestyle or culture from the earlier people. About 35,000 years ago, however, the rate of cultural change began to accelerate rapidly. This later period is generally referred to as the late Stone Age, or, in Europe, the Upper Paleolithic.

During the late Stone Age, prehistoric people made many advances in their way of life. The best-known type of human beings from this period are the *Cro-Magnons (kroh MAG nahnz)*. The Cro-Magnons lived in Europe from about 35,000 to 10,000 years ago. Scientists believe they resembled modern Europeans.

The improvement of tools was a major accomplishment of the Cro-Magnons and other late Stone Age people. New tool types and methods of manufacture appeared at a rapid pace. Stone tools made during this time were more refined and complex in design. Toolmakers invented new devices to serve specialized carving, cutting,

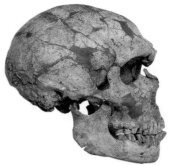

© John Reader/SPL from Photo Researchers

Neandertal

and drilling functions. Tools of bone, ivory, and animal horns also came into use. Archaeologists have found harpoons, fish spears, and needles made from bone that date from this period. These tools suggest the introduction of such activities as sewing close-fitting clothes and fishing with better equipment.

Upper Paleolithic fossil sites in Europe also indicate that these people had become skillful hunters. Some sites hold the remains of thousands of animals. In addition, the bones of mammoths, horses, and reindeer are common, suggesting these people hunted large animals successfully.

The Stone Age lasted until bronze replaced stone as the chief toolmaking material. In some areas, this change occurred about 5,000 years ago.

The appearance of art was one of the most spectacular developments of the late Stone Age. The oldest known works of art date from this period. Furthermore, the practice of creating art seems to have spread rapidly in Europe, Africa, and Australia.

Some of the oldest artworks from the Upper Paleolithic were ornaments, such as beads made from polished shells. After about 30,000 years ago, prehistoric people began to produce a variety of artwork. They excelled at carving—creating beautiful sculptures of animals and people, usually from ivory or bone. They also made engravings of people, fish, birds, and other animals on bone, ivory, and stone. In addition, the Upper Paleolithic people in Europe sculpted clay, ivory, and stone figurines of women, which may have represented fertility.

A number of caves in Europe are covered with paintings, drawings, and engravings from the Upper Paleolithic. Most distinctive of these are the paintings, which appear on the cave walls and ceilings. Most of the paintings are of the animals early people probably hunted, including bison, mammoths, and horses. Some of the paintings show animals that have been speared.

Many of the paintings are of a high artistic quality. Paleolithic artists used three basic colors: black, red, and yellow. They got these pigments from natural sources, including charcoal, clay, and iron and other minerals.

The development of speech. No one knows when or how spoken language developed. However, some anthropologists think that human beings may have first begun to speak sometime during the late Stone Age. These scientists believe that the many cultural developments that occurred at this time—especially the appearance of art—may be related to the development of speech. The beginnings of speech, the creation of artwork, and the making of complex tools all required advancements in human intelligence and cooperation.

The spread of settlement. Prehistoric people spread into new areas during the late Stone Age. Cultural and technological advances enabled them to migrate to such places as Australia, the Pacific Islands, and North and South America.

As early as 60,000 years ago, people used boats to reach Australia. About 20,000 years ago, people from Australia and Asia began to colonize the Pacific Islands. These people used sophisticated navigational systems involving knowledge of the stars, water currents, and wind direction. They also used simple navigational tools.

By 130,000 years ago, human beings had spread to the cold, harsh plains of western Siberia, but not until later did people move into the eastern part of the region. At that time, because so much water had been frozen as glacial ice, the level of the oceans and seas was lower than it is today. As a result, the Bering Strait was dry and formed a land bridge between northeast Asia and North America. Most scientists believe prehistoric people crossed this bridge and were living in North America by about 15,000 to 20,000 years ago. Eventually, through a series of migrations from Asia, modern people populated North and South America.

The most recent ice age ended about 11,500 years ago. As the ice receded, the environment of many prehistoric people changed and greatly affected their way of life. In some areas, such as Europe, forests began to spread across the land. The people of these areas learned to hunt new species of animals and gather new varieties of plants from the forests. In other parts of the world, people began to experiment with methods of controlling their supply of food. They learned that they could plant seeds from the plants they ate. They also learned that they could domesticate animals, perhaps by capturing young ones from the wild and raising them. These discoveries led to farming.

The rise of agriculture, according to most scientists, began in the Middle East about 10,000 years ago, or 8000 B.C. The first farmers lived in a region called the Fertile Crescent, which covers what is now Lebanon and parts of Iran, Iraq, Israel, Jordan, Syria, and Turkey. At first, these people probably did not depend entirely on the crops they raised. But as they improved their methods, farming became their most important source of food. The earliest plants grown in the Middle East were probably barley and wheat. Early farmers in the Middle East eventually raised cattle, goats, and sheep.

People were herding cattle and growing grain in northern Africa by 6000 B.C. By about 5000 to 4000 B.C., agriculture had developed independently in Asia. In the Yangtze Valley of China, and perhaps in what is now Thailand, farmers grew rice and a grain called *millet.* By the same time, people had begun to farm in the Indus River Valley of what is now Pakistan.

Between about 4500 and 4000 B.C., farming peoples spread from southeastern Europe into the dense forests of central and western Europe. These people brought wheat and cattle with them. Foraging people in Scandinavia learned how to farm from these newcomers.

Agriculture began to develop in southern Africa by about 3000 B.C. By 1500 B.C., people had begun to cultivate corn and beans in what is now Mexico. By 1000 B.C., peoples in what became the eastern United States were raising gourds and sunflowers. Farming began later in other parts of North America.

Changes in lifestyle. Prehistoric farmers, called Neolithic people, had a way of life that differed greatly from that of other late Stone Age people. In some ways, farming made life easier. It provided a steady supply of food and enabled people to live in one place for a long time. But farmers had to work harder than hunters and gatherers did.

Prehistoric farmers set up villages near their fields and lived there as long as their crops grew well. Most fields produced good crops for a few years. The land then became unproductive because the crops used up *nutrients* (nourishing substances) in the soil. The farmers did not know about fertilizers that could replace the nutrients. They shifted their crops to new fields until none of the land near their village was fertile. Then they moved to a new area and built another village. In this way, farmers settled many new areas.

Prehistoric farmers built larger, longer-lasting settlements than the camps that other late Stone Age people had built. In the Middle East, for example, early farmers constructed their houses of solid, sun-dried mud, sometimes on stone foundations. Dried mud was much more resistant to weather than the materials earlier people used, such as skins and bark. The early farmers also learned to build fences to confine and protect their livestock.

The end of prehistoric times. Neolithic farmers made inventions and discoveries at an even faster rate than other late Stone Age people had done. Early farmers developed a number of useful tools. These implements included sickles to cut grain, millstones to grind flour, and polished stone axeheads.

Perhaps as early as 9000 B.C. in Japan, and somewhat later in the Middle East, people discovered how to make pottery. Before then, they used animal skins or bark containers to hold water. To boil water, early cooks had to drop hot stones into the water because they could not hang animal skins or bark over a fire. Pottery containers enabled people to hold and boil water easily. Farmers also used pottery to store grain and other food.

The development of farming was an important step toward the rise of civilization. As farming methods improved and food became more plentiful, many people were freed from the jobs of food production. These people developed new skills and trades. In addition, the abundant food

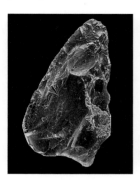
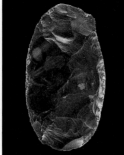

© Lee Boltin

Prehistoric tools were made chiefly of stone. The hand axe, *above left,* and scraper, *above right,* were made by Neandertals by chipping pieces away from a carefully selected stone.

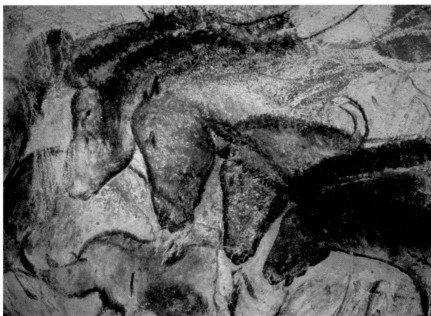

Cave paintings are among the most spectacular examples of art by prehistoric people. The cave paintings usually depict prehistoric animals, such as the horses and rhinoceros seen in this painting from Chauvet Cave in southern France. These animals were hunted by early human beings about 30,000 years ago. Human figures, however, are rarely depicted in European cave paintings.

Center for Information & Documentation (DRAC RhUne-Alpes)

supply enabled more people to live in each community. In time, some farming villages became cities. The first cities appeared by about 3500 B.C. These cities were the birthplaces of modern civilization.

No one knows when people made the first objects of metal. But metals became important only after metalworkers learned to make bronze, a substance hard and durable enough to make lasting tools. People of the Middle East made bronze as early as 3500 B.C. The Bronze Age began when bronze replaced stone as the chief toolmaking material. In some areas, such as the Near East, the Bronze Age began about 3000 B.C.

Archaeologists believe writing was invented about 3500 B.C. in cities in the Tigris-Euphrates Valley in what is now Iraq. People then learned to record their history, and prehistoric times came to an end.

Studying prehistoric people

Since the mid-1800's, scientists have learned much about prehistoric people and their ways of life. They have used various methods to obtain this knowledge.

Studying fossils of prehistoric people has provided anthropologists with much of their most valuable information. Human fossils give direct evidence of what prehistoric people looked like, what they ate, how long they lived, and how their lives differed from ours.

Unfortunately, fossil bones and teeth are scarce. They are rare because certain unusual conditions must be present for a fossil to form. An animal or person must be buried soon after death, and minerals from the soil must gradually replace the bony material to create a fossil. Also, the bones and teeth that do become fossils have often been broken, damaged, or distorted by the weight of the deposits in which they were buried. Soft tissues—such as skin, hair, and internal organs of prehistoric people—decay without leaving any fossil remains. As a result, scientists cannot determine certain characteristics of early hominids, such as the shape of their nose, the color of their skin, or the texture of their hair.

After a fossil is discovered, scientists first determine whether it came from an adult or a child and whether the individual was a male or a female. Anthropologists then compare the fossil with similar structures from other extinct hominids, living people, and apes. These examinations enable scientists to better understand the specimen's place in human evolution. Later, anthropologists study the fossil to determine a relationship between the individual's physical structure and its way of life. For example, looking at the way the teeth have worn down often provides clues about the foods the individual ate. The chemicals in fossil bones can also give clues about the diet of extinct hominids.

Examining prehistoric sites is another method that anthropologists use to gain information about prehistoric people and their way of life. Anthropologists spend a large amount of time surveying the landscape in search of prehistoric sites. These sites may be places where prehistoric people camped, made tools, butchered animals, or buried their dead.

The excavation of prehistoric sites is a complicated process. Archaeologists carefully scrape away soil, sand, or rock to reveal tools, bones, pottery, and other evidence of early human life. They make detailed notes and maps to record the exact position of all important items. They later use these records to precisely reconstruct the layout of the site. By studying the objects they find and the layout of the site, scientists learn how prehistoric people used the site and how these activities fit into their way of life.

Today, archaeologists avoid excavating the entire site they are working on. They try to leave enough of the ancient deposit so that future scientists, with more advanced techniques, can return to the site and learn still more about the people who lived there.

Where remains of prehistoric people have been found

The earliest fossils and other remains of prehistoric people have been found in Africa, Asia, and Europe. Most scientists believe our closest prehuman ancestors originated in Africa, and prehistoric people later spread to other parts of the world.

◇ Sahelanthropus tchadensis
◆ Orrorin tugenensis

○ Ardipithecus
● Australopithecus

□ Homo habilis
■ Homo erectus

△ Neandertals
▲ Homo sapiens

★ Uncertain classification

WORLD BOOK map

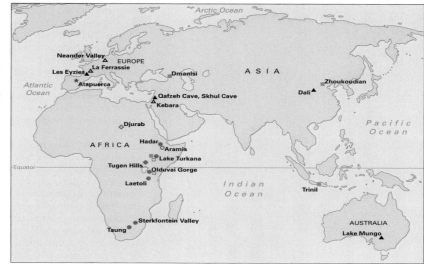

Important fossils of prehistoric people and their prehuman ancestors

Fossil	Location	Date found	Discovered or identified by	Importance
Prehuman ancestors				
Sahelanthropus tchadensis	Djurab Desert, Chad	2001	Djimdoumalbaye Ahounta (Chadian), Michel Brunet (French)	Oldest known hominid
Orrorin tugenensis	Tugen Hills, Kenya, near Nairobi	2000	Kiptalam Cheboi (Kenyan), Martin Pickford (British), Brigitte Senut (French)	Ancient bipedal hominid
Ardipithecus ramidus	Aramis, Awash River Valley, Ethiopia	1994	Tim White (U.S.), Gen Suwa (Japanese), Berhane Asfaw (Ethiopian)	Early apelike hominid
Australopithecus anamensis	Lake Turkana, Kenya	1994	Peter Nzube Mutiwa (Kenyan)	Oldest australopithecine
Taung child	Taung, South Africa, near Vryburg	1924	Raymond A. Dart (South African)	First australopithecine discovered
OH 5, nicknamed "Zinj"	Olduvai Gorge, Tanzania	1959	Mary D. Leakey (British)	First East African australopithecine found
Australopithecus afarensis "Lucy"	Hadar, Awash River Valley, Ethiopia	1974	Donald C. Johanson (U.S.)	One of the most complete australopithecine skeletons
Laetoli fossil footprints	Laetoli, Tanzania, near Lake Eyasi	1978	Mary D. Leakey (British)	Evidence that australopithecines walked erect
Early Homo and Homo erectus				
Olduvai Gorge Homo habilis	Olduvai Gorge, Tanzania	1960	Jonathan Leakey (Kenyan)	First H. habilis found
KNM-ER 1470	Lake Turkana, Kenya	1972	Bernard Ngeneo and Richard E. F. Leakey (Kenyan)	Oldest known H. habilis skull
Java fossils	Trinil, Indonesia, on the Solo River, island of Java	1891	Eugène F. T. Dubois (Dutch)	First H. erectus found
Peking fossils	Zhoukoudian, near Beijing	1921-1937 1949-1966	Davidson Black (Canadian)	Largest collection of H. erectus fossils found
Nariokotome boy	Lake Turkana, Kenya	1984	Kamoya Kimeu (Kenyan)	Skeleton of a boy, the most complete H. erectus found
Dmanisi fossils	Dmanisi, Republic of Georgia	1999	David Lordkipanidze (Georgian)	Early H. erectus found outside of Africa
Atapuerca fossils	Atapuerca Mountains, Spain	1976	Trinidad Torres and Emiliano Aguirre (Spanish)	Earliest human fossils from western Europe
Homo sapiens and Neandertals				
Neandertal	Neander Valley, Germany, near Düsseldorf	1856	Johann K. Fuhlrott (German)	First fossil recognized as remains of prehistoric people
La Ferrassie	La Ferrassie, France, near Les Eyzies-de-Tayac	1909	Louis Capitan and Denis Peyrony (French)	Most complete Neandertal skeleton
Skhul fossils	Skhul Cave, Mount Carmel, Israel	1931-1932	Theodore D. McCown and Hallam L. Movius (U.S.)	Early modern human beings (Homo sapiens), dating from 100,000 years ago
Qafzeh fossils	Qafzeh Cave, near the Sea of Galilee, Israel	1933-1975	René Neuville and Bernard Vandermeersch (French)	Early Homo sapiens, from 100,000 years ago
Cro-Magnons	Les Eyzies-de-Tayac, France, near Brive	1868	Louis Lartet (French)	First Cro-Magnon skeletons discovered
Lake Mungo fossils	Lake Mungo, New South Wales, Australia	1968	James M. Bowler (Australian)	Oldest human remains from Australia
Dali skull	Dali, Shanxi Province, China	1978	Wu Xinzhi (Chinese)	Early Asian Homo sapiens

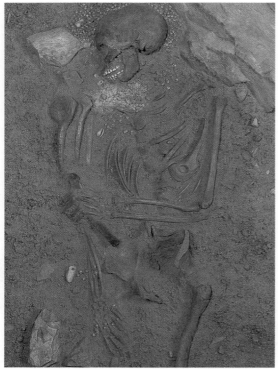

Giacomo Giacobini, University of Turin, Italy
Artwork adorns an Upper Paleolithic burial site at Arene Candide, Italy. This teen-aged boy was buried with a flint blade, shell beads, and other goods. The body was dusted with bright yellow and red pigments. The grave is about 20,000 years old.

Scientists have found much evidence of prehistoric people's lives at sites up to 100,000 years old. These sites have produced ancient tools, pottery, artwork, bits of clothing, traces of dwellings, and evidence of food, such as animal bones and plant material. Sometimes, burial sites are found. These clues enable anthropologists to form a fairly detailed picture of early people's lives. Unfortunately, scientists have found little of this type of evidence at sites older than 100,000 years. As a result, we know much less about hominids who lived before that time.

Placing prehistoric people in time is an important element of learning about human ancestors. To understand the significance of a newly discovered hominid fossil, scientists must determine how that hominid relates to others that have already been studied. This relationship can be determined by dating the newly found fossil—that is, by estimating when it lived.

Scientists have traditionally dated fossils by studying the deposit in which the fossil was found. Based on knowledge of geological history, scientists can determine the age of the deposit. They then interpret this information to provide an approximate age for the fossil.

Other dating methods are much more accurate. These methods are based on the fact that certain radioactive *isotopes* (unstable forms of chemical elements) decay at a known rate and form different isotopes. By measuring the amount of each isotope in a fossil, scientists can determine how long the decay has been going on and therefore how old the fossil is. The most commonly used dating methods of this type are *radiocarbon dating* and *potassi-*

um-argon dating. Radiocarbon dating is sometimes called C-14 dating. Potassium-argon dating is also known as K/AR dating. Other dating methods include *electron spin resonance* (ESR) *dating* and *thermoluminescence* (TL) *dating*. These dating techniques are based on the action of cosmic radiation and radioactive decay on rocks or tooth enamel.

Analysis of the genetic materials of living people is another method of studying prehistoric people. This method largely involves the study of the genetic material DNA.

Molecular biologists examine DNA from people and compare it with DNA from other people and from apes and other living primates. Such comparisons enable scientists to determine the evolutionary histories of species and groups of people more precisely. Using genetic samples, scientists study the rate of change that DNA appears to go through during evolution. From these studies, they have gained valuable knowledge about the relationship between living people and their ancestors.

Scientific comparison of the DNA among modern populations has shown that all living people share a similar genetic structure. Scientists have also compared the DNA from Neandertals and other prehistoric peoples to that of living human beings. Many scientists believe that these comparisons indicate that all modern people are a separate species distinct from prehistoric human beings like the Neandertals. However, not all scientists agree with this interpretation.

Most scientists believe that, as more is learned from genetic studies, they will be able to determine how physical features are related to specific genes. Scientists will then gain a better understanding of how our ancestors evolved into modern human beings over the last 7 million years.

Alan E. Mann

Alan E. Mann, Princeton University
An anthropologist excavates a site to recover fossil bones of Neandertals and the objects they left behind. This excavation is at Artenac, a site in France occupied about 100,000 years ago.

Rock music originated in the United States during the 1950's and rapidly gained worldwide popularity. The Irish rock band U2, *shown here,* achieved success internationally beginning in the 1980's.

Rock music

Rock music is the leading type of popular music in much of the world. Rock music exploded on the music scene in the United States during the mid-1950's. During its early history, it was called *rock 'n' roll* (also spelled *rock and roll).*

Much early rock was a rebellious style of music that particularly attracted young people who wanted an alternative to the musical tastes of the adult world. The creators of rock music were pioneers who turned away from the conventions of the music business, searching for a new sound. By the mid-1960's, however, rock dominated the music industry, and it remains one of the most important divisions of popular music.

Beginnings of rock music

Musical roots. Rock music originated primarily as a blend of two American musical styles—(1) country and western music and (2) blues. Much of the musical vocabulary of rock 'n' roll appears in recordings made during the 1930's by African American blues singers, such as Son House, Robert Johnson, and Charley Patton. At the same time, the Carter family and Jimmie Rodgers were making the first country music recordings, which provided another vital influence on rock.

By the late 1940's, a fast-paced blues style with an aggressive, driving beat emerged through recordings released by independent American record companies. This music, which was aimed primarily at a black audience, was known as *rhythm and blues.* Roy Brown recorded "Good Rockin' Tonight" (1947), and Wynonie Harris recorded "All She Wants to Do Is Rock" (1949), two rhythm and blues standards that helped shape rock 'n' roll. Big Joe Turner introduced the song "Shake, Rattle and Roll" (1954), which became a standard among rock music performers.

The Cleveland disc jockey Alan Freed is often credited with introducing the term *rock 'n' roll* as part of his radio show in the early 1950's. In black slang, the phrase had a sexual meaning, but Freed used it to describe the high-energy rhythm and blues he played on his program. The term soon became the name for the new music.

Early rock 'n' roll caused considerable controversy. Many people objected to the loudness of the music and its often rebellious or sexually suggestive lyrics and performing style. Some opponents of rock claimed that the music was corrupting young people.

Major record labels, such as Columbia and RCA Victor, ignored rock 'n' roll and focused on mainstream popular music during the early 1950's. Most of the musical developments that led to rock emerged from independent record companies, such as Atlantic, Chess, King, Specialty, and Sun.

Sun Records. In 1950, a radio announcer named Sam Phillips opened a recording studio in Memphis, Tennessee. The next year, his studio produced a song that many rock historians consider the first rock 'n' roll record. It was a song about an Oldsmobile, "Rocket '88" (1951) by Jackie Brenston with Ike Turner's band.

William McKeen, the contributor of this article, is Professor and Chair of the Department of Journalism at the University of Florida and the editor of Rock and Roll Is Here to Stay.

After "Rocket '88" became a success for Chicago's Chess Records, Phillips established his own label, Sun Records, to market his recordings. He recorded African American performers at first but sought a white singer with the sound and feeling of a black artist. With such a performer, Phillips believed, he could appeal to a large white audience and make a fortune.

Elvis Presley. In 1954 and 1955, Phillips recorded Elvis Presley, a teen-ager living in Memphis. Presley's first singles on the Sun label had a rhythm and blues song on one side and a country song on the other. The songs were only modest regional hits but became crucial to the development of rock 'n' roll.

Presley spent 18 months making innovative recordings for Sam Phillips at Sun. Then RCA bought Presley's contract in 1955 for $35,000, a remarkable sum at the time. Phillips needed the money to record his other discoveries—Johnny Cash, Jerry Lee Lewis, Roy Orbison, Carl Perkins, and Charlie Rich. They all went on to distinguished careers in rock or country music.

Presley gained mass success with his first RCA recordings, "Heartbreak Hotel" and "Don't Be Cruel" (both 1956), which led the music business to demand more songs in this new style. By the end of 1956, Presley had become a national phenomenon and established himself as rock music's greatest star.

Rock 'n' roll gains popularity

Rock 'n' roll gained in popularity during the middle and late 1950's. The first generation of rock 'n' roll artists emerged, and several different styles developed. Independent record producers played an important role in spreading the music and creating new sounds.

The first generation of rock 'n' roll artists were led by Presley and five other male performers—Chuck Berry, Little Richard, Bo Diddley, Fats Domino, and Jerry Lee Lewis. These artists appealed to black and white audiences alike, but only Presley and Lewis were white.

© Corbis/Bettmann

Elvis Presley, *center,* became rock's first superstar. His tough, rebellious manner and suggestive movements are apparent in this scene from the movie *Jailhouse Rock* (1957).

© Corbis/Bettmann

Chuck Berry helped define the rebellious spirit of rock 'n' roll in the 1950's. His rocking guitar rhythms and vivid lyrics effectively expressed the feelings and problems of youth.

Chuck Berry was one of rock's first great songwriters. His songs, aimed at teen-agers, combined lyrics with a squawking guitar and pounding rhythm. Such songs as "Maybellene" (1955), "School Day" (1957), and "Sweet Little Sixteen" (1958) dealt with themes that included cars, young love, and the frustrations of adolescence.

Little Richard was steeped in the rich tradition of black gospel music. But he had also played piano in striptease clubs, learning a sexier style of music. Little Richard's recordings for Specialty Records in New Orleans remain some of the most energetic records in rock history. They include "Tutti Frutti" (1955), "Long Tall Sally" (1956), and "Good Golly, Miss Molly" (1958).

Bo Diddley recorded for Chess Records beginning in 1955, issuing such hits as "Bo Diddley" (1955) and "Say Man" (1959). He used a guitar as a percussion instrument, and his characteristic pounding beat would influence rock bands for decades.

Fats Domino played piano with a driving rhythm and sang vocals in a rich voice that had mass appeal for white teen-agers. Domino began his career in rhythm and blues. He had more hits in the 1950's than any recording artist except Elvis Presley, beginning with his first pop music hit, "Ain't That a Shame" (1955).

Jerry Lee Lewis performed with great energy and excitement both as singer and pianist. Lewis recorded a pair of rock classics for Sun Records in 1957, "Whole Lotta Shakin' Goin' On" and "Great Balls of Fire." Lewis created controversy in 1958 when he married his 13-

year-old cousin, damaging his career for several years.

A variety of styles of rock 'n' roll emerged in the 1950's. One was the blend of country music (often called *hillbilly* music) and rhythm and blues popularized by Presley. It became known as *rockabilly.* Some rockabilly artists, such as Bill Haley and Buddy Holly, were former country music singers who altered their style slightly to succeed in the rock 'n' roll market. Haley recorded rock music's first huge hit, "Rock Around the Clock" (1954).

An African American vocal style known as *doo-wop* emerged from the streets of New York City and Philadelphia. Doo-wop, with its smooth harmonies, was the closest rock style to mainstream pop in the mid-1950's. The Orioles helped develop the doo-wop sound with their hits "It's Too Soon to Know" (1948) and "Crying in the Chapel" (1953). Other important African American doo-wop groups included the Coasters, the Drifters, the Moonglows, and the Platters. The style spread to white singing groups, such as the Capris, Dion and the Belmonts, the Earls, and the Tokens.

The major record companies, which had ignored rock 'n' roll at first, recognized the music's potential. The mainstream music industry rushed to create teen-aged idols. These young recording artists, all white, included Paul Anka, Frankie Avalon, Fabian, Connie Francis, Brenda Lee, and Ricky Nelson. Music publishing houses recruited young songwriters just out of high school, such as Neil Diamond, Carole King, and Neil Sedaka, to write songs for the youth audience.

The practice of white singers "covering"—that is, performing their own versions of—records by black artists was widespread throughout the early years of rock 'n' roll. For example, white mainstream singer Pat Boone rerecorded Little Richard's "Tutti Frutti" and "Long Tall Sally," Joe Turner's "Chains of Love," and Fats Domino's "Ain't That a Shame." Boone's "cover" versions cut into sales of the originals, costing the original artists money.

Setbacks. A number of setbacks hit rock music in the late 1950's and early 1960's. Little Richard left music and went into the ministry. Elvis Presley was drafted and served two years in the United States Army, effectively removing him from the music scene. Three important performers, Buddy Holly, Ritchie Valens, and J. P.

The Supremes were the most successful female vocal group in rock music history. The trio recorded with Motown Records, a company that popularized many black performers in the 1960's.

Richardson (the Big Bopper), were killed in a 1959 airplane crash. The next year, singer Eddie Cochran died in an automobile accident that crippled singer Gene Vincent. Chuck Berry went to prison in 1962, convicted of violating the Mann Act (transporting a minor across state lines for immoral purposes).

Independent producers brought strong creative drives to rock 'n' roll during its early years. Perhaps the first superstar record producer was Phil Spector. After working for record companies and as an independent producer, Spector founded the record label Philles Records

The Beatles, shown here at a 1965 press conference, earned a huge international following with their witty, sophisticated songs and whimsical humor. The Beatles were, *left to right,* Ringo Starr, John Lennon, Paul McCartney, and George Harrison. Their sensational popularity—called *Beatlemania*—resulted in mobbing fans, Beatle fashions, and tremendous media coverage of the band.

Bob Dylan became one of the most influential artists in the history of rock music. Dylan introduced an important new style known as *folk rock,* setting the poetic lyrics of his songs to a rock beat. Dylan, *in the print shirt,* performed at the 1965 Newport Folk Festival in Rhode Island, where he departed from the folk music tradition by switching from an *acoustic* (nonelectric) guitar to an electric one.

© David Gahr Photography

with producer Lester Sill in 1961. Spector specialized in "girl groups"—that is, vocal groups of young women—such as the Crystals and the Ronettes. He backed up their singing with what he called his "wall of sound," which consisted of blended recordings of multiple guitars, drums, and other instruments. Spector also recorded the Righteous Brothers, a popular singing duo consisting of Bill Medley and Bobby Hatfield.

In 1959, Berry Gordy, Jr., founded the Tamla record label in Detroit, which developed into the Motown Record Corporation in 1961. Gordy built Motown into a musical empire, recording such stars as Marvin Gaye, the Jackson Five, the Temptations, Smokey Robinson, Diana Ross and the Supremes, Mary Wells, and Stevie Wonder.

Brian Wilson was another record producer. Unlike Spector and Gordy, he had a major performing career as well as producing records. Wilson was a member of the Beach Boys, one of the most popular white singing groups of the 1960's. Most of Wilson's material depicted an ideal teen-age world centered in California. This world was filled with youthful romance, surfing, and fast cars. He created a complex harmonic blend in such songs as "Surfer Girl" (1963) and "I Get Around" (1964).

Brian Wilson produced the Beach Boys' album *Pet Sounds* (1966), which set a new standard for experimentation and sophistication in the recording studio. He gave the album layer upon layer of instruments and vocals to create a rich, symphonic sound.

The British invasion

In 1964, the arrival in the United States of the Beatles from England brought a rebirth to rock 'n' roll, now often called simply *rock.* The Beatles' appearance in the United States launched the visits of dozens of British rock bands that became known as the "British invasion." British acts dominated the American charts of best-selling records. Nearly all of the groups in the British invasion were actually reinterpreting American rock 'n' roll.

The Beatles were a quartet consisting of George Harrison, John Lennon, Paul McCartney, and Ringo Starr.

They came from Liverpool, an English port city where American music had a big influence. British sailors brought American rock 'n' roll records home through Liverpool, and the city's nightclubs and concert halls featured groups that accented a strong beat in the American style.

By the early 1960's, the Beatles had perfected their version of rock 'n' roll through appearances in British and German bars. Under the guidance of Brian Epstein, their manager, and the record producer George Martin, the group became hugely successful in the United Kingdom in 1963. When the Beatles brought their act to the United States the next year, they caused a sensation.

The Beatles were actually reinterpreting American rock 'n' roll from the 1950's. Their performances and recordings included songs by Chuck Berry, Buddy Holly, Carl Perkins, Little Richard, and other early rock 'n' roll stars. Lennon and McCartney soon began writing songs, and many of their compositions paid tribute to these early influences. Lennon and McCartney became one of the most successful songwriting teams in music history.

The Rolling Stones. The longest lasting of the British rock groups, the Rolling Stones, were even more steeped in American music than the Beatles. The Stones particularly liked the American blues singers Slim Harpo, Muddy Waters, and Howlin' Wolf.

The Rolling Stones formed in London in 1962. The quintet was led by singer Mick Jagger. Jagger and guitarist Keith Richards formed a songwriting partnership. Their aggressive, rebellious style can be heard in such rock classics as "(I Can't Get No) Satisfaction" (1965), "Sympathy for the Devil" (1968), and "Honky Tonk Women" (1969). The Stones rank among the most enduring rock groups. The band, with basically the same members, still performed in concerts in the early 2000's.

The Who ranked with the Rolling Stones among the top British rock bands expressing the dissatisfaction of young people. The quartet featured the songwriting of guitarist Peter Townshend. His song "My Generation" (1965) is a classic rock expression of youthful alienation.

Townshend and The Who created the first successful rock opera, the 90-minute *Tommy* (1969). The work began as an album and has been performed many times live. It was also made into a motion picture in 1975.

Other British groups followed the Beatles and the Rolling Stones and filled American music charts with their songs. They included the Animals, the Dave Clark Five, Gerry and the Pacemakers, Herman's Hermits, the Hollies (named for Buddy Holly), the Kinks, Manfred Mann, and the Moody Blues.

New styles and sounds

The 1960's became a time of peak creativity for rock music, which earned wide respect as a legitimate art form. Rock blossomed into many new styles and sounds. By the mid-1960's, rock music had become the dominant form of popular music.

Bob Dylan was a singer-songwriter who had emerged as part of a folk music boom in the United States during the early 1960's. At first, Dylan played his music on *acoustic* (nonelectric) instruments and wrote ballads calling for social change, such as "Blowin' in the Wind" (1963) and "The Times They Are A-Changin'" (1964). Then Dylan began playing his material on electric guitar with the classic rock 'n' roll accompaniment of electrically amplified instruments. Many of his original fans rejected the new electronic style, which he introduced at the Newport Folk Festival in 1965. But radio listeners were attracted to his new music.

Dylan's poetic lyrics set to a rock beat produced a style known as *folk rock,* which developed in the mid-1960's. Soon other American rock groups were recording Dylan songs, such as "Mr. Tambourine Man" (1965) by the Byrds. Other American artists who played folk rock included the Turtles and the Mamas and the Papas.

Fresh directions. Many prominent musicians of the 1960's returned to rock 'n' roll's early years for inspiration. After taking off time to recover from a motorcycle accident in July 1966, Bob Dylan recorded *John Wesley Harding* (1968). The muted guitar, bass, and drum music on the album reflected the instrumentation of the early Elvis Presley. The Byrds produced a country rock album called *Sweetheart of the Rodeo* (1968), exploring rock's roots in country music. Country rock remained popular during the 1970's. Such artists as the Eagles and Linda Ronstadt combined elements of rock and country music in their recordings.

The Beach Boys recorded a tribute to rhythm and blues in the album *Wild Honey* (1967). The British musicians John Mayall and Eric Clapton schooled themselves in the blues of Robert Johnson. John Mayall's Bluesbreakers and Clapton's group Cream played loud, fast blues rock. The American group the Doors established a dark, brooding blues rock style with their first album, *The Doors* (1967), and its hit single "Light My Fire."

Many rock artists brought diversity and experimentation to their music. The Beatles left behind the simple love songs of their early days and recorded the more personal album *Rubber Soul* (1965). The Beatles' next album, the famous *Sgt. Pepper's Lonely Hearts Club Band* (1967), was an interconnected series of songs with sound effects that were elaborate for the time. The Byrds' album *The Notorious Byrd Brothers* (1968) featured electronic instruments called *synthesizers* to combine, modify, and distort sounds. The Rolling Stones answered the *Sgt. Pepper* album with startling new music in *Their Satanic Majesties Request* (1967).

Psychedelic rock, also called *acid rock,* attempted to re-create the mind-altering effects of LSD and other drugs through music. Many psychedelic rock performances featured light shows and other special effects and deliberate use of *feedback.* Feedback is the sound distortion created when a microphone or electric guitar picked up sound from an amplifier and sent it back through that amplifier.

Many acid rock groups originated in San Francisco, including the Grateful Dead, Jefferson Airplane, and Big Brother and the Holding Company, which briefly had Janis Joplin as its lead singer. The Grateful Dead, led by guitarist Jerry Garcia, became the most popular live act in the history of rock music. Their devoted fans, known as Deadheads, filled stadiums and concert halls wherever the group appeared until Garcia died in 1995.

The heavy metal sound combined screaming guitars and crashing drums with dramatic vocals. The American guitarist Jimi Hendrix was a founder of the heavy metal sound. Hendrix became a celebrated rock guitarist with his flashy performing style, but he was also respected for his technical skill. Early in his career, Hendrix played and toured with many famous performers, including Little Richard. He gained fame after he moved to London and issued his first major recording, *Are You Experienced?* (1967). His band, the Jimi Hendrix Experience, exploited heavily amplified guitar and bass to produce an avalanche of sound.

One of the most successful heavy metal bands was the British group Led Zeppelin, which released four best-selling albums from 1969 to 1971. Other important heavy metal artists in the late 1960's and the 1970's included the American guitarist Ted Nugent, the British groups Black Sabbath and Deep Purple, and the American groups Grand Funk (also known as Grand Funk Railroad), Aerosmith, and Van Halen.

Soul music. Perhaps the most significant development of the late 1960's was the success of soul music, which was recorded primarily by black artists. Soul music developed from gospel music and the blues, but it had a smoother sound. The singer Sam Cooke launched the style, but he was shot to death in 1964 and did not live to see the success of the music he pioneered.

James Brown was the first major soul singer to cross over to a mass audience, with "Papa's Got a Brand New Bag" (1965). Brown concentrated purely on rhythm, discarding melody altogether. Like Brown, such soul artists as Aretha Franklin, Wilson Pickett, and Otis Redding gained a following among both blacks and whites.

Outdoor rock festivals began drawing huge audiences during the 1960's. The first major rock festival was the Monterey International Pop Festival in Monterey, California, in 1967. The most famous festival, however, was the 1969 Woodstock Music and Arts Festival in upstate New York. The event drew more than 300,000 fans and featured three days of top rock talent. It included such performers as the Grateful Dead, Jimi Hendrix, Jefferson Airplane, and Janis Joplin.

The 1970's

During the 1970's, the popularity of rock music spread

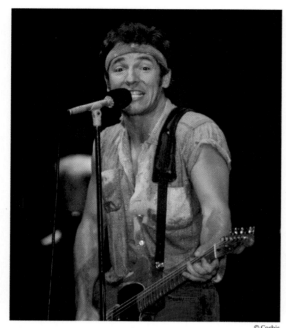

© Corbis

Bruce Springsteen has been one of the most dynamic and popular performers in rock music since the mid-1970's. He achieved success composing and singing songs that celebrate the dreams, relationships, and struggles of ordinary people.

among older as well as younger listeners, extending from preteens to middle-aged adults. As the audience for rock grew, a variety of new musical styles emerged.

The early 1970's were turbulent years in rock music. The Beatles broke up in 1970. A number of drug-related deaths shook the music world, including the deaths of Jimi Hendrix and singer Janis Joplin in 1970; and Jim Morrison, the lead singer and lyricist of the Doors, in 1971.

By the early 1970's, rock recording artists achieved a level of fame rarely gained by previous musicians. The British singer David Bowie described the ascent and decline of a rock star from outer space in his album *The Rise and Fall of Ziggy Stardust and the Spiders from Mars* (1972).

The success of The Who's rock opera *Tommy* opened the way for extended works for the stage by other rock composers. They included *Godspell* (1971) by Stephen Schwartz; *Jesus Christ Superstar* (1971) by Andrew Lloyd-Webber and Tim Rice; *Hair* (1972) by Galt MacDermot, James Rado, and Gerome Ragni; and *Grease* (1972) by Warren Casey and Jim Jacobs.

Progressive rock, also called *art rock,* was an attempt to combine rock with elements of classical music, jazz, and other forms of music. One of the most influential progressive rock bands was the British group Pink Floyd. The group's 1973 album *Dark Side of the Moon* became one of the most popular recordings in rock history. Other progressive rock groups—all from the United Kingdom—included Genesis, Jethro Tull, Yes, and the trio Emerson, Lake and Palmer.

Punk rock. Punk rock was simpler, faster, louder, and more energetic than mainstream rock. It developed pri-

marily in two cities, New York City and London. The movement was led in New York City by such bands as Blondie, the Ramones, Television, and the Patti Smith Group, and in London by the Sex Pistols, the Clash, X-Ray Spex, and many others. The punk rockers brought an angry, rebellious attitude unseen since the early days of rock 'n' roll. They were emotional and deliberately tried to offend audiences with their use of profanity and their rejection of mainstream values and lifestyles.

New wave. By the end of the 1970's, the influence of the punks had led to a more commercial brand of rock called *new wave.* The anger of the punks was present, but somewhat softened, in the new wave. Important new wave artists included the English singer-songwriter Elvis Costello, the British band the Cure, and the New York City band the Talking Heads, led by the singer and guitarist David Byrne. The new wave group the Cars achieved quick success with their first two albums, *The Cars* (1978) and *Candy-O* (1979).

Disco was a heavily rhythmic style that arrived in the late 1970's. In disco music, a steady dance beat was primary, and lyrics were of secondary importance. The success of the motion picture *Saturday Night Fever* (1977), with its best-selling soundtrack by the Bee Gees, popularized disco. The Bee Gees were a trio of English brothers—Barry, Maurice, and Robin Gibb—who began their music careers in Australia. Other disco stars included the American singer Donna Summer and the Swedish quartet ABBA.

The 1980's

A new element was introduced into rock music in the 1980's—the video. New wave music still dominated the rock music charts as the 1980's began. Rock drew strength from international musical influences, and rap music found wide acceptance.

© John Roca, Corbis

Madonna, one of rock's superstars of the 1980's and 1990's, gained fame for her recordings, videos, and live performances.

Rock videos and MTV. A cable television channel called MTV (short for Music Television) debuted in 1981, running 24 hours a day. Its initial programming consisted of short promotional films for songs and albums, called *videos.* Such films had been a part of popular music for many years. The Beatles and Bob Dylan had made memorable promotional clips for songs in the 1960's. However, with the advent of MTV, videos became a requirement for success. Many early stars of MTV, such as the British group Duran Duran and the American group Huey Lewis and the News, succeeded largely because of the style and creativity of their videos.

Many established artists, including the American bands Van Halen and ZZ Top, reached new levels of stardom though their videos. Bruce Springsteen solidified his position as one of rock's greatest stars with his best-selling album *Born in the U.S.A.* (1984). Springsteen made his first videos for this album's singles, including the hit "Dancing in the Dark." Another artist who made compelling videos was Prince. MTV's airing of Prince's video "Little Red Corvette" helped make the song and its album, *1999* (1982), a major hit. Prince became one of the top stars of the 1980's with his album and motion picture *Purple Rain* (1984) .

Madonna and Michael Jackson. Perhaps the first MTV-created rock superstar was Madonna, a dancer and singer whose sexuality dominated her cable TV appearances. Her album *Like a Virgin* (1984), with several hit singles including "Material Girl," helped make her a huge star.

Michael Jackson spent his childhood performing with his family band, the Jackson Five. Jackson found stardom as an adult with his best-selling albums *Off the Wall* (1979) and *Thriller* (1982). *Thriller* became the biggest-selling album in music history. The music video of the song "Thriller" is a 13-minute horror film that combines singing and dancing with spectacular visual and sound effects. Jackson also had hits with his dance-heavy videos "Billie Jean" and "Beat It" (both 1983).

New wave and mainstream rock remained influential. The American group the B-52's and the British group New Order blended new wave elements with dance music. The Police, a new wave group with British and American members, recorded the best-selling albums *Ghost in the Machine* (1981) and *Synchronicity* (1983). *Synchronicity* included the hit "Every Breath You Take" by the group's lead singer Sting, who later had a successful solo career. The Talking Heads, an American group, starred in the successful film *Stop Making Sense* (1984), a documentary based on their 1983 concert tour.

U2, a mainstream rock group from Ireland, gained international popularity in the 1980's. Their 1987 album *The Joshua Tree* sold millions of copies worldwide. In 1987 and 1988, and again in 1992, the group toured the world, filling arenas and stadiums with enthusiastic fans.

The American rock group R.E.M. also gained widespread popularity. R.E.M. incorporated influences ranging from folk rock to punk and new wave music. Many heavy metal bands became popular during the 1980's, including the American groups Bon Jovi, Guns n' Roses, and Mötley Crüe, and the British band Def Leppard. Bon Jovi's *Slippery When Wet* (1986) became one of the best-selling albums of the 1980's.

World music, a combination of rock and music from

© Dave Bennett, Getty Images

The Rolling Stones have been a popular and influential English rock band since the early 1960's. The group features the singing of Mick Jagger, shown on the left with guitarist Ron Wood.

other cultures, gained popularity with a large part of the rock audience. Rock artists looked outside American and European culture for other musical influences. The English rocker Peter Gabriel, a former lead singer of Genesis, and David Byrne, the Scottish-born vocalist of the American group Talking Heads, grafted African, Latin American, and Middle Eastern elements onto traditional rock. *Reggae,* a simple, pulsing form of rock music that originated in the West Indies, spread throughout the world. The passionate reggae music of Bob Marley of Jamaica became especially popular, even after Marley's death in 1981. The South African vocal group Ladysmith Black Mambazo participated in Paul Simon's 1986 *Graceland* album.

Rap is an African American form of rock that is spoken or chanted, rather than sung. Rap traces its origins to the streets of New York City in the 1970's. Rap's roots could also be heard in Jamaican music, where nightclub disc jockeys talked over the records they played. The talk was called *toasting.*

The Sugar Hill Gang scored the first major rap hit with "Rapper's Delight" (1979). Recordings by Kurtis Blow in the 1980's also found widespread acceptance. Perhaps the first rap super group was Run-DMC. Its 1984 album *Run-DMC* was the first rap gold record. The group collaborated with two members of the rock band Aerosmith on a remake of Aerosmith's hit song "Walk This Way" (1986).

Public Enemy became one of the most influential and controversial rap groups of the 1980's. Many of its raps dealt with racism and other social problems.

Early rap albums were issued by independent labels. By the end of the 1980's, such major labels as Columbia and Warner Bros. were recording rap music.

Rap remained a vigorous offshoot of rock music in the 1990's and early 2000's. With his band, Body Count, the rap star Ice-T recorded the album *Body Count* (1992), a blend of rap and heavy metal rock. The album featured a

© Alice Arnold, Corbis

Rap music consists of spoken words over a rhythm accompaniment. It emerged from black inner city culture in the 1980's and quickly became popular among young people. Arrested Development, *shown here,* became one of rap's most successful groups in the 1990's.

track called "Cop Killer" and dealt with murdering police officers. Outraged parents and public officials boycotted the album and put pressure on the record company, Warner Bros. In response, Warner eventually cut "Cop Killer" from the album. Ice-T released later albums on an independent label.

The 1990's

A style called *teen pop* dominated rock music during much of the 1990's. Artists on the fringes of mainstream rock music also brought new life to rock.

Teen pop, a pop music style aimed at preteen and teen-aged fans, achieved great commercial success in the 1990's and early 2000's. The music industry created dozens of teen-aged acts. Keeping in mind the demands of video, record producers and music-industry managers sought artists with high visual appeal. Groups of wholesome-looking boy singers gained popularity, beginning with the New Kids on the Block in the mid-1980's and continuing with the Backstreet Boys and 'N Sync, formed in the mid-1990's. Sexually appealing teen-aged girl performers, such as Britney Spears and Christina Aguilera, also gained enormous success, as much for their appeal on high energy videos as for their music.

Alternative rock. The term *alternative rock* referred to a variety of styles, usually aimed at teen-aged and young adult listeners. Much alternative rock was harsher and more experimental than mainstream rock. Many alternative rock groups were heavily influenced by the punk and new wave sounds of the 1970's and 1980's.

Alternative rock found a wide audience through such bands as Nirvana, Pearl Jam, and Soundgarden, all originating in Seattle. They played a forceful style of rock with an angry, rebellious message. The press called it *grunge rock.* Nirvana, the first grunge group to reach a wide audience, exploded onto the music scene with their second album, *Nevermind* (1991). A hit video for the album's single "Smells Like Teen Spirit" helped Nirvana gain a huge following. The group broke up in 1994 after its lead vocalist, Kurt Cobain, committed suicide.

Nine Inch Nails, an American alternative rock group,

mixed angry rock songs with heavy metal and synthesized electronic music. Other alternative rock groups that originated in the 1990's included the American bands Green Day, who were influenced by the punk rockers of the late 1970's; and No Doubt, who incorporated Jamaican popular music called *ska* into their sound. The Prodigy, a British group, combined aggressive messages with a hard-driving dance beat. Oasis, another British group, showed the influence of the Beatles in their melodies and harmonizing vocals.

Lauryn Hill mixed rap and soul music in new ways. Hill and her first solo album, *The Miseducation of Lauryn Hill* (1998), won five Grammy Awards.

Rock music today

Today, rock music takes many forms. Rock is so dominant that it can be defined as whatever music is played on popular radio stations. Some stations play *soft rock,* rock music that is slow and quiet. Others concentrate on older rock of the 1960's, 1970's and 1980's, often called *classic rock.* Still other stations focus on rap, or on alternative rock.

Rap music remains popular. Most leading rap artists, such as LL Cool J and Nelly, are black, but a few white rappers have emerged, notably Eminem.

Traditional rock maintains a foothold in the marketplace. The Rolling Stones and U2 remain huge concert draws decades after they first appeared on the rock scene. Such enduring artists as Eric Clapton, Bob Dylan, Paul McCartney, and Bruce Springsteen also continue to tour.

Alternative rock artists continue to provide some of the most creative and stimulating rock music today. The American electronic artist Moby combines, mixes, and distorts recordings of rock and other music. Another American, Beck, mixes influences from folk, soul, rap, and other types of music. Significant alternative rock groups include the British band Radiohead, who create futuristic electronic rhythms while retaining elements of traditional rock; and the American band Wilco, who blend folk and country songwriting styles with modern rock and electronic sounds.   William McKeen

Index

How to use the index

Each index entry gives the the page number or page numbers—for example, **Peter I, the Great,** 332-336, 341, 342, 345. This means that information on this topic may be found on the pages listed.

When there are many references to a topic, they are grouped alphabetically by clue words under the main topic. For example, the clue words under **Petroleum** group the references to that topic under numerous subtopics.

A page number in italic type means that there is an article on this topic on the page or pages indicated. For example, there is an Update article on **Poland** on page 318. The page numbers in roman type indicate additional references to this topic in other articles.

The indications (il.) or (ils.) mean that the reference on this page is to an illustration or illustrations only, as in **Porsche, Ferdinand.**

An entry followed by "reprint" refers to a new or revised encyclopedia article in the supplement section, as in **Prehistoric people.** This means that there is an article on pages 460 through 472.

The "see" and "see also" cross-references— for example, **Prime Minister,** refer the reader to other entries in the index.

Acknowledgments

The publishers acknowledge the following sources for illustrations. Credits read from top to bottom, left to right, on their respective pages. An asterisk (*) denotes illustrations and photographs created exclusively for this edition. All maps, charts, and diagrams were prepared by the staff unless otherwise noted.

8-14 AP/Wide World
17 © Joe Raedle, Getty Images
18-26 AP/Wide World
29 © Paul J. Richards, AFP/Getty Images
30 © Sandy Huffaker, Getty Images
33-34 AP/Wide World
39 AFP/Getty Images
46 AP/Wide World
48 © Wu Xiang, Imagine China
50-57 AP/Wide World
59 © China Photo/Reuters
63 J. Bell (Cornell University) and M. Wolff, (SSI)NASA
64 NASA/JPL/Caltech
65 NASA and The Hubble Heritage Team (STScI/AURA)
66 AP/Wide World
67 Debbie Mackall*; NASA/JPL/Caltech
68 NASA/NOAO/ESA, Hubble Helix Nebula Team, M. Meixner (STScI), and T. A. Rector (NRAO); NASA, ESA and J. Hester (ASU); Lockheed Martin Corporation/NASA
69 J. T. Trauger, NASA/JPL; NASA and The Hubble Heritage Team (STScI/AURA)
70 NASA/Goddard Space Flight Center
72 TRW Space and Technology Group/NASA; NASA/CXC/PSU
73 NASA/CXC; NASA/CXC/STScI/University of North Carolina
74 NASA/JPL/Caltech
77 © Chris McGrath, Getty Images
82 © Hulton/Archive/Getty Images; AFP/Getty Images
83 AP/Wide World
84 © Toyota
86 AP/Wide World
90 © Ray Stubblebine, Reuters
94 © James Nielsen, AFP/Getty Images
97-103 AP/Wide World
106-114 © Jim Young, Reuters; © Patrick Price, Reuters; © Andy Clark, Reuters
119 © Jeff Haynes, AFP/Getty Images
121 © Guang Niu, Reuters
127 © Janek Skarzynski, AFP/Getty Images
129 Apple Computer Inc.
136 AP/Wide World
138-139 © Ken Cole, Buffalo Field Campaign
144 AP/Wide World
146 © John Deane Photography
148 © Corbis/Bettman; © Corbis/John Springer Collection; AP/Wide World
149 © Lucy Nicholson, Getty Images; AP/Wide World; © Getty Images
150 AP/Wide World; Everett Collection
151 AP/Wide World; Corbis/Bettmann
152 Everett Collection
153 © HO/AFP/Getty Images; © Hulton/Archive/Getty Images

154 © Jerry Cooke, Corbis; AFP/Getty Images; AP/Wide World
155 © Richard Ellis, Getty Images
156-159 WORLD BOOK photo; AP/Wide World; © Corbis/Bettmann
163 © CNN/Getty Images
170-173 © PhotoDisc/Getty Images
174 © Image Bank/Getty Images
175 © PhotoDisc/Getty Images
177 © Shelley Gazin, Corbis; © PhotoDisc/Getty Images
179-187 AP/Wide World; PhotoDisc/Getty Images
192 © Tony Kyriacou, Rex Features/AFP; © Richard Young, Rex Features, AFP
198 © Bertrand Guay, AFP/Getty Images
201 Mark A. Kessler and B. T. Werner, University of California, Santa Cruz
203-207 AP/Wide World
209 © Mike Segar, Reuters
211-214 AP/Wide World
216 Roybal Corporation
219 Apple Computer Inc.
221 © Goran Tomasevic, Reuters
223 Kenneth Moll, U.S. Navy
224 © Oleg Popov, Reuters
226-227 AP/Wide World
228 © Scala/Art Resource
229 © AFP/Getty Images
231 © Reuters
232 AP/Wide World
233-239 © AFP/Getty Images
241 AP/Wide World
242 © Karim Sahib, AFP/Getty Images
243 © Reinhard Krause, Reuters
245-249 AP/Wide World
250 © New China News Agency/Sovfoto
254 © Aizar Raldes, AFP/Getty Images
259 American Library Association
264 © Photos.com; © Sandy Huffaker, Getty Images
267 © Hulton/Archive/Getty Images
271 WORLD BOOK photo*
272-279 AP/Wide World
284 Everett Collection
286 © Corbis/Bettmann
287 © Hulton/Archive/Getty Images
288 © Corbis/Underwood & Underwood
289 © Corbis/John Springer Collection/
291 © Chad Rachman
293-294 AP/Wide World; © Dick Hamilton, NHDTT
295 © Herman Beals, Reuters; © Dick Hamilton, NHDTT
296 © Mike Blake, Reuters
299 © Paul McErlane, Reuters
301 Auckland University of Technology, New Zealand

305 AP/Wide World
306 © Shaun Botterill, Getty Images
308 © Mario Tama, Getty Images
309 AP/Wide World
310 © Frank Micelotta, Getty Images
311 AP/Wide World
312 © Sven Nackstrand, Getty Images
313 © Spencer Platt, Getty Images; Thomas Coex, Getty Images
314 © Otto Greule, Getty Images
319 © Frank Micelotta, Getty Images
321 © Corbis/Bettmann
324 AP/Wide World
329 © Jim Bourg, Reuters
332-333 AP/Wide World
334 © Alexandre Orloff, Polaris Images; © Bernard Crochet Collection, Photos 12/Polaris
335 © Corbis/Bettmann
337 © Hulton/Archive/Getty Images
338-339 AP/Wide World
340 © Alexander Zemlianichenko, AFP/Getty Images
341 © Antione Giori, Corbis
342 © Mimmo Jodice, Corbis
343-344 © Yuri Belinsky, TASS/Sovfoto
346 AP/Wide World
347 © Ivan Milutinovic, Reuters
349 © Denis Balihouse, Reuters
354 AP/Wide World; NASA
355 NASA; AP/Wide World
356 © AFP/Getty Images
358 © Eric Gaillard, Reuters
364 EPA; AP/Wide World
367 © David Hume Kennerly, Getty Images
369-370 AP/Wide World
373 Garmin Ltd.
375 Family Communications Inc.
376 © Vince Bucci, Getty Images
378 AP/Wide World
381 © Joan Marcus
383 © Douglas Kirkland, Corbis
384 AP/Wide World
385 Active People
387-393 AP/Wide World
395 © Kieran Doherty, Reuters
397 AP/Wide World
398 U.S. Dept. of the Treasury
402-403 Art Explosion; Library of Congress; Hart Picture Archives
404-405 Library of Congress; Panhandle-Plains Historical Museum, Canyon, TX; Library of Congress
406 Library of Congress; AP/Wide World; Library of Congress; George Rodgers, Time Life Pictures/Getty Images
407 Johnson Space Center/NASA; © Corbis/Bettmann; Johnson Space Center/NASA
408 © Larry Downing, Reuters
410-412 AP/Wide World
413 © Heino Kalis, Reuters; AFP/Getty Images